The Economic History o

1860–1990

The Economic History of Italy 1860–1990

VERA ZAMAGNI

CLARENDON PRESS · OXFORD

Oxford University Press, Great Clarendon Street, Oxford OX2 6DP
Oxford New York
Athens Auckland Bangkok Bogota Bombay
Buenos Aires Calcutta Cape Town Dar es Salaam
Delhi Florence Hong Kong Istanbul Karachi
Kuala Lumpur Madras Madrid Melbourne
Mexico City Nairobi Paris Singapore
Taipei Tokyo Toronto Warsaw
and associated companies in
Berlin Ibadan

Oxford is a trade mark of Oxford University Press

Published in the United States by
Oxford University Press Inc., New York

First published in hardback 1993
First issued in new as paperback 1997

British Library Cataloguing in Publication Data
Data available

Library of Congress Cataloging in Publication Data
Negri Zamagni, Vera.
[Dalla periferia al centro. English]
The economic history of Italy, 1860–1990/Vera Zamagni.
p. cm.
Includes bibliographical references.
1. Italy—Economic conditions. I. Title.
HC305.N35913 1993 330.945—dc20 93-10775

ISBN 0-19-828773-9
ISBN 0-19-829289-9 (Pbk)

Printed in Great Britain
on acid-free paper by
Biddles Ltd, Guildford and King's Lynn

This publication was made possible through the co-operation of Biblioteca Italia, a Giovanni Agnelli Foundation for the diffusion of Italian culture

PREFACE

> For what more can be expected of any historical hypothesis than to have stimulated research to the point of becoming the stepping stone to a new hypothesis and to new research?
>
> A. Gerschenkron, *Economic Backwardness in Historical Perspective*

WHEN I started working on this book, I had something similar to Gerschenkron's conclusion in mind: that is, I wanted to bring together in a single volume those results of economic historiography pertaining to modern Italy in order to facilitate reflection on possible new directions for research. This task seemed to me to be rather urgent for two different reasons: first, the fragmentary nature of research in Italy, together with the stubborn narrow-mindedness and exclusiveness of individual schools of thought (which I have fortunately never been part of), have far too often impeded the circulation of ideas and research findings;[1] secondly, the difficulties that foreign scholars have in analysing the Italian case in comparative studies of long-term economic development—due, above all, to problems of a linguistic nature—has meant that Italy has not been dealt with as it should have been in a great number of European and world economic histories.[2]

If my aims, therefore, were to illustrate the case of industrial development in Italy, then on the one hand I would have to give an account of some important events that happened prior to the unification of Italy (to this aim the first section of the introduction is devoted), and on the other hand I would not be able to stop at the Second World War, as the industrialization process, which had started very late in Italy, was to witness some of its most crucial moments during the post-war years. The two chapters which I have devoted to this period (Chapters 11 and 12), however, have a different role to play in the book from that of the preceding chapters covering the period between unification and the Second World War (Chapters 1 to 10). The reason for this is that very little has

[1] There are some bibliographical essays on the economic history of post-unification Italy. The most recent are the following: L. Avagliano (ed.), *L'Italia industriale nelle sue regioni: bilancio storiografico* (Naples, ESI, 1988); L. De Rosa, 'La storiografia economica italiana nell'età contemporanea', in id., *L'avventura della storia economica in Italia* (Bari, Laterza, 1990); D. Bigazzi, *La storia dell'impresa in Italia: bilancio storiografico* (Milan, Angeli, 1990); G. Federico, 'La storiografia sullo sviluppo economico italiano negli ultimi trent'anni', in C. Cassina (ed.), *La storiografia sull'Italia contemporanea* (Pisa, Giardini ed., 1991); T. Fanfani, 'La storiografia economica contemporanea in Italia negli ultimi vent'anni: problemi e temi dello sviluppo industriale', in A. Grohmann (ed.), *Due storiografie economiche a confronto: Italia e Spagna dagli anni '60 agli anni '80* (Milan, Egea, 1991).

[2] In one of these histories, Italy (as well as Spain) is not included: P. Mathias and S. Pollard (eds.), *The Cambridge Economic History of Europe*, iii: *The Industrial Economies: The Development of Economic and Social Policies* (Cambridge, Cambridge University Press, 1989).

been written by economic-historians about the post-war period, with virtually all of the research so far available having been carried out by economists (with very few exceptions). I did not think it was necessary, therefore, to embark upon a detailed survey of the endless amount of economic research available, as this would first need to be systematically analysed by historians, dealing with different individual problems and economic sectors, before one could draw an overall picture. It seemed to me to be more useful, instead, to try to offer a long-term interpretation of those events that were more closely tied to the fundamental issues dealt with in the first ten chapters. In order to underline the long-term nature of the perspective offered in this volume, the second section of the introduction contains a survey of the main demographic and economic indices available for the entire period, that is, from 1861 to 1981 (and beyond).

This study adopts both macro- and micro-economic viewpoints: the latter consists, in particular, of detailed historical accounts of certain companies and banking institutions. As I am particularly interested in social history, I have also chosen to analyse income levels, consumption, standards of living, and education, as well as the provision of social services, with a view to establishing to what extent and in what ways economic development has enabled Italians to enjoy a better way of life. The book, which makes use of a considerable amount of quantitative data and contains a detailed methodological explanation of the techniques of estimation adopted, is aimed principally at students of economic history, who I assume have at least a basic knowledge of economic theory and of the statistical presentation of historical data.

Nevertheless, I have tried to make the exposition of the book as simple as possible, in order that it may also be read by the educated layman. Despite a deliberate attempt to maintain a certain balance between the different parts of the book, and to render it suitably informative, it was inevitable that it should to some extent reflect my personal areas of interest, in terms of the space assigned to the various topics covered and, above all, of the many other areas that I have chosen not to deal with.

On the other hand a textbook is not an encyclopaedia, and can hardly be judged in terms of how exhaustive it is, but should be evaluated from the point of view of its structural coherency, and its ability to stimulate the reader's interest, and while it should be as faithful as possible to source materials, it should also try to be as critical of such information as possible.

My task has undoubtedly been made easier by a natural intellectual inquisitiveness which has led to me being involved in many different fields of research, and which has been characterized by the same 'devilish frenzy, which forces me to express my opinion in the quickest and most succinct form possible' described by Cipolla in an autobiographical essay of his.[3] I have also

[3] C. Cipolla, 'Fortuna plus homini quam consilium valet', in id., *Saggi di storia economica e sociale* (Bologna, Il Mulino, 1988, 211; published with the same title in English in L. P. Curtis (ed.), *The Historian's Workshop* (New York, 1970)).

been helped by the contact I have had with numerous colleagues, both Italian and non-Italian, who, since my Oxford days (1969–73), have continuously contributed to the filling out and broadening of the theoretical and factual material which has gone to make up this present volume. This intellectual contact, through conferences and research carried out with others, has been for me the most fascinating part of academic life. I have also had the good fortune to be part of various intellectual circles outside my own speciality, and in particular the extremely stimulating one made up of economists. I have my husband to thank for having presented me with that particular opportunity: any recognition of the help he has given me, however, would be totally inadequate, because, to paraphrase Goethe, 'when faced with the superior talents of another person, love is the only thing that is left'.

I am very grateful to my many Italian and non-Italian students at the Universities of Trieste, Brescia, Florence, Bologna, and Cassino, and at the Bologna Center of the Johns Hopkins University, for having stimulated me with their many questions during my lessons, as well as for the great commitment and energy they have always put into their graduation essays and reports, and their postgraduate theses, some of which are cited in this book. The time and energy that I have dedicated to them has always been amply rewarded by their intelligence and affection.

The debt that I owe to my colleagues is so enormous that it would be impossible to repay them by simply publishing a list of their names. I leave it to my readers to judge the merits of the authors cited in the text. I would just like to express my thanks to those friends who read and made their comments on some of the chapters of this book: F. Amatori, P. Bolchini, T. Fanfani, G. Federico, R. Giannetti, F. Giusberti, C. Poni, L. Segreto, P. A. Toninelli, E. Sori, G. Lusignani—none of whom can of course be considered reponsible for anything written here.

Finally, many thanks go to Patrick Barr for his dedication to the delicate job of translating this book and to Anna Brizzi from the Economic Science Department of Bologna University for having patiently helped with the preparation of the final manuscript.

This book is dedicated to my daughters, Giulia and Elena, whose presence during the writing has made it all the more enjoyable.

V. Z.

University of Bologna

CONTENTS

LIST OF FIGURES

LIST OF TABLES

INTRODUCTION

It is not true to say that there are some countries with a propensity towards growth, while others are naturally inclined towards stagnation. Each nation has always tried to better its own position, only to be prevented from doing so by natural events, by political and military struggles, or by the creation of certain institutions and centres of power that have proved to be anathema to growth, as has again been underlined recently by E. L. Jones.[1] The history of Italy[2] from the Etruscans to the present day is a perfect example of this process, with the repeated appearance and disappearance, or alternation, of civilizations within the same geographical area but within different international contexts.

If the analysis developed in one of Jones's earlier works,[3] concerning Europe as a whole, is applied to the case of Italy, it could be said that Italy's great expansionist policies—involving the use of arms at the time of the Roman Empire, or trade and manufacturing during the Renaissance—were dictated by the necessity to escape from inevitable economic misery to which it had been condemned as a result of the country's meagre agricultural production and its almost non-existent reserves of raw materials. Of course, it is important to bear in mind that the Mediterranean was for centuries one of the main centres of civilization (the others being located in Asia)—as Braudel has proved beyond doubt in his famous writings[4]—and Italy had the good fortune of being situated in an enviable central position within the Mediterranean.

However, such 'favourable' conditions are certainly not enough in themselves to explain either Italy's periods of growth or its periods of decline. Furthermore, when geographical explorations during the Renaissance led to the discovery of the existence of enormous, previously undiscovered continents, such conditions soon represented an obstacle which Italy would later have to overcome.

[1] E. L. Jones, *Growth Recurring. Economic Change in World History* (Oxford, Clarendon Press, 1988).

[2] It is well known that the word 'Italy' was already used to denominate the peninsula during the 2nd cent. BC, but that its meaning was purely geographical until the Middle Ages, when the use of Latin gave way to that of another language, called Italian, used by the upper-class élite who lived on the peninsula now called Italy. The word only took on a political meaning, however, with the unification of the country. Nevertheless, we shall continue to use the word 'Italy' in this chapter in order to simplify things, although we are fully aware that this usage is not at all precise from a historical point of view.

[3] E. L. Jones, *The European Miracle* (Cambridge, Cambridge University Press, 1981).

[4] See in particular *Civiltà e imperi del Mediterraneo nell'età di Filippo II* (2 vols., Turin, Einaudi, 1973; Eng. edn., *The Mediterranean and the Mediterranean World in the Age of Philip II* (London, Collins, 1972)) and *La Méditerranée* (Paris, Flammarion, 1985).

Consequently, a more detailed examination needs to be made of the causes of Italy's periods of growth and stagnation.

1. FROM THE CENTRE TO THE PERIPHERY

In order to move away from too generalized an analysis, I would like to begin with the twelfth-century revival. According to C. M. Cipolla, 'from the twelfth to the fifteenth century, the Italians were in the forefront not only of economic development but also of technological progress'.[5] Many new changes were made, notably in textile (wool, cotton, and silk) manufacturing,[6] but also in the fields of navigation,[7] commerce,[8] and banking.[9] Venetians and Genoese dominated Mediterranean trade, Milanese and Florentines dominated manufacturing, and many other minor Italian towns also prospered. At the beginning of the fourteenth century, Venice, Milan, Genoa, and Florence already had populations of around 100,000 (within Europe this was perhaps only to be matched by Paris), and there were 26 other Italian towns with populations of over 20,000.

This blossoming of the Italian towns was due to a combination of economic and political factors: a marked improvement in agriculture led to an increase in agricultural surpluses, which in turn made a population increase possible as early as the eleventh century; the political situation at the time made it possible for the cities to enjoy a greater degree of autonomy in relation to the existing feudal order. The Italian cities' propitious geographical positions, from the point of view of foreign trade, promised to lead to important economic gains, and this promise was subsequently fulfilled largely as a result of these factors.

There was already a visible difference between the southern and the central-northern parts of the country at this time. A significantly minor growth in the southern towns, probably due to geographical-political factors, led to southern agriculture's specializing in sheep-farming and the extensive cultivation of cereals, as well as in the breeding of silkworms[10] and the cultivation of flax in certain areas, with the aim of exporting to the centre and the North. A proportionately larger increase in the prices of agricultural products compared

[5] C. M. Cipolla, *Storia economica dell'Europa pre-industriale* (Bologna, Il Mulino, 1974), 234. Eng. version, *Before the Industrial Revolution: European Society and Economy 1000–1700* (London, Methuen, 1976), 174.

[6] The most important were the fulling-mill (for the fulling of woollen textiles), the spinning-wheel, the horizontal loom, and the hydraulic spinning-wheel for silk.

[7] The compass (of Chinese origin), the rudder, canal locks—so carefully studied by Leonardo da Vinci during the time he spent in Milan.

[8] The introduction of double-entry bookkeeping, the formation of cartels and syndicates, the introduction of new forms of financing trade and shipping, such as the maritime loan, the 'commenda' (a form of shipping company), and insurance.

[9] The creation of money of account by means of the bank 'giro' system, which saw large sums of money being transferred by bankers from one merchant to another within the same commercial centre or, by means of a system of bills of exchange, from one commercial centre to others far away.

[10] The silk-cocoon was introduced into Sicily by the Arabs during the 10th cent.

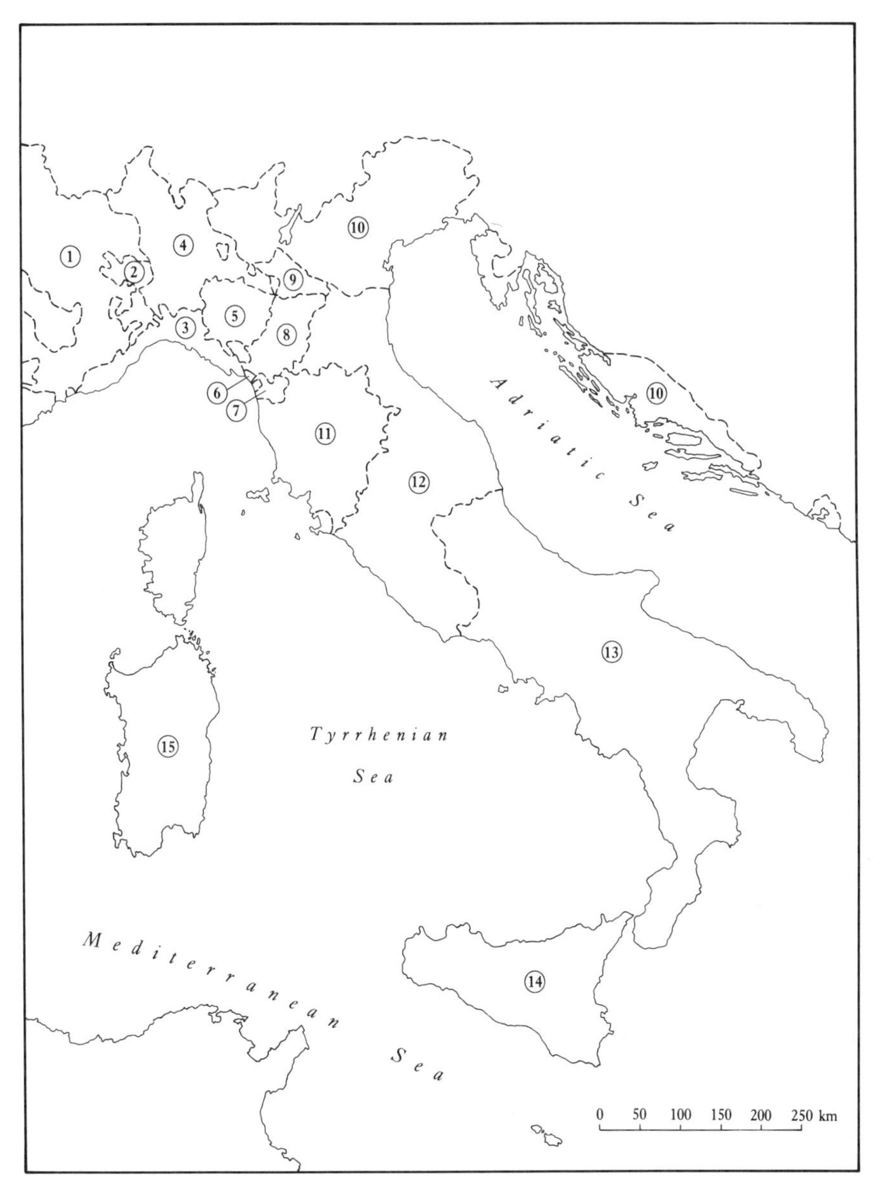

1. Duchy of Savoy
2. Marquisate of Monferrato (from 1566 joined with the Duchy of Mantua)
3. Republic of Genoa
4. Duchy of Milan
5. Duchy of Parma
6. Princedom of Massa
7. Republic of Lucca
8. Duchy of Modena
9. Duchy of Mantua
10. Republic of Venice
11. Grand Duchy of Tuscany
12. Papal State
13. Kingdom of Naples } under Spanish rule
14. Kingdom of Sicily } under Spanish rule
15. Kingdom of Sardenia } under Spanish rule

Fig. 0.1 Italy in the sixteenth century

with those of manufactured products, until the end of the sixteenth century, made such a policy appear to be both rational and advantageous in terms of southern Italy's economic position.[11]

Nevertheless such prosperity, whilst being both surprising and admirable in the eyes of latter-day observers and contemporary historians,[12] was not destined to last very long. Manufacturing and trade collapsed between 1580 and the second half of the seventeenth century. The woollen and shipbuilding industries almost disappeared; the major ports saw a dramatic decline in traffic, with the exception of Leghorn which became the chosen port of entry for goods, vessels, and other ships coming into the Mediterranean from northern Europe.

Cipolla writes: 'By the end of the seventeenth century, Italy largely imported manufactures from England, France, and Holland. At this stage she exported mostly agricultural and semi-finished goods, namely oil, wheat, wine, wool and especially raw and thrown silk. In the area of maritime services Italy was reduced to a passive role . . . Italy had begun her career as an underdeveloped area within Europe.'[13]

This reversal, this movement away from the centre back towards the periphery of economic development that happened within the space of one century, was so dramatic that it warrants a detailed examination as to its causes. The fact that the whole of the Mediterranean had become an underdeveloped area by the end of the seventeenth century is beyond question; however, if the geographical discoveries of this time are proffered as a reason for such a decline, one is ignoring the more important question of why there was no reaction to the external challenge that they represented.

As a matter of fact, the European markets remained the most important ones for a long time after these discoveries had been made, and yet it was these same markets that Italian producers lost control over as they persisted with their tried-and-tested methods of production, jealously guarded by the guilds, whereas in Holland and England 'rural' manufacturers had started to compete through the production of less refined articles at a lower cost. The rigidity of the guilds, which at first had proven to be an efficient and functional factor in the organization of urban manufacturing, but was later to become synonymous with

[11] On this point, see P. Malanima, *L'Economia italiana nell'età moderna* (Rome, Editori Riuniti, 1982), 89, and M. Aymard, 'Dal feudalesimo al capitalismo', in *Annali della storia d'Italia*, i (Turin, Einaudi, 1978), 1,145.

[12] See e.g. D. Sella, *L'economia lombarda durante la dominazione spagnola* (Bologna, Il Mulino, 1982), Italian version of *Crisis and Continuity. The Economy of Spanish Lombardy in the Seventeenth Century* (Cambridge, Mass., Harvard University Press, 1979), in which the author has the following to say about Lombardy: 'Overall, Lombardy's agricultural improvements, its clear superiority in many areas of manufacturing, together with the high degree of commercialization of its agricultural and industrial sectors, would seem to indicate that the economy and society of that region, with an exceptional lead on the rest of the world, had from certain points of view reached an advanced level of development in the modern sense of the word' (pp. 53–4 of the Italian edn.).

[13] Cipolla, *Storia economica*, 298–9; Eng. version, 243–4.

out-of-date production modes and too high wage-levels, has recently been cited as one of the recurrent factors in the decline of certain areas, to the advantage of others where labour flexibility is higher and relative costs are lower.[14]

However, scholars have pointed to other reasons for Italy's decline. In the first place, the wealth generated became polarised, with the benefits accruing to the few. As Romano noted, 'perhaps there is no other country in Europe that has had so many rich people (and so rich) as Italy has had'.[15] How were such riches spent, other than on ostentatious objects of desire? On churches, mansions, castles, villas, roads, and fountains. Fifty-four churches and about 70 mansions were built in Rome alone during the sixteenth century. Some believe that this type of unproductive capital investment was the result of the aforementioned polarization of incomes, since the vast majority of the population was kept at subsistence level, and so there was very little growth of the internal market for manufactured articles.[16] Others put greater importance on the aristocratic mentality of the wealthy, whereas others again underline the fact that 'productive investment opportunities were extremely limited' by the state of technology at the time.[17]

The problem of local strife was also an important factor during this period of decline. This was connected with the blossoming of the cities, which, being proud of their own independence from feudal power and other forms of domination, effectively prevented the setting up of a unified national State. In fact, the only area in any way unified was the South, a part of Italy that had a less deeply rooted urban culture. It could be said that Italy experienced that 'balancing of power' which developed on a larger scale in Europe during the nineteenth and twentieth centuries, and which led to a long series of debilitating wars and acted as an obstacle to the centralization of power, thus postponing the rationalization of markets. This political-institutional weakness cost Italy the leadership in Europe, in the same way that it has cost Europe the world leadership in more recent times. Furthermore, at that time a war meant famine, the danger of a plague epidemic, and also a decline in population, as portrayed in the novel *Promessi Sposi* (the most famous and well-known Italian novel by Alessandro Manzoni, poet and writer from Milan 1785–1873, that reconstructs life in Lombardy around 1628, at the time of Spanish rule) with all the attendant problems involved in a subsequent reorganization of the economic system. War also meant that the foreign armies that succeeded in conquering significant Italian territory then held on to that territory for a

[14] See H. Van der Wee, *Prosperity and Upheaval, The World Economy, 1945–1980* (New York, Viking, 1986), where the author makes the following interesting comparison: 'just as the merchant-entrepreneurs of the eighteenth century had shifted the locus of their industrial activity to the countryside, so multinationals began to look to the Third World, in particular to the newly industrialized countries' (p. 518).

[15] R. Romano, 'Una tipologia economica', in *Storia d'Italia. I Caratteri originali* (Turin, Einaudi, 1972), 298.

[16] Cf. Malanima, *L'economia italiana.*

[17] Cipolla, *Storia economica*, 183; the idea expressed is Postan's.

considerable length of time. Some scholars believe that the Spanish conquest of the South of Italy had seriously negative effects, with its punitive fiscal policy and deflationary monetary policy leading to the collapse of manufacturing and the paralysis of agriculture.[18]

Finally, I would like to look at a recently proposed explanation for Italy's decline, put forward by M. Aymard, in which the key factor is seen to be the limited elasticity of agricultural supply in relation to the demand created by national economic growth: cereal prices rose, producing an increase in wages (and consequently also in the prices of manufactured goods), whilst representing an incentive to invest in agriculture, although the fruits of such investment were too long-term. 'Agriculture is marking time and is even regressing, incapable as it is of reacting to the stimuli produced at higher economic levels.'[19] In this way, there is a reversal in the initial feudal relation between the towns and the countryside, with urban oligarchies now imposing their will upon the countryside; frequently such town-dwellers were oppressive absentee landlords, and this kind of relationship represented the basis for the mismanagement of much of the Italian countryside. Furthermore, the economic decline of the larger cities of north-central Italy, together with their increasingly close ties with the surrounding countryside, meant that the economy of southern Italy increasingly loosened its ties with that of central and northern Italy, as the latter no longer required wheat and industrial raw materials from the former.

> The premature economic unification of Italy is falling to pieces in the face of a new tendency towards the division of the whole into many autonomous parts: and in the eighteenth century, when trade resumes, northern Italian merchants will have lost control of southern exports, which will have passed into the hands of other commercial powers, such as England, France and the United Provinces. Old relationships of dependence will be replaced by new ones, thus reinforcing the breaking-up of the Italian peninsula's economic sphere and exacerbating existing internal divisions, which later on will be inherited by a united Italy, without however the North's regaining its former dynamism.[20]

Although it is not possible to credit one analysis more than another here, and it is inevitable to accept a rather eclectic interpretation of these historical developments, the concept of 'prematurity' does seem to be a common element in more than one explanation. That is, the commercial-manufacturing revolution in Italy would seem to have flagged as a result, on the one hand, of an inadequate level of support from other sectors of the economy, as well as from the political and international spheres, and on the other hand, as a result of its

[18] L. De Rosa, in *Il Mezzogiorno spagnolo tra crescita e decadenza* (Milan, Il Saggiatore, 1987), maintains that the excessive and ill-devised fiscal policy was due to the Spaniards' need for money to support their imperialistic wars.

[19] Aymard, 'Dal feudalesimo al capitalismo', 1180.

[20] Ibid.

own inability to offer alternative solutions to those already tried out, due to the limited nature of the revolution's base.

With its decline during the seventeenth century, Italy thus set out on its 'career as an underdeveloped area within Europe'. However, this was a particular kind of 'underdeveloped area', never having very much in common with other underdeveloped nations, whether those of pre-industrial Europe or those of other continents.[21]

First, Italian agriculture had freed itself for ever from the shackles of serfdom, having become highly commercialized, with strict limits to communal rights and with the introduction of paid labour over large areas of the country, even in the South. Significant investment was made in the area of the Po Plain, and in particular in Lombardy, with the construction of canals which subsequently made it possible to produce forage for livestock in place of the previously existing system of laying fallow the land. This enabled farmers to practise continual crop rotation, and allowed an increase in the scale of livestock farming which, as well as furnishing its own direct products, helped in the working of fields and produced fertilizer, leading to an increase in agricultural productivity. This 'virtuous circle' anticipated the agricultural revolutions in Flanders and England but was limited to the Lombard lowlands in Italy. Such practices remained an integral part of Italian agriculture in the centuries to follow, although they often had to coexist with important juridical and political vestiges of the feudal system (in some areas more marked than in others).

There has been, and still exists, an important division among scholars over a particular question: that is, whether or not there was a 'refeudalization' of the countryside during this period. Galasso[22] and Romano[23] are among those who maintain that there was, while the opponents of this thesis are Sella[24] and De Maddalena.[25] The latter's argumentation certainly seems the more convincing, at least as far as the North is concerned, in that it shows that the economic logic behind the exploitation of the land was essentially capitalistic in nature, even if 'rather important and commonly found structures and superstructures survived from the old feudal regime'.[26] Even in Cattini's very detailed study of an area of Emilia between 1500 and 1700, one sees that the admittedly slow transition that took place during this period transformed the area into one of increasingly

[21] It was in fact this reflection that led Aymard to talk of an Italian 'anomaly', as the transition from feudalism to industrial capitalism did in fact begin very early—and for this very reason Italy can not be defined as an underdeveloped country in the normal sense of the word—but was to last for five centuries.

[22] See G. Galasso, 'Le forme del potere, classi e gerarchie sociali', in *Storia d'Italia. I Caratteri originali.*

[23] Romano, 'Una tipologia economica'.

[24] Sella, *L'economia lombarda.*

[25] A. De Maddalena, *Dalla città al borgo. Avvio di una metamorfosi economica e sociale nella Lombardia spagnola* (Milan, Angeli, 1982); see also L. Faccini, *La Lombardia fra '600 e '700* (Milan, Angeli, 1988).

[26] De Maddalena, *Dalla città al borgo*, 351.

capitalistic production, with a move away from the sharecropping system towards one of tenancy and day labourers.[27]

The fact is that in a country like Italy, subsequent civilizations always arise out of a preceding one, and when the new civilization fails to fill completely all socio-economic spaces with its own innovations, there is no 'vacuum' as there might be in an underpopulated, recently colonized land such as Australia or the USA:[28] instead, there are the vestiges of the previous civilization, and these are sometimes deeply rooted, representing an obstacle to change. Each new civilization thus has to reckon with the previous one, through both compromise and conflict, and is therefore never completely 'pure' or 'consistent'. Contradictions and complications constitute the price that Italy has had to pay for the centuries of history that have been acted out on Italian soil. However, looking at events from the positive point of view, this continual contact between renewed traditions and new opportunities has been the foundation for unexpected and notable periods of economic revival.

In fact, the continued existence of manufacturing traditions is another characteristic factor of this uniquely Italian form of 'underdevelopment'; I am not referring so much to urban artisanal crafts, which never completely died out (they simply went from serving the merchant classes to benefiting those landowners who resided in the towns), as to the silk trade, which, as we shall see later, was to have a fundamental role in Italian economic renewal during the nineteenth century.

The cultivation of the mulberry tree and the breeding of silkworms had already expanded enormously in the countryside of central and northern Italy during the seventeenth century, while the activities of throwing and spinning the silk had taken root both in the countryside and in certain selected towns. The 'Bolognese mill', a complicated water-powered mechanism capable of activating a large number of spindles at the same time, became famous during this time, and was even copied by the English.[29] In 1683, there were some 119 working silk-mills in the city of Bologna—at that time, the most industrialized city in Europe.[30] Northern Italy's commercial ties were kept alive, despite the economic depression, thanks largely to the thrown and spun silk which was sold on all foreign markets, where it had no real competitors to speak of. By the end of the eighteenth century, Italian production of raw silk constituted more than

[27] M. Cattini, *I contadini di San Felice. Metamorfosi di un mondo rurale nell'Emilia dell'età moderna* (Turin, Einaudi, 1984).

[28] Forgetting the few natives, who were either massacred or isolated from the colonial population.

[29] A. Guenzi and C. Poni, 'Sinergia di due innovazioni. Chiaviche e mulini da seta a Bologna', *Quaderni Storici*, 64 (1987), 117.

[30] C. Poni, 'Espansione e declino di una grande industria: le filature di seta a Bologna fra XVII e XVIII secolo', in *Problemi d'acque a Bologna in età moderna* (Bologna, 1983) and the more recent work by the same author, 'Per la storia del distretto industriale serico di Bologna (secoli XVI–XIX)', *Quaderni Storici*, 73 (1990).

80 per cent of total European consumption.[31] It is true, however, that only a very small part of this intermediate product was then weaved into cloth in Italy, a sign of the weakness of the Italian manufacturing base at that time. Nevertheless, this intermediate product enabled the country to keep on trading, and thus accumulate capital, on the one hand, and on the other, it kept 'proto-industrial' activities alive in the countryside and in some northern cities which were later to become the birthplaces of industrialization.[32] 'A simple coincidence?', Vigo asks; 'It would be rather difficult to support the idea, since the centuries that separated early rural manufacturing from the construction of vast industrial plants during the nineteenth century were witness to the continual development (ups and downs notwithstanding) of a technological tradition that at one time had been at the forefront of European development'.[33] Unfortunately, the South failed to keep up with the North in the development of the raw silk trade: the Neapolitan silk-weaving trade, whose artisan membership had at one time numbered as many as 10,000 individuals, collapsed during the seventeenth century,[34] and all that remained in the South was a very modest artisan silk-throwing industry in the Catanzaro area, together with a limited production of luxury silk fabrics at San Leucio, which was also on the decline.

Lastly, Italy preserved the close cultural ties that it had always had with the rest of Europe, through the work of an élite group of scholars and thinkers, active in different fields, who quickly learnt again the lesson of humility which their Renaissance predecessors had forgotten, being used as the latter were to considering themselves as teachers and not students.[35] This élite managed to popularize the scientific innovations created in other countries, occasionally coming up with something original themselves. In the economic field as well, 'the exchange of ideas that took place between the Italian and European schools of thought was no less intense than that involving political thought, philosophy,

[31] Ibid.

[32] The most thorough study carried out so far of the proto-industrialization of Italy has been that of A. Dewerpe, *L'Industrie aux champs. Essais sur la protoindustrialisation en Italie du Nord (1800–1880)* (Rome, École française de Rome, 1985), which nevertheless is still somewhat imprecise and incomplete in parts. For a very good local study of this process, see R. Merzario, *Il capitalismo nelle montagne. Strategie famigliari nella prima fase di industrializzazione nel comasco* (Bologna, Il Mulino, 1989).

[33] G. Vigo, 'Alle origini dell'industrializzazione lombarda', *Rivista milanese di economia*, 23 (July–Aug. 1987).

[34] Cf. L. De Rosa, 'La deindustrializzazione del Regno di Napoli (secoli XVI–XVII)', *Rassegna Economica*, 49 (May–June 1985).

[35] Cipolla quotes an English writer's view of the Italians at the end of the 16th cent.: 'The Italians thincke themselves to have so much sweeteness, fruitfulness, and such monuments of arts and fabricks, as they seldome or never travaile into forayne kingdoms, but driven by some necessity ether to followe the warrs or to traffique abroade: this opinion that Italy doth afforde what can be seene or knowne in the world makes them only have home-bred wisdome and the proude conceete of their own witts.' *Storia economica*, 314; Eng. version, 263. The quotation comes from F. Moryson, *Itinerary*, ed. C. Hughes (London, 1903), 419.

mathematics and the natural sciences'.[36] Beginning with Bernardo Davanzati's publication of his *Lessons on Monies* in 1588, in which he revealed himself to be a forerunner of the quantitative theory of money and of the theory of utility value, and then going on to the seventeenth-century theorists Antonio Serra and Geminiano Montanari, one arrives at a substantial group of eighteenth-century thinkers, among whom the most original was without doubt Ferdinando Galiani, who even succeeded in disseminating his ideas, via Condillac, beyond Italy. Cesare Beccaria, Pietro Verri, Gianmaria Ortes, Antonio Genovesi, and Gaetano Filangieri were all part, to some degree or other, of the great enlightenment movement, even if their contributions were often of an eclectic and politically pragmatic nature. During the first half of the nineteenth century, a number of thinkers fought for a 'freer' and more modern economy: these included Melchiorre Gioia, GianDomenico Romagnosi, Carlo Cattaneo, Cesare Correnti, Angelo Messedaglia, Francesco Fuoco, Antonio Scialoja (who later became Minister of Finance and Minister of Education of the Italian Kingdom), and, most important of all, Francesco Ferrara. Their influence on Italian economic culture went far beyond academic circles and aristocratic drawing-rooms, as a result of the vast propaganda campaign conducted by some of them: in particular, involving publications such as *Il Caffè*, a newspaper founded by Beccaria and Verri in June 1764, the *Annali universali di statistica*, a review started by Gioia and Romagnosi in 1824, which was to survive until the year 1871, and *Il Politecnico*, another review founded by Cattaneo in 1839, which had the following to say in the preface to the first number: 'At this point in time, the need to promote all forms of industry is of paramount importance'.[37]

These ties were undoubtedly responsible, in large part, for the continued existence of Italy's close relationship with the rest of Europe, and they enabled the country to set out on the road to economic recovery, after the low point reached half-way through the seventeenth century. This was to represent a turning-point, and the economy subsequently began to show some positive signs of revival, even if progress often proceeded at a painstakingly slow pace, while during the same period the demographic problem once again was of critical importance. The population in 1700 was about one million more than it had been in 1600, at that time 12 million, and which had fallen to 11 million by 1660. From then on, there was a gradual and fairly constant rise in population, due, among other things, to the virtual disappearance of the plague, and by 1800 it had reached 18.5 million. This figure was to reach nearly 26 million by the time of Italian unification.

The population, which had doubled in the space of about 150 years, was fed

[36] A. Caracciolo, 'La storia economica', in *La storia d'Italia. Dal primo Settecento all'unità* (Turin, Einaudi, 1973), 692.

[37] See the essay by C. Cattaneo in C. G. Lacaita, *Sviluppo e cultura. Alle origini dell'Italia industriale* (Milan, Angeli, 1984).

by an increasingly productive agricultural system, although it has to be said that in many areas the growth in agricultural output was due more to the cultivation of previously uncultivated land or to an intensification of productive efforts rather than to an increase in productivity itself.[38] The diversity of agricultural production in different areas of Italy, whose origins can be traced back to the late Middle Ages if not before, continued to increase. Exactly the same

cultivation of new land had to be placed in different contexts. On the one hand, there was the straightforward destruction of forest and heathland, which meant that land traditionally reserved for 'public use' or for grazing animals on was sacrificed in order to increase grain production by a few hundredweight; on the other hand, there were cases of reclaimed land, where, for example, swamps were dried out and ambitious canal systems were built, or wetlands were reconverted to the production of forage and rice, or hilly terrain was rendered cultivable through costly investment in terracing and the growing of particular crops that improved the overall quality of the soil.[39]

In the Po Plain, and in Lombardy in particular, new crops were introduced, such as maize,[40] rice, and mulberry bushes, as well as flax and hemp (largely in the area around Bologna), while hilly areas saw the introduction of mulberry bushes, vines, fruit trees, and olive trees, according to each particular area's climate. In the South, however, the existing cereal monoculture was only partially complemented by the production of olive oil and wine and by the introduction of some citrus fruit groves in coastal areas, while the cultivation of mulberry bushes, and with it the breeding of silkworms, become less and less widespread, and became confined to a limited number of areas, most of which were to be found in Calabria.

Thus it can be seen that any discussion of the 'Italian economy' becomes more and more difficult, as the few scholars who have attempted to give an overall picture of economic development in Italy between the eighteenth and mid-nineteenth century have hastened to point out.[41] This is the main reason why writings in Italian economic history of this period are strongly tied to the economic and institutional reality of the pre-unification Italian States. Such strong structural differences were not even really affected by the arrogant forays into Italian political life made by representatives of the French Revolution, despite the fact that this historic event led to the final demise of the feudal

[38] L. Dal Pane, *Storia del lavoro in Italia dagli inizi del secolo XVIII al 1815* (Milan, 1958).

[39] Caracciolo, 'La storia economica', 545.

[40] On the cultivation of maize in Lombardy, see G. Coppola, *Il mais nell'economia agricola lombarda* (Bologna, Il Mulino, 1979).

[41] Caracciolo has the following to say on the matter, in 'La storia economica' (pp. 511–12): 'Our basic belief is that a single, structurally unified Italian economy (or at least one that is composed of fairly homogeneous parts) simply does not exist: there are, instead, a number of Italian economies, which often either exist in isolation, or when they do come into contact, all this contact does is to accentuate the respective differences and the "dualisms" of Italian economic life.' See also M. Romani, *Storia economica d'Italia nel XIX secolo*, pt. I (Milan, Giuffré, 1968).

privileges still in existence and to the partial privatization of Church and State land, together with varied attempts at setting up reform-minded governments.

We can therefore complete this section with a look at the main economic developments that took place in the various pre-unification States during the period between the end of the eighteenth century and the year of unification.[42] Economic diversification was, of course, more marked than that suggested by the political fragmentation which had become increasingly evident during the course of history, and which was formally recognized, with certain important modifications, by the rulings of the Congress of Vienna. Nevertheless, the articulation of the analysis offered in this chapter must avoid unnecessary details; we must, however, be aware that in many ways the only 'natural' dimension to the economic history of Italy remains that of the city and its hinterland, even long after unification.

1.1. *The Sardinian States*

Three regions were grouped together under this title—Piedmont, Liguria, and Sardinia—each having a rather different history, and with only the first two having formed an interconnected economic whole in the period prior to unification. Feudalism was abolished in Sardinia during the period 1835–9,[43] but in 1840 more than half of registered land had still not been privatized. *Latifundia* still dominated the economic panorama, and transhumant sheep-farming was the principal economic activity, with the lowest yield per acre in Italy, equal to one-tenth of average yield in Lombardy (see Table 0.1). The island's important mineral resources (in particular, zinc and lead) were exploited by either Genoese or foreigners (Belgians, French, English, and Germans), although this mainly took place after unification. This picture of the island's extremely low productive capacity was to change only marginally in the period up to the middle of the twentieth century.

While there can be no doubt that during the eighteenth century, wealth in Piedmont and Liguria (still politically separate States) was concentrated in the hands of the aristocracy, there is ample documentation to show that the middle classes' influence was growing, as was the interest of the aristocracy in economic activity when it involved agricultural improvements, manufacturing activity, or financial and commercial investment.[44] From a glance at the lists of Piedmontese taxpayers in the years 1734 to 1795, one notices a growth in

[42] I will not go into the developments of the dukedoms of Parma–Piacenza and Modena–Reggio for reasons of brevity: the agricultural evolution of these areas was similar to that of the Po Plain as a whole, whereas there was very little progress in other areas, with the exception of traditional artisan crafts and commerce tied to agriculture.

[43] Cf. G. Sotgiu, *Storia della Sardegna Sabauda* (Bari, Laterza, 1984).

[44] V. L. Bulferetti, *Agricultura, industria e commercio in Piemonte nel secolo XVIII* (Turin, 1963); L. Bulferetti and C. Costantini, *Industria e commercio in Liguria nell'età del Risorgimento 1700–1861* (Milan, 1966).

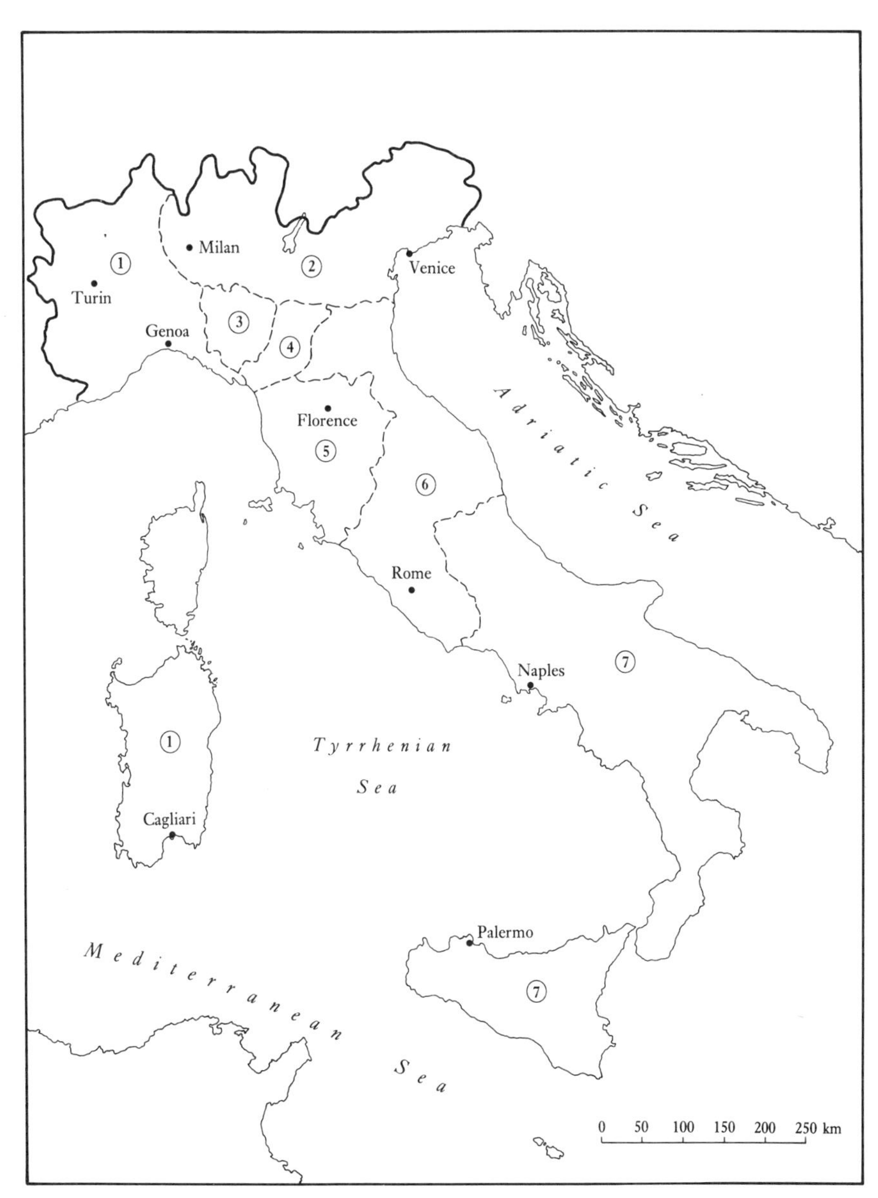

1. Sardinian States (or Kingdom of Sardenia)
2. Lombardy-Veneto Kingdom (under Austria)
3. Dukedom of Parma
4. Dukedom of Modena
5. Grand Duchy of Tuscany
6. Papal State
7. Kingdom of the two Sicilies

Fig. 0.2 Italy after the Vienna Congress, 1875

Table 0.1. The Italian States at the unification of the country

	Population in 1861 (millions)	Value of agricultural production (around 1857): Total (million lire)	Value of agricultural production (around 1857): Per hectare (lire)	Railways in operation in 1859 (km)	Roads in 1863 (km)	Letters received per inhabitant 1862	Illiteracy in 1861 (%)	Enrolment rate in primary schools % 1861
	(1)	(2)	(3)	(4)	(5)	(6)	(7)	(8)
Piedmont	2.8	516	169	850	16,500	6.1	54.2	93
Liguria	0.8							
Sardinia	0.6	48	23	—	986	. . .	89.7	29
Lombardy	3.3	435	238	522	20,901	5.3	53.7	90
Veneto	2.3	270	128		. . .	. . .	75.0	. . .
Parma–Modena	0.9	197	174	—	25,766[b]	2.7[b]	78.0	36
Papal State	3.2	264[a]	68[a]	101			80.0[c]	25–35[c]
Tuscany	1.9	242	117	257	12,381	3.1	74.0	32
Kingdom of the Two Sicilies	9.2	870	81	99	13,787	1.6	87.0	18[d]
Italy	25.0	2,842	104	1,829	. . .	. . .	75.0	43

Table 0.1 (contd.)

	Imports in 1858 (million lire)	Exports in 1858 (million lire)	Silk in 1857[e]: No. of basins in operation	Silk in 1857[e]: Value of raw silk produced (million lire)	Cotton spindles around 1867	Wool looms in 1866	Workers employed in metal-engineering industry, 1861	Value of paper produced, 1858 (million lire)	Leather produced (tons)
	(9)	(10)	(11)	(12)	(13)	(14)	(15)	(16)	(17)
Piedmont	303	217	25,000	59	197,000	2,700	2,204[f]	6.4	4,150
Liguria						350	2,255		

Sardinia	18	20	—	—	—	—	40	—	—
Lombardy	86	127	34,627	80	123,046	550	1,522	4.5	1,909
Veneto	90	60	20,000	33	30,000[c]	850	1,250	. . .	2,150
Parma–Modena	44	33	2,500	6	—	—	100	1.5	796[b] (Parma–Modena and Papal States)
Papal States	72	63	5,000	12	30,000[c]	400[b]	759	1.8	
Tuscany	79	45	3,300	8	3,000[c]	600	1,147	2.2	1,286
Kingdom of the Two Sicilies	128	139	14,400	35	70,000[c]	1,640	2,500	3.0	4,083
Italy	820	703	104,827	233	453,000[g]	7,100[g]	11,777	19.4	14,374

[a] The estimate offered by P. Maestri for the Papal State, based on private information, is certainly undervalued, but all the other estimates would also need a thorough reworking.

[b] Latium excluded.

[c] Approximate values.

[d] Sicily excluded.

[e] Output before the decline due to cocoon disease; the subsequent revival of production strengthens Lombardy's primacy and sees the decline of the South as a producer.

[f] According to Abrate, *L'industria siderurgica in Piemonte dal 1831 al 1861* (Turin, 1961), the metal-engineering industry in Piedmont had employed about 7,500 units.

[g] Rounded total.

. . . indicates a figure is missing.
— indicates a figure does not exist.

Sources: (1) SVIMEZ, *Un secolo di statistiche italiane: nord e sud 1861–1961* (Rome, 1961); (2)–(6) C. Correnti and P. Maestri, *Annuario statistico italiano* (Turin, 1864); (7)–(8) V. Zamagni, 'Istruzione e sviluppo economico: il caso italiano 1861–1913', in G. Toniolo (ed.), *L'economia italiana 1861–1940* (Bari, Laterza, 1978); (9)–(10) V. Zamagni, 'Ferrovie e integrazione del mercato nazionale nell'Italia post-unitaria', in *Studi in onore di Gino Barbieri*, iii (Salerno, 1983); (11)–(13) P. Maestri, 'Della industria manifatturiera in Italia', *Rivista contemporanea* (1858); P. Maestri, *L'Italia economica nel 1868* (Florence, 1868), 198; (15) F. Giordano, *L'industria del ferro in Italia* (Turin, 1864). Data coincide with those published in *Atti Parlamentari*, Camera dei deputati, session 1865–6, Documents no. 24A, 70–89; (16) P. Maestri, 'Della industria manifatturiera', 1859, 341; (17) P. Maestri, *L'Italia economica*, 199.

wealth among bankers, silk merchants, wool and cotton producers and salesmen, and wholesale merchants. It would seem that wealth in the Piedmont region was not as concentrated as in other regions, thus favouring a wider circulation of non-agricultural goods.[45] In Genoa, on the other hand, the enormous wealth that had been accumulated in the hands of the few was invested in the main European markets, after the downfall in trading activity. The Genoese were considered to be second only to the Dutch, and on a par with the Genevans, when it came to lending money.[46] However, the French Revolution put an end almost completely to such speculative financial activity, and in doing so it led to a grave crisis in the Genoese economy, which only recovered after Carlo Alberto's reforms during the 10 years from 1840 to 1850 had accelerated the process of economic unification between Piedmont and Liguria.[47]

The economy of these two regions subsequently took a qualitative leap forward in the two decades leading up to Italian unification. Agriculture continued to improve slowly, particularly in the plains, with the introduction of fertilizers and the expansion of irrigation and drainage schemes; however, the most important innovations were seen in the non-agricultural sectors. The mechanized spinning of cotton and wool became increasingly more common, and mechanized weaving also started to catch on (Table 0.1 gives a comparative picture, in quantitative terms, just before unification). The metallurgical industry's work-force reached the figure of 15,000, for the most part concentrated in the cities of Genoa and Turin, where important factories such as Ansaldo (opened in 1853), Cantiere della Foce, and the Arsenal were all situated, with their collective work-force of between 3,000 and 4,000 workers. They built ships, engines, weapons, railway coaches, and even the occasional locomotive, using a number of modern iron-casting furnaces.[48]

A great deal of capital went into the transport sector, and 40 per cent of the railway network already operative in Italy in the year of unification was located in the two regions, while Liguria's share of Italian freight amounted to one-quarter of total tonnage. In the banking sector, those private bankers already operating in this pre-unification period, who were to continue operations after unification (including the Genoese bankers Oneto, Parodi, and Croce—and those from Turin, like Barbaroux, Casana, Ceriana, Defernex, Deslex, Marsaglia, Nigra, and Segre), were joined by a joint-stock company, the Banca di Genova, which was founded under this name in 1845 and then amalgamated with a newly founded Turinese bank in 1849, to form the Banca Nazionale

[45] G. Prato, *La vita economica in Piemonte a mezzo secolo XVIII* (Turin, 1908).

[46] For a discussion of the financial activity of the Genoans following the decline in commercial activity, see G. Felloni, *Gli investimenti finanziari genovesi in Europa tra il seicento e la restaurazione* (Milan, Giuffré, 1971).

[47] G. Doria, *Investimenti e sviluppo economico a Genova alla vigilia della prima guerra mondiale. Le premesse (1815–1882)*, i (Milan, Giuffré, 1969).

[48] B. Caizzi, *Storia dell'industria italiana dal XVIII secolo ai giorni nostri* (Turin, UTET, 1965).

degli Stati Sardi, under the Genoese director Carlo Bombrini. It became the most important issuing bank in unified Italy, changing its name firstly to the Banca Nazionale nel Regno d'Italia, and then to the Banca d'Italia, as we shall see later on.

The period prior to unification, and in particular the 1850s when Cavour repeatedly held key positions in the government of the Sardinian States, saw the adoption of an 'English-style' economic policy, with a tendency towards the promotion of 'free trade' in the commercial field, together with the growth of the educational sector (especially that concerned with professional training) and the expansion of the railway network. Cavour, however, was more than the familiar figure one has of skilful politician: he can also be seen as symbolizing the attitude of rich, Piedmontese landowners, who took an interest in economic activity, both agricultural and non-agricultural, in order to increase personal wealth and the circulation of riches.[49]

1.2. *Lombardy*

Since the Austrian State of Lombardy-Veneto represented the amalgamation of two regions that continued to develop separately before and after Italian unification, an individual summary of each region will be given here, starting with Lombardy.

Repeated investment in irrigation projects across the Lombard Plain, together with the spread of mulberry groves and silkworm farming, particularly in the hills, had made agriculture highly intensive in Lombardy (as can be seen from the high yield per hectare at the time of unification).[50] The beneficial reforms introduced by the Austrians during the eighteenth century, and in particular Maria Theresa's land-register, had contributed towards the region's orderly growth. Agriculture provided the basis for other, non-agricultural activities, such as cheese-making, rice-cleaning, and, above all, silk production, with the area around Como maintaining its strong silk-weaving tradition. One statistic from 1829 showed that 14 'silk dealers and bankers' together with 13 'silk dealers and commission agents' were among the richest non-landowners in Milan at that time. In fact, at the time of unification, the region of Lombardy produced 40 per cent of total silk cocoons and one-third of Italian raw silk; there was a total of 94 weaving-plants, with 5,447 looms and 8,000 workers,[51] and raw silk constituted 86 per cent of total exports during the period from

[49] It is a well-known fact that Cavour took a personal interest in exploiting his own personal landholdings to the greatest possible degree, and that he was also directly involved in railway investments. See e.g. R. Romeo, *Cavour e il suo tempo, 1810–1854* (3 vols., Turin, Einaudi, 1969); and also M. Einaudi, 'Le prime ferrovie piemontesi e il Conte di Cavour', *Rivista di storia economica*, 3 (1938); and R. Romeo, *Vita di Cavour* (Bari, Laterza, 1984).

[50] See M. Romani, *L'agricultura in Lombardia dall'età delle riforme al 1859. Strutture, organizzazione sociale e tecnica* (Milan, Vita e Pensiero, 1957), for an analysis of agriculture in Lombardy before unification.

[51] P. Maestri, 'Della industria manifatturiera in Italia', *Rivista contemporanea*, 1858.

1851 to 1859.[52] According to Caizzi, 'agricultural and commercial activity provided the easiest paths to economic wealth in Lombardy at that time',[53] and even the outbreak of a serious silkworm disease—pebrine, which made the silkworm rigid and thus prevented it from forming its cocoon—did not compromise this situation very much. Although the silk sector went through a period of crisis, it managed to recover within the space of about 10 years (thus taking it into the post-unification era), by means of the substitution of an imported oriental seed variety for the infected local seed.

Although the Lombard economy was not in a position to reap the benefits of the geographical presence of a state capital, like Naples or Turin, it was nevertheless strongly diversified. Cotton-mills were already in operation[54]—see Table 0.1 for figures—as was the metallurgical industry, although this consisted largely of small or medium-sized firms. Firms such as Elvetica and Grondona in Milan, Como's Regazzoni, the Brescian arms manufacturers, and the iron manufacturers in the towns of Lecco and Dongo, where Giorgio Enrico Falk arrived from Alsace, and whose son later set up the Lombard Iron and Steel Works in Sesto San Giovanni (Milan). The road network was already very good at that time, thanks to considerable investment made during Austrian dominion, and although the construction of a rail network was at a very early stage, it made up about 30 per cent of the national total, in terms of kilometres, at the time of unification. Finally, the spread of education through schooling and the publication of newspapers and periodicals[55] needs to be mentioned, as does the Lombards' passion for technical invention (witnessed by the very early introduction of gas lighting, of steam navigation on the lakes, and of textile machinery), something that was to become a distinctive feature of life in Lombardy, as we shall see later on.[56]

Despite the fact that Austrian influence had been beneficial during the eighteenth century, the Lombard middle classes (made up mainly of rich tenant farmers and traders) joined together with the progressive aristocracy in the struggle against Austria, as the latter was seen as the principal obstacle to a better use of the region's economic potential.[57] This potential had hardly been

[52] I. A. Glazier, 'Il commercio estero del Regno Lombardo–Veneto dal 1815 al 1865', *Archivio economico dell'unificazione italiana*, 15 (1966).

[53] B. Caizzi, *L'economia lombarda durante la Restaurazione 1814–1859* (Milan, 1972), 102.

[54] S. Zaninelli, *L'industria del cotone in Lombardia dalla fine del Settecento all'unificazione del Paese* (Turin, ILTE, 1967).

[55] K. R. Greenfield, *Economics and Liberalism in the Risorgimento. A Study of Nationalism in Lombardy 1815–1848* (Baltimore, 1934). Working people were very much involved in the uprisings of the Risorgimento in Lombardy.

[56] N. Quilici, in his study *Origine, sviluppo e insufficienza della borghesia italiana* (Ferrara, 1932), sees the active economic role played by Lombard aristocrats as being the result of a lack of alternatives in the diplomatic and military world.

[57] R. Ciasca, 'L'evoluzione economica della Lombardia dagli inizi del secolo al 1860', in *La Cassa di Risparmio delle Provincie Lombarde nella evoluzione economica della regione* (Milan, 1923), 386–7.

exploited at all, if one considers the high level of per capita bank deposits existing at the time, together with the correspondingly low level of investment in joint-stock companies.

1.3. *The Veneto*

The economic history of the Veneto had been dominated since the seventeenth century by the decline of the naval and commercial strength of Venice, and this continued to be the case throughout the eighteenth century. As a consequence, guilds declined in importance, while the landed interests of the Venetian aristocracy and middle classes never prospered as they should have done, due to the relative lack of interest shown by these absentee landlords, who at the most spent a few summer months in their beautiful villas in the country.[58] With the Veneto passing into Austrian hands, agriculture began to show some signs of improvement, and a new land-register was established by the Austrians in 1839; however, this proved too late for it to produce results analogous to those given by the land-register set up by Maria Theresa of Austria in Lombardy almost a century earlier. The intensification of agricultural production was significant,[59] but there was no solid mercantile class involved in the exploitation of agricultural production, as was the case in Lombardy.

However, the most important element missing from the economic picture was that of productive diversification: admittedly, Venice still had its Arsenal, 'the largest factory in the entire State at the time of the Venetian Republic',[60] but this had been greatly reduced in size by the Austrians; a candle factory had been set up at Mira in 1835, and this was to have some economic success; Murano continued to be an important centre for traditional glass production; silk-throwing, wine and beer production, and other artisan trades existed in various areas throughout the Veneto. Nevertheless, the only factories of any importance in existence before unification were the wool-mills belonging to the Marzotto and Rossi families, and a couple of small cotton-mills.

1.4. *Tuscany*

The Austrian princes who governed Tuscany from 1765 to 1859 certainly left their mark on the region and its subsequent development, through their adoption of a policy of prudent reformism. This reformism, which rendered the existing economic equilibrium tolerable—an equilibrium involving the share-cropping system, with a mixture of cereals or leguminous crops cultivated in the same fields where tree crops were also planted—was responsible for the

[58] M. Berengo, *La società veneta alla fine del '700* (Florence, 1956), and D. Beltrami, *Storia della popolazione di Venezia dalla fine del secolo XVI alla caduta della Repubblica* (Padua, 1954).

[59] M. Berengo, *L'agricoltura veneta dalla caduta della Repubblica all'unità* (Milan, 1963).

[60] G. Zalin, *Dalla bottega alla fabbrica. La fenomenologia industriale nelle province venete tra '500 e '900* (Verona, Libreria Universitaria Editrice, 1987), 228.

slowing down of possible innovation; innovation which perhaps could[61] have led to an increase in agricultural production, thus making it possible to accumulate more capital and to expand markets.[62]

Apart from agriculture, some commercial and artisan activities continued to survive, but very few real manufacturing firms flourished in Tuscany, despite the geographically central position of the region and its abundance of raw materials (iron, copper, lead, marble, mercury, and borax) which were largely exported in their raw state.[63] There were some textile factories, some blast-furnaces (mostly government-owned); there was Marquess Ginori's pottery at Doccia (founded in 1738), which was later to merge with the Milanese pottery of Richard to form the well-known Richard–Ginori company; the Cini paper-mill (Cini's son Giovanni Cosimo was to become a famous financier after unification); the boracic acid factory founded in 1818 by the French refugee Francesco de Larderel; Pignone's casting furnace; and an extensive network of home-workers involved in the weaving of fabrics and straw. Not only were manufacturing activities not encouraged in Tuscany, they were positively discouraged by the region's free trade policy (the only one in Italy), whereby 'low-priced industrial products were imported into the state from Northern Europe, and in particular from England, thus leaving very little space for local industry, which could not exploit the internal market for its expansion'.[64]

The only place that benefited from this policy of favouring free trade was the port of Leghorn, which had become a free port in 1676, thus 'becoming one of the most important Mediterranean markets in a very brief space of time, a meeting place for rich merchants and unscrupulous dealers from every part of Europe and the Orient, as well as a kind of wealthy, cosmopolitan island—a separate State within the State', as Mori observed.[65] Several railway lines had already been built prior to unification, although they were limited to the area around Leghorn. As for the great Tuscan tradition in the field of banking, of the several important structures that had survived, hardly any had been modernized in keeping with historical developments.[66]

[61] The key-word is 'perhaps', since the Tuscan agrarian world is traditionally part of a wider Mediterranean panorama, where plains and watercourses are few and far between, and where continental 'high farming' techniques have traditionally been difficult to adopt.

[62] These hypotheses are developed in C. Pazzagli, *L'agricoltura toscana nella prima metà dell'800* (Florence, 1973), and in G. Giorgetti, *Capitalismo e agricoltura in Italia* (Rome, Editori Riuniti, 1977). I. Imberciadori, nevertheless, underlines the innovative efforts made by Cosimo Ridolfi and Raffaele Lambruschini, through their involvement in the periodical publication *Giornale agrario toscano*, founded in 1827, and in the context of the Florentine Academy of Agrarian and Economic Studies, see I. Imberciadori, *Economia toscana nel primo '800*, Florence (1961).

[63] G. Parenti, 'Il commercio estero del Granducato di Toscana dal 1851 al 1859', *Archivio economico dell'unificazione italiana* 8 (1959).

[64] G. Mori, 'Dall'unità alla guerra: aggregazione e disaggregazione di un'area regionale', in G. Mori (ed.), *Storia d'Italia. Le regioni dall'unità ad oggi. La Toscana* (Turin, Einaudi, 1986), 79.

[65] Ibid. 58–9.

[66] See e.g. the history of the Monte dei Paschi, in G. Conti, *La politica aziendale di un istituto di credito immobiliare: il Monte dei Paschi di Siena dal 1815 al 1872* (Florence, Olschki, 1985).

1.5. *The Papal State*

There was great economic variety within this State: from rich, capitalistic agriculture in the Bologna area (even though farms at this time were sometimes cultivated by sharecroppers, usually owning some farm capital), to the sharecropping system of the Marches and northern Umbria, and the *latifundia* of Latium and southern Umbria; the agricultural sector witnessed greatly diversified levels of productivity, which in turn had differing effects on the economic system as a whole. If we then turn to the city of Rome, we discover a singular kind of economy, with one-half of the population begging for a living,[67] while the other half (with the exception of the aristocracy and the clergy—who owned all the buildings in the city together with extensive farmland) included all those who lived from services provided for the rich, as well as for visiting pilgrims and foreigners (hoteliers and petty traders).

Manufacturing activity was almost non-existent: this was even true of the Bologna area, where silk production had declined during the eighteenth century (in contrast to its expansion in Lombardy), and in doing so, largely influenced the destiny of the whole city, which saw its industry 'reduced to a bare skeleton as a result of the destruction of a thousand fortunes' during the first half of the nineteenth century.[68] De Marco believes that there was a substantial decline also in the Papal State's other, non-agricultural activities during the first half of the nineteenth century, as witnessed by the fall in the number of factories producing woollen fabrics, the main manufactured product at the time. Scholars all agree that the blame lay with the papal administration, which had given exclusive power to the clergy, and which continued to operate using clientelistic methods, with only a very tentative opening-up witnessed during the years immediately prior to unification.

1.6. *The Kingdom of the Two Sicilies*

Although it cannot be said that a truly feudal system existed in southern Italy either before or after formal abrogation (in 1806 on the mainland, in 1812 in Sicily), nevertheless, the power wielded by southern 'barons' was still

[67] D. Demarco, *Il tramonto dello Stato Pontificio. Il Papato di Gregorio XVI* (Turin, 1949). The author adds: 'When charity failed to help out, the government tried to alleviate unemployment by getting the unemployed to do meaningless jobs' (pp. 97–8). See also M. Carnevale and A. Caracciolo, *Lo Stato Pontificio da Martino V a Pio IX* (Turin, UTET, 1978), and R. De Felice, *Aspetti e momenti della vita economica di Roma e del Lazio nei secoli XVIII e XIX* (Rome, 1965).

[68] L. Dal Pane, *Economia e società a Bologna nell'età del Risorgimento* (Bologna, Patron, 1969), 398. There are several accounts of begging in the city of Bologna: e.g. those given by Ricardo, in 1822, and by Goncourt, from 1855, which are cited in Zangheri, 'Bologna nell'anno dell'Unità', in R. Zangheri (ed.), *Bologna* (Bari, Laterza, 1986), 45. Agricultural investment had, however, been increased in the Bologna area during the first half of the 19th cent.

formidable. Villani estimates that at the end of the eighteenth century, when rent and other forms of income are taken into consideration, about 60 per cent of national income produced in the South went into the hands of the clergy and the families of southern barons, who numbered about 650, and that 90 of them 'controlled' two-thirds of the Kingdom's population, while about 20 'controlled' one-quarter of it.[69] De Meo draws a similar conclusion from his study of the South, where he perceives a massive concentration of wealth in the hands of the few.[70] The rural, landowning middle class struggled to affirm itself in this environment, and although property occasionally changed hands, the way that it was managed invariably remained the same. *Latifundia* dominated the agricultural panorama, most of them concentrating on cereal production using a work-force consisting of day labourers who spent most of the year unemployed. Yield per hectare was barely one-third of that produced in Lombardy, and the available work-force was severely underutilized, as the labourers lived together in impoverished villages miles away from the fields where they worked, and getting to work each morning often involved walking for hours. This was therefore a form of agriculture which could certainly support a few rich families, but which did not lead to any growth in the domestic market, either in terms of agricultural products—there was no opportunity for technological modernization—or of other consumer goods, as farm-workers were far too poor to be part of such a market. If this situation, which lay at the roots of the South's inability to play a positive role in the economic development of post-unification Italy,[71] was partly due to climatic and geographical conditions that were certainly not as favourable to 'high farming' as those present in the Po Plain, it cannot be said that these conditions inevitably condemned the South to its fate. As we have seen, historical events played their part in the development of the South, leading to the disappearance of silk production, together with the almost exclusive concentration on cereal production for the internal market, with only a limited production of olive oil and wine, together with citrus fruit in coastal regions; there was no attempt to make infrastructural investment in irrigation projects, for example, or in projects aimed at increasing productivity. If the agricultural fates of Lombardy, which in ancient times had consisted of nothing but unproductive heathland, and Sicily, once the grain store of Italy, were reversed, then the responsibility for this lies mainly with the men who made this history—from both within these regions and from outside—rather than with nature.

As agriculture, not very diversified and productive, was increasingly

[69] P. Villani, *Mezzogiorno tra riforme e rivoluzione* (Bari, Laterza, 1973), 195–7.

[70] G. De Meo, 'Distribuzione della richezza e composizione demografica in alcune città dell'Italia meridionale alla metà del secolo XVIII', *Annali di Statistica* 6 (1931). The author looks at the communes of Castellamare di Stabia, Foggia, and Barletta, and shows that the aristocracy and the Church between them received some 64% of total income.

[71] As we shall see in more detail later on.

incapable of providing merchandise for export abroad,[72] due to the pressure of domestic demand from a growing population, it hardly required a modern commercial and financial network to support it; similarly, an efficient transport system would have been superfluous in the circumstances. In fact, the road network was extremely poor,[73] as were the railways (only 99 km. of track had been put into use before unification), and banking facilities within the State were very primitive. There were no savings banks or joint-stock banks, and only a few private banks, together with two public banks, the Bank of Naples and the Bank of Sicily. These public banks only had one branch each at the time, in Bari and Messina respectively. There was also a network of grain banks (about 1,200 it would seem), which lent seed to peasant farmers on a barter basis.[74]

Industrial developments merit special attention here. It has been said that during the 1820s the Neapolitan government had attempted to encourage the industrialization of the kingdom by means of measures such as the reform of import tariffs, which were changed in order to protect domestic industry, a policy of public procurement and the public management of certain companies, such as the ironworks in Mongiana and the engineering works in Pietrarsa.[75] In fact, the area between Naples and Salerno did have a certain concentration of textile factories and metallurgy works at the time of unification,[76] although their importance should not be overvalued. The total number of mechanical cotton-spindles that had been installed was less than those present in Lombardy alone (see Table 0.1), the woollen-looms, most of them mechanical, numbered only half those present in Piedmont–Liguria, and the number of workers in the large metallurgy factories was only one-third of the estimated number employed in the same industry in Piedmont–Liguria.[77]

The really striking thing about these industrial developments, however, is the almost total dependence on the imported talent of foreign entrepreneurs: mainly Swiss in the textile industry (Vonwiller, Escher, Mayer, Egg, Zublin,

[72] A. Graziani, 'Il commercio estero del Regno delle due Sicilie dal 1832 al 1858', *Archivio economico dell'unificazione italiana*, 10 (1960).

[73] V. Giura, in 'Vie di comunicazione e vita economica nel mezzogiorno in età moderna', in *Mercati e consumi. Organizzazione e qualificazione del commercio in Italia dal XII al XX secolo* (Bologna, Analisi, 1986), writes: 'In my opinion, there can be little doubt that the South of Italy no longer possessed what could be really called a road network, from the fall of the Roman empire onwards' (p. 242). The great disadvantage for the South arising from this was partially alleviated by the use of coasting vessels.

[74] Cf. G. Muzzioli, *Banche e agricoltura. Il credito all'agricoltura italiana dal 1861 al 1940* (Bologna, Il Mulino, 1983), 30. The lack of banks was also responsible for the very low velocity of circulation of money (together with the weak capital mobility). Money in circulation in the Neapolitan provinces has been calculated as having been twice that in the rest of the country at the time of unification. Cf. D. Demarco, *Il crollo del Regno delle due Sicilie*, i. *La struttura sociale* (Naples, 1960), 86.

[75] Caracciolo, 'La storia economica', 691.

[76] F. Milone, 'Le industrie del Mezzogiorno all'unificazione dell'Italia', in *Studi in onore di G. Luzzatto*, iii (Milan, 1950).

[77] L. De Rosa, *Iniziative e capitale straniero nell'industria metalmeccanica del Mezzogiorno 1840–1904* (Naples, Giannini, 1968).

Wenner), and English in the metallurgy industry (Pattison and Guppy). Without doubt there were also a large number of foreign technicians who set up businesses in Piedmont and Liguria. However, they were not alone, and the local communities produced entrepreneurs who worked alongside the foreigners; in the Naples area, this was not the case, and there were very few local entrepreneurs (Polsinelli, Zino, and Ianuzzi were among the few). One has the impression that these manufacturing activities were something totally alien to the local economic milieu (as such, the Bourbon State often represented the main or sole market for such activities), in the same way that the railways were, the latter having been entirely financed and built by the French. In reality, 'Neapolitan industry was neither created by nor a creator of a local entrepreneurial class', as Davis concludes in his study.[78] Those aristocrats, foreigners, and few local 'self-made men' who made up the class of rich southern traders preferred to make their money through dealing in foodstuffs, or from somewhat paltry (given the Neapolitan State's modest finances) governmental contracts, rather than upset the economic equilibrium which provided them with a generous livelihood. Davis is unfortunately right in concluding that 'in the hands of the Neapolitan entrepreneurial class, the behaviour and interests of the traditional landed classes (as illustrated by the Duke of Terranova's preoccupation with "playing the usual tricks at the expense of the gabelotti")[79] were allowed to permeate down into all areas of economic activity within the Kingdom, thus acting as an obstacle to every attempt to modernize economic life, and blocking any possible effort aimed at creating a modern and efficient state. In effect, the southern entrepreneurs and capitalists were perhaps the only ones to stand to gain from the perpetuation of backward economic, social and political conditions in the South.'[80]

At this point, the only thing that remains to be done is to look briefly at Table 0.1. Since national income figures for the different States prior to unification do not exist, and those figures that do exist for the newly unified Italy, starting from 1861, are highly unsatisfactory, there was no choice left but to try and put together a number of somewhat disparate figures collected from various sources pertaining to the years immediately before and after unification. All the indicators we have show that there was a scarcity of manufacturing activity in pre-unification Italy: compared with the half a million cotton-spindles that Italy

[78] J. Davis, 'Oligarchia capitalistica e immobilismo economico a Napoli (1815–1860)', *Studi Storici*, 16 (1975), 379.

[79] The 'gabelotto' or 'gabellotto' was a southern tenant who, unlike his counterpart in the northern Po Plain, made his earnings from acting as an intermediary between the absentee landlord and the peasant farmers, rather than from any entrepreneurial activity involving the rational utilization of the farmland in question.

[80] J. Davis, *Società e imprenditori nel Regno borbonico 1815–1860* (Bari, Laterza, 1979), 323; Eng. version, *Merchants, Monopolists, and Contractors: A Study of Economic Activity and Society in Bourbon Naples, 1815–1860* (London, 1981). Cf. also A. M. Banti, 'Gli imprenditori meridionali: razionalità e contesto', *Meridiana*, 6 (1989), and A. Massafra (ed.), *Il mezzogiorno preunitario. Economia, società e istituzioni* (Bari, Dedalo, 1988).

had around the year 1860, the United Kingdom could boast 30 million, while France had five and a half million, and Germany 2 million; while Italy produced about 30,000 tons of pig-iron, England produced 3.8 million tons, France 1 million, and Germany 600,000.[81]

Moreover, all the figures underline the already existing divide between certain Italian regions and others, with the three regions of Piedmont, Liguria, and Lombardy at the top, Sardinia and the Kingdom of the Two Sicilies right at the bottom, and the other regions somewhere in between. Here I would like to comment only on the more important data that have not already been taken into consideration above. Columns 9 and 10 show that a half of all foreign trade was conducted by the three regions of Piedmont, Liguria, and Lombardy, while the Kingdom of the Two Sicilies, which had once been able to boast a large export surplus, now had a balance between imports and exports. Looking at columns 7 and 8, we can see a strong gap, perhaps the most significant of all, between the rates of illiteracy and schooling in the North and South of the country. While 'only' half of the populations of Piedmont, Liguria, and Lombardy were illiterate, and nearly 100 per cent of children attended primary school, the situation in the South was extremely disconcerting from both points of view, so much so that one can conclude that only the clergy, the aristocracy, and the bureaucracy were able to read and write.[82] Illiteracy was also a grave problem in central and north-eastern Italy, due to the lack of interest in popular culture shown by both governments and citizens. All of this hardly represented a promising point of departure for social and economic progress within the new Kingdom.

2. A LONG-RUN VIEW: POPULATION AND INCOME FROM 1861 TO THE PRESENT

Looking at events from the long-term point of view, the modernization of Italy started after that of many other countries, but it did not require a longer period of time: it took about one century, which was made up of an initial period in which the foundations were laid, followed by a second, rather difficult period of consolidation (taking in two world wars, a very serious international crisis, and a dictatorial regime), and finally a third phase which saw things flourish very rapidly, in connection with a period of intense international expansion. Before

[81] Another accurate collection of quantitative data (including the most relevant 1861 population census aggregates) is to be found, together with interesting remarks, in G. Mori, 'Industrie senza industrializzazione. La penisola italiana dalla fine della dominazione francese all'unità nazionale (1815–1861)', *Studi Storici*, 30 (1989).

[82] According to my calculations, in V. Zamagni, 'Istruzione e sviluppo economico. Il caso italiano 1861–1913', in G. Toniolo (ed.), *L'economia italiana 1861–1940* (Bari, Laterza, 1978), 139. As Cipolla points out in his study, *Istruzione e sviluppo* (Turin, UTET, 1969; Eng. version, *Literacy and Development in the West*, Harmondsworth, Penguin Books, 1969), already about one-half of the populations of the two most educationally advanced countries, England and Holland, could read and write in the eighteenth century.

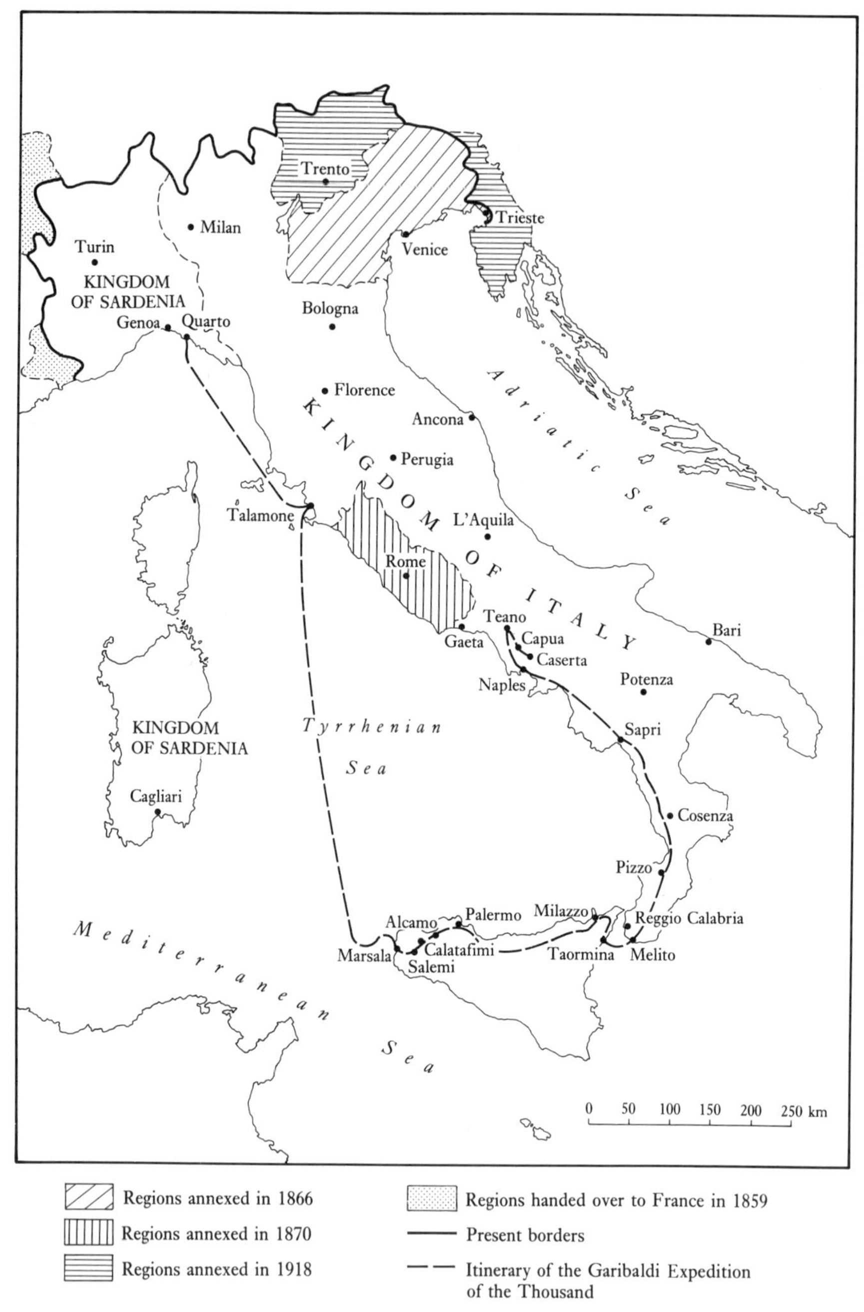

Fig. 0.3 Steps towards the unification of Italy

embarking on a detailed analysis of the various events that made up these historical phases, I would like to present a general overview, which will attempt to highlight the achievements and turning-points of the entire period under examination, and which should help to get rid of an illusory idea very dear to the hearts of certain economists: this is the idea that modern economic progress is self-propelling; it only needs to be started off, and it will continue under its own steam.

While it is undoubtedly true that once industrial, financial, and commercial structures have been organized under capitalism, they behave in accordance with dynamic laws of growth, none the less they exist in societies that are submitted to diverse politico-ideological pressures within an international context that can often produce highly unpredictable results. Consequently, strategies need to be continually revised, institutional changes are constantly necessary, and this in turn requires a continual input of fresh political ideas and commitment. If it is true to say that the beginning of any modernization process involves an enormous amount of effort in order to break the stranglehold of tradition, then it is no less true to say that the continuation of the initial momentum requires the co-ordination and finalizing of a great number of decisions taken at different levels, and this is often just as difficult. Unfortunately, many countries have yet to begin the transition from an economy based upon tradition to an industrialized one; others have begun the process, but have never managed to consolidate it; others again have completed the transition to an industrialized economy, but have proved incapable of withstanding subsequent challenges that have arisen.

In general, when a country is particularly successful at any one stage of the modernization process, it runs the risk of becoming too tied to those mechanisms which allowed it to build this success, and it thus becomes less flexible when it comes to those further changes that history continually demands. Paradoxically, we could say that the so-called 'second-best' countries find themselves motivated towards improving their position, while not having to pay the high price of leadership and of original research which world leaders are obliged to pay.

In order to compare different national examples of the modernization process, a suitable time-span is required (at least a century, as the modernization process has never been a fast one), remembering, however, to acknowledge the different features that characterize different stages of the process.

2.1. *A demographic profile of unified Italy*

Within the space of 120 years—from 1861 to 1981—the Italian population more than doubled, increasing at an annual growth rate of less than 1 per cent (see columns 1 and 2, Table 0.2), due to both a limited natural rate of growth and also the occurrence of large waves of emigration. During the same period, both the birth-rate and mortality-rate decreased (columns 3 and 5, Table 0.2), thus leading to a considerable increase in average life expectancy: from 30 years at the time of unification, to 75 years in 1981, and subsequently to 77 years at the time of writing (column 8, Table 0.2).

As can be seen from Table 0.3, Italy started off in 1861 from a relatively backward position compared with the other advanced countries of that period. Its birth- and mortality-rates were among the highest (including the infant mortality-rate, although this was higher not only in Russia but also in Germany and Austria); as a consequence, the average life expectancy at birth (or average life-span) was one of the lowest. One hundred and twenty years later, the birth- and mortality-rates are among the lowest of the advanced nations, and average

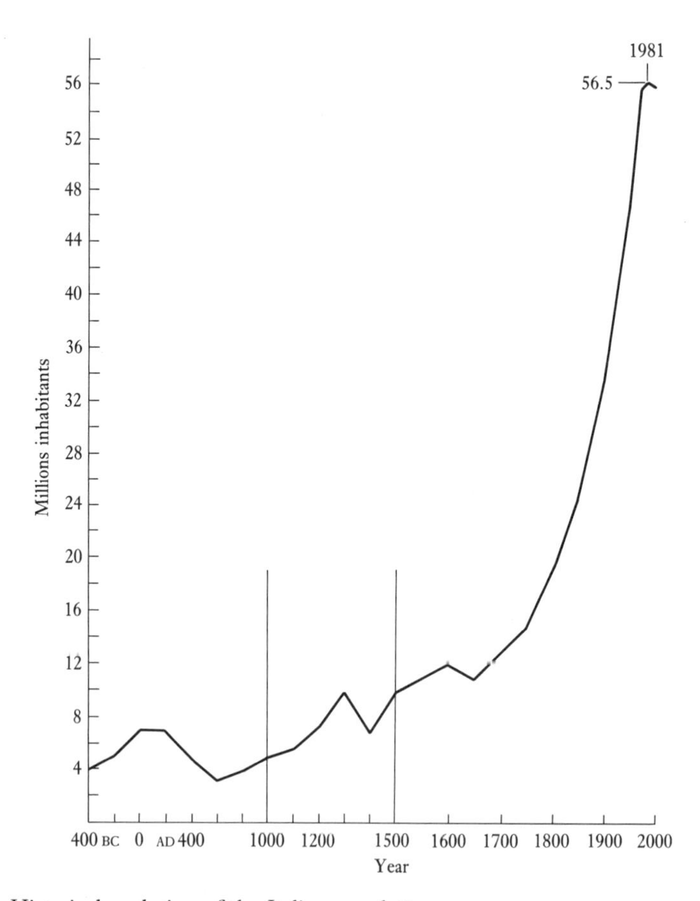

Fig. 0.4 Historical evolution of the Italian population

Table 0.2. Demographic figures, 1861–1981

	Population at present boundaries (000s) (1)	Annual growth rate of the pop. (%) 2)	Birth-rate (‰) (3)	Death-rate (‰) (4)	Mortality-rate during the the first year (‰) (5)	Marriage-rate (‰) (6)	Life expectancy at birth (7)	No. of members in the average family (8)
1861	25,756	—	—	—	—	—	30.5	—
1871	25,578	6.9	37.6	30.3	226.4	7.5	31.9	—
1881	29,278	6.0	36.9	29.9	214.8	7.7	35.4	4.5
1901	33,569	6.9	36.5	25.7	186.0	7.6	42.8	4.5
1911	36,184	6.5	32.7	21.6	159.7	7.7	46.6	4.5
1921	37,437	4.3	27.3	22.2	144.6	6.7	50.0	4.4
1931	40,921	8.7	28.6	16.9	122.6	8.3	54.9	4.2
1936	42,560	8.3	23.6	14.0	103.9	7.2	60.0	4.3
1951	47,159	6.9	20.5	12.7	92.4	7.2	65.5	4.0
1961	49,877	5.6	18.0	9.7	52.7	7.2	69.8	3.6
1971	53,725	7.5	16.8	9.7	28.5	7.6	72.0	3.3
1981	56,503	5.0	11.0	9.6	14.1	6.7	74.5	3.0

Source: ISTAT, *Sommario di statistiche storiche* (Rome, 1958 and 1983).

Table 0.3. An international comparison of demographic indices, 1861–1981

	Gt. Britain	France	Germany	Austria	Sweden	Spain	Russia	USA[l]	Japan	Italy
Birth-rate (‰)										
1861	34.6[a]	26.9	37.5	37.4[b]	32.6	39.0	49.7	41.4	...	38.0[c]
1913	24.1[a]	18.8	27.5	29.7[b]	23.2	30.6	43.1	39.5	...	31.7
1951	15.5[a]	19.5	15.7[d]	14.8	15.6	20.0	27.0	24.7	...	18.4
1985	13.3	13.9	9.6[d]	11.5	11.8	12.5	19.4	15.9	12.5	10.1
Death-rate (‰)										
1861	21.6[a]	23.2	25.6	29.8[b]	18.5	26.6	35.4	...	...	30.9[c]
1913	13.8[a]	17.7	15.0	20.3[b]	13.7	22.3	27.4	14.6	...	18.7
1951	12.5[a]	13.3	10.8[d]	12.7	9.9	11.5	9.7	7.9	...	10.3
1985	11.8	10.1	11.5[d]	11.8	11.3	7.8	10.6	8.7	6.2	9.5
Mortality-rate during the first year of life (‰)										
1861	153[a]	190	298[e]	264[b]	137	168	243[f]	...	...	232[e]
1913	108[a]	112	151	190[b]	70	155	237[g]	111	...	138
1951	30[a]	50	53[d]	124	22	63	84	25.8	...	67
1985	9.3	8	9.6[d]	11	6.7	10.5	28	10.5	6.0	10.9
Life expectancy at birth										
1861	42	...	42[h]	32[h]	...	...	...	...	...	30.5
1913	53	...	46[c]	40[i]	...	38[i]	32[m]	53	...	46.6
1951	69	...	66[d]	64	...	62	67[n]	69	61	65.5
1985	75	75	75[d]	74	77	76	70	75	78	77.3

[a] excluding Scotland; [b] besides Austria, this figure also includes Czechoslovakia, Dalmatia, Galicia, and Buchovine; [c] 1862; [d] West Germany; [e] 1863; [f] 1867; [g] 1911; [h] 1875; [i] 1900; [l] only whites; [m] 1895; [n] 1955.

Source: B. R. Mitchell, *European Historical Statistics, 1750–1970* (London, Macmillan, 1975); ISTAT, *Le regioni in cifre* (Rome, 1988)

life expectancy in Italy is among the highest, although differences between these nations are now relatively small. Italy has thus followed in the footsteps of the more advanced countries, demographically speaking, not only in recent years but also during the entire period of its existence as a unified nation, and in doing so has managed to get over the initial handicap it had at the beginning. It would be interesting to analyse regional differences from the demographic data available, but unfortunately there is not sufficient space to do so in this present study.

Instead, we can easily analyse the changes in the population's professional composition, even on a regional basis, with the help of Table 0.4. First of all, we should bear in mind that the share of the active population fell from 52.1 per cent in 1881 to 47.8 per cent in 1936, and by 1981 it had fallen even further to 36 per cent.[83] Table 0.4 shows the results of three of the ten censuses carried out between 1881 and 1981:[84] those of 1911, 1936, and 1981. These three were chosen for practical reasons, as they are placed towards the end of the three periods into which Italian economic history can be divided: the first 50 years, the inter-war years, and the post-war period. Note that the data contained in Table 0.4 are taken from a previous study of mine, which was aimed at rendering the census results homogeneous, using a grid system[85] in order to reclassify activities, so as to be able to make diachronic as well as synchronic comparisons.

One very important fact emerges from an analysis of the results contained in Table 0.4, and that is that Italy only became an industrial nation after the Second World War, though there had been a small increase in the numbers employed in industry and services during the inter-war years. Breaking these data down into regional figures enables us to qualify the statement just made, in that we can see that in 1911 there were already three industrialized regions in Italy. These three regions—Piedmont, Liguria, and Lombardy—constitute the country's famous 'industrial triangle'. Many other regions industrialized after the Second World War, as can be seen from a comparison between regional occupational figures for 1936 and those for 1981: regions such as the Veneto, Emilia–Romagna, Tuscany, the Marches, Umbria, and Friuli–Venezia Giulia.[86]

[83] V. Zamagni, 'A Century of Change: Trends in the Composition of the Italian Labour Force, 1881–1981', *Historical Social Research*, 44 (1987), Table A.1.

[84] In the above, national figures are given for all censuses, as well as regional figures also for the 1881 and 1961 censuses.

[85] The classificatory grid used in the case of the above-mentioned censuses is that pertaining to 1961, as has already been adopted by O. Vitali, in *Aspetti dello sviluppo economico italiano alla luce della ricostruzione della popolazione attiva* (Rome, Failli, 1970). The other changes made by Vitali have also been incorporated here, including an adjustment made to have all data at present boundaries.

[86] The percentage figures for industrial employment in this region were already slightly higher than the national average in 1911 and 1936, but this is not usually noticed as a large part of this area did not belong to Italy until after the First World War.

Table 0.4. Regional composition of the work-force, from population censuses of 1911, 1936, 1981, present-day boundaries (%)

	Agriculture			Industry			Services			Public administration		
	1911	1936	1981	1911	1936	1981	1911	1936	1981	1911	1936	1981
Piedmont–Val d'Aosta	58.4	47.4	8.0	26.4	31.7	50.3	13.3	18.2	32.7	1.9	2.7	9.0
Liguria	39.2	29.1	5.1	31.7	33.8	33.3	26.0	32.8	47.8	3.1	4.3	13.8
Lombardy	47.3	33.7	3.8	35.6	42.1	52.1	15.6	21.6	36.0	1.5	2.6	8.1
Trentino Alto Adige	66.5	56.3	10.7	15.5	19.6	34.0	15.4	20.0	42.3	2.6	4.1	13.0
Veneto	64.2	57.3	8.5	20.1	23.1	47.9	14.0	16.9	34.0	1.7	2.7	9.6
Friuli–Venezia G.	51.9	46.3	5.7	25.2	27.4	41.3	19.9	22.0	39.0	3.0	4.3	14.0
Emilia–Romagna	63.8	62.9	12.6	21.4	18.8	42.7	13.0	15.6	34.8	1.8	2.7	9.9
The Marches	71.6	69.4	11.5	17.0	16.6	46.8	9.6	11.3	30.0	1.8	2.7	11.7
Tuscany	56.9	53.2	6.7	27.4	25.5	45.7	14.0	18.2	35.1	1.7	3.1	12.5
Umbria	74.3	69.5	10.6	14.9	16.9	43.7	9.0	11.0	31.8	1.8	2.6	13.9
Latium	56.3	46.0	6.3	19.5	20.8	30.6	20.0	25.6	42.0	4.2	7.6	21.1
Campania	54.9	51.3	17.7	22.6	22.5	32.9	19.9	33.0	32.0	2.6	3.9	17.4
Abruzzi–Molise	80.3	76.7	17.2	10.0	11.4	37.9	8.4	9.5	29.3	1.3	2.4	15.6
Apulia	65.2	54.2	25.7	18.7	24.9	31.1	14.2	17.4	28.1	1.9	3.5	15.1
Basilicata	78.8	77.1	28.0	11.4	11.9	32.5	8.6	8.5	22.2	1.2	2.5	17.5
Calabria	73.7	69.5	24.0	14.3	15.0	28.9	10.5	12.9	27.7	1.5	2.6	19.4
Sicily	54.3	51.9	19.9	22.1	21.4	31.0	21.2	22.6	32.3	2.4	4.1	16.8
Sardinia	60.9	56.9	13.0	20.3	19.9	33.9	16.2	18.6	34.9	2.6	4.6	18.2
ITALY	59.1	52.0	11.1	23.6	25.6	41.5	15.3	19.0	34.4	2.0	3.4	13.0

Source: V. Zamagni, 'A Century of Change: Trends in the Composition of the Italian Labour Force, 1881–1981', *Historical Social Research*, 44 (Oct. 1987).

Fig. 0.5 The Italian regions today

These are the regions that make up the 'third Italy',[87] known for its own particular form of industrialization, which will be looked at later on.

Although the South was still clearly behind the rest of the country in terms of industrialization in 1981, the data do show a general increase in industrial and service-sector manpower, with surprising changes in certain cases, such as those of the Abruzzi–Molise region and, to a lesser extent, Basilicata. These are regions that saw a transformation from subsistence farming to a fairly diversified economy within the space of only 30 years or so.

Such profound changes in areas previously excluded from the modernization process have had important repercussions on agriculture; the percentage of people employed in agriculture fell from 52 to 11 per cent between 1936[88] and 1981, while the percentage employed in industry rose from 25.6 to 41.5 per cent, and in the service sector it went up from 22.4 to 47.4 per cent. Accordingly, urban population has grown, particularly in the North, without however producing a strong tendency towards polarization as can be seen in Fig. 0.6.

The industrial censuses shown in Table 0.5 are also of interest, as they throw further light on the evolutionary process that led to the modernization of the Italian economy. The data contained in this table have also been rendered homogeneous for comparative purposes, through the reclassification of those employed in manufacturing industry using the 1951 grid. One should bear in mind that the figures contained in the industrial censuses are always smaller than those present in the population censuses, since the first type of census only provides information about those people who are effectively employed in industrial firms; this excludes unemployed people, temporary workers, home-workers, and workers who are not officially registered as such, and yet declare themselves as being 'professional' in one form or another in the population censuses.[89]

The composition of manufacturing-industry employment can be seen to have changed quite radically from 1911 to the present time (see Table 0.5); on the one hand, there has been a sharp decline in the numbers employed in the textile industry (from 22.9 per cent in 1911 to 8.2 per cent in 1981) and in the food industry (from 13.8 to 6.5 per cent), while on the other hand, there has been a sharp increase in the numbers employed in the engineering industry (from 16.7 to 40 per cent), in the metallurgical industry (from 1.9 to 4.3 per cent), and in

[87] The first systematic analysis of the threefold division of Italy—into a first Italy (North-West or industrial triangle), a second Italy (the South), and a third Italy (the North-East and Centre)—was made by A. Bagnasco in his successful book, *Tre Italie. La problematica territoriale dello sviluppo italiano* (Bologna, Il Mulino, 1977).

[88] There was already a significant diffusion of industrialization, as we shall see, during the years leading up to the Second World War, and during the war itself.

[89] The discrepancy between industrial censuses and population censuses has tended to diminish, as is shown in Zamagni, 'A Century of Change'.

Table 0.5. Composition of the work-force employed in manufacturing industry, from the industrial censuses 1911–1981, boundaries of the time (%)

	1911[a]	1927	1937–9	1951	1961	1971	1981
Food and drink	13.8	11.4	14.0	10.3	8.8	7.1	6.5
Tobacco	0.9	0.9	1.4	1.5	0.6	0.4	0.3
Leather and hides	7.6	7.5	6.3	5.7	5.7	4.4	5.0
Textiles	22.9	23.0	17.6	18.6	13.1	10.2	8.2
Clothing	8.9	10.9	8.3	7.1	7.5	7.8	7.6
Wood, furniture	11.9	10.1	8.3	8.4	8.5	7.5	7.4
Paper	1.6	1.6	1.6	1.8	1.9	1.8	1.6
Printing and photogr.	2.1	2.3	2.4	2.4	2.9	3.1	3.6
Metallurgy	1.9	3.2	3.0	4.2	4.3	4.6	4.3
Engineering	16.7	18.0	24.9	26.0	31.1	36.6	40.0
Bricks, glass, etc.	8.5	6.1	6.0	5.9	7.1	6.2	5.6
Chemicals	2.6	3.0	4.5	5.7	6.0	6.0	5.3
Rubber	0.1	0.5	0.7	1.1	1.2	1.6	1.5
Other products	0.5	1.5	1.0	1.8	1.7	2.7	3.1
TOTAL	100.0	100.0	100.0	100.0	100.0	100.0	100.0
% of the active pop.	12.7	14.2	16.7	17.3	22.5	28.1	29.8

[a] Figures have been adjusted in order to take into account businesses with only one employee, excluded in the 1911 census.

Source: V. Zamagni, 'A Century of Change: Trends in the Composition of the Italian Labour Force, 1881–1981', *Historical Social Research*, 44 (Oct. 1987).

the chemical industry (from 2.6 to 5.3 per cent).[90] Such changes follow a fairly constant trend, although they happened faster in the period between the 1930s[91] and 1981. Italian industrialization was of a fairly 'classic' kind, with an initial emphasis on textiles and primary needs (food, clothing, housing, and home furnishings), followed by a move towards the engineering industry and metallurgy.

2.2. *The growth in Italians' incomes*

Every industrialization process leads to an increase in the capacity to produce consumer and investment goods, which gradually become more and more complex, and this in turn produces a progressive increase in personal incomes, and thus in spending power. While this is generally true, in order to obtain a historical illustration of the results of a specific process of industrialization, one needs to see whether a statistical representation of the nation's accounts exists. As is well known,[92] the figures which are available to us are those published in 1957 by ISTAT (Italian Central Institute of Statistics), which were subsequently revised and partially updated in the 1960s by a research group led by the economist Giorgio Fuà.[93] Although some scholars have for years been convinced of the need for a thorough revision of the ISTAT findings, only a few specific sectors have been successfully revised and results published so far.[94] While I shall take these latest results into account later on, for the moment I have used the data concerning national income for the period 1861–1945, taken from what I shall call the ISTAT–Fuà survey. It has not been easy to decide which subsequent data to use, as ISTAT has several times updated

[90] The chemical industry continues to remain relatively small when compared with that of other industrialized countries, even if we add a further 2% to the figure for 1981, as this represents those persons employed in the production of plastic goods included under the heading 'other manufacturing industries' because this was the way these persons were categorized according to the 1951 classification which has been used as a grid for the industrial censuses.

[91] The peak reached in employment in the food industry, shown by the 1937–9 census, is due, in fact, to the particular way this census was carried out: cf. Zamagni, 'A Century of Change'.

[92] See also G. Toniolo's comments on this in *Storia economica dell'Italia liberale 1850–1918* (Bologna, Il Mulino, 1988), chs. 1 and 12; Eng version, *An Economic History of Liberal Italy, 1850–1918* (London, Routledge, 1990).

[93] The main series were calculated by the statistician O. Vitali. To the same author we owe a recent report on the present state of Italian historical statistics to be found in G. Rey (ed.), *I conti economici dell'Italia. Una sintesi delle fonti ufficiali 1890–1970* (Bari, Laterza, 1991). A revision of the Italian GNP historical series has been advanced by A. Maddison, 'A Revised Estimate of Italian Economic Growth 1861–1989', *Banca Nazionale del Lavoro Quarterly Review* (June 1991). Substantially, the author has reweighted the years 1861–1913, producing a higher rate of growth and a lower starting level of GNP per capita in 1861.

[94] A study group, of which I am a member, organized by ISTAT's former president G. Rey, is now working on a fuller and more radical revision of our historical data, as part of a series of studies being financed by the Bank of Italy on the occasion of the celebration of its centenary year. The first results are now out: G. Rey (ed.), *I conti economici dell'Italia II, Una stima del valore aggiunto per il 1911* (Bari, Laterza, 1992).

GNP levels without tying them in with its previous series. Fortunately, a private research institute (Prometeia) has recently produced a thorough revision of the national income data from 1951 to the present. I have linked 1946–50 to this new revision through rates of growth and gathered the results in Table 0.6.

Having given this necessary technical explanation, we can now examine the data contained in Table 0.6. Italian national income in 1988 can be seen to be 19 times higher than it was in 1861, while per capita income increased eightfold in the same period. Unfortunately, there have been no studies of the long-term change in income distribution, which we shall briefly refer to in the chapters to come using the limited amount of data to which we have access.

We can identify the periods in which income grew fastest by looking at columns 2 and 4 of Table 0.6. There is no doubt that the total and per capita increases in income were much higher during the 1951–73 period than in any other period. The years between 1973 and 1988, despite being difficult ones, also produced much better results than those shown for the years before the Second World War. The next best period was that between 1896 and 1913—the 'Giolitti years'—which, together with the 1920s, can be considered to constitute a single period of economic development (despite the political and military events that separate the two) and was only brought to a halt by the 1929 crisis and the advent of the Second World War. The initial period until 1896 appears to have been the least satisfactory, with the ISTAT figures showing years of almost complete stagnation: however, this is also the period that would seem best to lend support to the argument of those who criticize the ISTAT

Table 0.6. Gross Domestic Product, 1861–1988, present-day boundaries (constant prices)

	GDP index (1861 = 100) (1)	Average annual growth rate of (1) (%) (2)	Per capita GDP index (3)	Average annual growth rate of (3) (%) (4)
1861	100	—	100	—
1896	131	0.8	104	0.1
1913	198	2.4	140	1.8
1922	231	1.7	157	1.3
1929	271	2.2	174	1.5
1938	315	1.6	187	0.7
1951	359	1.0	196	0.4
1963	719	5.8	365	5.3
1973	1249	5.5	589	4.8
1988	1965	3.1	893	2.8

Sources: P. Ercolani (ed.), 'Documentazione statistica di base', in G. Fuà (ed.), *Lo sviluppo economico in Italia*, iii (Milan, Angeli, 1969), and R. Golinelli and M. Monterastelli, *Un metodo per la ricostruzione di serie storiche compatibili con la nuova contabilità nazionale, 1951–1989*, *Prometeia*, report no. 9001 (Nov. 1990).

figures, since it includes the 1880s' boom, which does not appear at all in the ISTAT figures, not to mention the economic revival of the 1870s, which is also absent.

Table 0.7 shows the composition of gross domestic product according to the different productive sectors, for certain bench-mark years during the period under examination. The significant expansion of industry (column 2) can be clearly seen as having already got under way from the 1930s (this is not so clear if we look at Table 0.4), while agriculture shows in the same decade a sharp decline in productivity, together with a significant level of underemployment (with over half the population employed in agriculture, producing less than 27 per cent of total income). Also, column 3 clearly shows the large rise in income generated by the service sector during the 1970s. The second part of Table 0.7 shows a steady rise in investment and exports, with the latter only being interrupted temporarily during the 1930s, as a result of the 1929 crisis: in order to obtain more complex goods, economic processes needed to be more 'capital-intensive' (also in terms of human capital, as we shall see), whereas the Italian economy was gradually internationalizing.

Before looking at the Italian economic modernization process from a comparative point of view, I would like to offer a regional breakdown of this growth in income. While the national economic statistics are not always reliable, the regional per capita income figures for the years before the Second World War simply do not exist in many cases. Table 0.8 shows the figures that researchers have so far managed to produce. Note that income is given as earned income, and not disposable income (which has been higher after the Second World War in the South, as a result of government subsidies). Instead of presenting a series of figures for each region (which exist for those years shown in the table), I have chosen to adopt the previously mentioned

Table 0.7. Sectorial composition of GDP and destination of resources (GDP + imports) (%) (constant prices)

	GDP: Production				Resources: Destination			
	Agri-culture	Industry	Ser-vices	Public admin.	Consumption		Invest-ments	Exports
					Private	Public		
	(1)	(2)	(3)	(4)	(5)	(6)	(7)	(8)
1861	46.1	18.4	30.4	5.1	80.9	7.6	5.3	6.2
1913	37.6	24.9	32.0	5.5	65.4	7.1	15.1	12.4
1938	26.6	30.3	31.7	11.4	64.4	13.8	15.4	6.4
1963	16.5	49.5	26.0	8.0	52.8	9.9	20.9	16.4
1981	6.1	37.1	44.8	12.0	51.5	13.6	17.8	17.1

Sources: P. Ercolani (ed.), 'Documentazione statistica di base', in G. Fuà (ed.), *Lo sviluppo*; ISTAT, *Annuario statistico italiano*, 1981.

Table 0.8. Regional differences in per capita GDP, 1911–1984 (Italy = 100)

	North-West	North-East and Centre	South
1911[a]	136	100	75
1928[a]	147	95	69
1938[a]	152	95	67
1951	156	98	65
1984	130	107	68

[a] Excluding public administration.

Sources: 1911: V. Zamagni, *Industrializzazione e squilibri regionali in Italia* (Bologna, Il Mulino, 1978); 1928–51: SVIMEZ, *Un secolo di statistiche storiche italiane: nord e sud, 1861–1961* (Rome, 1961); 1984: ISTAT, *Le regioni in cifre* (Rome, 1988).

subdivision into the 'three Italies', which is amply sufficient for my purposes, as it illustrates the basic trends in the regional divide that separates these three different parts of the country:

1. the rapid development of the industrial triangle, already clearly visible in 1911, was even more evident during the years to follow, right up until the period of post-war reconstruction;
2. the North-Eastern and Central zone maintained its intermediate position, and only managed to gain ground in relation to the North-West after 1951;
3. in relation to the other two areas, the South's position worsened considerably up until 1951 (certainly from before 1911—even if we do not have figures for this earlier period), and although it improved slightly during the 1960s and 1970s, during the 1980s it slipped back almost to its pre-improvement standing; nevertheless, for the first time since unification, the South was able to maintain the same rate of growth as the rest of the country, during a period of 40 years of sustained economic improvement (see columns 8 and 9, Table 0.9).

Regional differences and, above all, the South–North divide (the North includes the Centre here) represents a structural characteristic of Italy which is further complicated by important socio-cultural differences. Some of these differences have been virtually eliminated with the passing of time, whilst others are as dramatically visible as ever, and the daily tension that they produce represents the real testing ground for Italian society's ability to find new solutions to old, unresolved problems. However, I do not support the view that 'the difference in incomes between the North and the South of Italy is exceptionally large and longlasting'.[95] This may seem to be the case when Italy

[95] Toniolo, *Storia economica*, 233.

Table 0.9. International comparison of GNP per capita at purchasing power parities, 1870–1989 (USA = 100)

						Average yearly rates of growth			
	1870 (1)	1913 (2)	1950 (3)	1973 (4)	1989 (5)	1870–1913 (6)	1913–50 (7)	1950–73 (8)	1973–89 (9)
France	70	56	48	73	76	1.3	1.1	4.0	1.8
Germany	58	54	39	72	76	1.6	0.7	4.9	2.1
Italy	54	43	33	61	71	1.3	0.8	4.8	2.6
North-West	—	58	52	81	88	—	1.2	4.1	2.1
North-East and Centre	—	42	32	64	81	—	0.8	5.2	3.1
South	—	32	21	42	48	—	0.4	5.2	2.5
United Kingdom	116	83	66	71	74	1.0	0.8	2.5	1.8
Spain	40	23	21	43	41	1.0	1.4	5.4	1.2
Japan	27	23	18	65	82	1.4	0.9	8.0	3.1
USA	100	100	100	100	100	1.8	1.6	2.2	1.6

Sources: Author's elaborations from A. Maddison, *Dynamic Forces in Capitalist Development* (Oxford, OUP, 1991) Table 1.1, and L. Prados de La Escosura, 'Crecimiento, atraso y convergencia en España e Italia: introducción', in L. Prados de La Escosura and V. Zamagni (eds.), *El desarrollo económico en la Europa del Sur: España e Italia en perspectiva histórica* (Madrid, Alianza Editorial, 1992).

is compared with Great Britain, or with smaller, more compact countries, or with France (which however does have its Midi), or Germany during the period of post-war division. Many other, larger nations (including the USA) do have parallel problems of regional disparity which show no signs of being resolved. It should be said that Italy has been more aware of its problem than other countries, and has shown the greatest interest in trying to resolve it, even if the means adopted have not always been the most efficacious. We shall examine this matter later on in this study.

One last thing remains before concluding this introductory chapter, and that is to try and place Italy's industrialization in an international context by comparing per capita income for different industrialized countries at different historical dates. It is clear that such an exercise, whilst in theory being of significant value, in practice is rather difficult to carry out: it involves the accumulation of diverse problems, which in turn makes it very difficult to establish a solid base for such a comparative analysis. In the first place, there are an infinite number of difficulties involved in trying to produce a set of reliable figures for each country; secondly, these figures then need to be translated from national currencies into an acceptable standard of value in order that they may be compared. The first of these 'obstacles' has been, and is still being, tackled by numerous historians, who have managed to produce various series of historical data pertaining to several different nations, some of which are more reliable than others. However, economists and statisticians have only taken the second obstacle into consideration in so far as it concerns the present-day period. They have concluded that the best method of evaluating comparative income is that of using 'purchasing power parities' (PPP).

Given that official exchange rates do not accurately reflect the respective purchasing powers of the citizens of those countries being compared,[96] an exchange rate has been calculated according to the direct evaluation of the cost of a predetermined basket of goods for each nation. This exchange rate at PPP can then be used in place of the official rate, when making a comparative international study of per capita income. Nevertheless, the methods used in arriving at an exchange rate at PPP are not without their problems,[97] and can sometimes lead to slightly different results. Moreover, the techniques involved in reconstructing figures according to PPP require an enormous quantity of information (which is not always readily available), as well as long periods of computer time spent elaborating data. The first major study to fully adopt this

[96] Cf. I. B. Kravis, 'Comparative Studies of National Incomes and Prices', *Journal of Economic Literature*, 22 (Mar. 1984), and R. Marris, 'Comparing the Incomes of Nations: A Critique of the International Comparison Project', ibid.

[97] For a discussion of alternative methods, see A. Maddison, 'A Comparison of Levels of GDP per capita in Developed and Developing Countries, 1700-1980', *Journal of Economic History*, 43 (Mar. 1983), and also I. B. Kravis, Z. Kenessey, A. Heston, and R. Summers, *A System of International Comparisons of Gross Product and Purchasing Power* (Washington, DC, World Bank, 1975).

technique was carried out by Kravis, Heston, and Summers for the World Bank:[98] it was originally designed to cover 15 countries, later extended to 30, and involved estimates for 1970 and 1975. These estimates were used to extrapolate and interpolate annual figures, applying income growth rates for each country to base-year figures.[99] Following this lead, the European Community's statisticians also began publishing regular comparative tables of per capita income in Community countries (as well as the USA and Japan), calculated using the PPP approach.[100]

Historians have not had the opportunity, until now, of carrying out a comparative study able to reconstruct original income figures, according to PPP, for selected historical base-years: instead, they have used the Kravis–Heston–Summers method of extrapolation. One historian, N. F. R. Crafts, started from the above-mentioned three authors' calculation for the year 1970, and extrapolated these data backwards in time, using the best available national figures for per capita income (1870–1910), in his justly famous essay on PPP-adjusted per capita incomes (in the case of some countries, he extended the extrapolation beyond 1870).[101] Of course, this technique does have some defects, the three principal ones being: (*a*) the Kravis–Heston–Summers estimates are based upon the adoption of a basket of present-day goods and services, which is not completely suitable for an evaluation of the cost of living in the nineteenth century; (*b*) these estimates cover a range of countries with very different economies, whereas Europe, the USA, and Japan in the nineteenth century represent a rather more homogeneous set; (*c*) during the course of time, certain important changes have taken place in the ranking of different countries' per capita incomes, and this has invariably altered the relative prices; however, Crafts' method maintains relative prices fixed at their 1970 pattern, as estimated at that date by Kravis, Heston, and Summers.

A thorough application of such method has been made by Maddison in his most recent volume,[102] from which I have compiled Table 0.9, adding data for Spain that I have extracted from a recent comparison of Italian and Spanish development.[103] The picture that it derives is extremely interesting: in 1989,

[98] I. B. Kravis, A. Heston, and R. Summers, *International Comparisons of Real Product and Purchasing Power* (Washington, DC, World Bank, 1978), and by the same authors, *World Product and Income: International Comparisons of Real Gross Product* (Washington, DC, World Bank, 1982).

[99] Naturally this is a less precise method, used in order to avoid the lengthy recalculation of PPP each year. Clearly, the further one gets away from the base year, the greater the risk that relative prices will be altered substantially.

[100] Cf. Eurostat, *Eurostatistics*, a monthly EEC bulletin.

[101] N. F. R. Crafts, 'Gross National Product in Europe 1870-1910: Some New Estimates', *Explorations in Economic History*, 20 (1983).

[102] A. Maddison, *Dynamic Forces in Capitalist Development. A Long-Run Comparative View* (Oxford, Oxford University Press, 1991). The Italian data embody the revision made by Maddison and quoted in n. 93 above.

[103] L. Prados de La Escosura and V. Zamagni (eds.), *El desarrollo económico en la Europa del Sur: España e Italia en perspectiva histórica* (Madrid, Alianza Editorial, 1992).

Italy had practically caught up with Great Britain, and lay just behind France and Germany, with Japan somewhat ahead of all the European countries, but still about 20 per cent below USA. The per capita income in the most advanced group of European countries was around three-quarters of that in the USA. A century before, Great Britain had a higher GDP than that of the USA (even if the method used to calculate GDP probably exaggerates the difference), while Japan had a much lower GDP (about one-quarter). France then stood at about the same distance from the USA as it does now, while Italy and Germany were much further behind. Spain started already in 1870 at a lower level than Italy and Germany, lost more ground by 1913, regaining its position only in the period 1950–73.

It is also very interesting to look at the figures for the intermediate years: all the countries in this study lose ground to the USA until 1950, when they then start to regain it. Great Britain and Italy lose more than the others, but, whereas Italy regains significant ground, Great Britain does so only to a limited extent. This is clear evidence of the change-over in world leadership, going from Europe (and in particular Great Britain) to the USA, that characterizes the first half of the twentieth century; it also illustrates Europe's recovery after the end of the Second World War, together with the powerful rise of Japan during this same period. There is no doubt that a more precise definition of the income data underlying a comparative picture, like the one in Table 0.9, could serve to produce a better model of the international industrialization process, with the above-mentioned leads and lags that characterize this process.

Now that a general picture has been drawn of Italy's economic development from 1861 to present, the following chapters will analyse in detail the various phases and features of this development, before offering some conclusive interpretative remarks.

PART I
The First Fifty Years

I

Agriculture and Regional Imbalances

1. THE LAND

ITALY is famous for its wide variety of geographical and climatic types, and as such this variety does not really need further illustration here: it has been an inspiration for poets and musicians, painters and town-planners, as well as a favourite topic of discussion for historians.[1] Perhaps what is not so well known is that there is no part of the Italian landscape that, for geological and historical reasons, has escaped man's efforts to manipulate it. This is true of the relatively scarce flatlands (only 20 per cent of the total land area), as they are frequently situated near to the sea, and as such consist of alluvial plains which are constantly being reclaimed only to be eroded again; what is more surprising is that the same is also true of the hills and mountains which make up the rest of the land area, as the pressure caused by an ever-increasing population has led to attempts to cultivate these areas even more intensely, and this in turn has led to the growing need for protective measures, as more and more of the fertile topsoil is washed away or subsides as a result of the rain.

Thus the whole of the Italian territory has continuously been subject to human intervention, in the form of large-scale reclamation projects, going right back to ancient times. It can be said that

> periods of growth, of expansion, of the supremacy of certain peoples, States or regions within the confines of the Italian peninsula, have repeatedly coincided with successful reclamation projects, which have helped agriculture enormously and led to new settlements in the former marshlands, thanks to the technical expertise utilized by men in order to control the waters' chaotic force. Each civilization, each great period of political and social organization, has left its hallmark on the land, the signs of man's endeavours, at times colossal, aimed at taming and modifying the adverse nature of the land and the environment. Similarly, each period of decline has been preceded, accompanied or followed by a weakening of man's power over nature, over the destructive force of the waters which have led to repeated losses of agricultural and habitable land.[2]

[1] See e.g. the well-written account given by R. Romanelli, *L'Italia liberale 1861–1900* (Bologna, Il Mulino, 1979), 122–229. A very eloquent survey of the diverse forms of agrarian society that existed in Italy in that period, from both a social and productive point of view, put together by the best specialists in the field, is P. Bevilacqua (ed.), *Storia dell'agricultura italiana in età contemporanea*, 3 vols. (Venice, Marsilio, 1989–1992).

[2] P. Bevilacqua and M. Rossi Doria, *Le bonifiche in Italia dal '700 ad oggi* (Bari, Laterza, 1984), 5–6. For a new kind of history of the environment, cf. A. Caracciolo, *L'ambiente come storia. Sondaggi e proposte di storiografia dell'ambiente* (Bologna, Il Mulino, 1988).

At the time of unification, the control over watercourses and the organization of reclamation was very different from one region to another. If we look at the Po Plain, we can see that for hundreds of years, man had been reclaiming large areas of the northern part (in the Lombardy and Piedmont regions) for his own purposes, through the canalization of water for irrigation and for the production of energy; this intervention resulted in the construction of certain works that have been recognized as being technically brilliant. Carlo Cattaneo could not really conceal his pride when, writing about Lombardy in 1844, he said that: 'one half of our plain . . . has been irrigated . . . A part of the plain, thanks to our work, is green even in winter, when everything else is covered in frost and snow. The worst swamps have been transformed into rice-fields, where, at the same latitude as the Vendée, or Switzerland, or the Tauern mountains, we have managed to grow an Indian crop.'[3]

Although there was no shortage of problems in controlling the Po's tributaries—the Adda, the Adige, and the Brenta—the major difficulty for the Po Plain was that created when the Po burst its banks at Ficarolo in the middle of the twelfth century, as that part of the river flowing in the vicinity of Ferrara changed its course as a result. This called for a series of public works, which unfortunately were not always beneficial, and sometimes they even worsened the already dramatic situation. The problem of land-reclamation in this vast area was still of urgent importance at the time of unification; however, such problems were directly connected to an economic calculation, that is, the economic benefit to be gained from the reclamation of the land against the cost involved.

There was not one area of flatland in Tuscany, either, that was not in part marshland, and these marshlands were invariably infested with malaria. The triangular-shaped Maremma, in particular, consisted of 245,000 hectares of marshland, swamps, and wild vegetation. Pietro Leopoldo and his successors had already started on ambitious public works programmes, based on the principle of reclamation, which, however, required incredibly long time-periods. In the Latium region, the areas of the Roman Campagna and the Pontine Campagna (208,000 and 20,000 hectares respectively) were largely covered by water, as a result of the irregular nature of the soil, the presence of numerous springs, and the chaotic structure of the watercourses. This represented a great loss in potential agricultural production, as well as being harmful to the local population. Of all the popes who committed themselves to trying to resolve this enormous problem, the effort of Pope Pius VI was of particular merit, although all work was brought to a halt on his death.

The South's problems were of a different nature, since the whole of its natural equilibrium, not only that of the plains, had been upset, and this was

[3] C. Cattaneo, 'Introduction' to *Notizie naturali e civili sulla Lombardia* (G. Bernardoni di Giovanni printer, Milan, 1844), p. xcix.

only partly due to natural factors. As the Bourbon engineer Carlo Afan de Rivera wrote in 1833:

Since the time when our plains, and in particular those along the coast, remained deserted and uncultivated as a result of political disaster, man's attempts to regulate the flow of those rivers and streams that cross the plains have ceased to exist. At the same time, the deforestation and ploughing-up of the mountain areas [carried out by those peoples who left the plains to go and live there], has greatly contributed towards exacerbating the already disastrous state of the waters that flow down into the plains.[4]

What was therefore required was an even more radical intervention than in the above-mentioned cases. Here, it was no longer simply a question of draining and reclaiming marshlands, or redirecting the flow of rivers; here, the plain had to be 'literally created, won back once more from nature and given back to man . . . to those populations who had abandoned it centuries beforehand, as a result of the lack of security they had felt living along the coast, or as a result of other historical reasons'.[5] At the same time, the random deforestation had to be stopped, in order to halt the soil erosion in the hills and mountains, as this simply exacerbated the poverty of those who carried on this practice. It is no wonder, then, that the Bourbons' concerted but disorganized and incomplete attempts to do something about this situation never had any long-term success. Unfortunately, the governments of a unified Italy were, for many decades, just as unsuccessful in their attempts to reclaim the southern soil.

At the time of unification, more than one million of the total of 26 million hectares of agricultural land and forest were still nothing more than swamplands, a large proportion being concentrated in the lower Po Valley and in the South. The total area of land that needed intervention of one kind or another was, however, much greater than this; but government intervention was only forthcoming after the passing of the so-called 'Baccarini law ' of 25 June 1882 (law no. 269)—Baccarini being the name of the engineer from Ravenna who proposed the law. This law introduced two categories of land-reclamation—categories 1 and 2—and made provisions for a financial contribution from central and local government (equal to 75 per cent of the total cost) for the first category, which included those projects of particular public interest.

[4] Afan De Rivera, *Considerazioni su i mezzi da restituire il valore proprio ai doni che ha la natura largamente concesso al Regno delle Due Sicilie* (Naples, 1833), 94.

[5] Bevilacqua and Rossi Doria, *Le bonifiche*, 37. In another essay, Bevilacqua has the following to say on this matter: 'The transfer and siting of demographic centres in this area has ignored the necessities and the logic of agrarian organization and agricultural production. The foremost, often dominant factor seems to have been one of defence, rather than economic advantage; this was the result of long periods of "foreign" domination, or the threat thereof, which the people living in that area had had to live through', P. Bevilacqua, 'Uomini, terre, economie', in P. Bevilacqua and A. Placanica (eds.), *La Calabria* (Turin, Einaudi, 1985), 117.

The Baccarini law was a great boost to land-reclamation in the Po Valley, especially that lying within the provinces of Ferrara, Modena, Rovigo, and Ravenna, where more than 400,000 hectares of land were reclaimed in the period up to the First World War, using for the best part a drainage technique involving a water-scooping pump.[6] The subsequent cultivation of this land was usually very profitable, as it gave a very high yield of wheat and other cereals.

In other areas of Italy (the Roman Campagna, the Maremma in Tuscany, and the South), public works did not produce anything like the same kind of results as those witnessed in the Po Plain. The initial problems were far more complex, and there was very little immediate financial reward, which in turn discouraged private investors from participating in such projects.[7]

Failures such as these were to lead the ruling classes under Giolitti's guidance to adopt stronger measures, and they moved towards an 'integral' programme of land-reclamation (the term was first officially used during the later period of Fascism, although it aptly evokes the motivation behind these early twentieth-century legislative measures). Of the 22 legislative measures passed between 1900 and 1914, the law of 31 March 1904[8] concerning the Basilicata region was the one that, more than any other, represented a turning-point. It made provisions for the complete reorganization of the area's woodland and waterways, taking in both hill and plain, together with numerous public works (roads, water supplies, sewers, the construction of farmhouses) and tax incentives for private persons investing in the redevelopment of the area. The Basilicata law was followed by a similar law for Calabria (25 June 1906), as well as other more modest measures for the rest of the South, including Sardinia. This legislation led up to the Luzzatti law of 2 June 1910, which provided for the extension of state-owned forestry land, and to the Nitti–Sacchi law of 13 July 1911, which made the State financially responsible for a reclamation project involving drainage areas in the mountainous parts of the South.[9] Although the far-sightedness of these laws has recently been

[6] G. Porisini, *Bonifiche e agricoltura nella Bassa Valle Padana* (Banca Commerciale Italiana, Milan, 1978). For Piedmont see L. Segre, *Agricoltura e costruzione di un sistema idraulico nella pianura piemontese (1800–1880)* (Milan, Banca Commerciale Italiana, 1983).

[7] G. Barone has the following to say: 'In reality, private initiatives in this field, as organized by farming consortiums, were only to have any real success in the area of the Po Plain, in the North of Italy. This does not, however, so much underline the level of absenteeism among southern farmers, as it does the large gulf that existed between the relative ease with which land-reclamation projects could be carried out in the northern plains (thus guaranteeing the profitability of such schemes), and the enormous geomorphological obstacles that stood between similar projects and their being put into practice in a worthwhile and profitable fashion in the South of Italy', *Mezzogiorno e modernizzazione. Elettricità, irrigazione e bonifica nell'Italia contemporanea* (Turin, Einaudi, 1986), 13.

[8] The special law for Basilicata was drawn up at the end of Giuseppe Zanardelli's visit to that area towards the end of the summer of 1902, during which the Prime Minister from Brescia (in Lombardy) was quoted as saying 'the incredibly sad conditions here are much worse than I had feared them to be': P. Corti (ed.), *Inchiesta Zanardelli sulla Basilicata* (Turin, Einaudi, 1976), 20.

[9] According to the famous agronomist, Arrigo Serpieri, this was in fact the first Italian law that made provision for a general programme of integral land-reclamation, A. Serpieri, *La bonifica nella storia e nella dottrina* (Bologna, 1948), 103.

recognized,[10] the projects themselves were only completed in part; however, this was more than had ever been accomplished before, and, more importantly, was conceived with the right objectives in mind. The amount spent by the State during the period 1900–18 was about twice as much as had been spent during the previous 40 years, and more than half went to projects located in the South. Of the 768,701 hectares of land reclaimed up to the year 1914, 52 per cent was situated in the North (75 per cent of this work having been carried out by farmers' consortia), 8 per cent in the Centre, and 40 per cent in the South (entirely at the State's expense).

This area of reclaimed agricultural land, won back from nature thanks to an enormous amount of hard work and fatigue, consisted around 1861 of the following: 45 per cent arable land, 4.3 per cent trees and shrubs, 26.6 per cent grazing land, 4.7 per cent uncultivated land, and the remaining 19.4 per cent woodland. Fifty years later, the percentage of arable land together with planted trees and shrubs had risen by about 8 percentage points, at the expense of grazing land, uncultivated land, and woodland. It should be pointed out that almost one-half of arable land was also planted with trees, and that 1.3 million hectares were irrigated (5 per cent of the total land area), of which 85 per cent was to be found in the North.

These figures are, however, somewhat approximate,[11] due to the rather unsatisfactory nature of land-registration at the time. At this point, it is worth looking again at the question of the differences between the various regions, in order fully to understand the weight of state intervention in the field of land-registration, a necessary step if the fiscal burden and other forms of agricultural intervention are to be fairly apportioned.

Immediately after the declaration of unification, a survey of land-registration was commissioned in order to enable the State to apply land-taxation equitably. The commission's findings are very interesting,[12] because on the one hand it managed to find a rather ingenious way of arriving at a 'provisional equalization settlement', which was put into effect in 1864, while on the other hand it uncovered the relative inequalities in land-registration throughout the country, and made a recommendation aimed at the standardization of land-registers. Table 1.1 gives an idea of the main characteristics of those land-registers in existence between 1871 and 1873. Basically, there were two types of register:

[10] Cf. G. Cingari, *Storia della Calabria dall'unità ad oggi* (Bari, Laterza, 1983).

[11] The figures given in the text are those calculated by E. Rossini and C. Vanzetti in *Storia dell' agricoltura italiana* (Bologna, Edagricole, 1986), 554—the first being based upon the work of C. Correnti and P. Maestri, *Annuario Statistico Italiano* (Turin, 1864), and the second (concerning 1910) on the *Catasto agrario del Regno d'Italia* (Rome, 1911–15, incomplete).

[12] *Atti della Commissione istituita con regio decreto 11 agosto 1861 per la perequazione dell'imposta fondiaria* (Turin, printed by Dalmazzo, 1863) in Atti Parliamentari, Camera dei deputati, Legislatura VIII, 1861–2, doc. no. 407.

Table 1.1. Principal characteristics of land-registers in existence, 1871–1873

Area	Denomination	Time	Geometric	Descriptive	Parcel
Piedmontese-Ligurian	1. Piedmontese	*	·		·
	2. Ligurian	1798–1808		·	
	3. French	1804–7	·		·
	4. French	1808–17	·		·
Lombard–Veneto	5. Old Milanese	1760	·		·
	6. Mantovan	1785	·		·
	7. New Lombard–Veneto	1846–73 and 1864	·		·
Parmesan	8. Parmesan	1830	·		·
Modenese	9. The Plain of Este	1791		·	
	10. The Mountain of Este	1817		·	
	11. Massese	1834	·		·
	12. Garfagnana	1533		·	
	13. Lunigiana	1826		·	
	14. Ancient Lucchese	1803		·	
Tuscan	15. The Mainland	1832–4	·		·
	16. Elba and the Plain	1840–2	·		·
	17. Modern Lucchese	1864–9	·		·
	18. Of the Giglio**	1875	·		·
Ex-Papal State	19. Roman	1835	·		·
Neapolitan	20. Neapolitan	1808–25		·	·
Sicilian	21. Sicilian	1835–52		·	·
Sardinian	22. Sardinian***	1855	·		

* A 1739 geometric register with maps dating from 1858–70.

** This register postdates the survey which provided all the other information (*Rendiconto dei lavori della sottocommissione per l'inchiesta sui catasti*, in *Atti Parlamentari*, Camera dei deputati, session 1873–4, Documents, no. 140, Rome, 1874).

*** The Sardinian register was organized according to territorial areas or group of properties.

Sources: M. Olivieri, 'I catasti all'unità d'Italia', in C. Carozzi and L. Gambi (eds.), *Città e proprietà immobiliare in Italia negli ultimi due secoli* (Milan, Angeli, 1981), 72.

the geometrical-parcel variety and the descriptive variety.[13] The first consisted in the measurement, by experts, of all parcels of land, thus enabling detailed maps to be compiled, together with the evaluation of the income that could be expected from the working of the various parcels of land, in accordance with prices calculated for a pre-established time period.[14] As A. Messedaglia has observed,[15] this kind of land-register was inspired by that 'precursor of modern land-registers', the famous State of Milan register created by Maria Theresa of Austria (1718–1757, with an interval between 1733 and 1749 due to the war). The other type, the descriptive register, was based on the individual declarations of landowners, which were sometimes checked by commissions using general criteria, and as such it could have been more or less accurate, but never 'objective'; it gave rise to inaccuracies and arguments, understandably enough, as it was not accompanied by a map. The prototype of this kind was the Neapolitan land-register: 29 per cent of the area appeared as either unproductive or had not been surveyed; in the provinces of Naples and Catanzaro, the surveyed area turned out to be greater than the geographical area. The Bourbon government only made provisions for a geometrical-parcel register in 1857, but failed to produce any real results.

The early governments of unified Italy had a further problem, in addition to that of the heterogeneous nature of different land-registers: the different time-scale used from one register to another, when evaluating the worth of land and buildings. In the first place, a decision was taken to impose a different duty on buildings from that to be imposed on land (18 April 1864), and thus a register of all buildings was begun (26 January 1865, law no. 2136). However, much more time and effort was required in order to get the new land-register under way, and it was only given final approval, as a geometrical-parcel register, in 1886, after it had overcome quite strong opposition, in particular from southern landowners. After a rather slow start, work finally got under way in earnest, and by 1914, 16.3 million hectares had been measured, 14.5 million had been evaluated, 9.2 million published as such, and 5.6 million had been taxed on the basis of the new regime. The best part of the remaining work was completed during the inter-war period, using modern techniques (Italy was the first country to use the aerial-photograph technique); however, the new land-register was not completed until 1956. Nevertheless, it was judged to be a great

[13] An exhaustive survey of the question of modern land-registration in Italy is contained in C. Carozzi and L. Gambi (eds.), *Città e proprietà immobiliare in Italia negli ultimi due secoli* (Milan, Angeli, 1981). For a discussion of the use of land-registers in analysing land-distribution and agricultural practices, see R. Zangheri, *Catasti e storia della proprietà terriera* (Turin, Einaudi, 1980).

[14] This evaluation should in theory have been updated on a regular basis in order to take account of any improvements made or of any worsening of the situation or of any changes in ownership of land, thus enabling taxes to be altered in accordance with such change.

[15] Cf. L. Messedaglia (ed.), *Catasto e perequazione. Discussione parlamentare sul riordinamento dell'imposta fondiaria (1885–1886)* (Bologna, 1941).

success (the entire operation had taken 70 years, although this was partly due to the interruptions caused by the advent of two world wars).

2. PRODUCTIVE RESULTS AND FARMING METHODS

During the course of an economy's modernization, agriculture has played a much more important role than simply that of provider of food supplies and raw materials. It has also played the part of catalyst for rural industry and its development has led to the growth of both internal and external markets, together with the attendant transport, credit, and insurance sectors. It has led the way towards capital accumulation and the development of an entrepreneurial spirit in the field of land-management. As agricultural techniques have improved, so productivity has increased, and this has meant that a greater proportion of the total labour-force could be freed from working on the land, in order to be used in other sectors. The agricultural surplus had in fact become sufficient to cover the basic needs of those that did not work on the land.[16] With a decrease in the need for individual self-sufficiency in the production of food, together with an increase in mechanization and the use of fertilizers, the agricultural sector has become a market for industrial production. Finally, agricultural (and mineral) exports have been invaluable in order to be able to pay for the importation of indispensable machinery and raw materials, during the early stages of the industrialization process.

It is important to bear such effects of agricultural modernization in mind when considering the great debate that took place, both in Italy and elsewhere, over the role of agriculture in the development process. It has even been suggested that in each industrialized country there had been an 'agricultural revolution' some 30–50 years before an 'industrial revolution' took place.[17] Even if a strict relationship between the two has still to be shown to have really existed, one can see the importance of analysing this question in the case of a country like Italy.

Firstly, it is important to note that there is as much diversity within Italian agriculture as there is in the country's geography. As Stefano Iacini concluded in his ambitious Agricultural Survey, commissioned by the Italian Parliament in 1877: 'there are still many different types of agriculture in Italy, not only in terms of the products they yield, but also because they have preserved more or less the same forms, the same appearance, the same shades that were bestowed upon them originally by the respective political, social and administrative structures in existence at the time of their creation, structures that have

[16] In pre-industrial societies, the average percentage of the working population employed in agriculture was around 80%.

[17] P. Bairoch, 'Niveaux de développement économique de 1810 à 1910', *Annales*, 20 (1965), and by the same author, *Rivoluzione industriale e sottosviluppo* (Turin, Einaudi, 1967). See also T. Kemp, *Industrialization in Nineteenth-Century Europe* (London, Longmans, 1969), ch. 2.

Table 1.2. Types of agriculture, 1913

	Hectares (000s)	%	Index of GSP per hectare (Italy = 100)
1. The Po Plain	3 590	13.6	216
2. Northern hills	1 945	7.4	169
3. Central-southern hills and plains	11 450	43.4	88
4. Mountain areas	9 415	35.6	56
TOTAL	26 400	100.0	100

Note: GSP = Gross Saleable Product at 1913 prices (average 1910–23).

however since disappeared.'[18] A breakdown of this diversity is inevitably going to overlook many details; however, the subdivision into four types as set out in Table 1.2 will be of use in the analysis that is to come.[19]

2.1. *The Po Plain*

It was well irrigated, and the crops grown were cereals (including rice), sugar beet, hemp, flax, and forage for livestock (which went together with the rearing of cattle and pigs).[20] Yield per hectare was very high by Italian standards (double the average), and was even favourable by international standards: for example, in 1913 wheat yield was 19.2 quintals per hectare (q.p.h., 1 quintal = 100 kg.), compared with a British average of 22 quintals; the yield for sugar beet was 455 q.p.h, which was well above the average in other European countries (Germany 338 q.p.h., France 265 q.p.h.); maize-yield was 25.3 q.p.h. (the nearest European yield was that of Hungary, with 17.4 q.p.h.).[21] There was a general system of crop-rotation, sometimes involving very complicated cycles, which in some zones had been introduced several centuries beforehand.

[18] S. Jacini, *Relazione finale* (Rome, Forzani, 1884), here quoted from G. Nenci (ed.), *I risultati della inchiesta agraria* (Turin, Einaudi, 1976), 78. A well-balanced and informed view of the material gathered by this agricultural survey is given by Caracciolo in *L'inchiesta agraria Jacini* (2nd edn., Turin, Einaudi, 1973). As far as the survey's results for the Veneto are concerned, as well as earlier materials for that region, see A. Lazzarini, *Contadini e agricoltura. L'inchiesta Jacini nel Veneto* (Milan, Angeli, 1983).

[19] The source is G. Zattini, 'Valutazione della produzione lorda dell'agricoltura italiana', *Notizie periodiche di statistica agraria* (Oct. 1924), and the figures refer to the average for the period between 1910 and 1923.

[20] Two-thirds of the cattle and one-half of the pigs were being reared in the regions of Piedmont, Lombardy, Veneto, and Emilia; two-thirds of butter and cheese were produced in those same regions at the time.

[21] The figures for European countries come from B. R. Mitchell, *European Historical Statistics* (London, Macmillan, 1975).

2.2. *The Northern hills*

The profitability of these areas was largely due to specialized crops—grapes, fruit, oil, and flowers, for example, in Liguria—and to the breeding of silkworms. Where cereals were grown, wheat and maize were rotated every year so as to avoid leaving the land fallow, although in the long run this led to an impoverishment of the soil, and thus a lower crop-yield.

These two highly productive areas (1 and 2) accounted for only 21 per cent of the total area of agricultural land in Italy, but produced 42 per cent of the entire GSP. They made up 85 per cent of total agricultural land in the North, with the remaining 15 per cent situated in the mountains.

2.3. *Southern hills and plains*

This vast area was mainly given over to the cultivation (sometimes highly intensive) of cereals, vines, olives, citrus fruit, pulses, vegetables, and tobacco; it was also an area in which there were great differences in crop-yields, some over and some under the previously mentioned averages. For example, Campania and the Marches produced yields per hectare that were above the national average, while those produced in Basilicata and in Sardinia (where transhumant sheep-farming was prevalent) were well below the average. Taken as a whole, however, the South was noticeably less productive than the other two areas mentioned above. Since crops were often mixed (soil and topsoil), productivity can best be measured in terms of monetary income (as has been done here) and not physical yield.

2.4. *Mountain areas*

More than one-third of the total agricultural area in Italy was composed of largely unproductive mountainous regions, which were stubbornly cultivated by the indigenous population, largely due to a lack of alternatives; these regions were responsible for only 20 per cent of GSP in the period 1910–23, and were gradually abandoned by the population.

It is interesting to consider whether the agricultural panorama at the beginning of the twentieth century, as described here, can be defined as being 'backward' or not, and to look at the various stages in its development. A recent study has provided us with a deeper insight into one important characteristic of this historical development, which could serve as a starting-point for an analysis of the matter: Italian agriculture was already heavily commercialized throughout the country at the time of unification.[22] In fact, Giovanni Federico has estimated

[22] G. Federico studied the levels of self-sufficiency on the basis of 255 case-studies of farming families between 1870 and the early 1930s. All the various types of farming structure are represented in this sample, as is the greater part of different geographical areas. The results have

that self-consumption accounted for only some 20–25 per cent of total food consumption, adding that:

This appears to be a direct result of the high proportion of urban population, and of rural families who had very limited possibilities, or no possibility at all, of consuming their own products (day labourers etc.). The resulting demand was satisfied by a supply coming from the sale of small farmers' products, as well as from rents paid in kind by the sharecroppers and from capitalistic farms. The long-run stability and low values of these percentages [of self-consumption] would suggest that there had been a process of commercialization of Italian agriculture prior to industrial development, and thus largely independent of it.[23]

The level of commercialization of Italian agriculture was similar to that of France and Switzerland, higher than that of Yugoslavia and Russia, and only slightly lower than the American equivalent (according to a 1910 estimate, self-consumption in the USA was equivalent to 17 per cent of total production). From this point of view, Italian agriculture certainly cannot be considered as backward. Furthermore, the findings of another recent study, this time comparing Italian and English agriculture around the year 1910,[24] tend to put the backwardness of Italian agricultural production into perspective. First of all, the usual comparisons made concerning physical yield per hectare have always put Italian agriculture in a bad light, as they have never taken into account its true nature: enormous areas were given over to the cultivation of mixed crops, and while this led to relatively lower yields for individual crops, it meant that the same area produced more than one crop at a time.[25] In terms of monetary income as opposed to physical yield, there can be no doubt that Italian agriculture was more intensive than its English equivalent. Value added per hectare was one-third or one-half higher in Italy than in England in the period 1909–14, and if we were to omit the Italian mountainous zone from our

been published in 'Azienda contadina e autoconsumo fra antropologia ed econometria: considerazioni metodologiche', *Rivista di storia economica*, 2 (1984); 'Autoconsumo e mercantilizzazione: spunti per una riflessione', *Società e storia* 27 (1985); 'Mercantilizzazione e sviluppo economico in Italia (1860–1940)', *Rivista di storia economica*, 3 (1986); and 'Contadini e mercato: tattiche di sopravvivenza', in *Società e Storia*, 38 (1987).

[23] G. Federico, 'Contadini e mercato', 883–4. Federico is referring to the 19th-cent. industrialization process; the link between the high level of commercialization of Italian farming and the flourishing commercial and manufacturing tradition of Italian cities from the 14th to the 16th cent. has already been mentioned in the introduction. Federico's conclusions throw a new light on the previously existing research carried out by E. Sereni into 'La formazione del mercato nazionale (1860–1900)', in id., *Capitalismo e mercato nazionale* (Rome, Editori Riuniti, 1981).

[24] P. O'Brien and G. Toniolo, 'Sull'arretratezza dell'agricoltura italiana rispetto a quella del Regno Unito attorno al 1910', *Ricerche economiche*, 40 (1986). On the fact that British agriculture was no longer particularly advanced from an international point of view in 1910, see the remarks by J. L. Van Zanden, 'The First Green Revolution: The Growth of Production and Productivity in European Agriculture, 1870–1914', *Economic History Review*, 44 (1991).

[25] If we only take the North into account, then it is no surprise that as early as the end of the 18th cent. the famous agronomist A. Young wrote that the richest countries in Europe were probably Piedmont and the Milanese and that this was due to the flourishing agriculture to be found there, *Travels during the Years 1787, 1788 and 1789* (London, 1792), 509–10.

calculations, then this superiority would be much greater.[26] However, Italian agriculture was at a disadvantage compared with its English counterpart if we consider the relative figures for value added per worker, which was in Italy 60–65 per cent of the English level, and this would indicate an excessively large work-force present in the Italian countryside. If a figure existed for income per unit of consumption, then this would also be much lower for the Italian population than for that of England, since the rural work-force in Italy contained a much higher proportion of women and children; their working hours and index of productivity were that much lower than those of men, whereas their level of consumption was not very much different. According to O'Brien and Toniolo: 'one can conclude that the Italian agricultural system was not particularly inefficient. The causes of rural poverty in Italy are, rather, to be found in the country's demographic history. . . . In 1911, Italy's agricultural labour-force was made up of some 10 million men, women and children, a large part of whom worked for a limited number of days during the course of a year, thus figuring out a situation well below that of full employment.'[27] Moreover, in order fully to understand the point, one needs to bear in mind the excessive amount of marginal land being cultivated in Italy at this time (large areas of infertile hills and mountains), and also the cultivation of cereals on land hardly suited to such crops, which substantially lowered the average yield per hectare, as we have seen, and resulted from the enormous pressure put on the land by a population that was disproportionately large when compared with the potential of the land.

If the data concerning agricultural productivity at the time of the First World War are sufficiently reliable for us to be able to reach the above-mentioned conclusions, this is due to the relatively advanced nature attained by land-registration, and to the noticeable improvement seen in statistical surveying methods, despite the inherent problems involved.[28] The development of Italian agricultural production during the period between unification and 1909–14 is a rather more difficult thing to ascertain. Mario Romani[29] notes, as others have done, that the first figures for agricultural production were produced between 1870 and 1874,[30] and they were 'subsequently rectified and given as representing average yields for 1876–81, followed by similar data for the five-year period 1879–83; annual estimates only began to appear in 1884'.[31] Local administrators were asked for checks and updating, but they often used

[26] A point already made by G. Biagioli, in 'Agricoltura e sviluppo economico: una riconsiderazione del caso italiano nel periodo preunitario', in *Società e Storia* 9 (1980).

[27] O'Brien and Toniolo, 'Sull'arretratezza dell'agricoltura italiana', 281.

[28] It is worth reading a short essay by Ghino Valenti, a well-known agronomist from the Italian Marches, on this point: 'Le vicende della statistica agraria in Italia', in *L'Italia agricola e il suo avvenire*, i (Rome, printed by Befani, 1919–20).

[29] M. Romani, *Storia economica d'Italia nel secolo XIX*, ii (Milan, Giuffré, 1976).

[30] They were published in MAIC, *Relazione intorno alle condizioni dell'agricoltura nel quinquennio 1870 1874* (Rome, Barbera, 1876–9).

[31] Romani, *Storia economica d'Italia*, 88–9. The annual estimates really start from 1880.

different criteria from one year to the next, and consequently there was very little real improvement in these estimates until reorganization was carried out in 1907: total production estimates were then based upon the productive use made of cultivated areas, and upon sample estimates of annual yields per unit area (the sample was progressively increased from 73 to 695 zones). Although this modification in the way statistical data were collected meant that Italy was now a leader in this field, those figures collected prior to this date need to be used with great care, if we also consider that there were no public surveys before 1870–74: of the private surveys that existed, the most famous one, conducted by C. Correnti and P. Maestri, and cited in Table 0.1 of the introduction, was published in 1864, but contains a large amount of information concerning much earlier years; furthermore, it was somewhat complicated by the vineyard crisis of the 1850s—caused by the presence of vine oidium—and the crisis in silkworm breeding that lasted for the second half of the 1850s and all of the 1860s, brought on by an outbreak of pebrine disease.

This is why it is very difficult to accept without qualifications the validity of ISTAT's annual figures for major products, produced years ago.[32] In the cases of the two most recent studies on the subject, concerning wheat[33] and silkworm cocoons,[34] ISTAT's figures have not proved to be infallible (see Table 1.3). The aggregate figures for GSP produced by ISTAT from such insecure foundations,[35] and given in Table 1.4, point to a slight increase in agricultural

Table 1.3. Estimates of wheat and silk cocoon output, 1861–1913

	Wheat (000 hl.)			Fresh cocoons (000 kg.)	
	ISTAT	Federico		ISTAT	Federico
about 1860	43,056	40,000[a]	1861–6	16,750	24,981
1870–4	50,898	47,000[a]	1873–7	37,392	35,180
1880–3	48,843	44,700	1883–7	38,956	48,580
1890–4	45,400	45,400	1893–7	55,800	58,971
1909–13	62,267	62,267	1908–13	44,979	62,250

[a] Average of the maximum and minimum estimates.

Sources: See notes 32 and 33 in the text and G. Federico, 'Il baco e la filanola. Il mercato dei bozzoli in Italia sec. XIX–XX', *Meridiana*, 15 (1992), 219.

[32] ISTAT, *Sommario di statistiche storiche dell'Italia, 1861–1955* (Rome, 1958).

[33] G. Federico, 'Per una valutazione critica delle statistiche della produzione agricola italiana dopo l'unità (1860–1913)', *Società e Storia*, 15 (1982).

[34] S. Fenoaltea, 'The Growth of Italy's Silk Industry, 1861–1913: A Statistical Reconstruction', *Rivista di storia economica*, 5 (1988). The series of figures shown in Table 1.2 have been obtained from Fenoaltea's series for dried cocoons, using a production coefficient supplied to me by G. Federico.

[35] ISTAT, *Indagine statistica sullo sviluppo del reddito nazionale dell'Italia dal 1861 al 1956* (Rome, 1957).

Table 1.4. GSP, 1861–1913, present boundaries (1938 prices)

	GSP (billions of lire)	Average annual growth rate of GSP (%)	Average annual growth rate of GSP per capita (%)	GSP per hectare (lire)
1861–5	23.9	—	—	934
1870–4	25.9	0.90	+0.2	1,012
1879–83	26.5	0.25	−0.4	1,023
1895–9	26.9	0.09	−0.6	1,023
1901–5	32.5	3.13	+2.5	1,226
1909–13	36.5	1.45	+0.8	1,377

Source: See n. 35 in the text.

production during the first 15 years of unification, followed by a period of stagnation at the time of the international agrarian crisis,[36] and a subsequent productive boom in the last 15 years of the period under examination. Although the data contained in Table 1.4 can only be considered broadly indicative of Italian agriculture's development during the first 50-year period after unification, we can nevertheless advance at least five observations:

1. It is impossible to support the idea that there was any kind of productive revolution during this period; Italian agriculture already had a very definite shape before unification, and this only changed marginally during the following 50 years.[37] The most interesting changes took place in the following sectors: citrus fruit, where production increased fourfold; sugar beet, whose production, almost non-existent prior to 1898, reached an annual total of 16–18 million quintals; wine and fruit, whose yield doubled. Italian agriculture thus moved towards more specialized forms of production, seen by many as being its true vocation, despite the warnings of one writer, Valenti, who suggested that the

[36] With the improvement in long-distance shipping made possible by the use of steam-vessels, American and Russian cereals became available at a low price on European markets, thus leading to a collapse in the profitability of European farming. As we shall see in Ch. 3, several years of crisis brought about the implementation of widespread protectionist measures.

[37] Many experts share this point of view, even for periods predating unification: see e.g. L. Cafagna, 'La "rivoluzione agraria" in Lombardia', *Annali*, 2 (Milan, Feltrinelli, 1959). However, on a local scale, change became noticeable during the second half of the 19th cent., e.g. in the countryside around the Lombard city of Cremona irrigation became widespread, as did the use of tenancy agreements, and yields increased considerably. Cf. P. L. Toninelli, 'Innovazioni techniche, mutamenti strutturali e accumulazione capitalistica nelle campagne cremonesi (1861–1914)', *Rivista di storia dell'agricoltura*, 12 (Aug. 1973), and A. Cova, *Cremona e la sua provincia nell'Italia unita*, i (Milan, Giuffré, 1984). For a similar analysis of the Brescian plain, see E. Braga, 'Un secolo di agricoltura bresciana 1880–1980', in *Dalla famiglia contadina all'impresa moderna* (Brescia, CAB, 1984).

growth of international and domestic demand for such 'luxury' products would necessarily be limited.[38]

2. The famous Romeo's thesis,[39] which enlivened historians' debates on the subject of the first 30 years of unification and the politics of the Destra Storica (Historical Right), can be seen to be devoid of all empirical content. This thesis starts from the premiss that the period 1861–80 was 'without doubt one of the periods during which Italian agriculture made the most progress',[40] and then goes on to conclude that the Historical Right's economic policy was extremely enlightened, since it not only aided agricultural development and, by limiting consumption, paved the way for the accumulation of capital, but it also employed taxation in order to channel this capital towards infrastructures first and then industrial objectives. While I shall look at the problems of industrial development in the next chapter, here I have to confirm that of the data so far available, nothing can be offered in support of Romeo's thesis.[41] If Italian agriculture was able to accumulate capital, this certainly did not happen primarily during the 1861–80 period,[42] and furthermore it was not due to the policies of the Historical Right. If Romeo's attack on the Gramscian concept of the 'failed agricultural revolution'[43] can be considered to be in some way justifiable from the point of view of the practical applicability of Gramsci's socio-political view, it cannot be justified from an historical-economical perspective, because the agricultural development that was supposedly based on political support (by the Historical Right) for existing working relations within agriculture has never been proved (the logical sequence itself could easily be questioned).

[38] G. Valenti, in 'L'Italia agricola dal 1861 al 1911', in Accademia dei Lincei (ed.), *Cinquan t'anni di storia italiana*, iii (Milan, Hoepli, 1912), p. lxi, wrote: 'It is true that our country is destined to become the orchard, the great allotment of Europe . . . but what we do not realize is that even if we only set about cultivating a further one million hectares of vegetable garden and fruit trees, we would have difficulty in ensuring a market in Europe for the produce yielded from such an area.'

[39] R. Romeo, *Risorgimento e capitalismo* (Bari, Laterza, 1963).

[40] Ibid. 120–1. Note that Romeo makes use of the ISTAT figures at the boundaries of the time, and in doing so, the gross saleable product (GSP) growth rate appears higher than it really is, due to the inclusion of the GSP of the Veneto and Latium, which became part of the Kingdom of Italy during that period.

[41] Subsequent efforts to give some extra weight to the empirical bases of Romeo's thesis, using figures obtained from farm studies carried out at the time, were somewhat inconclusive. Cf. G. Pescosolido, 'L'andamento della produzione agraria durante il primo ventennio post-unitario', *Nuova rivista storica*, 63 (Jan.–Apr. 1979). A more recent study of agricultural production in Lombardy from 1861 to 1914 accepts without qualifications the validity of the official figures and of the estimates provided by Correnti and Maestri concerning physical production. Cf. T. P. Barbiero, 'A Reassessment of Agricultural Production in Italy 1861–1914: the Case of Lombardy', *Journal of European Economic History*, 17 (1988).

[42] In fact, many agrarian scholars from Jacini onwards had a rather negative view of agricultural development during this period. Cf. among others G. Luzzatto, *L'Economia italiana dal 1861 al 1894* (Turin, Einaudi, 1968), ch. 4.

[43] This thesis was put forward by Gramsci in *Il Risorgimento* (Rome, Editori Riuniti, 1971), and figures in the works of E. Sereni.

3. The agrarian crisis that hit the rest of Europe towards the end of the 1870s arrived a few years later in Italy, as a result of the country being at the time outside the gold standard.[44] Prices for wheat and maize plummeted from 1883 onwards, followed by those for other agricultural products (hemp, butter, silk-cocoons, rice), and this led to an increase in the mortgage debt and to a process of readjustment; this involved a cut in the total area given over to the cultivation of rice and hemp, in favour of forage for animals (and, subsequently, sugar beet). Wine and oil production, spared from the crisis, spread in the South, whereas the marginal wheat-growing areas were reduced by a total of 450,000 hectares. A new class of modern agricultural entrepreneurs started to emerge, particularly in the Po Plain, and the innovations introduced by these agricultural entrepreneurs, such as the use of technically advanced machinery and chemical fertilizers, meant that the work-force, which was already severely underemployed, became even more so.[45] The persistence of the agricultural crisis eventually led to a general economic crisis, as agriculture was still the basis of the economy, and this led to both social unrest and emigration. The attempt to block this negative economic trend with the introduction of protectionist measures will be examined in Chapter 3.[46]

4. The adoption of new farming methods was further encouraged by the introduction of the new import tariff which brought about an increase in cereal prices; as a result, there was a consistent growth in agricultural productivity between the end of the nineteenth century and the First World War (continuing up until the mid-1920s); this expansion in the agricultural sector was an important aid to the concurrent industrial boom.

5. The last conclusion that can be drawn from the ISTAT figures (as offered by G. Orlando in his study)[47] concerns the relative performance of the different types of agriculture present in the nation as a whole, between the periods 1870–4 and 1909–13. Orlando subdivides Italy into four areas, which although different from mine, do have some things in common with them (see Table 1.5).

The first area, where yield per hectare is at its highest, is the one that best survived the period of crisis, managing to maintain an average yield twice as high as that of the other areas during the entire period. The various technological innovations introduced during this period are concentrated in this area, as we shall see below. The development of agriculture in the other three

[44] We shall be looking at the monetary policy that brought about inconvertibility of the lira in Ch. 5.

[45] For an illustration of these developments in the Bologna area, see my essay 'L'economia', in R. Zangheri (ed.), *Bologna* (Bari, Laterza, 1986), 250–4.

[46] The whole problem is dealt with in A. De Bernardi, *Questione agraria e protezionismo nella crisi economica di fine secolo* (Milan, Angeli, 1977).

[47] G. Orlando, 'Progressi e difficoltà dell'agricoltura', in G. Fuà (ed.), *Lo sviluppo economico in Italia*, iii (Milan, Angeli, 1969).

Table 1.5. Geographical breakdown of GSP estimates 1870/4–1903/13 (1938 billion lire)

	(1) Po valley hills and plains (5.6 million ha.)		(2) Intensive hills and plains in the Centre and South (7 million ha.)		(3) Appennine mountains and hills (9.3 million ha.)		(4) Alpine mountains (4.5 million ha.)	
	GSP	Yearly increase (%)	GSP	Yearly increase (%)	GSP	Yearly increase (%)	GSP	Yearly increase (%)
1870–4	7.76	—	8.03	—	8.16	—	1.98	—
1895–9	8.90	0.5	7.80	−0.1	8.31	0.01	1.90	−0.2
1901–5	11.10	3.7	9.01	2.4	10.30	3.60	2.14	2.0
1909–13	13.30	2.3	10.20	1.5	10.60	0.40	2.42	1.5
1870/4–1909/13	—	1.4	—	0.6	—	0.7	—	0.5

Source: See n. 47 in the text.

areas, however, differs only slightly from that of the first area.[48] If Orlando had chosen to separate the mountainous area from the others, then perhaps its marginal nature would have been more apparent. One would hope, in any case, that a further, more detailed study both of the trend of agricultural production in nineteenth-century Italy and of its territorial composition be carried out at some point in the near future.

Finally, a brief illustration of the technological advances made in Italian agriculture would be useful here. The most important period was that immediately following the start of the agrarian crisis, when the figure of the peripatetic agricultural instructor was established in order to give farmers technical help and instruction;[49] during the same period, farmers' associations were set up to provide farmers with modern agricultural productive factors, such as specially selected seeds, fertilizers, pesticides, and machinery. The first peripatetic post was created at Rovigo in 1886, while the first associations were set up in the Po Valley in 1889, and in 1892 these associations joined together to form the Farmers' Union. Both institutions proved to be invaluable for agricultural advancement in Italy; at first, posts for peripatetic experts only existed in the area of the Po Plain, but they were later created in both central and southern Italy, by the State in most cases. Farmers' associations and peripatetic instructors worked together to improve the technical level of agriculture. One sign of this was the relatively rapid adoption of chemical fertilizers during the 1890s, and this in turn was accompanied by a growth in their manufacture in Italy. In the 1880s, average annual consumption of fertilizers was about 30,000 tons, nearly all of this being imported from abroad; by 1913 this figure had risen to 1,278,486 tons, 78 per cent of this produced in Italy, and 70 per cent used in the Po Plain, where the main producers were also located (see Table 1.6).[50] The consumption of copper sulphate, employed as a fungicide, had previously been relatively insignificant, and demand had been satisfied through importation; by 1913 consumption had risen to 74,425 tons, 60 per cent of which was being produced nationally (with a heavy concentration in Piedmont, which accounted for about two-thirds of total national production). It is more difficult to furnish complete figures for farming machinery; however, we know that there had been a very sharp rise in imports, from about 10,000 at the end of the 1880s to roughly 170,000 just before the First World

[48] Of course this does not mean that studies conducted into more specific areas will not reveal extremely dynamic situations: see e.g. F. Galassi, 'Stasi e sviluppo nell'agricoltura toscana, 1870–1914: i primi risultati di uno studio aziendale', *Rivista di storia economica*, 3 (1986).

[49] On the diffusion of new agricultural practices, see the interesting volume edited by S. Zaninelli, *Le conoscenze agrarie e la loro diffusione in Italia nell'Ottocento* (Turin, Giappichelli, 1990).

[50] M. Pezzati offers a detailed study of chemical products used in agriculture, in 'I prodotti chimici per l'agricoltura in Italia nel periodo 1899–1929', in F. Amatori and B. Bezza (eds.), *Montecatini: capitoli di storia di una grande impresa* (Bologna, Il Mulino, 1991). The agricultural consortia themselves opened up fertilizer factories, and thus represented direct competition for private producers.

Table 1.6. Production and consumption of chemical products in agriculture (tons)

	1893		1901		1913	
	Prod.	Consump.	Prod.	Consump.	Prod.	Consump.
Phosphates						
superphosphates	72,095	112,243	378,774	390,225	972,494	1,025,217
Thomas meal	—	—	—	25,476	—	119,257
Potassium						
potassium chloride	—	4,748	—	3,453	—	7,061
potassium sulphate	—	158	—	1,411	—	9,454
Nitrates						
raw sodium nitrate	—	11,280	—	40,498	—	67,418
ammonium sulphate	328	4,500[a]	2,967	7,264	13,428	35,097
calcium cyanamide	—	—	—	—	14,872	14,982
Copper sulphate	881	9,890	15,734	47,772	44,497	74,425

[a] approximate value.

Source: See n. 49 in the text.

War, as well as a noticeable expansion in machinery production in Italy during the same period. Judging by the figures available for motor-driven equipment, again about 70 per cent of agricultural machinery of this kind was being employed in the sole area of the Po Plain.[51]

Before drawing any conclusions concerning the subject of agriculture's role in Italian economic development, brought up at the beginning of this section, we need to take a further look at its institutional aspects.

3. THE INSTITUTIONAL ORGANIZATION OF ITALIAN AGRICULTURE

Despite the fact that there had been a quickening in the pace of land privatization between the end of the eighteenth century and the Napoleonic period, some historical relationships continued to exist: for example, forms of perpetual service (emphyteusis, ground rents, annuities, and leaseholds), tithes and common rights, particularly in the South, *ademprivio* (common use) in Sardinia, and *fideicommissa* (no freedom of land sale). Large areas of public land (demesne), managed by both State and local government, together with extensive Church property, meant that potentially important agricultural land could not be worked privately. With unification, the new political classes made the complete privatization of agricultural land their prime objective, as a first step towards a fundamental revision of productive practices. Unfortunately, as A. Caracciolo noted when commenting on privatization during the Napoleonic period, in some areas (particularly in the South), 'even important changes that were made concerned more often than not the title deed and its owner, rather than the relationship between landowner and the use that the land was put to'.[52] Nevertheless, the entire privatization process, which went on for tens of years, was of enormous proportions, and is of interest for many different reasons. Although I cannot go into much detail here, the following represents a summary of the way privatization was carried out.[53]

The main laws concerning the abolition of 'common' land were all

[51] For further figures concerning the mechanization of Italian agriculture at the beginning of this century, cf. A. De Bernardi, 'Appunti sulle innovazioni delle tecniche agrarie in Val Padana tra Ottocento e Novecento', *Padania*, 2 (1988).

[52] A. Caracciolo, 'La storia economica', in *Storia d'Italia. Dal Primo Settecento all'Unità*, iii (Turin, Einaudi, 1973), 562.

[53] There is a methodical analysis of this question in G. Catalano, *La fine dei 'possessi plebei': svincolo e privatizzazione delle proprietà comuni della terra dopo l'unità d'Italia*, a graduation thesis written under my supervision in the Political Science Faculty of Florence University in 1985–6. For a discussion of the power of the Church in the Piedmont region, cf. A. Bogge and M. Sibona, *La vendita dell'asse ecclesiastico in Piemonte dal 1867 al 1916* (Milan, Banca Commerciale Italiana, 1987), and for the Campania region, see G. Montroni, *Società e mercato della terra. La vendita dei terreni della Chiesa in Campania dopo l'unità* (Naples, Guida, 1983). Another interesting analysis is that of E. Cerrito, 'Territorio, demani, comunità: per una interpretazione della questione demaniale. Il caso di Principato Citra nel XIX secolo', *Rivista di storia economica*, 5 (1988).

introduced immediately after unification, and they were invariably connected to some pressing financial need or other resulting from the State's budget deficit (see Chapter 5): the 1862 law, making provision for the sale of State property; the 1867 law which saw to the abolition of Church property; the 1861–2 laws that facilitated the division of local borough lands; finally, special laws concerning certain geographical areas—the Tuscan 'Maremma', the 'Sila' in Calabria, the Apulian 'Tavoliere', as well as Sicily and Sardinia. In all, these laws covered some 3 million hectares of land, more than 2.5 million of which were to be found in the South (equal to about 25 per cent of total farmland in the South, although this percentage was even higher in some areas such as Apulia). The revenue yielded in the State's favour from the application of these laws was particularly significant during the first few years, given that 70 per cent of sales took place between 1866 and 1875 (see Chapter 5).

The way in which privatization was carried out was criticized both at the time, and later on by historians, since its *raison d'être* was in one sense the urgent financial requirements of the seller; as a result, the laws were rushed affairs, and they led to six different methods of sale, together with a noticeable depreciation in the value of the properties being sold. As there was no real possibility (and/or the will was lacking) of creating supportive structures in order to help the setting-up of small farmholds, the property sold often went simply towards the enlargement of already existing properties (especially in the South), thus absorbing capital which could have been used to improve the productivity of existing farmland.[54] Moreover, while it is true that middle-class property in the South has its foundations mainly in this period in history—'at the expense of Church property'[55]—this does not mean that the structural nature of Southern farming changed to any significant degree (as we shall see shortly).[56] An invaluable opportunity was therefore missed to get a genuine process of reform under way, and the simple privatization of farmlands was not enough to encourage a real change in productive relations in the Italian South.

At this point, we can no longer avoid a more detailed analysis of the institutional structure of Italian agriculture. The ways of farming are as varied as the Italian coutryside itself. However, there are three basic models, each with innumerable variations, as well as different combinations of the three. These are the smallholding, the tenant farm, and sharecropping (see Table 1.7 for a region-by-region breakdown of the agricultural labour-force into those principal professional categories in existence, for the years 1881 and 1911).

[54] G. Valenti was also quick to point out that the hurried sale of land generated an enormous amount of speculation 'which, in diverting capital away from production, led to a halt in agricultural progress, at least for a period', 'L'Italia agricola dal 1861 al 1911', 56.

[55] E. Sereni, *Il capitalismo nelle campagne (1860-1900)* (Turin, Einaudi, 1947), 143.

[56] The most balanced view of this particular situation is still that given by Luzzatto in *L'Economia italiana*, 109, when he writes: 'where physical and demographic conditions favoured smallholdings, such sales contributed towards increasing the numbers thereof; where such favourable conditions were absent, the sales led to an enlargement of latifundia.'

Table 1.7. Professional composition of the agricultural labour-force in 1881 and 1911 (%)

	1881				1911					
	Owner-operators	Tenant farmers[a]	Share-croppers	Day labourers and others[b]	Owner-operators	Tenant farmers[a]	Share-croppers	Yearly labourers and skilled workers	Day labourers	Others[b]
	(1)	(2)	(3)	(4)	(5)	(6)	(7)	(8)	(9)	(10)
Piedmont	32	2.5	2.5	63	43	7.5	5	3.5	39	2
Liguria	31	5	7	57	39	8	14	1.5	34	3.5
Lombardy	12.5	9	11.5	67	18	10	18	11	39	4
Veneto	14	11	8	67	22	19	12	5	38	4
Emilia R.	10	4	28.5	57.5	13	9	31	6	38	3
Tuscany	10.5	2.5	42	45	12	2	55	1	25	5
Marches	7.5	0.5	53	39	12	1	58	0.5	25	3.5
Umbria	11	0.5	22	66.5	12	1	47	1	32	7
Latium	13.5	2.5	6	78	12	1.5	13	2	58	13.5
Abruzzi–M.	21.5	5	7	66.5	32	6	11	2	46	3
Campania	10.5	8	4	77.5	17	10	8	3	57.5	4.5
Apulia	13	2.5	0.5	84	8	5	1.5	3	76.5	6
Basilicata	15	5.5	0.5	79	16	9.5	3	4	61	6.5
Calabria	7.5	3	2.5	87	9	4	10	2	68	7
Sicily	12	3	4	81	7.5	5	8	4	68.5	7
Sardinia	20	7	5	68	12	3	4	5	53	23
ITALY	15.5	5	12.5	67	19	8	17.5	4	47	4.5

[a] The category of tenant farmers includes emphyteutas, mixed-tenancy sharecropping contract-holders, self-employed gardeners, fruit-growers, shepherds, livestock breeders, woodcutters; in 1911 it excludes emphyteutas, included in other categories.

[b] The category 'other' includes land agents, white-collar employees, and hired herdsmen and shepherds.

Sources: *Population censuses*, 1881 and 1911. The revision of population census figures operated by O. Vitali, *La popolazione attiva in agricoltura attraverso i censimenti italiani* (Rome, Tip. Failli, 1968), could not be employed here because the author has not recalculated the aggregates by profession. Such a revision has, however, been taken into consideration in the tables reporting the professional composition of the Italian labour-force in the Introduction.

Smallholdings were particularly common on farmland in the Alps (above all in Piedmont) and in the Abruzzo. Their numbers grew with the sale of public and church lands, although not in a uniform fashion throughout the country as a whole, as there were some areas where there was a relative decline, for example in Latium, Apulia, Sicily, and Sardinia. They often consisted in a form of subsistence farming, where the family also went to work outside the farm in order to supplement its income; in other cases, they were farms that specialized in highly profitable products, such as flowers, wine, or vegetables.

Tenancy was open to very different versions. Whether a small tenancy or a large one, there were basically, in the words of Jacini 'two different forms of tenancy in Italy . . . one [in which] the tenant is not a farmer, but takes on the role of speculator, whereas in the other form, he becomes an industrialist who exploits the land of another using his own capital. It should be noted that the former, deplorable model . . . is, in some cases, the result of the owners' laziness, and in others, due to the scarcity of circulating capital'.[57] The figure of the tenant entrepreneur was particularly common in the area of the Po Valley, whereas that of the speculator was to be found above all in Latium (in the person of the country dealer or trader), as well as in the South. In the South there were also so-called 'improvement' tenancy contracts, where the tenant farmer obtained land at a very low rent, but was obliged to plant certain kinds of tree in order to improve the land's value, and for which he received little or no compensation at the end of the period of tenancy. The tenant farmer employed farm-workers, who made up some 67 per cent of the total agricultural labour-force in 1881 (and 55.5 per cent of it in 1911). Some of these employees, usually those most specialized, were given annual contracts, while the rest were taken on as day labourers; it was the latter category of workers who suffered most from the the situation of underemployment present in the Italian countryside at the time, as they only found work for a relatively small number of days during the year, and were thus far from being fully employed (see Chapter 6 for a further discussion of the day labourers' situation).

Finally, we come to sharecropping, which usually took the form of métayage: this is a contract which consisted in the division of the products between landowner and farmer. In Tuscany, for example, this meant that all products were divided in half between landowner and farmer, and the landowner supplied all factors of production. Another kind of contract consisted in the division of products in different proportions according to the type of product, with the farmer supplying his own working animals—as in the case of livestock (*boaria*) contracts in Romagna; there were also innumerable other versions of the sharecropping system. Such contracts were particularly common in central Italy and in Romagna. In the dry, silk-growing areas of Lombardy, a mixture of

[57] Jacini, *Relazione finale*, 52–3. On the large capitalist tenancies of the Po Valley, see the very interesting book by M. Malatesta, *L'organizzazione degli interessi agrari padani (1860–1914)* (Milan, Angeli, 1989).

tenancy and métayage was common (the mixed tenancy). Sharecropping contracts, common to many Mediterranean areas, have traditionally been considered a residuary form left over from the preceding feudal order; as such, they have been seen as not really capable of adjusting to technological progress, and thus to an increasing level of productivity, but rather doomed to reinforce the farm's self-sufficient status, leading to a low level of commercialization and monetization of the system, and providing very little impetus to a growth in non-agricultural markets.[58] However, their longevity has led to a recent reappraisal of their traditionally negative reputation. It has been said that the sharecropping system has led to significant improvements in production in areas where this was feasible.[59] It has been seen as an elastic institutional structure from the point of view of those risks run during a period of crisis;[60] it allowed the peasant farmer to enjoy a modest living which was always better than that of a day labourer.[61] It also produced a level of commercialization that was not that low (although probably lower than in the case of the tenant farmer).[62] It has been considered to be the 'one agricultural form that has made some contribution towards preserving the fragile environment of the hill areas, through its avoidance of the impoverishing effect created by extensive monocultures, and its contribution towards the perpetuation of the topsoil's fertility'.[63] Finally, and most important of all, the sharecropping system has proved capable of producing entrepreneurial skills on a family scale.[64]

These important points concerning the consequences of the sharecropping system tend to bring up old problems once more; problems of why there is such

[58] See above all G. Giorgetti, *Contadini e proprietari nell'Italia moderna: Rapporti di produzione e contratti agrari dal secolo XVI ad oggi* (Turin, Einaudi, 1974); cf. also C. Pazzagli, *Per la storia dell'agricoltura toscana nei secoli XIX e XX* (Turin, Einaudi Foundation, 1979).

[59] Galassi, 'Stasi e sviluppo nell'agricoltura toscana'. In a more recent article, Cohen and Galassi argue that the backward elements that are to be found in sharecropping are not due to the institution, but to external constraints that are responsible, among other things, for the survival of sharecropping itself. See J. S. Cohen and F. L. Galassi, 'Sharecropping and Productivity: "Feudal Residues" in Italian Agriculture, 1911', *Economic History Review*, 43 (1990).

[60] J. S. Cohen, 'Rapporti agricoltura–industria e sviluppo agricolo', in P. Ciocca and T. Toniolo (eds.), *L'economia italiana nel periodo fascista* (Bologna, Il Mulino, 1976).

[61] V. Zamagni, 'Le radici agricole del dualismo italiano', *Nuova Rivista Storica*, 59 (1975).

[62] Cf. the already cited studies of self-sufficiency carried out by G. Federico.

[63] S. Anselmi, 'Caratteri dell'economia mezzadrile tra Ottocento e Novecento', *Proposte e ricerche*, 18 (1987), 132. See also S. Anselmi, 'Mezzadri e mezzadrie nell'Italia centrale', in P. Bevilacqua (ed.), *Storia dell'agricoltura italiana in età contemporanea*, ii (Venice, Marsilio, 1990) and *Proposte e Ricerche*, 25 (1990).

[64] C. Carboni, 'Mentalità, lavoro e classi sociali', in S. Anselmi (ed.), *Le Marche* (Turin, Einaudi, 1987); G. Becattini, 'Riflessioni sullo sviluppo socio-economico della Toscana in questo dopoguerra', in G. Mori (ed.), *La Toscana* (Turin, Einaudi, 1986). For example, Becattini writes (p. 907): 'First of all, the Tuscan sharecropping system, with its "farms" representing productive and second-order trading units, was not so far off from the capitalistic organization of production and commerce, as believed by some, after all. The "farm" was not only a productive unit, but together with village dances, parties, and the local market, represented an important unit of socialization for farmers and their families, and led to the formation of a collective consciousness among these people.'

a diversity of productive methods and institutional structures in Italy. Are we to accept Jacini's thesis, that sees all institutional and productive developments as being 'determined' by local climatic, geological, and environmental factors,[65] or are there important historical-cultural factors at play, which, over the centuries, are gradually transformed into environmental conditions? What would have been the costs and the advantages of institutional change at the productive level in different places and moments in history? It is clear that we can no longer afford to put off a comparative analysis of these problems, which have been considered solely at a local level up to now.

Before beginning our analysis of the long-term effects of different agricultural practices in Italy, we need to take a look at one last institutional aspect which is of vital importance for the improvement of productive practices: credit in agriculture. By agricultural credit I mean forms of credit specially devised for agriculture, besides the normal credit which was readily available but very expensive.

The Italian government had not shown any interest in agricultural credit until 21 June 1869,[66] when Parliament finally passed a law concerning this problem, although both contemporary commentators and historians criticized it for being unrealistic and ineffectual.[67] Subsequently, nothing was done to remedy the situation until 1887, a period which took in a good half of the agrarian crisis and of building speculation as well. This second law encouraged savings banks (Casse di risparmio), institutions already involved in supplying credit to farmers,[68] to open up special offices dealing exclusively with agricultural credit, but only six such offices actually became operative as a result of the law. Local co-operative banks (Banche popolari), and in particular rural savings banks (Casse rurali), which were founded from 1883 onwards almost exclusively in the North, also started to offer specialized credit to farmers, although this was usually limited to working capital credit. In the South the grain banks (Monti frumentari) continued operations (although they were in decline towards the end of the nineteenth century), as did the pawnbrokers (Monti di pietà), both of which were involved in giving working capital credit to farmers.

With the passing of special legislation for the South at the beginning of the twentieth century (as mentioned above), there was a move towards setting up institutions of credit that were to fill the gap left by the lack of local networks

[65] This 'deterministic' approach lay behind those arguments against the breaking-up of the southern *latifundia*, maintaining, as it did, that this was the only way that such land could be farmed: cf. A. Di Rudinì, 'Terre incolte e latifondo', *Il Giornale degli economisti*, 10, 2nd series (Feb. 1895). For an analysis of the relationship between the *latifundia* and droughts, cf. Barone, *Mezzogiorno e modernizzazione*, Ch. 4.

[66] L. De Rosa, 'Una storia dolente: le faticose origini del credito agrario', *Rivista storica italiana*, 76 (1964).

[67] For an analysis of the whole question, cf. G. Muzzioli, *Banche e agricoltura. Il credito all'agricoltura italiana dal 1861 al 1940* (Bologna, Il Mulino, 1983).

[68] In particular, the Cassa di Risparmio di Milano (1823) and the Cassa di Risparmio di Bologna (1837).

and by the failure of the grain banks. Unfortunately, there are no comprehensive quantitative figures giving the results of these legislative operations, but the available studies carried out in this field would suggest that the only geographical areas that had access to an adequate system of credit were, in fact, those that were already on a good economic footing; the other areas were virtually shunned by institutions of credit, receiving little financial help towards improving agricultural methods, and the figure of the usurer continued to be the scourge of farmers in such areas of Italy.[69]

4. SOME REMARKS ABOUT THE PERSISTENCE OF REGIONAL IMBALANCES

As one of the most enlightened historians of modern southern Italian history has pointed out, 'we should forget all those futile diatribes against the Italian State, for its having denied the South the economic assistance lavished on the North . . . the origins of the present-day economic imbalance are to be traced back to a period in history well before that of unification'.[70] If we accept that this analysis is correct, as I have done in the introduction to the present volume, what needs to be explained here is precisely what factors contributed to the persistence of this initial imbalance. I personally have been convinced for a long time[71] of the following: given the long-drawn-out decline of post-Renaissance manufacturing and trade and the increasing economic dependence of the country upon agriculture, which sometimes spawned activities that were not strictly agricultural (such as the raw-silk industry), the main reasons for the regional diversity of economic development after unification have to be located in this agricultural base. This must not hide the fact that, as has frequently been pointed out, the economic positions of the diverse agricultural bases, at the time of unification, were themselves the result of previously taken decisions that were not deterministic.

At the time of unification, we can clearly identify the diverse nature of the different types of Italian agriculture, and could classify them in the following way:

1. Profitable, intensive farming (Po Plain and northern hills), with a noticeably developed infrastructure, including transport, credit facilities, commercial and proto-industrial structures (sometimes involving ties with the old commercial and manufacturing activities). The home markets are wealthier,

[69] Cf e.g. E. De Simone, *Credito fondiario e proprietà immobiliare nell'Italia meridionale 1866–1885* (Naples, Stab. Arte Tipografica, 1883), together with the bibliography in Muzzioli, *Banche e agricoltura*.

[70] G. Barone, 'Stato, capitale finanziario e Mezzogiorno', in *La modernizzazione difficile. Città e campagne nel mezzogiorno dall'età giolittiana al fascismo* (Bari, De Donato, 1983), 28.

[71] Zamagni, 'Le radici agricole'.

manpower is more skilled and better trained, and underemployment is less common; capital accumulation and mobility is widespread; entrepreneurial ability is utilized over a wide range of activities.

2. In the typically Mediterranean mixed-farming areas, where smallholdings or sharecropping prevail, the above is also true, but either to a more limited extent and/or in a different form. In particular, entrepreneurial activity takes place on a family scale rather than on a large scale, as we have already seen.

3. In those areas of the Centre and the South which either have problems of a geological nature and/or are dry, the prevalent form of farming is that of the extensively farmed *latifundium* (often accompanied by smaller subsistence plots, *minifundia*); here, productivity is low; services such as transport[72] and commercial and credit facilities are primitive; there is an over-abundance of labour (most of it unskilled); the internal market is extremely poor; capital accumulation is limited;[73] entrepreneurial skills are hardly ever employed, and when they are it is in the worst possible manner; and finally, there is hardly any incentive to teach agricultural skills. At the time of unification, the situation was so bad that any kind of real change would have necessitated massive investment in land-reclamation and irrigation projects, together with revolutionary changes in the public infrastructure, credit facilities, and the deployment of labour: an enormous undertaking that would have far exceeded the potential of the resources available at the time.

4. A highly specialized type of farming, involving the cultivation of high-yield fruit and vegetable crops, was to be found in the coastal areas of the South, with the majority of these products destined for foreign export; as such, this form of agricultural production was one of the novelties of the first 50-year period following unification, even though it unfortunately involved 'a weak spreading effect and an inadequate self-supporting mechanism',[74] simply producing agricultural 'enclaves'.

It is clear, therefore, that it is of no use to draw general conclusions about the relationship between agriculture and economic development in Italy, since this relationship varies with the different farming areas. In some of these areas, agriculture furnished certain positive developmental impulses, in both the short and the long run; in other areas, agriculture proved to be incapable of

[72] Bevilacqua, in 'Uomini, terre, economie', has the following to say about Calabria: 'To reach Naples by land, at the time of unification, took at least 4 days from the nearest provincial capital, that is Cosenza. From Catanzaro, the journey took 2 or 3 days longer, and in the case of Reggio Calabria it was the case of a journey that took nearly 9 days' (p. 127). Further on, he writes: 'The mule and the donkey were . . . for a long time the chief protagonists of all journeys, whether of people or of foodstuffs' (p. 135). Cf. also L. Spoto, *Economisti e questione agraria in Sicilia: 1860–1895* (Palermo, Vittorietti, 1980).

[73] This did not prevent individual southern barons, who owned vast *latifundia*, from living sumptuously in Naples or in Palermo.

[74] Barone, *Stato, capitale finanziario*, 35.

contributing towards development, and the 'push' had to come from completely different sources.

Before concluding this chapter, I would like to make a final remark: this is, that the gap between those areas that had industrialized and the others that had not done so was to increase further, probably until the late 1940s, even if the quantitative data we have concerning this gap are somewhat scanty.[75] One of the main reasons for this limited geographical spread of development (until recent times) can be mentioned here, as it is intrinsically connected to the agricultural picture we have been looking at. As Luciano Cafagna first observed some years ago, North and South in no way complemented each other, and so were not able to grow together: 'In terms of resources . . . and of raw product supplies, whether mineral or agricultural . . . there was hardly any possibility for a complementary interweaving between the two different geographical areas.'[76] At the time of unification, less than 20 per cent of Italian States' trade was conducted between States; later, the whole of Italy became a net importer of wheat, while those specialized products that were produced in the South were, for the best part, exported to Central Europe. There was a greater degree of complementarity between the North-West and the North-East (in terms of sugar, wine, and meat). The same could be said for raw materials and industrial products, as well as for the labour-force: the North was self-sufficient (it had an excess, in fact) in these factors at least until the 1930s.[77] Other elements that contributed towards these regional gaps will be dealt with in the following chapters.

[75] A survey of existing studies in this area, together with an estimate of the development of this gap in terms of per capita income in the three areas—the North-West, the North-East and Centre, the South—during the period 1860–1980, can be found in V. Zamagni, 'Cuestión meridional o cuestión nacional? Algunas consideraciones sobre el desequilibrio regional en Italia', *Revista de Historia económica*, 5 (1987).

[76] L. Cafagna, 'Intorno alle origini del dualismo economico in Italia', in *Saggi in onore di Leopoldo Cassese* (Naples, Lib. Scientifica ed., 1971), 116—now to be found in L. Cafagna, *Dualismo e sviluppo nella storia d'Italia* (Venice, Marsilio, 1989).

[77] For details on these matters, see V. Zamagni, 'Ferrovie e integrazione del mercato nazionale nell'Italia post-unitaria', in *Studi in onore di Gino Barbieri*, iii (Salerno, IPEM ed., 1983). A recent study which underlines the importance of agriculture, in the province of Salerno, in as much as this is seen as constituting 'one of the principal factors forming an obstacle to balanced growth', is L. Rossi's *Dualismi economici nel Mezzogiorno liberale. La provincia di Salerno* (Salerno, Palladio, 1988), 279.

2

From Craftsmanship to Industrial Production

1. THE LOCALIZATION AND NATURE OF ITALIAN INDUSTRIAL DEVELOPMENT

At the time of the unification of Italy, industry, although not totally absent from the scene, was none the less of marginal importance: crafts, on the other hand, existed in proportion to local demand, and therefore to the different levels of income produced by the diverse forms of agriculture. Fifty years later, all the modern industries were present in Italy, some more some less advanced: from the metallurgical industry to the energy industry, from the production of tyres to that of cars, from chemical fertilizers to sugar. An industrial census was conducted at the end of this period in order to ascertain to what extent industrialization had been accomplished; it is not without its defects (there are no figures for the value of production, for example), but the data available for the intermediate stages of Italian industrialization are even more incomplete.

In fact, the Statistics Department of the Ministry of Agriculture, Industry, and Trade (MAIC—Ministero di Agricoltura, Industria, e Commercio) insisted for a long time on asking local prefects, councils, and chambers of commerce for the relevant information, rather than organizing direct surveys and/or proper censuses. The first attempt to conduct a survey of Italian industry goes back to 1862, but the only result it gave was the publication of two reports concerning the towns of Bergamo and Parma, together with a collection of figures from the silk-processing and mining industries.[1] A second, more ambitious attempt was launched on 7 September 1869, but again this was eventually limited to an examination of the effects of free trade on industrial enterprises, by means of the distribution of questionnaires (about 7,000 were given out, and 1,227 were returned), followed by a direct investigation by a specially appointed commission.[2] G. Are maintains that 'for the first time ever, political leaders were able to gain first-hand knowledge of businesses and their problems, and thus reconsider their own preconceived ideas, based for the best part on academic study, concerning the nature of Italian industry—and in doing so, they could acknowledge the complex series of obstacles that stood between

[1] A. Polsi, 'La "ṣtatistica dell'industria manifattrice" del 1862', *Quaderni Storici*, 45 (1980).

[2] Among the membership of such commissions there were men such as Antonio Scialoia, Alessandro Rossi, Luigi Luzzatti, the mines inspector Felice Giordano, and Vittorio Ellena.

the reality at that time and the coming-into-being of a truly European form of industry on Italian soil';[3] however, no statistical synthesis was forthcoming from this.

Another study, this time conducted by Vittorio Ellena in July 1876,[4] was something more of a success, although it did not cover the mining, metal and engineering, chemical, or brick industries, as engineers from the Mining Corps were responsible for these sectors: they eventually did cover with their surveys these areas of industry, with the exception of the engineering sector,[5] which, together with certain other sectors, such as the food, clothing, and printing industries, were left out of any kind of industrial survey. Ellena's figures only covered energy used and employment in factories, thus excluding the contribution made by home-workers and, at least in theory, by those employed in artisan trades.[6]

At the beginning of the 1880s, the Statistical Board decided to carry out another survey, this time on a provincial basis; however, the approach and the instruments used remained substantially the same as before, although this time they gave more comprehensive results. Between 1885 and 1903, 86 studies appeared (including second editions, together with five sectorial studies);[7] they were all different from one another, both in terms of the accuracy and the final conclusions drawn,[8] and therefore they were difficult to summarize, as can be seen from a look at the survey conducted by the MAIC in 1905–6:[9] the updating of all figures to 1903 appears, on closer inspection, to be a complete failure; and the picture of industry suggested by this survey, besides being very vague and inconsistent, almost certainly predates 1903.[10]

The final step in this lengthy process was taken on the 10 June 1911, with the carrying out of a true industrial census at the same time as a demographic one

[3] G. Are, *Alle origini dell'Italia industriale* (Naples, Guida ed., 1974), 12.

[4] V. Ellena, 'La statistica di alcune industrie italiane', *Annali di statistica* 2/13 (1880).

[5] The Mining Corps began annual publication of the report *Relazione sul Servizio Minerario* (later entitled *Rivista del Servizio Minerario*) in 1877. At first it only contained figures on the mining industry, but from 1890 onwards it also included production figures from the blast-furnaces and from the metallurgical plants, and eventually included data on chemical production as well (1893), data such as the number of workers, motive power, and other, less complete figures on various aspects of these industries (wages, strikes, technology, production etc.).

[6] On the differences between the terms 'factory' and 'workshop', which were and still are the subject of much debate, see Ellena's observations in the essay by M. Lungonelli (p. 915), 'Le rilevazioni statistiche sull'industria italiana (1876–1903): note introduttive', *Rassegna economica*, 45 (1981); see also id., 'Tra industria e burocrazia: gli esordi della statistica industriale in Italia', in *Studi Storici*, 28 (1987) and *La Magona d'Italia. Impresa, lavoro e tecnologie in un secolo di siderurgia toscana (1865–1975)* (Bologna, Il Mulino, 1991).

[7] These concern, respectively, the milling of cereals (1889), silk (1891), wool (1895), paper (1898), and cotton (1899).

[8] All of these monographs were published in *Annali di statistica.*

[9] The Statistical Office of the MAIC, *Riassunto delle notizie sulle condizioni industriali del Regno* (3 vols., Rome, 1905–6).

[10] M. G. Missaggia, 'Nota sulle statistiche ufficiali per l'industria in Italia: 1885–1903', *Rivista di storia economica*, 5 (1988).

was being conducted; despite its inevitable defects,[11] this census does provide us with the first real basis for an analysis of Italian industrial development in the years leading up to the First World War.

The lack of official statistics has led scholars to look further afield for sources of information: details supplied by private experts, various kinds of information drawn from technical literature, partial studies conducted on behalf of private institutions or other public bodies, company archives—all these sources have been used to reconstruct figures indirectly, and to fill the gaps left by the scant official figures available. One particularly useful source of information has been provided by industrial exhibitions, although this has only recently been discovered by academics.[12] The comparison between the first exhibition held in Florence in 1861 (one of the new Italian Parliament's first-ever projects), the second exhibition in Milan in 1881, and the one held in Turin in 1911 (for the fiftieth anniversary of Italian unity), has proved to be particularly useful.

The general report presented by F. Protonotari at the end of the first exhibition, after having noted that even in wine production Italy was some way behind its competitors, went on to conclude as follows: 'if we hope to salvage something from the economic disasters that continue to pile up around us, so as to be able to go on and build up a prosperous economy, then we desperately need to modernize and renew manufacturing machinery; we need to reorganize training procedures and techniques, together with the labour-force; we need to look for administrators and captains of industry with the right kind of knowledge and experience; we need a thorough reorganization of the industrial infrastructure, and we should avoid the encouragement of less serious firms and incompetent administrators'.[13]

The Milan exhibition was held in a completely different atmosphere. Industrial organization was much more pronounced; companies tended to imitate foreign technology much more; a number of brand-new modern companies had appeared on the scene—from Carlo Erba to Pirelli, from Salmoiraghi to Cantoni Krumm, from Veneta of Treviso to De Morsier of Bologna; technical training had become common practice (see Ch. 6). As F. Bertolini said in one of the conferences held during the exhibition, 'this show has proved to be a true revelation',[14] with its re-creation of workplaces and

[11] There is a detailed analysis of the census in V. Zamagni, *Industrializzazione e squilibri regionali in Italia. Bilancio dell'età giolittiana* (Bologna, Il Mulino, 1978).

[12] See P. Bolchini, 'Fiere, mercati, esposizioni: l'età contemporanea', in *Mercati e consumi: orgnizzazione e qualificazione del commercio in Italia dal XII al XX secolo* (Bologna, Analisi, 1986).

[13] A report republished in M. Romani, *Storia economica d'Italia nel secolo XIX*, ii (Milan, Giuffré, 1976), 628. On the Italian presence at the Great Exhibition in London (1862), cf. the interesting article by P. Bolchini, 'L'esposizione internazionale di Londra del 1862 e l'Italia', *Rivista di storia economica*, 3 (1986).

[14] F. Bertolini, 'L'industria nei suoi rapporti con la civiltà', the title of a lecture given on 17 Oct. 1881, and subsequently republished in Enrico Decleva (ed.), *L'Italia industriale nel 1881. Conferenze sulla esposizione nazionale di Milano*, with an excellent introductory essay by the editor (Milan, Banca del Monte, 1984), 337.

machinery, making it possible to observe complex work processes from close up, and with the opening experiment involving the electrical illumination of a part of the city of Milan. Above all, one could see that attitudes had changed. As Giuseppe Colombo wrote: 'Those producers who relied solely on experience have now realized that there can be no progress without the help of science, since everything can now be calculated in advance, using precise rules and formulas; from the construction of the steam engine to that of the simplest kind of machine—the successful combination of theory and practice is continual proof of the need for scientific knowledge'.[15]

The Fiftieth Anniversary Exhibition held in Turin was no longer just a sign of industrialization's healthy start and of the possibilities that existed for improvement; it was much more than this, in fact, as its very size (seven times as big as the one held in Milan) was a somewhat self-indulgent celebration of real industrial achievement. There was 'an entire pavilion given over to the "great" metallurgical companies, including the Terni, Falck and Breda factories';[16] there was a concrete-built Newspaper Palace; hydroelectric power was at the centre of one part of the exhibition dedicated to various energy sources; there were areas, either in the national or international pavilions (this time the exhibition was an international one), dedicated to all forms of modern machinery, different kinds of transport, including a conveyor belt, precision instruments, together with the latest chemical products.[17]

This enormous amount of source material, although not of a very well-organized or complete nature, has still to be utilized to the full: in fact, analyses dealing with the nature of Italian industrial development from 1861 to 1913 have so far only used a part of this material. Since these analyses only offer a partial picture, and often this varies from one analysis to another, we need to discuss them in comparative terms; this will then give us the possibility of illustrating the various interpretations that have been offered.

Table 2.1 shows the three versions of the industrial production index that have been produced up to now; two of them date back to the mid-1950s, while the third was calculated at the end of the 1960s, even though it was only published in 1983 by its author, Stefano Fenoaltea, who is currently working on a revised version (so far, only a few sections have been completed of this revised version, as we shall see in Section 2 of this chapter). This is not the right place to analyse the various strong and weak points of these three indices: Gerschenkron's is certainly the least complete of the three, based as it is on a very limited range of products and a less than satisfactory system of weights;

[15] G. Colombo, 'Sui progressi compiuti nell'industria delle macchine dall'epoca dell'esposizione di Firenze ad oggi', a lecture given on 15 Sept. 1881, ibid. 71.

[16] Bolchini, 'Fiere, mercati esposizioni,' 445.

[17] M. Picone Petrusa, M. R. Pressolano, and A. Bianco, *Le grandi esposizioni in Italia 1861–1911* (Naples, Liguori ed., 1988); see also R. Romano, 'Le esposizioni industriali Italiane. Linee di metodologia interpretativa', in *Società e Storia*, 7 (1980), and E. Decleva, 'Milano industriale fra mito e realtà: le esposizioni 1871–1906', *Museo scienza*, 22 (1982).

Table 2.1. Indices of industrial production, 1861–1913 (yearly increase, %)

	Gerschenkron (1)	ISTAT (2)	Fenoaltea (3)
1861–81	—	2.0	2.2
1881–1913	3.8	2.3	4.2
1881–8	4.6	1.0	6.2
1888–96	0.3	0.0	1.2
1896–1908	6.7	5.0	7.6
1908–13	2.4	1.5	2.3

Sources: A. Gerschenkron, 'Notes on the Rate of Industrial Growth in Italy 1861–1913', *Journal of Economic History*, 15 (1955); ISTAT, *Indagine statistica sul reddito nazionale dell'Italia dal 1861 al 1956* (Rome, 1957); S. Fenoaltea, 'Railways and the Development of the Italian Economy to 1913', in P. O'Brien (ed.), *Railways and the Economic Growth of Western Europe* (London, Macmillan, 1983).

however the other two, and in particular the ISTAT index, also have their weak points.

When comparing the three indices, we can see that there is one thing on which there is agreement, and yet another which would indicate strong disagreement: the first 20 years after unification were years of slow industrial growth—there would seem to be no quibbling about this, to judge from the figures available; however, the following period was characterized by an acceleration in growth, according to Gerschenkron and, even more so, according to Fenoaltea, whereas the ISTAT index shows no substantial variation in average growth during this period, although it was concentrated, to a large extent, during the years 1896–1908. If we subdivide the second period (1881–1913) into shorter sub-periods, we see that the contrast between the ISTAT figures and those of both Gerschenkron and Fenoaltea emerges above all in the 1880s. According to the ISTAT index, the rate of growth, rather than showing an increase in this period, actually fell in relation to the previous 20-year period. From this it would seem that neither the political support given to industry nor the new industrial activities created in the early 1880s had any positive effect, which is surprising to say the least. Qualitative accounts would seem to lend support to Gerschenkron's and Fenoaltea's figures, and thus to the overall picture of the 1880s that their indices give rise to.

The economic crisis, recognized by all as existing between the end of the 1880s and the mid-1890s, was triggered by various factors, involving both speculation at home and events internationally. Businesses, including the building trade, were seriously indebted, and this led to the tying-up of banks' assets; the international economic situation deteriorated during this period, leading to the withdrawal of foreign capital; the balance of payments went into the red, draining gold reserves. At the end, there was an enormous banking crisis (see Chapter 4), which prevented a normal flow of credit to industry for many years thereafter. Economic recovery began in 1896, and for a dozen years or so, Italian industry expanded rapidly, although this expansion once again slowed down, as a result of the 1907 international crisis.

However, we can only talk about economic recovery if we look at either Fenoaltea's or Gerschenkron's indices, because as far as the ISTAT figures are concerned, we have the *first* real period of intense industrial expansion, after 20 years of slow growth and 15 years of crisis. Only when we take the ISTAT index as our reference, can we identify a true *take-off* of industrial growth at the turn of the century; whereas the other two indices indicate a single cyclical process that began towards the end of the 1870s (1881 is here used as a dividing line between the first and second periods, primarily because it enables us to compare the other indices with that of Gerschenkron, which starts in 1881 only, although the choice of a slightly earlier date may have been more suitable).

It is this cyclical, or wavelike,[18] interpretation of industrialization (and not only of that of Italy) that seems to be the most popular nowadays. Its supporters underline the importance of the elements of continuity, as well as of the obstacles that arise from time to time to cause serious, albeit temporary, breaks in the developmental process. The cyclical view appears to point to a process which is much slower than that implicit in the previously evoked notion of industrial *take-off*, a notion which arose largely out of the search for some event or other that could be seen as a decisive 'break' with the 'stagnation' of the past, something that was to lead the economy along an irreversible path of stable and dynamic growth[19] through the so-called *big spurt* or *big push*. In contrast to this latter interpretation, more recent research identifies several periods of industrial growth which were all of crucial importance to the final outcome; that is, the initial period was not any more intense than the others, and together they contributed towards the complete industrialization of the nation. There were periods of crisis, some longer than others, in the intervals between one period of growth and another; some of these crises were very serious, and threatened not only the results achieved in the previous phase of growth, but also the adequacy of the means used up to that point, together with the will to continue in the process of modernization of the economy.

From this point of view, on the one hand it is easier to understand just how the important gains made by Italian industry after the expansion of the years 1896–1907 were still only partial ones; and why, on the other hand, many

[18] L. Cafagna, 'Protoindustria o transizione in bilico? (A proposito della prima onda della industrializzazione italiana)', *Quaderni Storici*, 54 (1983). V. Hunecke's study, *Classe operaia e rivoluzione industriale a Milan 1859–1892* (Bologna, Il Mulino, 1982), also gives ample evidence of the continuity of Milanese industrial development—which, if anything, picked up pace during the 1880s (452)—and of the growing numbers of small businesses.

[19] It is a well-known fact that the concept of 'take-off' was present in W. W. Rostow, *The Stages of Economic Growth* (Cambridge, Mass., 1960), and was used by A. Gerschenkron, with one or two variations, in *Economic Backwardness in Historical Perspective* (Cambridge, Mass., Harvard University Press, 1962).

subsequent growth periods were of equally 'fundamental' importance[20] for the complete industrialization of the country, as we shall see in later chapters. As far as the reasons behind the cyclical development of Italian industry in the period 1861–1913 are concerned, there are some scholars who put the emphasis on domestic policies, while others stress the fundamental importance of international events. Romeo figures among the first of these schools of thought: his thesis, cited above, concerning the role of agriculture in the capital accumulation of the first 20 years of unification, also points to the existence of a fiscal drag, which led to a part of this accumulated capital being employed in the building of infrastructures (intensified during the 1880s' boom), and thus created the vital foundations for the expansion of manufacturing industry that was to follow.[21] The second school of thought includes the recent thesis proposed by Fenoaltea, which connects the periods of growth in Italy with the cyclical nature of the export of English capital: he bases this on the examples of other countries' development, in the interpretation given by Kuznets and others.[22] This thesis sees the availability of foreign capital as responsible for the acceleration or slow-down of domestic industrial development in capital-scarce countries, like Italy. Both schools of thought are quite plausible and do not have to be mutually exclusive. Since the documentary material that we do have is still of a rather dubious nature, especially in the field of international capital flows, we have to postpone for the time being any definitive conclusions as to which of the two views is the most acceptable.

What we can do is to try and define Italian industrialization more accurately in terms of territorial distribution and scale. The diffusion of industrialization was limited to the areas that had shown substantial signs of modernization prior to unification: that is, the gap between the North (in particular the three regions of Liguria, Lombardy, and Piedmont that came to form the *industrial triangle*) and the rest of the country was reinforced during the industrialization process.[23] From here, industrialization 'spread according to proximity: from the

[20] There were many cases of abortive 'take-offs', some lasting longer than others: as far as Europe is concerned, the most important examples are documented in S. Pollard, *Peaceful Conquest. The Industrialization of Europe 1760–1970* (Oxford, Oxford University Press, 1981).

[21] See R. Romeo, *L'Italia liberale: sviluppo e contraddizioni* (Milan, Il Saggiatore, 1987). The main criticism of Romeo's thesis, already made by Gerschenkron in the early 1960s, concerns the excessively mechanical interconnection between agricultural surplus, tax revenue, and infrastructural (later industrial) investment.

[22] S. Fenoaltea, 'International Resource Flows and Construction Movements in the Atlantic Economy: The Kuznets Cycle in Italy, 1861–1913', *Journal of Economic History*, 48 (1988).

[23] A complete study of the industrialization of the regions within the industrial triangle exists so far for Piedmont (V. Castronovo, *Il Piemonte*, Torino, Einaudi, 1977) and Lombardy (S. Zaninelli (ed.), *Storia dell'industria lombarda*, ii: *Dalla unità politica all grande guerra* (2 vols., Milan, Il Polifilo, 1990–1)). For Lombardy, cf. the useful survey given by A. Moioli in 'L'industrializzazione in Lombardia dall'Ottocento al primo Novecento: un bilancio storiografico', *Annali scientifici del Dipartimento di Economia dell'Università di Trento*, 1 (1988). For Liguria, cf. G. Doria, *Investimenti e sviluppo economico e Genova alla vigilia della prima guerra mondiale* (2 vols., Milan, Giuffré, 1969 and 1973). On the role of the port of Genoa, cf. E. Bianchi Tonizzi, 'Traffici e strutture del Porto di Genova (1815–1950), *Miscellanea storica ligure*, 17 (1985).

industrial triangle it moved out into those regions that bordered on the triangle—the Veneto, Emilia–Romagna, and Tuscany. The Marches, Umbria and, anomalistically, parts of Latium represented the southernmost limits of industrialization'.[24] According to an estimate of mine relating to the year 1911, 55 per cent of industrial value added was produced in the industrial triangle, 29 per cent in the North-East–Centre, and only 16 per cent in the South;[25] the concentration of technologically advanced companies in the triangle was even greater than these figures would suggest. While there were already industrial districts with a solid tradition in the Veneto,[26] Tuscany,[27] the Marches,[28] and Umbria,[29] they were, however, lacking in a lot of the modern technology that had made its appearance in the industrial triangle.

There are two main reasons why the spread of industrialization in the South proved to be very weak, only really involving the Naples and Salerno areas,[30] together with a few isolated areas elsewhere:[31] on the one hand, the local communities were themselves generally incapable of setting up their own enterprises; on the other hand, there was very little interest shown in investing northern Italian and foreign capital in the South.[32] The discussion in previous chapters about the social and economic environment in the South—to which we turn in later chapters—explains why indigenous business enterprise was absent in this part of Italy; a little more needs to be said, though, about the lack of interest shown in the South by outside investors. The truth is that there was

[24] E. Sori, 'Della manifattura all'industria (1861–1940)', in S. Anselmi (ed.), *Le Marche* (Turin, Einaudi, 1987), 380.

[25] Zamagni, *Industrializzazione*, Table 56.

[26] G. Roverato, 'La terza regione industriale', in S. Lanaro (ed.), *Il Veneto* (Turin, Einaudi, 1984), 184–5. The undisputed leader of early industrialization in that region, Alessandro Rossi, used factory decentralization as one of the basic principles of his model of industrialization. On the Veneto, see also E. Franzina, *La transizione dolce. Storie del Veneto tra '800 e '900* (Verona, Cierre ed., 1990).

[27] G. Mori, 'Dall'unità alla guerra: aggregazione e disagregazione di un'area regionale', in G. Mori (ed.), *La Toscana* (Turin, Einaudi, 1986), 241.

[28] Sori, 'Dalla manifattura', 322 ff., as well as S. Anselmi (ed.), *L'industria calzaturiera marchigiana. Dalla manifattura alla fabbrica* (Unione ind. del Fermano, 1989).

[29] R. Covino, M. G. Fioriti, and G. Gallo, *Permanenza e modernizzazione: per una storia dell'industria in Umbria* (Foligno, Ed. Umbra, 1986); also R. Covino and G. Gallo (eds.), *L'Umbria* (Turin, Einaudi, 1989) and A. Grohmann, *Perugia* (Bari, Laterza, 1990).

[30] Cf. L. De Rosa, *Iniziativa e capitale straniero nell'industria metalmeccanica del Mezzogiorno 1840–1904* (Naples, Giannini, 1968). On the Campania, cf. also A. De Benedetti, *La Campania industriale. Intervento pubblico e organizzazione produttiva tra età giolittiana e fascismo* (Naples, Ed. Athena, 1990).

[31] See the excellent regional histories of Calabria and Sicily published by Einaudi. The first is edited by P. Bevilacqua and A. Placanica (Turin, 1985), and the second by M. Aymard and G. Giarrizzo (Turin, 1987). The volume concerning Apulia (L. Masella and B. Salvemini (eds.), *La Puglia* (Turin, Einaudi, 1989)) does not contain much economic history. The most recently published has been P. Macry and P. Villani (eds.), *Campania* (Turin, Einaudi, 1990).

[32] For an account of German investment in the South, see P. Hertner, *Il capitale tedesco in Italia dall'unità alla prima guerra mondiale* (Bologna, Il Mulino, 1984), ch. 4.

very little opportunity to exploit local resources in a big way, limited as these resources were.[33] Furthermore, the local market was small, the economic infrastructure was very spartan (despite some improvements made by the State since unification), and economies of agglomeration were almost non-existent. Even though the cost of manpower was probably lower in the South than elsewhere, there were too many disincentives for northern or foreign industrial oligopolies to be seriously interested in an investment drive in the South.[34]

All over Italy, industry remained very closely tied to the agricultural world that surrounded it, not so much because of the supply of raw materials (which agriculture supplied only in the cases of silk production, sugar-refining, and other food industries), but more so because of the very strong ties that existed between the working class and their peasant families of origin, ties that were not without their contradictions[35] and conflicts,[36] but which, nevertheless, constituted a 'buffer-like structure, a drip-feed enabling the transition represented by industrialization to be a gradual and gentle one'.[37] Moreover, a large part of industry was still somewhere between artisan production, family business, and home-working: a real mixture of diverse activities. Some enterprises gradually managed to pull away from this melting-pot, with the introduction of mechanization and other technological innovations; only the most modern sectors of industry ever saw the birth of larger companies, due to technical reasons which dictated the need for a minimum plant size. In this way, the larger, oligopolistic sectors of industry (metallurgy, electricity, sugar-refining, shipbuilding, rubber, gas, water, cement, modern chemicals, and cars) coexisted with other, more fragmented sectors; the latter were not only complementary to industrial production proper, but also acted as a reservoir of manpower—manpower that possessed some manufacturing know-how and practical ability: that of the Tuscan straw-weavers, for example, or of the women of Carpi employed in the production of baskets and hats woven from wood-shavings; that of the shoemakers of the Marches, or of the potters of Faenza; the list of these activities is never-ending. This work-force, having seen

[33] Hertner concludes (ibid. 327) that 'foreign capital was invested in the South ... in the exploitation of raw materials ... and ... in the infrastructures of some large cities', but to a limited degree, none the less. Similar forms of investment were also made by industrialists from the industrial triangle, who put their capital into mining in Sardinia, into the electrification of Sicily, or into the bauxite mines of the Abruzzi.

[34] Cf. Zamagni, *Industrializzazione*, 213 ff.

[35] P. Corti and A. Lonni show that work in the factory was sometimes seen as a way of reinforcing the ownership of land in their study 'Da contadini a operai', in V. Castronovo (ed.), *La cassetta degli strumenti. Ideologie e modelli sociali nell'industrialismo italiano* (Milan, Angeli, 1986).

[36] F. Ramella, in *Terra e telai. Sistemi di parentela e manifattura nel biellese dell'ottocento* (Turin, Einaudi, 1983), gives an example of such problems witnessed in the Biella area: the textile manufacturers complained about absenteeism among workers in their factories, as the latter needed to take time off from work in order to look after their crops on the land that they still owned.

[37] Cafagna, 'Protoindustria', 979.

the new economic opportunities on offer, slowly integrated into the industrialized environment.[38]

2. A SECTORIAL BREAKDOWN OF INDUSTRY

Although it is not possible to analyse all the indices that are available for each individual industry, in this section we can take a look at those revised figures, being prepared by Fenoaltea, that have already been published; in the remaining cases, we shall use the old ISTAT figures.[39] Table 2.2 is an attempt to illustrate these data in a clear fashion; the various sectors of industry have been divided into three groups, on the basis of technological criteria—horsepower per worker, shown in column 5, and the average size of firms in terms of the number of workers employed, shown in column 6—in order to highlight the changes that took place within Italian industry during the period from 1878 to 1911.[40] Since I decided not to limit this analysis to manufacturing industry, and have included mining, together with the production and distribution of electricity, gas, and water, I can also take into account the contribution made by the construction industry, which created demand for products from other sectors of industry. I should add that the initial period of very slow growth, prior to 1878, has not been included here and the starting-date is 1878 simply for practical reasons. Since we need to use ISTAT's figures for the base year of a great number of the industrial sectors, and these figures have only been supplied by ISTAT at current prices, I have chosen a year when average prices in the manufacturing sector were similar to those of 1911.[41] Furthermore, I have not included the intermediate cycle in the average growth rates shown in column 3, as I would rather take into consideration the overall results for the whole period.

Despite the approximate nature of many of the data, it is easy to see that the

[38] Many writers have given their accounts and interpretations of the process whereby small businesses continued to maintain an important presence on the industrial scene during the 19th and 20th centuries, until their recent technological transformation and organizational amalgamation with large industry. Two particularly important studies are: M. J. Piore and C. F. Sabel, *Le due vie dello sviluppo industriale. Produzione di massa e produzione flessibile* (Turin, Isedi, 1987, Ital. trans. of *The Second Industrial Divide: Possibilities for Prosperity*, Basic Books, 1984), and ASSI, *Piccola e grande impresa: un problema storico* (Milan, Angeli, 1987). On the links of industry with agriculture, see *Annali dell'Istituto 'Alcide Cervi'*, 11 (1989) dedicated to 'La pluriattività negli spazi rurali: ricerche a confonto'. On the Tuscan straw-weavers, cf. A. Pescarolo and G. B. Ravenni, *Il proletariato invisibile. La manifattura della paglia nella Toscana mezzadrile (1820–1950)* (Milan, Angeli, 1991).

[39] I am well aware that the use of figures from different sources can give rise to incorrect intersectorial comparisons; however, I could not avoid using more recent data than those of the ISTAT, as they came up.

[40] I have already used this type of approach in Zamagni, *Industrializzazione*, where a more detailed explanation can be found.

[41] Of course, this method can give way to over- and under-evaluations of individual sectors; however, overall these differences tend to balance each other out.

more advanced sectors of industry were those that on the whole grew the quickest, being overtaken only by the construction industry. Of these technologically advanced industries, the one with the highest annual growth rate was the electricity industry, while the textile industry was the one with the slowest growth rate (although Fenoaltea's figures revalue the importance of the silk industry). The 'intermediate' industries are fairly heterogeneous, with the glass, cement, and brick works growing at a faster pace than the construction industry itself, whereas the food industry virtually stagnated during this period.[42] There is very little one can say about the 'traditional' industries, since the figures so far available are of an even more arbitrary nature.

It would thus be useful to take a further look at the new industries, without aiming at covering either all of the literature available on this subject or all of the individual developments witnessed during this time.[43] My starting-point has to be the *textile* industries, which, although not the most technologically advanced of the modern industries, certainly predated the others (especially in the case of the silk industry), boasted a long tradition, and played a very important role in the rise of an industrial milieu in Italy, as we have already seen from the conclusions drawn from the Industrial Survey conducted during the first half of the 1870s.[44]

The first results of a major study of the *silk* industry being carried out by G. Federico have been published, covering the years from the 1850s' crisis up to the First World War, while the figures for value added, 1861–1913, have recently been revised by Fenoaltea, and the results are rather surprising: instead of a picture of stagnation, we see a period of growth from the end of the 1870s onwards, partly due to a revival in raw-silk production following the problems created by silkworm disease, and partly to a strong upward trend in the silk-weaving and silk-dyeing sectors, from the 1890s onwards; as a result, the percentage of total value added in silk due to these finishing stages of production rose from 20 per cent in 1890 to 38 per cent in 1913.[45]

According to Federico's research, the Italian silk industry managed to maintain an important share of the world market (about one-third) until the First World War; this was due to 'the highest quality of its products, guaranteed

[42] The relatively high level of horsepower per worker in this industry (col. 5) should not be misinterpreted, since it is largely due to the flour-milling industry, 61% of whose power capacity still consisted in hydraulic energy.

[43] Details of the development of the various industrial sectors can be found in R. Morandi, *Storia della grande industria in Italia* (Turin, Einaudi, 1966; 1st edn., 1931); B. Caizzi, *Storia dell'industria italiana dal XVIII secolo ai giorni nostri* (Turin, UTET, 1965); V. Castronovo, *L'industria italiana dall'ottocento ad oggi* (Milan, Mondadori, 1980). For a useful collection of essays not limited to industry, see G. Mori (ed.), *L'industrializzazione in Italia (1861–1900)* (Bologna, Il Mulino, 1977).

[44] Cf. R. Romano, *Borghesia industriale in ascesa. Gli imprenditori tessili nella inchiesta industriale del 1870–74* (Milan, Angeli, 1977).

[45] S. Fenoaltea, 'The Output of Italy's Silk Industry, 1861–1913: A Statistical Reconstruction', *Rivista di storia economica*, 5 (1988).

Table 2.2. Trend in industrial value added by sectors, 1878–1911, boundaries of the time

	1878 (million lire)	1911 (million lire)	1911 Fenoattea (million lire)	1911 industrial census		
				Employment	hp per worker	No. of workers per plant
	(1)	(2)	(3)	(4)	(5)	(6)
Textiles	473	643	429	505,806	0.50	70
Silk	46.5*	125*	125	...	...	...
Cotton	...	...	187	...	...	...
Wool	...	...	87	...	...	...
Metallurgy	19	129	90	42,663	2.62	38
Engineering	170	961	843	269,372[a]	0.51[a]	17[a]
Chemicals	20[b]	776	158	19,083[c]	2.53[c]	21[c]
Paper	18	112	67	36,102	1.36	21
Sugar	–	60	56	9,299	2.18	198
Electricity, gas, water	16*	183*	183	34,187	2.98	16
Advanced industry	716	...	1,826	916,512	0.79	30
Food industry	639	886	727	295,268	0.94	5
Mining, quarrying	60.5*	142[e]*	140[e]	98,362	0.27	22
Bricks, glass, cement	33	102	260	182,701	0.36	15
Printing, publishing	50	153	175	44,901	0.22	13
Other manufactoring			36	15,426[f]	0.24[f]	11[f]
Intermediate industry	782.5	...	1,408	674,584[c]	0.60[c]	9[c]

	(1)	(2)	(3)	(4)	(5)	(6)
Clothing	...	...	243	167,685	0.07	7
Leather	...	...	299	120,282	0.09	4
Furniture	...	...	386	220,674	0.24	4
Traditional industry	235	446	928	585,060[a]	0.15[a]	
Building	388*	1,201*	697	128,182[g]	0.13[g]	22[g]
TOTAL AVERAGE	2,121.5	...	4,859	2,311,529	0.53	9[h]

[a] 76,419 mechanical artisans with 0.17 hp per worker and 4 workers per laboratory have been moved into the total for traditional industry.

[b] ISTAT has neglected some traditional products.

[c] 37,926 workers in the production of traditional chemical products (soap, perfumes, candles, etc.) with 0.65 hp per worker and 15 workers per plant have been moved into the total for intermediate industry.

[d] Sugar excluded.

[e] Excluding reserves consumed.

[f] Including rubber.

[g] The industrial census was particularly unsuccessful in surveying the workers of the building industry, while the population census carried out at the same date registered 693,113 in the building trade.

[h] In order to evaluate this figure correctly, we need to bear in mind that shops with only one worker were not included in the industrial census.

Sources: Figures marked with * are derived from the following works by S. Fenoaltea: 'The Growth of the Utilities Industries in Italy, 1861–1913', *Journal of Economic History*, 42 (1982); 'Le costruzioni in Italia 1861–1913', *Rivista di Storia economica*, 4 (1987); 'The Extractive Industries in Italy 1861–1913: General Methods and Specific Estimates', *Journal of European Economic History*, 17 (1988); 'The Output of Italy's Silk Industry, 1861–1913: A Statistical Reconstruction', *Rivista di storia economica*, 5 (1988). The other figures for 1878 and 1911 are taken from ISTAT, *Indagine statistica sul reddito nazionale dell'Italia dal 1861 al 1956* (Rome, 1957); column 3 shows the latest estimates for 1911 by Fenoaltea ('Il valore aggiunto dell'industria italiana nel' 1911' in G. Rey (ed.), *I conti economici*. Data in cols. (4)–(6) are from R. Chiaventi.

by the use of steam power together with the ability of the work-force',[46] and by the flexibility demonstrated by the industry in adapting to changes at an international level which had led towards an increasingly protectionist market situation. However, this was an example of a technologically mature sector of industry, and a large part of its production was dedicated to an intermediate product (thrown silk) subsequently used by foreign weavers (see the analysis of silk exports—the only really important Italian export of that period—in the next chapter). Its value added was thus limited on the one hand by the high cost of raw material, silk-cocoons, which were produced less and less in Italy towards the end of the century, as a result of structural changes in agricultural production; and on the other hand by the violent fluctuations in silk market prices. The weak market position of raw-silk producers was certainly not helped by the fragmented nature of the industry, as well as by the fact that a large percentage of weaving was carried out in distant, richer countries, where markets for the final product existed; as a result, the industry was forced to seek state support, above all from 1906–7 onwards, but unfortunately this support was not forthcoming. The silk industry was seen as the 'natural' industry *par excellence* in Italy, the only one praised by the free-marketeers, as it had blossomed without any need for state intervention, and this certainly did not help to stimulate interest in economic policies that could have halted its fatal decline.

Nevertheless, the silk industry had played a very important role in maintaining Italy's position in world markets; it had also supplemented income from farming, encouraged the use of steam power through its use in the silk-throwing process (at the end of the 1880s, one-tenth of all steam-boilers in Italy were used for silk-throwing), and it had given work to a large number of people—above all to women—thus leading to an increase in the average family income (even though pay was very low—see Ch. 6). Furthermore, it led to an increase in accumulated capital, and furnished a trained work-force which proved to be invaluable in many ways later on in the history of Italian industrialization. It is also true, however, that an area such as that around Como, where there was a heavy concentration of silk-throwing, for a long time lacked any kind of economic diversification (an eventual increase in silk-weaving helped to remedy things slightly); as a consequence, this area was slow in participating in the real push towards industrialization (although it did manage to do so in the end). The advantages that the *industrial triangle* gained from the silk industry are, nevertheless, beyond question.

If we now take a look at the *cotton* industry, we can see that according to Ellena's figures, the situation had changed very little between the period prior to unification and the year 1876: the number of spindles had only doubled to a total of 900,000, while about 25 workers (mostly women) were required to

[46] G. Federico, 'Per una storia dell'industria serica italiana', *Annali di Storia dell'impresa*, 4 (1988).

operate 1,000 spindles; this is a figure that reveals the relative backwardness of the Italian cotton industry at that time, as only about four workers were necessary in the best English or Swiss factories. As Ellena explains, 'when a factory is unable to specialize in its working, then fewer, lower-quality goods are produced, since it is forced to use what could be called *generic* machinery . . . and has *generic* workers as well'.[47] With the introduction in 1878 of a protective tariff of between 10 and 30 per cent on cotton yarn and fabrics, together with a change in the economic climate during the 1880s, the cotton industry began to flourish; this state of affairs was further aided by an additional increase in import tariff in 1887 (see Ch. 3), and breaking off trade relations with France, which above all led to a fall in cloth imports.

Raw-cotton imports quadrupled between 1881 and 1890, fell back a little in 1891–2, only to pick up again afterwards, and continued to increase for several years thereafter (going against the prevailing trend in other sectors of the economy). The number of spindles increased as follows: from 1.2 million in 1887 to 2.1 million in 1900, 4 million in 1908, and 4.6 million in 1913. The number of looms went from 47,000 in 1894 to 78,000 in 1900, 90,000 in 1908, and 146,000 in 1911.[48] There was a problem of overproduction of cotton yarn from 1908 onwards, and various tactics were employed to try to tackle this: the implementation of short time, the promotion of exports, the raising of the average count of yarns, and the injection of new capital by means of the creation of joint-stock companies.[49] The industry had by now reached the point where production satisfied 'all of the nation's needs, with the exception of a limited number of luxury articles which continued to be imported from England or France';[50] however, productivity was still relatively low. There was still very little specialization in the organization of production, the female work-force was not always very efficient, and the commercial organization of the industry was still rough and ready. The entrepreneurs themselves often lacked the necessary ability to improve the standing of the industry, as Romano's studies have shown.[51] The cotton industry included certain 'giants' among its firms, such as the Piedmont cotton-mills,[52] the Cantoni cotton-mill, and the De Angeli dyeing and printing works,[53] as well as certain southern cotton-mills, all of which

[47] Ellena, 'La statistica', 64.

[48] E. Corbino, *Annali dell'economia italiana*, ii (Città di Castello, 1931), 207.

[49] Ibid. v (1938), 150–5.

[50] Ibid. 154.

[51] R. Romano, 'Le basi sociali dell'industria cotoniera lombarda nell'800', *Storia urbana*, 9 (1978), and M. C. Cristofoli and M. Pozzobon, *I tessili milanesi. Le fabbriche, gli industriali, i lavoratori, il sindacato dall'800 agli anni '30* (Milan, Angeli, 1981). On the influence exercised by foreign entrepreneurs and capital over the Italian cotton industry, cf. F. Bova, 'L'industria cotoniera piemontese fino al 1914', *Padania*, 4 (1988) and M. Gelfi, 'I cotonieri svizzeri a Bergamo tra il 1867 e il 1888', ibid.

[52] V. Castronovo, *L'industria cotoniera in Piemonte nel secolo XIX* (Turin, ILTE, 1964).

[53] Cf. R. Romano, 'La delega del potere: la struttura direttiva delle imprese cotoniere lombarde (1859–1914)', *Storia in Lombardia*, 5 (1986); and by the same author, 'Il cotonificio Cantoni dalle origini al 1900', *Studi Storici*, 16 (1975).

possessed the typical hierarchical structure of big corporations, involving owners and managers. However, the cotton sector as a whole was still dominated by the presence of family firms. While those family firms had certainly had interesting past histories, they often produced disappointing results when operating in a more modern context, with third and fourth generations sometimes struggling to carry on the family tradition, and the breaking-up of the family industrial patrimony that this invariably led to.[54]

The *woollen* industry, like the silk industry, had a much longer history than the cotton industry, as testified by its continued presence in country areas rather than in big cities: areas such as Biella, Schio–Valdagno, and Prato.[55] This longer tradition perhaps explains why the woollen industry had famous and important people, such as Venanzio Sella[56] (in the Biella area) and Alessandro Rossi (in the Vicenza area),[57] among its members, even before unification; people who were actively involved in the modernization of their companies, as well as in urging the government to take measures to help the woollen industry. A Wool Association had already been founded in 1877 (at the same time as the Association of Silk Producers and Traders was set up, and some time before the founding of the Association of Cotton Producers and Dealers in 1893), and already in 1878 the import tariffs asked for were implemented. However, this promising start did not lead to the expected

[54] See Romano's two histories of Lombard families: *I Caprotti. L'aventura economica e umana di una dinastia industriale della Brianza* (Milan, Angeli, 1980), and *I Crespi. Origini, fortuna e tramonto di una dinastia lombarda* (Milan, Angeli, 1985), together with the history of a Piemontese family as told by F. Levi, *L'idea del buon padre. Il lento declino di un'industria familiare* (Turin, Rosenberg & Sellier, 1984), which tells the story of the Mazzonis family, from 1852 until the year of the company's bankruptcy (1965), at which time it was being run by a fourth generation of Mazzonis. See also A. Canziani (ed.), *Il settore cotoniero italiano. La dinamica in situazioni varie di ambiente* (Milan, Egea, 1989).

[55] Other areas, such as that around Salerno, failed to survive as a result of the wave of foreign textile imports which followed the adoption of a free-market policy by the first governments of the newly unified State (see Ch. 3). See S. De Majo, *L'industria protetta. Lanifici e cotonifici in Campania nell'Ottocento* (Naples, Ed. Athena, 1989).

[56] The Sella family, of which details exist dating back to at least 1585, was one of the many families in the Biella area specializing in the drapery business, as can be seen from A. Fossati's study, *Lavoro e produzione in Italia dalla metà del secolo XVIII alla seconda guerra mondiale* (Turin, Giappichelli, 1951), 101. For an account of the activities of Venanzio Sella, grandson of that Pietro Sella who was the first person to introduce Belgian machinery in 1817, in his factory at Valle Mosso, see 'Una famiglia di pionieri industriali: i Sella', in V. Castronovo, *Grandi e piccoli borghesi* (Bari, Laterza, 1988).

[57] The Rossi family history does not go back quite so far, even though Francesco Rossi set up the family's first factory during exactly the same year, i.e. in 1817, in the wake of a business founded by Nicolò Tron in 1738. It was Francesco Rossi's son, Alessandro, who was to make his father's company a success, turning it into a joint-stock company in 1872, and combining its management with a very active public role, together with his involvement in various other industrial concerns. Cf. L. Avagliano, *Alessandro Rossi e le origini dell'Italia industriale* (Naples, Lib. Scientifica Ed., 1970); also G. L. Fontana (ed.), *Schio e Alessandro Rossi* (Rome, Ed. di Storia e Letteratura, 1985), and by the same author, 'Dall'"onda" tessile alle nuove industrie', in *Movimenti politici e sociali nel Veneto, dal 1876 al 1903* (Vicenza, Tip. Esca, 1986).

results, despite the increase in import tariffs in 1887. The industry struggled to modernize,[58] the strikes that took place in the Biella area had a devastating effect on wool production as a whole,[59] and there was only a marginal increase in the level of specialization; meanwhile, the smaller firms continued to dominate the scene.[60]

The changes that took place from unification onwards were continual, albeit very slow. At the time of unification there were less than 100,000 spindles installed in the woollen factories; by 1876 this number had risen to 284,000, by 1893 to 345,000, and by 1907 it had reached 490,000.[61] The number of looms installed (not including those in private homes) were, respectively: 7,000, 8,353, 10,267, and 12,467. Wool production continued to increase between 1907 and 1914, unlike that of cotton; woollen yarn production increased from 170,000 quintals to 240,000 quintals during this period, while the production of woollen fabrics went from up from 319,000 quintals to 340,000 quintals.[62] Certain long-established and rather fortunate companies were very successful during this period, such as the Marzotto Company—the details of which can be found in the case-study cited below.[63]

As already underlined, the textile industry was a very important element in the industrialization of Italy as it acted as a bridge between the agricultural world and the real industrial world: it kept the spark of industrialization alive for several decades; it saw the construction of the very first factories; the search for new sources of energy was a result of its growth; it led to the accumulation of capital; it supported the nation's balance of payments, first through the substitution of imports (cotton and wool) with home production, and secondly by means of a substantial flow of exports (silk products, followed towards the end of the period by cotton and wool, above all to the Balkan States and South America). In 1911, the textile industry employed one-quarter of manufacturing industry's entire work-force, mostly women, according to the industrial census carried out at the time (Table 2.2). Due to the lateness of the period in question, and the nature of industrialization in Italy, the textile industry was hardly going to be a leader in technological development; this role was reserved for other sectors of industry, as we shall now see.

I will start by looking at the one industry that revolutionized all previously existing energy production, not only in Italy, with the important consequences

[58] Cf. V. Castronovo, *L'industria laniera in Piemonte nel secolo XIX* (Turin, ILTE, 1964).

[59] Ramella, *Terra e telai.* There were no strikes of this kind in the Veneto, due to a widespread paternalism in the industry, which we shall be looking at in the following section.

[60] Above all in the Prato area, where big industry was a rarity. V. M. Lungonelli, 'L'industria laniera nella Prato postunitaria, 1861–1895. Nascita e sviluppo di un sistema di piccole imprese', in ASSI, *Piccola e grande impresa.*

[61] There were 5.5 million spindles in Gt. Britain in 1875, and 2.7 million in France.

[62] E. Corbino, *Annali*, v. 207.

[63] G. Roverato, *Una casa industriale. I Marzotto* (Milan, Angeli, 1986). See also P. Bairati, *Sul filo di lana. Cinque generazioni di imprenditori: i Marzotto* (Bologna, Il Mulino, 1986).

that this had for the organization and siting of factories: the *electricity* industry. Italy did not possess any of that one raw material that was indispensable to the first phase of industrialization centred as it was on the steam engine, namely coal: Italian factories were obliged to pay from between 5 and 8 lire for one quintal of coal, depending on their distance from the nearest port, whereas their English counterparts paid the equivalent of only 0.70 lire a quintal.[64] The low level of mechanization of the Italian economic system at the time of unification can be seen from the fact that only 357,000 tons of coal were imported in 1863, whereas by 1879 imports had already reached 1.4 million tons (see Table 2.3). The economic expansion of the 1880s led to a significant increase in coal exports, which had reached 4 million tons by 1890; there was a subsequent fall in exports due to the crisis, followed by a revival, which saw the figure for 1897 climb back to that of 1890; by 1913, imports had risen to 10.5 million tons. However, by this time coal imports were used in the main for transport (the railway system was still largely steam-powered), or as a raw material in certain industrial processes. Only 20 per cent of industrial energy took the form of steam power, a further 22 per cent was hydraulic, whereas 48 per cent was now generated by electric motors, which made it possible to decentralize factories and workshops, led to the use of smaller industrial machines, and gave birth to completely new productive processes.

Right from its rather uncertain early development, there were those who already foresaw the strategic role that electricity was to play in Italian industrialization; the first among these was Giuseppe Colombo, the founder of the Edison Company, who during a conference held in 1890 had the following

Table 2.3. Availability of energy sources in the Italian economic system, 1863–1913

	Total[a] (billion Kcal)	Fossil coal (million tons)	Electricity (million kWh)
1863	34,765	0.4	—
1879	48,423	1.4	—
1890	68,765	4.1	11
1898	68,089	4.2	105
1908	99,778	8.2	986
1913	118,911	10.5	2,077

[a] All sources and end-uses are included.

Source: C. Bardini, 'L'economia energetica italiana 1863–1913: una prospettiva inconsueta per lo studio del processo di industrializzazione', *Rivista di storia economica*, 8 (1991).

[64] A. Sapori, 'L'industria e il problema del carbone nel primo cinquantennio di unità nazionale', *Economia e storia*, 8 (1961).

to say: 'The utilization of electricity in the transmission of power over long distances is of such enormous importance for Italian industry that not even the most fertile of imaginations could begin to perceive the consequences it will have. It is something that could completely change the face of this country, bringing it one day up to the level of the strongest of nations'.[65] Colombo himself set up the Committee for the Advancement of Electrical Energy in Italy in the autumn of 1881 in Milan;[66] he then travelled to New York to see exactly how the Pearl Street power station worked, and on returning to Italy, was responsible for setting up the first European power station, in the building that once housed the Santa Radegonda Theatre in the heart of Milan; this power station became operative on 28 June 1883, illuminating the offices and shops inside the Milan Gallery, as well as the Scala Theatre and several surrounding streets.

This historical success was followed by the setting-up of the Edison Company on 6 January 1884, thus showing that 'the Italian electricity industry was, from its foundation, on a par with that of other international leaders'.[67] The incredible growth of the electricity industry, which can be seen from a glance at Table 2.3 and Fenoaltea's index given in Table 2.2,[68] was nevertheless subject to certain limiting factors, such as the need for foreign capital investment (see Chapter 3) and the backwardness of the national electromechanical industry, as well as certain technical choices that were made. In fact, hydroelectricity—the famous *white coal*—was the dominant choice in the big power stations built before the Second World War, and this acted as an obstacle to the utilization of the latest technological discoveries in the field of thermoelectrical generation, in Italy; it led to the orientation of the sale of energy towards a tariff structure that favoured the discontinous industrial use of energy 'surpluses' or 'waste'.[69] A further weak point in electrical energy's development in Italy was the late and badly organized setting-up of a unified

[65] G. Colombo, 'La trasmissione elettrica della forza e il suo significato per l'avvenire dell'industria italiana', in C. G. Lacaita (ed.), *Industria e politica d'Italia. Scritti scelti: 1861–1916* (Bari, Cariplo-Laterza, 1985), 356. The engineer Giuseppe Colombo (who in fact graduated in mathematics at the University of Pavia), started teaching at the Società d'Incoraggiamento d'Arti e Mestieri (SIAM) in Milan, and then went on to teach at the Milan Polytechnic from 1863 (the year it was founded). He was rector of the Polytechnic from 1897 to 1921.

[66] Cf. C. Pavese, 'Le origini della Società Edison e il suo sviluppo fino alla costituzione del "gruppo" (1881–1919)', in B. Bezza (ed.), *Energia e sviluppo. L'industria elettrica italiana e la società Edison* (Turin, Einaudi, 1986). See also P. A. Toninelli, *La Edison. Contabilità e bilanci di una grande impresa elettrica, 1884–1916* (Bologna, Il Mulino, 1990).

[67] Pavese, 'Le origini', 31.

[68] S. Fenoaltea, 'The Growth of the Utilities Industries in Italy, 1861–1913', *Journal of Economic History*, 42 (1982).

[69] This favoured energy-intensive chemical and metallurgical processes, but in the course of time it became increasingly more difficult to justify, as the amalgamation of the networks led to a reduction in 'surpluses', and other, cheaper productive techniques became available. For further discussion on this point and on the role and development of the Italian electricity industry, cf. R. Giannetti, *La conquista della forza: risorse, technologia ed economia nell'industria elettrica italiana (1883–1940)* (Milano, Angeli, 1985).

energy network.[70] Despite this, Italy's production of more than 2 billion kWh in 1913 compared favourably with Britain's 2.5 billion and France's 1.8 billion, with only Germany really leaving the others in its wake, with an annual production of 8 billion kWh.

Another energy industry that is very important in terms of private consumption, although not as well known or as strategically vital for industrial production, is the *gas* industry. It existed before the electricity industry, resulting as it did from one of the technical developments of the coal industry—the latter being the real driving force behind the first wave of European industrialization—when gas for lighting was produced during the distillation of anthracite; this gas was then used for both domestic and public lighting. London was already illuminated in this way in 1814–18, Berlin in 1828, and Paris in 1829. The first Italian gas company was the Joint-Stock Company for the illumination of the City of Turin by means of hydrocarbon gas, founded on 8 January 1838, which, despite its name, proved unable to light up Turin until the year 1846; it was, however, to become a large and powerful company, later called *Italgas*, which has survived to this very day. Subsequently, the gas industry became important for the production of metallurgical coke, for the retrieval of tar and ammoniacal liquids used in many important productive chemical processes, as well as for the production of heating and cooking-gas; whereas as far as lighting was concerned, electricity fairly soon became the most commonly used form of energy.[71]

While electricity can justly be considered to be a 'natural' industry in Italy, if one thinks of the great number of glaciers and waterfalls that nature has bestowed upon the country, certain people have expressed negative views concerning the 'naturalness' or suitability to the Italian environment of another of the more important and strategic industries that grew in this period, namely the *metallurgical* industry.[72] What is more, these critics were openly sceptical about the very economic viability of an industry that was not considered to be indispensable for engineering production in general in Italy. After one hundred years of a steel industry that has depended upon state support, both economic and political, for its continued existence within a symbiotic relationship (at times conflictual) with private entrepreneurs, perhaps one can still doubt its 'naturalness', but not the strategic role it has played in supporting all sectors of large-scale engineering production related to transport, to the war effort, the

[70] R. Giannetti, *La conquista della forza*, as well as 'I "sistemi" elettrici italiani, struttura e prestazioni dalle origini al 1940', in Bezza (ed.), *Energia e sviluppo.*

[71] Cf. V. Castronovo, G. Paletta, R. Giannetti, and B. Bottiglieri, *Dalla luce all'energia: Storia dell'Italgas* (Bari, Laterza, 1987); see also R. Franco, 'Industrializzazione e servizi. Le origini dell'industria del gas in Italia', *Italia contemporanea*, 171 (1988) and A. Giuntini, *Dalla Lyonnaise alla Fiorentina gas 1839–1989* (Bari, Laterza, 1990).

[72] For a survey of the criticisms of free-marketeers, cf. Zamagni, *Industrializzazione,* 44–9, as well as Ch. 3 of the present volume.

building industry, and heavy machinery. The State's blueprint for the steel industry, together with its subsequent support for it, was indeed guided by this awareness right from the beginning, and the Terni Blast-Furnace, Steelworks, and Foundry Company was founded with public money on 10 March 1884; its business was steel production in general, but in particular, it was to produce armoured plates for the ships of the Italian navy.[73]

Up to that point in time, steel production in Italy had been very traditional in nature, carried on in small workshops spread out over the country, and with a relatively insignificant annual output (little more than 120,000 tons in 1881, compared with Great Britain's 1.8 million tons of steel and 8.2 million tons of pig-iron, and Germany's 900,000 tons of steel and 2.6 million tons of pig-iron). A number of other companies were subsequently set up, following the introduction of import tariffs in 1887, the use of Elba's mineral ore for domestic consumption, and the financial intervention of the banks. The Elba Mining and Blast-Furnace Joint-Stock Company[74] and the ILVA were two of these new companies; other previously existing companies updated their technology, such as the Falcks' Lombard Steel and Iron Joint-Stock Company, which incorporated other ironworks belonging to the Falck family, but also set up a brand-new, modern steelworks at Sesto San Giovanni (Milan), opened in 1908.[75] The growth in steel production was quite remarkable, but it was also technically chaotic and had a weak financial base, and consequently it required several salvage operations, the first of which was co-ordinated by the Bank of Italy in 1911.[76] On the eve of the First World War, Italy had reached annual production figures of almost 1 million tons of steel and 400,000 tons of pig-iron, a very humble output when compared with the 17.6 tons of steel produced by Germany, but nevertheless of significance when seen within the context of the smaller-scale Italian industrial environment, and of importance as a basis for subsequent developments.

The *engineering* industry's expansion really got under way as a result of the new developments in the steel, electrical, and transport sectors. Prior to 1881, production was limited to steam-boilers and locomobiles (Ansaldo, Società Veneta, Cantoni and Krumm, Suffert, Naville, De Morsier of Bologna, Odero,

[73] F. Bonelli, *Lo sviluppo di una grande impresa in Italia. La Terni dal 1884 al 1962* (Turin, Einaudi, 1971).

[74] M. Lungonelli, 'Alle origini della grande industria siderurgica in Italia: la società "Elba di Miniere e Alti Forni" (1899–1911)', *Ricerche storiche*, 6 (1976).

[75] G. De Vecchi and L. Bosisio, 'Localizzazione e primo sviluppo dell'industria siderurgica a Sesto S. Giovanni', *Ricerche storiche*, 8 (1978): the whole volume is dedicated to 'La siderurgia italiana dall'unità ad oggi'.

[76] For details of the salvage operations, together with information about the Italian steel industry until the post-First World War period, cf. G. Scagnetti, *La siderurgia in Italia* (Rome, 1923). As for the financial affairs of the large industrial groups and the banks that were financing them, cf. A. Confalonieri, *Banca e industria in Italia, 1894–1906,* ii and iii (Milan, 1975–6), and *1907–1914*, i and ii (Milan, Banca Commerciale Italiana, 1982).

Balleydier, Guppy of Naples, and others), together with railway materials[77]—but very few locomotives[78]—and parts for various other industries. Colombo estimated the number of factories producing engineering parts to be no more than 150 in the year 1881, with a total of about 15,000 to 16,000 workers.[79] The industrial census carried out for the year 1911 put the numbers at more than 14,000 factories and 248,118 workers.[80] Production now included iron steamers, locomotives, automobiles, bicycles and motor cycles, electrical materials, precision instruments, turbine engines, farm machinery, and industrial machinery: all of this with hardly any form of government protection, and with only the occasional subsidy, in addition to a policy giving preferential treatment to Italian companies in public procurements, this latter being introduced in the 1880s (see Chapters 3 and 5). Italian industry continued to be in a rather weak position as far as the production of technologically advanced machinery was concerned, and so imports were still essential in this sector; however, there were no new inventions or technological developments that Italian industry did not try to produce, including the aeroplane.

Some branches of engineering have been better researched than others: for example, the work of Michèle Merger has given us a precise picture of the process involving the substitution of imported locomotives with Italian products.[81] While the locomotives bought from Italian producers numbered only 231 during the period 1861–4 (i.e. 17.8 per cent of the total), this figure grew to 808 (66 per cent of the total) in the years 1885–1904, and after the nationalization of the railways (see Chapter 5), sales during the period 1905–14 reached 2,124 (77 per cent). In addition to the Ansaldo and Pietrarsa works,

[77] In 1881, L. Loria had the following to say about the historical development of this sector: 'The production of railway coaches and tramcars represents a great victory, made possible thanks to the perseverance of several of our industrialists, who were not to be discouraged during a long and difficult battle, despite all the indifference, pessimism, and clear hostility often shown, which helped foreign competition to the detriment of Italian industry.' 'Il materiale ferroviario all'esposizione di Milano del 1881', in Decleva (ed.), *L'Italia industriale nel 1881*, 79.

[78] The technical capacities necessary for the construction of locomotives already existed, as could be seen from the prototypes present at the Milan exhibition. However, the locomotive-building industry had not taken off. Loria writes: 'The reason why the locomotive industry did not make any great progress was not that we did not know how to build them, but rather that railway management hardly ever turned to Italian producers to satisfy their requirements, and thus never gave them any encouragement to develop production any further. If our industrialists were to be given a continuous series of orders, then not only would they be able to produce all the locomotives required at a fair price, but in this way they would soon be able to compete with their foreign competitiors', ibid. 77.

[79] Colombo, 'Sui progressi compiuti nell'industria delle macchine dall'epoca dell'esposizione di Firenze ad oggi', in ibid. 53. His survey excludes the shipyards, which produced mostly wooden vessels, and artisan workshops.

[80] This does not include the artisan workshops, which numbered 25,983, with 98,444 workers.

[81] M. Merger, 'Un modello di sostituzione: la locomotiva italiana dal 1850 al 1914', *Rivista di storia economica*, 3 (1986); id., 'Le officine di costruzione e riparazione del materiale ferroviario nell'area padana dal 1850 alla prima guerra mondiale', *Padania*, 7 (1990) (the whole issue is dedicated to railways in the Po Valley); id., 'L'industrie italienne de locomotives, reflet d'une industrialisation tardive et difficile (1859–1914)', *Histoire, Économie et Société*, 3 (1989).

this period saw two other companies enter into the sector of locomotive production: one was the Breda Company, which was founded by an engineer, Ernesto Breda, on the site of an already existing Milanese workshop (the Elvetica Works, 1846); the second was the Saronno Engineering Works, set up in 1887 by the Kessler Company from Esslingen, who were afraid of losing their share of the Italian market.[82] Although Fenoltea is right when he says that, as a whole, 'the development of the railways [only] led to the substitution of a part of steel imports, and the positive effect it had on both industrial trend and cycle was thus of a very limited nature',[83] it should be added that it did, however, lead directly to the creation of jobs, and even to the birth of new companies—such as Breda[84]—that were to play a very important role in Italian industry.

The *naval* sector also witnessed a concerted effort to break away from the dependence upon foreign (particularly English) imports, with the substitution of wooden-built sailing-vessels with a new fleet of iron-built steamships.[85] Just before the start of the First World War, however, only one-third of the Italian navy's steam-powered fleet was composed of Italian-built vessels. The most important shipbuilding yards were owned by Genoese companies—Ansaldo, Odero, Orlando, and Cantieri Navali Riuniti—and they accounted for about 70 per cent of national production.[86]

The history of the *automobile* industry is undoubtedly more enthralling, and goes back to the end of the nineteenth century at a time when no country had either a regular or standardized production of cars. The Italian artisans' technical know-how and creative flair, which enabled them to produce excellent-quality automobiles that were a great success in international competitive events, has been recognized by many scholars working in this field. By 1907, the annual national production of automobiles had reached 18,000, with 61 companies involved in production. Some of these were to become legendary names, both in Italy and abroad: companies such as Isotta Fraschini

[82] P. Hertner, 'Capitale tedesco e industria meccanica in Italia: la Esslingen a Saronno 1887–1918', *Società e Storia*, 17 (1982).

[83] S. Fenoaltea, 'Le ferrovie e lo sviluppo industriale italiano, 1861–1913', in G. Toniolo (ed.), *L'economia italiana 1861–1940* (Bari, Laterza, 1978).

[84] On the affairs of the Breda company until its founder's death, cf. V. Castronovo, 'La millesima locomotiva di Ernesto Breda', in *Grandi e piccoli borghesi*, and *La Breda. Dalla società italiana Ernesto Breda alla finanziaria Ernesto Breda 1886–1986* (Milan, Pizzi, 1986).

[85] One-third of the Italian merchant navy still consisted of sailing-ships in 1913, whereas the Italian equivalent of the Royal Navy (la Marina Militare) was completely steam-powered by this time. For a case-study of a shipyard, cf. T. Fanfani, 'Per una storia della cantieristica in Italia: dallo "Squero San Marco" all'Italcantieri', *L'Industria*, 9 (1988). For the history of two important shipping companies, cf. G. Doria, *Debiti e navi. La compagnia di Rubattino 1839–1881* (Genoa, Marietti, 1990) and on the Florio's company (which after merger with Rubattino's formed the Navigazione Generale Italiana) G. Barone, 'Il tramonto dei Florio', *Meridiana*, 11 and 12 (1991).

[86] G. Doria, *Debiti e navi*, ii, 189. On the founder of the Perrone's dynasty who greatly enlarged Ansaldo at the turn of the century, see P. Rugafiori, *Ferdinando Maria Perrone. Da Casa Savoia all'Ansaldo* (Turin, Utet, 1992).

(Milan, 1904); Lancia (Torino, 1906); Alfa-Romeo (founded by English entrepreneurs in 1906 in Milan, its original name being the Società Italiana Automobili Darracq);[87] Bianchi (originally founded as a bicycle manufacturer in Milan in 1885, it also began producing cars in 1905); Itala (Turin, 1903); and Züst (founded in Brescia in 1904, but amalgamated with the OM (Officine Meccaniche, 1899) in 1918). The most famous of all, however, was FIAT (Fabbrica Italiana Automobili Torino), founded in 1899 by a group of entrepreneurs in Turin led by Giovanni Agnelli, and destined to control the future of the automobile industry in Italy.

The international crisis of 1907 was to have a devastating effect, however, partly as a result of the car industry's disorganized structure and weak financial foundations. Few manufacturers survived the crisis, whereas the FIAT company came out of it as a clear leader, with more than 50 per cent of total car production, which, however, consisted of a total of only 9,200 automobiles in 1914 (compared with about 500,000 produced at that time in the USA). This was once more a case of relatively disappointing overall results: the market was limited,[88] and production costs were high; the 1907 crisis had exacerbated the situation, as the losses involved had discouraged investment, and even FIAT only managed to get through this period with some difficulty, thanks to help from the Banca Commerciale Italiana (see Chapter 4).[89] However, the survival of a number of companies (albeit limited), active in the automobile construction industry, was of vital importance for the nation, as these were able to profit from developments following this period of crisis. FIAT in particular had already formulated plans to construct utility cars before the outbreak of the First World War, using more 'scientific' techniques and with an American-inspired standardization of parts (Agnelli had visited the Ford automobile plants in 1909); furthermore, the company had participated in setting up other related companies, ranging from the Villar Perosa ball-bearing factory to a company producing radiators, from producers of boat engines to producers of aeroplane engines. All of this led to the Piedmont region being to the present day synonymous with the specialized

[87] The early history of Alfa-Romeo, from its foundation until the year 1926 is described in an excellent volume written by D. Bigazzi, entitled *Il Portello. Operai, tecnici e imprenditori all'Alfa-Romeo 1906–1926* (Milan, Angeli, 1988).

[88] There were 18,857 cars on Italian roads in 1913, as well as 909 lorries, 1,459 public vehicles, 17,297 motor-cycles, and 1,225,000 bicycles. 90% of the bicycles and 85% of the motor-cycles circulated in the North and Tuscany; 83% of privately owned automobiles circulated in the North and Latium.

[89] For further details, cf. V. Castronovo, *Agnelli* (Turin, UTET, 1971). Fiat has recently sponsored the publication of a series of volumes based on the company's archives, of which five have already appeared: Progetto Archivio Storico Fiat, *I primi quindici anni della Fiat* (2 vols., Milan, Angeli, 1987); id. *Fiat 1915–1930* (3 vols., Milan, Fabbri ed., 1991). On the company Lancia, acquired by Fiat in 1969, see Progetto Archivio Storico Fiat, *Le carte scoperte. Documenti raccolti ed ordinati per un archivio della Lancia* (Milan, Angeli, 1990) and F. Amatori, *Storia della Lancia. Impresa Tecnologie Mercati, 1906–1969* (Turin, Fabbri, 1992).

production of cars and automobile parts.[90] The workers in the car factories were to become the avant-garde of the Italian working-class movement, in terms of both wages and union strength and action, in Turin and elsewhere.[91]

The *electromechanical* industry was another that got off to a promising start, only to find itself in difficulty soon afterwards. One area where Italy was not way behind the rest of the advanced world was that of the production of turbines, due to the ability of Franco Tosi, who bought up the Cantoni and Krumm Company in 1881—this had been founded in Legnano in 1875 with the principal aim of producing textile machinery—and then proceeded to convert it to the production of alternative steam-powered machinery, gas engines and motors, and turbines.[92] The Riva–Monneret of Milan (later to become the Riva–Calzoni, after merging with the Calzoni of Bologna) also produced turbines, two of these being installed at Niagara Falls. However, the production of other kinds of electrical products proved to be more difficult, as a result of the continually evolving technology within this sector, together with the delicate nature of some of the materials used, such as the magnetized sheets which the Italian steel industry was unable to produce for several decades. Although Italian industry was able to supply some 40 per cent of internal demand just before the First World War, the most important Italian producers were either offshoots of foreign companies (such as AEG Thomson Houston, a branch of the German giant AEG, and Westinghouse, which was an American concern) or local producers who had been bought up by a foreign multinational, as in the case of Tecnomasio Italiano Brown Boveri (TIBB).[93] In other cases, companies were of a highly specialized variety, such as Ercole Marelli, a company founded

[90] See P. Spriano, *Storia di Torino operaia e socialista. Da De Amicis a Gramsci* (Turin, Einaudi, 1972), and S. Musso, *Gli operai a Torino, 1900–1920* (Milan, Feltrinelli, 1980).

[91] The Milan car workers, both in the Alfa-Romeo plant and in others, were also among the best-paid workers in the city, as well as being the first to ask for a pay rise or better working conditions, striking if necessary. Cf. the above-mentioned volume by D. Bigazzi, who dedicates a number of pages to a very detailed analysis of workers' action.

[92] Cf. P. Macchione, *L'oro e il ferro. Storia della Franco Tosi* (Milan, Angeli, 1987). For an account of the Riva Company, see G. Bigatti, 'Commercianti e imprenditori nella Milano post-unitaria. Le origini della Riva 1861–1869', *Società e Storia*, 39 (1988). On the electrotechnical industry, see also M. Vasta, 'Innovazioni e sviluppo economico: l'uso dei brevetti nell'analisi del settore elettrotecnico italiano nel periodo 1895–1914', *Rivista di storia economica*, 7 (1990); R. Giannetti, 'Cambiamenti non adattativi della organizzazione industriale: l'industria elettromeccanica italiana 1883–1940', *Annali di storia dell'impresa*, 7 (1991) and S. Licini, 'Ercole Marelli e Tecnomasio Italiano dalle origini agli anni '30: un tentativo di comparazione', *Annali di storia dell'impresa*, 5 and 6 (1989–90).

[93] The Tecnomasio was founded in Milan, with the aim of producing physics and geodetics equipment. In 1878 it was bought by the engineer Bartolomeo Cabella (a graduate from the Polytechnic, who had already worked in the company since 1870), and from the end of the 1890s onwards moved into the production of electrical material, without having the plant or management suitable for this. The company went through a crisis, and as a result, Cabella left, and the remaining members drew up an agreement with the Brown Boveri Co. in 1903. The latter acquired 50% of the new company's capital, which then went on to buy up another Italian company, Gadda & Co., in 1908. See R. Giannetti, 'Cambiamenti non adattativi'.

in Milan in 1891, specializing at first in the production of small electric fans and later in small electric motors; this specialization helped it to win its share of the market. The situation was only to change with the advent of war. Now other companies began to establish a name for themselves, and the Italian producers' share of the home market rose to 80 per cent, although this did not mean the end of the multinationals' domination of the market, with companies such as TIBB and CGE (a branch of General Electric, set up in 1921) very much at the forefront in a highly specialized and technologically advanced sector of industry that needed vast markets for a company to be able to invest in research and development.

While the above-mentioned branches of the engineering industry were those that managed to develop to the greatest extent in Italy, many more companies involved in other areas of production were busy making their fortunes during this period: for example, Filotecnica of Milan (founded in 1865), later to be transformed by the engineer Angelo Salmoiraghi; the Galileo Works of Florence (1896, although originally founded under another name in 1870); the National Society of Savigliano Workshops (going back to 1789, although the Turin workshop was only set up in 1889);[94] the Nebiolo Foundries (Turin, 1878) which specialized in producing printing machinery; and also Olivetti (founded in 1908 in Ivrea).

The *rubber and cable* industry was closely tied to the automobile and electrical industries, and it developed early in Italy, thanks to the pioneering start made by the Pirelli Company, set up in the year 1872 in Milan by GiovanBattista Pirelli (an engineering graduate from Milan Polytechnic). With the help of Colombo,[95] Pirelli started by producing rubber goods, but by the beginning of the First World War the company had already become a powerful multinational, particularly advanced in the production of cables, a world leadership that Pirelli has retained to the present day. In 1888, the Todeschi Company of Turin, an electric cable manufacturer, became another member of this sector of industrial production. Richard Webster, in his detailed study of industrial and financial society in early twentieth-century Italy, was quick to point out the structural interdependencies that came to exist in this new industrial panorama:

> There was a striking development, from 1898 to 1914, of a whole string of interdependent industries, ranging from engine and automobile producers to those producing motor-boats, ball-bearings, rubber tyres, and insulated electric wires and cables. In fact, Italy stood in a class of its own when compared with other Southern European and Mediterranean countries because of this high-quality, highly diversified productive network. There was thus a marked difference between Italy's relatively

[94] These latter two companies were to become producers and/or installers of electrical systems.

[95] B. Bezza, 'Il viaggio di istruzione all'estero di Giovanni Battista Pirelli', *Annali di storia dell'impresa*, 1 (1985). On the Pirelli, cf. P. Anelli, G. Bonvini, and A. Montenegro, *Dalla prima guerra mondiale all'autunno caldo* and P. Bolchini, *Il gruppo Pirelli–Dunlop: gli anni più lunghi*, both published by Angeli (Milan, 1985).

precocious entry into these fields of industrial activity (coming in only just behind the great Western European and American industries), and its sluggishness during the early phases of the 'industrial revolution', when the 'steam–iron–coal' combination was the basis for the economic growth and success of newborn industry.[96]

Apart from those industries that were part of the first 'wave' of industrialization (textiles, metallurgy, railway materials, and steam engines), and those that constituted the new technological front (such as electricity, the combustion engine, and rubber), many other industries became either partially or wholly modernized as a result of technological progress. In the *milling* industry, the 1880s saw the introduction of cylindrical mills: these were first brought in by another of Colombo's ex-students, the engineer Cesare Saldini,[97] and were built in Italy from 1896 onwards at Alfredo Zopfi's factory in Monza (Milan). By 1914 there were 27 joint-stock companies operating flour-mills, including the enormous Stucky mills of Venice and the Alta Italia mills in Genoa, which managed to negotiate a cartel agreement in order to control flour prices. Enormous technological progress was also made in the following industries: paper, leather, cement, glass, and pottery, and these sectors gave birth to certain important Italian companies, such as the Italian Cement Corporation of Casale Monferrato, the Bergamo cement producers Fratelli Pesenti, and the famous Richard–Ginori pottery in Milan.[98] However, the full story of these industrial successes still has to be written, and only the occasional anniversary booklet has so far been published.[99]

Elisabetta Bianchi Tonizzi[100] has published a study of yet another industry, the Italian *sugar-refining* industry. This has to be considered an 'artificial' industry in the Italian context, regardless of the fact that sugar beet is cultivated nationally. The production of sugar, like that of steel, got under way after the introduction of protective import tariffs, which were much higher in the case of sugar than they had been for steel. Another similarity between the two was that the sugar industry, like the steel industry, was launched with the support of Genoese entrepreneurs (above all, that of Piaggio, Raggio, Bozano, and Ravano). At the beginning, life was rather difficult for the pioneering

[96] R. Webster, *L'imperialismo industriale italiano. Studio del prefascismo 1908–1915* (Turin, Einaudi, 1974), 259–60; Eng. shortened version, *Industrial Imperialism in Italy, 1908–1915* (Berkeley, Calif., University of California Press, 1975).

[97] M. Ferrazza, 'Cesare Saldini e l'industria molitoria', *Storia in Lombardia*, 6 (1987).

[98] The Richard–Ginori Co. was founded in 1896 in Milan, from the merger between Richard and Ginori; the former had been founded in Turin in 1824 by Giacomo Richard, and subsequently moved to Milan by Giacomo's son, Giulio, in 1842 (there were already 1,100 workers working for the company in 1873); Ginori had been founded by the Marquess of Ginori in 1737 at Doccia, in the province of Florence, and had a total of some 1,000 workers in 1880. The latter produced a more artistic line of pottery ware than Richard, whose products tended to be of a more industrial nature.

[99] For a picture of these industries in 1911, see Zamagni, *Industrializzazione.*

[100] E. Bianchi Tonizzi, 'L'industria dello zucchero in Italia dal Blocco continentale alla vigilia della grande guerra (1807–1914)', *Annali di storia dell'impresa*, 4 (1988).

companies Ligure–Lombarda and the National Sugar Refiners, founded in 1872. However, the industry experienced a change in its fortunes at the end of the century, as the farming crisis and land-reclamation had together combined to create the right conditions for the planting of sugar beet in the Po Valley, thus giving the sugar industry the possibility of resolving its raw-material problem. Twenty-four new companies were set up during the period 1898–1901, including Eridania, founded on 28 September 1899. Production of raw sugar increased from 5,972 tons in 1898 to 130,861 tons in 1903, a year in which there was already a problem of overproduction; this was solved by a series of cartel agreements and financial manœuvres, rather than by reducing protection which in turn would have lowered prices, thus enabling a more extensive level of consumption (Italy had one of the lowest per capita levels of sugar consumption in the world at that time).[101] Although the Italian sugar industry helped towards conserving the value of some areas of agricultural land, and acted as a kind of savings bank for some Genoese businessmen, it certainly did not benefit either Italian consumers or Italian industry, the latter being unable to produce the necessary machinery and plant until after the First World War.

Something finally needs to be said about the Italian *chemical* industry, which although unprotected by government, had already built up the foundations for its subsequent 'take-off', which came about throughout the First World War and the 1920s.[102] The only branch of the chemical industry to experience any substantial growth during the period between the 1890s and the beginning of the First World War was the manufacture of superphosphates and sulphuric acid (together with the traditional production of candles, matches, soap, and perfumes). The major companies were Unione Concimi (founded in Milan in 1903) and Colla e Concimi (Rome, 1899), both fertilizer manufacturers. This sector of the chemical industry also saw the setting-up of co-operative factories, under the aegis of the Federation of Agricultural Consortia,[103] and the overall result was a saturated market, with the subsequent organization of cartel agreements (that were not too effective) from 1910 onwards. Another branch of the industry—the electrochemical one—got off to a positive start at the beginning of the twentieth century, with the production of calcium carbide in electrical furnaces, from which another fertilizer (calcium cyanamide) and acetylene (used in lighting and welding) could then be obtained.

Other branches of the chemical industry were a long way behind the rest of the international field. Italy was totally dependent on imports for its supply of

[101] Per capita consumption in Italy in 1909 was 3.9 kg., equivalent to one-tenth of English consumption, one-fifth of that in Germany, a half of that in Russia, and even below that in Portugal and Turkey!

[102] I have taken details of the chemical industry from my essay 'L'industria chimica in Italia dalle origini agli anni '50', and from other essays published in F. Amatori and B. Bezza (eds.), *Capitoli di storia di una grande impresa: la Montecatini 1888–1966* (Bologna, Il Mulino, 1991).

[103] Cf. M. Pezzati, 'I prodotti chimici per l'agricoltura in Italia nel periodo 1899–1929', ibid.

caustic soda, chemical dyes, and azotic fertilizers, for example. In other cases, production was sporadic and badly organized. Factories producing explosives existed—such as Dinamite Nobel, founded in Avigliana in 1873, and SIPE, founded in Milan in 1891—and pharmaceuticals,[104] boric acid,[105] citric acid,[106] and tannic extracts were also produced; however, the problem of how to produce coal intermediates still had to be resolved, as did that of co-ordinating productive processes in the chemical industry as a whole. The company that was to be at the centre of such a programme of co-ordination after the war—Montecatini—already existed as a mining company in 1888 (copper and lead mining); but it was only in 1910 that it began to diversify, when it moved into the area of pyrites, thus enabling it to extend its noticeable influence into the chemical industry proper.

3. INDUSTRIAL MILIEU AND CULTURE IN ITALY

Historical research has undergone a considerable amount of change in Italy since the days when Gerschenkron wrote that 'what strikes the observer of the comparable Italian development is the absence of any strong ideological stimulus to industrialization'.[107] Nobody today would support the thesis that Italy was devoid of industrial ferment, or that there was a lack of interest in following the example that had been set by the English, although it was clear from the start, as Boccardo quite rightly pointed out, that 'instead of copying what the English do, our people [would be better off] . . . if they aimed at imitating the *way* the English did things in the past and do them now'.[108] The 'great movement in favour of industrialization'[109] which the Milanese politician G. Robecchi wrote about in 1868, and which many others from Milan and elsewhere had also underlined in their writings, was certainly not apparent all over Italy, as the required conditions for a transition to industry were only present in certain areas of the country. Where this was so, however, involvement in the great industrializing process was quickly forthcoming, and concrete projects to this effect were soon got under way, the first of these being the above-mentioned Industrial Survey. Lanaro would seem to be right when

[104] Some of those companies which were to become the top names in the pharmaceutical sector of Italian industry already existed at this time: e.g. Schiapparelli, founded in Turin in 1824; Carlo Erba, Milan, 1865; Istituto Farmacologico Serono, Turin, 1902; Lepetit, Milan, 1910; and Zambeletti, Milan, 1913.

[105] This industry was founded in Tuscany by Francesco De Larderel in 1818.

[106] This industry was founded in 1909 in Palermo by a German company, and produced citric acid utilizing calcium citrate found locally; cf. P. Hertner, *Il capitale tedesco*, ch. 4.

[107] A. Gerschenkron, *Economic Backwardness*, 86.

[108] G. Boccardo, *Il negoziante italiano. Manuale degli uomini d'affari* (Genoa, Fratelli Pallas Ed., 1863), 248.

[109] G. Robecchi, 'L'industria del ferro in Italia e l'officina Glisenti a Carcina', *Il Politecnico* (1868); re-published in M. Romani, *Storia economica*, ii. 698.

he claims that the year 1870 marked the birth of a 'long-term project' that became 'the guiding line of bourgeois culture'.[110]

There is an explanation for Gerschenkron's disappointment, however, which would also qualify the contrary and monolithic theory constructed by Lanaro in his 1979 publication:[111] that is, that we should acknowledge that there was no one single ideology of industrialization which had the upper hand over others; but rather that Italy, a nation of many different cities and different types of agriculture, is also a nation of many different ideologies—and not only of industrialization—which sometimes converge, whilst sometimes they conflict with one another, producing an inextricable tangle of ideas and policies. It may be noted in passing that the real meaning of nineteenth-century political 'transformism' (an expression used to characterize governments that changed their parliamentary majority according to the issues being discussed), as well as of the post-Second World War multiparty coalitions, lies in the search for converging operative modes that allow the country to be governed, in the presence of this pluralism of ideologies and interests.

We can identify at least three principal characteristics of late nineteenth-century Italian industrial culture: solidaristic populism, national economic prestige, and the technocratic ideal. I am not in a position to offer a systematic survey of this theme, as its study is still in the early stages; I will, however, give a brief outline. There can be little doubt that the Veneto was 'the home of a triumphant form of paternalism . . . during the early years of industrial development: . . . entrepreneurs endeavoured to make industrial plants blend in with the surrounding landscape, separating financial concentration from plant concentration, in order to pre-empt social unrest, and maintain a steady flow of cheap labour'.[112] On the other hand, their efforts were seen as supplementing the agricultural income of a growing population. This paternalism was often founded on a solid Catholic base and resulted in plants remaining relatively small in size[113] and scattered throughout the countryside; moreover, many entrepreneurs were committed to guaranteeing their workers an entire range of social services. These included mutual aid societies (that provided help above all in the case of illness), crèche facilities, boarding-schools for young girls, technical schools, savings facilities, company stores, factory canteens, and even

[110] S. Lanaro, *Nazione e lavoro. Saggio sulla cultura borghese in Italia 1870–1925* (Venice, Marsilio, 1979).

[111] Lanaro himself would seem to acknowledge the complex composition of post-unification Italian culture, in his most recent work, *L'Italia nuova. Identità e sviluppo 1861–1988* (Turin, Einaudi, 1988).

[112] Lanaro, 'Genealogia di un modello', in *Il Veneto*, 71.

[113] For an analysis of the fact that Italian small industry is often the result of industrial decentralization 'aimed at reconciling agriculture with the new form of industry, and the factory worker with his new future', cf. V. Hunecke, 'Cultura liberale e industrialismo nell'Italia dell'Ottocento', *Studi Storici*, 18 (1977), which includes this citation (p. 26). Of course, the lack of coal and the presence of a strong artisan tradition also had their role to play.

entire housing estates for workers. All of this, in return for the workers' loyalty and willingness to work very long hours.

This 'Catholic solidarism', which was an integral part of Alessandro Rossi's ideology[114]—too complex a character however to be confined within this one single category—was also present in the case of the Marzottos,[115] as well as in regions besides the Veneto, such as Lombardy,[116] Tuscany,[117] and probably elsewhere to a degree almost certainly greater than currently available research would seem to indicate, and this is something that was present not only in the textile industry.[118] The clear tone of social conservatism present in this ideology should be re-examined more closely today, in the light of the too abrupt process of change that elsewhere saw workers torn away from their peasant traditions, customs, and environment, as a result of total proletarianization of the work-force in factories concentrated in big Italian cities. It should also be reconsidered in the light of the different Japanese organization of the firm that is seen as the supplier of welfare services to its employees much in the same way as the Italian 'paternalistic' entrepreneurs had practised since the nineteenth century.

A second important inspiring motive in the industrialization of Italy was that of the technocratic ideal, based on a long tradition of mechanical-engineering expertise (including such famous names as that of Leonardo da Vinci) going back to well before industrialization, and aimed at creating an economic infrastructure and at reorganizing waterways and agricultural land in the Po Plain. The city of Milan is the most obvious illustration of this ideal, with the foundation of the SIAM (Society for the Promotion of Trades and Crafts) in 1839, followed by that of Milan Polytechnic in 1863—the latter being very active in the field of technology. It would be no exaggeration to say that the typical Milanese entrepreneur at that time was an engineer: men such as GiovanBattista Pirelli (one of the Polytechnic's very first graduates),

[114] Cf. G. Berta, 'Dalla manifattura al sistema di fabbrica: razionalizzazione e conflitti di lavoro', in *Annali della storia d'Italia*, i (Turin, Einaudi, 1978).

[115] G. Roverato, in *Una casa industriale*, 56–7 writes: 'this community in Valdagno [Vicenza] became accustomed very gradually and painlessly to the presence of industry: the latter offered a respite to hunger, led to the growth of a small mercantile class, and became part of the life of the community.'

[116] Cf. Macchione, *L'oro e il ferro*, 308 ff. for an analysis of the paternalism exercised by Franco Tosi. Cf. also *Villaggi operai in Italia. La Val Padana e Crespi d'Adda* (Turin, Einaudi, 1981), and L. Guiotto, *La fabbrica totale. Paternalismo industriale e città sociali in Italia* (Milan, Feltrinelli, 1979).

[117] The two largest workers' villages in Tuscany are Lardarello and Rosignano Solvay. The fact that a multinational like Solvay should decide to adopt a paternalistic approach to the factory and its work-force is highly significant.

[118] Cf. also G. Sapelli, 'Gli organizzatori della produzione tra struttura d'impresa e modelli culturali', in *Annali dell storia d'Italia*, iv (Turin, Einaudi, 1981). There is now a well-documented volume available analysing the socio-economic environment that existed to the north of Milan, an environment that was centred around a large number of small businesses, often 'paternalistic' in nature: R. Romano, *La modernizzazione periferica. L'Alto Milanese e la formazione di una società industriale, 1750–1914* (Milan, Angeli, 1990).

Salmoiraghi, Cabella, Prinetti, Riva, Tosi, Ettore Conti (a big name in the electrical industry), Cesare Saldini, and many others. Not only were these engineers active in the companies that they ran, but they were also very much involved in the life of technical associations, and in programmes organized for the promotion of industry.[119] An ideological position such as that of the technocrats, which often became amalgamated with a form of paternalism, was once more against the idea of accepting class conflict as an inevitable outcome of industrialization; instead, it preferred to promote the culture of the workplace[120] and class co-operation,[121] and only accepted class trade unionism at a later date.[122]

If Milan could be considered to have been at the forefront of this 'ideology of industrialization', the city of Turin was also of importance[123] in this context, as was the area of Piedmont in general. We have already mentioned the early development of the woollen industry in the area around Biella. A further example was that of the hydraulic engineer, Quintino Sella, who as a young man ran the family company, and who later became one of the most important post-unification politicians in Italy, 'the most able and logically coherent supporter of a strategy for industry within the Italian political and intellectual class of that period', according to the historian G. Are.[124] Vittorio Ellena, an important government bureaucrat, and a central figure in industrial surveys and trade agreements, was also from Piedmont (Saluzzo to be precise). In the introduction to his work *Industrial Statistics*, published in 1876, he wrote the following:

Once Italy was said to be a farming and seafaring nation, but not a manufacturing one. This belief failed to acknowledge Italy's great Renaissance tradition, and was founded on the recognition of the present poverty of Italian industrial production, as if the existence of decline and revival was foreign to the economic sphere. Political decline was

[119] For an analysis of other aspects and limitations of this engineering 'culture', see V. Zamagni, 'Il ruolo de "L'Industria" nella vita economica italiana: 1887–1942', *L'Industria*, 3 (1986). Cf. also G. Longoni, 'Una fonte per lo studio della borghesia imprenditoriale milanese: "L'Industria—Rivista tecnica ed economica illustrata" (1887–1918)', *Archivio Storico Lombardo*, 112 (1985). On the importance of associations in Milan, see M. Meriggi, ' "Lo spirito di associazione" nella Milano dell'Ottocento (1815–1890)', *Quaderni Storici*, 77 (1991).

[120] M. Berra, *L'etica del lavoro nella cultura italiana: dall'unità a Giolitti* (Milan, Angeli, 1981).

[121] G. M. Longoni's study is very good on this point, as it gives a description of the environment which gave rise to the first local organization of industrial patrons—the Federazione degli Industriali Monzesi (1902)—and to the model of co-operative industrial relations personified by these industrialists: G. M. Longoni, *Una città del Lavoro. Industria, associazionismo imprenditoriale e relazioni sindacali a Monza all'epoca della prima industrializzazione (1870–1930)* (Bologna, Cappelli, 1987).

[122] As noted by G. Baglioni, *L'ideologia della borghesia industriale nell'Italia liberale* (Turin, Einaudi, 1974), 174 ff.

[123] G. Are, *Alle origini*, 252.

[124] Turin also had its Istituto Tecnico, which was subsequently turned into a Polytechnic. In 1868, the Società Promotrice dell'Industria Nazionale (Society for the Promotion of Industry) was set up, followed by the opening of the Regio Museo Industriale (Royal Museum of Industry) in 1869.

associated with the low level of productivity in the factories, and even those few who had not given up hope of Italy regaining its dignity and pride, still did not believe that industrial production could make it wealthy once more . . . [But] how can agriculture be expected to prosper if it is not combined with a striving industrial production? . . . The great nations, both in terms of intellectual achievements and material wealth, are chameleon-like.[125]

However, the Piedmontese vision of factory organization was much more hierarchical and conflictual, perhaps as a result of old Piedmont's military tradition, or due to the strong influence of English culture. This produced an early tendency towards setting up trade associations, and in 1906 the Industrial League was founded from the old Society for the Promotion of Industry, and its first secretary was Gino Olivetti, who 'tenaciously pursued his aim of setting up an association of entrepreneurs, and was recognized as being the leader of Italian industrial organizations'.[126] This Turin-based League subsequently gave birth to the Piedmontese Industrial Federation in 1908, followed by that of the Italian Industrial Confederation on 5 May 1910 (which had 1,893 member companies, with 211,000 workers, by 1912—all of them located in the industrial triangle).

The third element of Italian industrialist culture is that associated with the country's national military prestige, and as such, is one of the most vociferous and thoroughly researched forms of ideology in Italy from this period in its history. Strong nationalistic tones can be found in the views of Alessandro Rossi, of Leone Carpi from Ferrara,[127] of the previously mentioned Milanese group of industrialists,[128] and of Vincenzo Stefano Breda from the Veneto, who was made head of the Terni Company. Furthermore, this ideology was an integral part of the plans of Ligurian industrialists (particularly those from Genoa), such as the Orlando, Bombrini, and Perrone families. Shipbuilding and metallurgy were the two central industries in the military and industrial structure created with the help of the State (see Chapter 5), and concentrated for the best part in the city of Genoa, which ended up becoming 'a productive centre almost exclusively geared to state production'.[129]

The involvement of politicians of very different political colours, such as Crispi and Nitti, in an ideological programme of this kind, can be put down to its forceful, but rather ambiguous connotations; it was also an important factor in the process that saw the 'nationalist' movement, which first appeared at the

[125] Ellena, *La statistica*, 3–5.

[126] M. Abrate, *La lotta sindacale nella industrializzazione in Italia 1906–1926* (Milan, Angeli, 1967), 41.

[127] Carpi had already declared in 1876 that it was necessary to 'use whatever means required, at whatever price, in order to transform Italy into a predominantly industrial and seafaring nation, with its own worldwide colonial possessions' (Lanaro, *Nazione e lavoro*, 23).

[128] See V. Zoppetti's warning about the lack of an Italian steel industry, in Decleva (ed.), *L'Italia industriale nel 1881*, 18–19.

[129] Doria, *Investimenti*, ii. 556.

beginning of the twentieth century, embrace the cause of economic independence with what was, at the time, astute reasoning.[130] Filippo Carli (Guido Carli's father) from Brescia argued that:

it is in the interest of nations to export mainly complex finished goods, as the foreign buyer is obliged to pay the extra amount represented by the labour that has gone into these goods: the greater the sum of such amounts, the quicker the nation as a whole becomes richer. Moreover, raw materials have no national identity: sulphur is the same the world over, be it from Sicily or from Louisiana; but a machine, a fabric, or an ornamental object each has its own particular form, incorporating the creativity and work of the labour-force, and thus can be said to possess a national identity.[131]

This political and economic nationalism was combined with a tentative form of imperialism, as described by Webster in his study of imperialism,[132] although it was to have very modest economic consequences.[133] What it did do was to push Italy towards its eventual participation in the First World War, the economic consequences of which will be examined in Chapter 7. While nationalism was to play a decisive role in the country's history only in the twentieth century, the aim of industrializing the economy was at the heart of government policy from the end of the 1870s onwards, and as a consequence the few supporters of free-market economics Italy had were destined to play out the role of a Cassandra, their views unheeded, and 'they had no influence over our country's economic policy, and could come up with no theory of industrialization'.[134] The only person among this group of free-marketeers who did not resign himself merely to criticizing everything that was happening at the time was Einaudi: he did criticize the immorality of certain kinds of relationships that existed between politicians and industrialists, but he also recognized that the state had a role to play as 'builder of an infrastructure and of external relations which would together aid development, as well as creator of wealth through public spending policy'.[135]

Nevertheless, I must admit that the phenomenon of industrialism was still a long way from influencing at large the labouring classes, or the middle-class

[130] On this subject, cf. L. De Rosa, 'Economics and Nationalism in Italy (1861–1914)', *Journal of European Economic History*, 11 (1982).

[131] F. Carli, 'La politica economica della grande Italia (1911)', cited in Lanaro, *Nazione e lavoro*, 176.

[132] Webster, *L'Imperialismo*.

[133] See the following: F. Grassi, 'L'industria tessile e l'imperialismo italiano in Somalia (1896–1911)', *Storia contemporanea*, 4 (1973); E. Sori, 'La penetrazione economica italiana nel territorio degli Slavi del sud (1896–1914)', *Storia contemporanea*, 12 (1981); A. Tamborra, 'The Rise of Italian Industry and the Balkans (1900–1914)', *Journal of European Economic History*, 3 (1974).

[134] A. Cardini, 'Economisti e politica in Italia tra il 1870 e il 1914', *Note economiche*, 13 (1984), 131. On the battle between the supporters of free-trade and those of protectionism in a less well-known case—which took place in Florence at the end of the 18th cent.—see R. Melchionda's interesting monographic study, *Firenze industriale nei suoi incerti albori. Le origini dell'associazionismo imprenditoriale cento anni fa. Esplorazioni e materiali* (Florence, Le Monnier, 1988).

[135] R. Faucci, *Einaudi* (Turin, UTET, 1986), 419.

and aristocratic circles in Italian society—all of whom continued to be for the best part agricultural in nature, as we have already pointed out. However, wherever there was an industrial presence, some degree of industrial 'culture' was inevitably to be found, even in the case of isolated and precarious forms of industry such as those present in the Neapolitan area, as De Rosa has shown in his study of the South;[136] but this industrial ideology was destined to remain incomplete and ineffective without the presence of a 'critical mass' of industrial enterprises.

Another interesting approach to the question of 'industrial ideology' in Italy would be to look at its connections with industrial reality beyond Italy's borders: that is, to identify its foreign roots, both ideological and economic, springing from flows of investment and technological ties between Italian entrepreneurs and foreign industry and technology. Likewise, one could attempt to sketch the social and cultural characteristics of the entrepreneurial class that instigated industrial change in Italy; however, the study of the Italian bourgeoisie is still in its early stages,[137] despite the existence of a number of biographies of entrepreneurs, such as that of Agnelli, or the rather interesting one of the engineer Vilfredo Pareto, who was the director of the Iron Industry Society (founded in 1872),[138] or others quoted above detailing the lives of some of the businessmen involved in the woollen and cotton industries. The Italian entrepreneurial class has always had to live with being labelled as a 'backward bourgeoisie', either as a result of the help given to it by governments, or because of its frequently reactionary stance, or because it was too slow and cumbersome in bringing about industrialization in Italy: perhaps this view of the Italian entrepreneurial class would change, in part at least, if a more detailed, comparative study were carried out. For the moment, we can conclude this chapter with an instructive quote from S. Lanaro, in whose opinion 'to talk of "backward" or "advanced" forms of capitalism should have no sense for the historian'.[139]

[136] L. De Rosa, *La rivoluzione industriale e il Mezzogiorno* (Bari, Laterza, 1973), chs. 2 and 3.

[137] The best work published so far on this argument is A. Banti, *Una borghesia padana dell'Ottocento* (Venice, Marsilio, 1989); another text that is quite valid, even though its essays are of a more varied nature, is G. Fiocca (ed.), *Borghesi e imprenditori a Milano dall'unità alla prima guerra mondiale* (Bari, Laterza, 1984).

[138] G. Busino, *Vilfredo Pareto e l'industria del ferro nel Valdarno* (Milan, Banca Commerciale Italiana, 1977).

[139] Lanaro, *Nazione e lavoro*, 15.

3

International Trade and Capital Flows

1. FROM FREE TRADE TO PROTECTIONISM

If there was one area in which Count Camillo Benso di Cavour's ideas were applied in full, it was that of free trade: the Sardinian customs tariffs and trade agreements, enacted by Cavour in the 1850s along the lines of the English example, were immediately extended to the newly unified Italy. Subsequently, tariffs were lowered even further following the navigation agreement signed on 13 June 1862 and the trade agreement signed on 17 January 1863 with France. As a result, Italy could boast 'the most liberal tariffs that had ever been adopted in Europe up to that time'.[1]

The political choices of the supporters of free trade have been seen by many as resulting from a wide variety of factors: the most important of these was the need to repay England and France for the political and military help they had given during the unification process opening up the Italian market to the industrial exports of these two countries; secondly, the free-traders wanted to guarantee the existence of unprotected foreign markets for Italian export products; the final motive was that of not wanting to see Italian industry excluded from the international flows of technological progress and investment, as these seemed to be part and parcel of the new international free-trade credo.

However, we can not ignore the fact that at that time there was also a widespread belief, often based on ignorance more than anything else, that, in the words of the southern Italian member of Parliament Carlo de Cesare (words pronounced in a parliamentary speech on 25 November 1863), 'Italy is an agricultural nation . . . The climate, the air, the sun and the Italian countryside will never, in my view, enable us to become a predominantly industrial nation like either France or England'.[2] A perhaps more interesting

[1] This was the belief at the time, as expressed in M. Romani, *Storia economica d'Italia nel secolo XIX*, ii (Milan, Giuffré, 1976), 7. For details of the domination of the English model in the newly unified Italy, and of the economic relations between England and Italy, cf. P. Bolchini, 'La Gran Bretagna e la formazione del mercato italiano (1861–1883)', *Miscellanea storica ligure* 1/2 (Genoa, 1968).

[2] Romani, *Storia economica*, 11. The idea that the Mediterranean was an area only suited to the production of raw materials and foodstuffs was so common outside Italy that even List adhered to it, which irritated Carlo Cattaneo enormously, causing him to comment: 'The entire North of Europe was for centuries a barbarous land, while Egypt, Persia, Sidon and Damascus were flourishing centres of trade and industry: nobody can say what the future holds for the peoples of this planet.

point, and one that is not generally known, is that the free-trade policy and legislation did not have an easy ride in Parliament. Concern about its adoption were expressed already during the last few months of Cavour's life. As a member of Parliament, Polsinelli, a woollen manufacturer from Arpino (Frosinone), succinctly put it in his speech to Parliament on 25 May 1861: 'France and England preach free trade having enjoyed a high level of protectionism for centuries—France has even experienced prohibition. They then say to us: let's trade freely—open up your markets to us. But this, gentlemen, is a battle between a giant and a baby.'[3] This sentiment was reiterated by the MP Lualdi, a cotton-manufacturer from Busto Arsizio (Varese), when he had the following to say during a speech to the House on 26 November 1863: 'Industry, like any other art or trade, needs a period of apprenticeship. The setting-up, together with the various trials and experiments, take time and effort, and lead to some amount of failure, which in turn can be learnt from in order to further improve methods and techniques, and so on. And what is it that you are doing right now? You are hitting industrialists just when the moment is ripe for reaping some of the rewards of such an experience. I believe that if one takes into account these factors, then it is not difficult to see that free-trade policies have to be put into practice very gradually'.[4]

Colombo also added his contribution to the debate when, not yet an MP, he wrote the following in his article on the Italian Exhibition held in Florence in 1861, to be published in the October–December 1861 number of the review *La Perseveranza*: 'Free competition is a wonderfully fertile principle, and can be certainly applied when industrial development has reached such a point where it is either no longer afraid of, or can reasonably hope to balance out, foreign imports; but until a country's industry has reached such a point in its development, until it is has reached a certain maturity and strength, then protectionism, albeit limited in nature, is not a dangerous practice, but a necessary one.'[5]

Although the supporters of this pragmatic point of view were in the minority during the early days of the new Italian Kingdom, they nevertheless continued to bring the problem up whenever and wherever possible: they did this rather timidly at first, during the period up to the end of the 1860s, which saw the newborn Italian nation involved in a number of political crises; but their voice grew louder after the publication of the Industrial Survey of 1870–4, when industrialists were united in their justified demands for some form of

Who would have ever told Caesar that an island inhabited by half-naked, painted barbarians was destined to colonize India while the other nations looked on helplessly?' 'Dell'economia nazionale di Federico List', contained in *Scritti economici*, ii (Florence, 1956).

[3] Romani, *Storia economica*, 392.

[4] Ibid. 481.

[5] Ibid. 690.

protection.[6] The industrialists, led by Alessandro Rossi,[7] were soon no longer alone in expressing their desire for protectionist measures, and consequently the abandonment of *laissez-faire* economic policies. In 1874 there was a heated debate among Italian economists which led to a split in two opposing groups, giving rise to two separate societies : the Società Adam Smith, based in Ferrara, which brought together all those economists who continued to believe in orthodox *laissez-faire*, and whose ideas appeared in the Florentine publication, the *Economista*; the second group was the Associazione per il progresso degli studi economici, founded by Lampertico and Luzzatti, and its members included both so-called 'socialists of the chair' and other personalities involved in Italian political and social life at that time.[8] This latter group at first wrote in various periodicals, and then set up the *Giornale degli economisti* in Padua in 1875, although this publication only survived until 1878.[9] In this periodical they sustained that a prudent form of state intervention in the economy was necessary, and not only in the area of protective tariffs.

As Cardini pointed out, 'while the ideas of Luzzatti and Lampertico were of scarce theoretical interest, they did inspire the policies of government and other milieux that effectively exercised economic power in the country'.[10]

It should be said that this turning-point came about before the agrarian crisis and before political power moved from the Historical Right to the Historical Left, though the latter two events were to reinforce the tendency towards protectionism. The first concrete results of the new economic thinking were to be seen when the existing trade agreements were changed, and a new tariff structure was introduced between 1875 and 1880; this took into account the technical criticisms made of the previous tariffs, and slightly increased the average duties for fiscal reasons, as well as providing better protection for certain industries—the textile, paper, porcelain, tiles, glass, and sugar industries.[11] The result of the agrarian crisis, on the other hand, was that it did put pressure on government to introduce an agricultural protectionist policy, something that had never really been seriously considered prior to the crisis. During the 1880s, 'many agricultural societies—the most important being the

[6] G. Are, *Alle origini dell'Italia industriale* (Naples, Guida ed., 1974).

[7] G. Zalin, 'Federico List e Alessandro Rossi. Considerazioni sulle origini e sulla natura del protezionismo in occidente', in G. L. Fontana (ed.), *Schio e Alessandro Rossi* (Rome, Ed. di Storia e Letteratura, 1985).

[8] Luzzatti himself recollects, in his memoirs, the involvement of Scialoja, Sella, Cossa, Sclopis, Messedaglia, De Vincenzi, Villari, Fortunato, and many others: cf. P. Pecorari, *Luigi Luzzatti e le origini dello 'statalismo' economico nell'età della Destra Storica* (Padua, Signum, 1983), 185–6.

[9] It would seem that this was due to insufficient finances. When the new series of *Giornale degli Economisti* came out in 1886, with its head office in Bologna, 'there was a general desire not to be associated with one particular school of thought', A. Cardini, *Stato liberale e protezionismo in Italia (1890–1900)* (Bologna, Il Mulino, 1981), 61.

[10] Ibid. 47.

[11] In E. Corbino, *Annali dell'economia italiana*, ii (Città di Castello, 1931), 206–14, the author cites some percentages which have been calculated, but as there is a lack of a more detailed evaluation of these results, I have decided not to enter into a discussion of them here.

one based in Milan—together with various northern farmers' associations, and, above all, southern absentee landowners, all moved towards a position that saw the need for some degree of protectionism in agriculture'.[12]

On 6 July 1883, a special commission was set up with the aim of establishing a basis for a newly revised set of custom tariffs. The most influential members of the commission were Luzzatti, Lampertico, Ferraris, Ellena, Monzilli, and Bonaldo Stringher, who was later to become governor of the Bank of Italy; they decided to make recommendations regarding the implementation of protective tariffs for several different industries, but not in the case of agriculture.[13] With a law passed on 14 July 1887, Parliament, on the other hand, decided to increase some of the existing industrial tariffs, but to ignore completely the commission's recommendations for agriculture. According to many historical texts, this decision was the result of an alliance between northern industrialists and southern landowners: apart from the fact that northern farmers were also demanding some form of protection, a more accurate interpretation of events, in my opinion, was that given by one of the protagonists, Stringher, when he subsequently wrote that 'at that time it would seem that a number of diverse groups were knocking on the doors of Parliament, and although they were very different in nature, they managed to lend each other considerable support, not through some premeditated plan or other, but simply because their motives and aims converged'.[14]

Since 'the 1887 duty was for the first time openly protectionist in nature, . . . [although] technically imperfect as far as the machinery, chemical and precision instruments industries were concerned',[15] then it would be a good idea to take a closer look at it. I do not propose to conduct a quantitative analysis, as Italian custom tariffs were specific ones, and the calculations that would be necessary in order to transform them into *ad valorem* rates have yet to be made, with the exception of one or two illustrative examples.[16] Moreover, the various commercial treaties, signed after the establishment of the general tariff in 1887, as well as the changes in import prices, could have made a significant difference to the real impact exercised by protection, making it necessary to calculate

[12] A. De Bernardi, *Questione agraria e protezionismo nella crisi economica di fine secolo* (Milan, Angeli, 1977), 33. An influential economic paper like *Il Sole*, issued in Milan since 1 Aug. 1865, had become favourable to protectionism in the second half of the 1870s. See P. Bairati and S. Carrubba, *La trasparenza difficile. Storia di due giornali economici. 'Il Sole' e '24 Ore'* (Palermo, Sellerio, 1990).

[13] Cf. D. Morelli, *Il protezionismo industriale in Italia dall'Unificazione del Regno* (Milan, Soc. Ed. Libraria, 1920), 118–27.

[14] B. Stringher, 'Gli scambi con l'estero e la politica commerciale italiana dal 1860 al 1910', in *Accademia dei Lincei* (ed.), *Cinquanta anni di storia italiana*, iii (Milan, Hoepli, 1911), 24.

[15] D. Morelli, *Il protezionismo*, 127. E. Del Vecchio, *La via italiana al protezionismo* (5 vols., Rome, Camera dei deputati, 1979–80).

[16] There are some figures relative to the incidence of protectionism in different sectors of the economy, in V. Zamagni, 'Commercio estero e sviluppo economico nell'Italia giolittiana' (in *Storia del Commercio Italiano* (Milan, Etas Libri, 1978), 102).

yearly rates of protection. However, we can say that the average level of nominal protection on industrial goods was somewhat limited, and was rarely higher than 21 per cent.[17]

The protected products were textiles, both yarn and cloth, including silk cloth, but excluding raw silk of course; pig-iron and steel; chinaware and pottery; glass; paper; raw and refined sugar; and a few chemical and engineering products, such as explosives and guns. The high level of protection given to wheat has been analysed by Federico (see Table 3.1).[18]

Thus the two major industries not to have any form of protection were the engineering and chemical industries, plus certain other less strategically important industries. In the case of the former two, their lack of protection was justified by the greater importance given to other industries, particularly the textile industry (which required machinery together with chemical products such as dyes), and also by the need to barter these unprotected markets against favourable international treatment when it came to the export of Italian agricultural products and Italian raw silk.[19]

The inconsistent nature of the system, together with the occasionally negative 'effective protection' produced by it, were well known at the time. For example, the Lombard Engineering Society complained that the total duty on the various parts that were needed to build a plating plant came to 142.69 lire, whereas the duty on a ready-built plant imported from abroad was only 126.67 lire, thus amounting to a 'negative protection' of 16.02 lire; and this was certainly not the only case. As far as the chemical industry was concerned, the long battle to obtain some form of protection was only won after the onset of war necessitated government intervention in the industry; protection was introduced in 1921, as we shall see later on. In some cases, it was supplemented

Table 3.1. Rate of grain duty, 1889–1913 (%)

	Durum wheat	Normal wheat
1889–92		23.9
1895–7		46.2
1899–1902	36.4	41.6
1903–7	38.1	42.8
1908–13	33.1	34.8

17 In 1911, this figure was higher in the case of duty on linen, cotton yarn, cardboard, iron- and steel-work, sheet glass, calcium chloride, chloroform, salicylates, explosives, paraffin, sugar, wheat, as well as in the case of fiscal duty on oils, coffee, and groceries.

18 G. Federico, 'Commercio dei cereali e dazio sul grano in Italia (1863–1913). Una analisi quantitativa', *Nuova Rivista Storica*, 68 (1984), 104.

19 The latter is F. Coppa's point of view, in G. Mori (ed.), *L'industrializzazione in Italia (1861–1900)* (Bologna, Il Mulino, 1977).

by state subsidies to the industry in question, together with preferential treatment when it came to public procurement (as was the case with shipbuilding, railway equipment, and armaments); from 1903 onwards, whoever exported machinery was eligible for a refund covering the duty previously paid on the steel used in the construction of this machinery. However, these were only very limited measures, and they failed to resolve the more fundamental problems. A special commission was set up to do so in 1913, with the aim of establishing a new customs tariff by 1917; but because of the war, this was postponed until 1921, when all sectors, including both the chemical and engineering industries, were given protection.

The incoherencies in the protective system set up in 1887, as well as the reluctance to justify the many public initiatives supporting the expansion of the Italian metallurgical industry, led Gerschenkron to comment that 'perfect inactivity of the government in economic affairs might have been more beneficial than what actually took place'.[20] A more objective analysis of the effects of economic protectionism in Italy will show that Gerschenkron's opinion was somewhat extreme when looked at from a present-day point of view.

First of all, the economic thinking that gave rise to the idea that *laissez-faire* always represents the best economic policy possible, has been shown to rest on unrealistic hypotheses; secondly, a comparative historical analysis shows that: 'the oldest and most important of prejudices is that protectionism is an exception in the history of international trade . . . whereas, in fact, the opposite is true—that is, free trade represents the exception to the protectionist rule'.[21] On the other hand, it has always been known that protectionism is not enough in itself to lead to the growth of a national industry, and that capital, entrepreneurs, technology, and easily accessible markets are also necessary. Bearing this in mind, we can now begin to understand why tariffs on textiles, paper, and ceramic products were far more successful economically speaking than similar tariffs on the metallurgical sector: the latter was a new industry in Italy, and had to be developed on a large scale, thus involving considerable risk and the employment of enormous amounts of capital. Nevertheless, it was a highly strategic industry for several reasons, for the completion of the Italian industrial sector and, above all, for the support it provided to the engineering and military sectors, and this was why it was protected from the beginning.

As for the engineering industry, Fenoaltea believes that 'Italy could have expanded a lot more quickly than it did if it had not reduced the relative

[20] A. Gerschenkron, *Economic Backwardness in Historical Perspective* (Cambridge, Mass., Harvard University Press, 1962), 117 (the italics are mine).

[21] P. Bairoch, 'Politiche doganali e sviluppo economico: miti e realtà del protezionismo', *Mezzogiorno d'Europa*, 6 (1986), 537. I would like to point out that the largest present-day industrialized nations all have a long history of protectionism. I am referring to the USA—more protectionist than European countries—to Germany, Japan—when it was allowed—and to England before 1844.

advantage it had in the engineering industry, and had instead increased its advantage by subsidizing exports in that sector'.[22] Well, a closer look will show that the engineering industry in fact developed at about the same pace as the metallurgy industry; furthermore, Toniolo has shown that even if we adopt all the more favourable assumptions concerning the engineering sector, in order to construct a 'counterfactual' model of that sector's development, then the maximum possible extra growth between 1898 and 1913 would have been of the order of 50 per cent, which in turn would have meant an increase in industrial value added at the end of the same period of only 4.6 per cent, and an increase in GNP of 0.9 per cent.[23] The fact is that the engineering sector was still relatively small in size at the time, and, as we have seen, a number of its component parts were not technologically advanced enough for it to be able to beat international competition. We can say, therefore, that more favourable customs tariffs would not have enabled the sector to grow much more than it did, although it was certainly a good idea to demand some form of protection.

Protectionism within the agricultural sector needs to be dealt with separately. The free-traders' vehement criticism of such a policy was also echoed in the reservations that many industrial protectionists had about it; in fact, it was clear that any increase in cereal prices due to a protectionist policy was going to have direct negative consequences for factory workers, as they would have to pay more for food, and thus wages would have to be increased, which in turn would represent an increase in production costs for industrialists. Furthermore, its critics maintained that a policy of protectionist tariffs represented an incentive to increase cereal production, which was a low-productivity crop in many parts of Italy. Nevertheless, as Federico's essay shows, 'given the weak market position of Italian exports at the time, the abolition of [cereals] tariffs would have had serious consequences for the country's trade balance'.[24] Also, the flight of peasants away from the countryside would have been even more serious than it already was (see Chapter 6).[25] In order to weigh up the government's policy, therefore, one also needs to take these latter points into account, as they were just as important as the personal interest that landowners might have had in the preservation of their rents through the application of protectionist tariffs to agriculture.

Overall, Italian protectionism can be seen to have been somewhat inconsistent, as its practical application through trial and error was determined

[22] S. Fenoaltea, 'Riflessioni sull'esperienza industriale italiana dal Risorgimento alla prima guerra mondiale', in G. Toniolo (ed.), *L'economia italiana 1861–1940* (Bari, Laterza, 1978), 90.

[23] G. Toniolo, 'Effective Protection and Industrial Growth: The Case of Italian Engineering, 1898–1913', *Journal of European Economic History*, 6 (1977).

[24] Federico, 'Commercio dei cereali', 85.

[25] The greatest agrarian economist of the time, Ghino Valenti, wrote that 'the duty on wheat, given the economic situation at the time, was a socially useful measure', in *Il dazio sul frumento e l'agricoltura italiana* (Bologna, 1898), 17. Cf. also E. Avanzi, *Influenza che il protezionismo ha spiegato sul progresso agrario in Italia* (Pisa, 1917).

by pragmatic motives rather than by the requirements of a previously agreed programme. It was just one of a series of instruments that were part of an economic policy that grew increasingly more industry-orientated from the late 1870s onwards. Although this policy did not always produce very good results, it was certainly preferable to the 'total inertia' of many other countries. We shall take a further look at the role of the State in the economic development of Italy in Chapter 5.

2. TRADE AND INDUSTRIALIZATION

Italy's foreign trade during the 50 years under examination seems at first sight to have progressed satisfactorily: the annual rate of growth of exports during the period between 1866[26] and 1913 was of the order of 3.1 per cent, while that of exports was equal to 2.7 per cent. However, Italy's share of world trade fell from 3.1 to 2.6 per cent during the same period, as it was unable to keep up with the pace of the other countries' trade expansion.[27] There were two cycles of expansion of exports during this period: 1867–76, with a growth rate of 3.7 per cent, and 1895–1912, with a growth rate of 4.5 per cent; in between these two cycles, there were 20 years in which the situation remained more or less stagnant, with a decline in exports after the breaking-off of relations with France after 1887.[28]

The weakness of Italy's position in the field of international trade can be clearly seen from its trade composition. Table 3.2 gives this composition only for 1886 and 1913—both very significant years however—so as not to complicate things unnecessarily. The trade conflict with France was still to come in the year 1886, as were the effects of protectionism introduced in 1887 and effective from 1888 onwards; 1913, on the other hand, being the final year of this period, enables us to see the effects of industrialization on the country's foreign trade. Table 3.2 shows 25 exported products, or groups of products, and 26 imported products, which represented more than two-thirds of imports and exports both in 1886 and in 1913. The enormous variety and the fragmentary nature of Italian foreign trade have made it impossible to present a more complete picture without the construction of an even longer and more complicated table.

As far as exports are concerned, one notices first of all the fall, or stagnation,

[26] The trade figures for the years 1861–5 are not compatible with those for subsequent years.

[27] G. Federico, 'Commercio estero e "periferie". Il caso dei paesi mediterranei', *Meridiana*, 4 (1988).

[28] This has been described as a 'tariff war' between Italy and France, following the introduction of the protectionist tariffs in 1887. In his *Annali*, iii, E. Corbino explains that it was not the tariff itself which prevented trade agreements being reached, as such agreements were stipulated with many other countries; the problem was one of a lack of goodwill, on both sides, which was necessary if an agreement were to be reached. This 'goodwill' was lacking on both sides, also for political reasons, and in the end this led to an escalation of retaliations and threats, which eventually subsided in 1892, and was finally forgotten with the reaching of the 1898 agreement.

Table 3.2. Main exports and imports, 1886 and 1913

Exports

	1886		1913		Growth % 1886–1913	
	Volume (tons) (1)	Value (million lire) (2)	Volume (tons) (3)	Value (million lire) (4)	Volume (5)	Value (6)
Rice	7,013	24.0	4,473	19.7	64	82
Pasta	41,679	2.0	70,992	34.1	170	1,705
Flour	5,327	1.7	113,351	41.9	2,128	2,465
Eggs	23,403	29.3	24,776	48.3	106	165
Cheese	3,901	6.6	32,804	73.6	841	1,115
Citrus fruit	124,879	24.9	436,541	85.7	350	344
Fruit and vegetables	49,310	26.6	371,490	145.0	753	545
Preserved food	—	—	68,530	54.0	—	—
Wine	2,566,790[a]	88.1	1,787,265[a]	82.5	70	94
Olive oil	64,801	77.8	31,218	42.3	48	54
Raw hemp	33,125	26.5	50,326	52.8	152	199
Raw hides	18,155	35.3	28,134	64.6	155	183
Marble	108,200	16.5	317,332	37.6	292	228
Sulphur	300,881	25.0	351,339	37.2	117	149
Metallic minerals	295,783	9.8	205,604	24.1	70	246
Cotton yarns	—	—	14,614	39.2	—	—
Cotton cloth	—	—	49.395	184.9	—	—
Wool cloth	—	—	2,023	21.7	—	—
Raw silk and schappe	6,412	302.7	11,359	407.5	177	135
Silk products	—	16.6	—	107.0	—	645
Cars	—	—	—	31.9	—	—

Boilers and machines	—	—	16,527	25.7	—	—
Rubber	—	—	4,116	51.0	—	—
Chemical products	—	37.6	—	78.4	—	209
Hats	3,991[b]	6.8	219,673[b]	39.4	5,504	579
TOTAL	—	757.8	—	1,830.0	—	—
TOTAL EXPORTS	—	1,028.2	—	2,497.0	—	244

Imports

	1886		1913		Growth % 1886–1913	
	Volume (tons) (7)	Value (million lire) (8)	Volume (tons) (9)	Value (million lire) (10)	Volume (11)	Value (12)
Wheat	936,233	192.0	1,810,733	399.5	193	208
Other cereals	47,362	10.3	526,207	89.1	1,110	865
Coffee	10,851	17.9	28,665	44.4	264	248
Tobacco	23,477	31.3	25,474	43.3	109	138
Oleiferous seeds	43,431	13.0	92,599	35.1	213	270
Preserved fish	47,602	31.2	65,224	58.7	137	188
Coal	2,927,092	67.3	10,834,008	373.8	370	555
Timber	789,800	59.1	1,367,875	133.8	173	226
Oil and petrol	71,268	12.8	150,034	32.0	211	250
Copper, brass, bronze	8,076	10.3	30,280	52.4	375	509
Scrap iron	115,705	7.5	326,231	29.4	282	379
Raw hides	18,155	35.3	24,526	67.1	135	190
Dressed hides	2,020	17.9	3,481	58.9	172	329
Raw silk	1,118	50.3	2,845	110.4	254	219

Table 3.2. (*contd.*)

Imports

	1886		1913		Growth % 1886–1913	
	Volume (tons) (7)	Value (million lire) (8)	Volume (tons) (9)	Value (million lire) (10)	Volume (11)	Value (12)
Wool cloth	5,242	51.0	2,955	52.9	56	104
Silk cloth	—	49.8	—	44.6	—	90
Cocoons	1,306	13.7	5,054	56.7	387	414
Linen, raw jute	8,635	4.2	57,141	39.7	662	945
Raw cotton	67,994	74.8	201,881	334.7	297	447
Raw wool	12,143	32.4	28,639	113.4	236	350
Chemical prods.	—	25.3	—	147.2	—	582
Pig-iron, cast iron	241,861	52.8	488,745	133.5	202	253
Copper prods.	870	2.2	9,297	27.4	1,069	1,245
Boilers and machines	33,766	41.3	86,939	130.4	257	316
Precision instruments	—	9.3	—	84.9	—	913
Rubber and rubber prods.	8,164	12.3	6,066	58.8	74	478
TOTAL	—	925.3	—	2,741.1	—	—
TOTAL IMPORTS	—	1,458.2	—	3,645.6	—	250

[a] Hectolitres.
[b] Number (hundreds).

Source: *Annuario statistico italia-10,* 1887–8 and 1914.

in raw-material exports (sulphur and metal ores) and exports of traditional agricultural products (oil, wine, eggs, and rice). Within that category, the only goods that showed any increase were raw hemp and raw hides. This is without doubt the result of the industrialization process that got under way between the 1880s and 1913, as this transformed the country's productive sectors on the one hand, and led to increased domestic demand for raw materials and food stuffs on the other.[29] A closer analysis of both imports and exports shows just how much the productive structure of the country changed during this period.

The enormous progress made in the textile sector can be seen from the increase in imported raw materials. In 1886, Italy still imported some 19 million lire's worth of linen yarn, together with 50 million lire's worth of cotton cloth; by 1913 these imports had completely disappeared, and instead Italy now exported a substantial amount of cotton yarn and finished fabrics, to the value of 224 million lire (equal to 9 per cent of total exports). Similarly, imports of woollen textiles fell by nearly 50 per cent during the same period, and the country slowly began to export woollen products. There were also changes in the silk sector, which had always been the strongest in terms of Italian exports: raw silk accounted for about 30 per cent of Italian exports in 1886, whereas finished-silk products were hardly exported at all, and imports of the same were inevitably high; by 1913 exports of raw silk had increased by almost 80 per cent (in volume), while exports of finished-silk goods were now fairly substantial, although they still made up only about one-fifth of the total value of all silk exports.

The food industry and agricultural sectors saw an increase in the exports of pasta, flour, cheese, citrus fruit, and fresh and preserved vegetables, while there was an increase in the imports of cereals, coffee, and preserved fish. It is interesting to note that sugar imports were of the order of 19 million lire in 1886, but they had completely disappeared by 1913, although this had not led to the beginning of sugar exportation. The reason for this was the emergence of a national sugar industry in Italy, which, although it had managed to cover the relatively limited internal demand for sugar, was not in a position to export because of international agreements that did not allow this. As for cereals, it is worth noting that imports doubled between 1886 and 1913, and at this latter date their value was roughly equivalent to that of silk exports.

Finally, looking at the group of metallurgical and engineering products one immediately notices the weakness of exports, which were non-existent in 1886, and had only just begun to emerge at the beginning of 1913 (the total value of all cars, boilers, and machinery exported in that year was no more than 58 million lire). Imports, on the other hand, were very substantial and rising continually. This gives us a fair indication of the state of industrialization in

[29] A detailed summary of raw-materials exports can be found in another work by G. Federico, 'Per una analisi del ruolo dell'agricoltura nello sviluppo economico italiano: note sull'esportazione di prodotti primari (1863–1913)', *Società e Storia*, 5 (1979).

Italy during the early stages that preceded the First World War. Only the textile industry was fully developed by this time, while the food industry had still not managed really to enter into the export market; the technological transformation had only just begun in the metallurgical and engineering industries, while the chemical industry was at an even more backward stage.

The weakness of Italian exports, itself an indication of the incomplete state of industrial transformation, together with the continued need to import the majority of raw materials, were the two main reasons behind the noticeable increase in imports at the very time the industrialization process had begun to gather momentum; it also explains the continual growth of a permanent balance of trade deficit. Exports were equivalent to about 70 per cent of imports in 1886; thereafter, the situation worsened before picking up in the 1890s. By 1905, the percentage had risen to roughly 84 per cent, but then there was a dramatic fall during the boom years, and by 1908 the relative position of exports and imports had reached its lowest level (59 per cent), before climbing back to 68.5 per cent by 1913. As Italy was tied to the gold standard, this meant that the country's balance of payments would have suffered greatly had it not been for the presence of balancing items, which we shall look at in the following section.

In order to complete the analysis of Italian foreign trade, we need to consider also its geographical aspects. In 1886, Italian foreign trade was almost totally concentrated within the confines of Europe (87 per cent of exports and 84 per cent of imports). Italy only imported a part of its cotton requirements, together with animal hides and some cereals, from outside of Europe, while its extra-European exports included marble, sulphur, and foodstuffs, mainly to the USA. Within Europe, Italy had very strong commercial ties with France, as can be seen from Table 3.3, with some 44 per cent of exports going to that country: of these, just under a half took the form of raw silk (France absorbed 61 per cent of total Italian silk exports), while the rest was made up of various products ranging from wine to hemp, from minerals to other agricultural products. It is interesting to compare this with Italian imports from France, which were much more limited; and France was closely followed by Britain as an exporter of goods to Italy (Italy mainly imported cotton goods, metallurgical and engineering products, and coal from Britain). In 1886, the other main importers of Italian products were Germany, Austria, and Switzerland, while the British market proved to be a difficult one to break into from the Italian point of view.

The situation changed dramatically in 1913, and one of the main characteristics of this change was the greater geographical variety of Italian export markets, as the previously existing domination by one single country was no longer present; even though Germany did have a slight advantage in comparison with other nations, Italy was no longer dependent on one country, as had been the case with France until 1887. The reason for France's 'decline' as a market for Italian exports, is connected to the previously mentioned breaking-off of trade relations between the two nations during 1887.

Table 3.3. Geographical composition of foreign trade, 1886 and 1913 (%)

	Exports (%)		Imports (%)	
	1886	1913	1886	1913
Austria	9.3	8.8	14.9	7.3
Belgium	1.4	2.3	1.9	2.1
France	44.3	9.2	22.9	7.8
Germany	10.0	13.6	8.6	16.8
Gt. Britain	6.6	10.4	18.2	16.2
Russia	1.7	2.4	6.3	6.5
Switzerland	8.3	9.9	6.3	2.4
Turkey	1.2	2.0	3.1	0.7
Rest of Europe	3.8	5.3	1.9	5.6
Africa	3.0	7.1	2.0	2.3
USA	4.9	10.7	3.7	14.3
Rest of America	3.5	11.4	3.0	7.9
Asia and Oceania	2.0	5.9	7.2	10.1
TOTAL	100.0	100.0	100.0	100.0

Source: *Annuario statistico italiano*, 1887–8 and 1914.

Regardless of the motive given at the time for this rupture, it has to be said that Italy could hardly have stood by and watched France consolidate its economic supremacy, which in turn would have led to a parallel political domination. The situation also has to be looked at in the light of the influx of foreign capital into Italy, which was in many ways tied up with the increase in foreign trade. Although, on the one hand, the worsening of relations between Italy and France was undoubtedly a major cause of the economic crisis that hit the country during the following years, with very serious consequences in particular for the southern countryside which was hardly prepared for such an eventuality, on the other hand Italy benefited in the long run from the increasingly 'international' nature of its economic relations with other countries.

This, then, is the background to the new commercial and financial relationship that emerged between Germany and Italy after the decline of French supremacy. The first thing to note is that Germany imported from Italy agricultural products (citrus and other kinds of fruit, fresh vegetables, and eggs), raw materials, and intermediate products (hemp, sulphur, and thrown silk), while its exports to Italy were made up of metallurgical, engineering, and chemical products—Germany was in fact Italy's major supplier of such products (more than 55 per cent being supplied by Germany, with the rest coming from various industrialized nations, according to their specializations). The commercial relationship between the two countries, in terms of the commodities exchanged, would therefore have been almost of a colonial nature had it not been for its limited importance in relation to Italy's overall foreign trade. The more far-sighted observers of the day—Lanino for example[30]—were perfectly aware of Germany's strategic importance for some types of Italian foreign imports, such as electrical goods.

A second important characteristic of this transformation in the geographical composition of Italian foreign trade was the enormous effort that went into finding non-European markets for Italian exports, which were not the most technologically advanced on offer at the time. Exports outside Europe rose from 13.5 to 35.1 per cent in the period between 1886 and 1913, an increase of roughly two and a half times, while imports increased from 15.9 to 34.6 per cent during the same period. Exports consisted mainly of cotton yarn, cotton and woollen fabrics, flour, pasta, and polished marble; the major importers of these products were the USA and Argentina (in the Americas), together with the African States of Egypt and Tripolitania. This change can be seen as representing Italian industry's attempt to break out of the 'difficult and almost inevitable role which saw it as merely "complementary" to that area where the "factory system" had triumphed';[31] this international division had become unbearable for an Italy that was inevitably seen as a supplier of foodstuffs and raw silk, in exchange for other countries' industrial products. However, the attempt to break with this stereotype was fraught with difficulties. The first of these, as we have already mentioned, was that the products Italy was trying to export were not technologically very advanced, and thus potential importers of such products had to be countries that were not industrialized to any great extent themselves; but such countries were, in general, neither very receptive nor stable trading partners. Italy had no problems in finding buyers for goods, such as cars, rubber, and silk fabrics, which were of a high technical quality—Britain, France, and Switzerland proved to be willing importers of such goods. The second problem was that even the potential markets of South America, the Balkans, and North Africa were the scene of fierce competition involving Italy's European competitors. As Webster has observed,[32] the Italian economic presence in North Africa had to contend with heavy opposition from the Germans, who incited the Turks to resist the development of the peaceful economic activities of the Banco di Roma in North Africa. Furthermore, the French had always been highly critical of the possibility of Italian colonial expansion in that part of the world. As far as the Balkans were concerned, England, France, Germany, and Austria-Hungary were all economically active in the area, and as we can see from Tamborra's accurate description,[33] cunning

[30] P. Lanino, *La nuova Italia industriale*, iv (Rome, 1916).

[31] G. Mori, *Il capitalismo industriale in Italia* (Rome, Editori Riuniti, 1977), 21.

[32] R. Webster, *L'imperialismo industriale italiano. Studio del prefascismo 1908–1915* (Turin, Einaudi, 1974).

[33] A. Tamborra, 'The Rise of Italian Industry and the Balkans (1900–1914)', *Journal of European Economic History*, 3 (1974).

diplomatic moves had to be made in order to give Italian interests a foothold against the prevailing tide of those stronger political connections held by other States: all for the meagre concession of the odd contract or two for the construction of sections of railway track which, because of the political and military instability of the area, were very rarely completed.

The success of Italian exports to the USA and to Argentina has been partly explained by the massive presence of Italian immigrants in these countries, who were unable to live without their traditional goods which, until produced by the host country or the immigrants themselves, were imported from Italy. The relatively poor prospects for such exports, limited as their life-span inevitably was, would thus seem clear. On the basis of the above analysis, we can now draw some conclusions about the relationship between foreign trade and economic development in Italy before the First World War.

Despite the sustained growth in the years between 1898 and 1906, Italian exports proved incapable of coming through the 1907 crisis unscathed (this was, in fact, the beginning of a five-year period of export stagnation), nor did they offer the Italian productive system sufficient substitutive (or complementary) markets for the very limited domestic market. Low agricultural productivity meant that the country was not even self-sufficient in food, as exports of agricultural products and foodstuffs were exceeded by imports (in 1911–13 the difference was roughly one-third more in favour of imports).

The backwardness of a vast area of the Italian economy is fairly clear from our analysis so far. Some geographical areas, such as the South, were worse off than others—the South was not even a net exporter of agricultural products, and in fact it is not true to say that Italy's very limited agricultural exports all came from the less industrialized zones. If we look at such agricultural exports, we can see that only about 60 per cent of them came from the South during the period 1911–13 (products such as citrus fruits, other kinds of fresh and dried fruit, vegetables, oil, wine, hides, and sumac for dyeing);[34] no area of the country was self-sufficient in cereals, since annual wheat production per head in 1908–13 was 1.4 quintals in the North, 1.7 quintals in the Centre, and 1.4 quintals in the South, whereas annual consumption per head was 1.9 quintals throughout the country as a whole.

As far as the reasons for this situation are concerned, one commonly held belief at the time was that the South's meagre agricultural exports were due not only to the general backwardness of agricultural production, but also to the high cost of transporting foodstuffs, the inadequate nature of credit facilities necessary for financing export activities, and the excessive diversification of products which made it impossible to have economies of scale, and rendered the standardization of products impossible. Another commonly cited factor

[34] Federico, 'Per una analisi', 393: the author takes into account a vast selection of raw material exports, and arrives at the conclusion that the percentage coming from the South of Italy fell from 44% (1863–7) to 33% (1908–13).

which was considered to represent a weakness was the low level of food preservation, which meant that exporters were potentially exposed to the threat of enormous losses during cyclical crises, as they were unable to preserve their stocks in order to sell them at a later date.

However, one thing that cannot be said to be true is that the South was unable to export very much because it had to supply the North. In the first place, the complementary nature of the North–South economic relationship was very limited: the South only produced a very limited amount of the raw materials required by northern industry (only wool and leather hides in any quantity); the majority of these raw materials were either imported from abroad or produced locally, as in the case of silk-cocoons, sugar beet, and hemp. Secondly, the South was hardly in a position to supply the North with basic foodstuffs (cereals and animal products) when these had to be imported from abroad to the South itself. As for specialized products such as fresh fruit and vegetables, their market potential was still very limited in the North, as their purchase presupposed an income level well above that to be found at the time.[35]

Finally, one can certainly not say that Italian economic growth was export-led. The only examples of sectors where exports were of strategic importance were that of the automobile industry—exports were equivalent to 55 per cent of total production in 1911 and 36 per cent in 1914—and that of rubber and cable production; and as such, these sectors had too limited an influence to be able to change the overall picture. It is, however, true that other countries that attempted to industrialize during the nineteenth and twentieth centuries often found themselves in much worse positions than Italy when it came to finding goods to export in exchange for the indispensable imports necessary to sustain this industrialization process. Italy was not the only country to utilize a staple (in this case raw silk) as a backbone for its exports; however, with its subsequent diversification of exports, Italy managed to avoid having to depend upon particularly favourable international situations or particular foreign markets.

3. BALANCE OF PAYMENTS AND FOREIGN INVESTMENT

Despite the positive note of the previous section's concluding remarks, it has to be said that Italy's balance of payments would have been considerably in the red had it not been for the presence of two important items which contributed towards offsetting the country's trade deficit: these two items were tourism and the remittances of Italian emigrants. Looking at Table 3.4, we can see that earnings from tourism and shipping (column 2) always constituted a positive item in the Italian balance of payments during the period we are looking at,

[35] There is a quantitative estimate of the flow of foodstuffs and textiles within the three Italian economic areas (industrial triangle, North-east and Centre, South) during the period 1911–13, in V. Zamagni, 'Ferrovie e integrazione del mercato nazionale nell'Italia post-unitaria', in *Studi in onore di Gino Barbieri*, iii (Salerno, IPEM ed., 1983).

Table 3.4. Balance of payments on current account, Average annual balances, 1861 and 1914 (million lire at current prices)

	Goods (1)	Services (2)	Factors income (3)	Total[a] (4)
1861–5	−300	47	−74	−325
1881–5	−154	169	−63	−41
1886–90	−368	189	−85	−255
1891–5	−126	218	−21	99
1901–5	−220	262	376	492
1911–14	−910	368	510	77

[a] Including current account transfers, which are not mentioned separately as they are relatively small.

Source: ISTAT, *Indagine statistica*.

producing a growing surplus. Only after 1900 were emigrants' remittances substantial enough to balance the negative flow of income from foreign capital investment in government bonds and private enterprise, as we can see from column 3, Table 3.4.[36] The overall balance of payments (column 4) was very negative during the years 1861–70 and 1885–90, extremely positive in the period from 1894 to 1906, and tended to oscillate during the remaining years.[37] So, although the general trend was not exactly encouraging, and in certain periods the deficit was actually very worrying, in particular during the first six years of the new Kingdom and the second half of the 1880s, there was no sign of a structural imbalance, thanks largely to both the growth potential of exports (as shown above), together with a substantial growth in tourist revenue and, above all, in emigrants' remittances. The 'industry' of the Italian people can rightly be seen as having contributed to the country's development, even when it was impossible to take advantage of this work-force in Italy itself (see Chapter 6 for an analysis of Italian emigration).

Let us now take a look at foreign investment in Italy. There are few quantitative figures available concerning foreign investment[38]—the most important ones that have so far been published are Corbino's,[39] and give us the situation as set out in Table 3.5.

[36] Cf. L. De Rosa, *Emigranti, capitali e banche 1896–1906* (Naples, 1980), and F. Balletta, 'Le rimesse degli emigrati italiani, 1861–1975', in F. Assante (ed.), *Il movimento emigratorio italiano dall'Unità nazionale ai giorni nostri* (Geneva, Droz, 1976).

[37] While many scholars have remarked that the reconstruction of the Italian balance of payments currently available is not reliable, the above conclusions are so general that they probably would not be affected by a revised version of it.

[38] For a detailed analysis of these data, see P. Hertner, 'Il capitale straniero in Italia (1883–1914)', *Studi Storici*, 22 (1981).

[39] Corbino, *Annali*, i–v. Corbino's figures are generally considered to be somewhat on the low side.

Table 3.5. Stock of foreign capital invested, 1870–1913 (billion lire at current prices)

	Government bonds	Other activities
1870	2	1
1880	1	1.5
1890	2.2	2.1
1900	0.8	1.1
1913	—	2.6

Table 3.5 shows an intense period of investment (mainly French) in government bonds during the first 10 years after unification, followed by disinvestment during the next decade.[40] During the 1880s, foreign investment in the private sector continued to grow, while there was a renewed interest in those government bonds issued in order to finance the public debt, and in particular the loan issue designed to cover the return to the gold standard (see Chapter 5). The crisis years saw a high level of disinvestment in both public and private sectors, while the first few years of the twentieth century saw the return of foreign investors to the private sector. Their interest in Italian government bonds, however, was never renewed, as a result both of the limited quantities made available by Giolitti's governments, and of the lower interest rates paid on them.

A detailed discussion of the public debt can be found in Chapter 5; here, I would like to consider the share of foreign investment in the Italian capital stock invested in industry and commerce (for which we have estimates from 1881 onwards).[41] If we adjust these figures in order to render them comparable,[42] then we can see that foreigners held some 15 per cent of all capital between 1880 and 1890; this then fell to 6 per cent in 1900, and had risen again slightly to 8 per cent by 1913. Even though these figures are very approximate, three conclusions can fairly safely be drawn from them: (*a*) foreign capital was never of fundamental importance for the industrialization of the country; (*b*) the first half of the 1890s was without doubt a crisis period for foreign investment in Italy; (*c*) the boom of the Giolitti years saw a marked growth in foreign

[40] The level of French investment in Italian government bonds was so high that a well-known French scholar decided to conduct an extremely detailed study of the Italian economy and financial sector during the first 25 years of the new Kingdom. This analysis remains even today one of the most important sources concerning the events of that period. Cf. I. Sachs, *L'Italie, ses finances et son développement économique depuis l'unification du royaume 1859–1884* (Paris, Librairie Guillaumin, 1885).

[41] O. Vitali, 'La stima degli investimenti e dello stock di capitale', in G. Fuà (ed.), *Lo sviluppo economico in Italia*, iii (Milan, Angeli, 1969).

[42] See the method used in V. Zamagni, *Industrializzazione e squilibri regionali in Italia. Bilancio dell'età giolittiana* (Bologna, Il Mulino, 1978), 147.

investment, although the pace of this was only marginally faster than that of domestic investment.

An increasing number of articles and studies have been published in recent years concerning foreign investment in Italy, and these enable us to qualify the above conclusions to some degree. First, a closer look at foreign investment reveals the existence of two separate parabolic curves: the first is dominated by a growing and then declining French interest, starting in the 1860s up until that country's virtual withdrawal from investing in Italy towards the end of the 1880s; the second parabola follows a similar pattern, although the kinds of investment are different, and this time the dominating force was Germany, which tried to establish a stronghold on Italian capital starting from the 1880s onwards, an influence that was consolidated during the 1890s and the first years of the twentieth century, only to be gradually lost during the years leading up to the First World War, at which point Germany had been virtually excluded from the Italian market. Foreign capital from other countries was present in both of these periods, although its relative influence was somewhat limited in each case: Swiss capital was invested mainly in the textile industry[43] at first, but subsequently in the electricity and electrical engineering industries;[44] English capital was invested in rail transport, the water and gas networks, and also the mining industry;[45] Belgian capital was mainly involved in the construction of tramway, gas, and water networks, together with sugar refineries at the end of the nineteenth century;[46] Austrian capital, finally, was mainly invested in merchant shipping and in insurance.[47]

French and German financial involvement were very different from each other in terms of both the different periods in which they were of importance, and their different objectives, as described above. French finance was heavily involved in government bonds (it possessed in 1884 80 per cent of those bonds

[43] Cf. P. A. Wavre, 'Swiss Investments in Italy from the XIXth to the XXth century', *Journal of European Economic History*, 29 (1988).

[44] P. Hertner, 'Les sociétés financières suisses et le développement de l'industrie électrique jusqu'à la Première Guerre Mondiale', in F. Cardot (ed.), *1880–1980: Un siècle d'électricité dans le monde* (Paris, 1987); L. Segreto, 'Capitali, tecnologie e imprenditori svizzeri nell'industria elettrica italiana: il caso della Motor (1895–1923)', in B. Bezza (ed.), *Energia e sviluppo. L'industria elettrica italiana e la società Edison* (Turin, Einaudi, 1986); and also, G. Bruno, 'Capitale straniero e industria elettrica nell'Italia meridionale (1895–1935)', *Studi Storici*, 28 (1987).

[45] During the periods before unification and immediately afterwards, English investors also showed interest in the Italian steel industry: first in the South (see L. De Rosa, *L'industria metalmeccanica*), and later, in joint-ventures with the Terni company (Vickers–Terni) and with Ansaldo (Ansaldo–Armstrong), see T. Row, 'Economic Nationalism in Italy: The Ansaldo Company, 1822–1921' (Ph.D. thesis, Johns Hopkins University, Baltimore, 1988) and M. Doria, *Ansaldo. L'impresa e lo stato* (Milan, Angeli, 1989).

[46] Cf. the essay by E. Bianchi Tonizzi, 'L'industria dello zucchero in Italia dal Blocco continentale alla vigilia della grande guerra (1807–1914)', *Annali di storia dell'impresa*, 4 (1988), and also M. Dumoulin, *Les relations économiques italo-belges (1861–1914)* (Bruxelles, Académie Royale de Belgique, 1990).

[47] See A. Leonardi, 'Gli investimenti austriaci in Italia 1861–1914. Primi risultati di un'indagine', *Economia e storia*, 30 (1983).

allocated to foreign investors), in the construction of the country's infrastructure (railways, tramways, gas, water), and to some extent in the metallurgical, mining, and banking sectors.[48] German finance, on the other hand, invested in the new mixed banks that were founded following the banking crisis (see Chapter 4);[49] it also invested in a series of new metallurgical and engineering companies, such as the 'Esslingen' company's subsidiary set up in 1887 in Saronno, for the construction of locomotives;[50] the 'Schwartzkopff' subsidiary set up in Venice in 1888, which made mines and torpedoes; and the Società tubi Mannesmann, set up in Milan in 1906 by the mother company 'Mannesmann' and involved in producing seamless tubes at its Dalmine works.[51] Above all, German financiers invested in the electrical and electrical engineering sectors.[52] This German involvement in Italian industry has been studied in detail by P. Hertner, and he has shown that it was of strategic importance in the latter two sectors of industry. He estimates that German capital made up some 40 per cent of the total capital invested in electricity in 1900; and if we take Swiss and French capital into account, then foreign capital amounted to 50 per cent of the total. As a consequence of new investment by former railway companies that had been nationalized (see Chapter 5), Italian capital won back a considerable share of capital investment in this sector; Hertner estimates that at the beginning of the First World War, German capital only controlled 16.5 per cent of the electricity sector (foreign capital as a whole some 25 per cent).[53] As we saw in the previous chapter, the penetration of foreign capital (particularly Swiss and German) in the electrical engineering sector was even greater.

Another important initiative, from the point of view of German involvement in Italian industry, was that of the Goldenberg Company's citric acid factory Arenella, set up in Palermo in 1912,[54] one of the rare cases of German investment in the Italian chemical industry. Hertner believes that this reluctance on the part of German capital to invest in the chemical sector was a

[48] B. Gille, 'Les investissements francais en Italie', *Archivio economico dell'unificazione*, ii (1968); and P. Milza, 'Les relations financières franco-italiennes pendant le premier conflit mondial', in J. Bouvier and R. Girault (eds.), *L'Impérialisme français d'avant 1914* (Paris, 1976).

[49] The early difficulties experienced by German capital in Italy are well described in P. Hertner, 'The Deutsche Bank in Italy and on the Italian Capital Market up to the Outbreak of the First World War', *Studies on Economic and Monetary Problems and on Banking History*, 21 (1986).

[50] P. Hertner, 'Capitale tedesco e industria meccanica in Italia: la Esslingen a Saronno, 1887–1918', *Società e Storia*, 17 (1982).

[51] P. Hertner, *Il capitale tedesco in Italia dall'unità alla prima guerra mondiale* (Bologna, Il Mulino, 1984), ch. 1.

[52] P. Hertner, 'Il capitale tedesco nell'industria elettrica fino alla prima guerra mondiale', in Bezza (ed.), *Energia e sviluppo*; and P. Hertner, 'Espansione multinazionale e finanziamento internazionale dell'industria elettrotecnica tedesca prima del 1914', *Studi Storici*, 28 (1987). On the German presence in Milan, cf. A. Schreiber von Oswald, 'Le iniziative economiche degli imprenditori tedeschi a Milano 1882–1914', *Annali di storia dell'impresa*, 5 and 6 (1989–90).

[53] Foreign capital was also present in other Italian electricity companies, but always in the form of a minority share.

[54] Hertner, *Il capitale tedesco in Italia*, ch. 4.

result of the lack of protection given to the chemical industry. It was more convenient simply to export the products rather than set up subsidiaries in Italy.[55]

Although from a quantitative point of view, Italian industry was not predominantly under the control of foreign capital, this capital did, however, have a strategic role to play in some of the more advanced sectors. In particular, this was true of German capital, and many people at the time saw this influence as being too overtly aggressive for their tastes. As a consequence, a nationalistic campaign against German influence was started, and this was almost certainly one of the reasons behind Italy's move away from its political alliance with Germany towards one with the Allied powers. With the advent of war, Italian businessmen managed to gain control over a large part of German investments in Italy, through the use of Swiss intermediaries. While the 'tariff war' of 1887 had seen Italy free itself from the economic hegemony exercised by the French, it was now the turn of the First World War to put an end to the economic hegemony of Germany on Italian industry, although in the latter case, the power exercised was far more limited, but also far more controversial in the view of the Italian people.

Before concluding this section, we need to look at Italian investment abroad which, although far more limited than foreign investment in Italy, certainly cannot be ignored. This particular topic has not been studied in any great depth by scholars so far, except when considered part of the Italian colonialist past, which we have briefly mentioned above.[56] Italy attempted to make inroads into the Balkans, and into some areas of northern and eastern Africa, but the results were disappointing and, more importantly, highly precarious. Several banks involved in this expansionist drive lost out as a result, in particular the Banco di Roma.[57] A more interesting feature was perhaps the flow of capital towards Argentina, described by Einaudi in a study concerning the activities of one textile entrepreneur in South America.[58] The most recent work on this topic underlines the important role played by Pirelli, together with Franco Tosi and TIBB, in setting up the Compañía Italo-Argentina de Electricidad in 1911. This company's objectives were 'the stipulation of supply contracts—piping and cables in the case of Pirelli, boilers and burners in that of Tosi, and alternators for Brown–Boveri'.[59]

[55] In the case of the Arenella factory, a locally produced raw material (calcium citrate) was used.

[56] Besides Webster, *L'imperialismo industriale*, cf. M. Bitossi, 'La componente economica dell'imperialismo italiano nel periodo liberale', graduation thesis, Florence University, 1986–87).

[57] Details of the Banco di Roma's involvement can be found in L. De Rosa, *Storia del Banco di Roma*, i and ii (Rome, 1982–3).

[58] L. Einaudi, *Principe mercante* (Turin, Bocca, 1900). This book tells the story of the activities of textile baron Enrico Dell'Acqua (from Busto Arsizio) in Argentina and Uruguay.

[59] B. Bezza, 'L'intervento del capitale italiano nell'industria elettrica argentina (1910–20)', in Bezza (ed.), *Energia e sviluppo*, 283.

The only company about which we have any real knowledge concerning pre-First World War expansionist policy abroad is the Pirelli Company. B. Bezza has reconstructed the network of companies that Pirelli built abroad at that time:[60] from the Spanish factory at Villanueva y Geltrú (1902) to the joint venture with General Electric—the Pirelli General Cable Works—at Southampton (1913), as well as numerous commercial subsidiaries set up in London, Vienna, Buenos Aires, Brussels, and Paris, some of which later led to the setting-up of a production plant. 'The main component in this rapid expansion abroad', Bezza believes, 'was represented by electric wiring and cable, the production of which, in terms of total sales, had risen from 23.9 to 49.2 per cent by 1899',[61] a field in which Pirelli was by that time the European leader. It would be easy to say that this case of early multinationalization of an Italian company was simply a precocious exception: however, we do not have sufficient evidence for excluding further cases of this kind, and more research needs to be done in this field before we can draw any definitive conclusions.

[60] B. Bezza, 'L'attività multinazionale della Pirelli (1883–1914)', *Società e Storia*, 35 (1987).
[61] Ibid. 70.

4

The Banking System: Its Evolution and Role

1. FINANCE AND DEVELOPMENT: A LONG-TERM VIEW

THE banking system of any country that is industrializing must, itself, undergo a series of important changes in line with that country's new needs: it becomes more important in quantitative terms, and also less uniform, qualitatively speaking, when compared with its pre-industrial form. According to Toniolo, who avails himself of Goldsmith's thesis,[1] 'In general, during modern economic development, the financial superstructure grows more quickly than income and real wealth itself . . . Growth in income is usually accompanied by an increased specialization and division of the savings process on one hand, and of capital formation on the other'.[2] Furthermore, an increasingly large part of savings is channelled through financial intermediation, while the cost of financial capital tends to diminish.

An authoritative study of this long-term phenomenon in Italy was carried out some years ago by experts from the Bank of Italy.[3] They worked out a series of financial and economic aggregates, which were then expressed in the form of different indices, two of which are given in Table 4.1. These are: (*a*) the ratio between the total volume of financial instruments in existence and total wealth at current prices (Financial Instruments Ratio, FIR); (*b*) the ratio between financial intermediaries' assets and total liabilities of the public sector, private companies, families, and foreign sector (Financial Intermediation, FIN).

As we can see from Table 4.1, both indices rose considerably between 1881 and 1971, but the FIR grew relatively slowly during the period that we are considering here, that is, 1881–1914; so much so, that Biscaini and Ciocca believe that 'the trend of FIR . . . does not confirm, from a simple quantitative point of view, the validity of the hypothesis according to which the overall role of finance was more important during the first period of rapid industrial growth

[1] R. W. Goldsmith, *Financial Structure and Development* (Yale University Press, New Haven, Conn., 1969, and id., 'The Quantitative International Comparison of Financial Structure and Development', *Journal of Economic History*, 35 (1975).

[2] G. Toniolo, *Storia economica dell'Italia liberale 1850–1918* (Bologna, Il Mulino, 1988), 40.

[3] A. M. Biscaini Cotula and P. Ciocca, 'Le strutture finanziarie: aspetti quantitativi di lungo periodo 1870–1970', in F. Vicarelli (ed.), *Capitale industriale e capitale finanziario: il caso italiano* (Bologna, Il Mulino, 1979).

in Italy . . . than during any other period'.[4] An international comparison carried out by Biscaini and Ciocca does, however, show that the FIR for Italy more or less reflects the trend shown in the case of other industrially advanced countries, bearing in mind the difference between Italian income levels and wealth and those of such countries.[5]

As far as FIN is concerned, the values calculated for the years 1881–1914 already 'demonstrate the validity of the thesis that sees the Italian case as one "orientated to the intermediaries" rather than one "orientated to the market"'.[6] Furthermore, the rapid growth of the FIN index during the Giolitti years would seem to suggest that the financial structures of the time were of strategic importance in qualitative rather than quantitative terms.[7]

An initial confirmation of this 'orientation to the intermediaries' thesis can be found in the work of Cesarini.[8] The latter calculated the incidence of share issues on the total flow of funds to private enterprises for each year between 1899 and 1913 (see Table 4.2). Shares and bonds only accounted for much more than half of total funds in five of these years (1900, 1905, 1906, 1907, and 1912); however, one must remember that some amount of shares and bonds were themselves acquired, in one way or another, through financial intermediaries, and this provides further support for the above conclusion (as we shall again see in Section 4.3 below).

While Italy can be said to have followed the general example of other

Table 4.1. Evolution of the financial structure, 1881–1971

	Financial Instruments Ratio (FIR)	Financial Intermediation (FIN)
1881	0.38	0.23
1914	0.47	0.41
1938	0.68	0.51
1963	0.81	0.70
1971	0.99	1.03

Sources: A. M. Biscaini Cotula and P. Ciocca, 'Le strutture finanziarie: aspetti quantitativi di lungo periodo (1870–1970)', in F. Vicarelli (ed.), *Capitale industriale e capitale finanziario: il caso italiano* (Bologna, Il Mulino, 1979), Tables 2 and 4.

[4] A. M. Biscaini Cotula and P. Ciocca, 'Le strutture finanziare', 67.

[5] Ibid., Table 4.

[6] Ibid. 70.

[7] It is clear, nevertheless, that the majority of financial flows were still outside the banking and stock-exchange circuit in 1914, which was inevitable in a country like Italy where the advanced forms of industry, agriculture, and services were still only present over a relatively limited area of the country.

[8] F. Cesarini, 'Il ruolo del mercato mobiliare nel primo trentennio del secolo', *Bancaria*, 41 (1985). On the Milan stock exchange, cf. S. Baia Curioni, 'Sull'evoluzione istituzionale della Borsa Valori di Milano (1898–1914)', *Rivista di storia economica*, 8 (1991).

capitalist countries in the field of finance—with a tendency towards financial intermediaries (in particular the banking sector), common to other capitalist nations (above all Germany)—the early years in question were characterized by the slowness of change, which can be explained if we take a closer look at the general evolution of the Italian financial system.

2. STRUCTURAL CHANGES IN THE ITALIAN BANKING SYSTEM, AND THE CONTRASTED RISE OF A CENTRAL BANK

The banking system inherited by the newly born Italian State had changed considerably since the days of its glorious past, and very little remained of the old system: occasional old Monti di Pietà, some of which only became real banks after the 1898 banking law; one or two old state banks with a troubled past;[9] and a fair number of private bankers, about whom we often only know the name.

Table 4.2. Value of shares and bonds issued by the private sector and net variation in credit obtained by the private sector from the banking system, 1899–1913 (millions of lire at current prices)

	Issue of shares (1)	Issue of bonds (2)	Total (1) + (2) (3)	Net variation in bank credit (4)	Overall total (3) + (4) (5)	(3)/(5)[a] (6)
1899	317.9	3.3	321.2	291.8	613.0	52.4
1900	217.8	1.1	218.9	124.0	342.9	63.8
1901	97.4	1.5	98.9	165.8	264.7	37.4
1902	69.4	8.2	77.6	155.7	233.3	33.3
1903	195.4	9.9	196.3	258.3	454.6	43.2
1904	299.4	52.9	352.3	306.8	659.1	53.5
1905	857.3	21.3	878.6	519.4	1398.0	62.8
1906	763.0	15.3	778.3	58.0	836.3	93.0
1907	617.4	53.2	670.6	142.9	813.5	82.4
1908	357.5	55.7	413.2	368.3	781.5	52.9
1909	324.6	109.1	143.7	392.7	536.4	26.8
1910	323.4	67.4	432.5	388.2	820.7	52.7
1911	338.3	95.5	128.8	314.9	443.7	29.0
1912	309.9	72.2	382.1	265.6	647.7	59.0
1913	293.2	43.8	337.0	273.4	610.4	55.2

[a] Results of this column are to be regarded with caution given the imprecision in the data, as Cesarini points out in his text.

Sources: Author's elaboration from F. Cesarini, 'Il ruolo del mercato mobiliare nel primo trentennio del secolo', *Bancaria*, 41 (1985).

[9] D. Demarco, 'Banca e Credito in Italia nell'età del Risorgimento: 1750–1870', in Società Italiana degli Storici dell'Economia, *Credito e sviluppo economico in Italia dal Medievo all'età contemporanea* (Verona, Fiorini, 1988).

The first half of the nineteenth century saw the appearance of two new types of bank:[10] savings banks and note-issuing banks, both of which carried out normal banking activities. In the South, 'grain banks' had existed since medieval times, and these gave loans in kind (cereals) to peasant farmers. At the time of unification, there were 130 savings banks, distributed as follows: 15 in Lombardy, 22 in the Sardinian States, 9 in the Veneto, 5 in the States of Parma and Modena, 27 in Tuscany, 51 in the Papal States, and only one in the South, which had, on the other hand, 1,560 grain banks (including the 360 present in Sardinia).

The most important and active of the note-issuing banks was the Banca Nazionale degli Stati Sardi, founded in Turin in 1849 from the merger between the Banca di Genova (1844) and the Banca di Torino (founded in 1847, but not to open its doors until 1849).[11] The other note-issuing banks included the Banca Nazionale Toscana, formed in 1857 from the merger of six note-issuing banks, themselves set up in Tuscany between 1816 and 1849; the Banca dello Stato Pontificio, which was founded in 1850 and was later to be called the Banca Romana; and finally three small banks that had been set up rather hurriedly, and had very few prospects, namely the Banca di Parma (1857), the Stabilimento Mercantile Veneto (1853), and the Banca delle Quattro Legazioni of Bologna (1855).[12] The Banco di Napoli, which had been reorganized in 1816, could not be considered to be a real note-issuing bank as it was only able to issue credit warrants, and not banknotes, at the time of unification. This institute had opened branches in Sicily, at Palermo and Messina, and these were to become independent in 1849, taking on the name Banco di Sicilia in 1860. The latter was also involved in the issue of credit warrants at the time of unification.[13] Although there were a large number of issuing banks in existence, paper circulation was very limited (about one-tenth of total money circulation), according to an estimate published by Toniolo[14]—and deposits with the savings banks were also rather small.[15]

Cavour proposed the unification of all existing note-issuing banks to form a single bank as was the practice in many advanced countries,[16] but his plan met with

[10] Several banks of this kind were set up towards the end of the 1850s, but the most important banks in this category were not founded until after unification, as we shall see.

[11] L. Conte, 'La Banca nazionale nel sistema del credito degli Stati Sardi', in *Credito e sviluppo*. See also by the same author, *La Banca Nazionale. Formazione e attività di una banca di emissione 1843–1861* (Naples, ESI, 1990).

[12] G. Porisini, *Condizioni monetarie e investimenti nel Bolognese: La Banca delle Quattro Legazioni* (Bologna, 1969).

[13] Le De Rosa, *Il Banco di Napoli nella vita nazionale, 1863–1883* (Naples, 1964)

[14] Toniolo, *Storia economica*, 93.

[15] In 1864 the savings banks only had about 230 million lire's worth of assets.

[16] Sweden had had a central bank since 1668, England since 1694, France since 1800, Holland since 1814, Denmark since 1818, Belgium since 1850, Germany since 1875, and Japan since 1882. Among the advanced nations, only the USA was left without a central bank until fairly late on: the Federal Reserve was set up in 1913, and with limited powers.

so much local resistance that in the end it did not get off the ground. The Banca Nazionale Sarda changed its name to the Banca Nazionale nel Regno d'Italia, and opened branches in Milan (1859), Naples and Palermo (1861), and in many other Italian cities. It took over the local banks in Parma, Bologna, and (at a later date) Venice, but was unsuccessful in its take-over bid for the Banca Nazionale Toscana, after a drawn-out, and eventually abortive, series of negotiations. Meanwhile, neither the Banco di Napoli nor the Banco di Sicilia would even hear of the idea of a take-over.[17] Thus, the project for the creation of a single Banca Nazionale was blocked, and this result received the approval of some economists of the time, such as Francesco Ferrara, who insisted on the need for a financial system with a number of different note-issuing banks. In the end, the advent of paper inconvertibility in 1866 (see Chapter 5) even led to authorization being given to the Banco di Napoli to issue notes. In 1871, the Banco di Sicilia received authorization to do the same, and in the meantime, a second Tuscan note-issuing bank—the Banca Toscana di Credito—had been founded.

It would seem that during the expansion in the supply of paper money, following the above-noted inconvertibility, the government preferred to have more than one institution issuing banknotes, even if this meant that the system was going to be more difficult to control. The real paradox was that the southern banks, which had been the strongest opponents of a single note-issuing institution, became note-issuing banks only after unification. This, however, did not prevent the Banca Nazionale from becoming the most influential and powerful of the note-issuing banks. At the time of the first banking act, passed in 1874, which placed a quantitative ceiling on the note-issuing of the six banks authorized to do so, the situation was as set out in Table 4.3.[18]

As we can see, the Banca Nationale held two-thirds of capital and about 60 per cent of circulation. In reality, the 1874 law simply represented the State's formal recognition of the existing situation, and was 'a compromise between the various disparate parliamentary positions taken up on this question at the time';[19] however, it did nothing to resolve the government's monetary and

[17] There is an interesting interpretation of the survival of different issuing banks in Italy in terms of regional interests, uses, and credit needs in V. Sannucci, 'The Establishment of a Central Bank: Italy in the 19th Century', in M. De Cecco and A. Giovannini (eds.), *A European Central Bank? Perspectives on Monetary Unification after Ten Years of the EMS* (Cambridge, Cambridge University Press, 1989). The author concludes that 'after re-examining the Italian events of the last century it would seem appropriate to conclude that the reasons for the continued existence of more than one bank of issue were due less to ideological hostility towards monopoly in note-issuing than to the defence of local interests, and it would be small-minded to interpret the latter either as purely private interests or those of restricted lobbies or to depict them as the typically chauvinistic attitudes common among large sectors of the population' (p. 271).

[18] C. Supino, *Storia della circolazione cartacea in Italia dal 1860 al 1928* (Milan, SEI, 1929), 61.

[19] Ibid. 62.

Table 4.3. Capital and note-issuing ceiling of banks, 31 December 1873 (million lire at current prices)

	Capital	Limit on issue
Banca Nazionale	150	450
Banco di Napoli	32.5	146.25
Banca Nazionale Toscana	21	63
Banca Romana	5	45
Banco di Sicilia	8	36
Banca Toscana di Credito	5	15
TOTAL	221.5	755.25

banking problems, which were only recognized as being serious problems at a later date.

In the meantime, the Italian banking system experienced one or two changes. Several joint-stock banks were founded in the immediate post-unification years, the most important being the Società Generale di Credito Mobiliare, set up first in Turin in 1863, and later moved to Florence, along the lines of the French Crédit Mobilier of the Pereire brothers; the Banco di Sconto e Sete (1863) of Turin; and the banche popolari, which were co-operative credit institutions, patronized above all by Luzzatti (following on from the German Schulze Delitsch model), the first of which was founded in Lodi in 1864. However, the real boom in new banks came between 1870 and 1874: the joint stock banks rose from 36 to 121, while that of banche popolari rose from 48 to 109;[20] both gained importance within a banking system that had begun to diversify, and this meant that the note-issuing banks' control over banking operations was reduced (see Table 4.4). One important addition to the list of new joint-stock banks was the Banca Generale, set up in Rome in 1871.

Following the 1870–4 period, a number of other changes were made concerning credit facilities: (*a*) Quintino Sella saw his project for the setting-up of post-office savings banks (casse di risparmio postali) sanctioned by a law passed on the 27 May 1875; these savings banks provided the Cassa Depositi e Prestiti (Cassa DDPP) with increasingly large sums which could then be used to support local finance and be invested in government bonds, as we shall see in Chapter 5; (*b*) several unsuccessful attempts were made to launch a specialized form of farmers' credit (as has been noted in Chapter 1); (*c*) the regulation of mortgage credit, with a law passed on 14 June 1886;[21] (*d*) the foundation of casse rurali (co-operative rural banks) from 1883 onwards, on Leone Wollemberg's initiative—these banks were organized according to the solid-

[20] The number of banche popolari continued to grow thereafter, and from a total of 140 in 1880, their numbers multiplied, reaching 738 ten years later, in 1890.

[21] For an account of land credit, see G. Dell'Amore, *Il credito fondiario in Italia* (Milan, 1946).

aristic principle of unlimited responsibility, following the Raiffeisen model, and were co-ordinated by Catholic joint-stock banks that came into existence towards the end of the century;[22] (*e*) some of the old Monti di Pietà were authorized to carry on banking activities by the banking act of 4 May 1898. It should be noted that we have no quantitative details of the private bankers' activities (they do not appear in Table 4.4); something is known only in the context of their collaboration with the big banks, in which the former sometimes had financial interests and often actively participated in the board of directors meetings.

Going back to Table 4.4, we can see that although the Monti di Pietà and the rural banks were socially useful, they were relatively unimportant during this period;[23] on the other hand, the savings gathered by the Cassa DDPP from the post-office banks continued to grow, reaching 16 per cent of the banking system's total assets, and these were used as described above; mortgage credit increased towards the end of the 1880s and during the following decade, for reasons which we will look at shortly, but remained limited. In order to understand fully the development of the Italian banking system from the 1880s onwards, therefore, we need to look at the other four types of bank that existed at that time.

The importance of the casse di risparmio (savings banks) within the banking sector was fairly constant, as they held about 20 per cent of total banking assets during the whole period; this shows that they were simply able to keep up with the general rate of growth of the banking system as a whole. In Confalonieri's monumental 2,500-page study of the Italian banking system in the period 1870–1914 (which we shall be looking at in more detail shortly), there are repeated references to the conservative nature of the investment policy adopted by these casse di risparmio. In the pages dedicated to the largest of these, the Cassa di Risparmio delle Province Lombarde (Cariplo), Confalonieri writes: 'the two pillars of the Cassa Lombarda's investment policy are mortgage loans and government bonds'.[24] He goes on to write about these banks' immobility, with the exception of those in Emilia,[25] an immobility that was only shaken at

[22] The Banco S. Paolo of Brescia (1888), the Piccolo Credito Bergamasco (1891), the Banco Ambrosiano of Milan (1896), and the Piccolo Credito Romagnolo (1896).

[23] There were 2,122 country savings banks ('casse rurali') in 1913, and while they were not particularly important in terms of the amount of credit granted, they nevertheless played an important role in those areas where Catholic co-operation was most widespread (the Veneto, Trentino, Lombardy, Emilia–Romagna). Cf. G. Tamagnini, *Le Casse Rurali* (Rome, 1952), and also L. Motta, *Credito popolare e sviluppo economico* (Milan, 1976).

[24] A. Confalonieri, *Banca e industria in Italia 1894–1906*, i (Milan, Banca Commerciale Italiana, 1974), 233.

[25] Ibid. ii (1975), 203. A confirmation of Confalonieri's views on the casse di risparmio in Emilia comes from G. L. Basini and G. Forestieri (eds.), *Banche locali e sviluppo dell'economia. Parma e la Cassa di Risparmio* (Milan, Giuffré, 1989). In a recent work of mine I have been able to find the same approach also in a cassa di risparmio in Romagna. See V. Zamagni, 'La Cassa di Risparmio di Rimini tra passato e futuro', in A. Varni and V. Zamagni (eds.), *Economia e Società a Rimini tra 800 e 900* (Rimini, Pizzi, 1992).

Table 4.4. Paper money in circulation and the structure of the banking system, 1862–1914

	Net paper money in circulation (million current lire)	Percentage composition of total banks' assets								
		Issuing banks	Savings banks	Banche popolari	Monti di Pietà	Rural co-op. banks	Joint-stock banks	Cassa DDPP	Land banks[a]	Total assets (million current lire)
	(1)	(2)	(3)	(4)	(5)	(6)	(7)	(8)	(9)	(10)
1864	122[b]	...	...	...	—	—	...	...	...	877[c]
1866	517[b]	...	...	...	—	—	...	...	...	1,627[c]
1870	929	66.9	18.2	2.3	—	—	10.9	—	1.7	2,192
1874	1,403	40.9	18.5	5.6	—	—	29.5	—	5.5	2,819
1880	1,527	36.5	21.2	6.8	—	—	20.7	6.5	8.3	3,841
1887	1,356	29.2	19.2	9.3	—	...	25.1	7.5	9.7	6,594
1894	1,576	31.2	22.6	7.7	—	...	13.7	10.4	14.2	7,145
1900	1,586	26.5	23.1	8.6	1.8	...	15.1	13.2	11.7	7,902
1907	2,272	24.8	21.5	10.2	1.8	0.5	18.4	15.7	7.1	11,979
1911	2,663	22.6	21.4	11.6	1.9	0.8	18.9	16.4	6.4	14,879
1914	3,526	26.4	20.1	9.3	1.9	0.7	19.3	16.0	6.3	17,096

[a] Agricultural credit is seen to be consistently of marginal importance.
[b] Gross circulation.
[c] Totals include only issuing banks and savings banks.

Source: R. De Mattia, *I bilanci degli istituti di emissione italiani dal 1845 al 1936* (Rome, 1967).

the beginning of the twentieth century with their accepting requests for credit in the case of investment that was aimed at the construction of public utilities or that came from selected operators who had the guarantee of established major banks.[26] With the decline in the availability of government bonds, and the beginning of the 1907 crisis (which we shall be looking at later), the Cariplo finally decided to increase the volume of rediscounted bills and bank advances on deposit of securities, with the customary prudence however, and it ended up by taking on the 'role of banks' bank, parallel to the Bank of Italy, [becoming] a sort of central bank for the "State of Milan"'.[27]

The banche popolari on the other hand were, from the very beginning, 'much more open than the casse di risparmio'[28] to the needs of the local economy. Whenever possible, they showed 'a tendency to get involved in medium- and long-term operations, departing from the principle of spreading risks, depending heavily on the use of rediscounting, and were inclined to throw themselves into risky financial operations involving industrial finance'.[29] Of course, this kind of behaviour meant that these banks were more vulnerable to the effects of a crisis, but at the same time they were more amenable to supporting new business initiatives. At first, the Banca Popolare di Milano was the most important among the banks of this kind, but it was subsequently superseded in this role by the more dynamic Banca Popolare di Novara.

It was, however, among the società ordinarie di credito—the joint-stock banks whose percentage of total banking assets was very changeable—that we see evidence of those banking institutions that were the most closely tied up with the financing of the nation's new economic activities: activities which were to determine the cyclical behaviour of the economy, and to challenge the configuration reached by the note-issuing banks.

At the end of the 1870–4 boom, several new banks went bankrupt, but others were quick to take their places in a sector that came to life again towards the end of that decade, after the Historical Left had introduced protectionism, had got the construction of railways and other infrastructures under way, and had reintroduced the gold standard (see Chapter 5 for a more detailed description of state intervention). As we saw in Chapter 2, this was a period of industrial revival, and the end of the 1880s also witnessed a building boom in Italy.

There were many banks that threw themselves headlong into these new economic activities, but the two most important cases were those of the Credito Mobiliare and the Banca Generale (the mention made above of their

[26] A. Confalonieri, *Banca e industria in Italia 1894–1906*, ii. 219.

[27] A. Confalonieri, *Banca e industria in Italia dalla crisi del 1907 all'agosto 1914*, i (Milan, Banca Commerciale Italiana, 1982), 166. For another example of similar behaviour, albeit on a more limited scale, see G. Pavanelli, 'Note sulle strategie creditizie della Cassa di Risparmio di Firenze tra la fine del secolo e la prima guerra mondiale', in *Credito e sviluppo*.

[28] Confalonieri, *Banca e industria in Italia 1894–1906*, i. 246.

[29] Confalonieri, *Banca e industria in Italia dalla crisi del 1907*, i. 229.

beginnings was far from casual). These were the two largest private banks in Italy,[30] although their growth has been altogether rather modest. The Credito Mobiliare was, in fact, similar in form to a modern investment bank that deals exclusively with securities, rather than to a bank involved in collecting deposits and in other normal banking operations. The Banca Generale placed more importance on normal bank activity than the latter, but was nevertheless again heavily involved in various long-term financial operations. Both had placed little or no importance on the necessity to develop a national network of branches, and as a consequence had to rely on so-called inter-bank current accounts, that is, on money borrowed from other banks, and in particular foreign ones.

The two banks got involved in the formation of syndicates selling government bonds, foreign bonds, railway debentures, banking and industrial shares. The Banca Generale also tried unsuccessfully to finance the modernization of the Italian Ironworks (Ferriere Italiane), and was involved in the Elvetica Company (which was later to become Breda); the Edison Company; the Venetian Cotton Mills; and the Terni Company. The Credito Mobiliare was also involved with the Terni, as well as with the Piombino Metallurgical Works, the Cuorgné Works, the Cirio Company, and the Condotte d'Acqua. However, both banks also decided to invest heavily in the real estate market, as they were highly ambitious investors, and saw very few openings elsewhere at that time. This they did either on their own or with other banks that were themselves involved in the real estate market, mainly in the cities of Rome, Turin, and Naples. When the rather fragile industrial boom started to slow down, the balance of payments situation worsened, and European economies began to see the first storm clouds on the horizon, the building trade also began to feel the pinch. As a consequence, a chain reaction was set in motion, and all the weaknesses of the Italian economic system were laid bare for everyone to see, including the fragility of the banking structure. The Banca Tiberina, the Società del l'Esquilino, and the Banco di Sconto e Sete all found themselves in grave difficulties, and the Banca Nazionale was urged by the government to intervene on their behalf. Thus the first salvage operations were got under way: that of the Società dell'Esquilino was performed in 1888 (and this also led indirectly to the salvage of the Banca di Torino); the Banca Tiberina was rescued in 1889, on the direct request of Crispi; and in 1891, all the note-issuing banks helped in rescuing the Società per il Risanamento di Napoli.

Confalonieri underlines the fact that the Banca Nazionale intervened in this crisis without knowing how to lay down an overall programme of intervention, and instead got involved in 'very risky operations aimed at helping banks that found themselves in extremely difficult positions, economically and financially

[30] In 1882, however, the Credito Mobiliare was only half the size of the Cariplo, and the Banca Generale (which was less than half the size of the Credito Mobiliare) had been overtaken in size by the Banca Popolare di Milano. This shows just how limited the banks' industrial business was at that time.

speaking'.[31] In this way, the Banca Nazionale had already used up most of its resources before the crisis reached its peak.[32] The Italian government intervened, and granted an increase in monetary circulation in order that the issuing banks had sufficient resources to be able to help out those banks that were in the greatest difficulties. However, one of the banks at risk, the Banca Romana, which had been more involved in loss-making operations than the other banks, had already exceeded the legal limits concerning circulation, and had also printed false copies of notes already issued—as proved by a parliamentary inquiry set up in 1889.

The results of the inquiry were at the centre of an enormous scandal,[33] as they were kept secret until the MPs Colajanni and Gavazzi finally revealed them in Parliament on 20 December 1892, a move that was designed to avoid any further possible delay in the parliamentary approval of a new banking law. Another parliamentary commission was set up to look into the Banca Romana case, and it very quickly found evidence of serious irregularities: however, news of this had already leaked out, and so the government was forced to underwrite the circulation of these notes so as to avoid panic, although it could no longer put off the question of a definitive solution to these problems. The directors of the Banca Romana meanwhile were faced with having to answer charges concerning the affair. Nevertheless, many months went by before the government finally passed the banking law of 10 August 1893, which led to the fusion of the Banca Nazionale nel Regno d'Italia, the Banca Nazionale Toscana, and the Banca Toscana di Credito into a single bank—the Banca d'Italia—which then took care of the question of the liquidation of the Banca Romana. The only other issuing banks left were the two southern banks, and together with the Banca d'Italia they were put under special surveillance from then onwards. As Giolitti, at that time a member of the government, had to admit, this solution was far from ideal, especially since the role of the Banca d'Italia (which became operative on 1 January 1894) was still not clear; however, the political situation did not allow for any better solution at the time. The rise to pre-eminence of the Banca d'Italia would have to be seen from eventual results, as was in fact the case (see Chapter 5).

The new law was not enough, however, to redress a very serious situation, as we can see from Corbino's description:

> On 30 November 1893 [the Società Generale di Credito Mobiliare], after lengthy and laborious attempts to overcome the crisis, was finally forced to close up shop and ask

[31] Confalonieri, *Banca e industria in Italia 1894–1906*, i. 188.

[32] For details of later developments in the events summarized here, see E. Vitale, *La Riforma degli istituti di emissione e gli 'scandali bancari' in Italia, 1892–1896* (Rome, Camera dei deputati, 1972).

[33] See the account given in A. Cardini, *Stato liberale e protezionismo in Italia (1890–1900)* (Bologna, Il Mulino, 1981), ch. 4; cf. also E. Corbino, *Annali dell'economia italiana*, iv (Città di Castello, 1934), ch. 7. For an account of the foundation of the Bank of Italy, see G. Negri (ed.), *Giolitti e la nascita della Banca d'Italia nel 1893* (Bari, Laterza, 1989).

the courts for a moratorium. The blow to the market was so great that several Chambers of Commerce thought they could suspend the monthly stock exchange settlement, due at that time. The result was that both industrial and bank securities plummeted, and continued to do so for a further two weeks. A few months later the market received another tremendous shock when the Banca Generale went bust; all of this happened at the same time as the banking scandals were being investigated, and the result was that the public was stupefied at the damage caused and the once-famous bank names involved.[34]

The two banks, which were tied up but hardly in a desperate position, both fell at the time of the change-over from the Banca Nazionale to the Banca d'Italia, as we have seen above. Evidently the power vacuum created at this time, together with the tying-up of banking assets, made intervention almost impossible. The government was forced to authorize a further increase in monetary circulation (23 January 1894), and on 21 February 1894 it declared the suspension of banknote convertibility, thus going back to the former position of inconvertibility of Italian currency that had been abandoned back in 1883 (see Chapter 5). This was to mark the end of a highly dramatic period in the economic life of the Italian nation; and together with the social unrest that characterized these years, with episodes of social protest up and down the country, the period 1889–94 has been called that of 'the new Kingdom's economy's darkest years'.[35]

The reorganization of the banking system's central structure—that of the banks of issue—represented an enormous operation for the government, and this operation was characterized by a series of delays and a certain amount of hesitation which, at the end of the day, caused the loss of the banking system's most prestigious members. Nevertheless, it did produce results, and suitable successors were quickly found for the Credito Mobiliare and Banca Generale. The strategic role played by the new banks born on the ashes of the former institutes in financing industrial development during the Giolitti years has warranted a large amount of interest from historians, and for this reason, I would like to devote the following section entirely to the question.

3. INDUSTRIAL CREDIT AND THE ROLE OF THE MIXED BANKS

The vacuum left by the departure from the scene of two important banks such as the Credito Mobiliare and the Banca Generale had to be filled, in the view of both industrialists and financiers, and so there was immediately talk of refounding them or replacing them, with the aid of foreign capital. In fact, some

[34] Corbino, iv. 359–60.

[35] G. Luzzatto, *L'economia italiana dal 1861 al 1894* (Turin, Einaudi, 1968), 177. The Banco di Napoli also had to be helped through an enormous salvage operation, in order to resolve the heavy losses due to its property investment.

members and directors of the two bankrupt institutions were the first to suggest such a move. A number of alternative plans were drawn up, with foreign bankers (Germans in particular) watching on with interest; in fact, an end was put to all obstacles when the interested German parties decided to set up a large bank without coming to any kind of preliminary agreement with those Italians interested in such a project. This was how the Banca Commerciale Italiana (Comit) was founded in Milan on 1 October 1894, exclusively with the help of foreign capital, mainly German, but also Austrian and Swiss.[36] The managing director of Comit was Otto Joel, a German who had emigrated to Italy at the age of 15, and had worked his way up to a top position with the Banca Generale;[37] his partner was another German-born banker, Federico Weil, who had previously been head of the Palermo branch of Credito Mobiliare. For these reasons, the Comit could be said to have been a continuation of the previous banking experience, as represented in the persons of its two initial directors, as well as having a German-style management.

Both Hertner[38] and Confalonieri provide us with a wealth of facts that show that it was never the intention of the German banks that financed the setting-up of Comit, nor that of its German managerial 'duo', to keep Comit in German hands. Italian and French groups very soon took an interest in the bank, and the share capital was divided up among a large number of shareholders, including the French Banque de Paris et des Pays Bas (Paribas), while a correspondingly large amount of German capital was withdrawn,[39] although this was not matched by an equally rapid reduction in the number of German members of the board of directors.[40]

Another new bank was set up in Milan just a few months after the foundation of Comit, this time by Genoese financiers, converting a local bank (the Banca di Genova) into a national institute with the help of other financiers from Italy, Germany, and Switzerland. The aim was to pick up where the bankrupt Banca Generale had left off, but nothing came of this plan.[41] The Credito Italiano (Credit) did not get off to a very good start, but it began to make a name for itself after Enrico Rava (already managing director of the Banca Generale) was appointed as managing director on 28 February 1897. The Credit subsequently followed the example set by Comit, in that it began to divide up shareholdings on a wider basis, with French and Belgian shareholders coming on to the scene, and a consequent reduction in German shareholdings.

[36] Conte Sanseverino Vimercati only owned a few honorary shares.

[37] He was vice-director of the Milan branch (1887) at first, then became director of the Genoa branch (1889) and of the Milan branch (1891), and finally inspector-general (March 1893).

[38] P. Hertner, *Il capitale tedesco in Italia dall'unità alla prima guerra mondiale* (Bologna, Il Mulino, 1984), 98–102.

[39] The German-Austrian-Swiss consortium that had founded Comit had already seen their share of the bank's capital reduced to a meagre 8.6% by 1901–2.

[40] By 1906, of the 31 directors, 14 were Italian, 4 French, 3 Swiss, and 7 German.

[41] Confalonieri, *Banca e industria in Italia 1894–1906*, ii. 41.

The other two banks that came into being at this time, and that were to make up the group of four large, so-called 'mixed banks', were the Banco di Roma and the Banca Italiana di Sconto. Neither had had any previous experience of industrial credit, and both got off to a relatively modest start compared with Comit and Credit: in the Banca Italiana di Sconto's case, this particular institute had been through a lot of problems, and also name changes, before establishing itself as part of the 'big four'.

The Banco di Roma was founded in Rome on 9 March 1880[42] by a group of local aristocrats who were joined by the very cream of the city's middle class. In June of that year, the Pope made the Banco responsible for looking after his liquid capital, for which he received a privileged rate of interest. De Rosa has the following to say on the affair: 'This event can hardly be ignored . . . [for] it is evidence of the fact that the Banco di Roma had had a relationship with the Pope from the very beginning of its existence.'[43] Nevertheless, the growth of the Banco was rather limited until the end of the century, with it going through a crisis period at the time of the banking scandals, followed by a period of slow recovery.[44]

The origins of the Banca Italiana di Sconto go back to the transformation of the banking institute Figli di Weil Schott e C. into the Società Bancaria Milanese, by a group of industrialists and bankers from Milan.[45] On 28 October 1904, the bank bought up the Banco di Sconto e Sete of Turin (which had gone bankrupt), and then changed its name to Società Bancaria Italiana (SBI), keeping this name until 1914, when it changed once more to become the Banca Italiana di Sconto (BIS).

Compared with Comit and Credit, the Banco di Roma and the SBI had no support from foreign banks, and their directors did not have the banking experience that those of the former two institutions had. Furthermore, neither bank could hope to have the most prestigious customers, due to the distance separating the Banco di Roma from the Italian industrial heartland, and the fact that the SBI had arrived on the scene after both Comit and Credit. This meant that they were both structurally weak, and thus vulnerable at times of crisis.

The spectacular progress of these four banks during the Giolitti years can be seen from the figures given in Table 4.5: the Comit stood out head and shoulders above the rest, while the Credit was forever second-best; the other two remained some distance behind, although the BIS went through a period of very fast growth (not documented in the table) during the First World War, which was to be a premonitory sign of its later collapse.

[42] L. De Rosa, *Storia del Banco di Roma*, i and ii (Rome, 1982–3).

[43] Ibid. i. 27–28.

[44] As shown by the figures elaborated and commented on by S. Sassi, *La vita di una banca attraverso i suoi bilanci. Il Banco di Roma dal 1880 al 1933* (Bologna, Il Mulino, 1986).

[45] F. Bonelli, *La crisi del 1907. Una tappa dello sviluppo industriale in Italia* (Turin, Einaudi, 1971).

Table 4.5. Assets of the four major 'mixed banks', 1895–1914 (millions of lire at current prices)

	Banca Commerciale (1)	Credito Italiano (2)	Banco di Roma (3)	Banca Italiana di Sconto[a] (4)	Share of total banking assets held by the 4 major banks (%) (5)
1895	78.7	49.8	3.7	2.6	1.9
1900	261.3	124.8	27.3	26.8	5.6
1904	498.3	251.1	72.4	85.0	9.1
1907	727.9	396.0	157.1	189.1	12.3
1911	921.9	561.9	497.7	264.3	15.1
1914	1,110.9	633.7	413.1	368.2	14.7

[a] Weil Schott & Co. until 1898; then Società Bancaria Milanese; then Società Bancaria Italiana from Oct. 1904; and finally Banca Italiana di Sconto from 30 Dec. 1914.

Source: V. Bava, *I quattro maggiori istituti italiani di credito* (Genoa, Valugani, 1926)

What were the characteristics of these banks that gave them their dynamism, and why were they called 'mixed banks'? The name 'mixed banks' was given to those banks that provided short-, medium-, and long-term credit at the same time; they were 'universal' rather than specialized in nature, providing all the services a client could possibly require—'from the cradle to the grave'—the prototype of which came into existence in Germany during the second half of the nineteenth century. Alexander Gerschenkron was the first to 'discover' the important role played by this kind of bank, so different from the British model which was based on specialization of services offered, and the separation of short- and long-term credit facilities,[46] during the period of growth of the German nation.[47] Gerschenkron identified the German 'mixed bank' as being a highly typical case of the creative 'substitution' of a prerequisite that was missing with a new factor. In Germany, the missing prerequisite for industrial investment was the existence of a sufficiently rich class of capitalists willing to take the risk of investing in industry—something that was certainly not absent in England at the time of the Industrial Revolution. The existence of the mixed bank served as a 'substitutive factor' because, on the one hand, it was capable of gathering large amounts of capital through the deposit of savings throughout

[46] See R. Cameron, *Banking and Economic Development* (New York, Oxford University Press, 1972), and K. E. Born, *International Banking in the 19th and 20th Centuries* (Oxford, Berg, 1983; German edn., 1977).

[47] A. Gerschenkron, *Economic Backwardness in Historical Perspective* (Cambridge, Mass., Harvard University Press, 1962).

the country, and on the other hand, was prepared to risk them in industrial investment.[48]

Some scholars argue that there was no substantial difference between the French banks like Crédit Mobilier—which was the model for the Italian banks Credito Mobiliare and Banca Generale[49]—and the German mixed banks; there can be no doubt, however, that a difference did exist. As far as collecting savings was concerned, the German mixed bank was very careful to distribute branches throughout the entire country, so as to maximize the quantity of savings collected; as for the use to which these savings were put, these banks were careful to use 'normal banking procedures' (discounting commercial bills) as well as, and sometimes in preference to, other financial activities. It is worthwhile taking a closer look at the nature of these mixed banks, particularly in view of the modern-day debate concerning the relationship between banking and industry.

First, it has to be said that the mixed bank is a bank and not an industrial holding, and as such is not primarily interested in acquiring shares in industry, or in managing such shares; on the contrary, its main objective is that of functioning as a bank. Nevertheless, in order to ensure the existence of 'a solid and faithful clientele'.[50] the bank perceives a need to take an active interest in the foundation and consolidation of businesses. The mixed bank has always devoted its time and effort towards this objective, and this has happened in the following ways:

1. The creation and/or extension of joint-stock companies was carried out by a placement syndicate led by the bank, which usually held on to a small percentage of the shares issued for strategic reasons (this gave customers an idea of the worthy nature of the business being supported, as well as allowing the bank to get one or two of its representatives on to the board of directors of the company, so as to follow the business's affairs 'in person'). The bank only took on more of the company's shares than it really wished to hold when this was necessary in order to cover up for the lack of response on the part of the public.

2. The medium- and long-term financing of the company was carried out by allowing its current account to remain in the red, and by accepting the deposit of shares against liquid funds for a predetermined period of time.

[48] See the study by R. Tilly, 'German Banking 1850–1914: Development Assistance to the Strong', *Journal of European Economic History*, 46 (1986). An interesting comparison with British financing—seen as a retardation factor in the British economy—is made in W. P. Kennedy, *Industrial Structure, Capital Markets and the Origins of British Economic Decline* (Cambridge, Cambridge University Press, 1987).

[49] Both the Credito Mobiliare and, above all, the Banca Generale tried towards the end of their days to spread their savings net, and to dedicate themselves more to 'normal banking operations', but it was too late. Nevertheless, it served as a useful lesson to Joel and Rava in their management of Comit and Credit.

[50] Taken from *Relazione all'assemblea degli azionisti del Credito Italiano* (1899), cited in Confalonieri, *Banca e industria in Italia 1894–1906*, ii. 320.

3. Business crises were often resolved through the direct intervention of the bank; when the crisis was too big to be resolved by a single bank, then a consortium was set up to do the job (we shall be looking at some examples later on).

4. The mixed bank could also get involved in other kinds of financial intervention: it acted as a catalyst for business initiatives; it acted as intermediary, by means of guaranty, to get funds from other banks (like the Cariplo) which were less inclined towards risk-taking; occasionally, it offered technical advice on the soundness of certain business projects.[51] None of these activities was, however, carried out with the regularity or systematic approach adopted in the three previous categories of activity cited above.

As Confalonieri has pointed out, industrial projects being financed by the banks were always proposed from outside: there was no sectorial strategy, at least in the Italian case, involving the mixed banks, with the possible exception of the case of the electricity industry, and, to a lesser extent, that of the steel industry.[52] This brings us back to the point made above, that is, that the mixed bank is a bank and not a holding company, and its job is that of providing financial rather than technical-commercial support, to businesses. It is unfortunately true to say that Italy was lacking in technical and commercial expertise on the part of businessmen, as can be seen from the large number of companies in difficulty at the time, with the implication of banking immobilization. However, one can hardly blame the private banking sector for not providing industrial business expertise along with banking services. It is proper, instead, to denounce the lack of technical and administrative ability in the mixed banks themselves, as is clearly obvious in the affairs of the SBI and the Banco di Roma (which we shall be looking at shortly). The one thing that was not missing in such banks, however, was the willingness to take risks.

In an extract from a letter written in August 1902 by Otto Joel to Noetzlin, a functionary of the Parisbas, we can see an illustration of this point. Noetzlin had criticized Joel for the latter's too keen interest in 'financial deals', and the answer given by Joel is of great significance, as Confalonieri has rightly pointed out:

I have never had any doubts about expressing the need for a prudent form of management, in the best interests of customers and shareholders; however, neither do I

[51] This happened when the bank possessed its own technical adviser: e.g. Comit had the engineer Carlo Esterle, who checked all of its manœuvres in the electrical sector, while Credit had the engineer Giovan Battista Pirelli, who was mainly responsible for checking the soundness of the bank's engineering interests. We now have an excellent account of the network of Comit's representatives in the boards of directors of corporations drawn by F. Pino Pongolini, 'Sui fiduciari della Comit nelle Società per azioni (1898–1918)', *Rivista di storia economica*, 8 (1991).

[52] J. Cohen mentions other, rather more limited plans for the superphosphates sector and for those sectors involved with the transport industry (steel-making, shipbuilding, shipping, railway companies); cf. 'Financing Industrialization in Italy, 1894–1914: the Partial Transformation of a Late Comer', *Journal of Economic History*, 27 (1967).

believe that the bank should sit back passively, as the great French banks have done (with the exception of the Banque de Paris, which is a different kind of institution from the rest). I would rather model things along the lines of the Deutsche Bank (which has demonstrated its ability, rising to number-one position among German banks): that is, a bank needs to be strong in the savings field, while at the same time able to look after all aspects of financial affairs, but without putting its own liquidity or its customers' deposits at risk.[53]

Since none of the other Italian banks was in a position to take such risks, then it is easy to see that the mixed banks were going to be of decisive importance for industrial development during the Giolitti years, as testified by both Hertner and Cohen in their writings on the subject.[54] They were also decisive in terms of their limits, both quantitative and qualitative; they were quantitatively limited from the point of view of resources, which were inadequate for the growth of particularly capital-intensive sectors;[55] their qualitative limits concerned management, and were something, unfortunately, that they had in common with industry.

We can now take a brief look at the more important stages in the development of the four mixed banks, as these will serve as concrete examples of the general points made above.

The Comit, although not averse to involvement in the more traditional areas of industry like cotton textiles, was mainly interested in financing railway companies and railway material manufacturers (Breda), metallurgical companies (Terni, Falck) and shipbuilders (Odero-Orlando), electrical companies (Edison, Sade), and also various engineering companies. Without any doubt, the most important of these from the bank's point of view was the electrical sector, and it is worth adding a little more about this particular relationship. Comit had had a relationship with Colombo's Edison Company from the bank's early days, when Edison had already been going for some ten years; however, the company did not really start its construction programme for power stations until the formation of its special connection with Comit, with which it hoped to be able to retain its independence from German influence. Comit also financed a German project, setting up the Society for the Promotion of Electrical Companies in Italy, otherwise known simply as Sviluppo. Both of these

[53] Confalonieri, *Banca e industria in Italia 1894–1906*, iii. 77.

[54] Hertner, *Il capitale tedesco*, stresses the wide range of banking experience possessed by Comit and Credit, together with their capacity to mobilize large amounts of capital. J. Cohen, in his essay on the Italian banks in Cameron, *Banking and Economic Development*, underlines above all the entrepreneurial aspects of the mixed banks.

[55] Confalonieri is right when, citing a debate on industrial credit held in 1911, he points out that the mixed banks were not capable on their own of satisfying the demand for this kind of credit in Italy, given the limited size of the stock market and thus the inevitably large request for bank credit from businesses. The problem only began to be resolved after the First World War, when institutes that specialized in long-term credit were set up. Cf. A. Confalonieri, 'Il credito all'industria in Italia prima del 1914', *Bancaria*, 41 (Feb. 1985).

companies were to become holding companies. Then in 1905, Comit joined up with Giuseppe Volpi, a financier from the Veneto region, to form SADE. In this way, Comit was sure of dominating the electrical sector, involved as it was in business activities managed by both Italian and foreign companies, although these activities required an ever-increasing amount of capital investment. This is the reason why the vice-president of the Bastogi (Società Italiana per le Strade Ferrate Meridionali, but called Bastogi after its founder), Cesare Mangili—who happened to be president of Comit as well—was so quick to suggest that the ex-railway companies, which were looking for investment opportunities after the nationalization of the railways, should invest in certain already existing electrical and engineering companies.[56] As Confalonieri says, 'the Italian electrical system would not have developed with such speed and in such an orderly fashion had it not been for the involvement of the large ex-railway companies'.[57] Despite the enormous efforts that had been made to find outside capital, at the outset of the First World War 'the Banca Commerciale ended up with its funds immobilized in its support for the electrical industry'.[58]

The Comit was also quick to support companies involved in Italian expansion in the Balkans (the Società Commerciale d'Oriente and the Antivari Company, both owned by the Venetian Volpi group), in Latin America (the Banco Commerciale Italo-Brasiliano di San Paolo, later to become Sudameris), and also in Africa; although the investments made were generally loss-making, the amounts involved were relatively insignificant.[59]

Finally, mention ought to be made of the nationalistic battle waged against Comit just before the advent of war. Despite the fact that a large proportion of German investment had already been withdrawn towards the end of the nineteenth century, and despite Joel's taking Italian citizenship in 1910, Comit was still very close to certain important international financial circles, and had failed to develop a close relationship with political circles in Rome. It was thus relatively easy for certain nationalistic groupings to mount an anti-Comit campaign, accusing the bank of trying to submit Italian industry to German interests; this campaign led to the resignations of both Joel and Weil at the outbreak of war (the former died in 1916). The campaign was really a pretext, however, as shown by the fact that the management of the bank had always declared its independence from the shareholders (Joel mentioned this more than once in his private correspondence), as well as by Comit's support for a number of exclusively Italian business projects.

[56] Minutes of the Bastogi's Board of Directors meeting, held on 21 Feb. 1907, cited in Confalonieri, *Banca e industria in Italia dalla crisi del 1907*, ii. 235.

[57] Ibid. 353. The other former railway company, the Mediterranea, decided on the other hand to stay in the railway sector, buying up branch lines and starting out on new building projects which were to lead to that company's financial collapse in 1914.

[58] Ibid. 371.

[59] For an analysis of Comit's investment within an 'imperialistic' framework, cf. R. Webster, *L'imperialismo industriale italiano. Studio sul prefascismo 1908–1915* (Turin, Einaudi, 1974).

Credit functioned in much the same way as Comit, although it was more interested in the chemical sector (Colla e Concimi, Unione Concimi, and Montecatini), in sugar refineries, and in steel production. Confalonieri points out that 'the entire weight of the financial requirements of one productive sector [pig-iron] had to be borne by a single bank';[60] that is, Credito Italiano was the sole supplier of credit to the Elba Company. In 1907, Credit formed a working relationship with Comit, and all the important salvage operations were carried out by the two banks working together, including that involving the steel industry in 1911, which we shall be looking at shortly. Besides the bank's director, Enrico Rava, the other important figure at Credit was GiovanBattista Pirelli, the founder of the famous tyre and cable company; Pirelli was always ready to procure business for the bank from his vast circle of business acquaintances, and was also in a position to act as technical consultant to the bank with regard to these business operations. Later on, he acquainted Agnelli with the bank's services, the latter having already turned to the Comit for help during the serious crisis of 1907.

The history of the other Milanese bank, which we call SBI in order to make things easier (it had a number of different names during the course of its existence), was rather different from that of the other two, in that it had a much more difficult and troubled life. As was mentioned above, SBI was in a weak position because 'it was not able to choose its clientele . . . and so was left with customers that the other bigger banks had chosen to ignore, with businesses and individuals who had not been able to find credit elsewhere'.[61] Furthermore, SBI's management was somewhat imprudent, and showed a clear tendency towards over-investing its funds in different business ventures. According to Confalonieri, the reasons behind SBI's early period of crisis 'were to be found in the administrative disorder present in the bank, and the extremely "tenuous" nature of the bank's resources',[62] as the bank had neither support from foreign banks nor an adequate supply of domestic savings.

Thus, when the 1907 international crisis erupted, and the Italian banking sector found itself involved in it, the SBI proved to be the weak link in the chain. It found itself with high liquid assets which would have meant bankruptcy in a short space of time had it not been for the intervention of the Banca d'Italia. The latter organized a consortium of banks, including Comit, Credit, and a series of smaller private banks, to rescue the SBI, which it did in two stages during October and November of 1907, helped by a significant increase in money circulation.[63] Bonelli suggests that 'the SBI, which was the main cause of the banking crisis, survived thanks principally to the goodwill of

[60] Confalonieri, *Banca e industria in Italia 1894–1906*, ii. 457.
[61] Bonelli, *La crisi del 1907*, 33.
[62] Confalonieri, *Banca e industria in Italia 1894–1906*, ii. 278.
[63] Full details of all the SBI salvage operations are contained in Bonelli, *La crisi del 1907*.

the Director General of the Banca d'Italia',[64] who believed in the need for a third, completely Italian banking institute in the industrial triangle. However, the SBI continued to live dangerously, as can be seen from the fact that it was the major beneficiary among the big banks of the rescue operation carried out in the steel industry in 1911.

Stringher had promised to strengthen the steel industry's financial position back in 1907, but it was only in 1910 that it was judged that the matter could no longer be put off. The seemingly bold, carefree nature of the steel companies' financial operations at the time did, in fact, hide a very different reality, a reality involving large investments, not always of a technically suitable kind, carried out very quickly, in an inadequate fashion, and sometimes at moments when the market was not at all favourable for such operations. If the SBI was the most vulnerable of them all, it has to be said that all the major banks were in one way or another involved, including the Banca d'Italia and the Bastogi. A Consortium for the Union of Italian Steel Companies was subsequently set up under the aegis of the Banca d'Italia. This consortium took the form of a cartel, but according to many, was incapable of resolving the steel industry's more important problems, despite its success in halting its financial crisis and in resolving the productive problems in the short term.[65] This is a clear case of the point made above about the bank's inability to produce enough people with the necessary technical and industrial knowledge and experience. Furthermore, there was a repetition here of the mixed banks' tendency to favour a market concentration, which they believed put the market in order, restricted the possibility of 'destructive' forces being unleashed, and ensured the profitability of investments.[66]

As for the SBI itself, its never-ending series of problems in the end led it to follow the tried-and-tested example of the other successful mixed banks, coming to a partnership agreement with a French bank, the Louis Dreyfus, in 1912, and increasing its territorial presence, through the amalgamation with a local bank, the Società Italiana di Credito Provinciale, to form the BIS (Banca Italiana di Sconto).[67]

[64] Ibid. 151. On this point, see also F. Bonelli, 'The 1907 financial crisis in Italy: A peculiar case of the lender of last resort in action', in C. Kindleberger and J. P. Laffargue (eds.), *Financial Crises. Theory, History and Policy* (Cambridge, Cambridge University Press, 1982).

[65] Mainly because it gave responsibility for the cartel companies' operations to the ILVA, without giving the latter the power to reorganize and technically co-ordinate them.

[66] Cf. F. Farina, 'Note sul ruolo della banca mista nello sviluppo italiano', in *Società e Storia*, 10 (1980). Gerschenkron (*Economic Backwardness*, 15) had also pointed out that 'the momentum shown by the cartelization movement of German industry cannot be fully explained, except as the natural result of the amalgamation of German banks. It was the mergers in the field of banking that kept placing banks in the position of controlling competing enterprises. The banks refused to tolerate fratricidal struggles among their children.' For other observations concerning this question, see V. Zamagni, *Industrializzazione e squilibri regionali in Italia. Bilancio dell'età giolittiana* (Bologna, Il Mulino, 1978), ch. 4.

[67] On the political consequences of the foundation of the BIS, the 'truly Italian' bank, cf. E. Galli Della Loggia, 'Problemi di sviluppo industriale e nuovi equilibri politici alla vigilia della prima

The history of the Banco di Roma is very different from that of the other banks, as it was the only mixed bank to operate largely outside the industrial triangle, although it did open a branch in Turin in 1901, and in 1905 bought a share in the Banco di Liguria e Genova, which it later took over. The Banco was involved in financing the few local agricultural and industrial projects that existed at the time. These included the Società Romana per le Costruzioni Meccaniche (a local engineering company); the Società Molini e Pastifici Pantanella (flour, bread, and pasta production); the Società Romana Solfato di Rame (copper sulphate producer); the Società Cines, which subsequently became involved in the manufacture of artificial silk; and the Società Albergo Minerva (a hotel business). However, the Banco only really found its true vocation in 1904, when it decided to open a branch in Alessandria in Egypt. 'This marked the beginning of the imperialistic policy of the Banco di Roma,' writes Webster. He continues: 'During the following six years of frenetic expansion, the bank seemed to be guided by one simple principle—that is, its policy was to increase its activities in the areas that international diplomacy had set aside for Italian control, in particular, Libya and (to a certain extent) Ethiopia.'[68] Branches of the Banco were opened in Malta, in Constantinople, Tripoli, and Benghazi.[69] Further branches were opened in Libya, and commercial and industrial operations were got under way there as well: a flour mill, a phosphate company, a company using the local esparto grass, and an edible-oil manufacturer. The bank was also involved in an operation designed to increase the number of shipping lines to and from Libya. Scholars agree that the interest shown in these colonial adventures by the Banco di Roma was largely due to the person of Romolo Tittoni, one of the bank's directors, who was the brother of Tommaso Tittoni, the Italian Foreign Minister until 1909.[70]

Foreign opposition to the bank's economic involvement abroad, together with war in Libya and the fragility of the bank's industrial operations, all contributed towards creating a situation in which the bank started to make large losses from 1911 onwards. It managed to hide these for a while, thanks to the inventiveness of its accountants who were busy making clearing entries and the like. The bank even tried to claim damages from the Italian State for the advent of war in Libya, but a final decision on the matter was continually put off, while the bank had to face heavy criticism from both its enemies and its shareholders. Tittoni resigned in May 1914, while the financial position of the Banco di Roma was near to collapse. The bank's president, Pacelli, informed the Vatican (the bank's major shareholder) of the situation, and an agreement was drawn up

guerra mondiale. La fondazione della Banca Italiana di Sconto', *Rivista storica italiana*, 82 (1970), and also A. M. Falchero, 'Banchieri e politici. Nitti e il gruppo Ansaldo–Banca di Sconto', in *Italia Contemporanea*, 146 and 147 (1982).

[68] Webster, *L'imperialismo*, 213.

[69] In 1912, there were 35 branches in Italy, and 12 abroad.

[70] De Rosa, *Storia del Banco di Roma*, i, ch. 5.

whereby the Catholic banks were to perform a salvage operation, through their newly founded central institute, the Credito Nazionale.[71] The bank devalued its own capital, but further losses were made in 1915, at which point Ernesto Pacelli (the president who had been the bank's guiding spirit since its foundation) and other members of the bank were forced to resign. So the Banco di Roma found itself in the position of having to undertake a thorough reorganization programme during the difficult war years. Confalonieri, in a damning conclusion, writes:

> Brought up in an environment lacking in industrial ideas, impregnated with the typical mentality of the landowning classes, and with no tradition of modern banking management, the directors of the Banco were under the illusion that direct involvement in entrepreneurial undertakings, together with the high rates of interest prevailing in African states and in the East, would together provide them with the profits that they could not make through 'normal' banking activities in Italy.[72]

We can thus sum up this chapter by saying that a certain equilibrium did exist in the relationship between banks and industry during the Giolitti years in Italy.[73] I do not believe, as Webster does, that 'high financial circles did not exercise control over the policy of industrialists, despite the support they gave to the latter';[74] neither do I share Cohen's view that 'Italian industry never achieved that freedom which German industrialists gained; the control of [the] banks was never challenged'.[75] It was, admittedly, a case of an unstable form of equilibrium, which was badly shaken by the advent of war, as we shall see in the next chapter. However, regardless of the reasons for this instability, one cannot say that it was an intrinsic feature of the mixed-bank system; on the contrary, the German example of such a system has clearly shown it to be potentially very stable. It is not my intention here to look at the relative advantages and disadvantages of different ways of financing productive activity, as the choice is not simply one between specialized banks or universal banks, but also involves the alternative between direct finance through the stock exchange or indirect finance through financial institutions, not to mention the increasing presence of holding companies.[76] What I have tried to underline here is that a mixed-bank

[71] Ibid. ii. 76–7.

[72] Confalonieri, *Banca e industria in Italia dalla crisi del 1907*, i. 265.

[73] This view is held by Toniolo, *Storia economica*; he writes that 'the symbiosis between banking and industry was to be typical of the 1920s rather than of this period' (p. 181).

[74] Webster, *L'imperialismo*, 210. For a general criticism of Webster's work, see G. Mori, 'Banche, industria e imperialismo nell'"età Giolittiana" ', in *Capitalismo industriale in Italia. Processo d'industrializzazione e storia d'Italia* (Rome, Editori Riuniti, 1977).

[75] Cohen, 'Financing Industrialization', 382.

[76] A recent article published on this question clearly sides with the mixed banks, which it maintains are much more capable of playing an active part in industrial development. Cf. R. Tilly, 'La banca universale in una prospettiva storica: l'esperienza tedesca', *Banca, impresa, società*, 9 (1990). See also Zamagni (ed.), *Finance and the Enterprise* (London, Academic Press, 1992).

system does not mean that banks and industry are inevitably 'Siamese twins' (except possibly when that system is in decline): this is not, therefore, where the difference lies between this kind of system and another based on the use of specialized banks (which can also be susceptible to immobilization of assets and overconcentration of risk).

5
State Intervention

1. A NON-LETHARGIC STATE

WHOEVER criticizes the Italian State's intervention in economic affairs, as Gerschenkron does,[1] at the same time implicitly acknowledges that the Italian State is an interventionist State, and is not at all 'lethargic', as Jones chooses to call those States that do not actively strive to improve their citizens' lives.[2] This was true of the Italian State as far back as the times of the Historical Right. G. Are wrote the following of Quintino Sella many years ago :

> he soon realized that, contrary to the mistaken idea of the spontaneous development of wealth, circumstances in fact dictated that the Italian State take on an uncommon and decisive role in the process of economic expansion: that is, it had to assume direct responsibility for the rapid construction of a basic civil infrastructure, which elsewhere was the result of decades and even centuries of labour, as little could be expected from private enterprise in this area; it also had actively to encourage the undertaking of certain industrial projects.[3]

In fact, Gerschenkron himself (followed by many others) recognized that an intensive programme of state intervention was necessary, as the State had to 'force' the pace of economic development through the use of 'substitutive' mechanisms in place of private enterprise in order that Italy could catch up with those countries that had industrialized first (the so-called 'first-comers'). Similarly, Bonelli wrote that 'Italian capitalism was soon to take on the form of state capitalism',[4] and he adds: 'the most important and characteristic aspect of capital accumulation in Italy, is the fact that it was not so much the result of the growth and interdependent nature of a range of productive sectors, but was due

[1] Besides Gerschenkron's criticism of protectionism introduced in 1887, he was also highly critical of Italian governments' lack of timing, incapable as they were of taking advantage of all those conditions which would have favoured the so-called 'big spurt' in Italy's economic development. A. Gerschenkron, *Economic Backwardness in Historical Perspective* (Cambridge, Mass., Harvard University Press, 1962), chs. 4 and 5. A revisitation of the Gerschenkronian interpretation of Italian economic development can be found in G. Federico and G. Toniolo, 'Italy', in G. Toniolo and R. Sylla (eds.), *Patterns of European Industrialization. The Nineteenth Century* (London, Routledge & Kegan Paul, 1991).

[2] E. Jones, *Growth Recurring. Economic Change in World History* (Oxford, Clarendon Press, 1988), 145–6.

[3] G. Are, *Alle origini dell'Italia industriale* (Naples, Guida ed., 1974), 253.

[4] F. Bonelli, 'Il capitalismo italiano. Linee generali d'interpretazione', in *Annali della storia d'Italia. Dal feudalismo al capitalismo*, i (Turin, Einaudi, 1978), 1,204.

rather to the deliberate creation of specific financial channels and forms of economic policy which were to facilitate the working of substitutive mechanisms'.[5]

While it is undoubtedly true to say that the role played by the Italian State in the industrial development of the nation was large, as we shall see in the following sections of this chapter, it has to be said that in all countries where economic development has been successfully brought about, such success has been due to the combination of private enterprise and public co-ordination, compensation, and regulation.[6] In fact, a 'pure' form of *laissez-faire* has only ever existed in the minds of some theorists, obsessed with the abstract perfection of their economic models or bitterly disappointed with certain government's behaviour, to such a point that they opted for total inaction, as in the case of Pareto who, in 1891, wrote:

Our politicians are possessed by a mania for interfering in everything, yet they are doomed to failure though acting with good intentions. Italy has always had a natural propensity for, and been successful in, producing goods for which it had lower comparative costs: it should have been left to do just that; but then our politicians had the idea of interfering with nature. In this way, they pronounced the death sentence on certain productive activities, while artificially supporting and expanding others with the public's money; and the only result thereof has been the destruction of a large part of the country's wealth.[7]

What prevents us from gaining a better theoretical understanding of the optimal balance between state intervention and private enterprise is the impossibility of fixing such a position of equilibrium in general terms, an impossibility that stems from the different historical situations which are found in different places and at different moments in time. Different precapitalistic traditions, involving different individual forms of behaviour and diverse kinds of institutions, in turn require different forms of state intervention in order to get the industrialization process under way. Furthermore, the problems produced

[5] F. Bonelli, 'Il capitalismo italiano', 1,237.

[6] The economist A. Sen rightly observes that cases of successful economic development 'are directly linked to deliberation and design, rather than being just the result of uncoordinated profit-seeking or atomistic pursuit of self-interest', in *Resources, Value and Development* (Oxford, Blackwell, 1984), 103.

[7] V. Pareto, 'Cronaca', *Giornale degli Economisti*, 3, 2nd series (1891), 23. R. Romeo observes, in a very vivid fashion, that 'a more profound historical analysis shows that those facts which historical observers had most vehemently condemned as being a sign of the pathological nature of Italian economic and industrial life, in fact represent the specific historical conditions which made it possible to force the pace of the Italian industrialization process: this, in turn, was to have a vital role in leading Italy towards membership of industrialized Europe, rather than seeing it being condemned to belong to that underdeveloped area of the Mediterranean of which it had been a fellow traveller for such a long time' (*Italia liberale: sviluppo e contraddizioni* (Milan, Il Saggiatore, 1987), 302).

by industrialization itself in capitalist societies—problems such as the exploitation of labour, the concentration of wealth in the hands of a few successful capitalists, pollution and the exhaustion of natural resources, the management of huge bureacratic machines—require further state intervention, which again varies according to the kind of problems involved, and which can be more or less critical depending on whether private enterprise is able to help out with a greater or lesser part of these problems.

Despite the difficulty involved in trying to categorize the role of the State in the economy, the recognition that it does have a genuine role to play implicitly means the refusal to accept for it the temporary and/or abnormal label it has been given by the disciples of theoretical *laissez-faire* or by those who support the more historically acceptable theory (neoclassical nevertheless) of the 'substitutive' role of such intervention (which then presumably becomes unnecessary once the country has reached, after 'forced' industrialization, a position of equilibrium). What this alternative vision requires, on the contrary, is a highly detailed study of each different historical situation in order to determine the best possible combination of private and public initiative for social and economic growth and well-being: in this way, both academics and politicians are freed from the stereotyped ideal of the optimality of the 'free market' as well as from the opposite ideal of the optimality of 'state planning', which has also proved to be tragically inadequate.[8] With Jones we can conclude that 'the strongest economy [is] the one in which a *balance* is secured between free markets and public intervention',[9] a balance that frees the creative force of man's intelligence and labour, and channels it into the building of lasting, worthwhile objectives, rather than repressing, distorting, and frustrating it through the degrading daily routine of mere survival.

After having clarified the contextual setting of a study of the State's intervention in Italian industrialization, in the subsections that follow I will be describing the road that this intervention took in the period up to the First World War. I would like to point out that all of the fundamental characteristics of state intervention in Italy were already present during this period.[10]

2. PUBLIC SPENDING AND ITS EFFECTS

The mass of available data concerning Italian public finances has recently been reorganized in series covering the years 1866–1980, which are in line with the current definition of 'public sector' including central administration, local

[8] There can be no sense in acclaiming either the advance or the retreat of the State, as any move in one direction or the other can be considered acceptable to a greater or lesser degree according to whether it helps reach those social aims shared by the majority of the nation's citizens.

[9] Jones, *Growth Recurring*, 78 (the italics are mine).

[10] The introduction of protectionism has already been dealt with in Ch. 3, while the creation of social legislation will be looked at in Ch. 6, for reasons of analytical coherence.

authorities, and social services.[11] The latter category was non-existent until the end of the First World War,[12] and so the public sector was made up of the first two categories only. According to the new series of figures, local authority spending made up some 30 to 32 per cent of total public spending during the period up to the First World War: this figure was stable over a long period, thus indicating a parallel growth in local government and central government spending.

Table 5.1 shows the most important of the results contained in this series (put together by G. Brosio and C. Marchese), which I shall be using together with other figures to illustrate the changes in the composition of public spending. Before doing so, it should be pointed out that column 1, which shows the ratio of public spending to gross domestic product (GDP) at factor cost constitutes an interesting indicator of the Italian State's active economic involvement. In comparison with similar indicators for France, Germany,

Table 5.1. Public expenditure, 1866–1913

	Total expenditure as % of GDP at factor cost	% composition of public expenditure			
		Public works	Education	Social	Military
	(1)	(2)	(3)	(4)	(5)
1866[a]	16.8	3.2	2.3	0.4	33.9
1870	14.4	14.2	3.2	0.3	14.1
1872	13.1	15.7	3.5	0.5	12.8
1880	13.7	13.3	5.0	0.5	14.9
1890	18.4	12.9	5.6	0.5	15.9
1900	16.2	8.2	6.5	1.0	15.0
1906	16.1	10.8	7.4	2.3	14.3
1912	18.3	11.4	8.7	2.1	21.1
1913	17.7	—	7.7	2.4	22.1

[a] The series starts with the year 1866 due to the difficulty encountered in finding data for local authority spending before that date.

Sources: For the public expenditure figures and their breakdown, G. Brosio and C. Marchese, *Il potere di spendere* (Bologna, Il Mulino, 1986); for the GDP figures, ISTAT, *Indagine statistica sul reddito nazionale dell'Italia dal 1861 al 1956* (Rome, 1957).

[11] G. Brosio and C. Marchese, *Il potere di spendere. Economia e storia della spesa pubblica dall'unificazione ad oggi* (Bologna, Il Mulino, 1986). I use this recent study rather than the traditional book by F. A. Répaci, *La finanza pubblica italiana nel secolo 1861–1960* (Bologna, Zanichelli, 1962), as the former also covers local government spending and welfare insurance, and it adopts a definition of spending which is more in line with the present concept of current public expenditure (expenditure on capital account is not included). Nevertheless, Répaci's study continues to be an extremely valuable source of information.

[12] Some social welfare legislation had already been passed, however, as we shall see in the next chapter.

Japan, The Netherlands, Great Britain, and the USA, Italy's public spending can be seen to have had a higher ratio to GDP, with the exception of Germany during the years leading up to the First World War, when the percentage was about the same. As far as the long-term trend is concerned, the annual figures, which have not been given here, show that public spending fluctuated between 12 and 14 per cent of GDP up until 1880 (with the exception of 1866, when there was an enormous increase in public spending, as can be seen by looking at column 5). In fact, the importance of public-spending programmes had already been recognized during the years of the Historical Right, as can be seen from the following statement by Quintino Sella during the parliamentary sitting of 14 April 1865):

> There were two paths that could be taken towards the construction of the Kingdom of Italy . . . Some people . . . and these were the least courageous . . . wanted to deny the existence of a pressing need for change that was to be witnessed all over the country . . . and were convinced that it was sufficient simply to match public spending to the limited resources that the old states had had prior to unification . . . We, instead, have chosen the completely opposite way; we have committed ourselves and our resources to satisfying the needs of civilization and progress which were those of the entire Italian population.[13]

With the coming to power of the Historical Left, the weight of public spending increased, and represented some 20 per cent of GDP in 1888–9;[14] it then fluctuated around the 19 per cent mark until 1897, when it began to decrease, reaching 14.2 per cent in 1907, and then finally rose once more to about 17–18 per cent in the immediate pre-war years. The fall in the weight of public spending during the first part of the Giolitti years was undoubtedly due to a rapid increase in GDP, which was not accompanied by a similar increase in public spending in the civil sector; the partial recovery in the subsequent period was due more than anything to an increase in the government's military spending.

The Historical Right's main commitments—apart from military spending during the numerous wars of independence, and the expense involved in managing the various public debts, which we shall be looking at shortly—were to the setting-up of a relatively well-organized administrative machine, and to the creation of infrastructures, and in particular that of the railway network. With regard to this latter topic, the Minister of Public Works, Stefano Jacini, had the following to say in his parliamentary speech of 31 January 1867:

[13] Q. Sella, *Provvedimenti finanziari*, in *Discorsi Parlamentari*, iii (Rome, 1888–90), 451.

[14] It should be noted, bearing in mind what was said in the introduction, that the ISTAT figures seem grossly to underestimate GDP for the 1880s; this, in turn, would imply a reduced rise in the incidence of public expenditure on GDP in that decade. On the nature of the Historical Left's public-spending policy, cf. P. A. Toninelli, 'Spesa pubblica e crescita economica dalla caduta della Destra alla Grande Guerra', in C. Pavese, P. Toninelli, and S. Violante, *Fiscalità e finanza pubblica in Italia (1861–1913). Saggi e documenti* (Milan, Unicopli, 1979), as well as G. Barone, 'Sviluppo capitalistico e politica finanziaria in Italia nel decennio 1880–1890', *Studi Storici*, 13 (1972).

In the past few years, we have had to give urgent attention to the question of making up for the inaction of past governments in the sector of public spending. This has involved: building new roads; fortifying the country's insecure ports and harbours; expanding and strengthening river banks and dams; channelling waterways in order to double the fertility of huge tracts of land; introducing that wonderful instrument of civilization, the locomotive, into the most remote corners of the land; drastically reducing the distances that separated thousands of Italian towns, through the introduction of the telegraph; increasing and modernizing the postal system; creating a national fleet of steamships. . . . All of this, which previously would have taken up the energies of a large nation for a considerable period of time, had to be achieved in Italy's case in the space of a few months; not so much for the benefit of public welfare and national wealth itself, but rather as a result of the nation's need to ensure its independence, . . . in order quickly to forget ancient quarrels and divisions, and to build a solid foundation for national unity and strong government.[15]

During the Right's administration, some 21,000 km. of new roads were laid down,[16] the telegraph network was increased from 9,860 to 21,437 km., that of the railways rose from 1,829 to 7,686 km., and the number of post offices increased from 2,220 to 2,907.

The Left further increased government commitment to building a solid infrastructural network; by the end of the century it had managed to double the length of the railways and the telegraph system; the total road network was increased in length by one-quarter; and the number of post offices rose by two-thirds. The public telephone service entered into operation in 1881, while some private companies were soon to be given contracts. After a further boom during the Giolitti years, the situation just before the First World War was as follows: there were 17,649 km. of railways, 148,380 km. of roads (not including local roads), 53,518 km. of telegraph lines, 9,837 post offices, and 89,843 telephone subscribers (two-thirds to the public telephone service).[17] Although these changes could hardly be described as miraculous, they are an indication of the Italian State's commitment to updating and modernizing the country's infrastructures, using the latest technological discoveries of the time.

The construction of a national rail network is worthy of a more detailed examination. Jacini, in his speech quoted above, cites the importance of a railway network connecting different parts of the country for the real

[15] S. Jacini, *L'Amministrazione dei lavori pubblici in Italia dal 1860 al 1867. Relazione del Ministro dei lavori pubblici S. Jacini presentata al Parlamento il 31 gennaio 1867* (Florence, 1867), 1.

[16] Unfortunately, the figures pertaining to the length of roads built in the years up to 1875 are somewhat imprecise, and should be cross-checked with those contained in the ledgers of the State and of local authorities. In fact, the aggregate data available for the post-unification period cannot be compared with those given in Table 0.1 of the Introduction, since the latter also include secondary roads, whereas such roads are largely absent from the post-unification figures, or are at most roughly estimated every now and then. The figure given in the text is, in fact, based on one such estimate.

[17] All data come from the *Annuario Statistico Italiano*, various years.

unification of Italy and for the mobilization of its resources; this was a commonly held belief at the time. The problem was how to go about constructing such a network. At first, the State thought that it could construct the lines using the Piedmontese method of direct state responsibility, but when it realized that it did not possess sufficient public funds to do so, it decided to contract out some of the work to private companies (including some foreign concerns).[18] In 1865, during a crisis period for public finances, it was decided to hand over the Ligurian-Piedmontese railway network, which the Italian State had inherited from the Savoyard State, to the Società Alta Italia; likewise, those sections of track that were under construction in Liguria and Campania were given over to the Ferrovie Romane. In all cases of this kind, the State committed itself to subsidizing the private companies in order that they were guaranteed an agreed annual profit.

However, the weakness of the privatization solution was soon fairly evident, as many lines did not prove to be profitable enough for the companies involved, due to the lack of traffic together with the high construction and running costs (this being a result of the difficult terrain involved). Once again, it was the Historical Right that had the task of redeeming two private companies: the Ferrovie Romane[19] and the railway inherited from Austria in 1866. This latter redemption took place in 1875, and led to a substantial increase in the State's debt.

When the Left came to power, it not only launched an ambitious building programme involving a secondary railway network in 1879,[20] to be financed by a public debt issue, but also passed a new law (1885) which led to the State taking on responsibility for the entire rail network, although three private companies were given renewable 20-year contracts for the use of that network. In this way, the State became responsible for the construction of new branches or lines, while the private contractors had to provide the necessary rolling-stock. This coexistence of private and public interest in the railways was heavily criticized at the time, and eventually led to the complete nationalization of the railways in 1905, when the initial agreement was due for renewal; as a consequence, the State had to pay these companies over 500 million lire as indemnity.[21] The new Ferrovie dello Stato immediately decided on a

[18] Founded with French capital.

[19] J. Tivaroni wrote that the Società delle Ferrovie Romane 'never managed to pay a dividend to its shareholders, and at the end of 1873 it left its debentures without any interest, and its railway lines in dire straits—including the one that hoped to reach the Kingdom's capital', in *Storia del debito pubblico del Regno d'Italia*, ii (2 vols., Pavia, 1908–10), 18.

[20] S. Fenoaltea maintains that the building of branch lines led to an improvement in the profitability of the entire rail network: see 'Railways and the Development of the Italian Economy to 1913', in P. O'Brien (ed.), *Railways and the Economic Growth of Western Europe* (London, Macmillan, 1983).

[21] The former railway companies became important financial companies that invested in the most advanced sectors of Italian industry, and especially in the electricity industry, as we have seen.

programme of modernization of rolling-stock, which meant a lot of extra work for Italian industry.

The overall result of the Italian State's commitment to the construction of railways was certainly substantial, but at the cost of spending during the period between unification and the First World War up to three-quarters of total spending on public works, to which the expenses of the public debt incurred for railway construction must be added.[22] Did the Italian railway network have the same catalytic effect on the industrialization process as railways had in other countries? We can hardly avoid this question, after the publication of Pollard's chapter on the 'differential of contemporaneousness'.[23] Starting from the well-known fact that industrial capitalism triggered off a series of important 'technological eras', and led to the introduction of social and economic institutions spreading throughout different societies that had a very different degree of preparation for such changes (because of the different stages reached in their economic development), Pollard goes on to illustrate this with reference to various examples, including that of the railways. The railways were an English invention, and as such corresponded to the mature industrial conditions present in England at the time: that is, their growth was made possible by the productive capacities of that country, and met the need for a fast and reliable form of transport. In the USA, France, and Germany, the railways were an important factor in starting the industrialization process.

In Italy, on the other hand, the railways did not play such a crucial role in the industrialization process. First of all, one must remember that it proved difficult at the beginning to develop an industry capable of supplying the necessary railway materials, and the metallurgical industry was even slower to respond to the demand for rails; as a consequence, the Italian railways were initially heavily dependent upon foreign imports in both these sectors. Fenoaltea has however pointed out that, as a result of the narrowness of the country and the limited areas covered by the railways, even if national history had been more technologically advanced, the extra demand coming from the railways would not have led to a substantial increase in engineering production over the period from 1861 to 1913.[24] The impact of the railways on the construction industry was more significant, however. During the two main cycles of investment in the

[22] The railway deficit made up a large slice of the total public debt at the beginning of the First World War (equal to about 40% of the total).

[23] S. Pollard, *Peaceful Conquest. The Industrialization of Europe, 1760–1970* (Oxford, Oxford University Press, 1981).

[24] Fenoaltea, 'Railways and Economic Growth'. Demand from the railways constituted 8% (1861–95) and then 13% (1896–1913) of value added in the engineering sector, and between 16% (1861–95) and 17% (1896–1913) of value added in the metallurgy sector. Gerschenkron thought that the effect produced would have been greater if railway construction had been concentrated more towards the end of the period; this probably undervalues the serious probem of supply elasticity which a heavy concentration of government orders would have brought about for Italian industry.

railways—during the 1860s and the 1880s—about one-third of value added in the construction industry was a result of demand from the railways.[25] Thus it comes as no great surprise to learn that, overall, the growth of the railways had a relatively insignificant 'expansion' effect on industry.

Results were also rather disappointing from the point of view of utilization of the railways: this was partly due to the fact that the South and the North did not complement each other, as we saw in Chapter 1, and partly because the main Italian export—silk—weighed very little; things were also further exacerbated by the backwardness of the country at that time. As a result, the profitability of the railways was always in question, as can be seen from the continual input of public money into the railways. This, together with other considerations, has led me, following Gerschenkron, to conclude that 'railway policy [was] excessively "forced" both in terms of timing and in the way it was financed'.[27] A few profitable lines were indispensable, and in particular those crossing the Po Plain. The others could have been built at a later and more propitious moment in time, and, more importantly still, could have been made part of a 'package' designed to help the more underdeveloped areas of the country. Left on their own as they were, the railways proved incapable of bringing progress as had originally been thought possible.

Going back to Table 5.1, if we look at column 5 we can see that military expenditure fluctuated between 13 and 16 per cent of total public expenditure, apart from the period during the war when it was obviously much higher. In this case, as well, the initial impact on the nation's industry as a whole was not important as a result of the low elasticity of supply of armaments by the Italian industry. To give one example: between 1870 and 1880, 70 per cent of the Royal Navy's orders went to foreign firms.[28] The arrival of the Historical Left represented a turn-around point in this state of affairs: during the 1880s, two inquiry commissions were set up, one to investigate the merchant navy's situation, and the other to conduct a survey of the engineering and shipbuilding industries. These commissions verified the backwardness of the Italian shipbuilding industry when it came to the construction of steel-hulled vessels,[29] and recommendations were made to provide the industry with subsidies and to help set up a modern steel-mill.

[25] The incidence of state demand on the construction industry remained at about the 70% level until the 1890s, when it fell very slightly to about 66%. Cf. S. Fenoaltea, 'Le ferrovie e lo sviluppo industriale italiano, 1861–1913', in G. Toniolo (ed.), *L'economia italiana 1861–1940* (Bari, Laterza, 1978).

[27] V. Zamagni, 'Ferrovie e integrazione del mercato nazionale nell'Italia post-unitaria', in *Studi in onore di Gino Barbieri* (Salerno, IPEN ed., 1983), 1,649.

[28] Cf. L. De Rosa, 'Difesa militare e sviluppo economico in Italia (1861–1914)', in *La rivoluzione industriale in Italia e il Mezzogiorno* (Bari, Laterza, 1973).

[29] See G. Roncagli, 'L'industria dei trasporti marittimi', in Accademia dei Lincei, *Cinquanta anni di storia italiana* (Milan, Hoepli, 1911).

The Terni steel-mill was thus founded on 10 March 1884 with funds made available by the government in the form of advances on subsequent production, and by large banks who were confident of the feasibility of an industrial venture with state backing. However, success was a long time coming in the case of the Terni works, which had a difficult time, partly because of the unusual form that management took, resulting from its 'artificial' birth,[30] partly because it was not followed by similar initiatives (until the early years of the twentieth century), and also because the plant was located a long way from the ports of shipment of the raw material and from the places where the finished products were to be used.[31] Nevertheless, the history of the foundation of the Terni works remains highly symbolic as it represented the first of a long series of acts of state intervention aimed at guaranteeing the country a basic steel industry; episodes of this kind were to be repeated in various forms throughout the history of Italy till recent times.

A law making provision for subsidies to the shipbuilding industry was passed on 6 December 1885; if we take into account the preceding subsidies given to shipping companies for certain lines and postal services, then we see that the shipping sector of the economy received an annual average of 22 million lire in the period between 1885 and 1913. The state intervention in the shipping sector and the birth of an Italian metallurgical industry, which followed on from the introduction of protectionism and the end of the early 1890s' banking crisis, together contributed towards the strengthening of the nation's war machine. In 1911, Italian military production covered some 90 per cent of all requirements, and public sector demand was equal to more than 20 per cent of total metallurgical and engineering production.[32]

Thus public spending, together with protectionism, contributed noticeably towards the build-up of a national metallurgical industry and supplied a not

[30] Engineer Vincenzo Stefano Breda, who was appointed director of the Terni company, had the following to say: 'the great steel plant at Terni was not the result of private enterprise; that is, it was not industrialists or capitalists who had the idea of creating this plant in order to make a profit. It was the work of the government. It was the government that got a large number of people involved in the project, through its appeal for the construction of an independent steel industry—at first without very much success, but then with the involvement of more able people, including some 1848 veterans—as if it were a question of carrying on the fight for the country's economic independence. It was the government that told these people: we will give you several million lire, we will guarantee you the job in order that you may amortize the capital that you put into this project; all we ask is that you have the courage to help us in this noble plan. And in this way the great Terni steelworks was built.' Quoted by Romeo in 'Lo stato e l'impresa privata nello sviluppo economico italiano', republished in *L'Italia liberale*, 296.

[31] The Terni was set up in Umbria for strategic reasons, as well as for the local availability of energy (hydraulic at first, electrical later). For further details, cf. F. Bonelli, *Lo sviluppo di una grande impresa in Italia. La Terni dal 1884 al 1962* (Turin, Einaudi, 1971).

[32] My estimate given in *Industrializzazione e squilibri regionali in Italia* (Bologna, Il Mulino, 1978), 65. For further details, see also P. Ferrari, 'La produzione di armamenti nell'età giolittiana', *Italia contemporanea*, 162 (Mar. 1986). If we include railway contracts as well, then public demand accounted for about one-third of total metallurgical production. This was to increase subsequently, as a result of the increase in war expenditure.

insignificant demand for the engineering industry, also acting as an incentive to the expansion of the Italian construction industry. As a result of such policies, the Italian State became involved, both directly and indirectly, in the industrialization process (indirectly, if one thinks of the use to which the ex-railway companies put their indemnity payments).

At this juncture, we might like to look at one of the operations carried out in the South at the beginning of the twentieth century by the Giolitti governments.[33] In July 1904, a special law was passed aimed at putting the financial affairs of the province of Naples in order, as well as providing economic and fiscal support to those companies who wished to set up business in the Neapolitan area. Furthermore, the law guaranteed local businesses a fixed quota of government contracts and an amount of iron ore from Elba. As a direct result of the new law, the Genoese company ILVA built a steel works at Bagnoli, near Naples.

As we shall not have a further opportunity to look at the policies of the Giolitti governments in relation to state intervention in the South, I would like here to give a summary of the other measures taken. These policies were really the idea of Zanardelli (from Brescia), who had decided to do something to try and alleviate the misery that he had witnessed on a journey to the South;[34] however, he did not stay in government long enough to see his projects materialize, and so the first practical steps were taken by Giolitti's first cabinet on 31 March 1904. Most of these measures, and of those that followed, concerned agriculture and the organization and reclamation of agricultural land, and have already been mentioned in Chapter 1. They included an expansion of the already existing land-reclamation, reforestation, and road-building programmes, as well as the introduction of fiscal incentives and an increase in agricultural credit.[35] As well as the helping hand offered to the Naples area, the State was also responsible for getting the building of the Apulian aqueduct under way (in 1904), and it decided to intervene in favour of the Sicilian and Sardinian miners in order to improve their appalling working conditions. The year 1906 saw another of those masterful surveys conducted by the Italian liberal State, in this case entitled *A Survey of Peasant Conditions in the Southern Provinces and Sicily*, and published in serial volumes between 1909 and 1911.[36]

[33] Giolitti revealed himself to be extremely aware of the needs of the South, and can rightly be seen as the Italian politician who did the most for the improvement of that part of Italy before the First World War. Cf. F. V. Coppa, 'Giolitti and the Mezzogiorno', in *Studies in Modern Italian History. From the Risorgimento to the Republic* (New York, Peter Lang, 1986).

[34] Cf. P. Corti (ed.), *Inchiesta Zanardelli sulla Basilicata* (Turin, Einaudi, 1976).

[35] See the details given in S. La Francesca, *La politica economica italiana dal 1900 al 1913* (Rome, Ed. dell'Ateneo, 1971).

[36] Cf. A. Prampolini, *Agricoltura e società rurale nel Mezzogiorno agli inizi del '900* (Milan, Angeli, 1981).

This packet of 'special measures' has still to be studied in its entirety,[37] although we know that they were unfortunately insufficient to remedy the backwardness of the Italian South: what remains to be answered is the question of whether this was due to their total inadequacy or rather to subsequent historical and military events. There can be no doubt that the government was distracted from its search for a solution to the 'southern problem' by the advent of war; subsequently, post-war economic difficulties meant that the government's spending power was severely curtailed, and the Fascist regime lost all interest in the South and its problems, except when it was necessary to intervene in order to maintain public order; and finally, the Second World War reared its ugly head. The only governments to pick up where Giolitti had left off were those formed in the new Italian Republic after the end of the Second World War, although this happened when the situation had worsened considerably from the South's point of view, as the North of the country had progressed significantly in the meantime. We shall be looking at this problem in more detail in Chapters 11 and 12.

If we ignore spending on redistribution of wealth, which added up to very little during these years, then we come finally to spending on education, which is, on the contrary, of significant importance. As can be seen from Table 5.1, resources originally destined for education were very meagre indeed, contrary to the beliefs and wishes of the more enlightened members of the Historical Right.[38] In order to grasp fully the importance of this fact, one must bear in mind that education in Italy has always been largely a state concern (more than 80 per cent).[39] The new Kingdom's first government passed a law (the Casati law) making primary education compulsory, if only for two school years, and local councils were made responsible for the financial burden involved. As a consequence, regional and local differences in tax revenue—which we shall be looking at in the next section—meant that it was impossible to create equal educational opportunities for those who lived in the poorer regions and in country areas.[40] The Left once again intervened, increasing educational

[37] The only two studies dealing with the special law for Naples available to date are: M. Marmo, 'L'economia napoletana alla svolta dell'Inchiesta Saredo e la legge dell'8 luglio 1904 per l'incremento industriale di Napoli', *Rivista storica italiana*, 81 (1969); and G. Acocella (ed.), *Lo stato e il Mezzogiorno* (Naples, Guida, 1986).

[38] During the parliamentary sitting of 27 May 1861, Cavour declared: 'I believe that in order to help Italian industry . . . we need to promote professional instruction, not only at the higher levels, but also among the lower levels of workers. We still lack a sufficient number of good engineering foremen in our factories; it is proving rather difficult to find mechanical engineers—the English simply call them engineers—and technical schools are necessary in order to have this kind of foremen', *Atti Parlamentari, Camera dei deputati,* leg. VIII, 1861 Session, Debates, 1,130.

[39] Zamagni, 'Istruzione e sviluppo economico: il caso italiano (1861–1913)', in G. Toniolo (ed.), *Lo sviluppo economico italiano 1861–1940* (2nd edn., Bari, Laterza, 1978), 142, Table 2. Cf. also E. Luzzatti, 'Introduzione allo studio delle spese pubbliche per l'istruzione (1862–1965)', in *Annali della Fondazione Einaudi*, iv (Turin, 1970), and G. Vigo, 'Il contributo della spesa pubblica all'investimento in capitale umano in Italia 1870–1914', *Annales cisalpines d'histoire sociale*, 1 (1970).

[40] Illiteracy and education are examined in Ch. 6.

investment by a substantial amount, and passing the Coppino law in 1877 which doubled the length of compulsory education to four years. Educational expenditure continued to rise rapidly during the Giolitti years, but the original defect of such a policy was never corrected, as can be seen from the 1910 Corradini report which highlighted 'just how inadequate those funds, given to the South with the aim of improving primary school organization, were . . . and it suggested that this system based on financial decentralization was in practice simply a way of increasing the concentration of government funds in the hands of large cities and councils who already had a sufficient number of schools'.[41]

The outcome of all this was that another piece of legislation, the Daneo–Credaro law of 1911,[42] finally made the State responsible for all primary schooling; as in the case of the banks of issue, this decision not to centralize control, which went against the general practice of the Italian State, was eventually abandoned as a result of the failure of the alternative solution.[43]

In aggregate terms, in 1911 Italy was not behind other developed countries (with the exception of Germany) in terms of the percentage of GDP spent on education, while at the time of unification it was among the lowest in Europe—with the exception of Piedmont, Liguria, and Lombardy[44]—but the low level of GDP per head in Italy meant that effective educational expenditure per head of the population was, relatively speaking, still inadequate.

3. THE FINANCING OF PUBLIC EXPENDITURE: TAXES AND THE PUBLIC DEBT

One of the most difficult problems that the Historical Right had to confront during the building of the new State was without doubt that of shaping a fiscal system capable of dealing with the relatively high level of public expenditure outlined above, and at the same time able to rectify the huge budget deficits accrued during its first few years.

It would be wrong to say that the new fiscal system was a mere copy of that already in existence in Piedmont, as the latter would not have been capable of generating the amount of fiscal revenue that the new State required. However, the new system was doubtlessly closer to the Piedmontese or Lombard systems than to that present in the Kingdom of the Two Sicilies, where the Bourbon State had always spent very little and consequently gathered very little in the way of taxes. The radical change in fiscal policy in the South, from the lethargic position of the pre-unification State to that of an active interventionist State after unification, was in fact one of the motives behind popular protest

[41] P. Frascani, *Finanza, economia ed intervento pubblico dall'unificazione agli anni trenta* (Naples, 1988), 51–2.

[42] D. Bertoni Jovine, *La scuola italiana dal 1870 ai giorni nostri* (Rome, Editori Riuniti, 1958).

[43] A good analysis of the institutional design of the new Italian state can be found in A. Caracciolo, *Stato e società civile. Problemi dell'unificazione italiana* (Turin, Einaudi, 1960).

[44] Cf. columns 7 and 8 of Table 0.1 in the Introduction.

immediately after unification (in the form of banditry), as well as that of later episodes of popular revolt involving, for example, the Fasci Siciliani (Sicilian peasant unions) during the early 1890s. Unfortunately, the activism of the State in the South was clearly visible when it came to collecting taxes, but not so much when it was a question of funding public works programmes.[45]

The new government dedicated a considerable amount of energy to its new scheme of income taxes, which included three different types of tax: a property tax on land, one on buildings, and a tax on personal non-property income . The first of these had already been implemented in all the pre-unification States, although the land-registers used for its calculation had differed from one State to another (see Chapter 1), as had the rates applied. Due to the logistic difficulties involved in an immediate unification of all land-registers, the new government passed a law (14 July 1864) introducing a provisional adjustment based on various indirect indicators of land value in different areas; this system survived longer than had originally been foreseen as a result of the lengthy and complicated process of drawing up the new register.[46] The tax on non-rural buildings was only in existence in the Piedmont and Lombardy regions, and the law passed on 26 January 1865 introduced it throughout the country at a fixed rate of 16.25 per cent of taxable income.

The tax on personal non-property income, on the other hand, was a completely new tax—no pre-unification State had ever imposed a tax of this kind—and it was modelled on the English income tax. Introduced on 14 July 1864, it was applicable to all forms of income apart from those already taxed separately, that is, land and buildings. There were very few exemptions from this tax, and one, concerning the interest earned on government bonds, was in fact abolished by a law passed on 7 July 1868.

A second group of taxes concerned transactions; these included a tax on inheritance, a registration duty, a stamp duty, and a series of other minor taxes, all of which were reorganized and standardized in this period. Consumer goods were hit by a third group of taxes which differed in some important ways from anything in existence prior to unification, in particular with the introduction of a new kind of duty on the manufacture of some goods; at first its application was

[45] Nitti was the first of several writers to argue that government fiscal policy was to have more harsh consequences for the South than for the North of the country, *Il bilancio dello stato dal 1862 al 1896–97* (Naples, 1900). The statistician Corrado Gini criticized Nitti's conclusions, underlining the fact that 'the statistical data available at the moment [1914] do not allow us to make an accurate comparison between the fiscal burden imposed by the State in the various regions, and the benefit accrued in those regions', *L'ammontare e la composizione della ricchezza delle Nazioni* (Turin, Bocca, 1914), 277. For a survey of existing studies in this field, together with an estimate for the tax year 1952/53, cf. G. De Meo, 'Un tentativo di determinazione del carico tributario nelle regioni italiane', *Moneta e Credito*, 29–30 (1955).

[46] However, during the course of the drawing up of the land-register, as each regional section of it was finished, so that section became effective. Cf. R. Nieri, 'Minghetti e il problema della tassazione agraria nell'Italia unita', in R. Gherardi and N. Matteucci (eds.), *Marco Minghetti statista e pensatore politico* (Bologna, Il Mulino, 1988).

limited to the production of beer and mineral water, but subsequently it was extended to the manufacture of spirits, of sugar, and the milling of cereals. This latter duty on the production of flour, introduced by law on 7 July 1868, was met by a wave of popular protest, as it hit at the foundation of the Italian people's diet, and was abolished in 1884. On top of these duties, there were also customs duties (although they only began to make a significant contribution to the State's coffers after 1878), a local excise on goods consumed which was increasingly paid directly to the councils, and finally a series of duties paid by consumers on products that were state monopolies, such as gunpowder, salt, tobacco, quinine, and the state lottery.

As for communal taxes, these included the above-mentioned excise tax, as well as other forms of personal taxation (such as taxes on the running of local pubs and shops, a family tax, and a tax on town animals). Furthermore, a law passed on 20 March 1865 gave local councils (and provinces) the power to introduce surcharges on top of national income taxes. This system, which could give local government the possibility to cover expenditure, was however modified by a further law, passed on 11 March 1870, which favoured state taxation at the expense of the local one; as a result, local government became heavily indebted, due also to the fact that is was financially liable for a whole range of expenses which would normally have been the responsibility of central government: the cost of local courts, primary schools and technical high schools, as well as communal and provincial roads.[47] Whereas a complete reorganization of local government finances would have to wait until 1931, despite the presentation of a whole series of projects before that date, the State was forced to do something about the debts incurred by local government: this it did by increasing the power of the Cassa Depositi e Prestiti (Cassa DDPP) to attract deposits. This institution had been set up on 17 May 1863, along the lines of a similar kind of institution in existence in Piedmont, in order to attract savings which it then lent out to local councils, provincial government, and charitable institutes, so that it could be used for carrying out works of public utility and public assistance. From 1876 onwards, the Cassa DDPP was given the greater part of post-office savings (deposited with a whole network of local post offices spread throughout the country), with the aim of increasing support to local councils and also investment in government bonds.

Despite some weakness as far as local government finances were concerned, on the whole the new fiscal system proved to be capable of supporting the new levels of public spending that governments were to establish until the First World War. It proved to be advanced in the field of income tax, but somewhat backward as far as duties on consumer goods were concerned (these were sometimes very old-fashioned and of a regressive nature).

[47] Cf. F. Volpi, *Le finanze dei comuni e delle province del regno d'Italia* (Turin, ILTE, 1962), and U. Rogari, *La crisi della finanza locale dal 1861 ai nostri giorni attraverso l'esame dei bilanci e dei conti consuntivi* (Florence, Sandròn, 1980).

Nevertheless, the weight of these regressive taxes was kept around 50 per cent until the Second World War,[48] which was not a particularly high level, comparatively speaking.[49]

The two creators of this tax system, Quintino Sella and Marco Minghetti (both members of the Historical Right), often disagreed on policy matters, but in this case, 'placing their trust in the nation's sense of public spirit, had the courage to get the heaviest taxes one could have imagined possible sanctioned by the State, and proceeded to go about collecting them with the greatest of energy'.[50]

Before looking in more detail at the situation in terms of tax revenue and budget deficit, we should mention that the tax collection system was also reorganized during this period. The model used by the State was the Lombard one, which involved the use of private tax-collectors who were obliged to leave a deposit which corresponded to the size of the area they were to cover;[51] however, the law in question had a hard passage as a result of local resistance, and was only passed, in an amended form, on 20 April 1871. As a result of this law, 78 per cent of all tax offices changed hands (the percentage was only 20 per cent in the North however), while only 30 per cent could at the time be assigned through the auction system (62 per cent of those in the North). The economic cost of the operation was very high, but the tax-collection system was at least guaranteed to be relatively safe and reliable. What could not be avoided, however, was the growth of clientelistic practices in the poorer parts of the country, with powerful tax-collectors abusing their powers at the expense of the local population, with the result that trust in the State remained weaker than ever among those who had already suffered at the hands of pre-unification governments.

Table 5.2 shows the trend in tax revenue for the period between 1866 and 1913. Italian public finance started off with a large governmental budget deficit, and some relatively minor imbalances in local finance: in 1862, State expenditure was only 58 per cent covered by revenue, whereas that of local government was 94 per cent covered in 1863. The situation worsened during 1866, a year of war, as we can see from the first line of Table 5.2, and in 1868, public expenditure was still only 73 per cent covered. However, by 1872 there was a dramatic improvement, and the State's budget was much healthier from

[48] Brosio and Marchese, *Il potere di spendere*, 202–3.

[49] France did not introduce an income tax until the First World War.

[50] A. Plebano, *Storia della finanza italiana nei primi quaranta anni dall'Unificazione*, ii (Turin, Roux e Viarengo, 1900; repr. Padua, Cedam, 1960), 2. Brosio and Marchese, seeing that the elasticity of total tax yield with respect to GDP was greater during the period 1866–1914 than in subsequent years, write: 'The impoverished Italy of the first 50 years of unification, governed by a political class belonging to a restricted élite, which was opposed, both in terms of ideology and interests, to an increase in taxation expressed a fiscal effort greater than that of the governments of the subsequent years' (*Il potere di spendere*, 85).

[51] Frascani, *Finanza, economia ed intervento pubblico*, ch. 1.

Table 5.2. Government and local authority revenue, and % coverage of public spending, 1866–1913 (millions of current lire)[a]

	State			Local authorities			Overall public sector			
	Revenue (1)	Non-tax revenue (%) (2)	Coverage of spending (%) (3)	Revenue (4)	Non-tax revenue (%) (5)	Coverage of spending (%) (6)	Coverage of spending (%) (7)	Non-tax revenue (%) (8)	Surplus (+) or deficit (−) (9)	Surplus or deficit as % of GDP at factor costs[b] (10)
1866	610	16.4	44	241	28.2	79	50	19.7	−836	−13.0
1868	741	16.3	73	275	28.1	73	73	19.5	−374	− 4.8
1870	787	11.1	73	321	32.2	79	74	16.9	−382	− 5.0
1872	1,152	14.1	105	358	31.1	75	96	18.1	− 60	− 0.7
1876	1,179	16.0	107	399	26.2	78	98	18.6	− 37	− 0.4
1880	1,297	19.8	109	432	23.6	79	106	19.5	+103	+ 1.1
1886	1,624	24.3	119	491	23.1	79	102	24.0	+ 44	+ 0.5
1890	1,604	19.0	99	534	19.5	68	89	19.1	−273	− 2.8
1896	1,646	17.4	99	522	17.4	77	99	16.2	−103	− 1.1
1900	1,742	18.5	106	568	20.8	82	99	19.0	− 27	− 0.2
1906	2,010	19.4	108	682	19.4	80	106	18.3	+155	+ 1.3
1912	2,495	19.4	93	1,015	27.1	65	82	21.7	−747	− 4.5
1913	2,573	19.9	93	1,040	27.9	73	86	22.2	−564	− 3.3

[a] Current revenue only (capital account excluded).

[b] In order to be consistent with the methods used in Table 5.1, the figures for GDP are those calculated at factor cost by ISTAT in *Indagine statistica.*

Sources: Author's calculations based on G. Brosio and C. Marchese, *Il potere de spendere*, F. Cavazzuti, 'Ricerca sulla dinamica della finanza locale in Italia', in *Studi di finanza pubblica* (Milan, Giuffré, 1967); Ministero del Tesoro, Regionera Generale dello Stato, *Il bilancio dello stato italiano dal 1862 al 1967* (Rome, 1969).

the point of view of current expenditure,[52] a situation which was to continue as such, if we disregard the occasional problem during the early 1890s and at the end of the Giolitti years. Minghetti and Sella's fiscal measures were thus a great success. Local government finances, on the other hand, continued to show a persistent deficit (column 6), which had a negative effect on the general position of public finances in Italy (column 7), although the conclusion reached above about the positive trend of Italian public finances remains largely unaltered.

There were thus three periods during which 'deficit spending' *à la* Keynes was carried out (see column 10): the first 15 years of this period, when the State was involved in reactivating the stagnant economy it had inherited; the crisis years between the end of the 1880s and the beginning of the 1890s, when state intervention again played a vital role, particularly in the context of the banking disaster; finally, the last years of the Giolitti governments, during which public expenditure rose noticeably, particularly in the military sector (as a result of the war in Libya). However, before presenting an overall judgement of the effects of this deficit spending, we need to consider the way the State went about financing it.

The decisive years were again the early ones, when decisions were made by the finance ministers of the Historical Right. Initially, a massive campaign was conducted with the aim of financing the public debt through the issue of the most common form of bond available at the time—consols, issued at a nominal interest rate of 5 per cent—subscriptions for which were also common outside Italy, in particular through the Parisian Stock Exchange. The circulation of one-year treasury bills increased in this period, although their importance remained relatively small. As a result of this policy, between 1861 and 1865 public debt climbed from the equivalent of 45 per cent to 78 per cent of the nation's GDP.[53] While the Italian Parliament was debating new tax legislation, aimed at balancing the State's budget, Sella decided to try and put a halt to the rise in public debt by selling off some of the nation's public property.

The period between 1864 and 1868 thus saw a massive operation, involving the privatization of common lands and the sale of Church property, which

[52] Note that capital account expenditure (and revenue) is not included in Tables 5.1 and 5.2. This capital account saw large positive balances between 1864 and 1868, due to the sale of government property; however, subsequent balances were always negative, particularly so during the years of the Left's railway programme and the nationalization of the railways carried out by Giolitti. For an analysis of the State's bookkeeping system, cf. R. Faucci, *Finanza, amministrazione e pensiero economico. Il caso della contabilità di Stato da Cavour al Fascismo* (Turin, Einaudi, 1975).

[53] All of the material concerning the public debt is taken from a research project of mine which is still largely unpublished. Only two sections have so far appeared in print: Zamagni, 'Debito pubblico e creazione di un nuovo apparato fiscale nell'Italia unificata (1861–1876)', in Ente Einaudi (ed.), *Il disavanzo pubblico in Italia: natura strutturale e politiche di rientro*, ii (Bologna, Il Mulino, 1992) and G. Salvemini and V. Zamagni, 'Finanza pubblica e indebitamento tra le due guerre mondiali: il finanziamento del settore statale', forthcoming in a collection of essays edited by F. Cotula (Bari, Laterza, 1993). See also M. De Cecco (ed.), *L'Italia e il sistema finanziario internazionale 1861–1914* (Bari, Laterza, 1990).

yielded large sums during these years, and somewhat smaller sums during the years that followed—at least up until 1875. The first part of this operation, planned back in 1862, was monetized in 1864 through the advances made by the Joint-Stock Company for the Sale of Public Goods: this company agreed to give the Italian government an advance of 150 million lire, and then to see to the sale of the property involved. The second part of the plan involved setting up another joint-stock company, this time the project of Ferrara during his brief spell at the Finance Ministry; Ferrara's project was not approved by Parliament and the sale was to be run directly by the State in collaboration with the Banca Nazionale, and yielded a slower, less concentrated flow of funds. Overall, more than 3 million hectares of land were privatized (as mentioned in Chapter 1), equivalent to 12 per cent of all farm land, and of this total, 2.5 million hectares were located in the South (representing one-quarter of total farmland in that part of Italy).[54] The pressing need to raise funds meant that the methods used to sell the land were often ill-conceived, and varied from one another: the law was not at all clear on this matter, and land prices fell as a result. However, perhaps the worst result of all was that these measures did not produce any noticeable increase in the number of small and medium-size landowners.

As well as selling off public lands, the State decided to sell the railway network in 1865, and in 1868 it granted a 15-year concession on the running of the tobacco monopoly—to an organization entitled Regìa Cointeressata dei Tabacchi (Profit-Sharing Tobacco Monopoly)—in exchange for an advance of 180 million lire. The government turned to all available potential sources of revenue, therefore, in order temporarily to dam up its budget losses, and to ensure that the public deficit did not get out of control. Naturally enough, this need to privatize fitted in conveniently with the economic philosophy of the Historical Right, which expected the private management of land, the railways, and the rest to lead to an increase in efficiency and profitability. This expectation was, however, not realized, as we know, because of the social and economic conditions existing in Italy at the time.

The international financial crisis of 1866, together with the outbreak of a third war of independence, meant that further state intervention was necessary: in April 1866 the price of consols fell to below 50 per cent of the nominal value on the Paris Stock Exchange, producing a real interest rate of around 10 per cent. As a result, the banks were forced to squeeze credit, and this led to a run to the banks' counters (to change lire for gold). The Finance Minister, Scialoja, declared the inconvertibility of the paper money in circulation, forcing the Banca Nazionale to provide the Treasury with a loan of 250 million lire. Subsequently, he also decreed the issue of a forced redeemable loan, which was very successful due to the patriotic fever sweeping through the country.

[54] G. Catalano, 'La fine dei "possessi plebei": svincolo e privatizzazione delle proprietà comuni della terra dopo l'unità d'Italia', graduation thesis, Florence University, 1985–6.

The most innovative decision, however, was that of monetizing a part of the debt: after the initial sum of 250 million lire, further agreements were drawn up with the Banca Nazionale and, subsequently, with a consortium of all banks of issue, taking the final total at the end of the 1870s to 940 million lire's worth of inconvertible 'state banknotes'. An end was put to what was seen as an anomalous situation in 1883 with the help of an international loan in gold, aimed at covering some 600 million of the 940 million banknotes that had been put into circulation.[55]

It is clear then that monetary policy was dictated by the State's financial needs during the first 20 years of Italian unity. A more comprehensive view of this monetary policy will be given in the next section; for the moment I would like to conclude this brief historical survey of the Italian public debt by looking at the period that followed the abolition of inconvertibility (see Table 5.3).

With the addition of the international loan in gold, the Italian public debt exceeded national income (see column 6 of Table 5.3), and was to remain at this level until the end of the nineteenth century as a result of the railway policy pursued by the Left together with their policy of extinguishing local government debts through state intervention. During the first years of the twentieth century, however, continual budget surpluses meant that there was no longer any need to issue government bonds to finance expenditure; consols rose above parity level as a result, thus making it possible to lighten the burden of the public debt on current public expenditure, through lowering the rate of interest from 5 per cent before tax (which was equivalent to 20 per cent) to 3.5 per cent net of tax. This operation, known as 'interest rate conversion', was successfully carried out on 1 July 1906. Looking at column 8 of Table 5.3, one can see that this produced a significant decrease in the burden of interest payments, which had at one point amounted to as much as one-third of total government expenditure. Central government spending seemed to have finally settled down into a position of equilibrium, with the budget balanced, the amount of public bonds held abroad at a lowest-ever level (see column 7), and the burden of interest payments finally at an acceptable level.

In his report on 'interest rate conversion', Luzzatti wrote with satisfaction:

> We can be patriotically proud of current developments! They represent the epilogue to what has been the heroic management of the country's finances and monetary circulation, made necessary by a certain fatal laxity in the past: they represent the long-suffering of Italian taxpayers' deserved reward for their role as the real heroes of financial consolidation. If we compare the present historic occasion with those days not long gone when public credit lay in ruins, and the premium on gold stood at the 20 per

[55] Details of the operation are given in C. Supino, *Storia della circolazione cartacea in Italia (dal 1860 al 1928)* (Milan, SEI, 1929). There are some interesting points on this international loan in G. Berta, *Capitali in gioco. Cultura economica e vita finanziaria nella City di fine Ottocento* (Venice, Marsilio, 1990).

Table 5.3. The public debt, 1861–1913

	Overall total (million current lire)[a]	Composition (%)			Effective rate of return on consols (%)[c]	Debt/GDP ratio (%)[d]	Debt in foreign hands (%)[e]	Share of interest payments on total state expenditure[f]
		Consols	Redeemable debt	Floating debt[b]				
	(1)	(2)	(3)	(4)	(5)	(6)	(7)	(8)
1861	3,102	82.02	16.72	1.26	7.11[g]	45	21.2	15.5[g]
1866	6,121	82.21	9.41	8.38	8.83	77	30.6	22.4
1870	8,342	59.23	29.53	11.24	7.98	96	25.1	38.7
1876	9,784	62.37	25.07	12.56	5.69	95	35.0	32.7
1880	9,999	66.18	20.49	13.33	4.66	87	33.9	35.5
1883	12,133	71.18	17.05	11.77	4.80	114	28.9	29.1
1889	12,613	68.60	24.46	6.94	4.53	116	41.5	29.0
1896	13,415	66.88	24.73	8.39	4.30	119	29.2	33.5
1900	13,921	69.05	22.10	8.85	4.01	111	23.1	33.5
1906	14,504	69.33	20.58	10.09	3.60	100	13.5	25.0
1913	16,462	61.05	25.64	13.31	3.60	80	20.2	16.6

[a] Not including bonds held by issuing banks.
[b] Includes Treasury bonds, advances made by the issuing banks, current account at the Banco di Napoli, and deposits collected by the Cassa Depositi e Prestiti (net of reinvestment made in govt. bonds).
[c] Taking into account Stock Exchange quotation of govt. bonds.
[d] GDP at market prices, provided by P. Ercolani (ed.), 'Documentazione statistica di base', in G. Fuà (ed.), *Lo sviluppo economico in Italia*, iii (Milan, Angeli, 1969).
[e] On the basis of public debt interests paid abroad.
[f] Actual yearly payments.
[g] 1862.

Source: V. Zamagni, 'Il debito pubblico in Italia 1861–1945', unpublished research.

cent mark, then we can all feel proud of recent developments, developments which show that we are part of a reborn nation guaranteed to attain greatness.[56]

However, Italy's involvement in the First World War inevitably meant a resurgence of serious financial problems for the State.

4. MONETARY POLICY AND SALVAGE OPERATIONS

Italy's monetary policy during the first 35 years after unification was, as we have seen, heavily influenced by the pressing needs of public finance, as well as by the difficulty of controlling circulation with the plethora of banks of issue that existed at the time. When both of these problems were on the way to being solved (see Chapter 4 and subsection 5.3), monetary policy became much more effective, and results were produced much more quickly.

Immediately after unification, an officially fixed exchange rate was established between the various coins in circulation and the Piedmontese lira. A law passed on 24 August 1862 led to the creation of the Italian lira, which was worth the same as the Piedmontese lira, and the French form of bimetallism was introduced, with a fixed ratio between silver and gold of 15.5.[57] This decision was taken in order to facilitate trading relations with France, Switzerland, and Belgium, who had similar systems. In fact, in December 1865 the Unione Monetaria Latina was set up so as to prevent a drain of silver coins during periods when the value of silver on international markets was higher than its legal worth: this Union, between Italy, France, Switzerland, and Belgium (with Greece joining in 1868), had the task of seeing to the standardization of government measures concerning the question of silver coins. It had a difficult life right up until the end of the nineteenth century, at which point the members of the Union themselves had opted for the adoption of the gold standard. Consequently, 'this Union, reduced to a mere façade, was to survive at least formally until the 1920s, simply because none of the members took the trouble to dismantle it'.[58] Nevertheless, the Union represented the first sign of the need for international co-ordination of monetary policies in a world that was becoming increasingly more interdependent.

Thus the new Kingdom of Italy started off within a financial system based on the convertibility of paper money into gold and silver; however, as we have already seen, this convertibility had to be abandoned on 1 May 1866 in order to stop the run to the banks and to finance the State with bank advances. The inconvertible system lasted until 1883, and this period saw an enormous expansion in that part of the paper money circulation issued for governmental needs: there were an estimated two billion lire in circulation in 1862, of which

[56] *Atti Parlamentari*, Camera dei deputati, 1904–6 Session, XXII Legislature, vol. 8, 9,343.

[57] M. Roccas, 'L'Italia e il sistema monetario internazionale dagli anni '60 agli anni '90 del secolo scorso', in *Temi di discussione del Servizio Studi della Banca d'Italia*, 92 (1987).

[58] Ibid. 27.

1,800 million consisted of coins, while only 200 million took the form of banknotes;[59] whereas by 1882, the coins in circulation amounted to only 1,300 million lire, while the value of the banknotes had risen to 1,500 million lire, of which 940 million had been issued on behalf of the State.[60]

This thus represented a rapid change-over from coins to paper money, and was to be a permanent characteristic of Italian monetary circulation; it also marked the growth in importance of the banks, as paper currency was not hoarded in the same way as coins were. Toniolo concludes that 'because this reduced transactional and intermediation costs, it can be considered a lasting contribution towards economic development'[61] to be attributed to the need to finance the State's budget deficit.[62]

These changes produced some inflationary effects, of course, which were more pronounced during 1872 (over 13 per cent) and 1873 (over 6 per cent); at the same time, the lira depreciated slightly against gold and consequently against other convertible currencies. If, as it would seem, the lira's depreciation was not completely compensated for by domestic price changes,[63] one would have expected Italian exports to have been more competitive: in fact, their volume did increase, although it is impossible to show exactly whether this was due to the depreciation of the lira, as no in-depth analysis of the question has been carried out so far. On the whole, however, both inflation and depreciation were relatively limited, although academics and politicians at the time were forever complaining about the situation and preparing plans for the lira's reversion back to convertibility.

It was Agostino Magliani, Finance Minister in the Depretis government, who saw to the passing of the law (in April 1881) which was to bring back the gold standard during 1883, as mentioned above. Although the operation was in itself a technical success, it happened to take place during the worst years of the agrarian crisis and at a time of great industrial expansion, which together led to a worsening of the balance of payments, to the immobilization of the banks, and to the reappearance of imbalances in public finance. This in turn quickly brought on the famous banking crisis (which we looked at in Chapter 4) and, from the monetary policy point of view, led to a series of measures between

[59] G. Toniolo, *Storia economica dell'Italia liberale 1850–1918* (Bologna, Il Mulino, 1988), 93.

[60] R. De Mattia (ed.), *I bilanci degli istituti di emissione italiani 1845–1936* (2 vols., Rome, Staderini, 1967). According to De Mattia's figures, the circulation of coins amounted to 1 billion lire in 1862, whereas paper circulation was equivalent to 125 million lire.

[61] Toniolo, *Storia economica*, 104.

[62] P. Masi, 'L'influenza del debito pubblico sulla costruzione dei sistemi finanziari: il caso italiano 1860–1893', *Rivista di storia economica*, 6 (1989). The author argues that the influence of the public debt went well beyond the creation and circulation of paper money, having an effect also on the profitability of financial intermediation, which in turn constituted an incentive towards the setting up of new banks and the reinforcing of those already in existence.

[63] For quantitative data, see M. Fratianni and F. Spinelli, 'Currency Competition, Fiscal Policy and the Money Supply Process in Italy from Unification to World War I', *Journal of European Economic History*, 14 (1985).

January and February 1894 which saw the suspension once again of the gold standard.[64] However, the 1893 banking act had bound the three remaining banks of issue to guaranteeing that 40 per cent of circulation was covered by metallic reserves. This, together with the fact that public finances were run along correct lines during this period—the State made no requests for an increase in legal (inconvertible) circulation—meant that the Italian monetary system did *de facto* remain tied to the gold standard, albeit with a greater degree of flexibility than before.[65] After the noticeable depreciation of the lira in 1893–4, the exchange rate improved, and reached parity in 1903. In the years to follow, it fluctuated to a limited degree; for a few years it even showed a slight tendency to appreciate, and then in the pre-war years this became a tendency to depreciate.[66]

After the strong immobilization due to the early 1890s' banking disaster had been eliminated, and the international situation had improved, the Banca d'Italia found itself in a position to get a stronger grip on the country's monetary policy, particularly when Bonaldo Stringher had become the Bank's director (in 1900). It was true that Stringher still had to look after the Bank's private interests, as it had preserved its private clientele and continued to compete with other banks on this level;[67] however, he became more and more involved in supervising the general financial affairs of the nation from his position in the Bank, especially at times of crisis on both the domestic and the international front. Ciocca has shown that the Bank of Italy succeeded in obtaining government permission to intervene freely in the foreign exchange market, and that it was also active in discount-rate policy-decisions, taking 'the agricultural and manufacturing situation as one of the variables taken into account when deciding the discount rate'.[68] If monetary policy during the period from 1910 to 1913 ended up having a somewhat restrictive effect at a time when business was not particularly flourishing, this cannot be attributed to negligence on Stringher's part, but rather to the fact that 'Stringher lacked the ability to assert

[64] For details, see Supino, *Storia della circolazione.*

[65] Italy only officially went back to the gold standard in Dec. 1927 (in the form of the gold exchange standard). M. Fratianni and F. Spinelli confirm what has been said here in the text when they conclude that 'Italian experience did not differ on the whole from what it would have been had the country adhered formally to the [gold] standard throughout' ('Italy in the Gold Standard period, 1861–1914', in M. D. Bordo and A. J. Schwartz (eds.), *A Retrospective on the Classical Gold Standard 1821–1931* (Chicago, Chicago University Press, 1984), 429; see also the same authors' study 'Una panoramica qualitativa della storia monetaria dell'Italia: 1861–1980', *Quaderni di economia e banca*, 9 (1989).

[66] See F. Spinelli, 'Le determinanti del cambio della lira italiana dall'unità al primo conflitto mondiale', *Annali scientifici del Dipartimento di Economia dell'Università degli Studi di Trento*, 1 (1988).

[67] P. Ciocca shows how Stringher tried to restrict excessive competition in the field of interest rates ('La ricerca di una politica monetaria 1900–13', in *L'instabilità dell'economia* (Turin, Einaudi, 1987). On the Bank of Italy evolution between its foundation and the First World War, see F. Bonelli (ed.), *La Banca d'Italia dal 1894 al 1913. Momenti della formazione di una Banca centrale* (Bari, Laterza, 1991).

[68] Ciocca, *L'instabilità dell'economia*, 157.

his views in the face of his "doctrinaire" colleagues, with whom he sometimes openly came to verbal blows'.[69]

Another of the Bank's roles during Stringher's time was that of heading salvage operations involving banks and industrial concerns. Since the policy of salvage operations did not originate during the Giolitti years, we need to go back a little further to find its origins. Toniolo has recently come up with the thesis that the introduction of inconvertibility in 1866 constituted 'the first important salvage operation put into practice by the lender of last resort in our country'.[70] Even if we have no proof to this effect, it is clear that the Italian government was already prepared at that time to intervene in a serious crisis. Less than 30 years later, there was another occasion on which this willingness to intervene could be put to the test: the intervention in the 1890s' banking crisis was built around the new banking act together with the foundation of the Banca d'Italia in 1893, as we saw in Chapter 4.

Once the Bank had been set up, it took over the important task of intervening in financial crises on the government's behalf. Its first successful operation was carried out in 1907, when a crisis originating abroad had particularly dramatic effects on the Italian Stock Exchange and on one of the most important banks of that time, the Società Bancaria Italiana (SBI). The Bank set up two consortia and, although not taking a direct part in operations, lent its support through the discounting mechanism: the first consortium lent support to the SBI, while the second helped support share values. In order to have a freer hand in circumstances of this kind, the Bank put forward a bill, which was passed on 31 December 1907, making existing limitations on monetary circulation more flexible, widening the range of activities that the banks of issue could be involved in, and reducing the fiscal burden of these banks.[71]

Within a short span of time, the Bank had to set up yet another banking consortium, this time with the aim of resolving the 1911 steel crisis; again, the Bank did not take an active part in the consortium, but it did help the SBI in lightening its debts. It was this experience, together with Italy's entry into war, that led Stringher to give the Bank an operative 'arm' in the event of further banking or industrial crises: on 20 December 1914, the Consorzio per Sovvenzioni su Valori Industriali (Industrial Loans Consortium)—CSVI—was set up.[72] This consortium, which was originally meant to be a temporary

[69] Ibid. 162. On Italian monetary policy, see also P. Ganugi, 'Financial deepening, risparmio forzato e accumulazione in Italia, 1881–1936', *Rivista di storia economica*, 6 (1989) and F. Spinelli, *Per la storia monetaria dell'Italia* (Turin, Giappichelli, 1989).

[70] Toniolo, *Storia economica*, 104.

[71] For full details of the 1907 crisis, see F. Bonelli, *La crisi del 1907. Una tappa dello sviluppo industriale in Italia* (Turin, Einaudi, 1971).

[72] A. M. Biscaini, P. Gnes, and A. Roselli, 'Origine e sviluppo del Consorzio Sovvenzioni su Valori Industriali durante il Governatorato Stringher', *Bancaria*, 41 (1985). The Bank of Italy succeeded in getting other banks to put up a part of CSVI's capital, but held on to the operative reigns (governing it through its own branches).

institution, dealing with short-term operations (4–6 months) and not involving enormous sums, subsequently grew in size and importance, to the point where it was involved in massive post-war banking and industrial salvage operations, which we shall be looking at later. It filled the role of 'the Bank of Italy's special branch, acting as a temporary, emergency measure aimed at resolving temporary emergencies',[73] but with an incredible ability to move from one 'temporary emergency' to another.

[73] Ibid. 166.

6

Society and Culture

1. URBAN SOCIETY: WORKING CONDITIONS AND HEALTH

DUE to Italy's glorious medieval and Renaissance traditions, the country could boast a greater number of cities and towns than other comparable countries even before industrial development had taken off; the process of industrialization, while leading to the growth of some cities and towns, never really brought about a polarization of industry in one industrial 'capital', as happened in many other countries. Between 1881 and 1911, the percentage of the Italian population living in towns with more that 10,000 inhabitants rose from 34 per cent to 42.4 per cent, with a large part of their number being attracted towards towns situated within the 'industrial triangle',[1] especially the medium-sized ones.[2]

There were still no great waves of internal migration, however. All those cities that attracted new inhabitants did so largely from the nearby countryside and villages, and to a lesser extent from surrounding provinces; only a very small part of the new town-dwellers came from other regions or from abroad.[3] The first few company towns began to appear: Schio (built around the Rossi woollen-mill), Collegno (the Leumann cotton-mill), Capriate d'Adda (the Crespi cotton-mill), and Piazzola sul Brenta. The latter is an example of an industrial town integrated within a landed estate: it was the project of a rich landowner with progressive ideas—Count Camerini—who had brought under cultivation some agricultural areas through land-reclamation projects, while at the same time setting up factories that were to produce a whole range of products, including bricks, sulphuric acid, fertilizers, jute, and silk. At the same time as these agricultural and industrial projects were being got under way, the Count saw to the building of a completely new town, whose population was later

[1] For an analysis of demographic mobility within the context of industrialization at the beginning of this century, cf. G. Federico, 'Sviluppo industriale, mobilità della popolazione e mercato della forza-lavoro in Italia: una analisi macroeconomica', in SIDES, *La popolazione italiana nell'Ottocento* (Bologna, Clueb, 1985).

[2] G. Alberti's study, 'Sviluppo urbano e industrializzazione nell'Italia liberale: Note su un modello d'interdependenza', *Storia contemporanea*, 6 (1975), provides us with an accurate analysis of these medium-sized towns (from 20,000 to 50,000 inhabitants, taking into account only the urban centres, in the year 1911). Cf. also L. De Rosa, 'Urbanization and Industrialization in Italy (1861–1921)', *Journal of European Economic History*, 17 (1988), including the bibliography, and also E. Sori, 'Assetto e redistribuzione della popolazione italiana 1861–1961', in *L'economia italiana 1861–1940*.

[3] See Federico, 'Sviluppo industriale', and for Milan see A. De Maddalena, 'Rilievi sull'esperienza demografica ed economica milanese dal 1861 al 1915', in *L'economia italiana dal 1861 al 1961* (Milan, Giuffré, 1961).

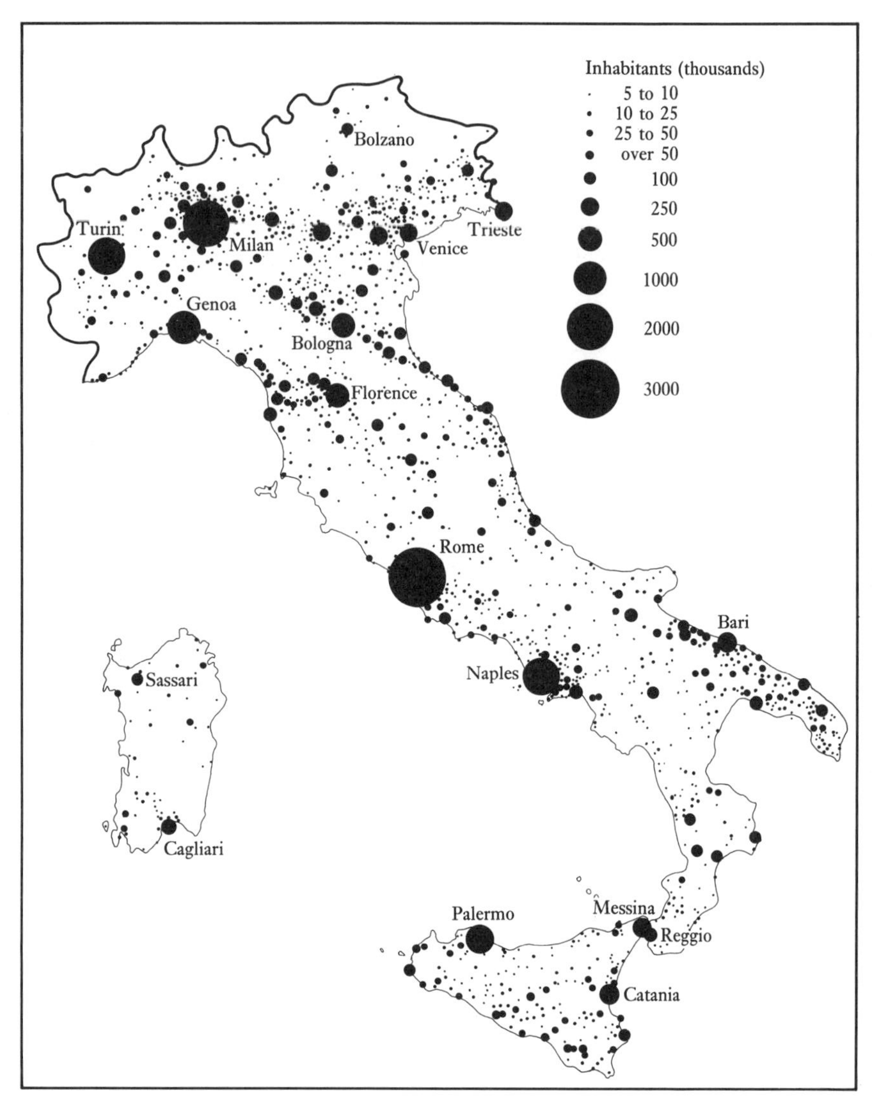

Fig. 6.1 Urban population, 1981

to reach 10,000.[4] In these new towns, electric lighting and drinking-water were an essential feature, together with a wide range of social services that were designed to care for the workers' health and education.[5]

The lot of working-class people was significantly harder in the large towns

[4] There is a detailed description in V. Fontana, *Il nuovo paesaggio dell'Italia giolittiana* (Bari, Laterza, 1981), 149 ff. Now the full history of the initiative is provided by C. Fumian, *La città del lavoro. Un'utopia industriale nel Veneto contemporaneo* (Venice, Marsilio, 1990).

[5] See *Villaggi operai in Italia. La Val Padana e Crespi d'Adda* (Turin, Einaudi, 1981).

and cities, however, as the latter were plagued with problems concerning the preservation of their historical centres, and consequently could offer very few solutions to the problem of working-class housing; as a result, one often saw a worsening of the housing situation (if only for a limited period in some cases). The first housing census, carried out in 1881, revealed that the cities were vastly overcrowded, with an average of 1.65 inhabitants per room,[6] although this figure was higher in cities such as Genoa, Naples, Rome, Milan, and Turin. More detailed data concerning the city of Milan show that there was a worsening of the situation between 1881 and 1911. In 1881, the number of inhabitants per room varied between 1.04 and 2.13, according to the zone; by 1911 there had been a considerable rise, with a variation from 2 to 3.78.[7] Many of the 'sad-looking housing blocks, veritable anthills where the working-class lives and proliferates'[8] were blocks of flats with communal toilets and no running water, which had to be fetched from the courtyard fountain. The efforts of the occasional co-operative society or charity made little difference to this situation.

The government finally decided to intervene in an effort to provide an incentive towards the construction of low-cost housing when it passed a law on 31 May 1903 which offered tax exemption, special credit facilities, and other favourable treatment to co-operatives, charitable organizations, and newly founded companies operating in this field. Twenty-two different organizations had already been founded by 1908,[9] and a great degree of energy went into low-cost housing projects, especially in the capital; during this period, blocks of flats were built in the Roman neighbourhoods of Testaccio, Garbatella, Monte Sacro, Trionfale, Flaminio, and Esquilino. The first projects of a similar nature to be got off the ground in Milan were the work of that famous charitable organization the Umanitaria, founded in 1893. The first 240 dwellings, finished in 1906,

> were equipped with lavatories, waste-disposal chutes, drinking-water, gas and electric lighting, the last of which was supplied at a reduced cost thanks to an agreement between the 'Edison Company' and the council. The typical one bedroom . . . was replaced by two rooms . . . A series of social services and facilities (a local library and open university, drawing-classes for men and domestic economics classes for women, a children's playschool, restaurants and co-operative shops) together with other facilities (toilets, showers, and wash-houses) were furnished in this urban experiment based on the principle of association, designed to fuel 'that great moral and economic force which we know as solidarity'.[10]

The alternative English model of urban development based on the small one-family dwelling situated in a garden suburb met with very little success in Italy. The president of the Milanese Unione Cooperativa, Luigi Buffoli, attempted to

[6] M. Casciato, 'L'abitazione e gli spazi domestici', in P. Melograni (ed.), *La famiglia italiana dall'Ottocento ad oggi* (Bari, Laterza, 1988), 528.

[7] V. Hunecke, 279.

[8] Taken from a manuscript of 1884, ibid. 280.

[9] It was only in 1935 that each province was forced to set up its own Istituto Autonomo per le Case Popolari.

[10] Casciato, 'L'abitazione', 556.

set up a new quarter just 10 km. from the heart of Milan's historical centre in a place called Cusano. His new development, called Milanino, got under way in 1909, but was gradually to run out of steam, and it finally came to a standstill in 1921, having found no new substantial support along the way. Old city walls, dating back to medieval or Renaissance times, were gradually pulled down in order to allow existing suburbs to be incorporated into the city's fabric, or to make space for the construction of brand-new urban quarters.[11]

The growth of the cities was obviously going to create significant organizational problems in the setting up and/or modification of public services. Services such as sewerage; water, gas, and electricity supplies; public lighting; urban transport; waste-collection; libraries and museums; and hospitals. While private companies were set up (sometimes with foreign capital—Belgian, French, German, English) with the aim of running some of these services, the predominant belief held at the end of the nineteenth century (especially among socialists and Catholics) was that municipal government would best ensure the fair and efficient running of public services; and this would also mean new blood for local government finances.[12] Both the working class and the middle class supported the request for 'the direct intervention of the local council in the production of local services'.[13] As a result, the government was forced to legislate on this matter, and it was law no. 103 of 29 March 1903 that gave municipal companies legal status;[14] and they were quickly set up to run the tram services, gas, water, and electricity supplies, the collection of rubbish, the building of low-cost housing, and were even involved in the opening of bakeries, pharmacies, and public baths.[15]

Some councils witnessed 'the beginning of that great tradition of municipal socialism which actively helped the lives of the less well-off, often through the realization of very ambitious projects'.[16] One example of such a council, which I have myself studied and written about, was that of Bologna: the city council brought the gas-supply under its control in 1900, and a section of the water-

[11] On the demolition of historical town walls and the gutting of historical centres, cf. I. Insolera, 'L'urbanistica', in *Storia d'Italia*, v: *I documenti* (Turin, Einaudi, 1973); on urban planning in general, see L. Gambi, 'Da cittá ad area metropolitana', ibid.

[12] R. Franco, 'Il dibattito sui servizi pubblici e le municipalizzazioni alla fine del sec. XIX', *Storia urbana*, 6 (1982). See also *Passato e presente*, 25 (1991), partly devoted to the provision of urban infrastructures, and C. Pavese, 'Dal cavallo al trolley: alle origini del trasporto pubblico urbano a Milano 1861–1989', *Annali di storia dell'impresa*, 7 (1991).

[13] G. Montemartini, 'Ancora di municipalizzazione', *Giornale degli economisti*, 38, 2nd series (1909), 325. On Montemartini and the 'Ufficio del lavoro' of MAIC, cf. V. Gallotta (ed.), *Cultura e lavoro nell'età giolittiana* (Naples, Guida, 1989) and id., 'Scienza economica e riformismo: Giovanni Montemartini e l'Ufficio del lavoro', in *La cultura delle riforme in Italia fra Otto e Novecento. I Montemartini* (Milan, La Pietra, 1986).

[14] Cf. G. Pischel, *La municipalizzazione in Italia. Ieri, oggi, domani* (Rome, 1965).

[15] Unfortunately there is no available general analysis of the results of this municipalization movement during the Giolitti years. For an example of an analysis of a specific area, see A. Berselli, F. Dalla Peruta, and A. Varni (eds.), *La municipalizzazione in area padana* (Milan, Angeli, 1988).

[16] G. Sapelli, *Comunità e mercato. Socialisti, cattolici e 'governo economico municipale' agli inizi del XX secolo* (Bologna, Il Mulino, 1986), 37.

supply was later municipalized; then during the socialist government it founded a local authority body (Ente Autonomo di Consumo) which ran 20 or so grocery stores, a wine store, a restaurant, a bar, an enormous bakery, and even bought a ship so as to guarantee a supply of coal to the municipal gas authority during the war.[17]

The administration of health care in Italy had been seen to by religious and civil institutions since the sixteenth and seventeenth centuries, as in other parts of Europe. It had been part of a whole series of social services, aimed at potentially or really marginalized segments of society that could have posed a threat to the existing order; these services included 'the hospitals, the homes, the religious associations, the charities, and the poor houses—which were set up to provide shelter for orphans and the terminally-ill, young maidens in danger from the unscrupulous outside world, the local poor, the "legions" of foreigners, convicts and prisoners, and for young women and widows who were in danger'.[18] Italian governments were slow at first to reorganize and regulate these kinds of charitable and religious institutions. On 20 November 1859, a law was passed setting up local health councils, but they had a merely consultative role to play.[19] The 1865 Local Authorities Act (mentioned above) created the figure of the municipal GP, while public health became the Home Secretary's responsibility (and thus that of prefects and mayors), and therefore no attempt was made to set up competent, specialized bodies in this field.

A National Health Board, provincial doctors, and local health offices were only created with the 1888 Health Act and the 1890 Charitable Institutions Act;[20] at the same time, the management and organization of hospitals was radically changed, so that they were now able to undertake medical experimentation, and could take in non-resident patients,[21] and local authorities were obliged to increase their financial contribution towards the running of these newly reorganized hospitals. These were the years of the great 'medical revolution',[22] which saw the discovery of those bacteria and parasites responsible for 'social' diseases such as malaria and tuberculosis, or for epidemic diseases like typhoid, cholera, and diphtheria; it also saw the

[17] V. Zamagni, 'L'economia', in R. Zangheri (ed.), *Bologna* (Bari, Laterza, 1986).

[18] J. S. Woolf, *Porca miseria. Poveri e assistenza nella età moderna* (Bari, Laterza, 1988), 31.

[19] G. Ognibeni, 'Legislazione ed organizzazione sanitaria nella seconda metà dell'Ottocento', in M. L. Betri and A. Gigli Marchetti (eds.), *Salute e classi lavoratrici in Italia dall'Unità al fascismo* (Milan, Angeli, 1982).

[20] F. Della Peruta, 'Sanità pubblica e legislazione sanitaria dall'Unità a Crispi', *Studi Storici*, 21 (1980), and S. Lepre, *Le difficoltà dell'assistenza. Le Opere Pie in Italia fra '800 e '900* (Rome, Bulzoni, 1988). On the transition from voluntary charity to public assistance, see A. Tonelli, *Per carità ricevuta. Povertà e assistenza in Romagna fra 800 e 900* (Milan, Angeli, 1991).

[21] P. Frascani, *Ospedale e società in età liberale* (Bologna, Il Mulino, 1986) and also id. (ed.), *Sanità e società. Abruzzi, Campania, Puglia, Basilicata, Calabria, secoli XVII–XX* (Udine, Casamassima, 1990). For a rural area, see L. D'Antone, *Scienza e governo del Territorio. Medici, ingegneri, agronomi e urbanisti nel Tavoliere delle Puglie 1865–1965* (Milan, Angeli, 1990).

[22] P. Melograni, 'Medicina e igiene tra Ottocento e Novecento', in P. Melograni and S. Ricossa (eds.), *Le rivoluzioni del benessere* (Bari, Laterza, 1988).

introduction of the first specific remedies, such as quinine against malaria,[23] and organic chemistry products, such as aspirin. Antiseptic medication was becoming standard practice in hospitals, thus making it possible to carry out more complicated surgical operations, and raising hygiene levels as a whole.[24] 'The number of patients cured in the new Kingdom's hospitals rose by 50 per cent between 1885 and 1902',[25] while the number of beds available increased by 58 per cent between 1885 and 1914.[26]

While in most cases 'the elimination of certain deadly diseases through medical-pharmacological control and a system of health care was more effective than economic and social change'[27] in lowering death rates, in the case of one very common 'social' disease—pellagra—its noticeable reduction between the end of the nineteenth century and the First World War was due to an improvement, if only marginal, in the living standards of those peasants living in the 'pellagra triangle' (Veneto, Lombardy, and Emilia–Romagna).[28] Although it was still not known at the time that pellagra was caused by a vitamin deficiency (in this case vitamin PP—niacin—which is not present in maize, the basic food of the peasant communities in these regions),[29] the fact that a richer and more varied diet was enough to prevent and cure pellagra was certainly common knowledge at the time.[30] The problem was that pellagra was an 'incurable' disease for this very reason: that is, in order to rid the countryside of pellagra, the social relations that existed in these areas would have had to be revolutionized, and this was something that only started to happen towards the end of the nineteenth century. The State only decided to do something in 1902, when it introduced a law prohibiting the sale of unripe or rotten maize, and forced the local authorities to take responsibility for the treatment of the worst cases of the disease.

The period between unification and the First World War was also marked by a battle against charlatans and witchdoctors, a battle conducted largely through

[23] G. Cosmacini writes: 'The control over, containment and reduction of mortality and illness caused by malaria are the results of a winning bet, made by the health authorities between 1900 and 1915 on the possibility of "human reclamation" through the generalized use of quinine', in *Storia della medicina e della sanità in Italia* (Bari, Laterza, 1987), 409. Cf. also F. Bonelli, 'La malaria nella storia demografica ed economica d'Italia', *Studi Storici* (1966) and V. A. Sironi, *Le officine delle salute. Storia del farmaco e della sua industria in Italia* (Bari, Laterza, 1922).

[24] The cramped conditions and the lack of effective methods of disinfecting the hospitals meant that there was a high risk of infection among hospital patients. Frascani, *Ospedale e società*, 155 ff.

[25] Ibid. 163.

[26] Ibid. 144.

[27] E. Sori, 'Malattia e demografia', in *Annali della storia d'Italia*, vii (Turin, Einaudi, 1984), 543. See also SIDES, *Popolazione, società e ambiente. Temi di demografia storica italiana (sec. XVII–XIX)* (Bologna, Clueb, 1990), sect. 2.

[28] This improvement was won at a high price, as can be seen in R. Finzi, 'Quando e perché fu sconfitta la pellagra in Italia', in Betri and Marchetti (eds.), *Salute e classi lavoratrici.*

[29] See the interesting table of human nutritional requirements, and the corresponding diseases that arise from a lack of a balanced diet, in M. Livi Bacci, *Popolazione e alimentazione. Saggio sulla storia demografica europea* (Bologna, Il Mulino, 1987), Table 5.

[30] A. De Bernardi, 'Pellagra, stato e scienza medica: la curabilità impossibile', in *Annali della storia d'Italia*, vii.

the spreading of municipal doctors throughout the country.[31] In 1861, there were local practices in three-quarters of all communes, benefiting about one-third of the total population. Twenty years later, 93 per cent of communes had a local practice, sometimes shared with the neighbouring communes, and there were some 9,000 general practitioners (10,263 by the year 1905).[32] Furthermore, the communes gradually saw to the provision of free health care for the poor, by means of the rather meagre salaries paid to local GPs, who were consequently allowed to round off their official pay with more lucrative visits to the wealthy (as stipulated in the 1888 Health Act).

As a consequence, the average life-span rose from 30 to 47 years, while the overall mortality rate dropped from 31 per thousand to 18.7 per thousand: during the same period, the infant mortality rate fell from 223 in a thousand to 138 in a thousand. Although these figures seem incredibly high from a present-day point of view, they were not really any worse than those of several other European countries, as can be seen from a glance at Table 6.1.

Another area where the need to look after the workers' health was intimately connected to the level of popular protest being voiced at the time was that of so-called social welfare legislation.[33] Industrialization had meant that vast numbers of workers—men and women, children, and adolescents—were squeezed into

Table 6.1. International demographic indices, 1913

	Life expectancy[a] (1)	Birth-rate (‰) (2)	Mortality-rate (‰) (3)	Mortality-rate during 1st year of life (‰) (4)
Gt. Britain	51	21.6	13.8	108
France	47	23.2	17.7	118
Germany	47	25.6	15.0	163
Austria	40	29.8	20.3	190
Sweden	56	23.2	13.7	70
Holland	52	28.2	12.3	91
Spain	38	30.6	22.3	151
Russia	32[b]	43.1	27.4	254
ITALY	45	21.7	18.7	138

[a] 1900.
[b] 1905.

Source: B. R. Mitchell, *European Historical Statistics* (London, Macmillan, 1978).

[31] A. Forti Messina, 'I medici condotti all'indomani dell'Unità', in Betri and Marchetti (eds.), *Salute e classi lavoratrici.*

[32] While, at the same time, the number of doctors operating privately rose from 8,973 to 12,375.

[33] The most complete study in this area, although limited to the 19th century, is that of T. L. Rizzo, *La legislazione sociale della nuova Italia (1876–1900)* (Naples, ESI, 1988).

cramped factories for very long hours (sometimes as many as 16 hours a day during the summer), factories with very little or no ventilation, often full of steam and/or dust as a result of the various operations carried out, sometimes right through the night; all this for a wage which in the case of women and children was nothing more than a pittance, and was not exactly large for the men, unless they possessed a specific qualification.[34] The 'savage' exploitation of the work-force has always been a feature of the early stages of industrialization, unfortunately, even in the case of the country that led the Industrial Revolution, Great Britain. This was partly due to the need to expand markets for basic consumer goods by keeping prices low, and partly due to the weak political position of the working-class who made up the best part of the work-force. Technological changes and social protest were later to put a limit to the more degrading aspects of this exploitation.

Despite the fact that social welfare legislation in Italy was very slow coming about, as many scholars have pointed out, Italy was not alone in having such shortcomings: the only country to have an early comprehensive social security system was Germany (set up between 1881 and 1889), while there was little or nothing in France at the time, and although England had made insurance against accidents in the workplace obligatory in 1880, the English had to wait until 1911 before a general National Insurance Act was passed, after a long and memorable battle in Parliament.

If we take into account Italy's late start in the industrialization race, then its social welfare legislation could almost be said to have been implemented more quickly than in other countries, even though state intervention now looks somewhat meagre from our present-day point of view. The following is a summary of the various measures taken by the Italian State in the area of social welfare legislation:

21 December 1873: law against the employment of children in pedlar trades and activities;
8 July 1883: foundation of a National Insurance scheme, optional in nature, aimed at providing insurance cover against accidents in the workplace;
February 1886: law raising the minimum working age to nine years (!), and banning children under 15 years of age from taking up employment of a dangerous or unhealthy nature;
15 June 1893: introduction of arbitration in industry;
17 March 1898: introduction of compulsory insurance against workplace accidents for several categories of workers;[35]

[34] The most vivid illustration of this 'life sentence' to which innocent people were condemned can be found in the two volumes by S. Merli, *Proletariato di fabbrica e capitalismo industriale. Il caso italiano: 1880–1900* (2 vols., Florence, La Nuova Italia, 1972 and 1973).

[35] The position of industrialists on the question of insurance against workplace accidents has been analysed in detail by R. Romano, in 'Sistema di fabbrica, sviluppo industriale e infortuni sul lavoro', in *Annali della storia d'Italia*, vii.

17 July 1898: setting up of a National Insurance Fund for illness and old-age, payment into which was again of a voluntary nature;[36]
19 June 1902 (subsequently modified in 1907): law raising the minimum working age to 12 years, and first controlling (then banning) the employment of women on night shifts, with the introduction of a maximum of 12 hours per day for women (!), and 11 hours for children between the ages of 12 and 15;[37]
17 July 1910: the setting up of a National Maternity Fund, contributions to which were compulsory.

Both the question of national insurance and that of universal suffrage were part of Giolitti's programme presented to the Chamber of Deputies on 6 April 1911, during his fourth ministry. Giolitti's proposal was to make life insurance a monopoly of the State in order to facilitate the establishment of a public fund aimed at the improvement in workers' pensions. The law that led to setting up the Istituto Nazionale delle Assicurazioni (INA) (National Insurance Company) was only approved after memorable battles had been fought in the Italian Parliament (1912), as a result of which the original objectives of the law had to be changed rather significantly.[38] In fact, the setting-up of the new institution was not accompanied by granting it a monopoly, which had to be postponed for 10 years (and was not subsequently finalized by Mussolini).

Thus national insurance provision was still largely inadequate at the outbreak of the First World War; this was particularly true of insurance against illness and unemployment, and also of pension funds, only existing at a voluntary level, which left a huge gap that could only be filled in part by mutual aid societies, numbering 6,535 in 1904, with roughly 1 million members,[39] or by organizations such as the Umanitaria in Milan.[40]

[36] The membership of this scheme increased from just over 40,000 in 1900 to half a million by 1914, partly also as a result of government contributions and the encouragement given to mutual aid societies to join the scheme. Compulsory contributions to the pension fund were introduced in the period after the First World War by the law passed on 21 April 1919. Cf. G. Geremia, 'La previdenza sociale in Italia nell'ultimo secolo', in *L'economia italiana dal 1861 al 1961* (Milan, Giuffré, 1961).

[37] Another law introduced in 1907 was to make it compulsory for employers to give their workers at least one day of rest (24 consecutive hours) each week.

[38] Cf. A. Scialoja, 'L'Istituto Nazionale delle Assicurazioni e il progetto giolittiano di un monopolio di stato delle assicurazioni sulla vita', *Quaderni Storici*, 18 (1971), and also F. Barbagallo, *Nitti* (Turin, UTET, 1984), 165 ff.

[39] *Annuario statistico italiano*, 1905–7.

[40] Cf. E. Decleva, 'Previdenza, disoccupazione, cultura popolare. La Società Umanitaria all'esposizione di Milano del 1906', *Archivio storico lombardo*, 111 (1984). See the following works for a mainly political interpretation of the fragmentary nature of social welfare provision during the period of liberalism: D. Marucco, *Mutualismo e sistema politico. Il caso italiano* (Milan, Angeli, 1981) and id., *Lavoro e previdenza dall'Unità al fascismo* (Milan, Angeli, 1984); the essay by F. Amoretti, 'Le politiche sociali in età giolittiana', *Stato e mercato*, 27 (1989).

2. THE GRADUAL SPREAD OF EDUCATION

Many economists and historians now share the belief that 'major changes in mass education are . . . likely to signal sizeable changes both in incentives structures and aptitudes favourable to modern economic growth',[41] above all because mass education allows an effective and widespread diffusion of technology, and a suitable understanding of how modern society works. While higher education for the élite together with the spreading of mass education can lead to technological excellence and the creation of suitable social and economic institutions, there are many examples to demonstrate how higher education by itself is not sufficient to guarantee overall economic progress. Easterlin has claimed with good reason that mass education was the result of three factors—humanism, Protestantism, and nationalism—and that all three were already influential in the spreading of primary education before there had been any significant improvement in personal incomes.[42] The result, in terms of economic and social development, was not exactly immediate, and neither did it represent a relationship that can be easily analysed over the short term; on the contrary, what has been seen is a long-term relationship between education and development.

This is the reason why Barbagli's analysis[43] of the phenomenon of intellectual unemployment (above all that of graduates) which has been an eternal feature of Italian history, does not in itself represent a contradiction of what we have said up to now, despite his conclusions.[44] It is primary education that plays an important role during the initial phase of development,[45] whereas secondary and higher education only become of crucial importance during the subsequent phases. It is also important to note that only certain branches of secondary and higher education are of strategic importance from the point of view of economic development.[46] As a result, it is quite easy to understand how intellectual unemployment and shortage of skilled labour can exist side by side when the composition of graduate (and high school) output does not correspond to demand. In fact, we should note that engineers, mechanics,

[41] R. A. Easterlin, 'Why Isn't the Whole World Developed?', *Journal of Economic History*, 41 (1981), 20.

[42] Ibid. Cf. also L. Sandberg, 'Ignorance, Poverty and Economic Backwardness in the Early Stages of European Industrialization', *Journal of European Economic History*, 42 (1982).

[43] M. Barbagli, *Disoccupazione intellettuale e sistema scolastico in Italia* (Bologna, Il Mulino, 1974).

[44] The author comes to the conclusion that during the post-unification period, 'the hypothesis of a direct relationship between economic performance and education can be adopted in the case of primary education, but loses its validity in the case of secondary and further education' (ibid., 114).

[45] For proof of this in the Italian case, see my study 'Istruzione e sviluppo economico: il caso italiano (1861–1913)', in G. Toniolo (ed.), *Lo sviluppo economico italiano 1861–1940* (2nd. edn., Bari, Laterza, 1978). A more long-term vision is offered in V. Zamagni, 'L'offerta di istruzione in Italia 1861–1981: un fattore guida dello sviluppo o un ostacolo?', forthcoming.

[46] Today there is, however, a tendency to re-evaluate the 'general culture' in terms of its methodological, conceptual, and formative importance for the development of a person's ideas and character.

dyers, skilled personnel with formal education in the electrical and chemical fields are of fundamental importance during the early stages of development, at least from the managerial point of view. Following this brief introduction to the question of education, I would now like to take a closer look at the Italian case.

As has already been mentioned, the position at all educational levels was very different from one area of Italy to another as a result of the different views of the ruling classes. For example, one can see an enormous contrast between the views of Melchiorre Gioia (an economist from Piacenza, Emilia), who claimed that 'education is important in all sectors of production, as light and warmth are for all manner of vegetation', and those of Cardinal Lambruschini, when he wrote: 'the present-day interest in the spreading of education and culture is not aimed at bettering society, but at making it considerably sadder. Let's fuel the pride of the lower classes . . . with a superficial knowledge and we shall see what results such an ill-advised system is destined to produce.'[47] General and technical education were widespread above all in Piedmont and Lombardy, with their technical schools and institutes designed to 'encourage trades and crafts', of which the most famous is the one founded in Milan in 1838.[48]

A short while after the end of the Second War of Independence, the task of drawing up new legislation for education in the new Kingdom fell to Count Casati, former mayor of Milan and a person professionally imbibed with German culture. The Casati law of 13 November 1859 remained in force, with one or two minor amendments, until Gentile's reform bill of 1923. It foresaw compulsory primary schooling for all children, followed by a division of secondary education into two branches, with two different types of school: the first being the grammar school, and the second a technical school (or normal school).[49] While the grammar school, which was the gateway to a university, was to be financed directly by the State, the technical school was to be the responsibility of the local authority. However the technical school, which was to be divided into various specialized branches, also allowed the way into some university faculties, unlike the German system, where such a possibility did not exist. Thus the Italian system was 'relatively "open-ended" . . . that is, it was structured in such a way as to allow a relatively large number of students the opportunity of going on to university',[50] especially when one takes into account that technical schools were both provided free of charge. Although technical schools were still not fully operative during the early days of the new law, partly because of the fact that they had been under the MAIC's supervision since 1865, things were to change after they became the Education Ministry's

[47] The quotes by M. Gioia and Cardinal Lambruschini can be found in C. G. Lacaita, *Istruzione e sviluppo industriale in Italia 1859–1914* (Monza, Giunti, 1974), 15 and 23.

[48] C. Patti, 'Strutture associative e formazione professionale', in G. Fiocca (ed.), *Borghesi e imprenditori a Milano dalla unità alla prima guerra mondiale* (Bari, Laterza, 1984).

[49] For the training of primary school teachers.

[50] Barbagli, *Disoccupazione intellettuale*, 81.

responsibility in 1877. There was also a growth in private vocational schools, subsidized by the MAIC.[51]

The only real novelties resulting from the introduction of the Casati law at the university level were two new institutions: one at Turin—the new Technical Engineering College attached to the Science Faculty of Turin University; the other at Milan—a new independent technical college,[52] both of which were to be highly successful, as we shall see.

This then was the school system which was to be the basis for Italy's cultural modernization in subsequent years. We can now have a look at the results achieved during the system's first 50 years, and in particular, at the regional distribution of these results (see Table 6.2).

As far as primary education is concerned, the three regions of the industrial triangle were still well ahead of the others in the year 1911: they had both low illiteracy rates and high levels of school enrolment. The other two northern regions (the Veneto and Emilia) and Latium had improved considerably, followed by the central regions of Tuscany, Umbria, and the Marches. Although school enrolment levels in the southern regions had doubled since unification, they were still very low in comparison with those of other regions. A more rapid improvement had been made virtually impossible by a combination of factors: widespread poverty, a lack of support from the ruling élite, and the financial problems of the local authorities, all worked against real improvement,[53] although these meagre achievements were, none the less, highly disruptive to the backward social conditions present in the South at that time.[54]

It is more difficult to interpret the data given for secondary and higher education, since almost all of the regions had their rich middle class that saw to its children's secondary and university education. The main difference lies in the subjects and curricula chosen by such students. The typical choice of the children of wealthy families in the South was classical studies followed by law or medicine at university: in the North, students opted more for vocational schools (see column 4, Table 6.2), technical schools and colleges, followed by

[51] C. G. Lacaita, 'L'istruzione tecnica e lo sviluppo economico in Italia, 1840–1914', *Rivista milanese di economia*, 19 (1986), and also S. Soldani, 'L'istruzione tecnica nell'Italia liberale 1861–1900', *Studi Storici*, 22 (1981).

[52] C. G. Lacaita, *Sviluppo e cultura. Alle origini della Italia industriale* (Milan, Angeli, 1984), ch. 5.

[53] There is considerable evidence to support the view that several southern councils were committed, though with little success, to educational reform, but it was only when the State was given responsibility for primary education that such an education became widespread throughout the entire country (with inevitable exceptions however). Cf. G. Vigo, *Istruzione e sviluppo economico in Italia nel secolo XIX* (Turin, ILTE, 1971), and also 'Il maestro elementare italiano nell'Ottocento. Condizioni economiche e status sociale', *Nuova rivista storica*, 61 (1977).

[54] G. Barone reminds us that the development of the Sicilian 'Fasci' movement was ascribed to the education of the peasants, and that as a result there was even a proposal made to abolish the free and compulsory nature of primary education. See 'Egemonie urbane e potere locale (1882–1913), in M. Aymard and G. Giarrizzo (eds.), *La Sicilia* (Turin, Einaudi, 1987), 259–60.

Table 6.2. Regional analysis of education, 1911

	Illiteracy rate (%)	School attendance (% of population in the age-bracket)			
		Primary (6–11)	Secondary (12–18)		Higher Educ. (20–25)[b]
			Total[a]	Vocational schools	
	(1)	(2)	(3)	(4)	(5)
Piedmont	11.0	98	9.8	3.9	
Liguria	17.0	99	13.0	4.6	
Lombardy	13.4	91	11.2	6.2	1.0
Veneto	25.2	81	8.5	4.6	
Emilia	32.7	93	8.9	3.2	
Tuscany	37.4	74	10.2	5.2	
Marches	50.7	70	7.5	1.5	1.6
Umbria	48.6	72	6.4	1.0	
Latium	33.2	86	15.4	5.5	
Abruzzi	56.7	63	3.5	0.7	
Campania	53.7	55	8.5	2.5	
Apulia	59.4	57	5.9	1.1	
Basilicata	65.3	50	3.4	0.7	0.9
Calabria	69.6	45	3.8	0.5	
Sicily	58.0	64	7.1	1.4	
Sardinia	58.0	60	6.7	1.8	
ITALY	37.9	76	8.6	3.3	1.1

[a] Including vocational schools.
[b] 20–25 age-group has been used due to lack of figures for 19–23 age-group.
Source: V. Zamagni, *Istruzione e sviluppo*, Tables 14 and 16.

chemistry, engineering, science, or commerce in their higher education. Forty-five per cent of all registered students studying for mathematics, engineering, or science degrees in Italy were at either Turin, Milan, Pavia, or Genoa University.[55] Generally speaking, an excessive concentration of students in the law faculties (31.7 per cent of the total in 1911–12) or in the medicine faculties (24.9 per cent) was inevitably going to lead to those forms of intellectual

[55] For a history of the universities during this period, see T. Tomasi and L. Bellatalla, *L'Università italiana nell'età liberale (1861–1923)* (Naples, Liguori, 1988). A. Aquarone also notes that 'in the South, humanistic, legal and, to a certain extent, medical studies were given priority, to the detriment of economic and technical-scientific subjects. In this way, continuity with that tradition of intellectual unemployment and frustration with one's social role—almost synonymous with the condition and backward function of the southern lower-middle classes—was guaranteed', see *Tre capitoli sull'Italia giolittiana* (Bologna, Il Mulino, 1987), 713.

unemployment which are well known in Italy, though somewhat over-emphasized by Barbagli in his study of this phenomenon.[56]

We ought to take a closer look at the two technical colleges in Milan and Turin, as they were to play a significant role in the process of industrialization in Italy. Milan's Politecnico opened in 1863,[57] intent on copying the German model whereby special emphasis was given to the industrial aspects of the college's programme, without however neglecting to devote sufficient attention to the preparation of traditional civil engineers.[58] In the year 1865 there were 25 graduates, all in civil engineering; by 1913 the number had risen to 156 per year, of whom 106 were industrial engineering graduates (85 specialized in mechanical engineering, 18 in electrical engineering, and 3 in chemical engineering). We have already seen (in Chapter 2) that the most famous names from the industrial milieu in Lombardy had graduated from Milan's Politecnico, but their role was to be much more than simply that of captains of industry: these men were intensely involved in spreading a new technical and industrial culture throughout the nation, in organizing technical and professional associations, and in the management of various public bodies.[59]

Turin's Scuola di Applicazione per Ingegneri had a harder time due to the rivalry of another institute in Turin—the Museo Industriale, founded in 1862—and this rivalry only came to an end in 1906 when the two colleges were amalgamated to form the Turin Politecnico.[60] Until 1881 there had been only 16 industrial engineering graduates (out of a total of 1,426);[61] subsequently, their numbers were to increase, although they only really rose significantly from 1900 onwards. The career histories of the Turin industrial engineers are less well known than those of their Milanese counterparts: perhaps the most famous of them all being Camillo Olivetti.

3. INCOME DISTRIBUTION AND STANDARDS OF LIVING

How did people live in Italy one hundred years ago? In order to provide a suitable answer to a question of this kind, researchers would have to conduct a much more in-depth analysis of both quantitative and qualitative aspects of Italian life at that time. While we have an idea, if only an approximate one, of

[56] Barbagli, *Disoccupazione intellettuale.*

[57] *Il Politecnico di Milano. Una scuola nella formazione della società industriale* (Milan, 1981).

[58] For an account of the important role played by engineers in pre-unification Lombardy, cf. C. G. Lacaita, 'La professione degli ingegneri a Milano dalla fine del '700 alla prima guerra mondiale', in *Lavorare a Milano. L'evoluzione delle professioni nel capoluogo lombardo dalla prima metà dell'800 ad oggi* (Milan, Ed. Il Sole 24 ore, 1987).

[59] See the ample coverage given to this matter in my essay 'Il ruolo de "L'Industria" nella vita economica italiana: 1887–1942', *L'industria*, 3 (1986).

[60] A. Ferraresi, 'La formazione degli ingegneri nella seconda metà del'Ottocento. Per una ricerca sulla scuola di Applicazione e sul Museo industriale di Torino (1860–1906)', *Nuova Rivista Storica*, 67 (1983).

[61] 175 engineering students had already graduated from Milan Polytechnic by 1881.

average income levels,[62] we do not have access to the kind of data that subdivides the population into deciles, and then assigns the relative percentage of income enjoyed by each decile, thus giving a clear idea of income distribution. Neither is it particularly easy to assemble a sufficiently accurate picture of the evolution of 'social classes', as the attempts made by Sylos Labini[63] and myself[64] demonstrate, without having to resort to a considerable degree of arbitrary estimates in doing so.

One way of looking at the question of living standards involves the concept of 'basic needs'; that is, what percentage of the population could be said to live above the 'subsistence level'? This approach is widely used in modern studies of growth and development in the underdeveloped countries,[65] and could thus be considered suitable in the case of the Italy of the late nineteenth century, given the low income levels at that time.[66] However, even this method has its problems, both theoretical and practical. The basic theoretical problem is that of establishing the minimum physical requirements of a person, as this will obviously vary according to weight, age, climate, and the kind of physical activity usually carried out.[67] Another difficulty is that of formulating a standard diet at minimum cost, while not forgetting to take into consideration the energy requirements and the cultural habits of the people in question. If we do not aim at one hundred per cent precision, but are more concerned with the use of this approach as a convenient point of reference, then we will find it to be extremely useful.

It is a well-known fact that food is by far the greatest need of poor people; and if one looks at the case of the Italian people during the first 50 years after unification, then one sees that food and drink made up some two-thirds of total consumption (both public and private). According to the information given in Table 6.3, the average daily calorie intake of Italians at the beginning of the twentieth century (columns 2 and 3) was close to the recommended figure (column 1). Since the average did not exceed that figure, however, it would seem to imply that there were a large number of people whose calorie intake was below the recommended amount. Although we do not know the distribution of individual cases around the average, we can try to identify those groups of people that fell below the subsistence level by comparing the cost of the diet given in column 3, Table 6.3 (last line) with the average incomes of

[62] Bearing in mind the criticisms raised in previous chapters of the reconstructed national income figures.

[63] P. Sylos Labini, *Saggio sulle classi sociali* (Bari, Laterza, 1974).

[64] V. Zamagni, 'Le alterazioni nella distribuzione del reddito in Italia nell'immediato dopoguerra (1919–1922)', in G. Mori and P. Hertner (eds.), *La transizione dall'economia di guerra all'economia di pace in Italia e in Germania dopo la Prima guerra mondiale* (Bologna, Il Mulino, 1983).

[65] For a critical account of the 'basic needs' approach, cf. A. K. Dasgupta, *Growth, Development and Welfare. An Essay on Levels of Living* (Oxford, Blackwell, 1988).

[66] The average per capita income in Italy in 1913 was about one-fifth of what it is today.

[67] For an excellent discussion of this problem, see M. Livi Bacci, *Popolazione e alimentazione*, ch. 2. Also see S. Somogyi, 'L'alimentazione nell'Italia unita', in *Storia d'Italia*, v. *I documenti*.

Table 6.3. Daily calorie requirements compared with calories available (averages for the period 1910–1914)

	Gross[a] recommended intake for a man in 1913 (1)	Calories available to the Italian population		Calories available to men in 51 Milanese working-class families (4)
		Men (2)	Per capita (3)	
Calories	3,300	3,220	2,696	2,853
Protein				
vegetable (gm.)	58	73	61	45
animal (gm.)	42	24	20	39
Fats (gm.)	75	63	53	70
Carbohydrates (gm.)	540	493	412	411
Average cost (lire)	—	0.76[b]	0.64[b]	1.07[c]

[a] The recommended gross quantity is 10% more than the net quantity.
[b] Bread and pasta consumption is included at the cost of flour.
[c] Bread and pasta prices are those to be found in co-operative shops in Milan.

Source: V. Zamagni, 'An International Comparison of Real Industrial Wages, 1890–1913: Methodological Issues and Results', in P. Scholliers (ed.), *Real Wages in 19th and 20th Century Europe* (Oxford, Berg, 1989), Table 5.6.

different groups. In order to do so, we should note that a man would have needed an average annual income of 290 lire in 1911 in order to pay for his dietary requirements, whereas a woman would have needed 217 lire; a child below the age of 7, 145 lire, whereas an adolescent would have needed even more than an adult.

We can begin by looking at the rural classes. There can be no doubt that the day labourers were the poorest of all rural classes, considering the precarious nature of both their work and housing, even though some tenant farmers, smallholders, and sharecroppers were not in a much better economic position. However, the latter certainly had a more stable position than the day labourer did, and they could also supplement their income with some revenue in kind, something which the day labourer was not in a position to do. Table 6.4, which shows the numbers of day labourers and their families, and the units of consumption according to age and sex, can be used to calculate roughly the economic position of this rural class. If we know the daily wage paid to such day labourers, then we can calculate whether this class managed to keep its head above the subsistence level or not by means of one all-important variable—the number of days worked during the course of the year. A very simple calculation[68] will show that 280 days of work a year would have been necessary

[68] 280 days of work at the average wage (1.59 lire) = 445 lire a year × 4,300,000 = 1.91 billion lire a year (total wage bill): 6,500,000 consumption units = 294 lire available for each person. As we have said, 290 lire was the cost of an ideal diet for a male adult.

Table 6.4. Daily budget of farm labourers about 1911

	Work-force (000s)	Daily wage (lire)	Estimated no. of day labourers and their families (000s)	
			Total	Male units of consumption
	(1)	(2)	(3)	(4)
Adult men	2,300	2.10	2,300	2,300
Adult women	1,430	1.10	2,000[a]	1,500[b]
Children and young people	570	0.80	3,870[c]	2,370[d]
Elderly people	—	—	830[e]	330[f]
TOTAL	4,300	1.59	9,000	6,500

[a] Ratio of 1 : 0.86 of men to women, given that many agricultural labourers were men with no families.

[b] Using a coefficient of 0.75.

[c] Ratio of 1 : 0.90 of adults (men and women) to children younger than 15 years of age (this is a little higher than the average of 0.75—for an explanation of this assumption, cf. M. Livi Bacci, *Donna, fecondità e figli* (Bologna, Il Mulino, 1980).

[d] Applying a coefficient of 0.50 to 3,000 youngsters and of 1 to the remaining 870,000 adolescents.

[e] Ratio of 1 : 0.20 of adults to elderly people, which is a little lower than the average.

[f] Applying a coefficient of 0.40.

Sources: *Population Census*, 1911; V. Zamagni, 'Le radici agricole del dualismo italiano', *Nuova rivista storica*, 59 (1975).

in order to guarantee an income above the subsistence level (solely in terms of food); however, we know that a day labourer never worked more than 180–200 days a year, and this figure was often lower in heavily populated areas or in areas where farming was particularly extensive in nature.[69]

The above calculation gives a good idea of why that class of 'regular' day labourers (that is, those who were guaranteed work for the whole year), particularly common in Lombardy, was less poverty-stricken than the rest, and also why poverty was less widespread amongst sharecroppers and small tenant farmers,[70] who were also provided with accommodation, and could rear farmyard animals if they wished. Furthermore, the 'complex' family, either extensive or multiple, was more widespread among sharecroppers, tenant

[69] My already cited study of the Bologna area shows how the number of working days a year fell to 100–120 during certain periods. For figures concerning the South, cf. A. Prampolini, 'L'inchiesta Faina e le condizioni di vita dei contadini meridionali all'inizio del Novecento', in Betri and Marchetti (eds.), *Salute e classi lavoratrici in Italia.*

[70] The larger tenants were members of the middle classes at that time. A. Serpieri estimates their numbers at about 100,000 in 1911, with an average income of 9,000 lire a year, in *La guerra e le classi rurali italiane* (Bari, Laterza, 1930).

farmers, and smallholders than among day labourers: this kind of family created a greater degree of solidarity among its members.[71] Finally, we need to emphasize the fact that the 1911 wage levels were the result of massive peasant struggles, together with some thinning-out of the work-force especially in the South, due to waves of emigration from the countryside (which we shall be looking at in the following section). This means that the daily wages of these labourers must have been even more miserable beforehand.[72]

A comparison can be made between agricultural labourers and factory workers. I have carried out a number of studies of industrial wages in Italy covering the period from 1890 to 1946. Table 6.5 shows the results for the period 1890–1913: from these, we can see that average real wages rose by 60 per cent, partly as a result of agreements drawn up for individual categories of workers following trade union action, and partly because of the greater number of higher-paid workers. If we compare column 1 with columns 2 and 3, we can also see that there was a great difference between the wages of women factory workers, who represented the greater part of the work-force in the textile industry, and their male counterparts, who dominated the engineering and building industries. We can now try and build up a picture of the economic

Table 6.5. Average daily wages of factory workers, 1890–1913 (lire)

	Textiles (1)	Engineering (2)	Building ind. (3)	Gen. average (4)	Average at 1913 prices (5)	Index of (5) 1890=100 (6)
1890	1.12	2.85	1.80	1.66	1.78	100
1896	1.20	2.90	1.70	1.71	1.93	108
1900	1.31	2.95	1.80	1.82	2.06	116
1904	1.36	3.25	2.27	2.03	2.22	125
1908	1.53	3.51	2.65	2.38	2.46	138
1911	1.61	3.88	2.95	2.67	2.70	152
1913	1.67	3.98	3.10	2.84	2.84	160

Sources: V. Zamagni, 'I salari giornalieri degli operai dell'industria nell'età giolittiana (1898–1913)', *Rivista di storia economica*, 1 (1984), and V. Zamagni, 'An International Comparison'.

[71] In *Sotto lo stesso tetto. Mutamenti della famiglia in Italia dal XV al XX secolo* (Bologna, Il Mulino, 1988), M. Barbagli points out that the complex family was a much more common phenomenon in Italy in the 19th cent., esp. in the Centre and North, where it accounted for 15 to 40% of the total, than in England, where it only accounted for 4% or less of the total. Also see A. Manoukian, 'La famiglia dei contadini', in Melograni (ed.), *La famiglia italiana* and M. Barbagli and D. I. Kertzer (eds.), *Storia della famiglia italiana 1750–1950* (Il Mulino, Bologna, 1992).

[72] The considerable amount of data collected by P. M. Arcari in his study, 'Le variazioni dei salari agricoli in Italia dalla fondazione del Regno al 1933', *Annali di statistica*, 6th series, 36 (1936) has yet to be elaborated for those years prior to 1911.

Table 6.6. Daily budget of factory workers in 1911

	Work-force[a] (000s)	Average daily wage (lire)	Estimated no. of factory workers and their families (000s)	
			Total	In male units of consumption
	(1)	(2)	(3)	(4)
Adult men	—	—	1,100[b]	1,100
Boys	1,270	3.25	750[c]	500[d]
Adult women			1,100[b]	825[e]
Girls	630	1.50	750[c]	500[d]
Elderly persons	—	—	450[f]	180[g]
TOTAL	1,900	2.67	4,150	3,130

[a] Workers who worked in a separate workshop employing at least 2 workers; the population census counted some 50% more, but they have not been included here as they almost certainly earned much lower wages than those given in Table 6.5.
[b] 10% less than the male work-force, so as to exclude boys, with a ratio of 1 : 1 of men to women.
[c] Ratio of 0.75 between adults and children below the age of 15 (Italian average).
[d] Using a coefficient of 0.75.
[e] Applying a coefficient of 0.75 to 1,000,000 children, and of 1 to the remaining 500,000 adolescents.
[f] Ratio of 0.20 between adults and elderly persons.
[g] Using a coefficient of 0.40.

Sources: *Industrial Census*, 1911; the sources used to construct Table 6.5.

situation of factory workers, in the same way as we have done for farm labourers, in Table 6.6. Most workers, with the exception of the occasional seasonal employee, worked a full year. Just to be safe, let us assume that they worked an average of 270 days a year, which, if we follow the procedure used in the previous example, gives us an annual income of 437 lire for each male unit of consumption: this is 50 per cent greater than the minimum cost of an ideal diet (290 lire). However, if we look at column 4 of Table 6.3, we can see that the real cost of the factory worker's diet was higher than this figure, since the factory worker ate bread and pasta bought from a shop (more expensive than home-made), and the composition of his diet differed from the norm. If we were to increase the minimum cost by 40 per cent (from the comparison between columns 2 and 4 in Table 6.3), then the cost of food alone would already account for 400 lire a year. Furthermore, the cost of housing (even of the worst kind) for the average factory worker would have been higher than that available in the countryside.[73]

[73] A survey conducted on behalf of the Umanitaria concerning working-class conditions in Milan in the year 1903 showed that rent accounted on average for 12% of a worker's family's budget.

Thus one can easily see that, while the average industrial factory worker in 1911 managed to earn enough to avoid falling below the subsistence level, that worker's expenditure on things other than food must have been very limited. What is more, the factory worker in industry was relatively well paid, and had some job security. Others, such as home-workers, seasonal workers, and temporary hands—which, according to census figures, meant another 2 million workers on top of those counted by the industrial census—must have been earning much less.

Thus the Italy of the Giolitti years was a country with many families living below the subsistence level. At the same time, however, there were already some privileged categories of workers, particularly in the engineering industry, as well as an active bourgeoisie[74] and growing middle classes. There has been no comprehensive study made of the incomes of this latter category, although we do have some figures for particular categories or companies. For example, a recent study has shown the position of various categories of non-manual worker at the Ansaldo company in the year 1904: 29 engineers received an average of 3,900 lire per annum; 59 draughtsmen 1,730 lire; 47 foremen 3,230 lire; 56 bookkeepers and secretaries 1,714 lire. These salaries compared with the average wage of an engineering worker of 877 lire (working 270 days a year). Directors earned between 10,000 and 60,000 lire a year, and some received a percentage of company earnings.[75]

In another study,[76] I gave the average earnings for the year 1910 of various categories of public employee:[77] full-time civil servants earned 2,033 lire a year; teachers 2,440 lire; servicemen 2,351 lire; railway employees 1,578 lire; while employees in various other public enterprises earned an average of 1,962 lire; this, when the average wage of a factory worker in industry stood at 688 lire (calculated for 270 days work a year).[78] The urban middle classes thus usually enjoyed a very reasonable standard of living, which was only reduced when families had many children.[79]

[74] There are a growing number of studies on the middle classes: cf. G. Fiocca (ed.), *Borghesi e imprenditori a Milano dall'unità alla prima guerra mondiale* (Bari, Laterza, 1984); *Quaderni storici*, 56 (1984); and A. M. Banti, *Una borghesia padana dell'Ottocento* (Venice, Marsilio, 1989).

[75] M. Doria, 'Colletti bianchi in età giolittiana: i lavoratori non manuali dell'Ansaldo', *Ricerche storiche*, 18 (1988).

[76] V. Zamagni, 'Distribuzione del reddito e classi sociali nell'Italia fra le due guerre', *Annali*, 20 (Milan, Feltrinelli, 1979–80), Table 7.

[77] A total of 283,136 employees.

[78] Since the vast majority of civil servants were men at that time, a fairer comparison would be that between the average wages of white-collar workers and that of government manual workers, who numbered 47,013 in 1910 and earned on average 1,068 lire a year.

[79] For an analysis of the qualitative aspects of middle-class life, see G. Montroni, 'La famiglia borghese', in Melograni (ed.), *La famiglia italiana.*

4. THE ALTERNATIVES OPEN TO THE POORER CLASSES: EMIGRATION, TRADE UNION ACTION, AND SOLIDARITY

As always, there were only two alternatives to the acceptance of what were intolerable living conditions: 'exit or voice'.[80] A third alternative—the creation of economic structures based on co-operation rather than profit—is generally less appealing, but was of some importance in Italy, as we shall see.

How many Italians chose to leave a country that was in no position to guarantee them an acceptable standard of living? Table 6.7 shows that an enormous number of people left (column 2), while fewer stayed abroad (columns 1 and 3), the percentage of those leaving permanently reaching more than 50 per cent during the 20-year period 1881–1900. In relation to the natural growth in population, emigration exceeded 50 per cent during the 10-year period 1911–20, and reached 42 per cent between 1891 and 1900 (with one and a half million Italians leaving the country for good during the course of the decade). One particularly interesting feature of this emigration was that the majority of those who left Italy fell into the category of 'men within the young age-groups, fitting in to a large extent with the idea of the purely physical labourer';[81] most were illiterate, and came from the peasantry.[82] At the beginning, they mostly made for other European countries, but later on the majority decided to leave for the Americas. They were mainly from the North of Italy during the early days of emigration, but the 1880s saw an increasingly

Table 6.7. Emigration, 1861–1920

	Net emigration (000s) (1)	Expatriated people (000s) (2)	(1)/(2) × 100 (3)	Natural pop. increase (000s) (4)	(1)/(4) × 100 (5)
1861–70	227	1,210	18.8	1,658	13.7
1871–80	334	1,180	28.3	1,946	17.2
1881–90	1,041	1,880	55.4	3,124	35.2
1891–1900	1,433	2,830	50.6	3,439	41.7
1900–10	1,021	6,030	16.9	3,778	27.0
1911–20	992	3,830	25.9	1,874	52.9

Source: E. Sori, *L'emigrazione italiana dall'unità alla seconda guerra mondiale* (Bologna, Il Mulino, 1979), Table 2.1.

[80] A. O. Hirschman, *Exit, Voice and Loyalty* (Cambridge, Mass., Harvard University Press, 1970).

[81] E. Sori, *L'emigrazione italiana dall'unità alla seconda guerra mondiale* (Bologna, Il Mulino, 1979), 32.

[82] However, relatively few Italians chose to work the land in the countries where they emigrated to.

greater number of southerners leave the country, while relatively few emigrants left from the central regions of Italy. In 1913, 39 per cent of emigrants were from the North, compared with 47 per cent from the South and 14 per cent from the Centre (their respective percentages of the population were 45, 38, and 17 per cent at the time).

The effects of emigration on Italy were the subject of a very lively debate at that time: various views were put forward, including that of wage increases caused by the scarcity of labour, of increasing productivity, of decreasing levels of usury, and of the formation of a class of small-scale farmers as a direct consequence of the return of some emigrants together with their foreign savings.

Recent studies have shown that all of these effects, when present, were of minimal significance, and could in no way compensate for the devastating social consequences of emigration: that is, the way in which villages became dominated numerically by women and elderly people when the menfolk went off in search of work. The only positive note concerned the savings that the men sent back to the families they had left behind in Italy, as we saw in Chapter 3. The Italian State had no choice but to try and facilitate the exodus of its impoverished citizens, and it tried, but with very little success, to render their journey more humane, treated as they often were like 'boat people', especially aboard the steamships bound for the Americas.[83]

A word will now be said about the second alternative—'voice'—which has been widely analysed in research on the history of the trade union movement (which is too extensive for me to give a worthwhile summary here). Whereas the second half of the nineteenth century was the setting for a great number of spontaneous popular revolts, beginning with the previously mentioned phenomenon of banditry, which were always put down by force, organized protest only began to take shape towards the turn of the century. The year 1891 marked the foundation of the first Camere del Lavoro (Bourses de travail), and trade union federations were organized between the end of the nineteenth and the beginning of the twentieth centuries, thus giving workers the possibility of expressing their grievances in an organized and modern way, through the use of strike action followed by direct negotiations between employer and workers (negotiations encouraged by Giolitti's well-known 'neutral' stance).[84] Wage

[83] See Sori, *L'emigrazione italiana*, 324 ff. On the matter of legislative protection for emigrants, cf. Rizzo, *La legislazione sociale*, ch. 10. On emigration in general, also see F. Assante, *Il movimento migratorio italiano dall'unità nazionale ai nostri giorni* (3 vols., Geneva, Droz, 1978) and R. Paris, 'L'Italia fuori d'Italia', in *Storia d'Italia*, iv (Turin, Einaudi, 1975). See also SIDES, *Popolazione, società e ambiente*, sect. 4.

[84] I will just mention two fundamental studies of the Italian trade union movement: G. Procacci, *La lotta di classe in Italia agli inizi del secolo XX* (Rome, Editori Riuniti, 1972), and I. Barbadoro, *Storia del sindacalismo italiano dalla nascita al fascismo* (2 vols., Florence, La Nuova Italia, 1973). See also L. Bordogna, G. P. Cella, and G. Provasi, 'Labour Conflicts in Italy before the Rise of Fascism, 1881–1923: A Quantitative Analysis', in L. H. Haimson and C. Tilly (eds.), *Strikes, Wars and Revolution in International Perspective* (Cambridge, Cambridge University Press, 1989).

improvements in both agriculture and industry, together with improvements in working conditions, were the direct result of a trade union militancy which also had political and social objectives, although the differences between the reformist and the revolutionary wings, at times unresolvable, meant that they only occasionally agreed on aims and programmes. In 1912, the Camere del Lavoro had about half a million members, the Federterra had 165,000, and the other non-agricultural federations had 198,000 members. In 1906 the Confederazione Generale del Lavoro (CGdL), a nationwide, general workers' trade union, was founded; and the immediate pre-war years were to be marked by a significant increase in trade union militancy.

A few final words will be devoted to the co-operative movement. The practical application of the concept of co-operation within the modern, industrial context can be traced back to the mutual aid societies, which began to appear in Italy during the second half of the nineteenth century. They represented 'the first organized answer to the challenge thrown up rather by the crisis of the old order than by the advent of the new radical economic and social change'.[85] There were 443 mutual aid societies in Italy in 1862; by 1885, their number had increased more than tenfold, to 4,896, and it continued to rise: there were 6,535 such societies in 1904, with 926,026 members. As well as offering sick pay, which was their main economic contribution, some of these societies also provided other forms of economic assistance, as well as pensions. Many began to get involved in other areas (particularly from the 1880s onwards), such as loaning money, finding work for the unemployed, opening co-operative stores and working-men's clubs, subcontracting, insurance, and also building houses for workers.

Another area of co-operation was represented by the work of the Mazzinian democrats, who set up a number of workers' associations which were themselves soon involved in a whole variety of co-operative activities, ranging from credit to consumption, from production to workers' education. Finally, we have the Catholic co-operative movement, which was behind the establishment of the country savings banks (casse rurali), and also that of the socialists; in the end, these diverse areas of co-operative interest came together to form a more united co-operative movement, although not without creating a number of internal problems.

The first Italian co-operative congress was held in Milan in 1886: 248 co-operatives of all different political colours, with some 74,000 members, took part in the congress, and the following year the Italian Co-operative Federation was formed. The Federation, which had its own magazine, was to change its name to the League of Co-operatives (Lega delle Cooperative) in 1893. In the meantime, the numbers of co-operatives (of all kinds) had been steadily

[85] R. Zangheri, 'Nascita e primi sviluppi', in R. Zangheri, G. Galasso, and V. Castronovo, *Storia del movimento cooperativo in Italia* (Turin, Einaudi, 1987), 6 and A. Varni (ed.), *Emilia–Romagna. Terra di cooperazione* (Bologna, Analisi, 1990).

growing, including one type which was unique to Italy, that of the farm labourers (these co-operatives were particularly common in Romagna). By 1901, there were more than 4,000 co-operatives: of the 1,714 which had furnished full details about themselves, we know that they had nearly 600,000 members (182,000 of whom were members of consumer co-operatives).[86] This number had risen to 7,429 by 1914 (excluding banking co-operatives), 4,222 of them accounting for more than 800,000 members. The bricklayers' co-operatives were taking on government contracts at this point, and the farm labourers' co-operatives were being given collective tenancies. In some areas of the country—above all, Emilia–Romagna, Lombardy, the Veneto, and Tuscany—co-operative activity took in all sectors of the economy; the South, on the other hand, continued to be a 'blackspot for Italian co-operative activity'.[87] The Istituto Nazionale di Credito per la Cooperazione was set up in 1913 (it was later to become the Banca Nazionale del Lavoro).[88]

While neither emigration, nor trade union militancy, nor the co-operative movement managed really to change the system in favour of the oppressed working classes, the combination of all three did help towards improving many people's standard of living, and it also kept alive a passionate belief in the need to promote personal dignity.

[86] Among the retail co-operatives of that time, there were such giants as the Unione Militare di Roma, the Unione Cooperativa di Milano, and the Alleanza Cooperativa Torinese. For a short history of these, see V. Zamagni, 'Dinamica e problemi della distribuzione commerciale al minuto tra il 1880 e la II guerra mondiale', in *Mercati e consumi* (Bologna, Analisi, 1986).

[87] A statement by Ruini, quoted in G. Galasso, 'Gli anni della grande espansione e la crisi del sistema', in Zangheri, Galasso, and Castronovo, *Storia del movimento cooperativo*, 281. On the co-operative movement in the Po Valley area, see *Padania* 2 (1987).

[88] See V. Castronovo, *Storia di una banca. La Banca Nazionale del Lavoro e lo sviluppo economico italiano 1913–1983* (Turin, Einaudi, 1983).

PART II
Between the Wars

7

State, Industry, Finance, and Society between the First World War and the Post-War Period, 1914–1922

1. THE STATE: THE WAR EFFORT AND THE SUBSEQUENT 'NORMALIZATION'

SOME sections of the Italian population were already on the warpath when war finally broke out in 1914. Although the parliamentary majority was neutral, there were many strong, vociferous groups crying out for Italian intervention in the war. Besides the nationalists, who were without a doubt the loudest and most cohesive group, there were democratic groups who took their lead from the struggles of the Italian Risorgimento, revolutionaries who thought that the war offered the opportunity to revolutionize the social order (among whom Mussolini was quick to make a name), cultural groupings of an anti-positivist and irrationalist nature, and also some industrial circles who saw the war as a possible answer to those problems of economic stagnation and excessive productive capacity which had materialized in 1913 and 1914. The industrialists became increasingly interested in the prospect of intervention, as they gradually realized the mistaken nature of the economic forecast which predicted that they, as industrialists, would prosper as a result of the manufacture of industrial products for the war effort of the belligerents. In fact, the Italian industrial machine was in need of those raw materials which the countries involved in the war were competing for; it was thought that Italy ran the risk of being isolated—which would have exacerbated an already serious economic crisis—if it did not take part on one side or the other, thus ensuring itself a place on international raw-material markets.

Despite the strong presence of German interests during the earlier 'Giolitti years', and the predominance of Comit (with its German financiers) in the banking sector, the interests of many Italian industrialists, particularly in the engineering and chemical industries, were diametrically opposed to those of the Germans. German competition was strong, and such industrialists feared that it would eventually come to control Italian production. On the other hand, the problem *vis-à-vis* France, concerning the late nineteenth-century clashes involving the two countries, had more or less been resolved; and the technological and financial ties between the two countries were strengthened during this period. In addition, the only way that Italy could be sure of adequate supplies of foodstuffs and raw materials was by allying itself with France and England. There were very few doubts, therefore, about who would be Italy's choice of ally: the only problem was that Italy's preparation for something as great as the First World War was far from adequate. While Italy's steel-producing capacity in 1914 was below 1 million tons, Germany could produce almost 18 million tons, England 8 million, France 6.6 million, and the Austro-Hungarian Empire 2.6 million tons; likewise, Italy had 618 machine-guns, whereas Germany had 3,000, France had 2,000, and the Austro-Hungarian Empire had 1,500. The entire Italian army had only 3,400 lorries, while there were not enough guns to go round, so that in the rear lines, only one soldier out of every ten received a rifle.[1]

So when Italy finally entered the war on 24 May 1915, the State was forced to put all its energies not only into financing and organizing war operations, but also into dramatically increasing production for the war effort, and in finding and allocating those resources that were not available nationally. Two of the three areas involving state intervention—the financing of the war effort and the management of supplies—will be dealt with in this section, while the third—the increase in industrial production—will be dealt with in the next section. The decision to analyse the war years together with the immediate post-war period follows from the fact that the post-war years (until 1922–3) were inevitably conditioned by the effects of war, at least (but not only) from an economic point of view .

We can see from the first column of Table 7.1 that the cost of war was extremely high, but not more so than in the other countries involved. The entire economy was involved in this war and up to as much as one-third of national income was spent on it during 1917–18, while public expenditure remained at a very high level for many years after the end of the war.[2] The three financial sources used were taxes, monetary circulation, and the public debt in ascending order of importance.

As far as taxes were concerned, very little was done during the war, and as a result the public budget deficit shot up (see column 2, Table 7.1). An increase in the rate of tax on profits did not produce a high enough yield, as the percentage of untaxable profits increased at the same time (see also section 7.2). According to calculations made by the League of Nations, Italy was the only country not to increase the fiscal burden (at constant prices) during the war, while Great Britain saw an almost fivefold increase in its tax burden, and it

[1] The period of less than one year during which Italy remained a neutral country was not, in fact, used to do something about Italy's lack of military preparation, partly because Parliament, which had adopted a neutral position on the war, refused to sanction any increase in military expenditure.

[2] France's experience was similar to that of Italy, whereas Gt. Britain managed not only to reduce civil expenditure fairly drastically, but also to increase tax revenues much more quickly than the other two.

Table 7.1. The cost of the First World War, 1914–1923

	War expenditure as % of GDP	% coverage of state expenditure by taxation	Paper money in circulation (million current lire)	Index of (3) (1914 = 100)	Public debt (billion lire)					
					Domestic debt	Foreign debt	Total	Composition of domestic debt		
								Consols	Redeemable debt	Floating debt
	(1)	(2)	(3)	(4)	(5)	(6)	(7)	(8)	(9)	(10)
1914	5.9	92	2,687	100	15.8	—	15.8	58.8	28.0	13.2
1915	18.3	48	4,443	165	18.4	—	18.4	51.1	29.9	19.0
1916	27.3	31	5,352	199	23.3	2.7	26.0	40.8	39.6	19.6
1917	33.1	29	7,180	267	32.3	6.8	39.1	50.9	22.1	27.0
1918	33.1	32	11,915	443	46.9	13.9	60.8	49.2	16.6	34.2
1919	24.8	38	14,171	527	58.1	22.3	80.4	39.5	18.1	42.4
1920	17.0	56	19,808	737	76.9	27.0	103.9	55.0	11.3	33.7
1921	19.1	69	20,028	745	84.5	31.1	115.6	51.4	12.1	36.5
1922	10.2	64	19,529	727	91.2	32.9	124.1	47.3	12.7	40.0
1923	3.9	67	19,375	721	94.2	34.0	128.2	45.4	15.8	38.8

Sources: (1) Author's calculations based on F. Repaci, *La finanza pubblica italiana nel secolo 1861–1960* (Bologna, Zanichelli, 1962) and P. Ercolani, 'Documentazione statistica di base'; (2) author's calculations based on Ragioneria Generale dello Stato, *Il bilancio dello italiano dal 1862 al 1967* (Rome, 1969); (3) R. De Mattia, *I bilanci degli istituti di emissione italiani dal 1845 al 1936* (Rome, 1967); (4)–(10) V. Zamagni, *Il debito pubblico in Italia 1861–1945*, unpublished study. Foreign debt is valued here at its collection price and not at its reimbursement price (the two differed in these years as a result of devaluation of the lira).

was increased by about 50 per cent in both France and Germany.[3] One likely explanation for this is that the government was afraid of lowering the incentive to increase production in a country in which the vast majority of people had a fairly miserable standard of living. Another possible explanation is that the country had undervalued the resources necessary for the preparation of a war of this kind.

The decision to introduce an extraordinary form of taxation was not taken until the immediate post-war period: this consisted in a wealth tax, introduced by two decree laws (one on 24 November 1919, the other on 22 April 1920), and a confiscation duty on war profits, introduced in September 1920. Ordinary taxation was also raised; however, one proposed decree that was very unpopular, and which was not adopted in the end, was Giolitti's proposal to register all securities in order that a progressive tax-rate could be applied to the income they yielded.[4]

The yield from extraordinary taxation was particularly high in the tax years 1920/21 and 1921/22, but it continued throughout the following years, as the payment of the wealth tax had been established over a 30-year period. The fiscal burden, however, only rose by a couple of percentage points on GDP. Many people have noticed that the State managed to increase taxes to the greatest degree, in fact, during those difficult years 1920–1, when the social, political, and economic crises already combined to render everyone's life that much more difficult. For this reason, the new fiscal measures were applied with less severity than had at first been planned.[5]

Since fiscal measures had proven to be rather insufficient, it was the turn of monetary circulation and the public debt to bear the weight of paying for the war. Paper circulation (columns 3 and 4, Table 7.1) quadrupled during the war, and went on growing during 1919 and, in particular, during 1920.[6] It is well known that this method is generally considered by economists to be inadvisable, as it invariably leads to inflation and depreciation of the exchange rate,[7] as can be seen clearly from a glance at Table 7.2. Nevertheless, it is often used for the simple reason that it quickly moves resources towards the one who spends the new notes printed by the note-issuing banks' mints, in this case, the State itself.

[3] P. Frascani, *Politica economica e finanza pubblica in Italia nel primo dopoguerra 1918–1922* (Naples, Giannini ed., 1975), 254.

[4] Cf. F. Balletta, *Per la storia della politica finanziaria in Italia. L'opera di Marcello Soleri* (Naples, 1983). On the characteristics of the tax on wealth and the debate among economists on this matter, cf. P. Ganugi, 'Il peso del debito nella dottrina e nella politica finanziaria degli anni '20 in Italia', *Rivista di storia economica*, 5 (1988).

[5] See Frascani, *Politica economica*, and Balletta, *Per la storia della politica finanziaria*.

[6] For details, see C. Supino, *Storia della circolazione cartacea in Italia (dal 1860 al 1928)* (Milan, SEI, 1929). For an analysis of the Bank of Italy's role in providing financial support for the war, see G. Toniolo (ed)., *La Banca d'Italia e l'economia di guerra 1914–1919* (Bari, Laterza, 1989).

[7] In order to be able to exercise a more effective control over exchange rates, Nitti set up the Istituto Nazionale dei Cambi con l'estero (INC) at the Treasury, which took charge of all foreign currency operations. After the war, the Bank of Italy took over the management of the INC.

Table 7.2. Inflation and foreign exchange rates, 1914–1922

	Indices of		Average annual exchange rate (lire)			
	wholesale prices (1914 = 100) (1)	cost of living (1914 = 100) (2)	US Dollar (3)	Pound (4)	French franc (5)	Gold[a] (6)
1914	100	100	5.28	25.86	103.21	105.80
1915	133	107	6.69	31.00	112.30	120.35
1916	193	134	6.86	32.62	117.30	128.85
1917	286	189	7.41	35.28	128.29	134.04
1918	431	264	7.85	37.60	140.18	149.49
1919	470	268	9.79	41.54	121.31	164.70
1920	617	352	21.19	77.46	145.76	307.06
1921	565	417	23.50	91.19	174.68	393.92
1922	569	414	21.19	93.74	172.94	408.75

[a] Lira value of one ounce of gold.

Sources: (1) and (2) ISTAT, *Il valore della lira dal 1861 al 1965* (Rome, 1966); (3)–(6) *Annuario statistico italiano*, 1913–1925.

One can say that the greater the public reluctance towards financing government spending through fiscal measures, the greater is the temptation to use monetary means to do so.

The history of the public debt is more interesting and more complex: as Table 7.1 (column 7) shows, it increased by more than 100 billion lire (at current prices), going from 81 per cent of GDP in 1914, to 125 per cent of GDP in 1920 (116 per cent in 1923). Five national loan issues were made during the war, starting with the first in 1914: the first three were redeemable, whereas the last two involved consolidated bonds. Column 10 of the table shows, however, that as savings gradually dried up and inflation rose, it became ever more difficult to increase the public debt through long-term bonds, and consequently more and more use was made of the floating debt, which by 1918 represented one-third of the total debt and continued to rise thereafter. This led to the debt being on the one hand a cause of inflation, and on the other a serious headache for the Treasury, which was forced to refund, within a short space of time, large quantities of government bonds; and this, against an extremely worrying social and economic climate. The problem dragged on for a long time, and was only resolved after Mussolini took over control of the situation (see Chapter 8).

Column 6 of Table 7.1 shows the value of that part of the debt which Italy had with foreign countries, in particular with Great Britain and the USA, which allowed Italy to finance its imports of foodstuffs and raw materials. Again, this part of the debt was only settled at a later date (during the mid-1920s), as part of a series of measures which we shall be looking at in Chapter 8. Frascani has remarked, following on from Stringher, that 'this mobilization of resources [through the use of the public debt] proved to be weaker than that carried out in other countries during the war'.[8] While there can be no doubt that England and France had a higher public debt / GDP ratio than Italy had, inflation had helped to reduce the burden of the debt in Italy, and savings were not nearly as high as in the other two countries, and could not be diverted in larger amounts from their normal use in the productive sectors. On the whole, all countries, and especially France, had difficulty in settling their enormous public debts, as Confalonieri and Gatti have shown in a recent study.[9] However, the legitimacy of the use of the public debt as a means of financing a war has been supported by many famous economists: they have underlined the fact that in doing so the State passes on a part of the cost of war to future generations, making them economically responsible in part for the sacrifices made by the previous generations who had fought the war.

We can now take a look at how the government tackled the problem of the provision of foodstuffs. At the beginning of the war in Europe, the problem of provisions had not been considered seriously: the few measures taken by government included a ban on cereal, animal, and meat exports. However, from the end of 1914 onwards, Italy was no longer able to import cereals from Russia and Romania, due to the closure of the Dardanelles and the Bosphorus. Government intervention became imperative at this point, and on 21 December 1914, voluntary consortia were authorized to organize cereal and flour supplies. A temporary office controlling the supply of wheat was set up on 26 January 1915 at the MAIC headquarters; but this office managed to do very little about the situation, and a serious crisis was already imminent by the summer of 1915, especially since that year's harvest was not very good (see column 11, Table 7.3). The State only managed to win control over domestic wheat production on 8 January 1916, including the power to make requisitions if necessary. The organization of foreign imports was co-ordinated with the Allies. On 10 January 1916, a central commission for supplying cereals was set up, and its temporary office became the decision-making body in such matters. In the meantime, however, other foodstuffs had become difficult to obtain, and the government was forced to assume the responsibility of buying and distributing them. March 1916 saw the introduction of governmental price lists for foodstuffs, despite opposition from several ministers.

Dentoni[10] writes that 'In reality, at the bottom of all this "pro-consumer"

8 Frascani, *Politica economica*, 43.

9 A. Confalonieri and E. Gatti, *La politica del debito pubblico in Italia 1919–1943* (2 vols., Bari, Cariplo-Laterza, 1986.

10 M. C. Dentoni, '"Questione alimentare" e "questione sociale" durante la prima guerra mondiale in Italia', *Società e storia*, 37 (1987), 621.

Table 7.3. Total exports and imports; availability of wheat, 1913–1922

	Exports					Imports					Wheat (million q.)		
	% GDP	Geographical composition (%)				% GDP	Geographical composition (%)				Domestic production	Net imports	Total availabilities
		France	Germany	UK	USA		France	Germany	UK	USA			
	(1)	(2)	(3)	(4)	(5)	(6)	(7)	(8)	(9)	(10)	(11)	(12)	(13)
1913	14.5	9.3	13.7	10.5	10.7	17.5	7.8	16.8	16.2	14.3	5.69	0.96	6.65
1914	13.6	7.9	14.5	13.9	11.9	14.2	7.0	17.2	17.3	15.2	4.49	0.82	5.31
1915	11.8	17.4	8.1	15.6	11.3	16.1	5.1	4.9	18.0	37.2	4.51	0.32	5.84
1916	9.2	24.2	—	14.6	10.3	17.7	7.1	0.1	23.6	40.7	4.68	1.44	6.12
1917	4.5	27.8	—	14.7	7.4	16.1	7.1	0.1	15.5	44.3	3.71	1.12	4.83
1918	4.9	36.5	—	22.0	5.1	13.5	7.7	0.1	16.6	41.4	4.86	1.78	6.64
1919	8.1	23.4	1.4	12.9	10.5	16.3	4.6	0.5	14.7	44.2	4.50	1.68	6.18
1920	12.1	14.6	4.9	11.9	8.1	23.0	7.1	4.1	17.1	32.4	3.74	1.96	5.70
1921	9.5	12.0	10.1	9.9	13.5	15.6	6.3	7.6	9.9	33.8	5.11	1.93	7.04
1922	10.0	14.9	10.6	12.3	11.1	14.1	7.3	7.9	12.8	27.9	4.26	2.32	6.58

Sources: ISTAT, *Sommario di statistiche storiche* (Rome, 1958); B. Barberi, *I consumi nel primo secolo dell'unità d'Italia 1861–1960* (Milan, Giuffré, 1961); P. Ercolani (ed.), 'Documentazione statistica di base', author's elaborations.

legislation concerning rationing there lay something that inevitably meant an obstacle to any possible positive effects it might have had, and this was the general lack of provisions in Italy, due in part, admittedly, to the effects of the war, but more importantly, a result of the mistakes made and the lack of confidence shown by the government in its running of the whole question—ranging from the goods bought abroad to the problems of exchange rates, freight, tonnage and so forth.' The government's rationing policy was finally reorganized and centralized with the passing of a decree law on 2 August 1916 which established for the first time ever the State's absolute responsibility for the provision of the nation's food supplies.

Even this piece of legislation proved to be insufficient, however, in so far as it did not produce the positive results hoped for: the Entente Cordiale (Britain, France, and Italy) continued to lose ships to enemy submarines, the army took large quantities of provisions for its own men,[11] and also the State's organization of buying and distribution was less than adequate; within a short space of time, it found itself having to play the part of wholesale merchant, a part for which it was ill-prepared, needless to say. In July 1917, the General Commissioner for food supplies, Canepa, put forward a proposal to set up a National Board for consumer goods, involving collaboration between the State, banks, public consumer-goods bodies, and large co-operatives. The proposal was opposed by traders, and failed to be put into practice on a nationwide scale, although it did have some success on a smaller scale, particularly in major cities. For example, a Consumer Goods Authority was set up in Bologna in 1917;[12] in August of the same year, a communal consortium was founded in Milan, 'involving all the city's charitable and friendly societies, together with all its consumer co-operatives'.[13] Foodstuffs were sold both in communal stores and in these consumer co-operatives. At the end of the war, there were some 250 consumer-goods authorities throughout the country, while all the major co-operatives had expanded,[14] receiving credit both from banks and from the newly formed National Co-operative Credit Institute (Istituto Nazionale di Credito per la Cooperazione, or INCC).[15]

The last novelty within this sector was the introduction of ration cards for all primary foodstuffs in September 1917 (introduced later in many cities). All these plans failed, of course, to prevent the existence of a black market, price increases, wastage, and a fall in farmers' motivation to produce (due to the low

[11] The majority of the 2,600,000 peasants who fought at the front received a more nutritional diet than they would normally have had back on the farm.

[12] V. Zamagni, 'L'economia', in R. Zangheri (ed.), *Bologna* (Bari, Laterza, 1988).

[13] M. C. Pedroni, 'Sviluppo e ruolo della cooperazione di consumo nel milanese durante la prima guerra mondiale', *Storia in Lombardia*, 16 (1987).

[14] Cf. V. Zamagni, 'Dinamica e problemi della distribuzione commerciale al minuto tra il 1880 e la II guerra mondiale', in *Mercati e consumi* (Bologna, Analisi, 1986).

[15] On the work of the INCC during the war, cf. A. Basevi, 'L'Istituto nazionale di credito per la cooperazione', in W. Briganti (ed.), *Il movimento cooperativo in Italia 1854–1925* (Rome, 1976).

prices paid for many requisitioned products). There were public demonstrations in Milan in May 1917, and in Turin in August of the same year (in which 50 people died and 100 were injured).[16] The system of rationing only became reasonably efficient when the industrialist Silvio Crespi was made Minister responsible for the provision and distribution of foodstuffs after the Caporetto defeat: at this point, however, the war was almost over.

At the end of the war it was believed that everything would quickly return to normal, and therefore, although the existing organization was not dismantled, it was again made the responsibility of an Under-Secretary, despite the continued presence of enormous unresolved problems. The most worrying thing was the increase in prices, which was no longer a result of scarcity of goods, but was tied up with monetary inflation, which had been partially held at bay by official price-fixing during the war, but which now rocketed upwards. For this reason, bread prices were maintained at a 'politically acceptable' level—something that cost the public purse a considerable amount of money—in order to bridge the gap between prices paid to producers for wheat and the cost of bread to the public. Also, plans were made to help co-operatives get by through the introduction of financial incentives in the hope that by doing so, 'the upward price spiral could be halted' to some degree.[17] In particular, the co-operatives were given generous credit terms by local banks, national banks, and the INCC, which was partly nationalized on 7 April of that year.

Nevertheless, the role of the co-operatives proved to be less effective than had been expected, partly due to their somewhat fragmented nature, and to the attacks perpetrated at first by the mob (many co-operatives were ransacked half-way through 1919), and then by the Fascists, and partly due to the fall in prices during 1921, which destroyed the already shaken financial position of many co-operatives.[18] In fact, it was only when inflation came to a halt in 1921 that Giolitti succeeded where Nitti had failed the year before: that is, he managed to put an end to wartime price-rationing. As Balletta shows,[19] the under-secretary for food distribution and provision from 1920 onwards, Marcello Soleri, managed to carry out one last difficult operation involving the acquisition of wheat on international markets that were still far from normal, and then to prepare the running-down of the rationing system. First, he limited the responsibility of the supply consortia to the provision of cereals (20

[16] These protests were to lead to the introduction of ration cards, and to the Government Food Supplies Office being transformed into a Ministry.

[17] V. Castronovo, *Storia di una banca. La Banca Nazionale del Lavoro e lo sviluppo economico italiano 1913–1983* (Turin, Einaudi, 1983), 48.

[18] The Unione Cooperativa di Milano, the biggest Italian retail co-operative in 1920, itself went through a crisis. When Mussolini took over power, he disbanded the Co-operative League, and its place was taken by the Ente Nazionale Fascista della Cooperazione, in Oct. 1925. The co-operative movement lost its momentum as a result, although it did not disappear altogether, and was to come to the fore again after the Second World War. Cf. A Caroleo, *Il movimento cooperativo in Italia nel primo dopoguerra 1918–1925* (Milan, Angeli, 1986).

[19] Balletta, *Per la storia della politica finanziaria*, 60.

November 1920), raised the price of bread (17 February 1921), and finally again liberalized the international trade in cereals and the import of maize and rye from abroad (wheat and sugar were partially freed, by a decree of 22 June 1921). The ration system was also wound up—all of this at a time when prices had begun to yield.

On the whole, despite delays, uncertainties, and mistakes, especially at the beginning of the war, there was no overall reduction in average food consumption: on the contrary, Barberi's figures[20] show that consumption was higher during the war years than it had been during the pre-war years,[21] and in 1922 was 15 per cent higher than before the war. This had been made possible by the agreement that Italy had with the Allies, by which it could import from abroad, especially from the USA and Canada, and pay for these imports using the loans that the Allies themselves had made. As Table 7.3 shows, Italian exports had fallen from 14 per cent of GDP to 4.5 per cent in 1917, whereas imports had remained more or less at pre-war levels (column 6), that is, between 14 and 18 per cent of GDP (reaching a maximum in 1920). Thus living standards and the availabilty of raw materials had been kept artificially high thanks to the Allies' help (in particular that of the USA), whose imports into Italy jumped from 14.2 per cent in 1913 to 44.3 per cent in 1917. As for price increases, these were only partly due to the scarcity of goods, as we have mentioned already; the real reason lay with the increase in monetary circulation necessary in order to pay for the war effort.

2. INDUSTRY: INDUSTRIAL MOBILIZATION AND POST-WAR RECONVERSION

Industrial mobilization got under way with the issue of law no. 993 on 26 June 1915:[22] this declared that the government had the right to bestow 'annexed' status on those industrial plants of use in the war, and it also set up regional committees for industrial mobilization, whose job it was to manage these plants, make decisions concerning production and prices, and implement military law within the confines of the plant. Particular importance was given to the importation of coal, which was hard to find on international markets at the time, and in February 1917 a general Coal Commission was set up. It proved

[20] B. Barberi, *I consumi nel primo secolo dell'unità d'Italia 1861–1960)* (Milan, Giuffré, 1961).

[21] It would be interesting to calculate whether per capita availability of food for the civilian population (having detracted soldiers' food consumption, which can be estimated to a fairly accurate degree) was still higher than it had been before the war.

[22] General Alfredo Dallolio from Bologna was the promoter and organizer of the mobilization of industry. He had gained a clear idea of the conditions of the engineering sector during his experience as General Commander of the Artillery and Engineer Corps from 1911 onwards, and he was fully aware of the fragmented nature of the business enterprises and the dire lack of vital raw materials needed for industrial production. Cf. F. Minniti, 'Alfredo Dallolio (1853–1952)', in A. Mortara (ed.), *I protagonisti dell'intervento pubblico in Italia* (Milan, Angeli, 1984).

impossible to avoid a fall in imports, although this was kept to a minimum, and the loss was partly made up by resorting to alternative domestic energy sources.

In this way, the State became of central importance even in the productive sectors, as one writer at the time observed:

> The country's economy resembles that of a besieged city, with the phenomenon of war polarizing every form of activity, every operation, every situation. The new role played by the State symbolizes the absolute dominance of this phenomenon. The State, as an entrepreneur of war, has become the focal point, the engine of the entire economy; it has become head of a gigantic business enterprise, upon which thousands of smaller individual enterprises depend for their existence; it employs, both directly and indirectly, millions of workers, animates a large part of the country's active industries, moves almost the entire merchant navy, carries on a vast trading operation, and, above all, consumes an enormous quantity of wealth.[23]

Industrial mobilization was the most important branch of the newly formed Ministero delle Armi e Munizioni (Ministry of Armaments and Ammunition) that had been the responsibility of an under-secretary until 1917. This Ministry was also responsible for general and technical services, administration, and the command of the artillery corps, the engineer corps, and the air force.[24] Besides operational tasks, industrial mobilization also set up an information service, with press and library facilities, and published a fortnightly news-sheet. Those plants that had been declared 'auxiliary' in order to serve the war effort were to be bases for control committees, military control offices, and for the important combined commissions for job arbitration, whose aim it was to prevent hiccups in the smooth running of things.[25] The number of companies that were declared 'auxiliary' during hostilities rose from 221 at the end of 1951 to 797 in June 1916, rising further to reach 932 at the end of 1916, and 1,976 at the end of the war. In June 1918, the workers in these establishments, together with those in the 60 or so military establishments, numbered some 902,000. Their regional and sectorial distribution is shown in Table 7.4. It should be noted that more than 70 per cent of them were directly involved in the production of arms (from the minerals to the explosives produced), and 56 per cent were concentrated in the industrial triangle (with 83 per cent of the metallurgical plants and 73 per cent of the engineering factories).

There is clear evidence to show that state production orders were in extreme administrative disorder, and that there was a tendency to accept the industrialists' requests without questioning them in any way, in terms of both prices and other important advantages offered to them by the State. Caracciolo

[23] R. Bachi, *L'Italia economica nell'anno 1916* (Città di Castello, 1917), 41.

[24] For a discussion of the political and institutional aspects of the Ministry, cf. L. Mascolini, 'Il Ministero per le armi e munizioni (1915–1918)', *Storia contemporanea*, 11 (Dec. 1980).

[25] Cf. L. Tomassini, 'Intervento dello stato e politica salariale durante la prima guerra mondiale: esperimenti e studi per la determinazione di una "scala mobile" delle retribuzioni operaie', *Annali*, 22 (Milan, Feltrinelli, 1982).

Table 7.4. Plants and factories declared to be 'auxiliary' to the war effort in 1918

	Mines (1)	Food (2)	Metall. (3)	Engin. (4)	Bricks (5)	Textiles (6)	Chem. (7)	Services (8)	Total (9)
Turin	19	44	50	141	15	15	61	26	371
Milan	28	54	87	215	20	28	80	33	545
Genoa	6	29	33	53	21	4	42	12	200
Venice	3	12	1	16	8	2	22	5	69
Bologna	12	9	5	17	3	4	46	8	104
Florence	49	21	11	23	11	18	33	5	171
Rome	22	19	7	36	11	3	24	17	139
Naples	17	28	6	37	6	—	22	12	128
Bari	—	1	—	5	4	—	16	6	32
Palermo	114	9	2	13	27	1	10	9	185
Cagliari	22	2	2	2	—	2	—	2	32
TOTAL	292	228	204	558	126	75	358	135	1976

Source: A. Caracciolo, 'La crescita e la trasformazione della grande industria durante la prima guerra mondiale', in G. Fuà (ed.), *Lo sviluppo economico in Italia.*

writes: 'on top of the profit obtained in terms of prices paid, there were two other types of benefit available, which were particularly important if the war industries were to be allowed to expand . . . the generous advances made, and the large subsidy given to cover the cost of the amortization of new plant',[26] made possible by means of considerable tax deductions. The expansion of industrial plants, although sometimes moving in an inconvenient direction from the point of view of the industry itself, was in the end stimulated by an increase in the untaxable part of profits reinvested, while there was a corresponding increase in the tax-rate on taxable earnings. It was no surprise then that there was a veritable boom in company profits, and that investment, which appeared to have sunk in aggregate terms, shot up in those sectors of the economy involved in production for the war, particularly the engineering sector. One calculation, made by Zugaro, shows that nearly 14 billion (pre-war) lire were spent on armaments between 1914–15 and 1919–20,[27] representing 12 per cent of income for those years (with a maximum of 20 per cent between 1917 and 1918). Despite wastage and differences between one company's productivity and another's, productive results were remarkable, as can be seen from Table 7.5.

Segreto writes: 'Italian industry managed to supply the army with the best part of its armaments during the war—this had not exactly been a foregone conclusion before the start of hostilities. . . . The help given by the Allies, indispensable as far as raw materials were concerned, became supplementary in nature, and only for some war materials, after the Caporetto defeat';[28] in fact, one would have witnessed even a limited flow of exports out of Italy.[29] In order to co-ordinate small and medium-sized companies' production, 'production groups' were set up, and well-known entrepreneurs were placed at their head. For example, Dante Ferraris (Fiat) was in charge of 25 companies, while Luigi Orlando (Italian Metallurgical Company) co-ordinated companies producing copper and copper goods. There were small companies, which, being very strong in their specialized areas, and having dynamic management boards, expanded at a surprising pace.

This was the case of the Alfa-Romeo Company which, with a total of 200 workers before the war, expanded to such an extent that the total work-force in November 1918 numbered some 4,130. This was due to its specialization in the production of munitions, hand-grenades, fuses, and aircraft engines, with the financial help of the BIS.[30] A similar case was that of the Franchi Company of

[26] A. Caracciolo, 'La crescita e le trasformazione della grande industria durante la prima guerra mondiale', in G. Fuà (ed.), *Lo sviluppo economico in Italia*, iii (Milan, Angeli, 1969), 211.

[27] F. Zugaro, *Il costo della guerra italiana. Contributo alla storia economica della guerra mondiale* (Rome, 1921).

[28] L. Segreto, 'Armi e munizioni. Lo sforzo bellico tra sperimentazione e progresso tecnico', *Italia contemporanea*, 146–7 (1982), 49.

[29] Ibid. 51.

[30] D. Bigazzi, *Il Portello. Operai, tecnici e imprenditori all'Alfa-Romeo 1906–1926* (Milan, Angeli, 1988).

Table 7.5. Armaments, ammunition, and other items for use in the war 1915–1918

	Stock in May 1915	Stock at Armistice	Total production 1915–18
Canons	2,038	7,789	11,789
Artillery bullets	...	...	69,835,000
Guns and muskets	2,474,700	3,143,416	24,230,000
Cartridges	...	...	3,616,000,000
Seaplanes	638	1,630	...
Aeroplanes	143	3,335	12,021
Aeroplane engines	...	...	24,400
Motor cars	400	2,510	...
Lorries	3,400	27,400	...
Motor cycles	1,100	6,000	...
Tractors	150	1,200	...
Ships	...	...	505
Submarines	...	...	71

Sources: L. Segreto, 'Armi e munizioni. Lo sforzo bellico tra sperimentazione e progresso tecnico', *Italia contemporanea*, 146–7 (1982); A. Caracciolo, 'La crescita e la trasformazione'.

Brescia, a small metallurgical company going back to the end of the nineteenth century, which amalgamated with the Gregorini Company in 1916, and subsequently took over the Brescian metal company Tempini and the Tubi Mannesmann in 1917, as well as other local electrical and mineral companies, and ended up with the grand total of 25,000 employees at the end of the war.[31]

However, the companies that were to gain the most from the war were in fact those that had already been fairly big before the war, as they had been better prepared both technologically and organizationally for the kind of orders that the State gave to them during the war, and were also in a better position to exercise political pressure on the government in order to obtain the best orders.[32] Such companies expanded their own productive bases, and also started to buy up other companies and expand into other areas of productive activity connected to their own, so that a process of concentration got under way, and for the first time ever in Italy one saw the growth of 'big business'

[31] R. Chiarini, *L'armonia e l'ardimento. L'ascesa del fascismo nella Brescia di Augusto Turati* (Milan, Angeli, 1988), 35. Both companies had a difficult time during the years immediately after the war, and there were a number of salvage operations conducted by various banks during this period. Even Mussolini got involved in Alfa's salvage operation, although it took the whole of the 1920s before the company was back on its feet. In the case of the Franchi–Gregorini, Comit at a certain point held the majority of the company's shares, and it decided to reorganize the company, removing Franchi from the management board in the process.

[32] The Ansaldo and the Caproni stood out from the rest due to their proven ability to gain 'admission' to governmental military and technocratic circles at the time of war.

and the formation of large industrial groupings. 'Within the space of a few years', Caracciolo writes,[33] 'the process of concentration in basic industries, and in the hands of the largest companies, was extremely quick.' This process can now be looked at a little more closely, as it was of fundamental importance for the subsequent development of the Italian economy. We shall take a look at each of the main productive sectors in turn.

The only figures available at the sectorial level are those given in Table 7.6, which show that there was a general increase in production until 1917, after which only a few sectors continued to follow this upward trend during 1918 (the aircraft industry, electricity, and gas), while from 1919 to 1921 all sectors were in decline, with the exception of the electricity industry, railways, and shipbuilding, which were clearly going against the general trend.[34] We can now take a look at some productive sectors and some of the companies involved.

2.1. ENGINEERING

Fiat. The number of people working at the Fiat factories grew from 4,300 in 1914 to over 40,000 by 1918,[35] partly as a result of the company's take-over of other companies and setting up new companies. While annual production of vehicles (including trucks) stood at 4,644 units in 1914, in 1918 Fiat produced 16,542 vehicles in all. The company also decided to diversify production, producing aeroplane engines (which counted for more than half the total number of engines produced) and boat engines, as well as machine-guns and ammunition. It set up its own steel plants, and built a brand-new plant at Lingotto, which was finished in 1922. At the end of the war, Fiat was the third largest company in Italy, behind Ansaldo and ILVA, and although the reconversion to civil production was difficult, it was rapid and thorough.[36]

ILVA. This company was responsible for the management of the main metallurgical plants in Italy, and these plants produced 90 per cent of the country's pig-iron and 60 per cent of its steel: the major plants were those at Bagnoli, Piombino, and Portoferraio, and there were a number of other smaller plants around the country. During the war, these plants enlarged and saw the adoption of Martin and electric furnaces,[37] while a brand-new productive complex was set up in 1918 at Marghera, near Venice. The companies managed by ILVA amalgamated on 11 July 1918 to form a new company, the ILVA Altiforni e Acciaierie d'Italia. This new company also took over a number

[33] Caracciolo, 'La crescita', 217.

[34] Some other productive sectors also went against the predominant economic cycle, thus compensating in part for the slump in heavy industry production.

[35] 60% of the total number of engineering workers in the Piedmont region.

[36] Cf. V. Castronovo, *Agnelli* (Turin, UTET, 1971).

[37] The number of electric blast-furnaces installed in Italy increased considerably, reaching a total of 187 by the end of 1917, which put Italy at the forefront in Europe in the use of this technology.

Table 7.6. Output of selected industries, 1913–1923

	Pig-iron[a]	Steel[a]	Cars		Aero-planes	Aeroplane engines	Loco-motives	Railway coaches	Ships[a]	Sulphuric acid[a]	Nitric acid[a]	Electricity produced[b]	Gas consump-tion[c]
			Total	Produced by Fiat									
	(1)	(2)	(3)	(4)	(5)	(6)	(7)	(8)	(9)	(10)	(11)	(12)	(13)
1913	427	934	6,670	3,251	...	...	210	5,258	60	645	13.6	2,200	391
1914	385	911	9,210	4,644	...	...	153	4,245	45	630	12.5	2,575	485
1915	378	1,009	15,420	7,646	382	606	153	2,982	24	626	15.8	2,925	455
1916	467	1,269	17,370	12,697	1,255	2,248	45	1,886	77	...	...	3,425	970
1917	471	1,332	25,280	19,184	3,871	6,726	160	1,931	37	...	...	4,000	798
1918	314	933	22,230	16,542	6,523	14,820	30	2,316	60	624	6.1	4,300	854
1919	240	732	17,900	12,591	...	...	268	7,422	93	584	6.8	4,000	731
1920	88	774	21,080	14,314	...	...	249	7,865	79	563	5.9	4,690	216
1921	61	700	15,230	10,326	...	...	261	3,084	143	672	6.0	4,540	254
1922	158	983	16,390	10,675	...	...	292	1,969	86	777	7.5	4,730	291
1923	236	1,142	22,820	15,162	...	...	220	662	60	993	8.7	5,610	339

[a] Tons (thousands).
[b] kWh (millions).
[c] m^3 (millions).

Sources: ISTAT, *Sommario di statistiche storiche italiane 1861–1955* (Rome, 1958); (3)–(6), A. Fossati, *Lavoro e produzione in Italia dalla metà del secolo XVIII alla seconda guerra mondiale* (Turin, Giappichelli, 1951) and D. Bigazzi, 'Un'impresa italiana sul mercato mondiale: l'attività multinazionale della Fiat fino al 1940', *Annali di storia dell'impresa*, 2 (1986).

of other enterprises, including the Neapolitan shipyards, the car manufacturer Isotta Fraschini, the Magona, and the Miani Silvestri engineering works, taking the total number of employees to 50,000 by the end of the war. Carparelli concludes that 'all of this was carried out with the final aim of creating one large, polymorphous company, with a high degree of horizontal and vertical integration, starting with pig-iron and finishing with production of the final product, which was to include ships, railway parts, electrical equipment, and automobiles'.[38]

However, the resulting financial strain, together with the directors' passion for speculative combinations, meant that this industrial giant was particularly vulnerable. The post-war slump in the steel industry (see columns 1 and 2, Table 7.6), partly due to the scarcity of coal, and the reduction in freight traffic (which hit Lloyd Mediterraneo, ILVA's fleet) put the company in a very difficult position, and its directors attempted to resolve the crisis by getting further involved in financial speculation.[39] The company publicly declared itself to be in a critical position during May 1921; the directors were removed from office, and with the help of Comit, Credit, the Banco di Roma, and the Banca d'Italia, the company was put back on an even keel in May of the following year, having sold off all of its non-steel-producing interests. Carparelli says that this solution, which had been Comit's idea, put an end, in fact, to any hope of freeing the company from its dependence on government contracts.[40] A similar attempt to free itself from state dependency, this time on an even larger scale, was made by the other steel giant, Ansaldo.

Ansaldo. Historians have been more interested in the affairs of Ansaldo than in those of any other company, because of the size of the company and its important relationship with the rest of the Italian economic system. The fact that at the beginning of the war the company had 6,000 workers, while at the end of the war they numbered some 56,000 (to which one must add the same number in affiliate companies), should be proof enough of this. Caracciolo notes that, 'starting from an engineering nucleus, the company created what was known as the "Ansaldo integrated vertical system", divided into three parts: steel-production, engineering, and ship building—all three of which were

[38] A. Carparelli, 'La siderurgia italiana nella prima guerra mondiale: il caso dell'ILVA', *Ricerche storiche*, 8 (1978), 152.

[39] The ILVA tried to take over Bastogi and Edison. On these events see G. Piluso, 'Lo speculatore, i banchieri e lo stato: la Bastogi da Max Bondi ad Alberto Beneduce (1918–1933)', *Annali di storia dell'impresa*, 7 (1991).

[40] Carparelli maintains that Comit resolved the ILVA case in this way, not because it was against the idea of adopting multi-sectorial strategies, but because it wanted to give 'its' company, the Terni, an advantage, and the Terni 'was in fact relaunched along multi-sectorial lines, thanks also to its taking on a part of ILVA's industrial activity when the latter was forced to sell', A. Carparelli, 'I perché di una "mezza siderurgia". La società Ilva, l'industria della ghisa e il ciclo integrale negli anni venti', in F. Bonelli (ed.), *Acciaio per l'industrializzazione. Contributi allo studio del problema siderurgico italiano* (Turin, Einaudi, 1982).

interdependent'.[41] A lot has been written about the Ansaldo system, and about the technology behind it that did not take into account the costs involved, which were of great importance for a country as poor as Italy at that time.[42] Ansaldo was very successful during the war, producing 46 per cent of all the artillery, as well as 3,000 aeroplanes, 1,574 aeroplane engines, 96 battleships, 200,000 tons of merchant shipping, and 10 million units of ammunition, etc. But this success led to a massive expansion programme which was totally out of proportion to the resources and markets in Italy at that time, despite being technologically valid and a model for similar projects which were to be successful later on. The important parts of this programme were: the Cogne mines, with their neighbouring electrical steel-mills and hydroelectric power stations, the steel-mills at Cornigliano operating on a complete cycle (these were built several years later), and a merchant fleet for the transportation of raw materials. All of this required an enormous amount of investment, and the Perrone brothers, who owned Ansaldo, tried to find the necessary capital through their banking connections, and by throwing their energies into unsuccessful foreign expansion projects.[43]

The crisis that hit Ansaldo also dragged one of the company's banks along with it, the BIS, and in doing so 'put an end, not only to the Perrone brothers' "national plan" . . . but also to the whole "Ansaldo vertical system", which the company's reorganizers were quick . . . to dismember'.[44] On the 3 December 1921, Bonaldo Stringher forced the Perrone brothers to resign, and gave the responsibility for the reorganization of the group, with financial help from the CSVI, to a committee made up mainly of representatives of the new ILVA, the Terni, and Fiat: these men were to 're-shape the Genoese group in such a way that it did not generate competition in those sectors of production controlled by its adversaries, and, in fact, to render its operations compatible with an eventual take-over by its competitors when they decided to do so'.[45] The new Ansaldo was set up on 15 September 1922.

2.2. THE AIRCRAFT INDUSTRY

It would not be wrong to say that the aircraft industry did not really exist before the war, even though one or two enthusiasts had built prototypes of aircraft and

[41] Caracciolo, 'La crescita', 222.

[42] The first essay written about this question was that of R. Webster, 'La tecnocrazia italiana e i sistemi industriali verticali: il caso dell'Ansaldo (1914–1921)', *Storia contemporanea*, 9 (1978).

[43] On the attempts made by the Perrones to find foreign markets for their products, cf. T. Row, *Economic Nationalism in Italy: the Ansaldo Company 1882–1921*, doctoral thesis, Johns Hopkins University, Baltimore, 1988.

[44] A. M. Falchero, 'La piramide effimera. Il sistema verticale Ansaldo dai primi passi alla distruzione', in *Studi in memoria di Mario Abrate*, i (Turin, Saste, 1986), 393.

[45] P. Rugafiori, *Uomini, macchine, capitali. L'Ansaldo durante il fascismo 1922–1945* (Milan, 1981), 28.

had drawn up several projects for their construction. During the war, this industry managed to produce more than 12,000 aircraft, 24,000 aircraft engines, and, according to a survey conducted at the time, employed a total of 100,000 workers. The most important companies were as follows: the Società Sviluppo Aviazione, run by the Caproni brothers; the SVA, belonging to Ansaldo; the Macchi Company of Varese; and the Società Idrovolanti Alta Italia (SIAI) of Sesto Calende (Varese). Aircraft engines were produced by Fiat, Alfa, Breda, and Isotta Fraschini. The excellent production figures, however, hid a real organizational mess, which was to be the cause of delays, wastage, and malfunctions, as ascertained by different inquiry commissions after the war had ended.[46]

2.3. THE CHEMICAL INDUSTRY

Some of the factors that had prevented the chemical industry from really taking off during the Giolitti years were eliminated as a result of the First World War. Protected from German competition, and spurred on by the requirements of war, the production of explosives was greatly increased through the enlargement of existing factories, and the setting up of new ones, and this in turn led to increased production of tar intermediates,[47] which had been produced in very small quantities up to that time, and which could be used just as well for the production of dyes and pharmaceuticals as for explosives. It is interesting to note here that whereas in Germany it was the large dye and pharmaceutical industries that were converted to the production of explosives, in Italy it was the need to produce explosives that led to setting up a productive sector that was later to be slowly reconverted to the production of dyes and pharmaceuticals, as we shall see in Chapter 9.[48]

Furthermore, the profits made during the war by the mining company Montecatini, a producer of pyrites that had already attempted to expand into the chemical sector (after Donegani had been appointed director in 1910), meant that the company now had sufficient liquid capital to be able to take over the two major fertilizer producers—Colla e Concimi and Unione Concimi—and in doing so, created a very powerful group which was to be at the centre of industrial development in the chemical sector from the 1920s onwards.

[46] Segreto, 'Armi e munizioni'. Also see A. Mantegazza, 'La formazione del settore aereonautico italiano', *Annali di storia dell'impresa*, 2 (1986).

[47] It was in fact the increased wartime consumption of carbon coke in the steelworks and of gas which led to a greater availability of tar.

[48] For further details of the development of the chemical industry during the First World War, see my study 'L'industria chimica in Italia dalle origini agli anni '50', in F. Amatori and B. Bezza (eds.), *Capitoli di storia di una grande impresa: la Montecatini 1886–1966* (Bologna, Il Mulino, 1991). It also gives details of the State's campaign in support of the industry.

2.4. ELECTRICITY

The history of the electricity industry is straightforward enough from the productive point of view: electricity production doubled during the war years, remained very high during the crisis years, and then continued to rise quickly from 1923 onwards (see column 12, Table 7.6). On the other hand, when looked at from a financial and political point of view, things seem much more complicated. First of all, those companies that had been controlled by German interests were 'Italianized', thus allowing the BIS—a mixed bank that had been kept on the sidelines of the electrical sector up to that point—to get involved in it.[49] Secondly, liquidity resulting from large profits, which had hardly been used at all for the construction of new plants (these had not increased in number during the war partly because directors feared that it could lead later to a productive over-capacity), could now be used in the attempt to free the major groups from their dependency on the banks, and Edison did in fact manage to accomplish just that.[50] Given that the nationalization plans for the hydroelectric industry had been abandoned for the time being (even by Francesco Saverio Nitti, their most famous supporter), the electricity companies proceeded to form the most powerful economic groupings of the 1920s and 1930s, thanks to their financial health and the absence of a production crisis in their sector.[51]

I would like now briefly to mention three other attempts at state intervention in industry. The first, which failed, was an attempt to obtain direct rights to the exploitation of certain raw materials, as payment for the country's victory: this involved Styria (which interested Fiat), Algeria, Greece, the Republic of Georgia, and Turkey.[52] The second form of intervention was represented by setting up the Inter-Ministerial Committee for the Settlement of the War Industries; although this committee proved capable of settling the State's outstanding debts with producers of materials used during the war, it failed to prevent a business crisis as it was incapable of devising a policy of gradual compensation, and in the end granted businesses too much liquidity that they used to further increase their speculative operations, given that there was no 'general programme for the regeneration of productive activity'.[53] Finally, the

[49] G. Mori, 'Le guerre parallele. L'industria elettrica in Italia nel periodo della grande guerra (1914–1919)', in *Il capitalismo industriale in Italy* (Rome, Editori Riuniti, 1977)

[50] Details of the operation are given in C. Pavese, 'Le origini della Società Edison e il suo sviluppo fino alla costruzione del "gruppo" (1881–1919)', in B. Bezza (ed.), *Energia e sviluppo. L'industria elettrica italiana e la società Edison* (Turin, Einaudi, 1986).

[51] R. Giannetti, *La conquista della forza. Risorse, tecnologia ed economia nell'industria elettrica italiana (1883–1940)* (Milan, Angeli, 1985).

[52] R. A. Webster, 'Una speranza rinviata. L'espansione industriale italiana e il problema del petrolio dopo la I guerra mondiale', *Storia contemporanea*, 11 (1980).

[53] A. Carparelli, 'Uomini, idee, iniziative, per una politica di riconversione industriale in Italia', in P. Hertner and G. Mori (eds.), *La transizione dall'economia di guerra all'economia di pace in Italia e in Germania dopo la prima guerra mondiale* (Bologna, Il Mulino, 1983), 247. The author gives a very clear account of the activity of famous engineers—Ettore Conti, Arturo Bocciardo, and Oscar

third form of intervention was that of commercial protectionism. A new set of tariffs had been prepared by a series of committees (which had already started work before the beginning of the war), and was passed by Giolitti's government on 1 July 1921; it was considered to be much better than the 1887 one, inasmuch as it 'formed an organic whole . . . [introducing] a general system of protection covering the entire range of agricultural and industrial production, including those sectors which had been developed during the war, as well as new areas which were only beginning to flourish at that time'.[54] As can be seen from Tattara's excellent study,[55] there was a lowering of effective protection in the textile industry, while protection in the steel industry was increased, and for the first time the engineering industry (in particular transport and electrical products) and the chemical industry (dyes and pharmaceuticals) were granted protection.

We can conclude that Pollard's idea of the 'differential of contemporaneousness' is particularly useful when considering the situation at the time of the First World War:[56] the same event, involving different economies at different stages of development, produces very different reactions and results. Compare Germany, which fought the war from a position of accumulated industrial strength, with Italy, which industrialized through the war.[57] We have also seen that the war accelerated the process whereby the basic industries, including engineering, were concentrated in fewer hands, and the country's industrial foundations were reinforced in stronger geographical locations, that is within the industrial triangle, with a significant spread effect in Emilia, the Veneto, and Tuscany. All of this, thanks to public expenditure—not only that concerning government war contracts, but also the salvage operations conducted after the war had ended. The war turned out to be an economic disaster for the South of Italy, as the policy of aid and development which had been part of Giolitti's policy prior to the war was abandoned in favour of state financial aid to those areas that were already industrially developed, that is, to the North. It was therefore inevitable that the North–South divide was to grow even wider as an indirect consequence of the war years. Other important consequences included a change in the very delicate balance between the banks and industry, as well as in the social and political make-up of the country. We can now take a closer look at these last two consequences.

Sinigaglia—who were quickly appointed to key positions on the Comitato. The full account of the working of another commission of industrialists can now be found in A. M. Falchero, *La 'commissionissima'. Gli industriali e il primo dopoguerra* (Milan, Angeli, 1991).

[54] F. Guarneri, *Battaglie economiche tra le due grandi guerre*, i (Milan, Garzanti, 1953), 49.

[55] G. Tattara, 'Protezione effettiva e sviluppo di alcuni settori dell'industria manifatturiera italiana dal 1921 al 1930', *Studi Economici*, 11 (1980).

[56] S. Pollard, *Peaceful Conquest. The Industrialization of Europe, 1760–1970* (Oxford, Oxford University Press, 1981), ch. 4.

[57] During the First World War, there was no case of countries involved simply in buying armaments from abroad, and getting heavily in debt as a result, as is frequently the case of developing countries today.

3. FINANCE: THE CONFLICT OVER THE LEADERSHIP AND THE CHANGING OF ALLIANCES

Unfortunately we do not have the kind of thorough, detailed study of the banking system, as supplied by Confalonieri for the previous period (see Chapter 5), for the difficult years we are dealing with here. However, the available literature does enable us to draw a general picture of the situation, and to give some detailed comments concerning the more important episodes. First of all, a few general points on the changes in the banking system due to the involvement in the war. Table 7.7 shows that the issuing banks regained for a brief period some of their earlier importance, as a result of the war, although by 1923 they had returned to the positions held in 1914 (column 1). Meanwhile, mixed banks gradually grew in importance, as their share of total banking assets rose from one-fifth to one-third (column 6). This occurred mainly at the expense of the savings banks and the land banks, although it also involved all other forms of banking institution. Of the other banks, the rural co-op banks were the ones that managed to hold on best to their percentage share during this period, although they were of relatively minor importance. Table 7.7, col. 9 also shows that two new institutions, dealing in long-term credit, appeared during this period: one was the CSVI (mentioned in Chapter 6), while the other was the Crediop founded in 1919, which we shall be looking at shortly.

The wartime growth in the issuing banks' assets was directly linked to the increase in monetary circulation mentioned above, and ceased from 1920 onwards (see column 3, Table 7.1); the mixed banks' success, on the other hand, was due to the fact that they were largely responsible for financing the war effort. The four major mixed banks' share of the total assets of joint-stock banks rose from 75 per cent (1914) to 90 per cent (1917), and it remained at this level until 1921, when the BIS went bankrupt (see Table 7.8). Table 7.8 also shows that Comit managed to hold on to first place during the entire period in question, Credit held on to second place until 1919–20, when it was overtaken by BIS, and the Banco di Roma remained in fourth place, with a period of stagnation until 1917 due to the problems mentioned in Chapter 5. As Cianci has written, if in a somewhat exaggerated fashion: 'The Banca Commerciale Italiana, the Credito Italiano, the Banca Italiana di Sconto, and the Banco di Roma formed an omnipotent banking quadrumvirate that was active in all areas of the Italian economy. They were behind every company and every speculative move made. The shareholders, the customers, and the savers of these four banks had inadvertently become partners in an enormous range of companies, as a result thereof'.[58]

It comes as no surprise then to discover that all the research carried out in

[58] E. Cianci, *Nascita dello Stato imprenditore in Italia* (Milan, Mursia, 1977), 20.

Table 7.7. The banking system, 1914–1923

	Percent composition of total assets									
	Issuing banks (1)	Savings banks (2)	Banche popolari (3)	Monti di Pietà (4)	Rural co-op. banks (5)	Joint-stock banks (6)	Cassa DDPP (7)	Land banks (8)	Long term credit institutes[a] (9)	Total assets (million lire) (10)
1914	26.4	20.1	9.3	1.9	0.7	19.3	16.0	6.3	—	17,096
1915	28.7	17.1	7.9	1.6	0.5	17.3	21.2	5.3	0.3	20,662
1916	29.5	16.3	7.9	1.5	0.6	21.8	18.7	3.4	0.3	24,117
1917	41.2	13.1	5.8	1.2	0.4	20.8	15.0	2.3	0.2	34,866
1918	36.4	13.1	8.0	1.1	0.4	24.3	14.6	1.8	0.2	43,550
1919	34.8	11.6	8.2	0.9	0.5	28.7	13.8	1.3	0.2	61,154
1920	32.9	11.1	7.5	0.9	0.5	30.7	14.8	1.1	0.6	75,900
1921	29.7	12.0	6.1	0.9	0.5	33.8	15.0	1.0	0.9	86,340
1922	27.1	13.3	6.9	1.1	0.6	33.2	15.4	1.1	1.3	88,695
1923	26.8	13.4	7.8	1.2	0.8	32.9	14.9	1.2	1.1	95,708

[a] Including the CSVI and the Crediop.

Source: R. De Mattia, *I bilanci degli istituti di emissione italiani dal 1845 al 1936* (Rome, 1967).

Table 7.8. Percentage share of total banks' assets held by the four major 'mixed banks', 1915–1923

	Comit (1)	Credit (2)	Banco di Roma (3)	BIS (4)	Total (5)
1915	5.5	3.9	1.6	2.3	13.3
1916	6.9	5.4	1.6	3.6	17.5
1917	7.2	5.6	1.7	4.2	18.7
1918	7.7	6.2	2.1	5.9	21.9
1919	8.2	6.6	3.9	7.1	25.8
1920	9.0	6.7	4.3	7.7	27.7
1921	8.6	6.1	4.7	. . .	19.4
1922	8.0	5.4	4.5	. . .	17.9
1923	8.0	5.3	2.4	0.7[a]	16.4

[a] Banca Nazionale di Credito.

Source: Author's calculations based on U. Bava, *I quattro maggiori istituti italiani di credito* (Genoa, Valugani, 1926).

this area concerns the four major mixed banks, and the changing nature of their relations with the larger industrial groups which had grown in status as a result of the war. It was, in fact, the war that threatened those unstable relationships that existed between banks and industry, and between the banks themselves, described in Chapter 5. What happened in the Giolitti years was repeated again here: the 'Trojan horse' that disrupted the existing order of things was again the bank that took over from the SBI—that is, the BIS. Partly because of its much publicized 'national' programme (perhaps more 'nationalistic' than 'national'),[59] and partly because it desperately needed to find some elbow-room for itself within the already limited space controlled by the large mixed banks, the BIS decided almost immediately to join forces with the Perrone brothers' Ansaldo, which up to that point had kept its distance from the banking sector's influence. The seeds of the fatal 'partnership' between Ansaldo and BIS had already been sown in 1916, when the Perrone brothers held 250,000 shares in the latter (representing 40 per cent of the bank's capital)[60] and BIS granted Ansaldo as much credit as it asked for: 49 million lire in 1916, more than 170 million in 1917, followed by increasingly large sums until 1921, when the company obtained some 780 million lire from the bank. 'The Ansaldo–BIS group was

[59] Nitti, who had supported the creation of the BIS, would have liked to have seen it called 'Banca Nazionale': cf. A. M. Falchero, 'Banchieri e politici, Nitti e il gruppo Ansaldo–Banca di Sconto', *Italia contemporanea*, 146–7 (1982), 69–70.

[60] Falchero, 'La piramide effimera', 408. Shares were bought up during the war, although the Ansaldo–BIS partnership began immediately.

growing rapidly . . . towards an objective which its directors had established beforehand, without trying to hide it from public attention, as early as mid-1914: that is, domination of the entire country's economy.'[61]

Despite the significant amount of liquid assets held by Ansaldo during the war years, the Perrone brothers' highly ambitious plans for the post-war period were such that the combined assets of Ansaldo and BIS did not seem to be enough. Consequently, the period between February and April 1918 (while the war was still on) saw the famous 'take-over' of Comit, almost certainly motivated by the Perrone brothers' desire (together with that of BIS's director Pogliani) to get their 'revenge' on Terni–Comit, their hated rivals. Almost at the same time, Fiat was involved in a similar kind of operation, when it joined forces with a rising star, Gualino, in order to make a take-over bid for Credit.[62] Just to make things more complicated, the Perrone brothers made a take-over bid for Fiat,[63] while Agnelli (of Fiat) had become an important member of the ILVA group (which was later to be of use at the time of ILVA's reorganization). Furthermore, the electrical sector was also going through troubled times, with the Edison company's director, Giacinto Motta (who had taken over from Carlo Esterle in 1916), trying to break free of Comit's influence by moving closer to BIS. As Mori says, this 'cross-fire' was in fact a form of 'parallel warfare'.[64] Within the complicated series of moves and countermoves being made at the time (which we cannot describe in full here),[65] there was a clear effort on the part of industrialists to sway the balance of the bank–industry equilibrium in their favour, and to consolidate their positions at the expense of their rival groups.

This complicated tangle of manœuvres and counter-manœuvres could only be resolved in a gradual fashion: in 1918, Agnelli and Gualino joined Credit's board of directors, although they did not hold power at that time. A second take-over bid was made by Gualino in 1920, but the result was even more disappointing from his point of view. A third and final attempt was made in 1924, and this finally brought the matter to a close, with the bankers on the winning side. As for the take-over bid made by the Perrone brothers for Comit, this technically came off in 1918. The fact that it failed to give the Ansaldo–BIS group complete control over Comit was due to Nitti's intervention, which was seen as either an attempt to 'put the house in order' or as an effective 'contribution [on Nitti's part] towards the group's [Ansaldo–BIS] attempt to

[61] Falchero, 'Banchieri e politici', 83.

[62] Gualino was a Piedmontese financier who, after one or two upsets, started to make his fortune by importing a large share of those goods that came into Italy from the USA during the war, and he set up the Società di Navigazione Italo-Americana (SNIA) on 18 July 1917, which was to be very successful in a completely different sector after the war, as we shall see in Ch. 9.

[63] Cf. Castronovo, *Agnelli*, 135.

[64] Mori, 'Le guerre parallele'.

[65] All the details are to be found in the literature cited earlier.

make sure it received the funds it required for its own "national program" '.[66] This intervention led to the transfer of large quantities of funds from Comit to Ansaldo, but at the same time it also forced the Perrone brothers to place their shares of Comit within a syndicated pact; co-operation between the former leaders and the new ones proved to be rather difficult, and as a consequence, the Perrone brothers attempted another take-over in 1920, and managed to get themselves nominated as directors of the bank (Pio Perrone was made Comit's vice-president). In fact, 'although the Perrone brothers had still not won the contest, they had nevertheless managed to get themselves into important positions within the most important Italian bank'.[67] However, this marked the beginning of the end for the Perrone brothers. Comit set up a consortium responsible for the placement of most of the bank's shares—the Consorzio Mobiliare Finanziario (Comofin)—and this was also given the Perrone brothers' shares. At this point, the bank's governing director, Giuseppe Toeplitz, felt safe enough, and so decided to revoke Pio Perrone's vice-presidency in March 1921, and in March of the following year both Perrone brothers were expelled from the bank's board.

Credit had similarly resolved the problem of Gualino's bids for power, through setting up, on 25 March 1920, a consortium—the Compagnia Finanziaria Nazionale—whose aim it was to protect the bank's shares. Such consortia were of strategic importance also in terms of their subsequent development. Their suscribers were often the bank's directors themselves, together with industrial and commercial companies financed by the bank, and other banks, which often led to agreements and secret financial manœuvrings. Furthermore, these consortia, which held the majority of the banks' shares and were run by the banks' directors, could be used towards fulfilling any needs that the banks might have had once they had been set up. Thus in order to defend themselves against possible take-overs by industrialists, the banks had armed themselves with a potentially double-edged weapon. For the moment, however, this battle between the banks and industry was clearly going in the banks' favour, as Luigi Einaudi also observed.[68]

Not all of the four banks were to take an equal share of this momentary glory. In fact, Ansaldo's power over BIS was such that the latter was forced to turn to rediscounting through the Bank of Italy. On 24 November 1921, immediately before the Perrone brothers were ousted from the board of directors of Ansaldo (on 3 December), the Bank of Italy had set up a consortium of banks involving Comit, Credit, the Banco di Roma, and the Bank of Italy, which then furnished BIS with 600 million lire in the hope of rescuing it from its immobilization in relation to Ansaldo; but this sum had already been used up by December, and a further one billion lire would have been necessary to get the bank out of trouble.

[66] Falchero, 'Banchieri e politici', 91.

[67] Cianci, *Nascita dello Stato*, 28.

[68] L. Einaudi, *La condotta economica e gli effetti sociali della guerra italiana* (Bari, Laterza, 1933), 274.

Comit and Credit were against further financial intervention,[69] and so the Bank of Italy had no choice but to stand by and allow BIS to declare itself bankrupt on 29 December. Several people have pointed out that the real reason behind Stringher's decision cannot be found in the excessive vulnerability of BIS, since in the similar case of the Banco di Roma, a salvage operation was in fact carried out, as we shall see.

Perhaps the most significant comment on the situation was that made by Guarneri, when he wrote: 'The weakness, the indecision, the untimeliness of the government, which did not know how (or did not wish) to evaluate the consequences that the downfall of a great bank would have had for the country's credit structure in terms of both domestic and foreign financial affairs, and the justifiable concern expressed by the bank's great rivals, worried about getting inextricably involved themselves in a disaster of these proportions, but also a fairly obvious degree of pleasure in seeing a powerful and troublesome rival removed from the scene: these were some of the circumstances which were directly responsible for BIS's downfall. BIS, during bankruptcy proceedings, managed to reimburse all customer savings, and honour 85 per cent of all its other outstanding financial commitments, showing that its energy and resources were far greater than its detractors would have people believe'.[70] BIS's bankruptcy proceedings were managed by a newly founded Banca Nazionale di Credito (set up in May 1922): one of the Bank of Italy's most trusted men was to be the head of the BNC.

According to De Rosa, 'the crisis of the Banca Italiana di Sconto had serious consequences for the Banco di Roma . . . which was busy resolving a liquidity crisis'.[71] In fact, the Banco had also had to turn to the Bank of Italy's rediscounting in order to try and resolve its own problems of tied-up capital, involving various kinds of securities, land-reclamation investments, and blocked foreign dealings, the latter an area in which the Banco had continued to maintain a considerable interest. By 29 March, the Banco di Roma owed the sum of 1,235 million lire to the Bank of Italy, while depositors were withdrawing their savings at an alarming rate. The Bank of Italy was pressured into keeping credit facilities open, despite Stringher's insistence upon a more radical solution to the problems of the Banco. De Rosa has thus shown that the Banco had already received considerable help even before Mussolini took over power: as Stringher wrote on 2 August 1922, this help was aimed at 'preventing a catastrophe which would also have hit a number of other concerns closely tied

[69] L. De Rosa, *Storia del Banco di Roma*, ii. 298. The author writes 'the 28 December Mr. Ghislotti from the Bank of Italy, after a series of checks made concerning the "Sconto", maintained that the bank could be saved. The Commerciale and the Credito were of the completely opposite opinion, as they thought that the loss would be greater than the capital.'

[70] Guarneri, *Battaglie economiche*, 53. A very thorough study of the BIS's affairs has just been published: A. M. Falchero, *La Banca Italiana di Sconto 1914–1921. Sette anni di guerra* (Milan, Angeli, 1990).

[71] De Rosa, *Storia del Banco di Roma*, ii. 299.

to the bank'.[72] However, a real plan to resolve the bank's problems had to wait until Mussolini's government gave the go-ahead in November 1922—Mussolini's first Treasurer was a member of the catholic Partito Popolare, and was thus keen to save the Banco di Roma—and this plan consisted in granting to a subsidiary company, the Società Finanziaria Industriale, control of the bank's equity interests. The salvage operation dragged on for some time, and was complicated by political problems; in particular, the Fascist assault on the Catholic banks, and the internal power struggle within the Banco. Despite such problems, the operation was basically a success, even though the losses were far greater than they had been during the winding-up of the BIS.

The CSVI proved to be vital in the Bank of Italy's salvage operations. This organization had been infrequently utilized during the war to fund securities and discount industrial bills of exchange, given the strong liquidity of the system at the time. From the end of 1920 onwards, Stringher decided to use the CSVI as the operational arm of the Bank of Italy in the case of intervention in the industrial and banking crisis. Furthermore, as the crisis continued to drag on, an independent section of the CSVI was set up (4 March 1922) with the job of sorting out BIS's and Ansaldo's obligations, as well as salvaging the Banco di Roma. According to a recent study, 'the section was completely autonomous, in that it answered directly to the banks of issue, and not to the members of the CVSI board',[73] thus freeing the CSVI from the salvaging operations which would have prevented it from performing its function as provider of credit to industry.

The CSVI was supported in this latter role by a new body created on 2 September 1919—the Consorzio di Credito per Opere Pubbliche (Public Works Credit Consortium), or Crediop—and funded entirely with public money (60 per cent of capital came from the Cassa DDPP, 20 per cent from the INA, and 20 per cent from the newly founded Cassa Nazionale delle Assicurazioni Sociali or CNAS). The Crediop was the idea of one of Nitti's entourage, a man destined for success—Alberto Beneduce—who hailed from Caserta, held a mathematics degree, was an expert in statistics, a socialist reformer, and had already held a post as Nitti's adviser at the time of the foundation of the INA. In 1919, he not only prepared the decree setting up the Crediop, but also became its president.[74] Beneduce's idea was to take away an easy source of income from the private sector, as had already happened in the case of the INA, through the financing of those large public works where public

[72] De Rosa, *Storia del Banco di Roma*, ii. 328.

[73] A. M. Biscaini, P. Gnes, and A. Roselli, op. cit., 165.

[74] L. De Rosa, *Banche e lavori pubblici in Italia fra le due guerre (1919–1939)* (Milan, Giuffré, 1979). On Beneduce, cf. also F. Bonelli, 'Alberto Beneduce (1877–1944)', in Mortara (ed.), *I protagonisti dell'intervento pubblico in Italia*, and *Alberto Beneduce e i problemi dell'economia italiana del suo tempo* (Rome, Ed. Industria, 1985).

funds predominated, by means of the creation of a long-term credit institute which would procure the necessary capital by placing tax-free bonds on the market: these could be bought by all those bodies that were obliged to invest part or all of their liquidity in government bonds or bonds guaranteed by the government. This still represented a drop in the ocean as far as the country's need for long-term credit was concerned, and it was not the answer to the mixed banks' difficulties; none the less, Beneduce's idea was to prove extremely useful later on, as we shall see in Chapter 9.

That these complicated banking adventures often ended in failure is fairly obvious, if one only thinks back to the problems that already beset the banking world during the Giolitti years: these latter crises occurred on a much smaller scale than was the case during the period immediately after the First World War, and so it is not surprising to learn that the crisis due to the post-war process of reconversion required a far greater degree of public intervention than was the case in Giolitti's time. If we look more closely at these salvage operations, we can see that their primary cause and final objective concerned the industrial interests backed by the banks, businesses that proved to be unbelievably difficult to organize and run as a result of the lack of training and experience of many entrepreneurs as well as of the patchy nature of the Italian economic milieu. While on the one hand the interrelationship between banks and industry favoured a large supply of credit (although this was distributed in a rather wasteful fashion), on the other hand it meant that the Bank of Italy's intervention became more difficult to avoid, as the latter was presumably more inclined to help banks than to intervene directly in order to salvage industrial concerns. Also the solution reached after the period of crisis was in many ways precarious: even those two banks that did not need to be salvaged found themselves in a difficult situation, with their assets heavily tied up; moreover, Ansaldo and the other companies associated with BIS and the Banco di Roma that had had their assets 'untied' were really struggling to find a coherent and adequate management.

The only thing that would have enabled the banks and industry to pick themselves up and to breathe again was a long period of prosperity; unfortunately, as we will see, this period of prosperity was all too short.

4. SOCIETY: THE SOCIAL STRUGGLES AND THE RISE OF FASCISM

There were many reasons leading to the involvement in social protest (sometimes violent) of various groups and classes during the post-war period: the sacrifices made during the war, without any form of material compensation; inflation, which threatened many people's standard of living; a job market which had been radically altered by the war, and which was slowly and visibly shrinking as a result of large numbers of workers being laid off;[75] and the lower-working-classes' enhanced expectations of a better life.[76] Above all, however, there was one thing at the centre of an increasingly bitter struggle between some social classes and the 'system'. This was the attempt to radically change the distribution of wealth, as the Russian revolutionaries had aspired to do in October 1917: many Italians saw the Russian revolution as an example of how to overthrow the power structure in existence at that time.[77]

There was a sudden rise in the number of unionized farm labourers and factory workers (see Table 7.9), and a whole series of strikes during the so-called 'red two years' (*biennio rosso*) (1919–20): 1919 was the year of occupation of farms, while 1920 saw factories being taken over by the workers, accompanied by acts of violence on the part of both the workers and their 'bosses'. The combination of inflation, economic crisis, and working-class protest had indeed the effect of changing the distribution of wealth to a certain extent. At the expense of those living on rent and the urban middle classes (particularly state employees) the beneficiaries were farm labourers, factory workers, sharecroppers, and the productive members of the middle classes (see Table 7.10). Then with the fall in prices during 1921, even the productive

Table 7.9. Trade union membership and strikes, 1919–1922

	Trade union membership (000s)		Days lost due to strike action (000s)	
	Agricultural labourers (1)	Factory workers (2)	Agricultural labourers (3)	Factory workers (4)
1919	...	1,500	3,437	18,888
1920	1,790	2,387	14,171	16,398
1921	1,113	1,510	407	7,773
1922	...	...	540	6,586

Source: Ministero dell'Economia Nazionale, *I conflitti del lavoro in Italia nel decennio 1914–1923* (Rome, 1924).

[75] Cf. L. Tomassini, 'Il mercato del lavoro in Italia fra guerra e dopoguerra (1918–1919)', *Ricerche storiche*, 18 (1988), and R. Cerri, 'Disoccupazione e lavori pubblici nel primo dopoguerra', in Hertner and Mori (eds.), *La transizione.*

[76] Einaudi had the following to say on the matter: 'Every class—the peasants, the factory workers, the middle classes, and the wealthy classes—had its own way of life, which changed very little from one year to the next; and each class or group considered the fact that its living standards were different from those of other classes or groups to be perfectly normal. It was the war, with the introduction of food-rationing, which led people to think about the idea of economic equity', *La condotta economica*, 390.

[77] See R. Vivarelli, *Il fallimento del liberalismo. Studi sulle origini del fascismo* (Bologna, Il Mulino, 1981), ch. 3, and the two large volumes by the same author, *Storia delle origini del fascismo. L'Italia dalla grande guerra alla marcia su Roma* (Bologna, Il Mulino, 1991).

Table 7.10. Trend in the income of various social categories, 1913–1922 (1913 = 100)

	Purchasing power (at constant prices)		Real wages					
	Income from property	dividends	Agric. workers	Factory workers	Miners	Railway workers	Civil servants	
							Level IV	Level XII
	(1)	(2)	(3)	(4)	(5)	(6)	(7)	(8)
1913	100	100	100	100	100	100	100	100
1914	100	93	103	102	100	101	100	100
1915	109	88	103	103	104	96	93	93
1916	96	72	109	92	104	80	75	75
1917	77	53	113	88	108	70	53	59
1918	55	42	107	79	99	74	44	58
1919	47	46	130	109	119	70	55	74
1920	60	36	118	137	137	122	61	80
1921	61	26	118	138	133	124	56	83
1922	70	36	123	134	138	130	61	93

Sources: (1), (2), (5), and (8) V. Zamagni, 'Le alterazioni nella distribuzione del reddito in Italia nell'immediato dopoguerra (1919–1922)', in *La transizione dall'economia di guerra all'economia di pace in Italia e in Germania dopo la prima guerra mondiale* (Bologna, Il Mulino, 1983); (3) id., 'Distribuzione del reddito e classi sociali nell'Italia fra le due guerre', in 20 *Annali* (Milan, Feltrinelli, 1979–80); (4) id., 'Industrial Wages and Workers' Protest in Italy during the "Biennio Rosso" (1919–20)', *Journal of European Economic History*, 20 (1991).

bourgeoisie and the rural middle classes found themselves in difficulty:[78] this is why 1921 marked not only an economic turning-point, but a political one as well.[79]

Until then the political panorama had been dominated by the existing two mass parties—the Partito Socialista and the Partito Popolare (founded by Don Sturzo on 18 January 1919)—a domination that had embarrassed the old-fashioned liberals in government, but that had failed to come up with any really radical democratic alternative to the existing liberal government. While it is true that Mussolini had founded his Fasci di Combattimento (Fighting 'Fasces' or Groups) in Milan on 23 March 1919, these were 'to be largely irrelevant, both politically and numerically, until the end of 1920 and the beginning of 1921, and were of an ambiguous and contradictory nature, being at the same time on the "right" and on the "left" ',[80] even though the phenomenon of the Fascist squads could already be seen in the countryside of the Po Plain. It was the economic crisis of 1921 that gave Fascism the opportunity to grow from a purely local movement based around these Fascist squads to a political movement that managed to join forces with the Italian nationalists, and win a considerable amount of support among the middle classes during that year. In the May 1921 elections, the National Fascists won 22 per cent of the vote, which was more than that won by the Partito Popolare, and only slightly less than the 26 per cent gained by the Partito Socialista: the latter had in the meantime lost the votes of its more radical wing, which had split off from the party to form the Italian Communist Party in January 1921 (they won 3 per cent of the overall vote).

The alliance with the Nationalists certainly proved to be useful to Mussolini, as on the one hand it enabled the Fascists to break away from their crude, rural reactionary stance, and on the other it meant that they were now able to obtain greater financial support;[81] it also fitted in nicely with one of the movement's basic aims, which was that of aiding the country's 'productive forces' in order to stand up to the industrial power of the richer nations (which were defined as 'plutocratic' by the Fascists). This apparently contradictory nature of Fascism, which saw itself as the champion of the rural upper classes (although with a distinct preference for those who produced rather than for the infamous absentee landlords), and at the same time proclaimed itself to be a supporter of national industry, still meant that it had to reckon with a country in which

[78] For an elaboration of this point, see V. Zamagni, 'Distribuzione del reddito e classi sociali nell'Italia fra le due guerre', in 20 *Annali* (Milan, Feltrinelli, 1979–80).

[79] For a survey of the economic and political situation at that time, cf. G. Sabatucci (ed.), *La crisi italiana del primo dopoguerra. La storia e la critica* (Bari, Laterza, 1976).

[80] R. De Felice, 'Le origini del fascismo', in Sabatucci (ed.), *La crisi italiana*, 292.

[81] The information available shows, however, that the financial support given to Fascism by the country's industrialists before the march on Rome was fairly limited. Cf. P. Melograni, *Gli industriali e Mussolini. Rapporti tra Confindustria e fascismo dal 1919 al 1929* (Milan, Longanesi, 1972).

agriculture was still very important, despite the rise of industry.[82] We shall take a closer look at this, however, in the following chapters.

Before closing the chapter, one or two further points concerning the relationship between industry and Fascism. First of all, Italian industrialists had tried to satisfy the workers' demands where possible. For example, in the introduction of the eight-hour working day and minimum wage-levels at a meeting with trade union representatives in Milan on 20 February 1919. This meeting also agreed officially to recognize the existence of shop-floor committees. However, as the workers' demands became increasingly more radical, and they began to think about the possibility of getting involved in the management of the factories, so the industrialists became increasingly more intransigent. On 8 April 1919, the Confederazione Generale dell'Industria Italiana (Confederation of Italian Industrialists, later called Confindustria) was founded, with sections for different industries. This employers' organization put a lot of energy into the matter of industrial relations without having to resort to using Fascist squads in dealing with the workers (or only marginally so).[83] However, the occupation of factories in August and September 1920, which ended from within and not because of outside intervention, left many Italian industrialists permanently embittered.

Abrate has written on this point: 'The behaviour of Giolitti's government—at first impartial and then decidedly negative from the industrialists' point of view—was the cause of violent recriminations and accusations, and even the more successful entrepreneurs began to lose faith in the political and economic situation. Certain industrialists were so shocked by the government's behaviour during the occupation of factories that they gradually lost all faith in a liberal State which had reached the end of a process of decay and degradation.'[84] If we then consider that, on top of all this, those liberal governments that held power after the war were weak and undecided also in economic matters, then it is easy to see how industrialists, who had never faltered in their support for a liberal State, could have been attracted towards Fascism. Fascism promised order,[85] decisive government, and, from the foundation of the Partito Nazionale Fascista in November 1921, it promised to support that free-market philosophy so dear to industrialists (as long as this included the possibility of salvage operations!): in fact, this had already been a manifesto pledge made by a group of industrialists, farmers, and Fascists before the May elections of that year.

[82] On this point, A. Lay and M. L. Pesante, *Produttori senza democrazia. Lotte operaie, ideologie corporative e sviluppo economico da Giolitti al fascismo* (Bologna, Il Mulino, 1981), ch. 5.

[83] M. Abrate, *La lotta sindacale nella industrializzazione in Italia 1906–1926* (Milan, Angeli, 1967).

[84] Ibid. 303.

[85] Melograni is another who underlines the fact that the industrialists saw 'Fascism as representing an exceptional means by which to re-establish order, but which was not to be allowed to take over the role of the traditional governing class', *Gli industriali*, 315. See also V. Castronovo, 'Il potere economico e il fascismo', in G. Quazza (ed.), *Fascismo e società italiana* (Turin, Einaudi, 1973).

It is true to say, however, that the industrialists preserved their independence from the Fascists, starting with the 'Confindustria' which, although inserting the word Fascist into its name after Mussolini's coming to power, kept the same secretary, Gino Olivetti, who had been there since before the beginning of the war (see Chapter 2).[86] It is also true that many industrialists' support for Mussolini was far from being unqualified,[87] although nothing was done to prevent him from carrying out his march on Rome, or to stop him transforming Italian political life into that of a dictatorial regime. Nevertheless, it would be difficult to justify the thesis that the support given to Fascism by the industrialists was in some way 'decisive'. In fact, despite their support, together with that of the farmers and of a part of the Italian middle classes, the Fascists' electoral success in 1921 was far from overwhelming. The incapacity of the country's political leadership, together with the total lack of commitment on the part of the King in guaranteeing the continued existence of democracy, were both crucially important in deciding the eventual historical outcome of events.[88] The day after the Fascist march on Rome (on 28 October 1922), Mussolini was given the job of forming a new government, and he travelled from Milan down to Rome in a railway sleeping-car.

[86] This thesis has been carefully developed in R. Sarti, *Fascism and the Industrial Leadership in Italy, 1919–1940* (Berkeley, Calif., University of California Press, 1971).

[87] For details of these reservations and conditions, cf. Abrate, *La lotta sindacale*, and Melograni, *Gli industriali.*

[88] The rise of Fascism was an extremely complicated process, difficult to interpret unequivocally. For another survey of the main interpretative theories, see R. De Felice, *Il fascismo. Le interpretazioni dei contemporanei e degli storici* (Bari, Laterza, 1970).

8

The Economic Policies of Fascism, 1922–1943

MUSSOLINI'S coming to power marked the beginning of a period in the economic history of Italy which is sadly noted for a number of dramatic episodes, from the international crisis of 1929 to imperialism, from the war economy to the collapse in production and consumption. The following three chapters will try to throw some light on this period in order to understand how the country's economic structure had changed from that of the first 50 years of unification. Despite this dramatic period of war and economic crisis, the process of industrialization that had begun earlier did not come to a halt, although it almost certainly followed a different path from the expected one.

This chapter will deal with the Fascist regime's most important economic policy decisions, with the exception of those concerning industry and finance, as these will be looked at in Chapter 9 together with an analysis of the industrial sector's development and of banking, and those concerning social policy, as these will be discussed in Chapter 10, as part of an overall survey of the growth of Italian society during the Fascist period.

1. FISCAL AND MONETARY POLICIES

The period of Fascism, from 1922 to 1943, followed a strong cyclical pattern of development. It began an inflationary economic revival, which was blocked in 1926 as a result of the need to stabilize the exchange rate of the lira. This was followed by the serious economic slump known as the '1929 crisis', which the economy struggled to overcome, choosing a policy of autarky and later beginning preparations for war; at the end of the period, the system simply collapsed. This cyclical development was sometimes helped by fiscal and monetary policies, while at other times they proved to have a damaging effect on growth. However, the Italian economy 'on the whole was part of the structural changes and developments that characterized world capitalism, to which it was tied in such a way that the policy of autarky could only slightly modify this relationship; furthermore, it was driven by an internal capitalistic logic which Fascism, with its particular brand of economic policies, did not in fact alter.'[1]

While monetary and fiscal policy was conditioned by the need to react to a

[1] P. Ciocca, 'L'economia italiana nel contesto internazionale', in P. Ciocca and G. Toniolo (eds.), *L'economia italiana nel periodo fascista* (Bologna, Il Mulino, 1976).

series of sizeable economic shocks, we can still identify certain characteristic general tendencies: monetary policy was, in the main, fairly 'orthodox', tied as it was to the philosophy of the gold standard, even when other approaches were being tried out elsewhere; fiscal policy, which at the beginning saw the government adopt an extremely low profile, in the attempt to balance its budget, was later to lead to an ever-increasing level of public spending.

Since there is a very strong interrelationship between fiscal and monetary policy, I propose to follow the developments of both in a single narrative account. The really big problem that the Fascist regime inherited from its predecessors concerned the government's budget deficit, which was still equivalent to about one-third of public spending in 1922, or to 12.1 per cent of GDP (see Table 8.1). We should here remember that the pre-Fascist governments, despite their political weaknesses, had in fact done something about both revenue and spending in an attempt to bring down the deficit, as was mentioned in section 7.1. It was exactly 'on the eve of the march on Rome that the reduction in extraordinary public spending together with the increase in ordinary tax yield, had together provided the first signs of an improvement in the nation's financial position'.[2] The new government, led by Mussolini, was extremely vague when it came to economic policy; however, it promised to balance the budget as soon as possible. This could be done either by restructuring the tax system in such a way as to increase the fiscal burden, or by further reducing public spending. Mussolini's Minister of Finance,[3] Alberto De' Stefani, tried to change tax legislation, but subsequently opted for the second alternative, and public spending was cut drastically—in particular, military spending (see Table 8.2)—which eventually led to the desired balanced budget in the tax year 1924/25.[4]

The label of free-marketeer that was quickly applied to the figure of De' Stefani has recently been criticized by Marcoaldi,[5] whose study shows that the Finance Minister's style was decidedly eclectic, as a result of his technological-productive conception of the economy, which was 'very different from that of theoretical liberalism'.[6] This concept was the inspiration for his fiscal policy, which saw a widening of the tax base, taking in several categories that had up to then been exempt from taxation,[7] together with a lowering of the rates of

[2] P. Frascani, *Politica economica e finanza pubblica in Italia nel primo dopoguerra (1918–1922)* (Naples, Giannini ed., 1975), 254.

[3] On the death of the Treasurer, Vincenzo Tangorra (31 Dec. 1922), a member of the Partito Popolare, the Treasury Ministry was incorporated with the Finance Ministry to form a single office; they were to be separated again after the Second World War.

[4] The overall public sector balance was always in deficit during the period of Fascist government as a result of the difficult situation in which local government finances invariably found themselves, as can be seen from Table 8.2.

[5] F. Marcoaldi, *Vent'anni di economia e politica. Le carte De' Stefani 1922–1941* (Milan, Angeli, 1986).

[6] Ibid. 14.

[7] Farm labourers, peasant farmers, tenant farmers, and sharecroppers. A progressive, supplementary form of income tax was introduced in 1925.

Table 8.1. State, local government, and social insurance fund revenue. Degree of coverage of public spending, 1922–1943

	State			Local government			Social insurance fund			Overall public spending			
	Current-revenue (million current lire) (1)	Non-tax revenue (%) (2)	Coverage of ex-penditure (%) (3)	Current revenue (million current lire) (4)	Non-tax revenue (%) (5)	Coverage of ex-penditure (%) (6)	Revenue (million current lire) (7)	Expenditure (8)	Coverage of ex-penditure (%) (9)	Coverage of ex-penditure (%) (10)	Non-tax revenue (%) (11)	Deficit (−) or surplus (+) (million lire) (12)	Deficit or surplus as % GDP at factor cost (13)
1922	19,507	28	67	2,440	26[a]	67	430	125	344	69	27	− 10,499	−12.1
1926	21,222	11	102	4,240	26[a]	67	720	275	262	94	14	− 1,694	− 1.3
1929	20,146	14	103	4,850	26[a]	67	990	431	230	94	16	− 1,877	− 1.6
1932	18,911	12	84	4,920	26[a]	76	880	778	113	84	15	− 4,927	− 5.8
1934	18,623	13	82	4,910	26[a]	79	1,060	910	116	83	16	− 5,209	− 6.6
1936	22,396	18	62	4,900	24	77	1,610	1,467	110	66	18	− 15,357	−16.1
1938	28,458	19	74	5,340	27[a]	71	2,560	2,143	119	76	19	− 12,286	−10.0
1940	34,403	17	44	. . .	. . .	70[b]	5,710	3,742	153	52	. . .	− 45,241	−28.2
1943	50,378	24	27	. . .	. . .	70[b]	11,690	11,000	106	35	. . .	−137,371	−41.7

[a] The % of non-tax revenue has been estimated for these years on the basis of data available for neighbouring years, due to the discontinuous nature of the figures available for the financial situation of local authorities at that time.

[b] The % coverage of local government spending for the years 1940 and 1943 has been assumed to be equal to about 70%.

Sources: G. Brosio and C. Marchese, *Il potere di spendere* (Bologna, Il Mulino, 1986); F. Cavazzuti, 'Ricerca sulla dinamica della finanza locale in Italia', in *Studi sulla finanza pubblica* (Milan, Giuffré, 1967); Ministero del Tesoro, Ragioneria Generale dello Stato, *Il bilancio dello stato italiano dal 1862 al 1967* (Rome, 1969).

Table 8.2. Public expenditure, 1922–1943

	Total expend. as % of GDP at factor cost (1)	Composition of total expenditure			
		Public works (2)	Educ. (3)	Social (4)	Military (5)
1922	27.6	8.0	4.2	19.8	46.0
1926	16.5	8.3	7.4	7.2	20.0
1929	19.4	9.8	7.6	6.7	19.2
1932	26.5	12.6	6.8	7.5	19.4
1934	28.4	9.0	7.3	7.6	17.0
1936	33.4	6.6	5.2	7.5	20.9
1938	29.2	10.8	5.6	8.2	19.4
1940	41.4	—	3.6	10.5	39.2
1943	46.6	—	1.2	16.6	34.7

Source: G. Brosio and C. Marchese.

taxation, especially as far as those more likely to invest were concerned.[8] The result was a slight drop in fiscal burden.[9] Similarly, the aim of public spending cuts in those cases where such spending was judged to be 'unproductive' was to stimulate and give support to private investment initiatives: this included making a number of public employees redundant,[10] opening up life insurance and the telephone service to private concerns,[11] and the reorganization of the management of some services through setting up *ad hoc* public bodies.[12]

[8] A number of different taxes were abolished: compulsory registration of bonds (with the name of the owner); the tax on profits paid by joint-stock company directors and by the directors and agents of business corporations; the tax on dividends paid on those bonds not issued by the State; inheritance duty, paid by members of the family, which was subsequently reintroduced in 1930; and, finally, property tax rates were lowered.

[9] As well as an increase in the regressive nature of the tax system. We should note here that in 1921 a general turnover tax was introduced, while taxes on consumer goods and on the production of some foodstuffs were altered accordingly.

[10] De Felice quotes a figure of more than 65,000 public employees who had been hired with a term contract (*Mussolini il fascista*, i (Turin, Einaudi, 1966), 397), and the total figure also included about 27,000 railway workers (P. Frascani, *Finanza, economia, ed intervento pubblico dall'unificazione agli anni trenta* (Naples, 1988), 150).

[11] The government monopoly of the life insurance sector that had to be in place in 1923 (this monopoly had been decreed at the time of Giolitti) was not enacted, while the entire urban telephone network was sold off to private concerns in 1925.

[12] The postal and telegraphic services, together with the telephone service, were organized along national lines in 1925, with the setting up of two companies responsible for these sectors; then in 1927, the state monopolies company and the forestry commission were set up, followed by the company responsible for the national road network (ANAS, 1928) and the state polygraphic institute (1928). De' Stefani was also responsible for a number of reforms concerning public finances, as well as the reform of the civil service career structure. Cf. R. Faucci, *Finanza, amministrazione e pensiero economico. Il caso della contabilità di Stato da Cavour al Fascismo* (Turin, Einaudi, 1975), ch. 4.

Although De' Stefani's tax programme succeeded in both eliminating the budget deficit and contributing towards the country's economic recovery (which had began before the march on Rome), his monetary policy was not such a success. As we saw in Chapter 7, the Bank of Italy (through the CSVI and its independent section) was heavily involved in giving support to some big banks and businesses that found themselves in trouble as a result of the post-war crisis. This commitment continued into the Fascist era, with the other banks being actively involved, and the result of all this was that 'monetary policy during the period between 1922 and 1925 had led to an increase in liquidity',[13] and this in turn produced an increase in inflation, which was further exacerbated towards the end of this period by a rise in the balance of payments deficit. De' Stefani, in an attempt to stop the situation escalating, issued measures blocking stock exchange speculation, followed by measures aimed at restricting the availability of domestic credit; the result was a crash on the stock exchange and a series of bankruptcies, while the fundamental problems that laid at the root of the nation's economic malaise remained unresolved. The resulting attacks on government policy by the country's industrialists[14] persuaded Mussolini to change the team's coach in June 1925. This account of De' Stefani's economic policy would seem to echo Toniolo's conclusion that we need to be 'very wary about labelling it in one way or another . . . and if we really have to classify it, then the view that it consisted in "continuity" with the previous financial, fiscal, and banking policy would seem to be much nearer the mark than the idea that it represented a form of free-market, liberal policy akin to that of the Manchester school, which is basically foreign to this country'.[15]

The new Minister of Finance, the Venetian Giuseppe Volpi, was a rich and famous financier who had come up from nothing during the Giolitti years with the help of Toeplitz (who was director of the Venetian branch of Comit at that time), through his financial dealings in the Balkans together with the starting of a company in 1905, the SADE, which was to be become one of the country's main electric companies.[16] During the war, Volpi had drawn up an ambitious plan for the economic renewal of Venice, which we shall be looking at in the next chapter, while the post-war period saw him being offered a number of diplomatic jobs, one of which was that of Governor of Tripolitania (given to him by Bonomi in July 1921), with the title 'Count of Misurata' (Misurata being the city in Libya where he resided at the time). So, with Giuseppi Volpi's nomination

[13] Frascani, *Finanza, economia*, 176.

[14] Cf. R. Sarti, *Fascism and the Industrial Leadership in Italy, 1919–40* (Berkeley, Calif., University of California Press, 1971).

[15] G. Toniolo, *L'economia dell'Italia fascista* (Bari, Laterza, 1980), 58. Toniolo's study contains numerous other details of De' Stefani's economic policies, as well as those of subsequent Fascist governments.

[16] S. Romano has written a very detailed biography of Volpi, *Giuseppe Volpi: Industria e finanza tra Giolitti e Mussolini* (Milan, Bompiani, 1979).

as Minister of Finance, '... the industrial "establishment" entered Government',[17] exactly at a time of crisis, when Mussolini 'needed to obtain that establishment's trust and support ... [which was essential] in order to give the regime some stability'.[18] Volpi's stay as Finance Minister was short-lived (from July 1925 to July 1928); nevertheless, it was marked by a whole series of important and contested decisions.

The halting of inflation, in fact, could not depend solely on those domestic measures adopted by De' Stefani, and had to take into account the international financial relations that had been created after the Treaty of Versailles. This treaty established that the European countries' debts to the USA and Great Britain, incurred during the First World War, were to be repaid, and special negotiations were to be opened to this end: this represented an indispensable move towards re-establishing a normal flow of foreign capital.[19] Germany, on the other hand, was to pay 'war reparations', while all European countries were to go back to the gold standard in order to eliminate unstable elements from the international financial system.[20] While it is generally acknowledged that a return to the gold standard could not, in itself, guarantee international stability,[21] the vast majority of economists at the time considered it to be an indispensable condition for stability,[22] and the USA had based its entire diplomatic programme on such a measure during the 1920s.[23] Since the question of German war reparations proved to be a long-drawn-out affair (a solution was only agreed upon in August 1924, with the introduction of the Dawes Plan), the European countries only had to deal with the problem of negotiating the settlement of the debt, and that of the stabilization of their currencies, from 1925 onwards.[24]

Thus Volpi had to start negotiations with the Americans at a difficult time for the Italian economy, with a strongly depreciated lira caused by the worsening of

[17] A. Lyttelton, *The Seizure of Power. Fascism in Italy 1919–1929* (London, Weidenfeld & Nicolson, 1973), 439–40. Lyttelton's lengthy volume is the best overall study of the origins of Fascism and of its coming to power in Italy during the 1920s.

[18] Ibid. 517.

[19] It was in fact the lack of foreign investment which meant that businesses had to obtain credit only on the domestic market, with the subsequent inflationary effects that this domestic demand brought on, as mentioned above.

[20] The most succinct short summary of the entire period can be found in C. Kindleberger, *The Great Depression 1929–1939* (London, Penguin, 1973).

[21] On this point, see D. P. Silverman, *Reconstructing Europe after the War* (Cambridge, Mass., Harvard University Press, 1982). The author writes of the 'poverty of traditional financial and monetary theory in an international economy which no longer functioned under the old laws of economics' (p. 298).

[22] A discordant voice, but one which went unheard, that of J. M. Keynes, *The Economic Consequences of the Peace* (London, Macmillan, 1920), trans. into Italian and published the same year.

[23] F. Costigliola, *Awkward Dominion. American Political, Economic and Cultural Relations with Europe 1919–1933* (Ithaca, NY, Cornell University Press, 1984).

[24] Cf. G. Falco and M. Storaci, 'Fluttuazioni monetarie alla metà degli anni 20: Belgio, Francia e Italia', *Studi Storici*, 16 (1975).

the balance of trade[25] and by speculative factors. On the domestic front, De' Stefani's credit restrictions had led to the uncovering of a problem that had lain hidden since the end of the war: that is, a public debt of enormous proportions (in 1922 it stood at 167 per cent of the nation's GDP at market prices!), only 30 per cent of which consisted of a long-term debt (see Table 8.3). February 1924 had already seen an attempt to substitute the short-term government bonds in circulation with 25-year bonds, but the operation had been a failure.[26] So the government's pressing need to squeeze credit was now complicated by the fact that it had to stand firm against an attempt by the banks and private individuals to obtain liquid funds by means of their non-renewal of government bonds, which on the one hand made it difficult to enact restrictive monetary measures, and on the other hand put the government in financial difficulty.

While the Bank of Italy, in the guise of the Istituto Nazionale dei Cambio, or INC, decided to lend its support to the exchange rate, Volpi finalized the somewhat difficult negotiations with the Americans,[27] which produced an agreement that was the most favourable, in absolute terms, among those reached between a European country and the USA; however, considering the country's economic situation, 'Italy was harder hit than its European allies'.[28] In order to lend support to the parallel policy of monetary stabilization, Italy was given a small inter-government loan (via the Morgan institute) in December 1925. In January 1926, similar negotiations were finalized with Great Britain, while German war reparations enabled Italy to balance its books, through the newly founded Cassa Autonoma di Ammortamento dei Debiti di Guerra (set up on 3 March 1926).[29]

The settling of Italy's foreign debt in record time did not, however, resolve the economy's inflationary tendencies or offer any relief to the Italian lira, which was losing ground: the reason for this was that expectations had not been reversed, as was hoped, but had become even more pessimistic as a result of the heavy depreciation of both the Belgian and French franc. 'The strategy of defending the lira was no longer feasible after April 1926, and the Treasury decided to suspend its policy of direct intervention; the result was a 17–18 per

[25] This was in turn a result of strong domestic expansion, of a decline in the competitiveness of exports, and of the mass imports of wheat caused by the suspension of import duty (which we shall be looking at in the next sections of this chapter).

[26] For details, cf. A. Confalonieri, 'La politica del debito pubblico in Italia e in alcuni paesi europei, 1919–1943', in A. Confalonieri and E. Gatti, *La politica del debito pubblico in Italia 1919–1943*, 2 vols. (Bari, Cariplo-Laterza, 1986).

[27] The entire question of American–Italian relations during the inter-war years has been analysed in G. G. Migone, *Gli Stati Uniti e il fascismo. Alle origini dell'egemonia americana in Italia* (Milan, Feltrinelli, 1980).

[28] Romano, *Giuseppe Volpi*, 139.

[29] As the repayment of debts owed to the USA and to Gt. Britain was more than covered by German war reparations paid to Italy (until 1931, when both forms of payment ceased as a result of international decisions taken following the serious crisis, and were subsequently abolished altogether), war debts have been eliminated from the figures given in Table 8.3 from the year 1926 onwards.

Table 8.3. The public debt, 1922–1938

	Total (billion lire)	Percentage composition			Foreign debt (%)	Effective yield on consols (%)	Ratio of debt on GDP (%)	Share of interest payments on total expend. (%)
		Long term bonds	Short term bonds	Other				
	(1)	(2)	(3)	(4)	(5)	(6)	(7)	(8)
1922	178.4	30.2	12.4	57.4	45.6	6.2	167	14.2
1926	92.3	61.1	15.2	23.7	2.4	5.6	57	17.4
1929	95.7	81.1	0.2	18.7	1.9	6.0	68	19.9
1932	102.7	78.7	0.1	21.2	1.7	6.1	95	21.2
1934	112.0	76.3	0.1	23.6	0.9	4.1	111	24.2
1936	127.6	67.7	2.7	29.6	1.3	5.3	105	10.3
1938	150.4	61.9	7.4	30.7	0.9	5.4	97	15.9
1940						5.5		9.1
1943						6.2		6.9

Source: G. Salvemini and V. Zamagni, 'Finanza Pubblica e indebitamente fra le due guerre mondiali', *Temi di discussione del Servizio Studi della Banca d'Italia*, 190, 1993. Foreign debt is calculated at the cost of reimbursement, which is higher in lire than the actual revenue up to 1926 as a result of depreciation of the lira.

cent depreciation in the value of the lira between May and August of that year, with fluctuations that followed those of the two francs.'[30] The Americans were worried about the way things were going, and Mussolini started to fear he might lose face as a result of his inability to stabilize the lira, when France and Belgium had already decided to introduce strong measures to stop the fall of their currencies. A law, issued on 1 July, established that there should be only one bank of issue, with the Banco di Napoli and the Banco di Sicilia losing their right to print money as a result. But Mussolini only decided to stabilize the lira in August, when he made his famous Pesaro speech (18 August 1926) declaring that the value of the lira was to be reset at 'quota 90' (in Mussolini's military jargon, 'quota' referring to the altitude reached during the First World War by Italian soldiers fighting against the Austrians over the mountains), i.e. 90 lire for 1 pound sterling, which was more or less the level at which it had stood immediately after the march on Rome.

Several people were surprised by this decision, as the lira at the time stood at 153 lire to the pound, and even before that summer's depreciation had stood at 120 lire to the pound (which was the level Volpi had tried to keep it at). There had been no pressure on the Americans' part to revalue the lira: they had, in fact, expressed their interest in seeing it held at a defendable level. Mussolini's decision had certainly been influenced by his wish not to lose national[31] and international prestige,[32] as well as by his concern not to lose the support of those sectors of the middle classes particularly hit by inflation,[33] and his aim of reducing the cost of imported raw materials.[34] What neither Mussolini nor Volpi had expected (the latter had been particularly sceptical about the 'quota 90' plan) was the fact that the lira settled at around the 90 mark, with a tendency to go even lower than this, within the space of a few months. It is true that some monetary measures, consistent with what Mussolini so pompously called 'the battle of the lira', were in fact introduced. On 7 September 1926, the proceeds from the Morgan loan were transferred from the Treasury to the Bank of Italy; on 6 November the forced consolidation of ordinary, five-year, and seven-year treasury bills was adopted, by means of the issue of the 'Fascist

[30] G. Falco and M. Storaci, 'Il ritorno all'oro in Belgio, Francia e Italia: stabilizzazione sociale e politiche monetarie (1926–1928)', *Italia contemporanea*, 126 (1977), 17.

[31] This is J. Cohen's thesis in 'La rivalutazione della lira del 1927', in G. Toniolo (ed.) *L'economia italiana 1861–1940* (Bari, Laterza, 1978), 336. The author concludes as follows: 'Through an upward revaluation of the lira, Mussolini was able to gain prestige for his regime and to demonstrate his absolute authority in political matters.' Eng. version 'The 1927 Revolution of the Lira: A Study in Political Economy', *Economic History Review*, 25 (1972), 654.

[32] Falco and Storaci, *Il ritorno all'oro.*

[33] Cf. Lyttelton, *Seizure of Power* and P. Baffi, 'La rivalutazione del 1926–27, gli investimenti sul mercato e l'opinione pubblica', in *Nuovi studi sulla moneta* (Milan, 1973).

[34] This point has already been underlined by P. Grifone, *Il capitale finanziario in Italia. La politica economica del fascismo* (Turin, Einaudi, 1945), who writes: 'Those groups interested in the imports were far more powerful than those interested in exports' (p. 57 of the 1971 edn.).

Loan' (Prestito del Littorio).[35] However, as Marconi's study shows, in reality monetary circulation only fell by a few hundred million lire as a result of these measures.[36] The year 1927 also saw a fall in domestic prices and an adjustment in the exchange rate, without a corresponding credit squeeze. Marconi writes that 'the expectations that arose and changed during the "battle of the lira" were thus ultimately reponsible for the system's performance',[37] and he points out that the velocity of monetary circulation fell to such a level that Volpi was forced to put off an excessive revaluation of the lira, at a time when industrialists were becoming more and more upset about financial and economic developments.[38] On 27 December 1927, the lira was tied once again to gold (at 92.46 lire to the pound). 'The gold exchange standard was thus officially reintroduced.'[39]

The new exchange rate meant adjustments in national wage and price levels and in the balance of payments, and these were far from easy to introduce; only a dictatorial government like the Fascist regime could have got away with the wage cuts of 1927–8, the reductions in rents, and the government employees' salary reductions introduced in that period. As Toniolo rightly observes:

> Even Keynes had been wrong on this point, when he wrote that 'the lira does not take heed even of a dictator, neither can this situation be remedied by a dose of castor oil' . . . The facts show that both dictator and dictatorship survived, without too much trouble, the period of deflation forced upon the country, and they show how a good dose of castor oil was enough to give them control of the exchange rate of the lira.[40]

Just when the Italian economy was in a position to shake off the effects of the crisis brought on by the revaluation of the lira (which we shall later examine more closely), the tidal wave of the international crisis hit home: its epicentres were located in the USA and Germany, but it soon swept right around the world. The Fascist regime made no attempt to free the economy from the gold standard in order to protect it from international deflation, not even when Great Britain abandoned it in September 1931, or when the USA did likewise in April 1933.[41] Italy, together with the other countries of the 'gold block'—

[35] Cf. P. Ganugi, 'Il peso del debito nella dottrina e nella politica finanziaria degli anni '20 in Italia', *Rivista di storia economica*, 5 (1988). The forced consolidation of the BOT (Treasury bonds) caused a sharp fall in the value of the funded debt, with consequent difficulties for those bondholders who needed access to liquid funds.

[36] M. Marconi, *La politica monetaria del fascismo* (Bologna, Il Mulino, 1982), 58. The author points out that circulation was kept up through massive private investment coming in from American investors during 1926 and 1927.

[37] Ibid. 64.

[38] Romano, *Giuseppe Volpi*, ch. 13, and E. Conti, *Dal taccuino di un borghese* (Milan, 1946), 375–8 (repub. in a new edn. by Il Mulino, Bologna, 1988).

[39] Toniolo, *L'economia dell'Italia fascista*, 121. On the working of the gold exchange standard in Italy in those years, see M. Storaci, 'Il gold exchange standard in Italia: 1927–31', *Rivista di storia economica* , 6 (1989).

[40] Toniolo (ed.), *L'economia dell'Italia fascista*, 113. Castor oil was forcibly given to the Fascist regime's opponents to discourage their intransigence.

[41] 25 countries followed Gt. Britain's example, while many others abandoned the gold standard later on.

France, Belgium, Holland, and Switzerland—saw its currency being strongly revalued once again, with negative effects on its already meagre exports, on its balance of payments, and on its gold reserves (see section 8.3). This obstinacy in persisting with orthodox monetary policy was certainly due to Mussolini's aversion to the idea of a devaluation of the lira, but it was also a result of his underestimation of the seriousness of the international crisis, at least until 1931. Positive intervention in this crisis took the form of a more active public spending policy, and above all an increase in spending on public works programmes (see Tables 8.1, 8.2, 8.3),[42] together with an enormous salvage operation involving banks and industry, which led to the setting up of IRI (Institute for Industrial Reconstruction, see Chapter 9). However, this did not definitively resolve the nation's problems, due to the strong deflationary tendency resulting from the lira being tied to the gold standard.[43]

It was during this period that the government decided to give local councils more autonomy in fiscal matters (particularly with the passing of a reform bill on 14 September 1931), at the same time relieving them of expenses such as the payment of primary schoolteachers. These measures, however, failed to produce any real change in the imbalances present in local authority budgets, as can be seen from a glance at column 6, Table 8.2.[44]

The economy only began to recover with Mussolini's Ethiopian campaign. Public spending shot up from the year 1935 onwards, and in order to pay for the increase, the regime decided to turn the previous fiscal policy on its head. The revenue from direct taxation increased noticeably as a result of a new series of extraordinary taxes: on joint-stock companies' dividends, on property, and on wealth. Even sales taxes were increased, and eventually the old tax on turnover was replaced by a general sales tax (Imposta Generale sulle Entrate, IGE) in January 1940; a tax that was to become one of the mainstays of the Italian taxation system after the war.[45] This policy was inevitably unpopular among the middle classes and the rich, and was one of the factors that led to the Fascist regime's loss of support among such social classes. Mussolini's rather drastic fiscal measures were not enough, however, to prevent the budget deficit from growing further, after its reappearance during the crisis period (see Table 8.2).

In order to bridge the gap between public spending and public revenue, new government bonds were issued. In some cases, they carried compulsory clauses

[42] For a comprehensive study of public works carried out during Fascism, see G .M. Sozzi, 'Le opere pubbliche nel regime fascista (1926–36)', graduation thesis, Faculty of Florence University, 1983–4.

[43] For an analysis of the crisis in Italy, cf. S. Lombardini, 'La grande crisi in Italia: politica od economica?', *Rivista milanese di economia*, 21 (1987).

[44] Cf. F. A. Repaci, *Le finanze dei Comuni, delle Province e degli Enti Corporativi* (Turin, Einaudi, 1936).

[45] For further details, see G. Maione, *L'imperialismo straccione. Classi sociali e finanza di guerra dall'impresa etiopica al conflitto mondiale (1935–1943)* (Bologna, Cappelli, 1979), and Repaci, *La finanza pubblica italiana nel secolo 1861–1960* (Bologna, Zanichelli, 1962).

in order to ensure their placement in a not particularly receptive market situation. In the meantime, other methods were adopted in an attempt to increase revenue, including the nationalization of foreign investment (1935) and the 'day of the wedding ring' in 1936, when the Italian population was asked to give its gold—including wedding rings—in the name of the Fascist cause (in doing so, the Fascists managed to collect some 400 million lire's worth of gold). However, it has been calculated that by mid-1937 at least 30 per cent of the preceding two years' deficit had been financed by printing more money, which naturally led to a reversal in the previous downward price trend. As a result, the gold standard was abandoned by the Italian government on 5 October 1936; Mussolini reluctantly accepted this move, on the condition that it be seen as bringing the lira into line with the dollar (the lira remaining closely tied to the dollar until well beyond the beginning of the war).

The Fascist government also tried to bring inflation to a halt through price controls. October 1935 saw the setting up of a National Prices Committee, whose job it was to keep the production and distribution costs of basic goods under observation, in order to establish the level of retail prices. Quality-controlled standard products were encouraged in order that they might be used as a basis for price-fixing, and this in turn led to the standardization of product terminology on a national scale for the most important products. Price-fixing was subsequently extended to cover all types of goods (October 1936), in the form of flexible price restrictions (flexible in that it could be modified in cases of proven necessity). In 1938, price restrictions on services were stiffened, followed by those on goods at the beginning of the war; however, these restrictions were not to last very long, due to the inflationary pressure caused by an increasingly large public budget deficit that was being financed more and more by monetary means.[46]

According to Repaci's calculations, the effort involved in the mobilization of resources, when compared to the nation's GDP, was at least as great during the Second World War as it had been during the 1914–18 War (see Table 8.4), but the strategical and military outcome was a failure, due to the enormous dispersion of resources (from Africa to Greece and then to Russia!) and to the economic and military might of the enemy powers which no longer consisted of the weak forces of the Austro-Hungarian empire. This time it was the USA and Britain who were the enemies, and Italy's strength was in no way comparable to theirs. Table 8.4 shows how inflation had been kept under control until the fall of the Fascist government in 1943, after which it simply took off as a consequence of the well-known political and military developments that were to divide the country into two halves, involving the nation in military occupations and internal struggles. Monetary order was only re-established in 1947 (see

[46] For further details on the fixing of prices, cf. V. Zamagni, *La distribuzione commerciale in Italia fra le due guerre* (Milan, Angeli, 1981), sect. 4.2.

Table 8.4. The cost of Mussolini's wars, 1936–1950

	War expenditure as % of GDP (1)	Money supply (billion lire) (2)	Index of (2) (1938 = 100) (3)	Rate of inflation: Wholesale prices (1938 = 100) (4)	Rate of inflation: Cost of living (1938 = 100) (5)
1936	11.5	22	89	80	85
1937	9.0	23	94	93	93
1938	5.4	25	100	100	100
1939	9.5	32	128	104	104
1940	21.0	40	160	122	122
1941	29.8	61	244	136	141
1942	31.4	91	364	153	163
1943	40.0	198	792	229	273
1944	34.7	368	1,472	858	1,215
1945	25.0	451	1,804	2,058	2,392
1946	14.1	613	2,452	2,882	2,825
1947	11.1	928	3,712	5,155	4,566
1948	10.0	1,123	4,492	5,435	4,854
1949	6.7	1,195	4,780	5,181	4,926
1950	5.0	1,322	5,288	4,902	4,854

Sources: Author's elaboration from F. Repaci, *Le finanza pubblica italiana nel secolo 1861–1960* (Bologna, Zanichelli, 1962); P. Ercolani, 'Documentazione statistica di base', in G. Fuà (ed.), *Lo sviluppo economico in Italia*, iii (Milan, Angeli, 1969); ISTAT, *Il valore della lira dal 1861 al 1965* (Rome, 1966).

Chapter 11), while the problem of the cost of the war, in terms of its being a burden to the nation's economy, was resolved relatively more quickly compared to the similar period after the First World War. This was made possible by the much higher rate of inflation (that drastically cut the real value of the public debt), together with the different international order that was to arise during the post-war period.

2. AGRICULTURE AND THE SOUTH

The First World War had had significantly unbalancing effects on Italian agriculture, and this had led to the social protest which we considered in section 7.4:[47] the decline in the use of working animals and the increase in the incomes of tenant farmers and sharecroppers had been accompanied by increased

[47] Also see the interesting article by P. P. D'Attorre, 'Conservatorismo agrario e fascismo negli anni venti: linee di ricerca sull'area padana', *Italia contemporanea*, 151–2 (1983).

Table 8.5. GSP 1913–1941 at 1938 constant prices, present boundaries

	GSP (billion lire)	Yearly rate of growth (%)		GSP per ha. (lire)	Sectorial composition of GSP (%)					
		GSP	GSP per capita		Cereals	Vegetables and fruit	Industrial crops	Oil	Wine	Animal products
	(1)	(2)	(3)	(4)	(5)	(6)	(7)	(8)	(9)	(10)
1909–13	36.5	—	—	1,313	23.5	10.8	11.5	3.7	17.3	33.2
1919–23	35.8	−0.2	−0.4	1,288	22.1	12.3	11.2	5.0	14.9	34.5
1924–8	39.6	+2.3	+1.3	1,424	23.5	14.0	11.0	5.0	14.7	31.8
1929–32	40.7	+0.6	−0.2	1,464	25.6	13.2	11.3	4.7	13.5	31.7
1933–6	39.5	−0.7	−1.5	1,421	...	...	...	...	...	...
1937–41	42.2	+1.5	+0.6	1,518	28.7	13.6	8.8	4.3	10.8	33.8

Source: ISTAT, *Indagine statistica sullo sviluppo del reddito nazionale dell'Italia dal 1861 al 1956* (Rome, 1957).

mechanization[48] and the formation of new small peasant-owned farms. A survey carried out by the National Institute of Rural Economics (INEA, founded in 1928) showed that nearly one million hectares of farmland was bought and sold during the post-war period, two-thirds of which were located in the North.[49]

However, the productive structure of Italian agriculture had changed very little, as can be seen from Table 8.5. The post-war composition of Gross Saleable Product (columns 5 to 10) remained the same as that of the pre-war period, with the exception of small fluctuations due to climatic factors. The growth rate of GSP also returned to its pre-war level, following a fall in 1919 and then a recovery in 1920–1. If we look at the breakdown of GSP into the various geographical areas (Table 8.6), we can see that the Alpine area was destined to experience a period of slow decline, the situation of the Appenine

Table 8.6. Geographical breakdown of GSP estimates, 1913–1941 (1938 billion lire)

	Po valley hills and plains		Intensive hills and plains in Centre and South		Appenine mnts. and hills		Alpine mnts.	
	GSP (1)	Yearly increase (%) (2)	GSP (3)	Yearly increase (%) (4)	GSP (5)	Yearly increase (%) (6)	GSP (7)	Yearly increase (%) (8)
1909–13	13.3	—	10.2	—	10.6	—	2.4	—
1919–23	13.8	+0.4	10.9	+0.7	8.7	−1.1	2.3	−0.4
1923–8	15.3	+2.4	11.3	+0.9	10.6	+4.5	2.4	+0.9
1929–32	15.8	+0.6	11.6	+0.6	11.1	+1.0	2.2	−1.5
1937–41	17.3	+1.0	12.2	+0.5	10.7	−0.5	2.1	−0.6
1909/13–1937/41	—	+1.0	—	+0.6	—	+0.04	—	−0.4

Source: G. Orlando, 'Progressi e difficoltà dell'agricultura', in G. Fuà (ed.), *Lo sviluppo economico.*

[48] G. Della Valentina writes: 'The First World War had a dynamic effect, pushing many farmers into buying tractors for the first time, and thus into gradually abandoning the use of draught animals on their farms', 'Il difficile cammino delle macchine nelle campagne lombarde', *Padania*, 3 (1988), 77.

[49] This was equivalent to 5.7% of total agricultural land. Cf. G. Lorenzoni, *Inchiesta sulla piccola proprietà coltivatrice formatasi nel dopoguerra*, xiv: *Relazione finale* (Rome, INEA, 1938). Many large aristocratic family estates were also bought up by those 'newly rich' tenant farmers who had made their fortunes during the war, and who were the first to enrol in the Fascist gangs sent in against strikers and the occupation of farmland. See e.g. A. L. Cardoza, *Agrarian Élites and Italian Fascism. The Province of Bologna, 1901–1926* (Princeton, NJ, Princeton University Press, 1982), and P. P. D'Attorre, 'Gli agrari bolognesi dall'età giolittiana al fascismo', in L. Casali (ed.), *Bologna 1920. Le origini del fascismo* (Bologna, 1984).

mountains and foothills was on the whole fairly stagnant, while only those hills intensively farmed, together with the plains, were to show any kind of productive dynamism (this was particularly evident in the Po Plain).

Mussolini's coming to power did not bring any immediate changes in the institutional framework of Italian agriculture, despite the passing of an act on 30 December 1923 concerning land-reclamation. This law was to 'completely change the legal situation *vis-à-vis* reclamation projects . . . [establishing that] reclamation did not stop at the drying out of the land and the reclaimed territory, but went beyond this, to incorporate the organization of watercourses in the mountains and valleys on the one hand, and on the other it was to be connected with the production of energy, with irrigation, with the road network and river navigation, not to mention the supplying of drinking water to the population, and the fight against malaria in such areas'.[50] In fact, this law was the natural consequence of years of research into the question of reclamation, which had seen a whole series of proposals by experts, going back to the Giolitti period; sadly, its practical application very quickly lost sight of the act's original objectives.

A more complete and unified concept of reclamation had been central to the work of men such as Angelo Omodeo,[51] an engineer who had already come up with the idea of a system of lakes in the Calabrian mountains (in the Sila) in 1906, and the agronomist Arrigo Serpieri, who had carried out a great deal of research into Italian agriculture: their idea of reclamation was also particularly suited to the Italian South. It was Serpieri, who had been nominated Agricultural Secretary in the new unified Ministry of National Economy, who issued a decree on 18 May 1924 concerning those changes made to landed property that were considered to be of public interest. This 'constituted the integration of the act as well as the explicit reconfirmation of the continuity between the reforming spirit of the last liberal governments and that of the Fascist regime in its early days'.[52] Absentee landlords were threatened with having their land taken away from them, while the way was paved for financial companies to undertake considerable investment programmes.

Comit and Credit, together with some electrical companies, were particularly involved in drawing up hydro-geological plans for selected areas in the

[50] G. Barone, *Mezzogiorno e modernizzazione. Elettricità, irrigazione e bonifica nell'Italia contemporanea* (Turin, Einaudi, 1986), 113.

[51] See A. Omodeo's essay from 1922, contained in P. Bevilacqua and M. Rossi Doria, *Le bonifiche in Italia dal '700 ad oggi* (Bari, Laterza, 1984). Other technicians collaborated in drawing up the new law on land-reclamation and drainage, leading M. Stampacchia to write: 'Without there being any change in the basic nature of the Fascist gangs' [and Fascism's] anti-peasant stance, a transformation was witnessed which saw the introduction of themes—as Serpieri had pushed for—concerning levels of productivity, and the modernization and technocratic development of agriculture, which had until that moment been completely alien to the nature of Fascism, and if anything the products of other political and cultural circles', *Tecnocrazia e ruralismo. Alle origini della bonifica fascista (1918–1928)* (Pisa, ETS, 1983), 67.

[52] Barone, *Mezzogiorno*, 116.

Calabrian Sila, Sicily, and Sardinia,[53] plans which could have completely changed the productive framework of such areas, involving them as they would have in a vast programme of capitalistic development. This was not to be, however, as southern landowners organized a grandiose counter-attack which led to the defeat of what Barone defines as the 'electro-irrigation' plan,[54] with the decree of 29 November 1925. This decree 'abolished the expropriation clause, and recognized the right of those landowners organized into consortia to have a preferential say in the assignment of contracts concerning works of an agricultural or hydraulic nature'.[55] This was not to mark the end of Fascist involvement in land-reclamation, which was in fact increased following this affair; however, it did compromise its more innovative features, which were the only ones that could have in some way changed the situation in the South. As can be seen from Table 8.6, the gap between agriculture in the Centre–South and agriculture in the North continued to grow wider. It was only when it was too late that something was done in order to reduce the power of those southern landowners who were part of the reclamation consortia, through the creation in January 1940 of an Authority for the Cultivation of the Sicilian Latifundia.[56]

Before giving further illustrations of other measures adopted by the Fascist regime regarding the reclamation and cultivation of land, which represented one of the main pillars of Fascist agricultural policy, I would like to mention the 'grain battle', started by Mussolini during 1925. Not only was this event motivated by a transient situation—that is, that half of the State's balance of trade deficit in 1924–5 was directly due to the importation of wheat[57]—but it also went against the views of the most highly respected agricultural experts (unlike the Fascists' policy on land-reclamation). These experts all agreed that Italian agriculture had increasingly to specialize in the cultivation of exportable products in order to finance the import of wheat, since so much Italian farmland was considered to be (and still is) unsuitable for cereal production.

Mussolini, on the other hand, decided on a more direct solution to the problem; his policy of revaluing the lira would have inevitably complicated matters, since it meant that imports were now cheaper, whereas exports were less competitive, being more expensive. This was another reason why he decided to set up his Wheat Committee and plan other supportive measures in 1925; but 'the battle soon discovered a major ally in the price support system',[58] which saw the reintroduction of the duty on wheat (suspended during the war and post-war years), thus guaranteeing profitable prices even for the most

[53] Cf. A. Checco, *Stato, finanza e bonifica integrale nel Mezzogiorno* (Milan, Giuffré, 1984).

[54] G. Barone, 'Capitale finanziario e bonifica integrale nel Mezzogiorno fra le due guerre', *Italia contemporanea*, 137 (1979).

[55] Barone, *Mezzogiorno*, 138.

[56] G. Lorenzoni, 'Trasformazione e colonizzazione del latifondo siciliano', *Economia*, 17 (1939).

[57] D. Preti, 'La politica agraria del fascismo: note introduttive', in *Studi Storici*, 14 (1973).

[58] G. Tattara, 'La battaglia del grano', in G. Toniolo (ed.), *L'economia italiana 1861–1940* (Bari, Laterza, 1978), 351.

marginal producers.[59] One or two interesting conclusions arise from Tattara's very detailed analysis: the South saw a 15 per cent increase in the area given over to the production of wheat between 1925 and the end of the 1930s—in spite of the South being the least suitable part of the country for this kind of crop—while yield per hectare increased by some 20 per cent throughout the entire country, thanks to an increase in the use of fertilizers (see Table 8.7). This, together with a fall in fruit production, led to an increase in the percentage share of Gross Saleable Product taken up by cereals at the end of the 1930s (as can be seen from Table 8.5), a result that went against the tide of history, and set back agricultural specialization tens of years. The increase in production only managed slightly to curb imports, until the Fascist regime decided to eliminate them altogether after the 1929 crisis, which in turn caused a fall in consumption. If Mussolini saw the 'grain battle' as the means whereby his 'soldiers and the Italian people' were to be ensured their daily bread, then his plan failed to achieve its aim.[60]

The Fascist regime's land-reclamation measures culminated in the so-called 'Mussolini law' of 24 December 1928 (which was completed by an act of 13 February 1933): this law officially used the term 'Integral Land Reclamation' (*Bonifica Integrale*) for the first time, although the concept had already been put forward towards the end of the Giolitti years. The Mussolini law led for the first time to the provision of substantial funds for land-reclamation projects: at the time, these amounted to 6.5 million lire (which can be compared with the Gross Saleable Production value shown in Tables 8.5 and 8.6, expressed in lire at 1938 prices). The best part of these funds had been used up by 1934, the year in which Serpieri was dismissed from his post as under-secretary for land-reclamation because he had once again presented a bill—with the Minister for Agriculture Acerbo who was also removed from office—which aimed at introducing the expropriation of absentee landlords.[61] As Cerri has underlined in his study of the problem, 'when the State was at the point of concluding its part of the land-reclamation programme between 1933 and 1934, and when, as Serpieri had already warned, the urgent problem came to the fore of getting the transformation of farming by the private landowners under way, then both private landowners and capitalist enterprises pulled out of lending their support to these projects.[62] So the financial responsibility for the integral land-reclamation project was left to the State, which ended up undertaking 'an ambitious public works programme which was orchestrated by, and was to the

[59] Also see P. L. Profumieri, 'La battaglia del grano: costi e ricavi', *Rivista d'agricoltura*, 3 (1971), and *Le campagne emiliane in periodo fascista. Materiali e ricerche sulla battaglia del grano* (Bologna, Clueb, 1982).

[60] On this point, see Preti, 'Politica agraria e "battaglia del grano" ', in *La modernizzazione corporativa (1922–1940)* (Milan, Angeli, 1987).

[61] Cf. R. Cerri, 'Note sulla politica della bonifica integrale del fascismo, 1928–1934', *Italia contemporanea*, 137 (1979).

[62] Ibid. 58.

Table 8.7. Average consumption per hectare of fertilizing basic elements, 1913–1939 (kg.)

	1913	1924	1929	1936					1939				
				North	Centre	South	Islands	Italy	North	Centre	South	Islands	Italy
Phosphoric anhydride	13.4	15.2	17.9	23.7	15.1	7.3	8.7	15.2	30.0	20.5	9.4	10.6	19.4
Nitrogen	1.1	1.7	4.0	9.5	4.2	2.8	1.5	5.3	16.2	7.4	5.2	3.4	9.4
Potassium oxide	0.7	1.2	1.7	1.6	0.1	0.1	0.2	0.7	2.2	0.1	0.1	0.2	0.9

Source: E. Rossini and C. Vanzetti, *Storia dell'agricoltura italiana* (Bologna, Edagricole, 1986), 646.

advantage of, the country's large landowners'.[63] It had very little effect on overall agricultural productivity,[64] although its 'technical' results should be borne in mind: that is, it led to a noticeable increase in the area of reclaimed land, three-quarters of which was located in the North (see column 2, Table 8.8).

In terms of tangible results in the Centre and the South, mention should be made of the Pontine marshes (south of Rome) and Porto Maccarese (west of the capital) in the Centre, as well as smaller areas of reclaimed land throughout the South.[65] One result of reclamation was that the incidence of malaria fell throughout the country.

If we compare the amount of public money spent on land-reclamation with that spent on non-agricultural policies, it soon becomes obvious that despite the rural demagogy of Fascism, agriculture was never really a number-one economic priority for Mussolini, who dedicated much more energy and gave far more economic support to the industrial and financial sectors of the economy, as we shall see in the following chapter. This was also true of prices (with the exception of that of wheat), as the ratio between agricultural prices and industrial prices invariably favoured the latter from the revaluation of the lira onwards.[66] This was not only true of Italy: the agricultural world everywhere was particularly hard hit by the 1929 economic crisis, being subsequently sacrificed in order to give preference to an industrial recovery. In this context, Mussolini's policies produced similar results to those obtained elsewhere.

Furthermore, all the institutions created during the liberal period and destined to aid agricultural development were 'used as peripheral terminals of the central authorities' orders' during the 1930s.[67] This was especially true of the peripatetic instructors, who were finally eliminated altogether in 1935, when provincial agricultural offices were set up under the aegis of the Ministry of Agriculture. The agricultural consortia (Federconsorzi) survived, and were very active during the 1920s. In 1921, the Banca Nazionale dell'Agricultura was set up, with the aim of improving credit facilities in the world of agriculture; and in 1927, a new law on agricultural credit was passed which, although not wholly

[63] Preti, *La modernizzazione corporativa*, 34.

[64] J. S. Cohen, 'Un esame statistico delle opere di bonifica intraprese durante il regime fascista', in Toniolo (ed.), *Lo sviluppo economico italiano 1861–1940*.

[65] For further details, cf. T. Isenburg, *Acque e stato. Energia, bonifiche, irrigazione in Italia fra il 1930 e 1950* (Milan, Angeli, 1981), and P. Bevilacqua (ed.), *Il Tavoliere delle Puglie. Bonifica e trasformazione tra il XIX e XX secolo* (Bari, Laterza, 1988).

[66] J. Cohen maintains that the exception constituted by the price of wheat 'favoured the large low-cost producers in the Po Valley, in the reclaimed marshlands around Rome, and in certain areas in the South (the central plateau in the Puglia)', leading to an increase in the concentration of farms and a slowing-down of capital accumulation elsewhere. See J. Cohen, 'Rapporti agricoltura–industria e sviluppo agricolo', in Ciocca and Toniolo (eds.), *L'economia italiana nel periodo fascista*, 406; Eng. version 'Fascism and Agriculture in Italy: Policies and Consequences', *Economic History Review*, 30 (1979), 86.

[67] G. Della Valentina, 'Enti economici e controllo politico dell'agricoltura', *Storia in Lombardia*, 8 (1989), 346. See also *Agricoltura e forze sociali in Lombardia nella crisi degli anni '30* (Milan, Angeli, 1983).

Table 8.8. Reclaimed and irrigated land, 1923–1980 (thousand hectares)

	Area reclaimed or under reclamation					Irrigated area			
	Before 1923 (1)	1923–49 (2)	1949–68 (3)	1968–80 (4)	Total (5)	1905 (6)	1931 (7)	1968 (8)	1975 (9)
North	566	766	321	657	2,310	1,100	1,194	1,500	1,650
Centre–South	353	286	1,026	175	1,840	200	248	800	900
TOTAL	919	1,052	1,347	832	4,150	1,300	1,442	2,300	2,550

Sources: (1) 1923 law on land-reclamation reported in E. Rossini and C. Vanzetti, *Storia dell'agricoltura*, 696; (2)–(5) P. Bevilacqua and M. Rossi Doria, *Le bonifiche in Italia dal '700 ad oggi* (Bari, Laterza), 67; (6)–(9) Ibid. 68–9.

Table 8.9. Professional composition of agricultural labour-force in 1911, 1921, and 1936, boundaries of the time

	1911	1921	1936
Owner-operators	19.0	33.6	33.5
Tenant farmers	8.1	6.8	18.6
Sharecroppers	17.5	15.6	20.4
Day labourers	55.1	43.8	27.2
Others	0.3	0.2	0.3

Sources: *Population Censuses*, 1911, 1921, and 1936.

satisfying farmers, represented a significant improvement on the past.[68] In 1925, the Utenti Macchine Agricole (Farm-Machinery Users' Organization) was founded; in 1926, it was the turn of the Federazione Agricola delle Cooperative Italiane di Esportazione (Confederation of Italian Agricultural Export Co-operatives). But later on, the Federconsorzi were placed under government control (despite disagreement over this move), and subsequently contributed towards the policy of pooling agricultural stocks, which then became law in 1936.[69]

One final feature of the development of Fascist agricultural policy was the move to eliminate the massive presence of farm labourers in the Italian countryside, as they represented a thorn in the side of the regime. Table 8.9 provides an illustration of how the post-war frontier changes (which saw Italy take over areas where smallholdings were common), together with the above-mentioned policy of increasing the number of smallholdings, led to an increase in the relative importance of small owner-operators in the 1921 census, at the expense of that of farm labourers. The last census carried out during the Fascist period (in 1936) shows that the number of smallholders had hardly changed since 1921, while there had been a considerable increase in the number of tenant farmers and sharecroppers, and a corresponding drop in the number of farm labourers (there were half as many in 1936 as there had been in 1911). In fact, sharecropping had been favoured in the new agricultural areas created by the practice of land-reclamation, while many labourers were given greater job stability, which in effect meant that they had tenancy status conferred upon them (although a tenancy of a particular kind); this explains the 1936 census results. However, none of this was able to bring a halt to the increasing overpopulation of the Italian countryside, which had already been a serious problem in the nineteenth century, and was now further exacerbated by the increasingly rapid mechanization (see Table 8.10), especially in the Po Plain. We shall see in Chapter 10 how the temptation to abandon the

[68] For details of the law, cf. G. Muzzioli, *Banche e agricoltura: Il credito all'agricoltura italiana dal 1861 al 1940* (Bologna, Il Mulino, 1983).

[69] Cf. A. Staderini, 'La Federazione italiana dei Consorzi Agrari (1920–1940)', *Storia Contemporanea* 9 (1978).

Table 8.10. The mechanization of agriculture, 1928–1942

	North		Centre		South		Islands		Italy	
	Tractors (1)	Other machines (2)	Tractors (3)	Other machines (4)	Tractors (5)	Other machines (6)	Tractors (7)	Other machines (8)	Tractors (9)	Other machines (10)
1928	13,243	1,386	2,913	600	1,374	461	654	437	18,184	2,884
1929	15,195	2,301	3,476	940	1,639	664	755	640	21,065	4,545
1930	17,245	3,460	3,838	1,438	1,998	917	963	884	24,044	6,699
1931	19,053	4,773	4,152	1,814	2,277	1,156	1,060	1,102	26,542	8,845
1932	20,115	6,163	4,490	2,322	2,446	1,459	1,110	1,310	28,161	11,254
1933	21,081	7,676	4,824	3,290	2,579	2,020	1,127	1,583	29,611	14,569
1934	21,676	9,360	4,792	3,999	2,646	2,313	1,096	1,706	30,210	17,378
1935	23,488	11,158	5,364	5,008	2,937	2,716	1,204	1,966	32,993	20,848
1936	25,420	13,331	5,818	5,934	3,193	3,044	1,332	2,368	35,763	23,677
1937	26,591	15,045	5,870	6,654	3,122	3,347	1,381	2,670	36,964	27,716
1938	27,762	17,739	6,268	7,641	3,179	3,740	1,412	3,023	38,621	32,143
1939	29,281	19.046	6,533	8,370	3,429	4,232	1,661	3,369	41,004	35,017
1940	30,298	20,074	6,680	8,745	3,660	4,518	1,731	3,479	42,360	36,816
1941	33,365	21,535	7,013	9,541	3,930	4,905	1,839	3,710	46,147	36,691
1942	37,101	23,853	7,535	9,918	4,222	5,263	1,898	3,952	50,756	42,959

Source: UMA, *Quarant'anni di motorizzazione agricola in Italia, 1928–1967* (Rome, Abete, 1968).

countryside was opposed by the Fascist regime, at times with the aid of force, only to grow even stronger in the post-war years. Despite the measures taken to contain this rural 'haemorrhage', the Italian industrial triangle, and Veneto, Trentino, Friuli, Latium, and Apulia all witnessed a continuous movement of people away from the land, towards the industrial and service sectors from the 1930s onwards (see Table 0.4).

3. TRADE, PROTECTIONISM, AND AUTARKY

The period between 1922 and 1925 definitely saw a boom in Italian exports, which according to Tattara's calculations[70] almost doubled during that time (see column 1, Table 8.11). Unfortunately, these new figures fail to link up the 1922–38 period with the year 1913. Using ISTAT's figures to build the linkage,[71] we can see that exports in 1922 would be equivalent to only 73 per cent of those reported in 1913, while by 1925, they were 42 per cent higher than they had been in 1913. However, this boom did not change the composition of Italian exports, which continued to be based upon agricultural and textile products, with one significant difference: the natural silk industry, which had already found itself in difficulty before the war, was slowly being scaled down, and its place taken by the production of artificial silk (which we shall be looking at in Chapter 11). Neither did Italian exports change very much in terms of their countries of destination.

Despite this considerable quantitative rise in exports, Italy's trade deficit, which had been enormous in 1922,[72] remained quite high during 1925, as column 1, Table 8.12 shows clearly. Income from services traded abroad and from labour employed abroad, which had traditionally been positive items in the country's balance of payments, was no longer sufficient to cover the deficit; neither could the gap be bridged by transfers (foreign aid and war reparations, see column 4, Table 8.12). Since the level of foreign investment in Italy was very low at this time,[73] due to the weakness of many European economies and

[70] G. Tattara, 'External Trade in Italy, 1922–38. Some Evidence from Trade Index Numbers', *Rivista di storia economica*, 5 (1988).

[71] ISTAT, *Sommario di statistiche storiche dell'Italia 1861–1965* (Rome, 1968).

[72] In 1922 imports exceeded exports by 73%, whereas in 1913 the difference had only been of the order of 41%; by 1925, the difference had returned to the latter level.

[73] For an interesting case of German investment (by the Siemens company), see P. Hertner, 'Un investimento tedesco in Lombardia tra le due guerre mondiali: le Officine Lombarde Apparecchi di Precisione', *Storia in Lombardia*, 5 (1986); for details of Swiss investment, see L. Segreto, 'Le nuove strategie delle società finanziarie svizzere per l'industria elettrica (1919–1939)', *Studi Storici*, 28 (1987), and G. Bruno, 'Capitale straniero e industria elettrica nell'Italia meridionale (1895–1935)', ibid. As far as Italian investments abroad are concerned, there are some new companies besides the already established ones that try to invest abroad. One such company is the Società Imprese Italiane all'estero, created 1 Aug. 1929 by Credit, Banco di Roma, and Banca Nazionale di Credito for the realization of large infrastructural works. The new company could not flourish at the beginning due to the world crisis, but in the 1930s was bought by Fiat and started to become active. Cf. G. Vigo, *Da banca a impresa. Fiat Impresit, 1929–1989* (Bologna, Il Mulino, 1991).

Table 8.11. Imports and exports, 1922–1938

	Volume		Geographical distribution									
	Exports (1922 = 100)	Imports	Imports					Exports				
			GB	France	Germany	USA	Other countries	GB	France	Germany	USA	Other countries
	(1)	(2)	(3)	(4)	(5)	(6)	(7)	(8)	(9)	(10)	(11)	(12)
1922	100	100	13	7	8	28	44	12	15	11	11	51
1925	194	100	10	9	9	24	48	10	12	12	11	55
1929	189	109	10	10	13	17	50	10	9	12	12	57
1932	142	72	9	6	14	13	58	11	8	11	10	60
1936	115	52	1	2	27	15	55	3	3	20	10	64
1938	162	58	6	2	27	12	53	6	3	21	7	63

Sources: (1)–(2) G. Tattara, 'External Trade', Table A.1, cols. (2) and (3); (3)–(12) ISTAT, *Sommario di statistiche storiche* (Rome, 1958), at current prices.

Table 8.12. Balance of payments on current account. Average yearly balances, 1921–1940 (million current lire)

	Goods balance (1)	Services balance (2)	Factors income balance (3)	Transfers balance (4)	Total balance (5)
1921–5	−6,656	+1,560	+1,986	+1,148	−1,962
1926–30	−6,268	+1,868	+1,794	+ 825	−1,781
1931–5	−2,133	+1,259	+ 216	+ 609	− 49
1936–40	−2,267	+1,076	− 145	+ 303	−1,033

Source: ISTAT, *Indagine statistica.*

the American government's ban on private investment in those countries that had still not negotiated the repayment of wartime debts, one can understand how the lira's exchange rate fell as it did at the time, and why Mussolini was so concerned about negotiating with the Americans, halting the fall in the value of the lira, and introducing policies that would curb this trade deficit.

Mussolini's policies, which we have been looking at previously, failed however to produce the desired results in terms of the trade balance, as exports declined marginally while imports increased (although only slightly) between 1925 and 1929.[74] Nevertheless, an influx of American capital, following Volpi's round of negotiations with the Americans, led to an improvement in the position of the Italian overall balance of payments.

Italy received a total of $316.5 million from the USA,[75] and this sum was divided up equally between public bodies and private concerns. The lion's share of foreign capital investment in the private sector went to the electrical industry (two-thirds of the total). Only the most important companies in the other sectors of industry were able to profit from this influx of American capital, companies such as Fiat, Pirelli, Montecatini, Snia, and a few others.[76]

This trend was very short-lived, however, as American investment in Europe had already begun to decline even before the advent of the international crisis which struck during the second half of 1929.[77] This crisis then put an end completely to such investment. However, the fall in trade during the crisis also

[74] However, the volume of imports reached in 1913 was not equalled again until 1929.

[75] Corresponding to more than 6 billion lire. Cf. Migone, *Gli Stati Uniti.*

[76] On this point, see C. Sartori, 'Giuseppe Volpi di Misurata e i rapporti finanziari del gruppo SADE con gli USA (1918–1930)', *Ricerche storiche*, 9 (1979), and S. Licini, 'La finanza americana nella storia della Ercole Marelli: il prestito obbligazionario del 1928', in P. Hertner (ed.), *Per la storia dell'impresa multinazionale in Europa* (Milan, Angeli, 1987).

[77] Cf. Costigliola, *Awkward Dominion.*

led to a drastic reduction in the trade deficit (see Table 8.12), and serious balance of payments problems re-emerged only from 1933 onwards. This was probably also due to the strengthening of protectionist measures (at least initially): an extra duty of 15 per cent on all goods was introduced in September 1931 (in reaction to the devaluation of the pound), while certain tariffs had already been increased in previous years.[78]

The new balance of payments problems, resulting not only from the sharp decrease in international trade, but also from the increasingly overvalued lira—as more and more countries abandoned the gold standard—could no longer be resolved by the influx of foreign capital or by reparations, as President Hoover called a moratorium on them. Consequently, the Fascist government was forced to turn to its reserves, which were thus reduced to a very low level, and to administrative measures (which were introduced in a number of other countries at the same time).[79] On 8 December 1934, monopoly control over currency exchange operations was reintroduced (this had been granted for a transitory period to the Istituto Nazionale Cambi during the war), while plans were drawn up that year for the introduction of clearing agreements which were already being used in several other countries.[80] In April 1934 a clearing agreement was signed with Bulgaria; another was signed, this time with Romania, in August of the same year; it was the turn of Germany the following month (this agreement was then renegotiated in April 1935).

In the meantime, preparations had begun for the war in Africa, which 'at least allowed Italy to shrug off the stagnation that had plagued all the economies tied to the gold standard'.[81] As preparations got under way, the Italian government introduced international trade controls: on 16 February 1935, a governmental import permit was introduced,[82] and in May 1935, the International Trade and Currency Supervisory Office was set up, later to become an Under-Secretariat (in December 1935), and then in November 1937 a Ministry. Mussolini put Felice Guarneri in charge of this new institution. Guarneri was one of those technocrats to whom the 'Duce' liked to give positions of responsibility as long as they did not interfere with his general political plans. Guarneri had been for many years a top-ranking functionary of the Confindustria before working for Mussolini in this new institution until 1939, when he resigned (prompted to do

[78] There is a detailed analysis of nominal and effective protection of the most important products, as witnessed during the period from 1921 to 1931, in G. Tattara, 'Protezione effettiva e sviluppo di alcuni settori dell'industria manifatturiera italiana dal 1921 al 1930', *Studi Economici*, 11 (1980).

[79] G. Gualerni, in *Industria e fascismo* (Milan, Vita e Pensiero, 1976), writes that the Italian government 'only introduced some forms of control too late, fearing the risk of insolvency' (p. 104).

[80] These clearing arrangements had been proposed for the first time by Austria in Nov. 1931, in order to regulate trade relations with those south-eastern European countries which had problems of currency reserves. For an account of how one of Italy's clearing agreements worked (that with Gt. Britain), cf. G. Tattara, 'Un esempio di countertrade: il clearing anglo-italiano', *Rivista di storia economica*, 2 (1985).

[81] Toniolo, *L'economia dell'Italia fascista*, 274.

[82] For further details, cf. S. La Francesca, *La politica economica del fascismo* (Bari, Laterza, 1972).

so by Mussolini), and shortly after became president of the Banco di Roma (until 1944). Guarneri himself wrote two extremely interesting, long volumes about his activity as first supervisory officer and then Minister in the Fascist government, which were published during the early 1950s.[83] A detailed biography of Guarneri is now available,[84] although this fails to give a clear idea of the merits and failings of Guarneri's decisions within the context of the needs and constraints of the Italian economy in the late 1930s.

There can be no doubt that Guarneri had to deal with extremely critical situations; in fact, as a result of the Fascist invasion of Ethiopia, which began on 3 October 1935, the League of Nations ordered sanctions against Italy starting from 18 November.[85] Although not all countries implemented sanctions, Italian trade suffered considerably during the first half of 1936 (sanctions were abolished on 4 July 1936): as a result imports fell by one-third that year, and exports diminished by 7 per cent. The geographical balance of Italy's international trade moved towards Germany: 27 per cent of imports came from that nation in the period 1936–8, and this figure had increased to 40 per cent by 1940. Italy proved incapable of increasing exports to Germany to the same degree,[86] and a considerable amount of tension arose between the two countries,[87] which was never completely settled during the Fascist regime years.

Guarneri's answer to these emergencies was to tie up Italian foreign trade in a muddle of rules and regulations which even led to the sale of import permits on the black market, while exports continued to shrink. The figures given in column 1, Table 8.11 do not seem to support this last point, but the fact is that they include exports to the Italian colonies, and we need to say something here about such exports. Exports to the colonies, like imports, had always been negligible; however, by 1935 they represented some 14.3 per cent of the total, which subsequently rose to 31 per cent in 1936, dropping to 24.7 per cent in 1937, and reaching 23.3 per cent in 1938. A good percentage of these exports was made up of advanced engineering products, chemical products, motor

[83] F. Guarneri, *Battaglie economiche tra le due grandi guerre* (Milan, Garzanti, 1953; repub. by Il Mulino, Bologna, 1988, in a new edn. ed. by L. Zani).

[84] L. Zani, *Fascismo, autarchia, commercio estero. Felice Guarneri. Un tecnocrate al servizio dello stato nuovo* (Bologna, Il Mulino, 1988).

[85] F. S. Northedge, *The League of Nations: Its Life and Times 1920–1946* (Leicester, Leicester University Press, 1986).

[86] This was a problem that many countries had with Germany. Cf. D. E. Kaiser, *Economic Diplomacy and the Origins of the Second World War* (Princeton, NJ, Princeton University Press, 1980), and also I. Berend and G. Ranki, *Economic Development in East-Central Europe in the 19th and 20th Centuries* (New York, Columbia University Press, 1974).

[87] G. Tattara, 'Power and Trade: Italy and Germany in the Thirties. A Critical Revision of Albert Hirschman's Thesis' (mimeo, University of Udine, 1989). Tattara's excellent study clearly shows that Italy did not interest Germany either as a market for the latter's exports, since Italy asked for too much raw material in return, or from the point of view of imports, as Italy offered mainly non-strategic goods (fruit, silk, etc.).

vehicles, and rubber.[88] Understandably enough, these exports did not really help the country's balance of payments, as they had been paid for by the Italian government itself in its attempt to conquer and organize these colonies.

In this way, Italy's capacity to import remained at an extremely low level, even after sanctions had been lifted. If we link Tattara's figures for the volume of imports between 1922 and 1938 (Table 8.11) with the ISTAT figures for the previous years, we see that Italy's import capacity in the period 1936–8 was about one-half of what it had been in 1913! On top of this, the country had a significant trade deficit (see Table 8.11), which brought about a dramatic import crisis in Italy; this was so bad that in 1939 the government was forced to sell off part of its already scarce production of armaments to those countries who were already at war with its ally, Germany, to earn enough foreign exchange to acquire at least some indispensable raw materials.[89] If Italy's decision not to go to war at its ally's side immediately was dictated by the its lack of military preparation, this in turn was largely the result of the great shortage of raw materials which confronted Italian industry. No policy of autarky would have been capable of resolving such a problem; in fact, domestic production still only covered about one-fifth of the country's raw material needs in 1939, and Germany was not in a position to resolve Italy's problem, as it also had problems of a similar kind (although of course at a much higher level of production).[90]

Thus we see that Italy's new ally was not only unreliable politically speaking, but was also incapable of lending material support to Italy's new war effort (and showed very little inclination to do so). This represents an important difference between the two wars, as Italy was given a great deal of allied aid during the First World War, but not so by Germany during the Second World War. It also became evident just how vulnerable the Italian economy was in the face of a forceful reduction in foreign trade; this knowledge, obtained at a rather high cost to the Italian economy and society, was to be a key element in the economic policy of post-war governments.

[88] For further details of flows of trade towards the colonies, cf. M. Paradisi, 'Il commercio estero e la struttura industriale', in Ciocca and Toniolo (eds.), *L'economia italiana nel periodo fascista.*

[89] Italian industrialists concentrated their efforts on producing goods for export for several months after the signing of the non-belligerency pact.

[90] The role played by raw materials in Germany's defeat was first underlined by B. H. Klein, in *Germany's Economic Preparations for War* (Cambridge, Mass., Harvard University Press, 1959).

9

Industry and Finance, 1923–1943: From Siamese Twinship to Separation

1. ITALIAN INDUSTRIALIZATION: CONTINUITY AND NEW DEVELOPMENTS

THERE are a variety of indices of industrial production available for the 20-year period of Fascism, 1923–43, with one often contradicting another, and it is virtually impossible to choose one as being more reliable than the others, as there are no recent studies covering this area. There are three series of overall figures for manufacturing industry, three for the gas and electricity industries, and one for the building industry: some of them do not, however, cover the entire period of Fascism. They are presented together in Table 9.1, and have enabled me to construct the following overall picture of developments.

As far as the manufacturing industry is concerned, we first need to look at the indices in columns 1–3: there are two, virtually identical indices available for the years from 1923 to 1929, and they show a period of rapid growth between 1923 and 1925, although 1926 is a little uncertain, as the ISTAT index indicates stagnation in that year, whereas the OEEC index shows production to be still on the increase; 1927 saw a slight fall in production due to the deflationary policy of 'quota 90', and this was then followed by a recovery in 1928. The average annual growth rate between 1923 and 1929 was more than 5 per cent. When it comes to the 1929 crisis, however, there is a large discrepancy between one index and another. The worst year was 1932: production levels dropped by one-third according to the ASI index, by one-quarter if we take the OEEC index, and by only 14 per cent according to the ISTAT figures. This discrepancy is undoubtedly due to two factors: (*a*) the differing sectorial coverage of the indices; and (*b*) the difference in the behaviour of raw material prices during the crisis years compared with that of finished-goods prices. As Tattara and Toniolo's essay suggests,[1] it is likely that those indices that allow

[1] G. Tattara and G. Toniolo, 'L'industria manifatturiera: cicli politiche e mutamenti di struttura (1921–37)', in P. Ciocca and G. Toniolo (ed.) *L'economia italiana nel periodo fascista* (Bologna, Il Mulino, 1976), 197. Also G. Toniolo, *L'economia dell'Italia fascista* (Bari, Laterza, 1980), 139–46, where the author presents a comparative analysis of the impact of the international crisis on different countries. On the basis of the ISTAT figures, Italy would seem to be one of the countries the least hit by the crisis, whereas the OEEC figures put Italy in a middle-to-low position, and the ASI figures place Italy among those countries the worst hit by the crisis (the others being Austria, Germany, and the USA).

Table 9.1. Industrial production indices (1929 = 100)

	Overall			Manufacturing								Electricity, gas, water			Building
	ASI	OEEC	ISTAT	Textiles ASI	OEEC	Metallurgy ASI	OEEC	Engineering ASI	OEEC	Chemicals ASI	OEEC	ASI	OEEC	ISTAT	ISTAT
	(1)	(2)	(3)	(4)	(5)	(6)	(7)	(8)	(9)	(10)	(11)	(12)	(13)	(14)	(15)
1923	...	74	73	...	75	...	56	...	...	...	55	...	53	54	70
1924	...	81	81	...	82	...	66	...	...	...	63	...	61	61	78
1925	...	89	92	...	92	...	82	...	...	...	75	...	70	72	82
1926	...	93	92	...	91	...	83	...	...	...	84	...	80	80	87
1927	...	88	89	...	82	...	80	...	...	...	93	...	83	87	83
1928	92	99	98	98	90	90	91	96	90	...	97	94	92	96	88
1929	100	100	100	100	100	100	100	100	100	100	100	100	100	100	100
1930	92	92	94	90	82	84	87	91	91	...	99	104	104	112	104
1931	78	82	86	81	70	71	74	80	79	...	90	103	103	109	92
1932	67	75	86	66	75	65	75	68	68	...	84	104	103	110	86
1933	74	80	91	75	85	79	79	69	69	...	96	112	114	120	92
1934	80	82	89	72	79	82	84	73	72	...	115	118	121	129	104
1935	94	96	96	76	81	101	100	98	97	96	119	128	135	143	125
1936	88	97	96	70	69	95	98	115	115	107	133	132	133	144	127
1937	100	111	111	82	89	103	110	127	127	124	152	145	150	153	115
1938	99	110	111	82	88	109	115	129	128	131	149	148	152	162	103
1939	113	...	121	87	...	110	...	145	...	138	...	166	...	193	111
1940	111	...	122	90	...	110	...	167	...	122	...	176	...	209	111
1941	96	...	114	77	...	106	...	186	...	114	...	195	...	221	101
1942	84	...	99	58	...	98	...	190	...	107	...	195	...	218	89
1943	...	...	77	...	...	96	...	...	...	...	...	...	...	179	68

Sources: ASI: *Annuario statistico italiano*, for different years; OEEC: OEEC, *Statistiques industrielles 1900–1955* (Paris, 1956), Addendum; ISTAT: in the version published by Ercolani, there are no deflated series for individual sectors.

for variation in the incidence of value added on production, according to the relative prices of raw materials and finished goods, tend to show a smaller percentage fall in production; this is due to the much more pronounced fall in raw material prices compared with the prices of finished goods during the crisis years. The subsequent recovery appears to have been quite strong; however, whereas the OEEC and ISTAT indices give a 10–11 per cent increase in production from 1929 to 1938, the ASI index shows production to be at the same level in 1938 as it was in 1929. The year 1939 was one of rapid growth, and this continued throughout 1940; but 1941 marked the beginning of the slippery downward spiral for the Italian economy, which was to end in its total collapse a short time after.

There are also strong discrepancies between the ASI and OEEC sectorial indices—those concerning the textile, metallurgical, engineering, and chemical industries (columns 4–11)—although we can nevertheless see a strong movement towards the engineering and chemical sectors, which had already begun during the 1920s, and was to continue after the 1929 crisis. The rapid growth of these sectors was accompanied by an even faster rate of growth in the electricity industry (columns 11 and 12), which, as we have seen, is strongly connected with the engineering and chemical industries. Finally, the building industry seems to have followed the overall trend, with a slight difference in that it experienced a quicker post-crisis recovery than the other sectors did (column 15).

We can now draw the following conclusions, notwithstanding the differences seen in the documentary sources available:

1. The Fascist period did not represent a standstill in the industrialization process, despite all the rural rhetoric that frequently accompanied the Fascist regime: those anti-Fascist theses that depicted Fascism as equivalent to stagnation, that saw Mussolini's downfall as having been partly a result of the dictatorship's economic failings, have been critically reappraised since the 1970s.[2] Nevertheless, one thing is certain, and that is that Fascism failed to narrow the economic gap between Italy and the other industrialized countries.[3] Gualerni believes that this was due to the fact that 'the Italian economy was so enmeshed in the general Western economic system that, despite any differences it may have shown in relation to other economies, it was very difficult for it to follow a different path from that of the general flow; and given

[2] E. Fano Damascelli, 'La "restaurazione antifascista liberista". Ristagno e sviluppo economico durante il fascismo', *Il Movimento di Liberazione in Italia*, 23 (1971).

[3] This was the conclusion reached by a group of researchers who had carried out a study of 'L'economia italiana nel periodo fascista' in 1973–4, which was published in *Quaderni Storici*, 29–30 (1975), 337. This conclusion cannot lend support to the later thesis by A. J. Gregor in *Italian Fascism and Developmental Dictatorships* (Princeton, NJ, Princeton University Press, 1979). Gregor argues that Fascism was intentionally a 'developmental dictatorship' and not simply that under Fascism development did not stop. For a criticism of Gregor's view, see J. S. Cohen, 'Was Italian Fascism a Developmental Dictatorship?', *Economic History Review*, 41 (1988).

its size, it would have been very difficult for it to have influenced the general trend of world economic development'.[4] Others have pointed to the dearth of domestic demand, which was a result of low wage-levels and limitations on private consumption: we shall take a look at this point in the next chapter.

2. The continuous forward march of the industrialization process did not slavishly follow previous lines, but was open to new developments and change; the shock-waves of the First World War and the changing international context, followed by Mussolini's dream of building an empire, all contributed towards the appearance of a whole series of new initiatives in the more technologically advanced industries. These were to prove vital in Italy's post-war reconstruction period, and we shall now look at them in more detail.

1.1. *The chemical industry moves forward*

The First World War led to the removal of those constraints that had prevented the chemical industry's take-off up to that point. In fact, the immediate consequences were the development of the existing explosives factories and the setting-up of new plants, together with the beginning of production of tar intermediates, which had previously been imported from abroad; these were used for the production of explosives, but could also bc uscd in the manufacture of dyestuffs and pharmaceutical products (from aspirin to sulphonamides, from saccarin to phenacetin), which had also been imported before the war.[5]

The war had also forced the State into paying more attention to the plight of the chemical industry; this is immediately apparent if we consider that the State had included all the main chemical products in its list of protected goods, when it introduced the new customs tariff in 1921 (see section 7.2). The war was also responsible for the fact that capital was made available to some companies for new investment projects[6] and mergers, which made it possible for such companies to become big corporations.

The projects that had already been got under way during the 1920s were consolidated during the period of Fascist 'autarky' (not without bankruptcies, mergers, and salvage operations during the crisis years), leading to experiments into synthetic materials (textiles, cellulose, elastomers, and synthetic resins), as well as into the use of those raw materials that Italy produced (aluminium, zinc, alcohol, and lignite). The Fascist period also witnessed the foundation of an

[4] G. Gualerni, *Industria e fascismo* (Milan, Vita e Pensiero, 1976). The author maintains in this book that there was very little room for independent economic policies, and that the Fascist regime's economic policies roughly followed the 'kind of economic intervention witnessed in several other countries during that period' (p. 83).

[5] For complete technical details concerning production, cf. my essay, 'L'industria chimica in Italia dalle origini agli anni '50', in F. Amatori and B. Bezza (eds.), *Capitoli di storia di una grande impresa. La Montecatini 1886–1966* (Bologna, Il Mulino, 1991).

[6] Italgas tried to diversify its activities in the field of chemical production during the 1920s.

Italian oil industry. The best way to analyse the various developments that took place is in terms of the products.

Artificial fibres. Although production had already started in one or two areas before the war, it was Riccardo Gualino's SNIA (later to become SNIA-VISCOSA) that really got the production of artificial cellulose fibres (so-called artificial silk or rayon) under way on a large scale in Italy.[7] By the mid-1920s, the Italian industry was second only to the American industry in terms of quantities produced, and was the first in terms of exports. The SNIA then went through a difficult period of financial problems, leading to Gualino's dismissal and the company's loss of international leadership. However, the SNIA remained one of the industry's front-runners, being the first company to produce flock (in 1931), a short fibre that could be spun using traditional methods, and to undertake the production of cellulose from reeds (in the name of national autarky). Several competititors arrived on the scene—Châtillon,[8] Rhodiaceta (later called Rhodiatoce), Gerli, and Orsi Mangelli—but SNIA still held on to some 80 per cent of total national production in 1938 (production statistics are given in column 8, Table 9.2).

Dyes. The Società Italiana Prodotti Esplodenti (SIPE), founded in 1891 and expanded during the war in the area of Cengio (Savona), was the most important of the companies first to produce synthetic dyes. However the conversion from the production of explosives to that of dyes proved to be difficult from a technical and organizational point of view, and as a consequence the company very soon found itself in a critical position. It was reorganized in 1924, and then merged with other companies between 1925 and 1927, until it became the ACNA, controlled by Italgas, in 1928. This was not to be the end of the company's organizational adventures, however, as Italgas was badly shaken by the 1929 crisis, and as a result decided to sell off its interests in the chemical industry. In this way, ACNA came under Montecatini's control; the latter then set about reorganizing ACNA together with other chemical companies it had acquired. Despite all these rather dramatic episodes, the company's productive results proved to be satisfactory, especially during the 1930s (see column 11, Table 9.2).

Nitrates. While the production of phosphate fertilizers had already reached a high level before the First World War (see Chapter 2), the Montecatini Company got involved in the production of nitrates during the 1920s; these proved to be more difficult to produce for the Italian chemists, but Montecatini had the good fortune to have a very capable technician, the engineer Fauser, and with his invaluable help was able to produce synthetic ammonia on a large

[7] Riccardo Gualino was a Piedmontese financier and friend of Giovanni Agnelli, who had made his fortune by importing American goods into Italy during the war, using the Società di Navigazione Italo-Americana (SNIA), as has already been mentioned in Ch. 7.

[8] Details of the Châtillon can be found in A. M. Falchero, ' "Quel serico filo impalpabile". Dalla "Soie de Châtillon" a Montefibre (1918–1972)', *Studi Storici*, 33 (1992).

Table 9.2. Output of main industries, 1923–1943

	Textiles		Metal-engineering					Chemicals					Aluminium (000 tons)	Metallurgical coke (000 tons)	Petrol (000 tons)	Electricity (million kWh.)	Gas consumed (million m³)
	Cotton yarn, flock and mixed (000 tons)	Cotton cloth (000 tons)	Pig-iron (000 tons)	Steel (000 tons)	Cars		Ships launched (000 tons)	Cellulose fibres[a] (000 tons)	Sulphuric acid (000 tons)	Nitric acid (000 tons)	Artificial dyes[b] (tons)	Sodium carbonate (000 tons)					
					Total no.	No. produced by Fiat											
	(1)	(2)	(3)	(4)	(5)	(6)	(7)	(8)	(9)	(10)	(11)	(12)	(13)	(14)	(15)	(16)	(17)
1923	164	105	236	1,142	22,820	15,162	60	5	993	9	1,815	63	1	275	1	5,610	339
1924	173	122	304	1,359	37,450	24,393	74	10	1,011	9	1,685	85	2	310	1	6,450	375
1925	199	134	482	1,786	49,400	19,720	126	14	1,280	12	2,000	138	2	512	7	7,260	806
1926	199	130	513	1,780	63,800	51,762	250	17	1,317	11	2,140	147	2	592	10	8,390	955
1927	179	116	489	1,596	54,300	47,513	94	24	1,312	22	1,895	185	3	578	17	8,740	958
1928	196	130	507	1,960	57,600	47,765	67	25	1,127	30	2,987	193	4	636	14	9,630	1,097
1929	220	141	671	2,122	55,100	46,187	72	32	1,335	40	3,324	200	7	792	22	10,380	1,198
1930	184	114	537	1,743	46,400	35,120	96	30	1,330	75	3,107	181	8	813	82	10,670	2,192
1931	153	100	510	1,409	28,400	19,382	167	34	1,012	60	2,630	181	11	740	133	10,470	1,957
1932	169	101	461	1,396	29,600	22,012	49	33	899	109	3,250	174	13	714	157	10,590	1,958
1933	191	117	518	1,771	41,700	32,227	19	38	1,085	160	5,023	195	12	730	163	11,650	1,966
1934	173	112	529	1,850	45,402	36,927	27	49	1,239	209	4,941	220	13	817	126	12,600	1,994
1935	171	119	633	2,209	50,493	37,355	32	69	1,287	228	6,441	272	14	998	103	13,800	2,471
1936	140	107	762	2,025	53,144	41,053	14	89	1,532	194	5,169	295	16	1,211	130	13,648	2,873
1937	187	131	801	2,087	77,708	64,157	42	109	1,642	275	7,576	351	23	1,703	289	15,430	3,039
1938	178	135	864	2,323	70,777	56,053	106	119	1,721	305	6,222	352	26	1,739	422	15,544	3,074
1939	192	141	1,005	2,283	68,907	55,701	136	140	2,055	385	8,798	406	34	1,986	518	18,417	4,282
1940	178	145	1,062	2,258	48,674	34,231	102	163	2,008	437	9,642	400	39	1,988	287	19,430	5,393
1941	115	109	1,038	2,063	38,798	26,371	109	181	1,818	467	8,705	390	48	1,833	75	20,761	5,339
1942	76	78	887	1,934	30,507	21,776	85	144	1,225	414	7,197	331	44	1,668	88	20,233	5,608
1943	49	54	648	1,727	21,134	15,745	69	102	875	344	6,392	333	46	1,581	34	18,247	. . .

[a] Yarn and flock.
[b] Excluding those made using sulphur, whose production had got under way before the war.

Source: ISTAT, *Sommario*.

scale, thus eliminating the need to import it. One indication of growth in this area of the chemical industry is provided by the production of nitric acid, which increased rapidly during this period (column 10, Table 9.2); on the other hand, the production of sulphuric acid, which is a basic ingredient in the production of phosphate-based fertilizers, was stagnant (column 9). The Italian Calcium Carbide Company, which was taken over by the Terni Company in 1921, also produced synthetic ammonia, under a different patent which involved the use of vast quantities of electrical energy.[9]

Pharmaceuticals. Of all the Italian companies producing pharmaceutical products, only two—Carlo Erba and Schiapparelli—managed to transform their production into something more than just an artisan activity: this was something that was to weigh heavily against the Italian pharmaceutical industry's competitive strength after the Second World War, when the big foreign multinationals started to appear on the scene. The Carlo Erba Company, which was well managed by the chemist Giovanni Morselli, produced antipyretics, pain-killers, tranquillizers, and chemotherapeutic products. The Schiapparelli Company, which had been taken over by Italgas in the 1920s, was to be heavily involved in the crisis that afflicted the latter company; its plant at Settimo Torinese was taken over by Montecatini, which then proceeded to reorganize it, with the help of the French company Rhône-Poulenc, under its new name of Farmitalia.[10] The Schiapparelli was to survive nevertheless, although with great difficulty, and was recently launched once again by a Bolognese businessman, Golinelli.

Sodium carbonate and caustic soda. Sodium carbonate (soda) was one of the typical mass-produced chemical products of the nineteenth century, together with sulphuric acid, as it was widely used in the textile industry. Italian industry had never managed to organize its production before the Belgian multinational Solvay stepped in to do so directly, on Italian soil, when it set up its Rosignano (Leghorn) plant in 1913. This plant began production in 1919, and together with another Solvay plant at Monfalcone (Gorizia), still managed to provide 84 per cent of Italian demand for soda in 1938 (see column 12, Table 9.2). The Solvay Company was also heavily involved in the production of caustic soda and chlorine (used in making artificial fibres), as were other companies such as the Caffaro Electrochemical Company, the Rumianca (founded in 1915), and ACNA.[11]

[9] The Fauser system also used electrical energy in order to obtain hydrogen. On Fauser and his activities cf. P. P. Saviotti, L. Simonin, and V. Zamagni, *Dall'ammoniaca ai nuovi materiali. Storia dell'Istituto di Ricerche Chimiche Guido Donegani di Novara* (Bologna, Il Mulino, 1991).

[10] The Carlo Erba company was bought up by Montedison in 1971, and then merged with Farmitalia (a 49% share in Farmitalia having been bought back off the French chemical giant Rhône Poulenc by Montedison).

[11] On the activities of Solvay, cf. A. Brogi, 'L'industria in Toscana fra le due guerre con particolare referimento al settore chimico e alla Solvay di Rosignano', graduate thesis, University of Florence, 1986–7.

Aluminium. Although aluminium is a metal, it does not exist as such in nature, but is obtained from bauxite by means of electrolysis involving an enormous amount of electrical energy, which often meant that aluminium producers were tied to the hydroelectrical industry and/or the electrochemical industry. Although some aluminium was produced before the war at Bussi (in the Abruzzi), production did not really take off until the 1920s, when plants were established at Porto Marghera by the SAVA Company (owned by the Swiss AIAG), and at Mori (Trentino) by the SIDA Company (set up by Montecatini and the German firm VAW).[12] The real leap in production took place during the second half of the 1930s (see column 13, Table 9.2), when the Fascist policy of autarky encouraged Italian production of 'national' metals (aluminium, lead, cadmium, and zinc), without however really leading to any great savings on imports.[13]

Oil products. While the nation's organic chemical industry struggled to get on its feet, and only really managed to make a significant advance during the 1930s (both in terms of the working of intermediate and finished products, and in that of its raw materials),[14] the oil products industry was quicker off the mark. The first move made by the government was to set up the Azienda Generale Italiana Petroli (AGIP) in April 1926, a public company whose task it was to explore for oil within the confines of Italian territory, to buy the rights to exploit oilfields abroad, and to sell oil products.[15] By 1939, AGIP supplied 28.5 per cent of national demand for such products, and had embarked upon some interesting prospecting programmes on Italian soil which were to prove of strategic importance in the period following the Second World War. The second step taken in this field was again motivated by the philosophy of self-sufficiency, and it saw the creation of the Azienda Nazionale Idrogenazione Combustibili (ANIC) in 1936—a partnership between Montecatini, AGIP, and

[12] See M. Rispoli's excellent study, 'L'industria dell'alluminio in Italia nella fase di introduzione 1907–1929', *Annali di storia dell'impresa*, 3 (1987), where the Italian aluminium industry is placed within an international context. Some more recent details of the Italian aluminium industry can be found in another essay by the same author, 'L'industria dell'alluminio', *Economia e politica industriale*, 14 (1976).

[13] The effects of autarkic policies in the energy sector have been analysed in great detail in R. Petri's essay, 'Acqua contro carbone. Elettrochimica e independenza energetica italiana negli anni trenta', *Italia contemporanea*, 168 (1987). The increase in the quantities of lead, zinc, lignite, antimony, manganese, and kaolin extracted from Sardinian mines has been well documented in M. S. Rollandi, *Miniere e minatori in Sardegna. Dalla crisi del primo dopoguerra alla nascita di Carbonia (1919–1939)* (Cagliari, Ed. della Torre, 1981). There is a general account of the question of energy and raw materials during the period between Fascist autarky and the war, in a graduation thesis by C. Checcucci, entitled 'Trasformazioni strutturali dell'industria pesante italiana durante l'economia di guerra (1936–1943)', Florence University, 1984–5.

[14] Carbon coke distillation capacity was doubled when the Società Cokitalia was set up in 1935 at San Giuseppe di Cairo in the province of Savona, by Montecatini and Italgas. See col. 14 of Table 9.2 for details of metallurgical coke production.

[15] For a complete analysis of Italy's early oil policy, cf. M. Pizzigallo, *Alle origini della politica petrolifera italiana 1920–25* (Milan, Giuffré, 1981), and id., *L'Agip degli anni ruggenti (1926–1932)* (Milan, Giuffré, 1984).

other public bodies—which led to a considerable increase in productive capacity as far as petrol (column 15, Table 9.2) and other oil products were considered. However, as soon as Italy entered into war, the possibility of utilizing this increased capacity was strongly limited by the dearth of raw material.

Rubber. While the Pirelli Company continued its successful reign as the Italian leader in the production of both tyres and cable, one important new development was the setting-up of the SAIGS (Società per Azioni Industria Gomma Sintetica) at Milan in September 1939. This company, which aimed at the production of synthetic rubber at its Terni and Ferrara plants, was founded by IRI and Pirelli; but between 1942 and 1944, only 13,027 tons of this type of rubber were produced, at the Ferrara plant,[16] although both plants were to become important after the war for their production of synthetic fibres and plastics, made possible by the accumulated expertise of the company and its founders.

1.2. *Electricity and economic power*

The inter-war period witnessed a new phase in the development of the electricity industry on a world scale; the aim of this was to rationalize production into integrated national systems, and to expand the use of electricity in the communications field, that is, in relation to the telephone and radio.

The electricity system 'suffered . . . from the different criteria used by the companies in developing their plants. Transmission using different periodicity, together with a multiplicity of lines, meant that it was very difficult to connect up one system with another.'[17] Government legislation, the financial problems involved in connecting up those different systems already in existence, in particular the famous 'backbone' which was to travel the length of the country, and finally the differences that existed between the main Italian groups, together contributed towards the failure of all plans aimed at setting up an integrated electricity system, until beyond the end of the Second World War.

A closer look at the nature of the main electrical groups may provide an explanation for this failed 'unification' of the electricity network. If we ignore municipal companies, local producers, and one or two smaller concerns, then we are left with the three major Italian groups: EDISON, SIP (Società Idroelettrica Piemontese), and SADE. The Edison group was reinforced by the take-over of Ettore Conti's company during the early 1920s and was guided by Giacinto Motta, an engineer who became managing director of the company on

[16] Full details can be found in R. Petri, 'Il polo chimico ferrarese dagli anni trenta agli anni cinquanta', *Annali dell'Istituto Storico della Resistenza dell'Emilia Romagna*, 7 (1990).

[17] R. Giannetti, *La conquista della forza. Risorse, tecnologia ed economia nell'industria elettrica italiana 1883–1940* (Milan, Angeli, 1985), 85.

the death of Esterle in 1918, and who was to be the real 'boss' until his death in 1943. Edison's international connections ranged from the American companies International Power Securities and General Electric to the Swiss company Motor-Columbus, and it adopted the typical strategy of a holding company, with its lack of interest in technical matters or questions of production, opting to concentrate its energies on the administration side.[18]

The SADE, which was firmly run by Giuseppe Volpi, remained tied to the German company AEG, through the Swiss Bank für Elektrische Unternehmungen,[19] and reigned supreme in Tuscany and Emilia. The creation of the industrial complex at Porto Marghera (see section 1.4 in this chapter), together with the setting-up of other electrochemical and aluminium production plants in the area, all helped to further SADE's position; and its relationship with the world of American finance enabled it to survive quite brilliantly the crisis caused by the 'quota 90' policy.

The SIP, led by Giangiacomo Ponti, was undoubtedly the most dynamic of the three groups, and it had very strong ties in the South with the SME (Società Meridionale di Elettricità), as well as being strongly involved in the telephone sector.[20] It made the most serious attempt of all to set up a national electricity network, only to see this fail as a result of revaluation of the lira during the mid-1920s. Its ties with the Swiss company Brown Boveri (through the TIBB) and with Panzarasa's Italgas certainly did not contribute towards the company's financial stability. Hit by the 1929 crisis, SIP became part of IRI in the autumn of 1933 (more about this in the next section), and its telephone companies were dismembered and then taken over by the newly founded STET. The project to sell the company back to private business was discarded,[21] whereas the shareholdings of Edison and SADE taken over by IRI were quickly reprivatized, and the SIP's electricity companies were to remain part of IRI until 1963, when all electrical companies were nationalized to form the ENEL.

While differences between the groups, and particularly between EDISON and SIP,[22] were to prevent the establishment of a national electricity network,[23]

[18] R. Giannetti, 'Tecnologia, scelte d'impresa ed intervento pubblico: l'industria elettrica italiana dalle origini al 1921', *Passato e Presente*, 2 (1982).

[19] L. Segreto, 'Le nuove strategie delle società finanziarie svizzere per l'industria elettrica (1919–1939)', *Studi Storici*, 28 (1987).

[20] Mussolini privatized the telephone service in 1924–5.

[21] For details of the crisis at the SIP, cf. A. Castagnoli, 'La crisi economica degli anni trenta in Italia: il caso della SIP', *Rivista di storia contemporanea*, 4 (1976). For an account of the STET, see B. Bottiglieri, *STET. Strategia e struttura delle telecomunicazioni* (Milan, Angeli, 1987).

[22] These differences of opinion led to a split in the electrical industry's organization, the AEIE, in 1922 (Ponti had been elected president of this organization). Subsequently, Motta set up a rival organization, the ANIEL, with its own periodical. The two rivals were only reunified in 1927, forming a single organization, the UNFIEL, with Motta as its president: Ponti's decline had already started, and he was to be sacked from the SIP during the crisis. For a general account of these events, and for a portrait of Motta, see P. Bolchini, 'Giacinto Motta, la Società Edison e il fascismo', *Storia in Lombardia*, 8 (1989).

[23] Giannetti, in *La conquista della forza*, underlines the fact that the inability to unify the country's

another development, the use of thermoelectric power, which was proving very successful at an international level, failed to get off the ground in Italy. Virtually all the energy being produced in Italy at the time was of a hydroelectric kind (about 92 per cent of the total), and Italy had become highly specialized in this field. Although this did not prevent further expansion of energy production during this period (see column 16, Table 9.2),[24] such expansion was becoming more and more expensive; and this was not perhaps the most negative aspect of such specialization. The real problem was the extremely expensive storage of hydroelectric energy, which thus favoured 'the simpler uses such as those involving industrial processes which required a high quantity of energy and [the use of] loads that corresponded to water resources available. . . . For this very reason, the most dynamic industrial sectors of that period were the electrochemical and electrometallurgical sectors, which accounted for 43 per cent of total consumption in 1940, compared with 14 per cent in 1925.'[25] This led to a differentiation in electricity tariffs which favoured the intensive use of energy (the metallurgical and chemical industries specialized in electric-intensive forms of production as a result thereof, often choosing not to invest in alternative technology more in line with international developments); and it penalized domestic consumers and those sectors of industry that used electrical energy as motive power, especially the engineering industry.

This period saw a fairly rapid process of electrification of the railways in Italy, but these electrified lines continued to use rather out-of-date systems of traction which also proved to be more expensive; 14.6 per cent of track had been electrified in Italy by 1927, which made it a European leader in this field. By 1939, this figure had increased to 31.5 per cent, covering 56 per cent of total railway traffic at the time.

There were some fairly important developments in the telephone and radio sectors during the 1920s and 1930s, although, in quantitative terms, they were somewhat limited. The first attempts at organizing public radio broadcasts were made by Enrico Marchesi's Radiofono Company in 1923. The Unione Radiofonica Italiana (URI) was set up the following year, and its first broadcasts began on 6 October 1924 from Rome. Subscribers numbered only 26,855 by 1926, but in the meantime more capital was found in Rome and Milan, and on 15 January 1928, the Ente Italiano Audizioni Radiofoniche (EIAR) was founded, which led to an increase in the number of broadcasting stations.[26] By 1937, the number of subscribers had risen to 806,000, and this reached

electricity network was largely due to the priority given to hydroelectric power, which made it 'difficult to formulate projects that would have been compatible with the best possible utilization of economies of scale, due to the presence of various restrictions which were absent in the case of thermically generated electricity' (p. 206).

[24] Problems were already visible, however, during the second half of the 1930s.

[25] Giannetti, *La conquista della forza*, 206.

[26] A. Fossati, *Lavoro e produzione in Italia dalla metà del secolo XVIII alla seconda guerra mondiale* (Turin, Giappichelli, 1951), 527–9.

1,757,000 by 1943. The number of telephone subscribers had risen from about 90,000 in 1913 to some 150,000 by 1925, and at the end of the 1930s there were more than 600,000 subscribers throughout Italy.

The production of electrical material, which had been the Achilles heal of pre-war Italian industry, improved significantly during the inter-war years, although the country remained heavily dependent upon foreign imports, and Italian industry continued to be highly fragmented. Germany reappeared on the scene, exporting goods to Italy and also assembling them at the Siemens plant in Milan: this last activity led to setting up the OLAP, a precision tool company, in November 1927,[27] whose main activity was the production of telephones and exchanges, and which was particularly busy during the second half of the 1930s. A continued Swiss presence in Italy was guaranteed by the activity of the TIBB, one of the main companies in this sector, particularly in the production of parts for hydroelectric plants. The United States were also represented in Italy, in the form of the Compagnia Generale di Elettricità (CGE), set up by General Electric in 1920. This company has nearly always been among the top four in this sector during the inter-war years.

The two major Italian companies were Ercole Marelli and Ansaldo, the first specializing in small electric motors, while the second specialized in electric-traction, machinery of different kinds, and electric ship-engines. All companies producing in Italy managed to cover 80 per cent of national demand for electrical goods in 1927; this figure had risen to 99 per cent by 1937, although a large number of products were still produced under licence, and some, such as large generators and alternators, continued to be imported from abroad.[28]

At the height of the crisis in the early 1930s, attempts were made to concentrate production in fewer hands, as production was too dispersed for the size of the Italian market. A plan to this end was drawn up, involving Ansaldo, CGE, and General Electric, but fell through as a result of opposition from Ansaldo's directors. In 1934, Benni, the president of Marelli, began talks with CGE about an eventual merger which would also have involved Ansaldo; these talks fell through, at which point CGE attempted a similar move with the management of Ansaldo, but nothing came of this either. According to Marco Doria, 'these repeated failures were due to political calculations that won over a rational economic approach';[29] that is, the desire not to see the electrical and technical side of Ansaldo's operations dismembered, as they were of strategic importance for the war effort. This is why research and development in the

[27] Siemens' activities in Italy in the inter-war years are detailed in P. Hertner, 'Un investimento tedesco in Lombardia tra le due guerre mondiali: la Officine Lombarde Apparecchi di Precisione', *Storia in Lombardia*, 1 (1986).

[28] R. Giannetti, 'Cambiamenti non adattetivi della organizzazione industriale: l'industria elettromeccanica italiana (1883–1940)', *Annali di storia dell'impresa*, 7 (1991).

[29] M. Doria, 'Una "via nazionale" all'industrializzazione: l'Elettrotecnico Ansaldo dall'inizio del secolo alla seconda guerra mondiale', *Annali di storia dell'impresa*, 4 (1988), 205.

industry continued to be minute in proportion to that of its foreign competitors, and why mass production of electrical goods continued to be the bread and butter of the industry, with very little space dedicated to technologically advanced products.[30]

A quick reference to the production of the telephone industry that continued to be controlled by companies set up in Italy by foreign multinationals (e.g. OLAP, FACE of Milan, and FATME of Rome), while the production of radiophonic goods involved certain important Italian companies, such as Ducati of Bologna (1926), and the Compagnia Italiana Marconi.

This section of the book is concerned with electricity and economic power because several writers have pointed out that the leadership in Italian industry and in the economy in general changed 'during the years of Fascism, through the substitution of the mixed-bank/steel-industry grouping with an extremely powerful constellation of interests led by the electrical giants and Montecatini, and allied with the important figure, and various industrial concerns, of Senator Giovanni Agnelli'.[31] This supremacy of the electrical companies can certainly be seen from the developments that took place within the industry itself, starting with the Bonomi decree (October 1916) which ensured the industry's members preferential treatment in water-supply contracts and government subsidies for the construction of aqueducts, reservoirs, and power lines. The same conclusion can be drawn from the episode of the consumers' failure to obtain a reduction in electricity prices during the 1930s, or that of the reprivatization of Edison and Sade shares (but not those of SIP).

It is not so easy instead to show whether this supremacy extended over the rest of industry and the economy. Those studies carried out so far only give us one or two examples.[32] We shall shortly be looking at one of these—the building of Porto Marghera on Giuseppe Volpi's project. Here I would like to consider another example: the role of the electric companies in the South of Italy, which has already been mentioned in the section on land-reclamation (Chapter 8), with particular reference to a company set up in Naples in March of 1899, the Società Meridionale di Elettricità (SME), by the Swiss–French company Société Franco-Suisse pour l'Industrie électrique. This company, with its large Swiss shareholding, was nevertheless partly owned by the mixed banks, and it ended up in the hands of IRI,[33] which then proceeded to strengthen its financial and economic position, with Giuseppe Cenzato

[30] Giannetti, 'Cambiamenti non addattativi'.

[31] G. Mori, 'Per una storia dell'industria italiana durante il fascismo', in *Il capitalismo industriale in Italia* (Rome, Editori Riuniti, 1977), 234.

[32] A. M. Falchero has recently begun work on an in-depth survey of those industrialists operating in the electrical sector during the early 1920s, with the aim of establishing the importance this sector had for the country's overall productive and financial framework: cf. ' "Foto di gruppo": gli elettrici dopo la marcia su Roma', forthcoming.

[33] G. Bruno, 'Capitale straniero e industria elettrica nell'Italia meridionale (1895–1935)', *Studi Storici*, 28 (1987).

directing operations. In fact, the company's ambitions had always been frustrated by the underdeveloped industrial environment of the Italian South, and it was very glad to see the State getting directly involved in the electrification of the southern railway network. In a letter he wrote to Beneduce (IRI's president) in 1934, Cenzato pointed out that the plan to consolidate financially the position of the SME, which Beneduce himself had pushed for, was in fact a move aimed at exploiting the economic potential of the South.[34] The fact is that the electricity industry found itself 'in a very strong position with respect to other entrepreneurial forces operating in the South . . . This was evident from the fact that its most influential members [Maurizio Capuano first, followed by Giuseppe Cenzato] were the undisputed leaders of the Industrialists' Organization.'[35] A number of projects for the industrialization of the South emanated from the SME, but very few of them were to materialize:[36] those that did included the aircraft works at Pomigliano d'Arco (set up with the help of Alfa Romeo and Cantieri Riuniti dell'Adriatico), the Navalmeccanica, the Naples oil refinery, and the Montecatini chemical plants.[37] Some of the other projects were put off until after the war, when interest was renewed in them.

1.3. *Engineering and armaments*

Both the steel and engineering industries recovered strongly during the 1920s, following a period of deep crisis after the First World War, only to find themselves in serious trouble again in the 1929 economic crisis; they then recovered once more during the 1930s, as a result of the Fascist war effort. This recovery was much stronger in the engineering industry than in the steel industry, however, and the latter had great difficulty in increasing productive capacity at the time (see columns 3–7, Table 9.2).

Let us first of all consider the development of the steel industry during this period. The 1920s' upsurge in production was largely founded upon the widespread working of scrap iron: the imports of scrap 'grew . . . at an incredible rate, reaching 1,000,000 tons in 1929'.[38] The ratio of pig-iron to

[34] A. De Benedetti, 'Napoli tra le due guerre: sistema produttivo, proletariato industriale e regime fascista', in *Annali*, 20 (1979–80) (Milan, Feltrinelli, 1981) and id, 'L'equilibrio difficile. Politica industriale e sviluppo dell'impresa elettrica nell'Italia meridionale: la SME, 1925–1937', *Rivista di storia economica*, 7 (1990). For an account of the activities of Cenzato, cf. M. Fatica, 'Giuseppe Cenzato 1882–1969', in A. Mortara (ed.), *I protagonisti dell'intervento pubblico in Italia* (Milan, Angeli, 1984).

[35] De Benedetti, 'Napoli tra le due guerre', 783.

[36] G. Savarese, *L'industria in Campania (1911–1940)* (Naples, Guida, 1980).

[37] On the poor results given by industrialization in the South during the inter-war years, see G. Toniolo, 'Politica economica fascista e industrializzazione nel Mezzogiorno: alcune considerazioni', *Ricerche economiche*, 31 (1977); and V. Castronovo, 'La politica economica del fascismo e il mezzogiorno', *Studi Storici*, 17 (1976).

[38] A. Carparelli, 'I perché di una "mezza siderurgia". La società Ilva, l'industria della ghisa e il ciclo integrale negli anni venti', in F. Bonelli, *Acciaio per l'industrializzazione* (Turin, Einaudi, 1982), 43.

steel production, which had been 50 per cent in 1913, fell to 29 per cent in the period 1926–9. Italy became the world's number one scrap iron importer (between 1921 and 1936, it absorbed one-third of all the scrap iron exported in the world). Carparelli has traced this peculiarity of the Italian steel industry to two factors: on the one hand, the difficulties experienced by Italy as a latecomer on the scene were predictable enough; on the other hand, there were the failings of the ILVA, which should have been a leader in the field of integrated steel production, but which, on the contrary, has been seen as responsible for the fact that Italian products were twice or three times as expensive as those of other industrialized countries.[39]

A recent study by Ranieri,[40] however, emphasizes the importance of the kind of recovery in Italian industrial production that was witnessed during the 1920s. According to this study, recovery centred on light engineering and private demand, thus favouring steel production based on recycled materials; there had also been a fall in international scrap prices, which was another factor in this particular trend in steel production in Italy. After the crisis, there was a massive growth in the nation's demand for steel, and this, together with the concentration of a large part of steel production in the hands of IRI, led to a renewed call for expansion of the integrated production-cycle. Subsequently, pig-iron production increased a little, although Oscar Sinigaglia's ambitious plan for expansion during his period as president of ILVA (1932–5) had to struggle to get off the ground as a result of the strong differences of opinion that it provoked (and which finally led him to resign).[41] Sinigaglia's plan was taken over by Agostino Rocca,[42] managing director of the Dalmine Company, of SIAC, and of Ansaldo from 1935 onwards, and later to become general manager of the newly founded FINSIDER in 1938; however, work on the integrated production-cycle plant at Cornigliano, which had been designed to produce 300,000 tons of steel a year, only began in September 1938.[43] It has been pointed out that the argument about whether to expand this form of

[39] A. Carparelli, 136.

[40] R. Ranieri, 'Fattori nazionali ed internazionali nella ricostruzione della siderurgia italiana in una prospettiva di lungo periodo', published in Spanish in L. Prados de la Escosura and V. Zamagni (eds.), *El desarrollo economico en la Europa del Sur: Espãna e Italia en perspectiva historica* (Madrid, Alianza, 1992).

[41] Cf. G. Toniolo, 'Oscar Sinigaglia (1877–1953)', in Mortara (ed.), *I protagonisti*, and L. Scalpelli, 'L'ILVA, alla vigilia del piano autarchico per la Siderurgia (1930–1936)', *Ricerche storiche*, 8 (1978).

[42] P. Rugafiori, 'Agostino Rocca (1895–1978)', in Mortara (ed.), *I protagonisti*, and L. Offeddu, *La sfida dell'acciaio. Vita di Agostino Rocca* (Venice, Marsilio, 1984).

[43] The delay was due to a difference of opinion over where to locate the new plant, which some people wanted to see built at Bagnoli. On the divergencies over the 'autarkic plan for the steel industry', cf. F. Bonelli, A. Carparelli, and M. Pozzobon, 'La riforma siderurgica IRI tra autarchia e mercato 1935–1942', in F. Bonelli (ed.), *Acciaio per l'industrializzazione. Contributi allo studio del problema siderurgico italiano* (Turin, Einaudi, 1982), and V. Castronovo, 'L'industria siderurgica e il piano di coordinamento dell'IRI (1936–1939)', *Ricerche storiche*, 8 (1978).

production or not depended not so much on subjective opinion as on the fact that 'the advantages of the integrated cycle during the inter-war years, and in particular those of the first Cornigliano project, were far from self-evident'.[44] This was a result of the exceptionally low price of scrap iron up until the mid-1930s, as well as the difficulties Italy had in obtaining a regular supply of coal suitable for producing smelting coke, and also the size of the Cornigliano plant, which was still too small to be really economically viable.[45]

The fact of the matter is that the high cost of Italian steel production was not so much due to technical reasons as to the bad management and utilization of existing plant, as well as the fragmentary nature of the demand for steel[46] and the lack of an efficient organization of steel production in general. The new Cornigliano plant never began production because 'when building work was completed, the Germans stepped in and dismantled everything'.[47]

These developments fully explain why Italy's steel production failed to increase during the second half of the 1930s, and why those private businesses producing steel in electric furnaces were granted increasingly favourable conditions by the government.[48] The problem was only tackled again during the post-1945 period, this time with concrete results.

Turning now to a survey of the engineering industry, it has to be said, first of all, that although the data we have (columns 8–9, Table 9.1) say nothing about the 1920s, there can be no doubt that this was a period of expansion for the engineering industry, with the exception of the short period 1926–7.[49] This expansion was particularly strong amongst those small and medium-sized companies that specialized in the production of a limited range of goods, many

[44] V. Wengenroth, 'Il mito del ciclo integrale: considerazioni sulla produzione di acciaio in Italia', *Società e Storia*, 30 (1985), 909.

[45] Plants twice as big as the one that had been planned for Cornigliano were already considered to be barely profitable by the 1930s.

[46] The composition of demand for steel products changed during the 1930s, with a move towards the engineering sector, and stagnation (and in some cases a decline) in demand for the building industry. This would explain how it was that at a time of very modest growth in the steel industry, the engineering industry was able to grow at a disproportionately fast rate. Cf. G. Federico, 'La domanda siderurgica italiana negli anni Trenta', in Bonelli (ed.), *Acciaio*.

[47] L. Scalpelli, 'Razionalizzazione e sviluppo della siderurgia pubblica alla fine degli anni trenta: lo stabilimento di Cornigliano', *Rassegna economica*, 45 (1981), 1,251. The ILVA plant at Bagnoli and the modern section of the plant at Piombino were also detroyed by the Germans, thus reducing the productive capacity of pig-iron produced in the blast-furnaces by some 50%.

[48] Steel production in the electric furnaces, which had been equivalent to 25% of total production in 1935, had risen to 31% by 1939, and subsequently to 40% in 1943 (52% by 1944).

[49] A confirmation of this can be had through the following exercise involving the reconstruction of another production index for the engineering industry. Using ISTAT's figures for value added (*Indagine statistica sullo sviluppo del reddito nazionale dell'Italia dal 1861 al 1956* (Rome, 1957), at current prices, together with the engineering industry's price index as given by Vitali ('La stima degli investimenti e dello stock di capitale', in G. Fuà (ed.), *Lo sviluppo economico in Italia*, iii (Milan, Angeli, 1969). Taking the year 1929 as equal to 100, this index is as follows: 1923, 59; 1924, 81; 1925, 96; 1926, 103; 1927, 99; 1928, 108; 1929, 100; 1930, 90; 1931, 86; 1932, 74; 1933, 76; 1934, 79; 1935, 99; 1936, 114; 1937, 117; 1938, 123; 1939, 136; 1940, 136; 1941, 142; 1942, 129; and 1943, 109.

of which were completely new to the scene; but it was also true of some larger companies, such as Fiat, Marelli, and Olivetti. It would be interesting to carry out a fresh study of these new small and medium-sized companies: I can only give one or two examples of this kind of productive expansion here.

Italian production of sewing-machines had been tried before, but it was not until the Necchi company of Pavia started to produce them in the 1920s that this sector could be said to have made progress.[50] This company had been a foundry since the eighteenth century, and after its wartime expansion it was obliged to convert to some other form of production—hence the idea of producing sewing-machines—and by 1925, the company was producing some 20 machines a day. The Weber Company, founded in Bologna in 1923, produced carburettors. Other companies that were founded in Bologna at the time included the GD, which produced motor cycles (founded in 1924), and the ACMA which specialized in the manufacture of automatic packaging machinery, not to mention a whole series of other small companies that sprung up in the Bologna area during the 1920s.[51] Tractor production also boomed during the 1920s, thanks largely to the success of Fiat, which started production in Turin and then transferred its tractor division to Modena in 1928, following the take-over of the Officine Costruzioni Industriali (OCI). In 1939, the OCI supplied 35–40 per cent of all tractors built in Italy. Other kinds of farm machinery were also being built, and national production covered about 85 per cent of domestic demand in 1939.

In new areas such as aircraft production, specialized companies were still too small to be able to make a 'qualitative leap', while the larger companies such as Fiat, Breda, Piaggio, and Reggiane furnished the greater part of the aircraft engines. Although on the one hand mass production never really got under way, on the other hand Italian aircraft broke a series of national and international records, at the same time as the cars produced by Alfa-Romeo (and Lancia) were breaking records on the racetrack. The fact is that the Italian population's standard of living, which we shall be looking at in the next chapter, was not high enough for either the automobile or aircraft industries to be able to nurture any great economic hopes as far as mass production was concerned. Even Fiat, which dominated the domestic market to such an extent that it was capable of blocking a move made by Ford in 1930,[52] was 'very wary about concentrating its

[50] S. H. Wellisz, 'Studies in the Italian Light Mechanical Industry: The Sewing Machine Industry', *Rivista Internazionale di scienze economiche e commerciali*, 4 (1957).

[51] V. Zamagni, 'L'economia', in R. Zangheri (ed.), *Bologna* (Bari, Laterza, 1988).

[52] Towards the end of the 1920s, the Ford company bought a majority shareholding in the prestigious Milanese automobile company Isotta Fraschini, a company that produced excellent luxury-class vehicles, but which had had some serious financial problems. This move was aimed at getting around the Italian government ban on setting up a Ford assembly plant at Leghorn. Agnelli blocked the move in 1930, when he persuaded the government to pass a law which prevented the expansion of existing plants without the War Ministry's prior agreement. The Isotta Fraschini was transformed into a factory producing engines for aeroplanes and lorries. Cf. A. Bellucci, *L'automobile italiana 1918–1943* (Bari, Laterza, 1984).

efforts on mass production'.[53] Despite the opening of a new, modern plant at Lingotto, Fiat produced 29 different models between 1919 and 1929, and furthermore it decided to diversify production into ship and aircraft engines; although this was to prove extremely useful to the company during the 1929 crisis and after the Second World War, it certainly did not mean short-term savings in the running costs of the company.[54] While in 1929 the USA produced more than 5 million cars, Great Britain and France produced 250,000 each, Germany 130,000, Italian production was limited to a total of 55,000 cars, 27,000 of which were for export. The number of motor vehicles in circulation in Italy at the time was just over 200,000, which explains the survival of such artisan-type producers as Alfa-Romeo, Bianchi, Lancia, and Maserati.

Recovery in the engineering industry, after the shock of 1929, took place at the time of reconversion to a wartime economy.[55] The old wartime producers, Ansaldo, Breda, ILVA, Terni, OTO,[56] who had struggled to survive during the 1920s (most had been absorbed into IRI), reorganized their production, while Fiat, together with several other new companies, expanded its work-force as a result of the wartime contracts they were given by the Fascist government.[57] Despite an overall increase in production, most commentators at the time (as well as present-day scholars) agreed that 'the Fascist regime ... led an inadequately prepared country into war'.[58] There were many reasons for this:

[53] G. Volpato, 'L'evoluzione delle strategie di marketing nell'industria automobilistica internazionale', *Annali di storia dell'impresa*, 2 (1986), 176.

[54] It was the wave of protectionism witnessed after the 1929 crisis that persuaded Fiat to defend its foreign influence by opening up production plants in other countries: through the Simca in France (1934), NSU in Germany (1929), the Pzinz in Poland (1931)—although Fiat had already been present in Poland since 1920, with its Polski Fiat subsidiary—together with other agreements with Spain, Austria, Hungary, and Latin American countries. Although these ventures did not prove to be particularly profitable, they 'were to be extremely important in the period after the Second World War', D. Bigazzi, 'Un'impresa italiana sul mercato mondiale: l'attività multinazionale della Fiat fino al 1940', *Annali di storia dell'impresa*, 2 (1986), 259.

[55] For a thorough examination of the question of industrial reconversion, cf. R. Covino, G. Gallo, and E. Mantovani, 'L'industria dall'economia di guerra alla ricostruzione', in Ciocca and Toniolo (eds.), *L'economia italiana nel periodo fascista.*

[56] The Odero–Terni–Orlando (OTO) company emerged at the end of the 1920s from the reorganization of Vickers–Terni, the Odero shipyard at Genoa, and that of Orlando at Leghorn, together with the Fiat–San Giorgio; cf. L. Segreto, *Una joint-venture fallimentare. La Vickers, la Terni e l'industria italiana degli armamenti (1905–1933)* (Ancona, 1989).

[57] The Ducati company, which had employed 400 people in 1934, ended the war with some 7,000 employees; the Reggiane, from having 1,512 employees in 1935, had expanded to such an extent that by 1940 its work-force numbered some 10,000 employees. For an analysis of these important industrial changes in the region of Emilia, cf. P. P. D'Attorre, 'Una dimensione periferica. Piccola industria, classe operaia e mercato del lavoro in Emilia–Romagna, 1920–1940', *Annali* (Milan, Feltrinelli, 20, 1979–80).

[58] F. Minniti, 'Il problema degli armamenti nella preparazione militare italiana dal 1935 al 1943', *Storia contemporanea*, 9 (1978), 6. This view has been echoed in the writings of one American scholar, J. J. Sweet, in *Iron Arm. The Mechanization of Mussolini's Army, 1920–40* (Greenwood Press, Westport, Conn., 1980), where the author concludes: 'The Italian defeat in a mechanized war ... resulted from the failure of the army as technical expert and military advocate, the failure of the

1. First, the regime's military objectives were themselves not really very clear: the Fascist government had opened up campaigns on diverse fronts; decisions were invariably late in coming; and the declaration of 'total' war exposed a structurally weak nation to the risk of attack from the combined forces of its very strong enemies.[59] As a consequence, the government did not possess the capacity to organize and plan for coming events.

2. The country's military chiefs proved to be blinkered and disorganized, plagued by an inability to define the roles that the various armed forces were to play and by bureaucratic red-tape, which in the end was to lead to delays in the undertaking and co-ordination of important projects.[60]

3. Not only was the Italian industrial apparatus insufficiently developed, but it was far from being suitable for the kind of 'total' war envisaged by Mussolini, due to the absence of large companies capable of mass-producing reliable, standard products for an indefinite period of time.[61] We shall be looking at one or two illustrations of this point in this chapter.

4. Raw material supplies were totally insufficient to keep the war effort going.[62] According to General Favagrossa, not more than one-half of the raw materials considered to be necessary were made available.[63] There were numerous breakdowns in production, and the meagre productive capacity of Italian industry was in any case not used to the full. The fact is that the alliance with Germany, a country with similar problems though on a different scale—did not help towards solving the problem of Italy's lack of raw materials,[64] and the process of substituting the missing raw materials with artificial products was a slow and expensive one.

5. Finally, the willingness of businesses and the Italian people in general to collaborate with the regime's war effort continued slowly to decline as it became more and more obvious that the country was totally incapable of fulfilling the commitment asked of it by the Fascist regime.

government as overseer of national needs and planner and enforcer of national policy, and the failure of Italian industry as supplier of national needs' (pp. 186–7).

[59] In contrast, the First World War was fought against a single, not too powerful enemy, i.e. the Austro-Hungarian empire.

[60] Cf. F. Minniti, 'Due anni di attività del "Fabbriguerra" per la produzione bellica (1939–41)', *Storia contemporanea*, 6 (1975), and id., 'Aspetti organizzativi del controllo sulla produzione bellica in Italia 1923–1943', *Clio*, 12 (1977). On the overall problem of war preparations, cf. also M. Di Sabatino, 'L'industria bellica italiana dal 1939 al 1943. Aspetti tecnologici e problemi organizzativi', graduation thesis, Florence University, 1986–7.

[61] It is no coincidence that the highest quantitative levels were reached by American industry.

[62] V. Castronovo, 'Il "partito degli affari" e la guerra di Mussolini', in *Grandi e piccoli borghesi* (Bari, Laterza, 1988).

[63] C. Favagrossa, *Perché perdemmo la guerra. Mussolini e la produzione bellica* (Milan, Rizzoli, 1946); also see F. Minniti, 'Le materie prime nella preparazione bellica dell'Italia 1935–1943', *Storia contemporanea*, 17 (Feb. 1986 and Apr. 1986).

[64] The differences between this war and the First World War are also evident in this area: during the earlier war, Italy received significant financial aid from the USA and Gt. Britain, as well as food supplies and military supplies.

Despite the nation's heavy military defeats, the war effort was to leave a significant mark on the Italian industrial framework. It led, once again, to the further concentration of heavy industry in the North;[65] it led to a 50 per cent increase in the productive capacity of the engineering sector, especially in branches such as machine-tools, aircraft construction,[66] engine construction, and electrical engineering; it also produced an increase in the productive capacity of the chemical and rubber industries, as well as those manufacturing oil-based and coal-based industries. This new industrial capacity was to furnish the basis for the reconstruction of Italian industry in the post-Second World War period.

1.4. *Centres of industry: old and new*

As we have seen, the expansion of heavy industry during the inter-war years, particularly towards the end of the period, contributed to reinforcing the hegemony of the northern industrial triangle. While this is undoubtedly true, we cannot ignore other developments that took place, and which can give us a clearer picture of industrial progress in the country as a whole.

I am in agreement with Segreto when he writes: 'A strange tale, that of Italian light industry: it has always constituted the basis of the nation's productive capacity . . . and yet has almost always failed to catch the attention of modern economic historians.'[67] Now, while it is undoubtedly true that private consumption increased very little during the inter-war years (as we will see in the next chapter), this did not prevent important improvements in the organizational and technological nature of light industry, which in some cases led to the substitution of imports with Italian products. This little-known process made it possible for traditional artisan crafts to survive, and in some cases to begin the transition towards small and medium-sized industries. This was, of course, the basis for important post-war success stories, such as that of the clothing industry, of leather goods manufacturing, and of furniture. In many cases, these branches of manufacturing were geographically located outside the industrial triangle, for example in Tuscany, in the Veneto, in Emilia, and in

[65] That part of Italy produced 100% of all tanks, 94% of naval tonnage, 100% of naval engines, 85% of aircraft, and 50% of total artillery weapons.

[66] Cf. A. Jacoboni, *L'industria meccanica in Italia* (Rome, Istituto Poligrafico dello Stato, 1949). On the aircraft industry, which employed 11,000 workers in 1934, and some 150,000 in 1943, see F. Minniti, 'La politica industriale del Ministero dell'aeronautica', *Storia contemporanea*, 12 (Feb. 1981 and April 1981); A. Mantegazza, 'La formazione del gruppo Caproni', *Storia in Lombardia*, 5 (1986); and, finally, P. Macchione, *L'aeronautica Macchi. Dalla leggenda alla storia* (Milan, Angeli, 1985).

[67] L. Segreto, 'L'industria calzaturiera in Italia. La lunga rincorsa marchigiana, 1914–1960', in S. Anselmi (ed.), *L'industria calzaturiera marchigiana. Dalla manifattura alla fabbrica* (Ancona, Tecnostampa, 1989), 247. See also M. L. Blim, *Made in Italy: Small Scale Industrialization and its Consequences* (New York, Praeger, 1990).

the Marches. The textile industry's historical bases were strengthened—at Prato,[68] Valdagno, Biella, and Brianza—although no great leaps in production were witnessed (see columns 1–2, Table 9.2). The only industry to show real signs of decline was the silk industry.[69] We know very little about developments in the food industry, with the exception of one or two individual case-studies, e.g. Perugina-Buitoni,[70] and these happened outside the industrial triangle (as was the case of the sugar industry).

Secondly, the inter-war period witnessed the birth of some brand-new centres of industrial production and trade. The first, and most widely studied, is that of Porto Marghera (Venice). This centre was first conceived back in February of 1917, when Volpi set up the 'Port of Venice Research Centre for the Electrometallurgical and Shipbuilding Industries'.[71] This was followed by the foundation of the Industrial Port of Venice Company in June of that year; this organization signed an agreement with the government concerning the work to be carried out, and another with the Venice City Council aimed at the building of streets, housing, and public services in the area. The project was held back by the advent of war, and work was finally begun in 1919. The first factories were built in 1922, and there were already 5,000 workers at Porto Marghera by 1928, a figure which had risen to 15,000 by 1939.[72] As Petri has pointed out, 'the industrial area's main characteristic is the complex and widespread interaction between the principal productive cycles in the chemical and electrometallurgical industries'.[73] At the end of the 1930s, Porto Marghera produced 88 per cent of Italian aluminium, 59 per cent of alumina, between 90 per cent and 100 per cent of cadmium, 33 per cent of zinc, 47 per cent of ammonium phosphate, 100 per cent of plexiglass, and 100 per cent of the nation's propane and butane gas. 'It had gained an important place in the Fascist autarky project',[74] at times through foreign investment as well, and

[68] See G. Mori (ed.), *Prato: storia di una città*, iii: *Il tempo dell'industria (1815–1943)* (Florence, Le Monnier, 1988).

[69] S. Angeli, 'Il comparto serico: appunti su mercato, organizzazione d'impresa e lavoro in un caso di deindustrializzazione', *Storia in Lombardia*, 5 (1986).

[70] See G. Gallo (ed.), *Sulla bocca di tutti. Buitoni e Perugina. Una storia breve* (Perugia, Electa, 1990) and F. Chiapparino, 'Nascita di una grande impresa: la Perugina 1907–1923', *Proposte e ricerche*, 23 (1989).

[71] C. Chinello, *Porto Marghera 1902–1926. Alle origini del 'problema di Venezia'* (Venice, 1979); and S. Peli, 'Le concentrazioni finanziarie industriali nell'economia di guerra: il caso di Porto Marghera', *Studi storici*, 16 (1975).

[72] F. Piva and G. Tattara, *I primi operai di Marghera. Mercato, reclutamento, occupazione, 1917–1940* (Milan, 1983).

[73] R. Petri, *La zona industriale di Marghera 1919–1939. Un'analisi quantitativa dello sviluppo tra le due guerre* (Venice, Centro Tedesco di Studi Veneziani, 1985), publication 32, p. 10.

[74] R. Petri, 'Strategie monopolistiche e "Veneto industriale". Porto Marghera alla vigilia della seconda guerra mondiale', *Venetica*, 2 (1984); this essay contains an exhaustive list of all the advanced products produced at Marghera (where there were also some more traditional forms of manufacturing plant). See also R. Petri, 'Un laboratorio di nuova tecnologia: il polo industriale di Marghera prima e durante la seconda guerra mondiale', *Annali di storia dell'impresa*, 4 (1988), 136.

using some of the most advanced forms of technology available at the time, which were to play a strategic role in Italy's post-war recovery.

The foundation of other industrial complexes was encouraged by the Fascist policy of creating 'industrial development zones' during the 1930s; the incentives granted by the State ranged from subsidies for infrastructures to tax exemption. Two such areas have been studied by R. Petri, and these are Bolzano[75] and Ferrara.[76] The decree pertaining to Bolzano goes back to 28 September 1934, while that of Ferrara was dated 26 December 1936. By the end of 1942, 20 industrial plants had been set up at Bolzano, employing some 6,500 workers. The most important of these was a Lancia factory, a steelworks, and an aluminium plant belonging to the Montecatini group. Twenty-four companies had established factories in Ferrara by 1942, employing more than 4,200 workers. These included a factory producing light alloys, a Fiat factory producing ball-bearings, and, more importantly, chemical factories, producing soda, cellulose, and synthetic rubber.

Petri has lately reorganized all his previous works, plus a new set of case-studies, in a volume where he traces public intervention aimed at the development of new industrial areas back to the 1904 special laws for Naples and shows an interesting line of continuity through the inter-war measures up to the economic policies for the South in the post-Second World War period, especially after 1957 and the industrialization attempts. In all cases State intervention produced advanced plants with the latest technology, often incapable of merging with the local economic environment.[77] During the 1930s, one of the instruments of this planned industrial relocation was the law of 12 January 1933, concerning the so-called 'regulations governing the new industrial complexes', which were related to the construction of new plants and the expansion of old ones. Gualerni points out that 'particular attention was paid to the areas of Marghera, Livorno, Carrara, Ferrara, and Bagnoli'.[78]

2. THE BANKING UPHEAVALS OF THE 1920S, THE BIRTH OF IRI, AND THE NEW BANKING ACT OF 1936

The economic boom of 1923–5 was financed in the main by the banks, who had no liquidity problems at the time, given the salvage operations carried out by the Bank of Italy (through the CSVI). This involvement of the banks contributed towards the inflation we mentioned in Chapter 8, which in turn necessitated

[75] R. Petri, *Storia di Bolzano* (Padua, il Poligrafo, 1989).

[76] Petri, 'Il polo chimico'.

[77] R. Petri, *La frontiera industriale. Territorio, grande industria e leggi speciali prima della Cassa per il Mezzogiorno* (Milan, Angeli, 1990). At p. 313, the author writes: 'The creation of the Cassa per il Mezzogiorno, the reform of ISVEIMER and other interventions in the South after 1957 were a re-edition with some innovations of policies that had a very long history behind them.' See also R. Petri, 'Industria, territorio, intervento speciale. Riflessioni su una tradizione non solo meridionalista', *Meridiana*, 11–12 (1991).

[78] G. Gualerni, *Industria e fascismo*, 178.

monetary intervention on the part of the government, culminating in the famous 'quota 90' operation. The 1925 stock-market crash, together with the financial difficulties of many companies following 'quota 90', had meant that many banks now found themselves in difficulty, and the 1929 crisis hit when they had already been weakened. Consequently, the crisis had an extremely damaging effect on the existing banking system, so much so that a drastic cure had to be found. The solution proposed by the government at this point was quite novel and was to alter significantly the structure and role of the Italian banking system.

The process of transformation in the banking system during the 1920s consisted in three diverse moves: (*a*) an increase in the number of special credit institutions; (*b*) the 1926 banking act; (*c*) the transformation of the biggest banks from mixed banks into holdings.

The Crediop (founded in 1919) and the CSVI (1914) were two special credit institutions that already existed in 1923; the latter subsequently attempted to become a 'normal' industrial-credit bank, without any real success, due to the difficult economic and financial circumstances of the time.[79] It was Beneduce, who had been one of the founders of the Crediop and had become a central figure within the industrial and financial world, who had the idea of setting up a new credit institution which would provide long-term credit to the rapidly expanding electricity companies. This institute was the ICIPU (Istituto di Credito per le Imprese di Pubblica Utilità), which began business in 1924,[80] and was headed by Beneduce until 1939. Both the Crediop and the ICIPU financed themselves directly, through the emission of state-guaranteed bonds, and were to set an example for those institutes set up afterwards.[81] The famous financial house of Bastogi, which had been through a difficult period during the early 1920s due to an internal battle for its control, appointed Beneduce president in 1926, and subsequently went back to being an investment trust (a role it had had during the Giolitti years).

The foundation of the ICIPU was followed by that of the Credito Navale in 1928, and then by the much more important IMI (Istituto Mobiliare Italiano) in 1931, which was set up as part of the reorganization of banking which we shall be looking at shortly.[82] Sabino Cassese has pointed out that the 'Beneduce institutes'—as they were to be known—all had certain things in common: they were all conceived in accordance with the plan to increase state intervention in

[79] In 1926 the Independent Section of the CSVI became the Liquidation Office, which should have seen to selling off its industrial shareholdings, including Alfa-Romeo and Ansaldo, to private business, something which in fact it did not do.

[80] P. Baratta, 'Alberto Beneduce e la costituzione e gestione del Crediop e dell'ICIPU', in *Alberto Beneduce e i problemi dell'economia italiana del suo tempo* (Rome, Ed. Industria, 1985).

[81] The two institutes merged—ICIPU was incorporated into Crediop in 1981.

[82] Not forgetting the creation of the ISVEIMER (Institute for the Economic Development of Southern Italy) in 1938, and of the EFI (Industrial Financing Institute) in 1939.

the Italian economy; they all saw the Cassa DDPP, the INA, and the National Social Security Fund (CNAS, later to become the Istituto Nazionale per le Previdenza Sociale) as sources of funds (as alternatives to the Treasury and the Bank of Italy, whose share in the total financial assets of Italian banks had plummeted, as can be seen from Table 9.3). They all put bonds on the market, thus getting around the problem of the reluctance of the private sector to invest in shares, at a time when the share market was still trying to recover from the crash of 1925.[83] These institutes' share of total banking assets can be seen in column 10, Table 9.3.

Something still needs to be said about other public institutes of credit, such as the Liquidation Institute, the first institute of this kind, set up in 1926 in place of the autonomous section of the CSVI. This, however, was set up as a temporary body, and it was in fact to disappear from the scene later on, although in a different manner from the way that had been intended, as we shall shortly see. The second public institute of credit proved to be more long-lasting: this was the Istituto Nazionale di Credito per la Cooperazione, which went through a crisis period after the First World War, and was then transformed by Arturo Osio[84] into the Banca Nazionale del Lavoro e della Cooperazione in 1927 (in 1929 the name was changed once more to the Banca Nazionale del Lavoro, BNL). The first transformation permitted the institute to act as a savings bank for Fascist trade union organizations, and social welfare and other public bodies,[85] while the second change led to the further extension of the bank's activities, making it a banker for the various public authorities and for the artisan trades and small industry; this enabled it to expand rapidly, becoming very quickly one of the top eight Italian banks (see column 7, Table 9.3).

The second change in direction was tied to the 1926 Banking Act, a decree issued on 6 May, revoking the note-issuing powers of the Banco di Napoli and the Banco di Sicilia (this power lay exclusively with the Bank of Italy from then on), and transforming these banks into public institutes of credit. Some restrictive measures were introduced in September of that year, at a time when banks were still very possessive about their freedom of movement. These measures were aimed at the safeguarding of savings: they introduced a licence for the opening-up of new banks and new branches of already existing banks;

[83] S. Cassese, 'Gli aspetti unitari degli statuti degli enti Beneduce', in *Alberto Beneduce*. For an analysis of the whole question of long-term credit institutes and banking developments during the 1920s, see A. Innocenti, 'Crisi del sistema bancario e nascita dello stato "finanziere": la politica creditizia del fascismo negli anni venti', graduation thesis, Florence University, 1986–7.

[84] Osio, who had been a Catholic trade unionist and a militant of the Partito Popolare, then got involved with Fascism; cf. A. Scialoja, 'Arturo Osio, 1890–1968', in A. Mortara (ed.), *I protagonisti dell'intervento pubblico in Italia* (Milan, Angeli, 1984).

[85] V. Castronovo, *Storia di una banca: La Banca Nazionale del Lavoro e lo sviluppo economico italiano 1913–1983* (Turin, Einaudi, 1983).

Table 9.3. Percentage composition of Italian banking system's assets, 1923–1943[a]

	Issuing banks (1)	Savings banks (2)	Banche popolari (3)	Monti di Pietà (4)	Rural co-op. banks (5)	Joint-stock banks (6)	Public banks (7)	Banks of national importance (8)	Long term credit institutes (9)	Land banks (10)	Cassa DDPP (11)	Total assets (million lire) (12)
1923	26.8	13.3	7.8	1.1	0.8	32.9	—	—	1.0	1.4	14.9	95,708
1926	22.0	13.8	7.4	1.1	1.2	33.5	3.7	—	1.7	1.8	13.8	122,964
1929	16.3	15.6	7.3	1.1	1.1	33.7	4.1	—	2.6	4.0	14.2	136,287
1931	14.8	17.0	5.6	1.3	1.0	30.1	4.4	—	3.2	5.5	17.1	137,763
1933	12.3	17.8	4.7	0.7	0.8	24.7	5.5	—	6.5	6.4	20.6	142,987
1936	13.9	16.0	4.4	0.7	0.6	21.0	8.6	—	6.5	6.0	22.3	146,817
1938	14.0	13.2	3.9	...	0.7	7.2	9.8	13.6	7.2	6.4	24.0	168,460
1940	17.9	11.8	4.5	...	...	7.6	10.8	12.7	6.1	5.1	23.5	218,700
1943	37.1	7.7	3.7	...	...	6.3	7.9	9.8	10.6	2.6	14.3	564,700

[a] Excluding private banks.

Source: A. M. Biscaini Cotula and P. Ciocca, 'La struttura finanziaria: aspetti quantitativi di lungo periodo (1870–1970)', in F. Vicarelli (ed.), *Capitale industriale e capitale finanziario: il caso italiano* (Bologna, Il Mulino, 1979).

they imposed the setting-up of reserve funds; they set a ceiling on the ratio of deposits to assets, and of overdrafts to deposits; and finally, the Bank of Italy was given the power to control the activities of the other banks. The Bank of Italy had not yet been prevented from having financial dealings with private individuals (or companies) at this time, but such relations were becoming less and less important in comparison with the Bank's other activities. This law put an end to 'wild finance', although the 1929 crisis subsequently created the need for an even greater measure of government intervention, which took the form of a much more radical and long-lasting banking act 10 years later.

In order to complete this survey of the Italian banking system at the end of the 1920s, we still need to look at the development of the mixed banks. In Chapter 4 we saw that a balance between banks and industry had been established towards the end of the Giolitti years, and that this equilibrium was disrupted by the advent of war, moving in favour of industry during the war, and then back towards those banks that had survived the crisis, during the period of industrial reconstruction (see Chapter 7). The events of the 1920s are not wholly clear in their details,[86] although the main trend is well known enough, as can be seen from the account given by Raffaele Mattioli at the time:[87]

> The structure of the big Italian mixed banks had been transformed, or rather had been 'incredibly' deformed, just before the crisis of 1930–1 hit the banking world. The best part of the credit they furnished . . . went to a limited number of companies—a hundred or so in all—who were then able to expand their activities greatly, but who were so dependent upon this credit that they would have found it impossible to carry on without it. In other words, they were being controlled by the banks, who in turn were investing all the savings placed with them, together with a significant portion of rediscount operations, in these companies' activities (the 'less important' clientele had a negligible share of banks credit . . .). The physiological symbiosis had been transformed into a monstrous Siamese twinship: the banks were still 'mixed' officially speaking, but in reality they had become a sort of merchant bank, that is, they were finance houses doubly tied to their client industries' fortunes. This is not all, however, as in order to insure against the obvious risks involved in a situation of this kind, the banks had virtually bought back all their capital; they owned themselves by dint of their ownership of the

[86] Confalonieri is in the process of preparing complementary volumes to those five already published dealing with the pre-war period. An anticipation of his work has been published in the essay 'Considerazioni sull'esperienza del Credito Italiano 1914–1933', in *Il Credito Italiano e la fondazione dell'IRI* (Milan, Scheiwiller, 1990). Confalonieri confirms that 'banks had largely become holding companies, without being able or willing to adopt the techniques and structures of the holding companies' (p. 79). He also supports the view that the Bank of Italy was sometimes seen to encourage such behaviour, but in any case was not opposing it, and that it was the First World War and its consequences that were the main cause for the unbalanced relationships between industry and finance.

[87] Raffaele Mattioli, who had been given a job with Comit in 1925, became its managing director after Toeplitz (1933), a position which he was to keep until 1960. Cf. G. Malagodi, 'Raffaele Mattioli (1895–1973)', in Mortara (ed.), *I protagonisti.*

holdings they themselves had created and financed in order to ensure control over their capital. The initial deformation led to another. The Siamese twinship had become a form of 'catoblepism'.[88] Abyssus vocat abyssum.[89]

The developments that Mattioli outlines here were certainly reinforced by the effects of 'quota 90', which necessitated the larger banks' continual support of share prices and the financing of companies who were already in debt. By the time the international financial crisis that had exploded in Europe in 1931[90] hit Italy, several salvage operations had already been carried out. As well as those involving a number of local banks, which were helped by means of their merging with other, stronger institutes, the most important salvage operation was that involving the Banca Agricola Italiana. This bank, connected with the name of Gualino, was salvaged during the first few months of 1930, and was subsequently taken over by the BNL (in 1932), as were other small Catholic banks. Cianci points out that 'Osio's clever policy enabled him to gain credit through this salvage operation, for his support for the Fascist regime's economic policy, while at the same time presenting the bank with an entire network of branches nationwide without involving it in any form of capital outlay'.[91] Another case was that of the Credito Italiano, which had set up a holding company—the new Banca Nazionale di Credito[92]—during the spring of 1930, to which it had passed on its parcel of industrial shares; a year later, it signed an agreement with the Bank of Italy whereby its shareholdings were liquidated and handed over to a new holding company, the Società Finanziaria Italiana (SFI)—set up on 27 January 1931. This operation was funded through the Liquidation Institute, and the Credito Italiano subsequently committed itself to becoming a truly mixed bank once again. The new Banca Nazionale di Credito changed its name to Società Elettrofinanziaria, and only held electricity, telephone, and real estate companies' shares. The tie between the Credit and these two holding companies nevertheless remained quite strong, involving interlocking directorates and also current banking credit. The fact that the convention remained a secret one at the time, and did not involve either the Comit or the Banco di Roma, has led some experts to claim that it demonstrated the 'greater influence of the Motta-Pirelli-Feltrinelli triad [allied

[88] The word 'catoblepism', of unknown origin, is used here to express the concept of 'the owned-owning-the-owner', i.e. the idea of a bank which owns companies which, in turn, are joint-owners of the bank.

[89] R. Mattioli, 'I problemi attuali del credito', *Mondo Economico*, 15 (1962), 28. This citation opens the fine volume written by G. Rodano, *Il credito all'economia. Raffaele Mattioli alla Banca Commerciale Italiana* (Milan and Naples, Ricciardi, 1983).

[90] Cf. C. Kindleberger, *The Great Depression 1929–1939* (London, Penguin, 1973).

[91] E. Cianci, *Nascita dello stato imprenditore in Italia* (Milan, Mursia, 1977), 71.

[92] Confalonieri in 'Considerazioni' argues that the incorporation of the (old) BNC (administering the left-overs of BIS) into the Credit in 1930 worsened the situation of the Credit, that had not been too bad up to then.

to Credit] on political hierarchies, Fascist and governmental'.[93] However, the international financial crisis then frustrated Credit's timing in this matter.

The salvaging of the mixed banks, in fact, proved to be much more difficult: as Rodano points out, 'it is a well-known fact that Comit . . . initially tried to stand up to the impact of the crisis . . . relying solely on its own resources and the help of friends'.[94] Relations between Mussolini and Toeplitz had in any case never been particularly good. However, the seriousness of the situation meant that some kind of 'surrender' was necessary in the end, and so Toeplitz met Mussolini on 11 September 1931, in order to discuss a salvage project for Comit. The Banco di Roma also accumulated a series of tied-up assets, despite its management's extremely prudent policy.[95] We now have some accurate details concerning the subsequent plans for financial reorganization, drawn up by the Minister of Finance and Beneduce,[96] although they do not cover every single point of these plans. We know that the first project was presented by Toeplitz himself, and that its main ideas and proposals were probably the work of Mattioli:[97] the core proposal was that a similar operation to that which had involved Credit should be carried out, but within the context of a much vaster programme of public intervention. The convention was subsequently signed on 31 October 1931 (the details are too complicated to go into here).[98]

This was not all, however. Neither Credit's SFI nor Comit's holding company Sofindit was in a position to convert tied-up assets to liquid assets in a short period of time. What was needed, therefore, was a body capable of funding industry, but separate from the banks which, although they had been salvaged, were still heavily tied up. At first, the idea of a new independent section of the CSVI was considered,[99] but then it was decided that a completely independent institute was what was required, and this took the name of the Istituto Mobiliare Italiano (IMI), founded on 3 December 1931. This was not to be the final act of this complicated story, however. Using the same principles tried out in the case of the Beneduce institutes, 'IMI's directors made it known that they were not interested in buying shares or carrying out salvage operations, but would be restricting their range of activities, concerned as they were about the safety of investments and, above all, about remunerating the

[93] G. Mori, 'Nuovi documenti sulle origini dello "Stato industriale" in Italia', in Mori, *Il capitalismo*, 272. See also G. Toniolo, 'Crisi bancarie e salvataggi: il Credito Italiano dal 1930 al 1934', in *Il Credito Italiano*.

[94] Rodano, *Il credito*, 14.

[95] See Gabriele De Rosa, *Storia del Banco di Roma*, iii (Rome, Coragraf, 1984), chs. 2 and 3.

[96] In his role as plenipotentiary Minister under Mussolini.

[97] G. Rodano, *Il credito*, 15; G. Malagodi, 'Il "salvataggio" della Banca Commerciale nel ricordo di un testimone', in G. Toniolo (ed.), *Industria e banca nella grande crisi 1929–1934* (Milan, Etas Libri, 1978).

[98] They can be found in Rodano, *Il credito*.

[99] Cianci, *Nascita dello stato imprenditore*, 137 ff.

initial capital investment of those banks who were to fund this new body'.[100] The position of the three large mixed banks was even worse, however, by the year 1932. Memoranda and projects were produced at an ever-increasing rate, until finally a plan of action was decided on. In January 1933, the Istituto per la Ricostruzione Industriale (IRI) was set up, and was then divided into two separate departments—the Industrial Investment Department and the Industrial Disinvestment Department.

Recent historical research agrees on the following points concerning these developments:

1. The adopted solution was dictated more by the need to resolve a problem that threatened to disrupt the solidity of the Bank of Italy, rather than by a determined plan aimed at nationalizing the Italian economy.[101]
2. The birth of IRI meant the death of the mixed bank experience, and it was Beneduce who signed its death warrant.[102]
3. The State's assumption of responsibility for the running of businesses was originally conceived as a temporary measure, aimed at reorganizing these companies in order that they might then be returned to the private sphere, via the Disinvestment Department.

Let us consider for a moment the size of this operation, which involved IRI taking over the shareholdings of Comit, Credit, and the Banco di Roma, for a total of 10 billion lire, equal to 21.5 per cent of all capital belonging to joint-stock companies in Italy. The chain-like nature of shareholding meant that IRI was the major shareholder in companies representing some 42 per cent of all joint-stock company capital. It controlled 100 per cent of steel production for the war effort, of arms manufacturing, and of coal production; 90 per cent of shipyards; 80 per cent of shipping companies and of companies building locomotives; 40 per cent of general steel production; 30 per cent of electricity; most of the telephone companies; several engineering firms (including Alfa-Romeo), together with smaller shares of other sectors; it also had control over a large amount of property and, of course, over the three former mixed banks.[103] However, the cost of the salvage operation exceeded the nominal value of IRI's 'shareholdings' by more than 2 billion lire; the 'real' value of the latter was given as 7.7 billion lire, and the resulting overall loss was some 4.6 billion lire. IRI took over the Liquidation Institute and was extremely busy yielding up

[100] F. Cesarini, *Alle origini del credito industriale. L'IMI negli anni '30* (Bologna, Il Mulino, 1982). In another of Cesarini's essays ('Le origini e la gestione dell'IMI', in *Alberto Beneduce*), the author maintains that 'Beneduce was the main inspiration behind the creation of the IMI' (p. 63), which was conceived originally as being a means of salvaging Comit, which in the end was not the case.

[101] Rodano, *Il credito*, 72–3.

[102] F. Bonelli, 'Alberto Beneduce, il credito industriale e l'origine dell'IRI', in *Alberto Beneduce.*

[103] Toniolo, *L'economia dell'Italia Fascista*, 249–50; and id. 'Crisi economica e smobilizzo pubblico delle banche miste (1930–1934)', in *Industria e banca.* The former mixed banks were to be called 'banks of national importance' (col. 8, Table 9.3.).

companies to the private sector (among the most important privatized companies are Italgas, Bastogi, some electricity shareholdings including the majority shareholding in the Edison Company). However, these privatizations were compensated for by other investments and acquisitions, and in June 1937 a decision was taken to transform IRI into a permanent body with its own endowment fund. At the same time, the Disinvestment Department was closed down, while the Investment Department was merged with the IMI.

Beneduce became president of IRI, while Donato Menichella, an ex-functionary of the Bank of Italy who had been subsequently made a director of the SFI, was nominated general manager; he was to stay with IRI until 1943, and was later to become governor of the Bank of Italy (in 1947).[104] These two men were aided by a number of managers from private enterprise[105] in their reorganization scheme for Italian companies, which followed a sectorial pattern. In 1933 the STET was founded, with the task of controlling the telephone companies; in 1936 it was the turn of the FINMARE, which reorganized the shipping companies; this was then followed by the FINSIDER, set up in 1937 to control the activities of the steel companies. These various holdings were funded through the issue of bonds, many of which could be converted into shares. A special effort was made to train new managers and to draw up development programmes for these various industries, such as the integrated production cycle for the steel industry mentioned in the previous subsection.

Was the solution represented by IRI an inevitable one? According to Menichella, 'there was no choice left but to face up to the consequences of what had been done in the past, and to acknowledge that the State was the real owner of the banks, and of the shares in the banks' possession; and thus it was the State's duty to manage that capital as best it could'.[106] In Saraceno's opinion, setting up IRI corresponded to 'the intention to put a stop to the kind of government involvement which had up to that point only been requested in order that the bill be paid for expenses incurred as a result of decisions taken privately; this kind of involvement had to be replaced by another form, which gave the State the responsibility for making the choices which it would have had to pay for in any case'.[107] This solution was not, therefore, triggered by the 1929 crisis. Even in Germany—the birthplace of the mixed banks—the banks were unable to avoid the consequences of the 1931 financial crisis, and had to be rescued by the State, which did not attempt to change the mixed banking system, however, and this has survived in Germany until the present day. The

[104] Cf. *Donato Menichella. Testimonianze e studi raccolti dalla Banca d'Italia* (Bari, Laterza, 1986).

[105] On this half public, half private technocracy, see M. Maraffi, *Politica ed economia in Italia. La vicenda dell'impresa pubblica dagli anni Trenta agli anni Cinquanta* (Bologna, Il Mulino, 1990).

[106] D. Menichella, 'Le origini dell'IRI e la sua azione nei confronti della situazione bancaria (2 July 1944)', reported in Cianci, *Nascita dello stato imprenditore*, 316.

[107] P. Saraceno, 'Nuovi assetti introdotti nel nostro sistema economico dalle misure richieste dalla grande crisi 1929–1935', in Toniolo (ed.), *Industria e banca*, 8; also see P. Saraceno, 'L'intervento dell'IRI per lo smobilizzo delle grandi banche: 1933–1936', in *Alberto Beneduce*.

fact is that the intervention of the Italian State had been necessitated by far less serious crises than that of 1929, thus demonstrating the existence of a structural weakness, rather than a temporary one, of both a large number of companies and of the banks to which they were tied. In order to get around this weakness, which was not an inherent feature of the system of mixed banks, but rather of the Italian economic system, the proposed solution was to substitute 'the State for the mixed bank, as the linchpin of the system of financial intermediation',[108] and to create public companies; these have continued to be characteristic features of the Italian economic system up to this very day. Whether or not this solution be considered a definitive and irreversible one is a question that is hotly debated today, given the evolution of the Italian economic system since that solution was first proposed.

In concluding this section, I would like to reiterate the fact that the final act in this drama consisted in the passing of the banking bill on 12 March 1936. This nationalized the Bank of Italy (which could no longer have economic relations with private clients); the Bank's powers over the other banks were strengthened; and the separation of short-term credit from medium- and long-term credit was officially sanctioned.[109] As far as this separation was concerned, we shall see that it did not mean that the Italian financial system was to function in the way that the Anglo-Saxon system did, and neither was such a separation rigorously adhered to in practice, as it was possible to argue at length about the exact meaning of 'short-term credit activity'.[110]

[108] Toniolo, *L'economia dell'Italia fascista*, 268.

[109] Cf. S. Cassese, *E' ancora attuale la legge bancaria del 1936?* (Rome, La Nuova Italia, 1987). Also see M. Porzio (ed.), *La legge bancaria. Note e documenti sulla sua storia segreta* (Bologna, Il Mulino, 1981), and P. Caranza, F. Frasca, and G. Toniolo, 'Cinquanta anni di legge bancaria', *Temi di discussione del Servizio Studi della Banca d'Italia* (1986).

[110] Rodano, *Il credito*, 115.

10

The Slow Social Progress under Fascism

1 AUTHORITARIANISM AND CULTURE

ONE of the first reforms introduced by the Fascist regime as soon as it came to power was in connection with education. The urgency with which this reform was carried out has been interpreted in different ways by various scholars; some of them point out that plans for educational reform had been bandied about for over 20 years prior to this, and that therefore the educational world was waiting with bated breath for some kind of change. Others underline the fact that Mussolini had himself been a schoolteacher, and was therefore particularly interested in this area, and especially in the possibility of a Fascist school system forming the basis for a true Fascist society. One must also take Giovanni Gentile, Education Minister in Mussolini's first 'cabinet', into account. He was an idealist philosopher, determined to see that his élitist and humanistic ideology be considered as the basis for this reform.[1] Barbagli maintains that 'the Gentile reform was *also* a reactionary answer to the imbalance between education and the job market, which was evident from the overproduction of educated manpower, and from the social and political tensions that resulted from this'.[2]

Gentile's reform, which was passed during the summer of 1923, not only reinforced the authoritarian and hierarchical nature of the school system, but also led to a higher level of selection through the introduction of school admission exams, various diplomas and certificates, and above all, through stopping students from technical (renamed subsidiary) schools going to university. These schools, like the girls' grammar schools, were thus transformed into a blind alley within the educational system as a whole. Access to university[3] was also restricted in the case of students from technical colleges as only those studying economics, commerce, and statistics were admitted and the so-called 'normal' schools, which were renamed teacher training colleges (scuole magistrali), were reduced in number from 153 to 87, and a new, more humanist curriculum was introduced; finally, Gentile's reform gave birth to the

[1] A. Lyttelton, *The Seizure of Power. Fascism in Italy 1919–1929* (London, Weidenfeld & Nicolson, 1973).

[2] M. Barbagli, *Disoccupazione intellettuale e sistema scolastico in Italia* (Bologna, Il Mulino, 1974).

[3] D. Bertoni Jovine, *La scuola italiana dal 1870 ai giorni nostri* (Rome, Editori Riuniti, 1958), 274.

science-orientated grammar schools (licei scientifici), which were also to have a strongly humanistic curriculum.[4]

The reform proved to be very unpopular, not only among the regime's opponents, but also among Fascists themselves, as they realized that it would limit the possibility of social mobility for their children. The subsidiary schools were such a flop that they were abolished by the 1929–31 law, and their place was taken by vocational schools;[5] some students were given the possibility of then going on to technical college or teaching college. The policy of restricting the number of admissions to secondary schools, another of Gentile's reforms, was also gradually abolished. In fact, his reforms were something of a disaster for the educational system, as can be seen from Table 10.1, as all educational indices available for the year 1926 were lower than those of the pre-reform years. This crisis had already been shored up by the early 1930s, while the following decade was to be witness to a veritable boom in educational standards in the middle- and high-school categories. (Very little research has been carried out into the reasons for this boom.)[6] Thus Gentile's reforms proved to be a rather serious set-back to educational improvement in Italy, although they did not stop it altogether. They led education towards a more humanistic future, but failed to suffocate completely the development of technical and scientific studies that had become too deeply rooted in Italy since the Casati law.

The composition of the university population during this period is further proof of this. Table 10.2 shows that university admissions increased by 350 per cent between 1913–14 and 1940–41. This increase is largely explained by the phenomenal rise in the number of students admitted to economics faculties and teacher-training colleges; the increase in admissions to literature faculties

[4] Norberto Bobbio has written that 'the universities and the Fascist regime learned to live with one another: the universities were left alone (no attempt was made to transform them into Fascist institutions, as some of the hardliners would have liked to do) as long as they themselves did not attempt to interfere with the regime's business. . . . Faced with the changing nature of the Italian State, the academic world was neither fawningly complimentary nor particularly critical of this process: it accepted this *fait accompli* and its consequences, while continuing to work away relatively undisturbed in the little niche it had carved out for itself. When it came to the acid test, and 1,200 university lecturers and professors were called up to swear allegiance to Fascism (during the academic year 1931–2), only 11 did not agree to take the oath . . . The real blow came much later, when in 1938, as a result of the racial laws, all of the numerous Jewish members of the universities' academic staff were sacked from their jobs', 'La cultura e il fascismo', in *Fascismo e società italiana* (Turin, Einaudi, 1973), 214.

[5] In July 1928, the engineer Giuseppe Belluzzo from Milan Polytechnic was appointed Minister for Education, and in this role he came up with a plan for a rather ambitious technical 'counter-reform', which was subsequently cut down, but not completely ignored, following the objections of Gentile. Belluzzo was only to remain in his job at the Education ministry for 14 months. Cf. I. Granata, 'Un tecnocrate del fascismo: Giuseppe Belluzzo', in *Il Politecnico di Milano nella storia italiana (1914–1963)*, with an introduction by E. Decleva, Supplement to *Rivista milanese di economia* (Milan, Cariplo-Laterza, 1988).

[6] Barbagli, *Disoccupazione intellettuale*, puts this down to the high levels of unemployment, in accordance with his cyclical theory, which underestimates the importance of an underlying upward trend in school enrolment which is independent of the economic cycle.

Table 10.1. Trend in educational levels, 1911–1940

	Illiteracy (%)	School enrolment rates		
		Primary (6–11)	Secondary (11–18)	Higher (19–23)
	(1)	(2)	(3)	(4)
1921	27.4	87	...	1.4
1926	...	73	5.6	1.2
1931	20.9	93	7.0	1.2
1936	17.0	99	10.9	2.0
1940	...	95	14.1	3.4

Sources: *Population Censuses*, 1921, 1931, and 1936; *Annuario statistico dell'istruzione italiana*, various years.

Table 10.2. Breakdown of university students by faculty, 1913/14–1940/1

	1913/14	1920/1	1926/7	1930/1	1936/7	1940/1
Law	9,382	9,766	8,871	10,073	14,097	20,937
Economics	1,379	7,212	5,886	8,285	13,008	23,011
Literature and languages	1,908	3,586	2,501	2,709	7,756	15,779
Teacher training	282	941	1,070	1,456	6,229	13,800
Medicine	5,342	10,208	8,865	9,991	13,829	13,781
Engineering	6,332	12,362	6,567	4,290	4,472	9,331
Science	1,325	4,030	2,906	2,269	3,347	8,840
Pharmacy	1,080	2,350	3,228	2,734	2,266	2,567
Agricultural science	547	1,391	1,027	1,130	1,382	2,533
Applied chemistry	—	—	152	121	127	450
Others	449	1,393	1,791	3,204	4,999	16,029
TOTAL	28,026	53,239	42,864	46,262	71,512	127,058

Source: ISTAT, *Statistica dell'istruzione superiore nell'anno accademico 1945–46* (Rome, 1948).

was also more than proportional to the overall rise in student numbers, while the law and pharmacy faculties (highly 'traditional' choices in Italy) saw a proportionately lower increase in their numbers. Engineering, on the other hand, went through something of a crisis after the high enrolment of 1920–21, and it only started to recover from this during the second half of the 1930s; the growth of pure sciences, as well as some very specialized faculties (see 'others' in Table 10.2), was also fairly healthy during this period. Thus we can see that neither sciences nor 'new' subjects were marginalized at the time, while engineering had a very cyclical performance (no specific study of this phenomenon has yet been carried out).[7]

Another new project which was eventually realized by the Fascist regime was the establishment of a National Research Council (CNR) in December 1923, although it was not to become truly operative for at least a decade, despite Gugliemo Marconi's presidency. Other special bodies and foundations were also set up, but their programmes and resources were fairly limited. Maiocchi concludes that 'by the beginning of the Second World War, the position of the sciences had certainly improved, both from the organizational and the ideological point of view in comparison with their plight during the Giolitti years; however, they had failed to make up any of the ground that separated them from their foreign counterparts, and scientific methods and values still had a long way to go before they could be said to have really permeated the fabric of Italian society'.[8]

One important development from the humanistic point of view was the foundation of the Istituto Giovanni Treccani on 18 February 1925. This institute was to be responsible for compiling the *Enciclopedia Italiana*, launched as a 'national project' that same year and aimed at involving the entire body of Italian academics and researchers in a grandiose representation of Italian culture. It has been proved that a number of Italian academics who disagreed with Fascism did in fact collaborate on this project, which in turn caused certain extreme Fascists to protest at their involvement, and the result was that the encyclopaedia did not turn out to be a Fascist work as such, even though the pages concerning Fascism were written by members of the party faithful.[9] The encyclopaedia was published regularly, four times a year, for a period of eight years—from 1929 to 1937—and involved a considerable economic expense for the government, which paid for its compilation and publication.

Apart from this rather isolated case, education in general was forced to conform to the wishes of the Fascist regime to an increasingly great extent. On 1 November 1928, a single government textbook was introduced into the

[7] The decline in the status and role of the engineer, which was witnessed from the 1920s onwards, is illustrated in V. Zamagni, 'Il ruolo de "L'industria" nella vita economica italiana: 1887–1942', *L'industria*, 5 (1986). The Milan Polytechnic, nevertheless, continued to grow in importance, partly as a result of its move to a new site (eight times as big as the previous one) in 1927. Cf. C. G. Lacaita, 'Il Politecnico e il fascismo', *Storia in Lombardia*, 8 (1989), together with the previously mentioned two volumes on the Milan Polytechnic. In a recent article, Maiocchi describes the transformation of the Polytechnic during this period as the passage from 'a well-established and professionally competent training college to an important centre for technological and scientific research', R. Maiocchi, 'L'attività di ricerca nel Politecnico di Milano tra le due guerre', *Storia in Lombardia*, 8 (1989), 33.

[8] R. Maiocchi, 'Scienza, industria e fascismo (1923–1939)', in *Società e storia*, 2 (1978), 315; cf. another study written by the same author, 'Il ruolo delle scienze nello sviluppo industriale italiano', in *Annali della storia d'Italia*, iii: *Scienza e tecnologia* (Turin, Einaudi, 1980).

[9] G. Turi, *Il fascismo e il consenso degli intellettuali* (Bologna, Il Mulino, 1980), ch. 1. Also see G. Lazzari, *L'enciclopedia Treccani. Intellettuali e potere durante il fascismo* (Naples, Liguori, 1977).

classrooms of all Italian primary schools; in February 1929, all primary schoolteachers were forced to pledge their allegiance to the Fascist regime; and young people were organized into various groups, including the Opera Nazionale Balilla, the Fascist Youth Movement, and GUFs (Fascist University Students' groups). Any independence that teachers had left was taken away in 1935, and in 1939 the Carta della Scuola (School Charter) was introduced, which united the wholesale Fascist transformation of society with the 'movement towards the people', dear to the anti-bourgeois spirit of one section of the original Fascists, which was to make its reappearance towards the end of the Fascist era. However, the School Charter was not to have any practical repercussions on the school system, due to the war.

In rounding off this brief survey of cultural developments during Fascism, I would like to say a brief word about publishing. The Giolitti years had witnessed some very important developments in the publishing world, with a number of the most important Italian publishing houses being founded at that time, including Laterza (1901), Ricciardi (1907), Rizzoli (1909), and Mondadori (1911), and the number of titles being published each year rising to about 11,000 by 1914.[10] These boom years were then followed by a post-war crisis in publishing, due to economic, cultural, and technological factors,[11] as a result of which the number of titles fell by half; recovery from this crisis was very slow after 1927, and the number of books published only returned to its original level during the period between 1930 and 1935.

While the publishing market more or less stagnated from a quantitative point of view, there were one or two novelties during this period, despite the presence of the keen eye of Fascist censorship, which was exercised from the Journalism and Propaganda Office at first (1934), and was then made the responsibility of the Ministry for Popular Culture (the famous Minculpop, set up in 1936). The main protagonists of such innovations were two publishing houses: on one side there was the new publishing company Einaudi, founded in 1934, which, although it had a very limited number of titles (a total of 212 published between 1934 and 1944), still managed to be something of a dissident voice with respect to certain areas of Fascist thinking, and in particular in the field of economics;[12] on the other side there was the Mondadori company which, through its support for the regime, found itself in the position of being able to introduce certain novelties from abroad on to the Italian market, ranging from detective stories to Walt Disney's mickey mouse, as well as the Medusa series, which consisted of some of the best titles from modern foreign literature translated into Italian.

[10] Cf. M. Curia, 'L'editoria italiana tra le due guerre', graduation thesis, Florence University, 1984–5. G. Tortorelli has produced a well-informed survey of research carried out to date on the history of publishing in Italy entitled 'Studi recenti di storia dell'editoria in Italia', *Storia in Lombardia*, 8 (1989).

[11] Mass-production technological methods, which meant a dramatic reduction in costs, were not readily implemented due to the limited size of the market.

[12] Cf. Turi, *Il fascismo*, ch. 1.

The content of such writings was often 'a long way from the political and cultural line as dictated by the Fascist hierarchy'.[13] However, such innovations were very limited, and although they meant that Italian culture did not completely lose sight of international developments at the time, they failed to penetrate very deeply into the national consciousness, and made very little impact even among the nation's intellectual and ruling élites.

2. UNEMPLOYMENT, WAGE-LEVELS, AND THE STANDARD OF LIVING

According to Barberi's figures,[14] set out in column 1, Table 10.3, personal consumption only increased 6 per cent between 1923 and 1939. If we compare this with the pre-war level (1913), the increase remains a rather modest one, equal to 21 per cent over a period of 26 years! The fluctuations due to the First World War and the 1929 depression were small enough, whereas there was a dramatic fall in incomes between 1943 and 1945. There had already been a reduction of about 15 per cent between 1939 and 1942, and by 1945 income had fallen to such an extent that consumption stood at 54 per cent of its 1939 level. Even if we ignore the years after 1939, the picture still remains one of virtual stagnation in individual consumption.[15] It is worth noting, however, that the consumption of non-foodstuffs changed considerably. In absolute terms and at constant prices, the latter more than doubled between 1913 and 1939, and in doing so contributed towards creating additional outlets (together with government consumption, which more than quadrupled) for Italian industrial producers.[16]

The main reason for this overall stagnation of individual per capita consumption can be traced back to the economic and demographic features of the inter-war period: the adverse economic climate, the impossibility of emigrating, and the process of rearmament meant that wages and salaries could not increase, while savings were reduced by inflation at first, then by unemployment, and then by inflation again. Table 10.3 gives us a more precise picture of these developments. The first thing to note is that of the three categories of workers that had won an improvement in wage-levels after the First World War—farm labourers, factory workers, and railwaymen—the

[13] M. Zerbini, 'Arnoldo Mondadori. Tra impresa e organizzazione della cultura', *Storia in Lombardia*, 5 (1986), 135.

[14] B. Barberi, *I consumi nel primo secolo dell'unità d'Italia, 1861–1960* (Milan, Giuffré, 1961).

[15] For futher details, cf. V. Zamagni, 'Dinamica e problemi della distribuzione commerciale al minuto tra il 1880 e la II guerra mondiale', in *Mercati e consumi* (Bologna, Analisi, 1986), 16.

[16] In order to have a clear idea of the distorted nature of Italian consumption, one should bear in mind the fact that in 1939 public consumption was equal to three-quarters of the private consumption of non-foodstuffs, although the comparison is not totally accurate, as public consumption includes food for the troops and for the army's animals, which should be excluded from calculations.

Table 10.3. Consumption, wages, and salaries, 1923–1938 (indices 1913 = 100, constant prices)

	Total per capita individual consumption	Daily wages of			Annual salaries of civil servants	
		agric. workers	factory workers	railway workers	IV cat.	XII cat.
	(1)	(2)	(3)	(4)	(5)	(6)
1923	115	129	133	145	67	94
1925	116	113	126	135	75	80
1927	118	123	125	140	75	78
1929	122	130	110	155	85	80
1931	114	132	110	162	109	95
1934	115	135	119	160	114	106
1936	112	125	105	158	103	99
1938	120	120	106	153	100	95
1941	111	...	...	...	86	95

Sources: B. Barberi, *I consumi nel primo secolo dell'unità d'Italia, 1861–1960* (Milan, Giuffré, 1961); V. Zamagni, 'Distribuzione del reddito e classi sociali'; id., 'La dinamica dei salari nel settore industriale', in P. Ciocca and G. Toniolo (eds.), *L'economia italiana nel periodo fascista* (Bologna, Il Mulino, 1976).

factory workers were those who saw the largest slice of their hard-won gains eroded, while farm labourers lost purchasing power chiefly during the two inflationary periods—from 1923 to 1926, and then from 1935 onwards. The well-known privileges enjoyed by the railway workers are confirmed by a glance at column 4: the improvement in their pay was the most consistent of all during this period (although their numbers were decimated immediately after the Fascists came to power).

The second point concerns working conditions. Whereas the situation in the countryside was one of increasing underemployment, forcing many peasant farmers and labourers to migrate, the industrial sector of the economy witnessed a new development in terms of work organization. The movement towards the rationalization of the working process, known as 'Taylorism', began slowly to spread to Italy, and in fact had already been witnessed in some industries during the First World War. Although 'the Italian situation did not exactly represent fertile ground for the rational organization of work',[17] due to the limited expansion of large industry during the period in question, none the less there can be little doubt about the spreading of the piece-rate system, and about the interest shown by the Confederation of Italian Industry in such developments. In fact, a body called the Italian National Authority for the Rational Organization of Labour (ENIOS) was set up in 1926 with the task of studying specific forms of intervention in this field, not only technical but also legislative, such as the plan to unify steel products. Slowly but surely the concept of 'fluid working' (as it was defined by one expert at that time) became part and parcel of the productive process, as illustrated by the assembly-line system; but this 'fluidity' or rationality also incorporated the use of conveyor belts for transporting raw materials, finished goods, parcels, letters, etc., as well as the reorganization of office work. The organizational aspect of company management started to move slowly towards the creation of a multi-divisional system, although at the time this 'Americanization' process was still very limited in Italy, and did not really take off until after the Second World War.[18]

The third point to be made concerning wage-levels is that civil servants, although recovering the purchasing power that they had lost during the period 1915–21, saw hardly any improvement in their position compared with the pre-war years. This produced a reaction on their part against the tendency towards a redistribution of income along more egalitarian lines (as seen in the years 1919–21), and the result of this was that by the end of the 1930s the wage differential between civil servants and factory workers had increased marginally

[17] G. Sapelli, *Organizzazione, lavoro e innovazione industriale nell'Italia fra le due guerre* (Turin, Rosenberg & Sellier, 1978), 122. Also see F. Steri (ed.), *Taylorismo e fascismo. Le origini dell'organizzazione scientifica del lavoro nell'industria italiana* (Rome, Ed. Sindacale It., 1979).

[18] V. Zignoli, 'I trasporti interni di fabbrica e la razionalizzazione', in *Organizzazione scientifica del lavoro*, 8 (1933), cited in Sapelli, *Organizzazione*, 244.

compared with 1911.[19] During Fascism, therefore, we can talk not so much of an 'improvement for the middle classes' as of the reaffirmation of their 'advantage' over the working classes, which merely enabled them to gain a little more ground in terms of relative status than they had had before the outbreak of war.

The factors that had the greatest influence in limiting the purchasing power of the working classes were, as we have already mentioned, unemployment and the standstill in emigration. It is difficult to say exactly how widespread unemployment was, given the significant level of underemployment during 'normal' times and the large number of home-workers in Italy, not to mention the inaccuracy of statistical surveys at that time. A recent study made by Piva and Toniolo[20] gives industrial unemployment during the worst years (1931–4) as fluctuating between 11.4 and 15.5 per cent of the total work-force. Unemployment in the cities was undoubtedly higher than this figure suggests, while the disastrous plight of the Italian countryside was hidden to an extent by the existence of solidarity networks deeply rooted in rural areas, as well as by the government's numerous public works programmes located in the countryside. Several writers have expressed doubts about the effectiveness of the public works policy that the Fascist regime had heralded as the 'productivistic' answer to the problem of unemployment. Piva and Toniolo estimate that the total number of jobs created (including those pertaining to land-reclamation projects) numbered about 60,000, equivalent to 9 per cent of the total number officially unemployed at the height of unemployment. The figures for public spending on such projects confirm the fact that there was an increase, but that it was not particularly large.[21]

As regards emigration, we can see from the figures available that it was very quick to take off again after the First World War, with a total of 2.6 million people deciding to leave the country during the 1920s (net emigration amounted to 1.5 million during this decade).[22] Emigration had begun to be directed more towards Europe than previously had been the case, in particular towards France and Belgium, as a result of the United States' decision to put a halt to immigration into the country, a decision originally taken in 1921, but toughened up in 1924, leading to a collapse in the average annual emigration

[19] The estimates I made of the ratio between salaries earned by office-workers and wages earned by factory workers, given in the already mentioned 'Distribuzione del reddito e classi sociali nell'Italia fra le due guerre', *Annali*, 20 (Milan, Fetrinelli, 1979–80), 42, are as follows: 1911, 2.42; 1921, 1.54; 1925, 2; 1931, 2.93; 1938, 2.60.

[20] F. Piva and G. Toniolo, 'Sulla disoccupazione in Italia negli anni '30', in *Rivista di storia economica*, 4 (1987).

[21] Cf. G. M. Sozzi, 'Le opere pubbliche nel regime fascista (1926–1936)', graduation thesis, Florence University, 1983–4.

[22] The level of voluntary expatriation was lower than it had been during the period from 1891 and 1920, whereas the level of net emigration was higher than even the peak previously reached during the 1890s (see Ch. 6).

figures for Italy, which fell to 41,916.[23] The Fascist regime started to resent this constant wave of emigration towards the end of the 1920s, but the numbers were only drastically reduced as a result of the Great Depression.[24] Thus the effects of the closing of this 'safety-valve' were only felt during the 1930s, when wages, employment, and consumption suffered as a result. One by-product of this drastic reduction in emigration was a rise in internal migration from certain areas of the country to others, studied by Treves[25] and also by Sori. The evidence shows that there was a substantial flow of migrants from the Veneto, and to a lesser extent from Emilia–Romagna and Tuscany, towards the country's industrial triangle during the 1920s and in the period between 1932 and 1937. Rome also attracted a fair number of migrants from many Italian regions, including the southern regions, migration from the South towards the North really taking off during the 1930s, above all during the second half of the decade. 'Apulians, Sicilians, and Calabrians were present in many central and northern regions before the Second World War: in Liguria, Piedmont, and Lombardy, in Rome, but also in regions like Tuscany',[26] despite the regime's numerous laws banning this labour mobility.[27] Evidently the countryside around the industrial triangle could no longer supply sufficient numbers of workers for industry—which was being developed almost exclusively in that part of the country—during the years of economic recovery following the First World War.

The process whereby the Italian population found itself increasingly concentrated in towns and cities was to continue, therefore, during the Fascist period. The government was very much involved in town planning, and massive inner-city renewal programmes were put into operation in many cities, whereby old quarters were gutted, and new, more 'respectable', and often very pompous constructions were erected in place of the old buildings that had been pulled down. This was hardly a new practice, as there had been similar operations during the Giolitti years and even beforehand,[28] nor did it stop with the fall of Fascism. The difference was that in the case of the Fascist programme of urban renewal, all was done in the name of a Fascist ideology of 'purification' and 'progress', and this policy of renewal through demolition has, by extension,

[23] E. Sori, *L'emigrazione italiana dell'unità alla seconda guerra mondiale* (Bologna, Il Mulino, 1979), ch. 10.

[24] A total of 113,000 people emigrated during the course of the 1930s.

[25] A. Treves, *Le migrazioni interne nell'Italia fascista* (Turin, Einaudi, 1976).

[26] Sori, *L'emigrazione italiana*, 461.

[27] The most drastic being that of July 1939, which declared it illegal for those who did not already have a signed contract of employment to migrate or change their place of residence; this contract, according to another law passed in 1938, could be given only to persons registered at the local employment office, and to be registered one had to be a resident of that town or city. The circularity of the two measures was intentional. This law was abolished in 1961, after having been largely ignored for years.

[28] e.g. the new cathedral square in Milan, built between 1860 and 1865, and the dramatic alterations made to the lay-out of the city of Florence during the same period.

become synonymous with Fascism.[29] The fact that thousands of working-class families were moved out of the old city centres meant that the government was forced to build inexpensive housing in the city suburbs; this kind of housing spread like wildfire, and consisted of poor-quality terraced houses and large apartment buildings, of little worth both from the architectural and the qualitative point of view, and was often accompanied by the growth of shanty towns, which sadly became widespread during the 1950s. The expansion of the suburbs included the building of sports stadiums, hospitals, mental asylums, polytechnical colleges, and university laboratories, and all of this meant a reduction in the urban green belt. The architecture was rather eclectic in style, frequently taking in classical themes with a huge waste of space and marble (for example, ridiculously tall arcades and floors), although there was an attempt at 'functional' architecture, particularly in the new towns (Mussolinia—now Arborea, in Sardinia—Carbonia, Guidonia, Arsia, Torviscosa, and the EUR neighbourhood of Rome).[30]

Several steps were taken to modernize the retail network in Italian cities, although it hardly represented a revolution in retailing practices.[31] Besides the co-operative stores, many of which survived both the post-war crisis period and the attacks of Fascist gangs, although with some difficulty,[32] this period in history saw the beginnings of a modern retail trade in Italy. The Rinascente department store was born out of what remained of the old Bocconi store in Milan in 1917, although it had a hard time at first, due to the war and to the fire which destroyed the building at the end of 1918. However, the store was rebuilt by its promoter, the Milanese industrialist Borletti, who then decided to open up branches in other Italian cities such as Florence, Rome, and Naples.[33] The chain of Rinascente department stores expanded very quickly, thanks to the work of the managing director Umberto Brustio, and 10 years later there were 19 stores throughout the country.

In the meantime, Rinascente's directors had decided to introduce a new sales system into Italy, and the year 1928 saw the foundation of the UPIM (Unico Prezzo Italiano Milano), which was a 'single price' store along the lines of other similar stores which had been a huge success abroad. These stores sold cheaper goods than the Rinascente stores did, goods that were arranged on different counters, each counter having a single price (1, 2, 3, 4 lire) for all goods. Not only was the UPIM a success, but it also helped the Rinascente to get over the

[29] Cf. L. Borlotti, *Storia della politica edilizia in Italia* (Rome, Editori Riuniti, 1978).

[30] R. Mariani, *Fascismo e 'città nuove'* (Milan, 1976).

[31] For full details concerning commercial distribution and its organizational network, cf. V. Zamagni, *La distribuzione commerciale in Italia fra le due guerre* (Milan, Angeli, 1981).

[32] In 1938 the sales made by Italian co-operatives were estimated as making up 3% of total commercial consumption, compared with a figure of 10% in Gt. Britain. For information concerning the Fascist period, see M. Degl'Innocenti, 'La cooperazione dalle origini alla seconda guerra mondiale', in *Storia della Società Italiana*, xvii (Milan, Teti, 1987).

[33] F. Amatori has written an excellent history of the Rinascente company, entitled *Proprietà e direzione. La Rinascente 1917–1969* (Milan, Angeli, 1989).

crisis years of the early 1930s, and as a result, 14 of the 19 Rinascente branches were transformed into UPIM stores. There were 35 branches of UPIM in 1939, and 55 by 1943.[34] In 1930, UPIM even found itself with a competitor, the Standard (later STANDA), which had opened 39 branches by 1943.[35] However, this form of modern retailing was to remain of marginal importance in Italy, and in 1938 represented only 1 per cent of total retail sales. Only the strength of the Borletti, Brustio, and Monzino families made it possible to continue with this retailing experiment during such difficult times, when individual consumption was virtually stagnant while the number of petty retailers and distributors never stopped increasing.

Another aspect of the Fascist period concerned developments in the transport sector. Apart from the electrification of some railway lines, this period saw the opening of new stations, together with that of some 'direct' lines, including the very important Bologna–Florence line, which meant that the journey took one and a half hours, whereas before it had taken some five hours (via Porretta and Pistoia).[36] The slow beginnings of a spread in the use of the motor car meant that Mussolini's government had to do something about the road network. An official body was set up in 1928 to take on responsibility for the construction and upkeep of the roads; and this body, the AASS (which later became the ANAS), was given its own budget to this end. The year 1925 saw the first stretch of motorway in Italy—the Milan–Lakes motorway—which was the beginning of a policy of motorway construction that was to see 500 km. built by the end of the Fascist period. The pay-tolls were high,[37] but then so were petrol, road tax, and the cars themselves. At first, the cheapest Fiat car was the Balilla, launched in 1932 at a price of 10,800 lire (subsequently lowered to 9,900 lire), and then the Topolino arrived in June 1936 at 8,900 lire. These prices compare with an average annual wage for a factory worker of 4,000 lire, while an office-worker in the private sector earned about 12,000 lire in 1938,[38] and a full-time secondary schoolteacher about 16,000 lire. It is no surprise, then, that there were only 290,225 cars on the road in 1939.

3. THE FASCIST 'WELFARE STATE'

Contrary to what the Fascists would have had people believe, their record on

[34] Also see V. Zamagni, 'Alle origini della grande distribuzione in Italia', *Commercio*, 10 (1982).

[35] Set up by the Monzino brothers, who were both managers of the Rinascente chain. The Standard changed its name in 1937 to STANDA (Società Anonima Tutti Articoli Nazionali dell'Arredamento e Abbigliamento—a clothing and home-furnishing chain), as a result of Mussolini's criticism of the foreign-sounding name Standard.

[36] A. Giuntini, *I giganti della montagna. Storia della ferrovia direttissima Bologna–Firenze (1845–1934)* (Florence, Olschki, 1984).

[37] A. Bellucci, *L'automobile italiana 1918–1943* (Bari, Laterza, 1984), 188 ff.

[38] The famous 'one thousand lire a month'. Cf. G. F. Vené, *Mille lire al mese. Vita quotidiana della famiglia nell'Italia fascista* (Milan, Mondadori, 1988). See also G. Aliberti, *L'economia domestica italiana da Giolitti a De Gasperi 1900–1960* (Rome, 50 & Più Ed., 1992).

social security provision was not particularly impressive. In fact, it was the work of liberal governments during the immediate post-war period that led to the establishment of the Cassa Nazionale per le Assicurazioni Sociali (CNAS, the national social security body) in April 1919, with a law that made national insurance contributions for pensions compulsory, and set up 37 provincial social insurance offices.[39] In October of the same year, another form of compulsory insurance was introduced, this time against unemployment, and the management of this was subsequently transferred to the CNAS (in 1923). The Fascist years, on the other hand, saw the reorganization of the CNAS, the introduction of health care and family allowances, and the establishment of an institution that paid those workers who were laid off temporarily, or whose working hours were reduced, through a fund set up by the employers themselves, the Cassa Integrazione Guadagni (CIG).

A few words should be said about the reorganization of the CNAS. In March 1933 it was transformed into a public body called the Fascist National Institute for Social Security—the INFPS (Istituto Nazionale Fascista della Previdenza Sociale, presently INPS)—which incorporated the national maternity fund,[40] unemployment insurance, and insurance against the risk of tuberculosis (which we shall refer to shortly). The INFPS was then also given the responsibility for family allowances and for the Cassa Integrazione. Tables 8.1 and 8.2 show details of the INFPS's financial structure (revenue and expenses), while its policy of investing in public holdings and state industry is described in Chapter 9.

The regime's health policy was of far greater importance, and many studies have been published on this topic. All of them unanimously agree that the '20 years of Fascism were responsible for the fragmented nature of the organizational and administrative structure of the country's health care'.[41] Mutual aid societies had previously been responsible for the provision of insurance against illness and disease: these organizations were persecuted by the Fascists, and their job was slowly taken over by company bodies set up by Fascist trade unions; however, the latter proved incapable of guaranteeing a decent service[42] and, as there was no central co-ordinating body, were often highly unreliable from the point of view of both the insured workers and the doctors themselves. It was only in January 1943 that a national health authority

[39] INPS, *Settant'anni dell'Istituto Nazionale della Previdenza Sociale* (Rome, 1970), 241 ff.

[40] Besides improving insurance provisions for women giving birth, Fascism also set up a special body to provide health care and education for the very young—L'Opera Nazionale Maternità e Infanzia (ONMI)—which was created with a Fascist law passed in Dec. 1925, although its foundation had already been planned by a commission set up before the coming to power of Fascism. The ONMI acted as a means whereby the Fascist regime could put into effect its policy of demographic expansion, although it has to be said that it also proved effective in helping to reduce the infant mortality rate.

[41] D. Preti, *La modernizzazione corporativa (1922–1940)* (Milan, Angeli, 1987), 119.

[42] M. Soresina, 'Mutue sanitarie e regime corporativo', *Storia in Lombardia*, 8 (1989).

was set up—the Istituto per l'Assistenza di Malattia (INAM)—although this only managed to unify the various forms of health insurance to a limited extent, and many of them survived until September 1978 (and beyond in some cases), when the National Health Service (Servizio Sanitario Nazionale) was finally set up.[43]

Fascism also decided not to carry out a complete reorganization programme as far as hospitals were concerned (in this case, it would have involved the exclusion of religious charitable organizations, which had been begun by Crispi, in favour of state-run hospitals). Therefore 'the entire problem of hospital finances . . . remained dramatically unresolved, and was left between two unsatisfactory poles—one being represented by the limited resources that charity could provide, and the other by the hardly reassuring support of local government finances.'[44] For this reason, hospitals opened their doors to wealthy private patients, with all the speculation that this entailed. The overall result was an enormous imbalance in health care throughout the country. Impressive new hospitals were built in some places, for example the Molinette in Turin (1935), the Gaslini in Genoa (1938), and the new Ospedale Maggiore at Niguarda, Milan (1939), whereas, on the other hand, 5,000 out of a total of 7,000 Italian communes had no hospital facilities whatsoever. In 1936, there was a national average of 3.3 hospital beds for every 1,000 inhabitants. This compared with 6.4 beds in Liguria, 5.6 in Venezia–Giulia, and 5.2 in Tuscany and Piedmont, whereas the southern regions of Basilicata and Calabria were right at the foot of the national table, with 0.6 and 0.7 beds per thousand, followed by the Abruzzo and Campania, which each had 1.4. This extremely precarious position of the hospitals did not prevent hospital doctors (and surgeons in particular) from sometimes receiving enormous sums for their services, according to the results of research carried out by Preti.

The Fascist regime proved to be a little more adept at tackling the problem of 'social illnesses'; although it did not manage to prevent their outbreak to any great extent, it offered some help to patients suffering from this kind of disease; and tuberculosis cases were given particular assistance in the form of a compulsory health insurance scheme set up in October 1927. Cosmacini writes that 'in the fight against tuberculosis, it was the ideology of therapy, involving patient care in clinics and hospitals, that prevailed over the preventive ideology of hygiene and environmental improvements',[45] despite the fact that the regime was, at the same time, involved in vast rehousing projects. In the case of tuberculosis, like those of malaria and syphilis, it was the advancement of

[43] M. Soresina, 'La tutela della salute nell'Italia unita (1860–1980)', in *Storia della Società Italiana*, xvii.

[44] Preti, 201–2.

[45] G. Cosmacini, *Medicina e sanità in Italia nel ventesimo secolo. Dalla spagnola alla 2a guerra mondiale* (Bari, Laterza, 1989), 201.

medical science rather than social and economic improvements that was to lead to a lowering of the high mortality rates in Italy.[46]

One measure that reflected the demographic policy of the Fascist regime was the introduction in 1934 of family allowances, along the lines of the previously introduced Belgian and French versions (something that was subsequently passed on to the post-war generation). These payments were made in order to supplement the wages of workers who had to maintain a wife and children, and although they were at first only paid to factory workers, the scheme was later extended to office-workers and farm-workers as well.

Other forms of allowances were awarded to those families whose men had been conscripted (in June 1936 and June 1940), as well as to those factory workers whose working week fell below a total of 40 hours due to the war (June 1941, Cassa Integrazione dei Guadagni degli Operai dell'Industria, already mentioned above). In this way, the Fascist regime tried to rebalance the purchasing power of Italians, which had suffered as a result of the war, and at the same time to buy the continued support of the working classes.

The highly proclaimed 'Fascist social policy' was therefore a mixture of measures that had already been put into practice by the previous liberal governments, and others, badly co-ordinated and taken for either ideological or pragmatical reasons, which demonstrates just how little real social progress was made during the years that separated the two World Wars. The decision to devote an entire chapter to such modest developments was taken not so much because of any particularly interesting features these developments have, but rather to underline the deplorable length of time it took to get anything of this kind done. The period of social reform took a long while coming in post-war Italy, and the social security system inherited from the Fascist regime was not substantially changed until the 1970s.

[46] Ibid. 211. Cosmacini writes: 'penicillin was to strike a body blow to the biological problem, and thus to the social problem, represented by syphilis. The same thing happened in the case of DDT and malaria, and also in the case of tuberculosis, which was virtually eliminated through the use of streptomycin and PAS.'

PART III
The Post-War Boom

11

The Building of New Foundations, 1946–1952

1. 'MAKING BOTH ENDS MEET': POST-WAR RECOVERY (1946–7)

ACCORDING to a survey carried out by the Bank of Italy, and subsequently sent on to the newly founded International Bank for Reconstruction and Development in the autumn of 1947, wartime destruction had failed to seriously damage Italian industry's productive capacity. Only 8 per cent of industry's capital existing in 1938 had been lost,[1] although with important differences between one industrial sector and another (for example, losses in the metallurgical industry were estimated at some 25 per cent). This would thus seem to support Petri's view that 'the changes witnessed during the second half of the 1930s were undeniably responsible for the formation of that technical, geographical, and social order which was to enable the performance of the so-called "economic miracle" and the definitive transformation of Italy into an industrialized country'.[2]

The engineering industry had grown substantially during the Second World War, as it had done during the First, thanks largely to the significant level of state demand for engineering products: this already took up 28 per cent of total production in 1938 (not including the production of parts by smaller companies),[3] and was to increase to 50 per cent during the following years. Productive capacity had increased by 50 per cent, net of those losses sustained as a result of war damage; and if we allow for the fact that a part of this could not then be reconverted to peacetime production, there was still a significant increase in productive capacity between the pre-war and post-war periods, which Jacoboni estimates to be of the order of at least 15–20 per cent between 1938 and 1947. The peacetime market's recovery was, of course, not exactly an easy process; however, as we shall see, the international situation was a lot more

[1] There are different sets of figures for this period. Cf. C. Daneo, *La politica economica della ricostruzione 1945–49* (Turin, Einaudi, 1975), 3–7. However, they all support the view that the destruction caused by the war was of a limited nature in the case of Italian industry. Since they mostly make use of 1938 as a point of reference, the productive capacity given for 1945, after the war had taken its toll, is quite often higher than that previously existing in 1938, as a result of investment made during the 1939–42 period.

[2] R. Petri, 'Acqua contro carbone', *Italia contemporanea*, 168 (1987), 63.

[3] A. Jacoboni, *L'industria meccanica italiana* (Rome, Poligrafico di Stato, 1949).

favourable towards recovery (followed by expansion) in the engineering industry during the post-Second World War years than it had been in the period immediately after the First World War.

The metallurgical industry found itself in a much more difficult situation, following the loss of the Cornigliano plant and the serious damage sustained by the Bagnoli complex, although it still possessed a rich technological and managerial heritage. The other industries were all ready to repair the damage and start up production again as soon as possible, but this was made somewhat difficult by the damage that communications and transport had suffered as a result of the war: only one-sixth of the merchant navy fleet had survived; railway lines had been cut (between one-third and a half of all bridges, overhead wires, and track had been destroyed); roads were often unusable, and only about a half of the lorries had got through the war unscathed. Furthermore, supplies of raw materials were extremely limited, for both national and international reasons. If, on top of all this, we add the political problems involved in trying to reorganize and reunite a country that had only just come out of a period of dictatorship followed by civil war, split in two and invaded by foreign military powers,[4] then it is easy to see why Ferruccio Parri, the first Prime Minister of liberated Italy, chose to use the expression 'to make both ends meet' during a radio broadcast on 1 July 1945, an expression that sums up very well the first few months of the post-war period, economically speaking.

In the meanwhile, the so-called 'governments of national solidarity' were witnessing a very heated debate about Italy's future, which was to result in the country's definitive placement into the Western capitalistic world headed by the USA. Even the Italian Communist Party leader Togliatti, writing in the party newspaper *L'Unità*, referred to the Communist Party's struggle in the following terms: 'The struggle must be conducted not against capitalism in general, but against all forms of theft, speculation and corruption, without however prejudicing private enterprise.' The coalition governments managed to implement very few measures to help the nation's economy, as on the one hand they were too busy dealing with the emergency situation and with serious political problems, and on the other they were not homogeneous enough to produce any kind of consistent policy, not even when De Gasperi became Prime Minister (in December 1945). This explains the quasi-liberal line adopted within these governments by the Treasurer, Corbino, and the Bank of Italy's Governor (later Budget Minister), Einaudi. It was not a line shared by the majority of politicians, who nevertheless were still in no position to intervene directly, and so let the liberalization of the economy take place.

A northern industrial committee (Consiglio Industriale Alta Italia, CIAI) was

[4] The restrictions imposed by the Allied Commission on the Italian government were only lifted during 1946, e.g. foreign trade restrictions were done away with on 28 Jan. 1946. Cf. Mariuccia Salvati, *Stato e industria nella ricostruzione. Alle origini del potere democristiano (1944–1949)* (Milan, Feltrinelli, 1982), 70.

at work during this period, although its responsibilities were eventually limited to the collection of data concerning the position and necessities of northern industry,[5] rather than its original task of planning the development of industry in the North; 'first-aid plans' were formulated, asking the Americans to see that the most urgent imported goods were guaranteed, through the UNRRA.[6] Apart from this, very little else was achieved. On 26 March 1946, free exchange of the lira was partially introduced for exporters in order to facilitate exports, but which in many people's opinion also led to speculation, capital flight, and inflationary spirals.[7] The stock exchange and banks were allowed to operate freely, which also contributed towards inflation, while there was a strong governmental budget deficit (despite the overall positive trend)[8] which constituted a further inflationary factor.[9]

Two communist politicians, Scoccimarro and Pesenti, were the first to come up with an anti-inflationary proposal; that of a 'change in the currency' together with a wealth tax and other harsher fiscal measures.[10] It was in fact this combination of a monetary measure and heavier taxation that was to be the downfall of the communist proposal. The 'currency change' never came about, and there was no halt to galloping inflation (see columns 4 and 5, Table 8.4), partly a result also of the lack of raw materials, which in turn led to bottlenecks in production and in the supply of energy.

The living standards of Italians, meanwhile, continued to suffer from the economic and political situation: per capita income had been halved and food rations had been reduced by one-third compared with pre-war levels; black-market prices were astronomically high, and the lucky ones were those who had something to barter for foodstuffs. Volpi writes[11] that 'the years 1945 and 1946 were the hardest . . . two years of hunger . . . as seen not only from the alarming drop in the average calorie intake already mentioned, but also from the fall in consumption of individual products, all of which stood at much lower levels than had been the case prior to the war. There was a net improvement in the situation during the two-year period 1949–50, but average per capita

[5] The interesting data collected by the CIAI have been used by G. Maione in the study *Tecnocrati e mercanti. L'industria italiana tra dirigismo e concorrenza internazionale 1945–1950* (Milan, Sugarco, 1986).

[6] For details of these plans, see P. Saraceno, in P. Barucci (ed.), *Ricostruzione e pianificazione, 1943–48* (Bari, Laterza, 1969), and also P. Saraceno, in L. Villari (ed.), *Intervista sulla ricostruzione 1943–1953* (Bari, Laterza, 1977).

[7] Among others, cf. M. De Cecco, 'Sulla politica di stabilizzazione del 1947', in *Saggi di politica monetaria* (Milan, 1968), and U. Ruffolo, 'La linea Einaudi', *Storia contemporanea*, 5 (1974).

[8] In 1945/6, revenue only covered 26% of expenditure; in 1946/7, this had risen to 41%.

[9] Another cause of inflation was the issuing of the so-called 'AM-lire', which the Italian and American governments had agreed upon in order to pay the American troops stationed in Italy.

[10] The American government favoured this proposal, and the fact that it was never put into practice led to disagreement between the latter and De Gasperi's cabinets.

[11] R. Volpi, *Storia della popolazione italiana dall'unità ad oggi* (Florence, La Nuova Italia, 1989), 135.

consumption of foodstuffs was only higher than it had been before the war in the case of sugar and milk, whereas meat consumption stood at 24 per cent below its pre-war level.' The poverty of Italy during the reconstruction period was not wholly due to the destruction[12] and expense of war, but this had exacerbated things to such an extent that a parliamentary investigation into poverty (1951–2) was commissioned.[13] The findings showed that 11.8 per cent of Italian families were below the subsistence level, while another 11.6 per cent were poor; only one-half of housing had an inside toilet, and little more than 10 per cent a bathroom; less than a half had running water. They also underlined the enormous differences in living standards that existed between central and northern Italy on the one hand, and southern Italy on the other.

Faced with such a situation (which had already improved somewhat by the time this inquiry was carried out), the Italian government decided to ask for help. De Gasperi went to the USA in January of 1947 with the aim of asking for extra financial help, but his visit was only a partial success, with the concession of a modest 100 million dollar loan from the Export-Import Bank (which was only delivered in October of that year). However, this visit and other meetings with the Americans did give De Gasperi reason to believe that the Americans were not very happy with the presence of left-wing parties in the Italian government.[14] On 13 May 1947, he provoked a split in the governmental coalition, and his fourth cabinet was set up on 31 May, comprising the Christian Democrats (DC), the Italian Liberals (PLI), and the Republicans (PRI). The Socialist Party went into opposition together with the PCI. It was the end of the governments of national solidarity.

A few days later (5 June 1947) the American Secretary of State, George Marshall, announced the American plan for the reconstruction of Europe (we shall be looking at this in the next section). Participation in this plan meant that the economic policies of the European nations had to be co-ordinated, and plans for development had to be drawn up and presented.[15] This was a highly opportune (and decisive) moment in which to attempt to launch Italy's economic reorganization once and for all.

The manœuvre attempted by the Italian government became known as the 'Einaudi line', as it was Einaudi who had formulated it. Bank reserves were increased between July and November of 1947, the discount rate increased

[12] Among other things, some 1.9 million habitable rooms were completely destroyed, while a further 5 million were seriously damaged (from a total of 33.6 million rooms in existence at the end of 1941).

[13] For a comprehensive summary, see P. Braghin (ed.), *Inchiesta sulla miseria in Italia (1951–52). Materiali della Commissione parliamentare* (Turin, Einaudi, 1978).

[14] Daneo, *La politica*, 218–22.

[15] This point is underlined in G. Gualerni, *Ricostruzione e industria. Per una interpretazione della politica industriale nel secondo dopoguerra 1943–1951* (Milan, Vita & Pensiero, 1980), 62–9.

from 4 to 5.5 per cent, while the lira exchange rate against the dollar, after climbing from 225 to 350 lire by November, had reached 589 lire. These measures were highly effective in the battle against inflation, which was halted completely, thus representing a blow to financial speculation.[16] However, many scholars claim that the 'Einaudi line' severely hit the nation's recovery in productive terms, and led to a further wages squeeze.[17]

The claim that the Einaudi measures led to productive stagnation has never, in fact, been completely proved, as I have tried to show in an essay on this topic,[18] while it is generally accepted that his monetary measures marked the beginning of a period in which several rather important economic decisions were to be taken following an approach somewhat distant from that of the liberal free-marketeers. I would like to a look at two of these measures here, as the others can be more appropriately dealt with in the sections that follow. In September 1947, the FIM—a fund for the engineering industry—was set up. Its role was that of financing the restructuring of those sectors of the engineering industry which found themselves in the greatest difficulty. In February 1948, IRI received a new statute, which allowed it to proceed with new sectorial redevelopment plans, free from the worries about whether it was going to be privatized or not, as this option was shelved. The Einaudi measures marked the end of the emergency and the beginning of a new period in which the foundations for economic development could be laid down.

2. THE MARSHALL PLAN AND THE EUROPEAN OPTION

Contrary to what happened after the First World War, the post-1945 period was marked by a continued American presence in Europe after hostilities had ceased. In the first place, the Americans stayed on in a Germany that was torn apart and that needed help on a daily basis, due to the absence of a sovereign State. However, they also maintained a political and military presence in many other areas of Europe, and continued to supply emergency aid, above all through UNRRA (United Nations Relief and Rehabilitation Administration). By 1947 the material reconstruction of Europe was well advanced, but all the same the Americans realized that this kind of aid was not enough to put Europe back on its own feet. In particular, there appeared to be two serious, unresolved problems: (*a*) the European nations' acute lack of dollars with which to pay for raw materials and foodstuffs on international markets, which was soon to

[16] P. Baffi, 'Memoria sull'azione di Einaudi', in *Studi sulla moneta* (Milan, Giuffré, 1965).

[17] Cf. B. Manzocchi, *Lineamenti di politica economica in Italia (1945–1959)* (Rome, 1960); De Cecco, 'Sulla politica di stabilizzazione'; Daneo, *La politica*—just to mention a few.

[18] V. Zamagni, 'Betting on the Future. The Reconstruction of Italian Industry, 1946–1952', in V. Becker and F. Knipping (eds.), *Power in Europe. Great Britain, France, Italy and Germany in a Postwar World, 1945–1950* (Berlin, Walter de Gruyter, 1986), 287–90.

constitute an obstacle to the continuation of economic recovery;[19] and (*b*) the impossibility of beginning the reconstruction of Germany without first having solved the extremely delicate problem of the payment of war damages,[20] which began to reproduce the situation at the end of the First World War, which in the end had had very damaging consequences for all the countries involved. Besides these two extremely urgent problems, there was also the fact that the Americans were worried about the possibility of the economic and political collapse of Western Europe, as it would have had serious consequences for the USA. It could have provoked the onset of a perverse chain of events which may have led to the kind of economic depression experienced in 1929, while, at the same time, Russian imperialist expansion would have been able to get past the buffer represented by Western Europe.

These and others were the reasons behind the Americans' decision to launch a multilateral aid programme, with a duration which was later fixed at four years (1948–52), aimed at dealing with the balance of payment problems of various European nations, and at the reintegration of the German economy into Europe. This also had the long-term aim of guiding the European continent towards a new era of economic co-operation.[21] Several studies have been published on the European Recovery Programme (ERP, otherwise known as the Marshall Plan), and so I shall not go into any great detail here.[22] Basically, it was a plan to transfer goods (not dollars) free of charge from the United States to Europe, on the basis of a yearly request from each European country formulated in accordance with its four-year development plan. The sale of these goods within individual European countries led to the formation of 'counterpart funds' in the national currency, which were then to be used according to a bilateral agreement between the country's government and the American government. Obviously the 'saving' in currency which such free imports implied could then be used either to increase imports, or to build up reserves.[23]

This meant that Italy had to come up with a long-term development plan

[19] A. Milward has given perhaps the best interpretation of this point in *The Reconstruction of Western Europe 1945–51* (London, Methuen, 1984). G. Fodor in 'Perché nel 1947 l'Europa ebbe bisogno del Piano Marshall?', *Rivista di storia economica*, 2 (1985), showed that the 'dollar gap' got worse as a result of the inflationary process which saw American prices rise considerably during the course of 1947.

[20] See J. Gimbel, *The Origin of the Marshall Plan* (Stanford, Calif., Stanford University Press, 1976).

[21] See Milward, *Reconstruction of Western Europe*, for the link between the Marshall Plan and the beginning of European economic co-operation; also cf. M. J. Hogan, *The Marshall Plan and European Integration* (Cambridge, Cambridge University Press, 1987).

[22] Cf. I. Wexler, *The Marshall Plan Revisited* (Greenwood, Westport, Conn., 1983); R. J. Donovan, *The Second Victory. The Marshall Plan and the Postwar Revival of Europe* (Lanham, Md., Madison Books, 1987); and C. Meier (ed.), *Germany and the Marshall Plan* (New York, Cambridge University Press, 1991).

[23] Italian governments opted for the latter choice, worried as they were about the Bank of Italy's total lack of reserves.

between the summer of 1947 and that of 1948, and the responsibility for this fell on IRI's tiny Centro di Studi e Piani Tecnico-Economici, run by Pasquale Saraceno.[24] The plan, presented to the OEEC in the summer of 1948, is generally considered to have been very hurried, inconsistent, and ineffectual. However, a more impartial observer would agree that it was not totally lacking in inspiration, and that it did have some effect on the economic policy of the governments of the day.

The 'philosophy' behind the plan was, in fact, very simple: to force productive investment, especially in the economic infrastructure and in capital goods, in order to squeeze costs and increase exports; this would then allow improvement in the balance of payments, and would lead to a more competitive economy in view of the imminent liberalization of international markets. This obviously implied a freezing of consumption, together with a refusal to bow to the temptation to introduce demand-support Keynesian measures. The plan even contained certain predicted results, which are compared with the results actually achieved in Table 11.1.

First, one sees that the estimated figures contained in the plan (column 1) predicted a 50 per cent increase in the output of capital goods over the four-year period, whereas the production of consumer goods excluding foodstuffs was due to increase by only 14 per cent and the per capita consumption of foodstuffs was actually going to remain at just under the 1938 level. These estimates thus correspond perfectly with the philosophy behind the plan.

As for the results actually achieved (column 2), we can see that in the case of two of the four more general forecasts—population and national income—the estimates proved to be correct, whereas in the other two cases—industrial production and agriculture—the first result went beyond the predicted figure, while the second fell short of the plan's target. The government's industrial strategy was therefore further strengthened by the results achieved over this four-year period. Foreign trade also went well beyond the target, partly as a result of the Marshall Plan itself, partly due to the consistent support given by subsequent governments to the project for the liberalization of Italian trade,[25] but also as a result of the Italian engineering industry's ability to win over foreign markets.[26]

Individual per capita consumption increased more than had been expected,

[24] Cf. P. Saraceno, *Elementi per un piano quadriennale di sviluppo dell'economia italiana* (Rome, 1948), and id., *Elementi per un piano economico 1948–52* (Rome, 1948), the latter being a revised version of the former. On the continuation in the 1950s of these programming efforts and the 'Vanoni plan' see A. Magliulo, *Ezio Vanoni. La giustizia sociale nell'economia di mercato* (Rome, Ed. Studium, 1991).

[25] For an extremely informative and well-documented summary of Italian trade policy during these years, cf. M. L. Cavalcanti, *La politica commerciale italiana 1945–1952. Uomini e fatti* (Naples, ESI, 1984).

[26] Exports of engineering goods rose from 6% of total exports (excluding colonies) in 1938 to 20% in 1947, and 26% in 1948.

Table 11.1. Comparison between forecasts of the long-term plan 1948/9–1952/3 and results actually achieved by 1952 (index 1938 = 100)

	Plan's projections for 1952/3 (1)	Results achieved in 1952 (2)
Population	109	110
National income	117	117[a]
Industrial production	140	149[b]
Output of capital goods	150	. . .[c]
Output of consumer goods	114	. . .[c]
Rail transport: passengers	200	233
goods	125	89
Shipping[d]	85	173
Imports	156	221
Exports	160	186
Consumption of food[e]	97	110
Consumption of industrial goods[e]	105	121
Agricultural output[e]	115	105[g]

[a] GDP at constant prices.
[b] Including mining and the building trade; if building is excluded, the index does not change.
[c] There are no indices available to compare with those of the plan, so I can only give a sectorial breakdown: engineering, 155; chemicals, 185; textiles, 108; food and drink, 117
[d] Merchant shipping tonnage.
[e] Per capita.
[f] Base year 1934/8 = 100.
[g] Including the products of the forestry and fishing sector.

Sources: OEEC, *Interim Report on the ERP*, ii: Italy (Paris, Dec. 1948); Ercolani, 'Documentazione statistica di base'; ISTAT, *Sommario*; B. Barberi, *I consumi nel primo secolo dell'unità d'Italia* (Milan, Giuffré, 1961).

due to an increase in imports and in the production of consumer goods other than foodstuffs, thus minimizing those sacrifices called for in the plan. The only result which at first sight appears to be totally unsatisfactory is that of transport of goods by rail. However, during this period there was a noticeable increase in the volume of goods being transported by road: the number of trucks increased from 80,589 in 1938 to 266,285 in 1952, while the number of articulated lorries rose from 8,389 to 28,508. This was only the beginning of the process whereby road transport began to take the place of rail transport, a process which was to gain considerable momentum in subsequent years.

The plan opted to concentrate investment in the engineering, energy (electricity and oil), transport, and communications industries (about 60 per cent of the total), while agriculture only received 29 per cent of the total amount invested.

In the *metallurgy* sector, the aim was to create three vertically integrated plants in order to reduce the cost of steel for engineering purposes.[27] This was

[27] *Interim Report on the ERP*, ii: *Italy* (Paris, OEEC, 1948), 577.

attempted through the implementation of the 'Sinigaglia plan', which in turn was based upon the Cornigliano project drawn up by IRI towards the end of the 1930s, with important technical modifications. The Sinigaglia plan had a difficult time: first of all, the heated pre-war debate concerning the choice between a nationalized and a private steel industry was repeated for a second time during the immediate post-war years; it was further complicated by vested political interests and by the high cost of continuous-cycle plants.[28] Secondly, other European countries were extremely reluctant to accept Italian steel production on a large scale, as this would have inevitably meant a reduction in their own exports to Italy. The supply of iron ore to Italy was also cause for some debate between Italy and the other European countries who established the first inter-European organization—the European Coal and Steel Community (ECSC) (April 1951).

Furthermore, the Italian government had to placate the Americans' worries about public enterprises (which were responsible for the Sinigaglia plan and for the future of the Italian steel industry). An important part in the strategy adopted in order to persuade the Americans to finance the Sinigaglia plan was played by the Fiat Company, represented by its president Valletta (nominated after the death of the founder Giovanni Agnelli in 1945), who committed the company to absorbing a sizeable portion of the steel produced by Finsider's new continuous-cycle plant at Cornigliano.[29] The complicated negotiations involved meant that the Sinigaglia plan was put into practice late, but they nevertheless guaranteed the plan's total success. By 1952, Italian steel production was already half a million tons over the 3 million tons envisaged by the plan.

The *engineering* industry was seen as the most important sector of Italian industry, and consequently it was this sector that received the greatest financial help. Besides the FIM which we mentioned earlier,[30] IRI set up a holding—the Finmeccanica—to organize the financing of its vast engineering sector.[31] Half of the Eximbank loan went to engineering companies, as did 23 per cent of the IMI-ERP soft loans approved before December 1951 (counted against

[28] On this matter, cf. M. Pozzobon and R. Mari, 'Le acciaierie e ferriere lombarde Falck (1945–48)', in *La ricostruzione della grande industria. Strategia padronale e organismi di fabbrica nel triangolo industriale 1945–48* (Bari, De Donato, 1978), and G. Toniolo, 'Oscar Sinigaglia', in *I protagonisti dell'intervento pubblico in Italia* (Milan, Angeli, 1984). On the whole question of the Italian steel industry during the reconstruction years, particularly within the context of the ECSC negotiations, an extremely well-documented doctoral thesis now exists, 'L'espansione alla prova del negoziato. L'industria italiana e la Comunità del Carbone e dell'Acciaio, 1945–1955', by R. Ranieri (Florence, European University Institute, June 1988); the same author has also published 'La siderurgia italiana e gli inizi dell'integrazione europea', *Passato e presente*, 7 (1985) and 'L'Italia e i negoziati del Piano Schumann', in E. Di Nolfo, R. H. Rainero and B. Vigezzi (eds.), *L'Italia e la politica di potenza in Europa (1945–1950)* (Milan, Marzorati, 1988).

[29] P. Bairati, *Valletta* (Turin, UTET, 1983).

[30] On the FIM, see R. Tremelloni, 'Premesse e compiti del Fondo per il finanziamento dell'industria meccanica', *Moneta e Credito*, 1 (1948).

[31] IRI controlled between one-quarter and one-third of the sector's productive capacity.

counterpart funds).[32] The restructuring and reorganization of the engineering industry was naturally carried out along less unified lines than had been the case with the steel industry, and it proceeded at a slower pace as it required much wider national and international markets, which it only won gradually. The industry attempted to produce just about everything that was possible at the time: from cars to tractors, from sewing-machines to paper presses, from cash registers to electrical material, from refrigerators to washing-machines, from typewriters to packaging machinery. The engineering companies tried to produce a vast variety of goods, in some cases successfully, in others not quite so successfully, but always at an opportune moment.[33]

The *energy* industry was also given special treatment during this period. New hydroelectric plants were built, and, more importantly, machinery for huge thermoelectric power stations was imported into Italy from the USA. The production of electrical energy doubled in the period between 1938 and 1952. The construction of new oil-refineries was also given high priority, and as a consequence refining capacity quadrupled between 1938 and 1952, while AGIP stepped up its natural-gas prospecting in Italian territory.[34] AGIP's success under Mattei's management was to lead to bitter argument between the Italian state-owned company on the one hand and Italian and American private companies on the other, and the latter tried desperately (and in vain) to eliminate AGIP from the contest. Mattei proved to be very much their match, and in fact led the company into a new partnership with the SNAM and ANIC to form the state holding-company ENI (Ente Nazionale Idrocarburi) in 1953,[35] a company that was to have a brilliant future.

Unfortunately, the plan's long-term capital-intensive projects could not offer a short-term solution to the problems of unemployment and underemployment which blighted Italy. This is evident from a comparison between the industrial censuses of 1937–9 and 1951 (see Table 11.2): whereas the total number of employed remained more or less the same, the horsepower installed doubled during the same period. Industry's transformation in favour of the metal, chemical, and energy sectors is also confirmed by these data. The Italian government was well aware that the plan's contribution towards creating jobs would only have been visible in the long-term, and that the immediate problem of unemployment could only be solved by emigration and the implementation of government assistance programmes.[36]

[32] Cf. CIR, *Lo sviluppo dell'economia italiana nel quadro dell'economia europea* (Rome, 1952).

[33] An overall study of post-war reconstruction in the engineering industry has been completed by M. Doria, 'Note sull'industria meccanica italiana nella Ricostruzione', *Rivista di storia economica*, 4 (1987).

[34] AGIP's annual distribution of methane gas rose from 12 million cu.m. in 1946 to 2 billion cu.m. in 1953.

[35] M. Colitti, *Energia e sviluppo in Italia. La vicenda di Enrico Mattei* (Bari, Laterza, 1979).

[36] Cf. P. Rontini, 'Il dibattito post-bellico sull'emigrazione come valvola di sfogo alla disoccupazione', graduation thesis, Florence University, 1986–7.

Table 11.2. Comparison between industrial censuses of 1937/9 and 1951 (1937/9 = 100)

Industry	Workers	Horsepower installed
Mining	86	210
Food manufactures	75	158
Tobacco	108	176
Leatherwear and shoes	93	220
Textiles:	108	158
Cotton	142	190
Wool	163	282
Clothing	88	172
Wood	103	258
Paper	113	191
Printing	106	180
Photo./radio	109	99
Metallurgy	141	182
Engineering	106	173
Non-metallic minerals	100	187
Chemicals	131	194
Rubber	154	278
Other manufactures	124	175
Building	95	197
Electricity	220	907[a]
TOTAL	102	199

[a] The large difference between installed hp in the electrical sector from one census to another is mainly due to the different criteria adopted in the collection of data.

Source: *Industrial Censuses*, 1937/9 and 1951. Figures have been made sectorially homogeneous using the 1951 classification.

In my opinion, it was in fact the unemployment problem which constituted the central issue in the disagreements between the Italian and American governments over the use of Marshall Aid funds. These differences of opinion, which cropped up at regular intervals, were formally recognized in the so-called 'Country Study', which was prepared at the end of 1948, but only discussed by the US Congress in February 1949. A close inspection of the American report on the state of the Italian economy during the first few months of the Marshall Plan reveals something of an obsession with the serious problem of unemployment. In analysing the plan's long-term investment proposals, the Country Study declared its dissatisfaction with the low rate of increase in employment that seemed to result from the plan, and in fact suggested that priority should be given to public works programmes for political reasons.[37]

[37] See D. Ellwood, 'Il piano Marshall e il processo di modernizzazione in Italia', in E. Aga Rossi (ed.), *Il Piano Marshall e l'Europa* (Rome, 1983). For an analysis of the logic behind the positions taken up by the Americans on this question, cf. P. P. D'Attore, 'Il Piano Marshall. Politica,

Table 11.3. American aid to Italy

	UNRRA ($m.)	ERP ($m.)	Average exchange rate ($–lire)	Billions of current lire	% of GNP
1946	380	—	331	126	4.2
1947	245	—	485	119	2.0
1948	218	114	570	189	2.7
1949	—	350	570	200	2.6
1950	—	273	625	171	2.0
1951	—	292	625	182	1.9
1952	—	208	625	130	1.3

Sources: author's elaborations for 1946 from ISE, *Annuario della congiuntura economica italiana, 1938–1947* (Florence, 1949), 186; for 1947–52, F. Masera (ed.), *Bilancio dei pagamenti dell'Italia, 1947–1969* (Rome, 1970).

After that, the Italian governments proceeded to soften their position *vis-à-vis* the Americans' position on this question, although they continued to stick fairly closely to their original line, led by Pella (after Einaudi's nomination as President of the Republic),[38] while making certain steps forward in the field of regional development in the most backward areas of the country, which we shall be looking at in the next section. Table 11.3 gives the total figures for American aid to Italy during the period 1946–52. Of course, the strategic value of such aid went well beyond the quantitative amount shown in the table. As well as alleviating the balance of payments problem and providing the country with essential supplies of foodstuffs, raw materials, and vitally important means of producing energy, it is important to emphasize the fact that 90 per cent of counterpart funds were used for investment purposes, which in turn enabled Italian industry to renew a massive amount of plants with the aid of mainly American technology.

At the end of the reconstruction period, Italy found itself inextricably tied to the process of European integration under the leadership of the Americans. If this process were to prove a success, then Italy would be part of it, although inevitably from a position of weakness (due to the constraints imposed by its historical development) that was not, however, considered to be an unresolvable

economia, relazioni internazionali nella ricostruzione italiana', *Passato e Presente*, 7 (1985); and also J. Harper, *L'America e la ricostruzione dell'Italia 1945–1948* (Bologna, Il Mulino, 1987). Most scholars agree that the Country Study was influenced by Keynesian thinking.

[38] On the 'Pella line', cf. B. Bottiglieri, *La politica economica dall'Italia centrista (1948–1958)* (Milan, Comunità, 1984), and the collection of essays *La ricostruzione economica italiana dopo la seconda guerra mondiale* (Geneva, Droz, 1985).

hindrance. This was the gamble that the governments of the time decided to take, and it was to prove a winning move.[39]

3. A SEASON OF REFORMS

While the industrial option had been reconfirmed as the strategic choice of the first governments of the new Italian Republic, agriculture was still a very important sector of the economy during the reconstruction period, although more so in terms of people working the land (44 per cent of the total labour-force) than in terms of value added (23 per cent). The peasant revolts at this time were extremely violent, the reasons being that there was still a chronic excess of labour in the countryside, the Italian *latifundia* still extended over vast areas of the country, and the farm-workers and peasants had finally won back their trade union rights. During these revolts more than 80 farm labourers were killed, and prison sentences totalling more than 10,000 years were given out to those who were arrested.[40] There were two immediate consequences of these revolts: on one hand, laws were passed with the aim of providing employment and increasing productivity; on the other hand, the Christian Democrats supported setting up small farms (breaking up *latifundia*).[41] A Federazione dei Coltivatori Diretti (Union of Small Farmers) had already been set up in 1944, and was headed by Paolo Bonomi; then on 7 May 1948, the Federconsorzi was reprivatized, and the year after Bonomi also took charge of this body. Finally, the Cassa della Piccola Proprietà Contadina (a fund to help small farmers) was set up on 22 September 1948. Its activities were originally limited to the South, but were subsequently extended to the rest of the country (on 23 April 1949).

The most ambitious aim of the peasant revolts was undoubtedly agrarian reform, which had even been mentioned in the Italian Constitution (article 44). However, complete agrarian reform never came about: what did happen was that a series of laws[42] led to some important measures being taken in those

[39] Several people have criticized the speed with which Italy opened up its economy to international influence: cf. M. De Cecco, 'Lo sviluppo dell'economia italiana e la sua collocazione internazionale', *Rivista internazionale di scienze economiche e commerciali*, 18 (1971). The inevitability of such an opening was instead acknowledged by the economists of the time, as is evident from the following passage from an article by Papi: 'One thing is certain: our country has to face up to the competition of other countries; if, as has happened in the past, an attempt were made to model the economy along independent and autarkic lines, then this would lead to the eventual destruction of the economic structure and to progressive economic misery. If a country is forced to import goods, as in Italy's case, then it must be in a position to export goods as well', 'Una condizione di successo dell'European Recovery Program', *Rivista di politica economica*, 38 (1948).

[40] P. Villani and N. Marrone, *Riforma agraria e questione meridionale. Antologia critica 1943–1980* (Bari, De Donato, 1981).

[41] Cf. T. Fanfani, *Scelte politiche e fatti economici in Italia nel quarantennio repubblicano* (Turin, Giappichelli, 1987), pt. 1, sect. 11.

[42] The principal measures were the following: extraordinary measures for the settlement of the Sila plateau and of the adjoining eastern territories, 12 May 1950; regulations concerning the

areas with the highest percentage of *latifundia* and absentee landlords. Eight 'reform zones' were created, taking in some 8.5 million hectares of land (equal to about 30 per cent of total land area) and covering 36 different provinces. Roughly 700,000 hectares of land were confiscated, 70 per cent of this total being located in the South. The economist Mario Bandini has written that '99 per cent of this total consisted of land where there was nothing—no roads, no houses, no stable residents, no water, and therefore, as they stood, areas which offered no possibility of being farmed'.[43]

These areas were slowly transformed; between 1948 and 1970, within the provinces subject to the law, those communes that had not had land expropriated witnessed a reduction in the area being farmed by peasant-owners, whereas those communes where land had been expropriated saw a 30 per cent increase in the area farmed by them.[44] This was to mark a definitive break in the tradition of the *latifundia* in Italy.

A new authority was subsequently set up to provide aid to the underdeveloped areas of the country. This was the Cassa per il Mezzogiorno (Southern Development Fund), founded in August of 1950 with the aim of helping to resolve one of the Italian economy's oldest structural problems, the problem of the North–South divide. The truth is that the problem of the South's underdevelopment had received very little attention during the immediate post-war years. As Barucci shows in his study, in the long debates at the legislative assembly drawing up the new Italian Constitution, the South only comes up during debates on regional regulations, the *latifundia*, and agrarian reform, and government only put aside very modest sums for the development of the South.[45] Real change had to wait until the 'growth of what is commonly known as "new southern politics" (*nuovo meridionalismo*), which coincided with the creation of the SVIMEZ'.[46]

The SVIMEZ was founded on 2 December 1946 by a group of people who had been connected with IRI during the 1930s—Donato Menichella, Francesco Giordani, Giuseppe Cenzato, and Pasquale Saraceno—and by Rodolfo Morandi, a member of the Socialist Party, as well as by southern and northern businessmen. The 'new southern politics' of the SVIMEZ was mainly

expropriation, reclamation, transformation, and assignment of plots of land to peasant farmers, 21 Oct. 1950; subsequent laws, passed in December 1950 and April 1951, extending the new agrarian measures to other areas of Italy, involving the Tuscan Maremma, Fucino in the Abruzzi, the Po Delta, the areas bordering the Volturno and Sele rivers, as well as the regions of Apulia, Lucania, Molise, Sicily, and Sardinia.

[43] M. Bandini, *La riforma agraria* (Rome, 1956), 43.

[44] INSOR, *La riforma fondiaria trent'anni dopo* (Milan, Angeli, 1979).

[45] P. Barucci, *Ricostruzione, pianificazione, Mezzogiorno. La politica economica in Italia dal 1943 al 1955* (Bologna, Il Mulino, 1978). Cf. F. Barbagallo, *Mezzogiorno e questione meridionale 1860–1980* (Naples, Guida, 1982).

[46] V. Zamagni and M. Sanfilippo, *Nuovo meridionalismo e intervento straordinario. La SVIMEZ dal 1946 al 1950* (Bologna, Il Mulino, 1988), 13.

of an industrial and pragmatic nature, less concerned with ideological considerations and the problem of the *latifundia*, and modelled more along the lines of the American Tennessee Valley Authority of the New Deal era. The SVIMEZ's theoretical and cultural base[47] was undoubtedly the point of departure for the proposal to set up an extraordinary body, which Menichella baptized Cassa per il Mezzogiorno, and the project for which was presented before parliament in March 1950.[48] The Cassa was financed by the BIRS[49] and by the central government, and it started operating in the agricultural sector, and on the South's infrastructures, thus going against the original objective of building up an industrial base in the South that lay at the heart of the 'new southern politics'. This was, however, to re-emerge at a later date. It was then the beginning of a new era for the South, and although it has yet to produce any really self-sustained economic results, nevertheless it marked the end of the South's separation from the rest of the country, which had continued to exist throughout the new nation's history (with the few exceptions we have looked at in previous chapters).[50]

Apart from agrarian reform and the Cassa per il Mezzogiorno, mention should also be made of the social measures taken at the time. In reality, what measures were taken were very heterogeneous, although they were all inspired by that Christian Democrat ideology which stresses the importance of Christian solidarity[51]—measures such as the law setting up the Social Solidarity Fund (29 July 1947) for pensioners; laws in favour of charitable institutions, social assistance authorities, professional training centres, wages funds (between 1947 and 1952), work-training programmes; and finally the INA-Casa project (or Fanfani plan 1949) aimed at the construction of popular housing for the working classes. The fact that such projects were not part of a unified programme was partly due to the poor state of public finances, which made it impossible to carry out costly social reform programmes, and partly due to the

[47] For a collection of the main works produced by the various members of the SVIMEZ until 1951, see the study cited in n. 46.

[48] Cf. M. Finoia, 'Il ruolo di Donato Menichella nella creazione della SVIMEZ e della Cassa del Mezzogiorno', in the collection of essays *Donato Menichella. Testimonianze e studi raccolti dalla Banca d'Italia* (Bari, Laterza, 1986), and S. Cafiero, *Tradizione e attualità del meridionalismo* (Bologna, Il Mulino, 1989). See however what R. Petri has to say on the previous Italian experiences of relocalization of industry in his book *La frontiera industriale. Territorio, grande industria e leggi speciali prima della Cassa per il Mezzogiorno* (Milan, Angeli, 1990).

[49] On this point, see P. Baffi, 'Via Nazionale e gli economisti stranieri, 1944–53', *Rivista di storia economica*, 2 (1985).

[50] Obviously the enormous numbers of southerners who moved to the North of Italy to look for work from the 1950s onwards helped to bridge the gap between the two cultures.

[51] Cf. G. Mori (ed.), *La cultura economica nel periodo della ricostruzione* (Bologna, Il Mulino, 1980), and in particular the essay by P. Roggi, 'Il mondo cattolico e i grandi term della politica economica'. See also P. Roggi, *Scelte politiche e teorie economiche in Italia nel quarantennio repubblicano* (Turin, Giappichelli, 1987).

break up of the trade union movement,[52] which found itself involved in the political 'taking sides' of the period, and which was to continue to be an obstacle to any united trade union action on social issues for about 20 years.

[52] The Confederazione Generale Italiana del Lavoro had rebuilt with the federative Rome Pact of 3 June 1944. The Catholic wing of the CGIL, however, split to form its own organization under Giulio Pastore's leadership in Oct. 1948, under the name of 'free CGIL' at first, and then the CISL (in 1950), while the Social Democrats and Republicans were to set up the UIL the following year (1949).

12

Economic Miracle: Crises and Recovery

THIS final chapter has a very different role to play from that of the preceding chapters. The process of economic development in Italy went through a decisive stage during the years after the Second World War, and for this reason it is essential to consider this period in order not to lose sight of the long-run interpretation of economic growth which I heartily believe in. However, these past 40 years or so have still not been analysed in depth by historians, although a growing number of studies of an increasingly more specialized nature have been produced by economists interested in the period.[1] I myself have never taken the opportunity to do research on this period, with the exception of one study which I shall be mentioning shortly. Thus, while an even more detailed study should have been made of this very important period than has been made of the first 50 years of the newly unified Italy, it is not possible to do it here.

Consequently, I have chosen to try to sum up in one single chapter the country's main economic and social achievements during the period stretching from the early 1950s until the present day. In doing so, I have paid special attention to the institutional aspects of the continuity/discontinuity with the past, as well as to the problems that still lie unresolved.

1. CYCLES AND STRUCTURAL CHANGE

The reconstruction years were to represent the start of a 40-year period of sustained growth for the Italian economy, a period dotted with crises, some of them rather serious from the point of view of their effects on Italian society, but not so serious as to bring that growth to a halt. Italy continued to be an important member of the Western economic world during each of the cyclical phases which the West went through; it remained a member of a small group of

[1] Few studies have tried to give an overall view of post-war developments. Moreover, most of them cover too short a time-span and suffer from a lack of research into the development of the various sectors of the economy. Among the best of those works currently available, see A. Graziani (ed.), *L'economia italiana 1945–1970* (Bologna, Il Mulino, 1979); V. Valli, *L'economia e la politica economica italiana dal 1945 ad oggi* (Milan, Etas Libri, 1983); M. D'Antonio, *Sviluppo e crisi del capitalismo italiano: 1942–1972* (Bari, De Donato, 1973); Michele Salvati, *Economia e politica in Italia dal dopoguerra ad oggi* (Milan, Garzanti, 1984); G. Gualerni, *Economia e politica industriale: il caso italiano*, ii: *1945–1972* (Turin, Giappichelli, 1988); together with T. Fanfani, *Scelte politiche e fatti economici in Italia nel quarantennio repubblicano* (Turin, Giappichelli, 1987). On the 1980s, see R. Brunetta, *Il modello Italia: analisi e cronache degli anni '80* (Venice, Marsilio, 1991).

countries which proved to be the most dynamic in terms of growth in both incomes and exports.

At the beginning, this period was marked by years of rapid growth, with an annual growth rate which stood at nearly 6 per cent up until 1963. The period contrasted markedly with the years of sacrifice and misery during the war and the earlier squeeze in consumption (analysed in Chapter 10), and for this reason it earned the title of 'economic miracle', although, as the reader who has followed the history of Italy's long and difficult march towards industrialization knows, it was hardly a case of a miracle. Industry, new constructions, exports, and investment all grew at a rate of between 9 and 11 per cent a year, thus increasing the industrial character of the country's economic system, and opening it up further to exchange with other economies. The bigger companies, which had up to then been so only in relative terms, finally began to take on the size which had until then been only a dream.

The year 1963 marked the end of this initial 'miraculous' phase. It was the year of the first round of wage-claims, of inflationary price rises, and of a loss in competitiveness of Italian exports, which in turn had serious repercussions for the country's balance of payments. A credit squeeze was introduced in order to slow down inflation, and this, making Italian products again competitive internationally, reduced the growth rate only slightly. The growth rate in income stood at about 5 per cent during the following 10 years, and the most important developments were of a social rather than an economic nature: this was to be the decade of the famous 'hot autumn' of 1969, when protests were aimed at securing improvements in social services, better conditions for the workers, a change in the structure of industrial relations to guarantee workers greater job security. This marked an upheaval in Italian society, which was to lead to very important changes for the better, but which was also to have serious repercussions during the subsequent period of Italian history. A new workers' statute was passed in May 1970. The Italian social security system was greatly improved, with an increase in pensions (in 1969), and a better deal for the unemployed and for mothers and children (1968–72); government policy on council housing was substantially revised (1972); and, finally, a series of measures were introduced, which were to lead at last to setting up a National Health Service (Servizio Sanitario Nazionale) in 1978.[2] The subsequent increase in public spending was not met, however, by a tightening of fiscal measures, which politicians at the time thought would have been best left to a later date, when the social fervent of that moment had died down. Unfortunately, it was then the turn of international events to aggravate the already difficult position of public finances, and for this reason, the Italian government found it impossible to reduce the gap that had been opened up by

[2] On the transformation of the Italian welfare system, see M. Ferrara, *Il welfare state in Italia. Sviluppo e crisi in prospettiva comparata* (Bologna, Il Mulino, 1984).

the early 1970s' programme of spending on social welfare measures. Furthermore, the extreme wing of the Left produced a movement called the Red Brigades which turned to terrorism, and the 1970s and 1980s were dotted with violent and bloody attacks against the state apparatus.

The 1973 oil crisis hit Italy roughly one year later, and was responsible for the only real fall in income during the entire post-war period; in 1975, Italian national income fell by 3.6 per cent. This crisis, which had other causes besides the fourfold increase in crude oil prices, caused problems for the entire Western world at a time when exchange rates were in a state of flux after the demise of the gold exchange standard in 1973. The freeing of the exchange rate initially prompted different reactions from each country. Italy decided to follow an inflationary policy which would allow businesses to rebuild their profit margins. This was a dangerous option, but one which, if carefully administered over a short period of time, could prove to be effective. Italy was lucky in that the end of inflation was not dictated by time-limits set internally, but by the establishment of the European Monetary System (EMS) in 1978, of which Italy became a member in 1979. The EMS—an agreement supporting fixed but adjustable exchange rates (which could only be changed by means of negotiation) between those EEC currencies which chose to participate in the agreement—was introduced in order to save European integration which proved to be at risk from fluctuating exchange rates. These developments led to a fall of at least another percentage point in the average rate of growth of national income in Italy between 1973 and 1980, reducing it to 3.7 per cent. Nevertheless, this was still higher than the equivalent rates for other European countries and for the USA, and was equal to that of Japan.[3]

The following three years (1981–3) were characterized by economic stagnation, during which the average rate of growth of national income was only 0.6 per cent. These were difficult years for Italian big industry, which on the one hand was hit once more by the repercussions of a second oil crisis, and on the other was no longer able to count on inflation to help its profit margins; furthermore, mechanisms such as 'wage-indexing', which had been revised in the workers' favour in 1975, contributed towards pushing wages upwards.[4] This period saw some important changes in the organization of Italian industry, with the introduction of automation, a thinning-out of the industrial work-force (the number of people employed in large industry fell by 21 per cent between 1980 and 1984, with the support of the fund for 'temporarily' laid-off workers or those put on short-time working—the Cassa Integrazione Guadagni—and an early retirement scheme), and an increase in productivity which resulted from these radical changes. The continual growth of

[3] C. D'Adda and B. Salituro, 'L'economia italiana negli anni settanta e ottanta', *Rivista di Politica Economica*, 79 (1989).

[4] It was not until 1984 that the inflationary effects of index-linked wage rises were largely eliminated through a government decree.

small industry was helped by the tendency of larger companies to decentralize, giving some of the more labour-intensive work to smaller subcontractors.

As a consequence of these changes, growth in national income started to pick up again in 1984 (it now stood at about 3 per cent), and although this was only half the growth rate witnessed during the 'miracle years', it was still one of the highest internationally. The reorganization of large industry continued until the tendency to rationalize the labour-force gradually came to an end, while there was a growing concern about the production of new technology, and both public and private spending on research increased as a result.

This was the background against which there was to be a structural transformation of the Italian economy. A period of change but without any deep shocks for the Western world; shocks tended to be confined to the Third World and the Eastern block countries. From its original industrial base, which had been quantitatively limited, Italy had leapt forward to take its place as one of the industrial powers and now stands in fourth position among the Western economies as far as the size of the industrial sector is concerned, immediately behind the USA, Japan, and Germany, while the growth in services has continued, including services for export, such as tourism. The percentage of GDP provided by the agricultural sector fell to 5 per cent, while GSP more than doubled. Public spending relative to GDP grew considerably during this period (from 30 to over 50 per cent), while the Italian economy degree of opening rose from 11 to 26 per cent.[5] Average annual income approached that of the most advanced European countries, as we saw in the introduction, despite the continued presence of large areas of the country where economic development was far from satisfactory. Finally, the population growth rate fell almost to zero.

While it is true that the foundations for such a transformation already existed, as the previous chapters have illustrated, it is just as important to recognize that new opportunities had to be taken as they presented themselves, and traditions had to change in accordance with those new challenges which confronted Italian society at the time. Those who, like myself, lived through this period, will know exactly how much of a battle had to be fought, and how much energy was needed in order to grasp such opportunities and to respond to the new challenges. They will also know about the terrible waste, the never-ending delays, and the human tragedies that were all part of this process of change. It thus comes as a great surprise to discover that other countries, certainly better organized, with better applied civil rights, and apparently more united than Italy, were not, in general, capable of sustaining such a high rate of growth as Italy had managed to do during these post-war years. The fact is that a country's degree of 'civilization' cannot be measured solely in terms of national

[5] ((Exports + Imports)/2) : GDP.

income, but must also take into account other aspects of life: aspects such as the quality of its public services, the suitability of its educational system, the stability of its political system, and the degree to which that system represents the wishes of the people, as well as guaranteed liberties—both negative (i.e. not being prevented from doing) and positive (i.e. being put in a position to do). Not all of these aspects of life are directly connected to the maximization of growth in national income, even if there are numerous ties, especially indirect ones, between them and economic prosperity. Therefore, it is quite possible that a country be very successful at producing goods, but prove to be slow in producing more 'civilized' institutions and vice versa: this is a point I will be coming back to a little later in this chapter.

2. FISCAL AND MONETARY POLICIES

Donato Menichella[6] was to follow the so-called 'Einaudi line' until 1960. This policy gave priority to the exchange rate, which had been fixed at 625 lire against the dollar after its slight devaluation in 1949, and to checking inflationary tendencies in the economy. Many experts have stressed the fact that Menichella's job was made easier by particularly favourable historical factors, such as a very elastic labour supply, and the interest in Italian goods shown by international markets. The budget deficit was gradually reduced in size, and the government subsequently managed to keep it at a very low level. Menichella, however, continued to ignore the possibility of a more Keynesian form of monetary policy, persuaded as he was that unemployment in Italy was largely of a structural nature, and as such could only be dealt with in the long run through an expansion of the nation's productive base. Multilaterality of international payments was declared in 1956, and the convertibility of the lira was officially sanctioned on 28 January 1960, at the exchange rate that had already been tested during the 1950s.

Overall, Menichella's monetary policy can be deemed to have been both consistent, effective, and firm. But it has been criticized for its lack of concern about unemployment, and for its excessive reluctance to utilize monetary incentives. The fact is that Menichella's monetary policy was simply a reflection of the economic stance taken up by the governments of the day. Toniolo writes that 'the acceptance of the basic political choices made in 1947 as a given fact . . . means that it is doubtful whether a different monetary policy . . . could have reconciled the stability of prices and of the exchange rate and the rate of capital accumulation which was in fact achieved with a much higher increase in private consumption'.[7]

[6] On Menichella's days as Governor, and those of his two successors, Carli and Baffi, see F. Spinelli and M. Fratianni, *Storia monetaria dell'Italia. L'evoluzione del sistema monetario e bancario* (Milan, Mondadori, 1991).

[7] G. Toniolo, 'La politica monetaria degli anni '50 (1947–60)', in G. Franco (ed.), *Sviluppo e crisi dell'economia italiana* (Milan, Etas Libri, 1979), 70.

Guido Carli took over Menichella's job in the mid-1960s, and at first carried on with the latter's policy of growth accompanied by cautious monetary measures. When prices and wages started to rise rapidly during the course of 1962, while the balance of payments went into the red, the new Governor made no attempt to introduce a monetary squeeze, choosing on the contrary to support the existing productive expansion. However, it was impossible to avoid a monetary squeeze the following year, and when it came it proved to be rather drastic. The economy's reaction consisted in a fall in domestic demand, the stagnation of investment, and a flight of capital; exports, however, quickly recovered, and maintained this trend for several years afterwards.

Monetary policy after 1964 became far less rigid than it had been up to then, although it still reflected a certain caution with regard to the risk of inflation. It was at this time that the Bank of Italy attempted to provide the Treasury with an alternative source of finance, in the form of support given to government bond prices; this measure did, in fact, manage to channel twice the amount of private savings into these bonds during 1966–7, compared with the equivalent flow during the previous two-year period. However, this support could not have continued indefinitely were the economic situation to take on a more inflationary tone; and, in fact, it eventually had to be withdrawn during the spring of 1969, with serious repercussions for the monetary base.[8] The Bank of Italy was subsequently criticized for having taken on the responsibility for establishing measures which it deemed 'compatible' with governmental policy, when the government itself ignored such 'compatibility'. Amato writes, 'in taking on this responsibility, the Bank of Italy failed both to achieve such compatibility and to force the government to enact the necessary measures to achieve it. Had it not assumed responsibility in this case, perhaps the government would have been forced to react in a different fashion and to adopt different measures, when there was still time to do so to the economy's advantage.'[9] Indeed, it is commonly acknowledged that Governor Carli attempted to increase the Bank of Italy's influence over the Italian economy, envisaging it as in some way constituting a 'clearing-house' for power struggles between members of the nation's ruling class.[10]

This strategic role of monetary policy, which Carli had given to it as a result of the almost total absence of a governmental fiscal policy, continued to exist even when conditions inside and outside of the country changed radically,

[8] For further details, cf. A. Fazio, 'La politica monetaria in Italia dal 1947 al 1978', *Moneta e Credito*, 127 (1979); G. Mengarelli, *Politica e teoria monetaria nello sviluppo economico italiano 1960–1974* (Turin, Boringhieri, 1979); and also F. Cotula (ed.), *La politica monetaria in Italia: il sistema finanziario e il contesto internazionale* (Bologna, Il Mulino, 1989).

[9] G. Amato, *Economia, politica e istituzioni in Italia* (Bologna, Il Mulino, 1976), 137.

[10] B. Jossa and C. Panico, 'L'intermediazione bancaria negli anni della crisi economica italiana (1964–1984)', in B. Jossa and C. Panico (eds.), *Teorie monetarie e banche centrali* (Naples, Liguori, 1988), 273. Also see M. De Cecco, 'Banca d'Italia e conquista politica del sistema creditizio', in the collection, *Il governo democratico dell'economia* (Bari, De Donato, 1976).

following the 'hot autumn' of 1969. There were a number of occasions on which it was necessary to implement credit squeezes (such as on the occasion of the 'spring thaw' of 1970), while monetary policy attempted to use inflationary measures as a means of rebuilding those margins of profit and of self-financing that companies had lost as a result of higher costs, while at the same time having to satisfy the ever-increasing financial requirements of the Treasury, thus increasing inflation even more. This inflationary tendency, which had been partially contained as long as Italy had had to maintain fixed exchange rates, exploded with previously unseen force from 1973 onwards. The rate of growth of the consumer price index was higher than 10 per cent for a period of 10 years, hitting 19.4 per cent in 1974, dropping to 12.4 per cent in 1978, then rising to a record 21.1 per cent in 1980, before beginning its final descent during the following year.

By the time Carli stepped down as governor of the Bank of Italy (during the summer of 1975), and his place was taken by Paolo Baffi, it was generally agreed that monetary policy alone could not hope to resolve the domestic and international problems of the country. Baffi's governorship, together with that of his successor Carlo Azeglio Ciampi,[11] led to the direct intervention of the Bank of Italy in the most dangerous cases of economic imbalance, but also to a general reduction in the Bank's role in economic affairs, rendered possible by making the various pressure groups responsible for the effects their actions had on the economic system. Structural forms of intervention were introduced, aimed at making the normal channels of financial intermediation more efficient, and at improving control over monetary aggregates. The two major decisions taken were: (*a*) the above-mentioned one to take Italy into the EMS in March 1979, which meant that inflation had to be brought down; and (*b*) the 'Treasury–Bank of Italy divorce' of June–September 1981, which, through the elimination of the Bank's obligation to take up all the state bonds not subscribed to by the public, gave the Bank an indispensable instrument with which to control the monetary base. In this way, Italian monetary policy was able to follow a more orthodox course. The level of inflation was brought down by adopting a 'softer' line, despite the need to cover a massive public deficit, which in turn was made possible by the increasingly large flow of private savings—fortunately abundant at that time—that were channelled towards this target. The option of adjusting the exchange rate in order to accommodate inflation was gradually abandoned, until the opposite policy aimed at the maintenance of a fixed exchange rate so as to push inflation further down was adopted in 1987, and in 1990 the wide margin of fluctuation (6 per cent on both sides) was also abandoned (this had been conceded at the time of Italy's entry into the EMS). With the monetary situation on a more even keel, the Bank of Italy was now able

[11] Ciampi took Baffi's place in 1979 after the latter and his general director Sarcinelli had been the target of an unjustified attack by Italian judges on the basis of their having given excessive credit to Rovelli's chemical company, SIR, which subsequently went bankrupt.

to dedicate its energies to the serious problem of the reorganization of the Italian financial system in view of the fast-approaching Single European Market (we shall briefly mention this reorganization in subsection 5).[12]

While this inflationary monetary policy was judged very harshly by the experts at the time, it has since undergone a re-evaluation. In a recent study, Giavazzi and Spaventa[13] conclude that, together with other measures introduced by the government of the day, it aimed at helping the restructuring of large companies, and helped to keep the profitability of such companies at a higher level than that of their European rivals, thus contributing indirectly towards that investment which was to form the basis of their recovery. The fall in inflation did, it is true, bring about a recession (1981–3), but it was one of relatively limited proportions, and in any case, following on as it did after the investment boom, it was easier to overcome without having to witness any spectacular bankruptcies. According to the authors, it is not the case that the price paid for the implementation of this policy was a very considerable rise in the public deficit, since fiscal policy at the time was very productive in terms of revenue as well. In order to understand exactly how Italy managed to accumulate the enormous budget deficit that it has at present, we need to take a closer look at recent fiscal policy.

After an initial period of improvement in the State's fiscal position, the public deficit once again began to widen during the second half of the 1960s, although this was due solely to the deficit in public spending on investment (capital account spending, see column 4, Table 12.1), which could no longer be covered by the current account surplus existing up to 1964 (column 3, Table 12.1). While revenue remained fairly steady percentagewise until 1975, Table 12.1 (column 3) clearly shows the appearance also of a current account deficit from 1971 onwards; this latter deficit was to increase in size until it finally peaked in the disastrous year of 1975 at some 7 per cent of GDP. Similarly, the ratio between public debt and GDP, which had fluctuated around the 30 per cent mark during the entire post-war period, reached 55 per cent in that same year (see column 5, Table 12.1).

While the rapid rise in public spending during this period was mainly due, as we have seen, to an increase in welfare expenditure, which rose from 13 to 16 per cent of GDP, it was also exacerbated by the need to pay off interest—interest payments rose from 2 to 4 per cent of GDP—whereas the considerable growth in the number of public sector employees only produced a marginal increase in the percentage of public spending on GDP, because of a decrease in their real wage-level.[14] Some kind of tax reform became indispensable at this

[12] For details of changes in the structure of Italian banking during the 1980s, cf. P. Ciocca, *Banca, finanza, mercato* (Turin, Einaudi, 1991), ch. 5.

[13] F. Giavazzi and L. Spaventa, 'Italy: the Real Effects of Inflation and Disinflation', *Economic Policy*, 5 (1989).

[14] F. Reviglio, *Spesa pubblica e stagnazione dell'economia italiana* (Bologna, Il Mulino, 1977).

Table 12.1. Public finances, 1960–1987 (% of GDP)

	Current revenue (1)		Current expenditure (2)		Balance (1–2) (3)		Balance of capital account (4)		% ratio public debt/GDP (5)	
1960	29.5		26.7		2.8		−3.7		31	
1961	28.9		26.0		2.9		−3.8		29	
1962	29.8		27.0		2.8		−3.8		29	
1963	30.2		28.1		2.1		−3.3		28	
1964	31.3		28.7		2.6		−3.4		27	
1965	30.7		31.2		−0.5		−3.5		30	
1966	30.7		31.3		−0.6		−3.3		31	
1967	31.7		30.7		1.0		−3.5		31	
1968	32.2		31.6		0.6		−3.6		33	
1969	31.3		31.2		0.1		−3.4		33	
1970	31.2		30.9		0.3		−3.9		34	
1971	31.8		33.8		−2.0		−3.3		40	
1972	31.5		35.7		−4.2		−3.5		43	
1973	31.0		35.0		−4.0		−3.2		45	
1974	31.4		35.0		−3.6		−3.5		47	
1975	31.8		38.9		−7.1		−4.7		55	
1976	33.6		38.6		−5.0		−4.1		54	
1977	35.2		39.1		−3.9		−3.7		58	
1978	36.5		42.3		−5.8		−4.1		65	
1979	36.1	b	41.6	b	−5.0	b	−4.2	b	65	b
1980	38.5	33.4	43.6	37.8	−5.1	−4.4	−4.6	−4.0	62	52
1981	40.1	34.2	48.1	41.1	−8.0	−6.9	−5.2	−4.4	65	55
1982	43.0	36.3	50.4	43.3	−7.4	−7.0	−4.9	−4.2	69	59
1983	46.0	38.2	52.8	44.9	−6.8	−6.8	−4.5	−3.8	76	65
1984	45.3	37.9	53.2	45.0	−7.9	−7.1	−5.1	−4.5	81	69
1985	45.8	38.4	53.5	45.2	−7.7	−6.8	−6.5	−5.6	92	78
1986		39.3		45.8		−6.5		−4.9		83
1987		39.7		45.4		−5.6		−4.9		92

[a] Public Administration includes the State, local authorities, and social insurance funds.
[b] These columns utilize the revisions of GDP carried out by ISTAT in 1986.

Source: Ministero del Tesoro, *Il debito pubblico in Italia 1861–1987* (Rome, Istituto Poligrafico dello Stato, 1988) i. 63 and 90.

point, and this was in fact what happened in 1973–4, although the effects of such a reform were only to be felt since 1976;[15] the increase in taxation only succeeded in stopping any further growth in the current account deficit, counterbalanced as it was by another bout of increased public spending during

[15] The problem of the Italian tax system is not in its overall design, which is modern enough, but rather in the high level of tax concessions granted to particular categories of taxpayer (farmers, artisans, etc.) and in the high level of tax evasion among other categories (professional people, shopkeepers, hoteliers, and other small operators in the service sector).

the early 1980s. Once again, the incidence of welfare expenditure on GDP increased, this time by 3 per cent (between 1980 and 1985), interest repayments also rose by 3 per cent on GDP, and all other forms of public expenditure were to increase marginally during the same period. Due to the considerable and persistent budget deficit, the ratio of the public debt to GDP inevitably rose each year, and will continue to do so unless some measures to limit public spending[16] and/or increase normal and extraordinary tax revenue[17] are implemented. This cannot be put off much longer, in view of the Maastricht agreements on the introduction of a single European currency and the establishment of a unified monetary policy among member countries of a United Europe.

There has been a lot of argument about 'sustainability' of the public debt. It is certainly true that the present ratio of public debt to GDP has been larger on more than one occasion in the past—in the case of Italy itself (see Chapters 5 and 8), not to mention that of other countries—without any particularly dramatic consequences; and it is also true that it has been possible until now to finance this debt relatively easily through private domestic savings (a very small part of the Italian public debt involves foreign creditors). What is worrying, however, is not so much the level reached as the existence of a mechanism which, if not halted, will mean that the public debt/GDP ratio will go on increasing, at a time when Italy's finances become increasingly entwined with those of other countries, thus exposing it to the repercussions of international financial events, as the hasty devaluation of the lira in the summer of 1992 has demonstrated.

3. THE LATE AND INCOMPLETE MODERNIZATION OF AGRICULTURE

There can be little doubt that the Italian agricultural sector has gone through a phase of radical transformation since the Second World War. During this period, the number of persons employed in agriculture has dropped from 8.6 million to 2 million; similarly, agriculture now represents only 5 per cent of GDP, compared with 23 per cent immediately after the war; the GSP, on the other hand, has roughly doubled; more than half is now concentrated in the plains, although the division between the North–Centre and the South has remained as it was at the beginning of this period (50 per cent in the North, 16

[16] It cannot be said that nowadays the ratio of public expenditure to GDP is much different in Italy from other advanced European countries. However, many critics are worried about the effectiveness of much Italian public expenditure, and about the quality of those services offered. Cf. G. Brosio and C. Marchese, 'The Growth of Public Expenditure in Italy since the Second World War', in J. A. Lybeck and M. Henrekson (eds.), *Explaining the Growth of Government* (Amsterdam, North-Holland, 1988).

[17] Such as a wealth tax and/or the privatization of a considerable slice of public property.

per cent in the Centre, and 34 per cent in the South).[18] The percentage of GSP represented by cereal cultivation has been halved, whereas livestock farming and fruit production have risen in importance, the latter from 14 to 25 per cent of GSP. The modernization process has involved the entire country, although it has been much slower in the South, where the value added per worker has dropped from 75 per cent of the equivalent value in the North (1951) to 54.5 per cent in 1982.

In this section I will be surveying those economic policies aimed at the agricultural sector, and will conclude with the question of whether or not the undoubted progress made by farming in Italy during this period can be considered to have kept up with international developments in this field, and with the food requirements of the nation.

First, agriculture was never a priority issue for the post-war governments of the Italian Republic, as it had failed to be for both Giolitti and for the Fascists, despite the rural rhetoric of Mussolini, as was seen in the preceding chapters. The Christian Democrat governments saw it basically as a reservoir of both resources and labour (and votes as well), and while they made some attempts at modernizing it, they were mainly concerned about alleviating the misery and poverty of rural life in order to avoid a mass exodus from the countryside. The 12-year plan laid down by law no. 949 (1952)—entitled 'Measures for the development of the economy and growth in employment'—contained eleven articles concerned with agriculture; these covered the concession of soft loans in order to buy agricultural machinery, build new rural housing, and set up irrigation projects, while the Southern Development Fund (Cassa per il Mezzogiorno) provided other funds for the creation of infrastructures of a mainly agricultural nature. These measures were updated in the 1960s by the two so-called 'Green Plans' (the first in June 1961 and the second in October 1966), which were improvised sets of measures failing to contribute to the modernization of agriculture, and although productivity increased, this was more a result of the number of people leaving the countryside than of any other factor.

In the meanwhile, Common Market agricultural policy decisions began to have their effect on Italian agriculture, although Italy did not gain any real immediate advantage from the CAP (Common Agricultural Policy), as this was aimed above all at supporting cereal and livestock prices. It was not until the end of the 1970s that the CAP really began to help fruit and vegetable production as well. At that time, national agricultural policy awoke from a period of hibernation which had lasted roughly six years, since the end of the second Green Plan, and law no. 984 (the so-called 'four-leaved clover' law) was passed in December 1977. This law was 'aimed at sectorial intervention (four

[18] Cf. G. Fabiani, *L'agricoltura italiana tra sviluppo e crisi (1945–1985)* (Bologna, Il Mulino, 1986).

sectors at first, and then seven) which was to last for several years, and which was to see the division of those resources made available on the basis of production goals defined according to the type of land'.[19] This law produced a substantial flow of funds to the agricultural sector, but it failed to bring about any of the more ambitious structural changes. Furthermore, the fact that responsibility for agriculture had been handed over to regional government in July 1977 now meant that there was far less interest in a national agricultural programme. During the 1980s, the CAP was under pressure to reduce the level of price subsidies, given the accumulation of enormous surpluses of some products,[20] and the improvement in the competitiveness of many European agricultural enterprises.

Italy is very concerned about the reductions being made in CAP subsidies as it is still in a relatively weak position despite the fact that a number of agricultural improvements have undoubtedly been made. First of all, the level of homogeneity (from both the territorial and the farms' point of view) is not nearly as high as in other European countries: the weight of small, inefficient farms is still disproportionately large in Italy, while the gap between the regions is in fact widening. The level of domestic subsidization of Italian agriculture needed to support marginal farms in the presence of declining EEC monetary support has recently become difficult to sustain and the institution which had been used to such a purpose—the old Federconsorzi, reorganized in the late 1940s—suffered heavy losses in 1991.

Secondly, the agricultural balance of trade deficit has steadily worsened in monetary terms, while in relation to the value of exports it worsened in the mid-1970s, and has since picked up to return to its initial level. This deficit is mainly the result of the imports of large quantities of animal feedstuffs, without a correspondingly adequate increase in exports (especially of prepackaged goods), which is in turn a result of organizational weaknesses within the Italian food industry.[21] As the policy of price support favours a country in proportion to the quantities it produces, then the continual presence of a trade deficit means that the sacrifice asked of Italian consumers, who have to spend more on food in order to support farmers' income levels, does not in fact all accrue to Italian farmers, but is partially absorbed by farmers in other EEC countries. One final point that ought to be mentioned is the existence of an ecological problem caused by the excessive use of chemical fertilizers and pesticides in agriculture; the latter leads to pollution of rivers and streams, contributes to the

[19] Fabiani, *L'agricoltura italiana tra svilluppo e crisi (1945–1985)* 391.

[20] Remember that agricultural exports from EEC countries represent a heavy burden for the Community's budget, since they require subsidies to cover the difference between EEC prices (much higher) and international prices.

[21] See G. Medici and G. Fabiani (eds.), *La bilancia agroalimentare italiana* (Bologna, Il Mulino, 1987).

proliferation of dangerous forms of algae in the sea, and is generally harmful to health.

Italian agriculture, therefore, has still a long way to go before it can be considered to be in a position of equilibrium, and rather more ambitious forms of structural intervention are going to be necessary before it can hope to reach such a position.

4. LARGE INDUSTRY VERSUS SMALL INDUSTRY, PUBLIC VERSUS PRIVATE: WHAT DIRECTIONS HAS THE DEVELOPMENT OF INDUSTRY TAKEN?

Post-war Italy was a country of small businesses, partly as a result of the widespread artisan tradition inherited from the past, and partly due to the limited size of its markets. Many of the relatively few large companies had had such a difficult life that, as we have seen, they had been brought under direct government control as a result of the numerous salvage operations they had undergone in the past. However, when markets started to expand rapidly during the 1950s and 1960s, and Italy, like all European countries, found itself influenced by an influx of technology and managerial methods imported from the great US corporations, then most economists began to predict the disappearance of the small Italian firm, or at least the limitation of its operations to the domestic economic scene, where it would be out of reach of the dangers of international competition.

In fact, the movement towards the creation of large production plants which could benefit from important economies of scale started during the 1950s in the steel industry, in oil-refining, in petrochemicals, and in some branches of the engineering industry; and sometimes this involved an overestimation of the capacity of the market to absorb increased production, as happened in the case of a number of steel and chemical plants.[22] Public enterprises competed with private companies in this process of enlargement of plant and production,[23]

[22] This could in fact be described as the 'Americanization' of Italian industry, which is a process which also took place in other countries during this period; cf. V. R. Berghahn, *The Americanization of West German Industry 1945–1973* (New York, Berg, 1986). One famous economist had the following to say about developments at the Fiat company: 'The management of Fiat ... already knew in the 1930s everything about American methods of automobile production. They did not introduce them, because the size of the Italian market did not justify mass production. When the Italian economy grew into a sufficient size, the previously known methods were introduced', P. N. Rosenstein-Rodan, quoted from 'Technical Progress and Post-War Rate of Growth in Italy', in *Il progresso tecnologico e la società italiana. Effetti economici del progresso tecnologico sull'economia industriale italiana 1938–1958* (Milan, Giuffré, 1962), 163. On the question of the Americanization of Italian industry and economy, cf. V. Zamagni, 'The Italian "Economic Miracle" Revisited: New Markets and American Technology', in E. Di Nolfo (ed.), *Power in Europe? II* (Berlin, Walter De Gruyter, 1992).

[23] The evolution of nationalized industry in post-war Italy is analysed in B. Amoroso and O. J. Olsen, *Lo stato imprenditore* (Bari, Laterza, 1978); G. Maggia and G. Fornengo, *Appunti sul sistema delle participazioni statali in Italia* (Turin, Giappichelli, 1976); and M. Leccisotti (ed.), *Le*

while a number of foreign multinationals (American ones in particular) set up branches in Italy—sometimes buying out Italian companies in the process—and in certain cases these were to grow enormously, so that Italian big industry now could be divided into three, almost equal areas of ownership: the private sector, public enterprises, and foreign-owned industry.

It was inevitable that a process of vertical integration and co-ordination would take place within those companies located in urban areas which were already heavily industrialized. The result was that big industry became even more concentrated within the confines of the northern industrial triangle, which witnessed an enormous influx of migrant workers from the poorer areas of the country, especially from the South. These waves of migration were to become a feature of the years of the so-called 'economic miracle'. The rather weak spread effects of this phase of industrial development were felt above all in the areas immediately outside the 'metropolitan zones', where a number of medium-sized firms carried out contract work for large industry. Traditional industrial activity underwent some technological improvement, although the firms remained more or less of the same size and continued to produce from their original geographical locations.

This process led to predictions that the South would quickly be stripped of its native population,[24] and that the rest of the country would end up living and working in increasingly large metropolitan areas. However, things began to develop in a different direction from the 1960s onwards. At first the change was very gradual, but was to gain speed during the 1970s. Technological and economic conditions began to favour a revival in the fortunes of small businesses, which helped the North-East and Centre in particular, as these were the areas where the best conditions existed for such businesses. At the same time, the State decided to try to help the South through the location and development of nationalized industry, while granting tax incentives to private businesses setting up plants there. The purchasing power of its inhabitants also rose during this period as a result of emigration, the extension of the Welfare

participazioni statali: obiettivi e realizzazioni (Milan, Angeli, 1980). As well as IRI and ENI, another public holding, the EFIM, was set up in 1962 with the aim of managing those FIM companies which the State had not been able to reprivatize (companies such as Breda, Ducati, Reggiane OMI, and Caproni). A fourth government body, the EGAM, was set up in 1958 with the aim of running the mining companies, but it only entered into operation much later, in 1971, and it had already been dismantled in 1977 as a result of the mismanagement of the companies under its control. These companies were subsequently put under the control of ENI and IRI. In March 1971, the EFIM, IRI, ENI, and IMI together founded the GEPI (Società per la Gestione di Partecipazioni Industriali), whose aim it was to provide temporary aid to companies in difficulty. Finally, mention should be made of the nationalization of the electrical energy industry on 6 Dec. 1962, which led to the formation of the ENEL. See *La nazionalizzazione dell'energia elettrica. L'esperienza italiana e di altri paesi europei* (Bari, Laterza, 1989).

[24] The well-known position of the economist V. Lutz is clearly stated in her book, *A Study in Economic Development* (Oxford, Oxford University Press, 1963).

State, and the measures passed by the government aimed at assisting agriculture.

I would like to take a closer look at the technological and economic changes that produced such unexpected results.[25] Improvements in the transport and communication networks meant a decrease in the diseconomies connected with distance from the main centres, while the electronics revolution led to a reduction in the importance of the integrated production cycle. Different phases of the production cycle could now be located in different places; the amount of multi-purpose machinery increased—machinery which could be programmed to carry out different tasks, thus avoiding having to substitute it completely for each new task. From the market point of view, the demand for standardized products began to diminish with the rise in income levels and the greater instability which was witnessed, especially during the 1970s. The new forms of market demand favoured small-scale production, and thus flexibility in the use of both capital and labour, which are typical characteristics of smaller companies; these latter were able to update their technological know-how and specialize in customized products.

Crivellini and Pettenati summarize the consequences of this transformation as follows: 'As a result of this . . . the previous tendency towards the centralization of production was inverted. In fact, this new situation favours a form of development based on the creation of new, much smaller companies . . . over a much vaster area than before. The new tendency towards decentralization . . . is accentuated even further by the difficulties encountered by northern industry due to having reached the "saturation threshold".'[26] There are, of course, many other reasons why the new opportunities for growth possessed by smaller companies were taken advantage of so quickly in Italy (and not to the same extent in Great Britain, for example), and in some areas of Italy rather than others (mainly in the North-East and Centre).

Two factors are of particular importance in this context. First, there is the existence of local traditions, which tend to encourage the development of micro-entrepreneurial skills, in so far as they offer kinship structures which are both strong and extensive, and capable of making up for the lack of various elements present in large company structures, for example, control over working times. A vast literature exists now about these local traditions, which are above all evident in the so-called 'industrial districts', and it makes very interesting reading[27] as it enables one to understand the complex historical

[25] Cf. M. Crivellini and P. Pettenati, 'Modelli locali di sviluppo', in G. Becattini (ed.), *Modelli locali di sviluppo* (Bologna, Il Mulino, 1989).

[26] Ibid. 49–50.

[27] See above all G. Fuà and C. Zacchia, *Industrializzazione senza fratture* (Bologna, Il Mulino, 1983); G. Becattini (ed.), *Mercato e forze locali. Il distretto industriale* (Bologna, Il Mulino, 1987); A. Bagnasco, *La costruzione sociale del mercato* (Bologna, Il Mulino, 1988); C. Trigilia, *Grandi partiti e piccole imprese* (Bologna, Il Mulino, 1986); E. Goodman and J. Bamford (eds.), *Small Firms and*

reasons for the formation of such districts. Among these, one important factor that stands out is that of the ties to markets, both domestic and foreign, that developed out of home-working going back as far as the nineteenth century. A recent case-study which illustrates this point is that of the small town of Carpi, in the province of Modena, in Emilia, where there was a tradition of straw-weaving for the manufacture of hats going back to the nineteenth century. After the Second World War, manufacturing switched to shirts and sweaters, involving numerous small businesses, and with a great deal of the work being done by home-workers.[28] Another aspect stressed by the available literature is that the sense of belonging to a community is one of the characteristic features of these districts, as is the importance of the family, not only as a consumer unit but also as a producer, with an important interrelationship existing between productive activity and daily life.[29] The organization of the district is not the responsibility of a hierarchical mechanism, but is carried out through market mechanisms and various unwritten local rules. Conglomeration 'favours the rapid spreading of innovation'[30] through the circulation of information and also labour—the labour-force being highly skilled in terms of both 'ability and knowledge pertinent to the working processes that characterize their industrial district'.[31]

The second factor that played an important role in the success of small businesses was the conflictual character of industrial relations in big industry, which was to emerge from the so-called 'hot autumn' of 1969 onwards. According to a number of writers, these conflictual relations caused big industry to decentralize some phases of production in order to minimize high employment and training costs, the cost of making workers redundant, of production control, and of the high level of union conflictuality.[32] However, it has been shown that the development and growth of small businesses largely took place outside this decentralization process.[33]

Industrial Districts in Italy (London, Routledge, 1989); G. Becattini, 'Piccole e medie imprese e distretti industriali nel recente sviluppo italiano', *Note economiche*, 18 (1989); F. Pyke, G. Becattini, and W. Sengenberger, 'Distretti industriali e cooperazione fra imprese in Italia', *Banca Toscana Studi e Informazioni* 34 (1991).

[28] L. Cicognetti and M. Pezzini, 'Dalle paglie alle maglie. Carpi: la nascita di un sistema produttivo', in P. P. D'Attorre and V. Zamagni (eds.), *Distretti, imprese, classe operaia. L'industrializzazione dell'Emilia Romagna* (Milan, Angeli, 1992).

[29] This is the background against which the system of home-working is created—a type of labour known as 'working on the black', since it lies outside the reach of labour legislation and tax legislation. Cf. L Frey, *Guida all'analisi economica dell'occupazione* (Rome, Ed. Ceres, 1979); and L. Frey, G. De Santis, and R. Livraghi, *Lavoro a domicilio e decentramento della attività produttiva nei settori tessile e dell'abbigliamento* (Milan, Angeli, 1975).

[30] M. Bellandi, 'Capacità innovativa diffusa e sistemi locali di imprese', in G. Becattini (ed.), *Modelli locali di sviluppo*, 160.

[31] Ibid.

[32] F. Barca and M. Magnani, *L'industria fra capitale e lavoro. Piccole e grandi imprese dall'autunno caldo alla ristrutturazione* (Bologna, Il Mulino, 1989), including the bibliography.

[33] Among the factors that contributed towards the development of the small company besides the growth in services, there is what could be called the fiscal savings factor (which is sometimes

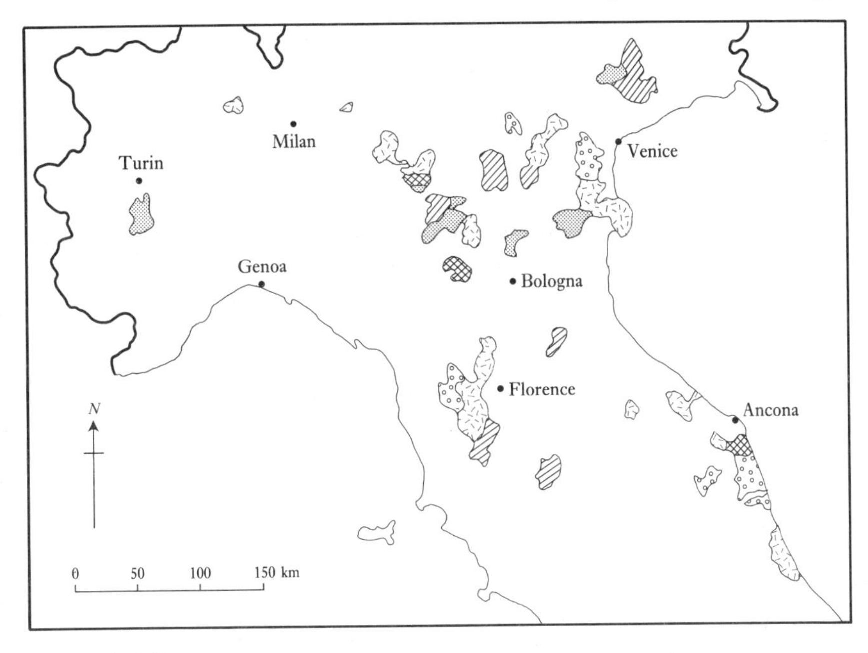

Metal goods: Carmagnola (Piedmont). Rivarolo Mantovano (Lombardy).

Mechanical engineering: Suzzara (Lombardy). Novellara (Emilia-Romagna). Cento (Emilia-Romagna). Copparo (Emilia-Romagna).

Electrical and electronic engineering: Conegliano (Veneto). Guastalla (Emilia-Romagna).

Textiles: Urgnano (Lombardy). Quinzano d'Oglio (Lombardy). Asola (Lombardy). Carpi (Emilia-Romagna). Prato (Tuscany).

Clothing: Oleggio (Piedmont). Manerbio (Lombardy). Pontevico (Lombardy). Verolanuova (Lombardy). Ostiana (Lombardy). Noventa Vicentina (Veneto). Piazzola sul Brenta (Veneto). Adria (Veneto). Porto Tolle (Veneto). Mondolfo (Marche). Urbania (Marche). Corinaldo (Marche). Filottrano (Marche). Roseto degli Abruzzi (Abruzzi). Castelfiorentino (Tuscany). Empoli (Tuscany).

Leather tanning: Arzignano (Veneto). Santa Croce sull'Arno (Tuscany).

Leather goods: Tolentino (Marche).

Footwear: San Giovanni Ilarione (Veneto). Pieve di Sacco (Veneto). Civitanova Marche (Marche). Fermo (Marche). Grottazzolina (Marche). Montefiore dell'Aso (Marche). Montegranaro (Marche). Monte San Pietrangeli (Marche). Torre San Patrizio (Marche). Lamporecchio (Tuscany). Montecatini Terme (Tuscany).

Wooden furniture: Viadana (Lombardy). Bovolone (Veneto). Cerea (Veneto). Nogara (Veneto). Motta di Livenza (Veneto). Oderzo (Veneto). Montagnana (Veneto). Sacile (Friuli-Venezia-Giulia). Modigliana (Emilia-Romagna). Saltara (Marche). Poggibonsi (Tuscany). Sinalunga (Tuscany).

Ceramic goods: Sassuolo (Emilia-Romagna). Casalgrande (Emilia-Romagna).

Toys: Canneto sull'Oglio (Lombardy).

Musical instruments: Potenza Picena (Marche). Recanati (Marche).

• Most important towns.

Fig. 12.1. Marshallian industrial districts, according to principal economic activity

Finally, the post-war governments' southern development policy helped towards the growth of industrialization in the South, involving big industry of all kinds, and in particular nationalized industry, but including private and foreign-owned industry to a lesser extent; and this thus represented an extension of the country's industrial base over a much wider area. We shall be taking a closer look at the industrialization of the South, in terms of the course it took and the results obtained, in section 7 of this chapter. For the moment, we can conclude this particular section with a summary of the strengths and weaknesses of present-day Italian industry.

In 1981, 59 per cent of workers in manufacturing industry worked in factories or workshops with less than 100 employees; this was roughly equivalent to the situation in Japan in 1978, but represented a far higher proportion of the total than that of the United States (23 per cent in 1982), Great Britain (25 per cent in 1979), France (29 per cent in 1979), and Germany (30 per cent in 1977).[34] Small Italian companies proved themselves capable of exporting goods, but to a slightly lesser extent than medium-sized companies (from 100 to 500 employees) and large companies (more than 500 employees), both of which have similar exporting capacities. Gross product per worker—productivity, in other words—is slightly lower than in medium-sized and big industry, but the gap has narrowed considerably, as has that between small industry and the other two categories in terms of investment per worker. The gross operating margins of small industry are much higher than those of large industry, and slightly higher than those of medium-sized industry. Small industry has also proved to be very good at adapting to technological change,[35] whereas its capacity to generate technological innovation, although not totally absent, is fairly low. Thus small Italian companies are, on average, fairly efficient and competitive, as well as being dynamic and creative,[36] although they

hard to separate from fiscal evasion). The financial factor, on the other hand, does not seem to have made much of a contribution, due to the limited amount of cheap credit available to small companies, and their use of mainly short-term (thus more expensive) credit. However, it is true that small companies were frequently self-financed themselves, and the existence of a local banking network meant that they nearly always had access to the basic financial services necessary. Cf. M. Onado (ed.), *Sistema finanziario e industria* (Bologna, Il Mulino, 1986).

[34] M. Samek Lodovici, 'Le piccole imprese manifatturiere in Italia e negli altri maggiori paesi industriali', in I. Cipolletta (ed.), *Struttura industriale e politiche macroeconomiche in Italia* (Bologna, Il Mulino, 1986). Also see A. Daems, 'The Size of the Firm. Theoretical and Empirical Reflections on European Industrial Hierarchies', in the collection of writings, ASSI, *Piccola e grande impresa: un problema storico* (Milan, Angeli, 1987).

[35] See the conclusions of the article written by E. Santanelli, A. Sterlacchini, and F. Quaglia, 'Investimenti in macchine e innovazione nelle piccole e medie imprese', *L'Industria*, 12 (1991): 'The main empirical conclusion of this study is that the widespread use of micro-electronics and information technology during the course of the last ten years has led to considerable change even in those industries which are generally considered to be already mature technologically speaking, such as the fashion industry, furniture manufacturing, or the shoe industry' (p. 315).

[36] There are two excellent studies of the widespread nature of entrepreneurship in Italy: cf. P. Mariti (ed.), *La formazione di nuove imprese* (Milan, Angeli, 1990), and G. Mussati (ed.), *Alle origini dell'imprenditorialità* (Milan, Etas Libri, 1990).

cannot be considered as constituting the driving force of the Italian industrial sector.

Italian big industry, both private and state-owned, went through a considerable crisis during the second half of the 1970s and the early 1980s. Many jobs were lost during this period,[37] but industry managed to get back on to a competitive footing, state-owned companies doing so at a slower pace, as they were heavily involved in such basic industries as steel and shipbuilding which were going through a crisis throughout Europe, and were finding it much more difficult to lay off large numbers of workers. Government policy proved to be an important factor in the reorganization and rationalization of big industry. This consisted in monetary policy (see above), a policy of labour flexibility introduced in the years 1980–4,[38] the watering-down of the policy of wage indexation (in 1984), and the so-called industrial policies.[39] Another element was the attempted reorganization of the Italian industrial power system, through the implementation of mergers and the building up of large industrial groups.

The presence of such groups is not something that was witnessed for the first time in the 1980s, although it was undoubtedly reinforced during this period due to their appetite for buying up other companies, both in Italy and abroad: this involved both small and large private companies as well as large public enterprises. The growth of these industrial groups in Italy was so considerable that it was deemed necessary for the first time to draw up some form of anti-trust legislation, and a law limiting their size and their activities was passed by Parliament on 10 October 1990 (law no. 287).[40]

A full account of the historical growth of these industrial groups and of their relative importance for the industrialization of Italy has still to be written, particularly since neither the census data nor the information we have concerning joint-stock companies would be of any use in constructing such an account. According to the most recent study in this field, 'the Italian groups are hierarchical . . . Each group is headed either by a holding company, in the case of the private groups, or by a government body functioning as a holding company in the case of the three state-controlled groups.'[41] The private holding companies are mostly controlled by families, although other associate groups or

[37] Those companies with more than 200 employees lost about one-quarter of their work-force, while smaller companies continued to expand. Cf. L. F. Signorini, 'Grandi e piccole imprese negli anni ottanta: la ristrutturazione dell'industria in un'analisi di dati di bilancio', *Temi di discussione del Servizio studi della Banca d'Italia*, 157 (1991).

[38] The already mentioned CIG, the fiscalization of social benefits, the mechanism governing early-retirement benefits, and restrictions on the index-linking of wages and salaries.

[39] Cf. P. Bianchi, 'Politiche industriali di settore', in V. Balloni (ed.), *Esperienze di ristrutturazione industriale* (Bologna, Il Mulino, 1985); P. Ranci, 'Italy: the Weak State', in F. Duchêne and G. Shepherd (eds.), *Managing Industrial Change in Western Europe* (London, Pinter, 1987).

[40] See the annual report of the commission that was set up at the time of the anti-trust law in order to guarantee competition and market transparency, in *L'Industria*, 12 (1991).

[41] F. Brioschi, L. Buzzacchi, and M. G. Colombo, *Gruppi di imprese e mercato finanziario. La struttura di potere nell'industria italiana* (Rome, NIS, 1990), 38.

companies also have some shareholdings, which has led the above-cited authors to comment that 'the Italian industrial grouping system is characterized by a considerable level of interlocking, which leads to a collusive reaction to many problems that arise. Interlocking between different groups is of an asymmetrical nature, in the sense that some groups rely on the support of other groups and/or that of Mediobanca, while others are self-sufficient as far as control is concerned.'[42] In 1987, the top five groups (of the 100 quoted on the Milan Stock Exchange, excluding the secondary market) held some 72 per cent of the total gross capitalized value of all such groups.[43]

Some remarks finally need to be made about public enterprises. In 1981, public enterprises accounted for about 12 per cent of the turnover of manufacturing companies with more than 20 employees, and it had a much bigger proportion in some branches such as metallurgy (37 per cent) and construction of means of transport (27.5 per cent). In other sectors, this percentage was considerably higher: sectors such as mining (82 per cent), electricity, gas, and water (93.5 per cent), and transport and communications (77 per cent).[44] An attempt was made to sell off a number of state-owned companies to the private sector, but this proved to be largely unsuccessful. The few successful privatizations included a number of steel plants, with the result that the nationalized steel industry slowly returned to being a profitable concern, and also the sale of Alfa-Romeo to Fiat in 1986. The numerous failures included the attempted merger between the state-owned Italtel and Elettra (owned by Fiat) in the field of telecommunications; the De Benedetti group's attempt to buy up the SME (IRI's holding company in the food industry), after having already bought up IBP-Perugina, with the aim of creating a powerful group within the food industry (in the end, the Perugina Company was sold to the Swiss giant Nestlé); and the joint-venture in the field of basic chemical products, which saw ENI and Montedison (owned by the Ferruzzi group) form a company, Enimont, which in turn, as a result of the unsolved problem of managerial responsibility, was sold back to the ENI (which changed its name back into Enichem, the former chemical division of ENI).

The failure of these privatization moves has given rise in the last few years to

[42] Ibid. 39.

[43] These were the Agnelli group, IRI, Assicurazioni Generali (the only Italian public company), Ferruzzi, and De Benedetti. For details of the Agnelli group, cf. A. Enrietti and G. Fornengo, *Il gruppo Fiat. Dall'inizio degli anni Ottanta alle prospettive del mercato unificato del '92* (Rome, NIS, 1989); on the Ferruzzi group, see G. C. Bianco, *Il gruppo Ferruzzi. Formazione di una global company* (Rome, NIS, 1988); on IRI, see N. Acocella, *L'impresa pubblica italiana e la dimensione internazionale: il caso dell'IRI* (Turin, Einaudi, 1983); and for details on the Montedison group, see A. Marchi and R. Marchionatti, *Montedison 1966–1989* (Milan, Angeli, 1991).

[44] The Italian State Railway Company has never been a part of the Italian nationalized industries network, and has been a branch of the Ministry of Transport, which until recently managed it in the worst bureaucratic manner possible. A more independent and entrepreneurial approach to management has only been adopted in recent years, with the aim now being that of converting it into a joint-stock company with substantial private shareholding.

a different approach, that of wholesale privatization, with state-owned companies being first converted into joint-stock companies. A new law was passed to this end in January 1992, after heated debate among the various political parties, who would like to keep their own men in key positions in public enterprises. The law leaves a considerable margin for doubt as to the eventual outcome of such an operation, despite the fact that the government can obtain some very useful revenue from the sale of nationalized companies, which could then be used in reducing a part of the sizeable public debt. Only EFIM, which is the only one of the three public holding companies to have suffered from serious mismanagement, and to find itself heavily in debt as a result, was put into liquidation in the summer of 1992.

Finally, a note on the dynamism (not always successful) of Italian big industry within the international context, where it has tried to win a place among the leaders, and in some cases has worked together with important foreign companies in domestic and international markets. Some figures relating to the results of these activities will be given in section 6 of this chapter.

5. THE EVOLUTION OF THE BANKING SYSTEM

The 1936 Banking Act, whose effects were only felt after the end of the Second World War, failed to lead to a conversion from a bank-oriented financial system to the kind of system prevalent in other countries whereby companies are financed through stock markets (market-oriented systems).[45] There have been at least two periods during which the stock market grew in importance during the last 40 years in Italy: at the end of the 1950s and during the mid-1980s. However, Italy has always remained in that group of countries with a bank-oriented system, due largely to the repeated episodes of company unprofitability, together with the small size of the country's Stock Exchange, which represents both the cause and effect of the all-important relationship between companies and banks.[46]

The Banking Act did, however, lead to the specialization of the banks in short-term or long-term credit. While it is true that Italian banks offer a variety of services which, if looked at from the American or Japanese point of view, would justify their being classified as 'universal banks',[47] nevertheless, at least

[45] Cf. G. Conti's survey, 'Alternative Financial Systems in Industrial Economies 1970–1986', in V. Zamagni (ed.), *Finance and the Enterprise* (London, Academic Press, 1992), including the extensive bibliography.

[46] There are many writings on the post-war development of the Italian credit system, although a lot of this literature is very fragmentary. Cf., among others, G. Carli (ed.), *La struttura del sistema creditizio italiano* (Bologna, Il Mulino, 1979); F. Bruni and A. Porta, *Il sistema creditizio: efficienza e controlli* (Bologna, Il Mulino, 1980); Onado, *Il sistema finanziario italiano*; and also the collection by various authors, *Banca e mercato. Riflessioni su evoluzione e prospettive dell'industria bancaria in Italia* (Bologna, Il Mulino, 1988).

[47] C. Conigliani, 'Recenti indagini empiriche su aspetti strutturali dell'industria bancaria', *Note economiche*, 21 (1991), 26.

officially speaking, they respected the difference between short-term and medium/long-term credit until the 1980s. Long-term credit institutions had come into existence after 1914 (see preceding chapters dealing with banking and finance), but separation between short-term and long-term credit was sanctioned only by the 1936 Act.

Some interpretations of this 1936 Act have recently been given. Masera declares that

> the legislators in 1926, and again in 1936, did not intend to impose normative measures concerning the specialization of credit. The explicit introduction of special [i.e. long-term] banks and the definition of their set of rules did, it is true, correspond to the need to define the operational limits of the non-deposit institutes that had been created, but more importantly, it arose out of a desire to circumscribe as much as possible the interdependencies that had been created between banking institutions and businesses. In fact, the excessive involvement of one in the other, in both directions, led to the crisis of the mixed bank, which necessitated the intervention of the government—hence the two laws of 1926 and 1936.[48]

Another economist, Onado, adopts a similar position when he writes: 'specialization is not based so much upon the need to establish a balance relating to the length of credit, as to the need to establish a distinction between the financers and the financed',[49] which is very much a worry shared also by present-day observers, as a result of the negative historical example set by the mixed banks during the 1920s and 1930s, and which lies at the roots of the recent anti-trust legislation limiting the possibilities of reciprocal shareholdings between banks and industry. From the long-term point of view, however, this temporal specialization probably does not constitute either a characterisic or a definitive trait of Italian banks.

In the first place, those banks whose names had previously been connected with the financing of industry, that is, the three large former mixed banks, called banks of national importance, as well as the co-operative banks, quickly came together during the immediate post-war period to form two new long-term banks, Mediobanca and Centrobanca, both of which were founded in 1946.[50] Mediobanca remained the property of the three former mixed banks until the end of the 1980s, when it was privatized (thus representing one of the few

[48] R. Masera, *Intermediari, mercati e finanza d'impresa* (Bari, Laterza, 1991), 49–50. The author states that it was only with the law passed in July 1990 (and the relative decree of Nov. 1990)—the so-called Amato law, Amato being the Minister who drew it up—that the separation between banks and business was explicitly referred to. For a discussion of the relationship between banks and industry, also see P. Ciocca and F. M. Frasca, 'I rapporti fra industria e finanza: problemi e prospettive', *Politica economica*, 3 (1987).

[49] Onado, 'Introduzione', in *Banca e mercato*, 476. See also by the same author, 'Banche e altri intermediari: specializzazione o concorrenza?', *Note economiche*, 16 (1986), an issue devoted to the 50th anniversary of the 1936 banking bill.

[50] Cf. G. Nardozzi, *Tre sistemi creditizi a confronto. Banche ed economia in Francia, Germania e Italia* (Bologna, Il Mulino, 1983).

successful privatization operations carried out so far in Italy), and has had a very important role in the financing of the large private industrial groups in Italy.[51] The exact relationship between Mediobanca and the three former mixed banks, who supplied short-term credit and lost some of their market share to medium/long-term financial institutes, will be an interesting subject for future historians.

Secondly, other banks of a more local nature that were traditionally less involved in the financing of industry, such as the savings banks (casse di risparmio), got together during the 1950s to set up regionally based medium/long-term credit institutes called Mediocredito (followed by the name of the region),[52] which were in turn financed by a central institute, the Mediocredito Centrale. However, it would seem that these banks were mainly involved in dispensing soft loans,[53] so that the normal medium/long-term credit requirements of small and medium-sized businesses 'fell to . . . those banks that were present locally . . . [which] easily managed to satisfy the demand for long-term financial loans through credit channels that formally provided only working capital. In this way, long-term loans came to be covered by banker's ordinary credit'.[54] The long-term banks' normal method of financing involved instead the placing of bonds on the market, which were also bought up by the deposit banks. Only Mediobanca was allowed to collect term deposits directly from the public.

Finally, during the 1980s the Bank of Italy, a fierce supporter of the distinction between short-term and medium/long-term credit, had to recognize that such a rigid separation was untenable in view of world developments towards universal banking. It then started to encourage the creation of merchant banks by deposit banks[55] and the mergers between banks with different specializations, to create multi-functional groups which managed to

[51] An interesting biography has recently been published of Enrico Cuccia, who has been undiscussed head of Mediobanca from its very foundation: cf. F. Tamburini, *Un siciliano a Milano* (Milan, Longanesi, 1992).

[52] In Sardinia the institute was set up directly by the State in 1953, under the name of Credito Industriale Sardo (CIS); the already existing Istituto per lo Sviluppo Economico dell'Italia Meridionale (ISVEIMER) and the Istituto per il Finanziamento Industriale in Sicilia (IRFIS) were reorganized through the 'Cassa per il Mezzogiorno'.

[53] Cheap credit has been used since the times of the first post-war governments in order to help the artisan sector and small businesses in general, as well as to give financial support to large companies reconverting from wartime production (through loans given out by the IMI against Marshall Plan counterpart funds) and to provide incentives to the agricultural modernization and industrialization of backward parts of the country. Such 'soft' loans are still largely used in Italy.

[54] Nardozzi, *Tre sistemi creditizi a confronto*, 62. The exact relevance of this involvement of ordinary banks in the provision of medium-term credit still remains largely concealed, despite the fact that experts interested in the banking world during the 1950s and 1960s were all aware of it. See F. Cesarini (ed.), *Economia della banca* (Bologna, Il Mulino, 1971) and also A. Macchiati, *Il finanziamento delle imprese industriali in Italia* (Bologna, Il Mulino, 1985).

[55] On the setting-up of Italian merchant banks, see M. Onado, 'Le merchant banks. Nuove forme di intermediazione per le imprese italiane', in M. Onado (ed.), *Sistema finanziario e industria* (Bologna, Il Mulino, 1986).

keep some separation in banking functions but acquired the synergies typical of a universal bank. This was aimed at encouraging the concession of credit to new businesses, and was also an attempt to bring Italy into line with the international trend away from specialization in banking, which was to be the subject of EEC legislation on banking.[56]

Another aspect which is considered to be typical of the Italian banking system is its low degree of concentration of banks, on which, however, some qualifications need to be made. It is widely accepted that the Bank of Italy, in order to avoid the formation of dominant groups in the banking sector, discouraged any kind of move which would have increased the degree of concentration of banks in the immediate post-war years. The number of banks fell slightly, from 1,378 to 1,274 between 1946 to 1966, while the number of branches increased from 7,200 to 10,200. By 1966, there were fears that the system was too fragmented, and this led to a temporary suspension of setting up new banks, which was to last, with one or two exceptions in the case of artisan and rural banks, until 1985, when the first EEC directive on banking was issued. No new bank of any importance was set up during this 20-year period, and at the end of 1988 the number of banks stood at 1,100,[57] with 15,447 branches between them. Given the significant increase between 1946 and the present day in the assets being handled and the services provided, in the face of the admittedly slow reduction in the number of banks operating in Italy, is the thesis of the low concentration of banks still a valid one?

I would like to emphasize the fact that Italian markets were territorially highly segmented, and therefore the presence of a large number of banks nationwide did not necessarily mean that there was a competitive situation throughout the country; in fact, in some areas businesses only had access to one branch of a particular bank. Policy concerning the increase in the number of branches aimed at modifying this situation during the 1970s through the granting of permission to open further branches in those areas where competition was lacking,[58] which led to protests from some local banks faced with an increase in competition in areas they had until then jealously guarded.

We can now draw a comparative picture of the international situation in order to see how Italy is placed in relation to the other major powers. Table 12.2, which reports figures for the top 500 European banks in 1988, shows that Italy is well represented, with more than double the number of British banks, more banks than France, and only fewer banks than Germany. The subdivision of the banks according to size, however, reveals that Italy is underrepresented in the top category of the largest 100 banks, and this would

[56] Cf. J. Dermine, *European Banking in the 1990s* (Oxford, Blackwell, 1990).

[57] C. Conigliani, *La concentrazione bancaria in Italia* (Bologna, Il Mulino, 1990).

[58] This policy was to lead to the installation in the South of the important banks from the Centre and North of Italy, while the opposite tendency was witnessed to a lesser extent. Cf. Banca d'Italia, *Il sistema finanziario nel Mezzogiorno* (Rome, 1990).

Table 12.2. Average size of the European banks ($ million)

	Within the 500 largest banks			Within the top 100			Between the 101st and the 300th			Between the 301st and the 500th		
	No.	Assets	Average size	No.	Assets	Average size	No.	Assets	Average size	No.	Assets	Average size
Belgium	9	273,777	30,420	4	191,880	47,970	3	66,042	22,014	2	15,855	7,927
Denmark	8	103,265	12,908	—	—	—	4	69,393	17,348	4	33,872	8,468
France	20	1,188,873	59,444	10	1,073,709	107,371	3	65,486	21,829	7	49,678	7,097
Germany	44	1,490,562	33,876	11	986,586	89,690	23	429,845	18,689	10	74,131	7,413
Italy	33	851,221	25,794	8	519,314	64,914	13	245,088	18,853	12	86,819	7,234
Netherlands	5	323,862	64,772	4	292,808	73,202	1	31,054	31,054	—	—	—
Spain	13	291,502	22,423	2	102,955	51,477	7	165,460	23,637	4	23,087	5,772
United Kingdom	15	693,060	46,204	5	557,563	111,513	5	106,228	21,246	5	29,269	5,854

Source: *The Banker*, July 1988.

Table 12.3. Banking concentration within the major industrialized countries (excluding USA). Share of deposits held by the five major banks in each country (%)

	1987
Belgium	57.8
Canada	73.2
Denmark	73.6
France	70.9[a]
Germany	22.4
Japan	24.7
Italy	29.1
Netherlands	83.3
Spain	48.6
Sweden	81.9[a]
United Kingdom	37.7

[a] 1986 figures.

Source: C. Conigliani, *La concentrazione bancaria in Italia* (Bologna, Il Mulino, 1990).

lead one to conclude that Italy has a good number of medium-sized banks, but a lot fewer larger banks than its European neighbours. However, it is also important to bear in mind the importance of the country's largest banks in relation to the size of the national financial market. Table 12.3 shows the most accurate indicator of such a relationship currently available; if we look at the levels of concentration for each country given in this table, we see that Italy is more or less on a par with Japan and Germany, and that all three have a much lower level of banking concentration than the other countries reported.[59] In relative terms, therefore, the Italian banking system cannot be considered to be 'bottom of the class', but is, on the contrary, in very good company. The similarity between Italy, Japan, and Germany would seem to be due to the existence of a considerable number of small and medium-sized businesses that are linked with small and medium-sized banks.[60]

This does not alter the fact that, according to recent studies, an increase in the size of Italian banks, and above all in the value of their branches' turnover, would probably lead to increased economies of scale,[61] as is in fact believed by the banks themselves in their rush to organize mergers and to strengthen their networks of branches. However, recent legislation in this field indicates that

[59] The USA are not included since the figures indicating national banking distribution, i.e. concentration of banks, are not wholly comparable, because bank branching has for a long while been regulated by laws that prevented national networking.

[60] Even though they have sometimes been grouped together in extremely large industrial groupings, as was mentioned above.

[61] There is a convincing analysis of banking costs in Italy in A. Landi, *Dimensioni, costi e profitti delle banche italiane* (Bologna, Il Mulino, 1990).

such operations should proceed with some caution, in that there should be time and opportunity enough to ascertain whether the banks who intend to merge are suitable or not, and also to establish whether the system as a whole can withstand such changes. The fact that the Italian banking system has until now been so profitable is not simply due to the high costs borne by its customers, but also to the fact that its roots are part and parcel of the nation's economic fabric. This in turn means that it needs to be coaxed into opening up to that inevitable internationalization which will result from the unification of European financial and monetary markets already well under way.[62]

If we turn to the reasons for the Italian population's consistently high level of savings deposited with banks, one could perhaps be the existence of these strong local ties which characterize the Italian banking system; another could be the fact that Italians have a particularly high saving propensity, or it may be that until recently there were very few alternatives to the banks.[63] Bank deposits certainly tended to diminish during the 1980s as a result of the strong competition provided by the issue of enormous amounts of government bonds, which was necessary in order to fund the public debt.[64] Thus the Italian banking system was not only very profitable, but it was also remarkably stable, and it succeeded in getting through the crisis of the 1970s very successfully, with few salvage operations, most of which involved banks whose directors had been indicted for criminal activities, such as Calvi's Banco Ambrosiano and Sindona's Banca Privata.

One last aspect of the Italian banking system that needs to be mentioned here is the involvement of the State. With the foundation of the Istituti di Diritto Pubblico (most of which are banks providing medium- and long-term credit),[65] and the inclusion of the three former mixed banks in the IRI, all the major national banks were owned by the State. If we now add the casse di risparmio, the banche popolari, and the co-operative banks to these two categories (because they are also run with non-private capital and are either non-profit making or co-operative societies), then the result is that between 70 and 80 per cent of banks' assets is under public control. This is what has produced the undercapitalization of Italian banks noted in various international comparisons. The last 10 years have seen some progress made towards the privatization of

[62] On the subject of internationalization, in 1988 Italian banks accounted for 11% of the international activity of all European banks, compared with 13% in the case of British banks, 19% in that of German banks, and 21% in that of French banks. However, the trend is an upward one.

[63] See the interesting survey of the formation of private wealth and the use to which it is put, in E. Fornero and O. Castellino (eds.), *Formazione e impiego della ricchezza delle famiglie. Confronti internazionali e analisi della situazione italiana* (Turin, Collana Giorgio Rota, 1990).

[64] On the effects of the public debt on family savings and bank deposits, see T. Jappelli (ed.), *Bilancio pubblico e risparmio privato* (Milan, Angeli, 1991).

[65] For a list of Italian banks, subdivided according to their legal definition and historical background, see R. Camaiti, *Le istituzioni creditizie italiane. Linee evolutive e strutturali* (Bologna, Ed. Libreria Minerva, 1979), which also includes an extensive bibliography.

the Italian banking system, and the transformation of the public banks into joint-stock companies[66] as the first step towards privatization. However, there is a lot of opposition from certain political quarters, as the Italian political parties are accustomed to having their own men nominated as presidents and directors of the various publicly owned banks. As a consequence, the true privatization of the Italian banking system is still far from having been accomplished.

6. THE INTERNATIONALIZATION OF THE ECONOMY

As we have seen in Chapter 11, there had already been a considerable growth in Italian exports during the reconstruction period and in the 1950s. There was a change in the overall composition of exports during these years, with an increased emphasis on manufactured products (60 per cent of total exports in 1938, but 75 per cent in 1948, 83.5 per cent in 1953, and 90 per cent in 1963), and within this category there was an increase in the percentage of engineering products (11.7 per cent of total exports in 1938, 28.5 per cent in 1948, and 39.4 per cent in 1963) and of chemical products (5.3 per cent in 1938, 8.2 per cent in 1948, and 14.3 per cent in 1963). Customs duties were gradually lowered during the course of the 1950s and 1960s, and brought into line with those of other EEC countries, and Italy very quickly opened up to foreign trade: in 1950, the degree of opening was equal to 11 per cent, but this had reached 14 per cent by 1950, 18 per cent by 1970, and stood at 28 per cent in 1980,[67] a level at which it has since settled, save for the occasional small fluctuation.

The rapid growth in exports, which saw Italy win an increasingly large share of the international market until the end of the 1970s (see Table 12.4),[68] led some economists to talk of export-led growth. This thesis was advanced by Stern[69] and Graziani[70] during the second half of the 1960s, but it was subsequently qualified and limited to the period 1959–63,[71] which were the years immediately after the birth of the EEC. It should be said that the foreign

[66] Cf. F. Merusi, *Trasformazioni della banca pubblica* (Bologna, Il Mulino, 1985).

[67] For an analysis of Italian trade at the end of the 1970s, see P. Alessandrini and G. Conti, *Commercio estero e allargamento della CEE. Prospettive per l'industria italiana* (Bologna, Il Mulino, 1981).

[68] In the period between 1958 and 1978, the trend of Italian exports was second only to that of Japan and Spain. Cf. D. Ciravegna, *Cicli e tendenze del commercio estero dell'Italia (1952–1978)* (Bologna, Il Mulino, 1982), 11.

[69] R. M. Stern, *Il commercio estero italiano e la sua influenza sullo sviluppo economico nazionale* (Milan, Etas Libri, 1968).

[70] A. Graziani, *Lo sviluppo dell'economia italiana come sviluppo di un'economia aperta* (Turin, Agnelli Foundation, 1969), and A. Graziani et al., *Lo sviluppo di un'economia aperta* (Naples, ESI, 1969).

[71] P. Ciocca, R. Filosa, and G. M. Rey, 'Integrazione e sviluppo dell'economia italiana nell'ultimo ventennio: un riesame critico', *Contributi alla ricerca economica* (Rome, Banca d'Italia, 1973).

Table 12.4. Percentage share of world exports of selected countries, 1951–1987 (at current prices)

	1951	1960	1970	1982	1987
USA	20.3	18.9	14.8	12.2	10.5
Japan	1.9	3.8	6.7	8.2	9.9
Germany	5.4	12.2	11.9	10.4	12.7
France	3.7	5.7	6.2	5.5	6.2
Great Britain	8.8	8.4	6.7	5.7	5.7
Italy	2.2	3.4	4.6	4.4	5.0

Source: GATT, *International Trade Statistics*, various years.

market never became more important than the domestic one, and investment was extremely lively even in sectors where exports were neither particularly important nor on the increase. However, the fact remains that the real novelty of this period was provided by the prospect of an increasingly wider opening-up of foreign markets, thanks largely to both the GATT negotiations and the foundation of the EEC. These developments stood in stark contrast to the previous decades of economic difficulty and the narrowing of international markets, which were considered in Chapters 7–10. In order to find another period favourable to international trade, we would need to go back to the years before the First World War.

The Italian economy's specialization within the context of world trade was already clearly visible at the end of the 1960s, and it was to be reinforced during the years that followed. There are some very sophisticated analyses available of the international specializations of various countries, and I have reported one of these—a comparative analysis of the USA, Japan, the EEC, and Italy with reference to the years 1970 and 1987—in Table 12.5. The index used in making this comparison measures the relative contribution made by each productive sector to the overall balance of trade of each country or area. If the sector contributes either positively or negatively to the balance of trade in direct proportion to its relative weight in that country's foreign trade, then the value of the index is zero. Thus positive (or negative) values of the index are an indication of sectors whose contribution to the balance of trade is disproportionately positive (or negative), hence revealing comparative advantages (or disadvantages) and strong (or weak) points of that country's specialization.[72]

[72] The formula for the working out of the index is as follows:

$$I_i = \frac{(X_i - M_i)}{(X - M)/2} \times 100 - \frac{(X - M)}{(X + M)/2} \times \frac{(X_i \times M_i)}{(X + M)} \times 100$$

where X_i = total exports of country j of the group of products i, M_i = total imports of country j of the group of products i, X = total exports of country j, M = total imports of country j.

Table 12.5. Evolution in the international specialization of advanced countries, 1970 and 1987

	USA		Japan		EEC		Italy	
	1970	1987	1970	1987	1970	1987	1970	1987
Agricultural food products	−2.04	−0.45	−2.17	−5.68	−1.71	−1.24	2.15	−0.13
Agricultural products for food industry	7.26	3.82	−7.32	−3.53	−2.98	−1.08	−7.25	−3.74
Agricultural raw materials	1.61	1.92	−15.34	−6.55	−2.50	−0.61	−4.83	−2.72
Energy raw materials	−1.52	−5.91	−16.74	−20.71	−7.68	−4.80	−13.22	−9.80
Other raw materials	−1.71	0.17	−13.25	−3.86	−2.40	−0.90	−1.68	−0.88
Food industry	−2.84	0.91	−2.59	−4.83	−2.10	−0.14	−5.30	−4.27
Alcoholic and non-alcoholic drinks	−1.76	−0.71	−0.18	−0.50	0.56	0.53	0.82	0.58
Refined tobacco	0.40	0.86	−0.04	−0.33	0.12	0.10	−0.13	−0.48
Textiles, clothing, leather, shoes	−5.69	−6.37	9.52	−3.24	2.11	−1.32	14.21	13.64
Wood, furniture, paper, and printing	−3.01	−0.89	−0.63	−3.16	−2.94	−1.91	−1.25	0.85
Chemicals, pharmaceutical, and rubber	4.94	5.28	4.44	−0.94	3.52	2.87	0.75	−2.14
Oil products	−1.95	−1.12	−3.94	−4.81	0.75	−0.74	4.27	−1.95
Ceramics, glass, and building materials	−0.37	−0.63	1.54	0.32	0.59	0.44	1.67	2.61
Basic metals	−2.97	−2.05	7.41	0.02	−1.20	0.43	−10.11	−1.86
Metal products	−0.04	−0.58	3.06	0.90	1.30	0.70	1.89	2.90

Farm and industrial machinery	4.50	0.85	0.87	5.03	4.06	2.57	5.31	5.83
Electrical engineering and components	4.50	1.16	2.80	3.48	1.83	1.50	2.75	3.68
Office machinery and computers	2.67	2.96	−0.01	6.21	−0.18	−0.90	1.32	−1.15
Telephones and electrical components	−1.04	−1.73	9.31	12.92	0.71	−0.71	0.43	−1.78
Electrical appliances	0.94	−0.04	2.98	4.50	1.46	0.66	2.54	1.59
Cars and engines	−5.83	−8.22	10.07	24.37	5.82	2.59	5.17	−1.33
Ships, trains, and aeroplanes	6.85	6.55	5.74	0.47	0.53	0.77	−0.31	0.25
Optics and precision instruments	1.30	1.82	2.38	1.90	0.42	0.14	−0.35	−1.09
Other manufactured goods	−3.64	1.34	1.62	−1.88	0.41	0.47	2.16	1.97
Residual items	−0.56	1.07	0.46	−0.08	−0.54	0.55	−1.00	−0.58

Source: P. Guerrieri and C. Milana, *L'Italia e il commercio mondiale* (Bologna, Il Mulino, 1990), Tables 2.3, 2.14, 2.18, 3.3.

The table shows, for example, that the USA lost some ground in the engineering sector between 1970 and 1987, but gained some in the chemical and aircraft-building sectors; Japan consolidated its advantage in the electronics and automobile sectors, and gained an advantage in machinery manufacturing; the EEC failed to display any consistent advantage in any of the sectors, but its disadvantages were also relatively small.[73]

As far as Italy is concerned, the most consistent advantage can be seen in the textile, clothing, leather goods, shoe-manufacturing sector, followed by the machinery sector; furthermore, none of the disadvantages appears particularly serious, with the exception of that of raw materials for the generation of energy. There is a sharp decline in the position of only one sector, that of the automobile industry. If we look at another classification, that of Pavitt,[74] we can say that Italy is deficient in the science-based industries and in the scale-intensive ones, but it is highly specialized in the supplier-dominated or traditional industries, where the design, quality, and price of the product count, that is, in textiles, clothing, furniture, leather goods and shoes, and ceramics, and in the specialized-suppliers' sectors, with a high level of diversification and economies of scope (machine-tools and industrial machinery). In both cases, competitive companies are generally fairly small, artisan traditions are clearly evident, innovation is of an incremental type, but productive processes are usually very advanced.

This type of specialization certainly does not put Italy into the group of the most competitive nations, as it has never been capable of creating technologically advanced goods. Italy has therefore never had a very large positive balance of trade. This is also due to the fact that it has always been totally lacking in raw materials, and has consistently had an agricultural products deficit. However, the external constraint has never been such as to prevent Italian growth.[75] Its deficits have always been of manageable proportions, even in recent years, as can be seen from a glance at Table 12.6.[76]

Another reason for Italy's relatively weak international position has been the limited presence of Italian companies abroad. The small size of Italian companies, together with the country's productive specialization, have hardly favoured foreign investment, which in 1986 stood at only a little more than 2 per cent of the world total of foreign investment (compared with Germany's

[73] For further details, cf. P. Guerrieri and C. Milana, *L'Italia e il commercio mondiale. Mutamenti e tendenze nella divisione internazionale del lavoro* (Bologna, Il Mulino, 1990).

[74] K. Pavitt, 'Sectoral Patterns of Technical Change: Towards a Taxonomy and a Theory', *Research Policy*, 14 (1984).

[75] G. Conti, 'L'integrazione internazionale dell'economia italiana: opportunità e vincoli', in A. Graziani (ed.), *Il dollaro e l'economia italiana* (Bologna, Il Mulino, 1987). The author maintains, however, that this constraint is going to get stronger in the future, partly as a result of foreign competition.

[76] For a more sophisticated analysis of Italy's international specialization, see F. Onida (ed.), *Specializzazione e integrazione internazionale dell'industria italiana* (Milan, Angeli, 1989).

Table 12.6. Current balance as a percentage of GDP in leading industrial countries

	1983	1984	1985	1986	1987	1988	1989
USA	−1.2	−2.6	−3.0	−3.4	−3.6	−2.6	−2.1
Japan	1.8	2.8	3.6	4.3	3.6	2.7	2.0
Germany	0.8	1.6	2.6	4.4	4.1	4.2	4.6
France	−0.8	−0.2	−0.1	0.3	−0.5	−0.4	−0.4
United Kingdom	1.2	0.6	0.8	—	−1.0	−3.2	−3.8
Italy	0.4	−0.6	−0.8	0.4	−0.1	−0.7	−1.2

Source: IMF, *Balance of Payments Statistics*, various years.

4 per cent, Japan's 8 per cent, Great Britain's 10 per cent, and the USA's 30 per cent).[77] Furthermore, Italy's foreign investment has been of a different nature compared with that of other countries. According to Acocella and Schiattarella, 'we can . . . say that the multi-nationalization of Italian industry always seems to be connected to the labour skills factor, and not to any particular innovative capabilities in the strictly technological sense'.[78] Moreover, Italian foreign investment usually involves some form of joint venture, both in the case of those developing countries that wish to adapt tried-and-tested technology to local needs, and in the case of advanced countries, where Italian companies are interested in studying and reproducing the advanced technology of others. Italian industry is very active in buying up foreign companies, but such operations are often of a limited size and therefore have a limited overall weight.

7. THE SOUTHERN CHALLENGE

As we saw in the previous chapters, the gap between the South and the North of Italy has continued to grow since unification. Few readers of Italian literature will ever forget the descriptions of the malaria-infested countryside of Basilicata, in Levi's *Cristo si é fermato a Eboli*, or the dreary existence of the peasants in the Abruzzi, depicted in Silone's novel *Fontamara.*[79] In Chapter 11 we mentioned the post-war period, during which the Giolittian tradition of 'special intervention' in favour of the South was revitalized, with the creation of the Cassa per il Mezzogiorno (Casmez). The Casmez was not the only form of government intervention, however. This period also witnessed the introduction

[77] Cf. N. Acocella (ed.), *Le multinazionali italiane* (Bologna, Il Mulino, 1985).

[78] N. Acocella and R. Schiattarella, 'Vantaggio di proprietà e imprese multinazionali: il caso italiano', in Onida (ed.), *Specializzazione e integrazione*, 407.

[79] Cf. C. Levi, *Cristo si é fermato a Eboli* (Turin, Einaudi, 1946); I. Silone, *Fontamara* (Milan, Mondadori, 1949).

of welfare provisions, public works programmes, and from the 1960s onwards, a massive investment programme on the part of public enterprises, as we have already mentioned. All these forms of intervention have been criticized for one reason or another, and we shall be shortly looking at their undoubted limitations. However, as one of the most fervent experts on the 'southern question' has recently remarked, 'the fact that the economy of the South has kept up with that of the North during the period in which the latter has experienced its greatest expansion ever, has to be considered an extremely important result: a result that would never have been possible without the extraordinary intervention of the State.'[80]

In fact, the indices available show that the gap between GDP per capita in the South and that in other parts of the country has been reduced slightly in the last 40 years. The GDP per capita in the South, which was equal to 56 per cent of that in the Centre and North in the period 1951–5, had risen to 62 per cent of the latter in the period 1971–5, only to fall to 58 per cent in 1986–8.[81] The rate of growth of employment in industry was also slightly higher in the South than in the North during the period 1951–81.[82]

While the combined effects of emigration (important until the end of the 1960s),[83] extraordinary government intervention, and the international expansionary trend were to keep the South of Italy in line with changes taking place throughout the country and the rest of Europe, the fact remains that more could have been achieved, and a particularly disappointing aspect of this is that the self-propelling form of economic growth, which has been so evident in the North-East and Centre areas during recent years, never managed to get off the ground in the South. Admittedly the gap between the NEC area and the industrial triangle has always been smaller than that between the latter and the South; nevertheless, some parts of the NEC have managed to do much more than bridge that gap.

[80] S. Cafiero, *Tradizione e attualità del Meridionalismo* (Bologna, Il Mulino, 1989), 110.

[81] P. Saraceno, 'Si é iniziata l'industrializzazione del Mezzogiorno?', *Rivista economica del mezzogiorno*, 3 (1989), 650. Note that there is a smaller difference between the Centre and North and the South when it comes to disposable income, as a result of strong transfers made by the State in the South. For up-to-date figures, cf. E. Wolleb and G. Wolleb, *Divari regionali e dualismo economico* (Bologna, Il Mulino, 1991), and E. Wolleb, 'I paesi del Sud Europa: un'analisi comparata', *Rivista economica del mezzogiorno*, 4 (1990). Taking the European GDP per capita average (of the 12 EEC countries) to be 100, then Italy stands at 104.8, the South of Italy at 72.3, the Centre and North at 123.3, Spain at 75.7, Greece and Portugal at 54.5, Germany (before unification) at 113, and France at 108.5.

[82] L. Bruni, 'L'industrializzazione del Mezzogiorno: tendenze di lungo periodo', *Rivista economica del mezzogiorno*, 2 (1988) and 3 (1989). Also see F. Silva and G. Viesti, 'Problemi dell'industrializzazione del Mezzogiorno', in G. Fuà (ed.), *Orientamenti per la politica del territorio* (Bologna, Il Mulino, 1991).

[83] Net emigration (taking into account those emigrants coming back to Italy) between 1942 and 1971 was of the order of 2.5 million persons: those who left the country between 1951 and 1970 numbered 5.6 million, of whom 62.3% from the South. About 2.5 million southerners changed their region of residence during the period between 1951 and 1972. Cf. R. Volpi, *Storia della popolazione italiana dall'unità ad oggi* (Florence, La Nuova Italia, 1989).

Who and what can be held responsible for this disappointing missed opportunity? I do not believe that there can be one answer to such a question. First of all, let us examine the question of extraordinary intervention to see where its weak points lie. The first 5 years of the Casmez's existence saw a largely agricultural programme of intervention, accounting for 77 per cent of total funds made available, with other funds being used in the building of infrastructures in the South. The second five-year period marked the beginning of a programme of industrialization, which saw the designation of special areas for industrial growth, and the use of two main instruments which were to form the basis of this intervention: the concession of financial incentives and investment on the part of nationalized industry. A vast amount has been said and written about the forms that such financial incentives should take; however, the main aim has always been that of drastically reducing the cost of investing in the South. Basically, the critics have always held that such a policy has led to the building of capital-intensive plants in the South (the so-called 'cathedrals in the desert'), and that it has also encouraged unprofitable investment projects, or projects of dubious profitability, such as the SIR and Liquichimica chemical plants in Calabria and Sardinia.

As for the investment by public enterprises in the South, this continued at a significant level until the 1973 oil crisis, but even this has been criticized for having been insufficient and badly mismanaged. It has only been reinterpreted in a more generous fashion just recently. Di Maio and Fausto write:

> In our view, this intervention [of public enterprises in the South] has had a significant impact on economic life in this area. We do not agree, therefore, with the negative views, often very vague, simplistic and contradictory, that have been expressed concerning the operations of public enterprises in the South . . . If we evaluate this intervention in terms of employment, then the results have admittedly been somewhat limited. Nevertheless, one has to bear in mind that this policy has been deliberately aimed at investment in basic production and infrastructures.[84]

In the period between 1957–9 and 1970–4, 57 per cent of investment made by public enterprises went into the steel, chemical, and oil industries, while 25 per cent was invested in the construction of motorways and telephone lines, and the rest, amounting to 18 per cent, on the remaining sectors, of which the most important was engineering, with the creation of Alfa-Sud.

The fact is that the industrialization of the South was the work of companies, both state-owned and private, particularly Fiat and Montedison, who came from outside that area of Italy. Del Monte and Giannola comment as follows on this:

> a very strange form of industrial revolution has happened in the South during the past few years. It has no roots in any form of existing social milieu, but on the contrary, has

[84] A. Di Maio and D. Fausto, 'Il ruolo delle imprese pubbliche nello sviluppo del Mezzogiorno', in ASSI, *Piccola e grande impresa: un problema storico* (Milan, Angeli, 1987), 245–6.

been imported from outside. Instead of acting as a catalyst to the long-awaited-for spread effects of industrialization, it coincides with the crisis of local industry and business. Self-propelling industrial development having failed, the emphasis was placed upon the role of oligopolistic groups and, above all, on that of public enterprises.[85]

Further funds were given to the Casmez in 1971, and above all in 1976, with the aim of rectifying this situation of capital-intensive development, and more incentives were provided for medium-sized and smaller companies;[86] social security contributions were made tax-deductible, and there was an attempt to rationalize the credit they received from various southern banks and financial institutes.[87]

However, the Casmez's public image had been tarnished for ever, and despite it being conceded a reprieve every year for four years from 1980 onwards, it was finally closed down in August 1984. At the beginning of 1986, its place was taken by another southern development agency, the Agenzia per la Promozione dello Sviluppo del Mezzogiorno (until 1993), which differs from the Casmez in that it works on the basis of three-year plans (an approach that had already been put into practice by the Casmez in 1983), it arranges the contracting-out of parts of the programmed operations to private companies along French lines, and it involves local authorities from the South.[88] This involvement, which different groups had pushed for, has shown itself to be a double-edged weapon. In fact, local authorities in the South have been seen to be extremely ill-prepared from the point of view of planning and putting plans into operation.[89] The incapability of complying with some of the obligations concerning projects financed by the EEC aimed at regional development is

[85] A. Del Monte and A. Giannola, *Il Mezzogiorno nell'economia italiana* (Bologna, Il Mulino, 1978), 257. For details of the local multiplier effects of a large company, see M. Florio, 'Interazioni tra grandi e piccole imprese nello sviluppo locale: una riconsiderazione e alcune implicazioni per le politiche pubbliche', *L'Industria*, 3 (1991).

[86] Cf. M. D'Antonio, *Struttura economica, stabilità e sviluppo del Mezzogiorno* (Naples, Liguori, 1979).

[87] Some scholars have identified a recent expansion of small and medium-sized businesses in the South, and in particular along the Adriatic coast. Cf. G. Lizzeri (ed.), *Mezzogiorno possibile: dati per un altro sviluppo* (Milan, Angeli, 1983); A. Salghetti (ed.), *Potenziali di sviluppo nel Mezzogiorno d'Italia* (Padua, Marsilio, 1985); M. D'Antonio (ed.), *Il Mezzogiorno negli anni '80: dallo sviluppo imitativo allo sviluppo autocentrato* (Milan, Angeli, 1985). The question is still a debatable one, however. See also A. Giannola, *Industria manifatturiera e imprenditori nel Mezzogiorno* (Naples, Guida, 1986), and P. Sylos Labini, 'L'evoluzione del Mezzogiorno negli ultimi trent'anni', *Studi SVIMEZ*, 38 (1985).

[88] Cf. F. Silva and G. Viesti (eds.), *Il difficile sviluppo dell'industria nel Mezzogiorno* (Milan, Angeli, 1989).

[89] A recent study concludes: 'the negative experience of law no. 64 leads one to believe that it is unlikely that local authorities will be called to intervene, as this would be of little or no use. In fact, local administrative structures in the South are generally characterized by a degree of inefficiency which is even greater than that generally associated with the central administrative apparatus of our country' (G. Bodo and P. Sestito, *Le vie dello sviluppo. Dall'analisi del dualismo territoriale una proposta per il Mezzogiorno* (Bologna, Il Mulino, 1991), 241).

more than proof of this worrying aspect of southern local authority behaviour.[90]

We can conclude that the most successful years of extraordinary state intervention in the South correspond to those years in which the South was most successful in bridging the gap separating it from the Centre and North. It is true that these were also the years of mass emigration from the South, and of rapid growth of the Italian economy as a whole. However, southern industry continued to remain weak, not only in relation to the process of European integration—not more than 10 per cent of total Italian exports come from the South[91]—but also in relation to industry in the Centre and North itself. This would seem to be further justification for concluding that 'special aid is still necessary', as one famous southern expert has recently written,[92] although this intervention has to be organized in a different manner.[93]

While the type of extraordinary intervention was partly responsible for the lack of establishment of any self-propelled form of economic development, I think that two other factors were also responsible, and as such need to be examined here. The first is emigration, and the second concerns the social conditions in the South. As those scholars who analysed emigration at the beginning of the century pointed out,[94] emigrants are generally young people, mostly male, and are the ones enterprising and willing to try something new. The result is that these waves of emigration impoverish society, depriving it of some of its most dynamic elements, and changing the sexual composition and age of that society. I can personally testify that a good proportion of the best students I have taught so far at universities in the Centre and North of Italy were from the South; their career prospects in their regions of origin were not sufficiently interesting for them to consider returning to the South after having completed their studies, in the presence of highly attractive job offers in the Centre and North. If the other conditions in the South were more favourable, then I believe that it would be the less attractive job markets of the North in the last few years which could paradoxically enable the South to hold on to its best young people, who would thus be able to fill qualified jobs locally.

However, many believe that even this opportunity will go by the board unless civil society—the social and political environment which exists in the South—changes radically. I am, of course, referring to organized criminal activity,

[90] Cf. F. Moro, 'Gli incentivi finanziari regionali nella Comunità europea: aspetti amministrativi', *Rivista economica del mezzogiorno*, 4 (1990), and C. Buresti and G. E. Marciani, 'L'esperienza dei programmi integrati mediterranei', *Rivista economica del mezzogiorno*, 5 (1991).

[91] See F. Caracciolo (ed.), *Mezzogiorno e Italia nell'Europa del 1992* (Milan, Angeli, 1991), and M. D'Antonio, *Il Mezzogiorno nella struttura dell'economia italiana* (Milan, Angeli, 1990).

[92] N. Novacco, 'L'intervento "speciale" é ancora necessario', *Rivista economica del mezzogiorno*, 3 (1989); also see the interesting article written by D. Fausto, 'Etica, politica ed economia nella questione meridionale', *Mezzogiorno d'Europa*, 8 (1988).

[93] A clear and concise picture of the characteristics that such intervention must have can be found in A. Graziani, 'Mezzogiorno oggi', *Meridiana*, 1 (1987).

[94] See e.g. F. Coletti, 'Dell'emigrazione italiana', in Accademia dei Lincei (ed.), *Cinquant'anni di storia italiana*, iii (Milan, Hoepli, 1911).

which is very powerful in Sicily and Calabria, but also widespread in Campania and, more recently, in Apulia. Criminal organizations condition negatively the profitability of businesses, with the practice of systematically imposing 'protection money', form an obstacle to free political, cultural, and economic life, render daily activities even more frustrating in terms of waste in time and energy, and, above all, corrupt the young. From the moment that such criminal organizations discovered the drugs gold-mine, many youngsters have been attracted by the promise of easy money in exchange for the criminal services rendered, and they thus learn the lessons of abuse and violence.

Adam Smith believed that 'little else is required to carry a state to the highest degree of opulence from the lowest barbarism, but peace, easy taxes and a tolerable administration of justice'.[95] While it has been observed that Adam Smith was over-simplifying the problem, and that a modern State's task is much more complex, nobody has ever proved that the elements cited by Smith are not indispensable. Peace guarantees accumulation of wealth, fair taxes ensure that there is a continuing incentive to invent new things and work hard, and an 'acceptable' administration of justice means that individual rights are not abused, or only in exceptional circumstances. When, by contrast, citizens' rights are continually abused, for example in the case of those criminal organizations that choose to challenge the State and terrorize ordinary people, then the motivation to start up business activity is severely diminished, and those who are already involved in some form of business activity can do no more than attempt to survive. Only the very large corporations are in a position to limit the blackmail threats of the criminals. Small local businesses can never hope to prosper in an environment of this kind.[96]

The problem of the South has, for these reasons, become even more complicated than before. It is no longer simply a question of economic intervention, as it is no longer one undifferentiated problem. Those areas of the South that lie along the Adriatic coast, and in particular the Abruzzi and Molise, and where organized crime either does not exist or is relatively small in scale, have progressed enormously in recent times. In the other areas, the industry that has grown the most has been the so-called 'illegal industry', and this has extended its branches in the North and even abroad in recent years. While the old southern agrarian politics has had its place taken in the post-war

[95] Quoted from J. A. Hall, *States in History* (Oxford, Blackwell, 1986), 154.

[96] The most interesting recent studies on the mafia are the following: P. Arlacchi, *La mafia imprenditrice. L'etica mafiosa e lo spirito del capitalismo* (Bologna, Il Mulino, 1983); N. Dalla Chiesa, *Il giano bifronte* (Milan, Etas Libri, 1987); R. Catanzaro, *Il delitto come impresa. Storia sociale della mafia* (Padua, Liviana ed., 1988); S. Lodato, *Dieci anni di mafia* (Milan, Rizzoli, 1990). Also see *Meridiana*, 7–8 (1990), which are dedicated to the question of the mafia, P. Pezzino, *Una certa reciprocità di favori. Mafia e modernizzazione violenta nella Sicilia post-unitaria* (Milan, Angeli, 1990); C. Fava, *La mafia comanda a Catania, 1960–1991* (Turin, Einaudi, 1991); N. Tranfaglia, *Mafia, politica e affari, 1943–1991* (Bari, Laterza, 1992).

years by a new form of southern politics, based on industrial development, perhaps the time has come to switch to a third form, based on civil rights.

8. SOCIETY, CONSUMPTION, AND LIVING STANDARDS

The population of Italy has grown from 47 million (in 1951) to the present figure of little more than 57 million, with a strong tendency to even out during recent years as a result of the drastic drop in the birth-rate. Average life expectancy has increased from 63 to 71 years for males, and from 67 to more than 78 years for females. Employment and production has moved towards the service sector,[97] where more than 60 per cent of income is earned. A new industrial and professional bourgeoisie has established itself, while the ranks of the middle classes have swollen in numbers.[98] Nevertheless, one-seventh of the Italian population lives below the poverty line as defined in modern terms, that is, their annual income is less than half the national average.[99] While income distribution in Italy is certainly not ideal, it is, however, slightly less unequal than in the other advanced countries of Europe.[100]

Educational levels have risen: the percentage of the population with a middle-school certificate increased from 6 to 24 per cent between 1951 and 1981, those with a high-school certificate increased from 3 to 11 per cent, and those with a degree increased from 1 to 3 per cent. School attendance levels also rose dramatically: in the period between 1951 and 1986, the percentage of children aged between 11 and 13 attending lower middle school increased from 30 to more than 100 per cent; those 14–18-year-olds going to high school went up from 11 to 59 per cent; attendance at higher educational establishments (19–23-year-olds) increased from 3.5 to 17.2 per cent (excluding those students who had to repeat one or more years). Illiteracy had dropped to only 3 per cent of the population above the age of 6 by 1981.

How has the population's lifestyle changed? Table 12.7 gives some indication of the differences between life in 1951 and in 1987. While real per capita income increased by a factor of 4.4 during this period of time, some forms of consumption increased disproportionately, whereas others were left behind. Among the latter we can see that the number of rooms in the average house did not even double during this period, the number of hospital beds per head of

[97] Many services are complementary to industry, as has been shown in F. Momigliano and D. Siniscalco, *Mutamento nella struttura del sistema produttivo e integrazione fra industria e terziario* (Bologna, Il Mulino, 1976).

[98] See P. Sylos Labini, *Le classi sociali negli anni ottanta* (Bari, Laterza, 1986), and L. Gallino, *Della ingovernabilità: La società italiana tra premoderno e neo-industriale* (Milan, 1987).

[99] G. Sarpellon, *Secondo rapporto sulla povertà in Italia* (Milan, Angeli, 1992). 26% of the population lives below the poverty line in the South, compared with only 9% in the Centre and North.

[100] In the mid-1980s, Gini's coefficient of concentration of disposable income was equal to 0.399 for France, 0.338 for Great Britain, 0.352 for West Germany, and 0.301 for Italy. See G. Wolleb (ed.), *La distribuzione dei redditi familiari in Europa* (Bologna, Il Mulino, 1991), Table 1.4.

Table 12.7. Changes in living standards and lifestyles between 1951 and 1987

	1951	1987	1987/1951
Income per capita (1987 lire)	3,835,227	16,875,000	4.4
No. of rooms per 100 inhabitants	73.8	127.4	1.7
Energy consumption per capita (kWh)183	858	4.6	
Cars per 100 inhabitants	0.9	42.4	47.1
Bank branches per 100,000 inhabitants	16.5	26.8	1.6
Telephones per 100 inhabitants	2.9	40.1	16.9
Airplane passengers boarded	223,000	18,691,000	83.8
Mortality rate during the first year of life per 1,000 born	66.6	9.5	0.1
Hospital beds per 1,000 inhab.	8	7.3	0.9
Doctors and nurses per 10,000 inhab.	16.4	56.9	3.5
Classrooms per 1,000 inhab. 6–18 years	25.3	42.2	1.7
Secondary schools pupils per 100 inhab. 14–18 years	10.6	60.2	5.7
University students per 10,000 inhab.	46	190	4.1
TV licences per 100 inhab.	7.8	25.6	3.3
Spending on entertainment per capita (1987 lire)	29.4	44.8	1.5

Source: S. Gattei, 'Evoluzione del divario Nord–Sud nelle condizioni civili e sociali nel periodo 1951–87', *Rivista economica del Mezzogiorno*, 3 (1989).

population actually diminished, and entertainment expenditure per capita only increased very slightly, but consumption of cars, telephones, and televisions increased dramatically.

It is interesting to point out that the gap between the North and the South in terms of consumption and living standards is generally narrower than the gap in terms of per capita production as a result of the redistribution of income through public spending. Table 12.8 offers an interesting attempt to measure the standard of living in the various Italian regions on the basis of 43 different indicators; these measure standards of health and hygiene, living conditions, education, availability of services and infrastructures, information and cultural services, as well as environmental and social problems. If we calculate the average of all 43 indicators, then we see that the level of the standard of living in the South is 70 per cent of that in the Centre and North, whereas per capita income in the South is less than 60 per cent of that in the Centre and North. However, certain indicators given in the table—such as the murder rate, or the level of unemployment, or the number of newspapers read—are particularly

Table 12.8. Selected indicators of living standards in the different areas of the country, about 1989

	Unemployment rate	Households with a bathroom (%)	Branches of banks for every 10,000 inhab.	Newspapers sold per 100 inhab. > 14 years	Murders per 100,000 inhab.	General index of the quality of life (Italy = 100)	GDP per capita (Italy = 100)
North-West	5.4	88	32	14.4	0.9	110	126
North-East	4.8	92	37	14.8	0.7	119	117
Centre	9.9	92	29	12.6	1.3	108	111
South	19.7	77	18	6.1	6.1	82	67
Italy	11	86	27	11.3	2.9	100	100

Source: S. Gattei, 'Qualitá'della vita nelle regioni meridionali e divario rispetto al Centro–Nord', *Rivista economica del mezzogiorno*, 5 (1991).

significant, in that they make clear the relative social and civil backwardness of certain areas of the South.

Thus Italian society suffers from the presence of a great number of imbalances, together with new forms of poverty, as well as from a series of unnecessary political and social conflicts that prevent it from functioning as it could.[101] It has problems of an irrational and stubbornly ill-organized bureaucracy, of unscrupulous political practices, and it continues to suffer from the problems of a country with very limited natural resources and not widespread enough popular education, while sharing with all advanced countries the worrying problem of continuously keeping positive life-values going in society. There is, as always, enormous room for improvement: the results seen so far are just an indication of what widespread commitment could achieve.

[101] G. Sapelli writes: 'Contradictions are nowadays openly flaunted: the most obvious example is the way the conflict has taken on an added dimension, with the user taken hostage in the service sector', *L'Italia inafferabile. Conflitti, sviluppo, dissociazione dagli anni cinquanta ad oggi* (Venice, Marsilio, 1989), 133.

Conclusion: From the Periphery to the Centre?

GENERALLY speaking, Italian economic development has not been seen in a very good light. It has been considered to be incomplete and anomalous, and more often than not has been ignored in international comparisons of economic growth. Apart from the difficulty represented by the language, there are a number of other reasons which help to explain why this has been so. First, there is a theoretical reason. As long as the English model of industrialization continued to be taken as a standard, Italy appeared to be the foolish imitator, as Italian economic development proved incapable of following the English pattern. This helps to explain why Gerschenkron dedicated so much energy to the Italian case after he had decided to put forward his 'imitation-with-variation' interpretative approach. However, Gerschenkron ended up by overemphasizing the importance of the take-off period of economic development, which prevented him from looking at Italian industrialization and that of other countries over a longer period of time. In my view, this is a powerful reason that has prevented scholars from really understanding the Italian case.

In fact, as we have seen, the take-off of the Italian economy at the turn of the century was far from overwhelming: it was limited, territorially speaking, and incomplete, although it has to be said that it was not as unsatisfactory as Gerschenkron would have us believe; his index of industrial production represented a pioneering foray into unchartered waters, and was later modified for the better. Subsequently, however, Italy managed to keep its head above water, even during the extremely difficult inter-war years when all European countries were going through serious periods of crisis, and the two world wars proved even to be advantageous for the Italian industrial base. One has to admit that the Italian economy drew some benefits from Fascism too, which gave priority to national industry, propping it up in a number of ways, this being epitomized by the enormous salvage operation which led to the foundation of IMI and IRI. (As I have repeatedly underlined, this operation represented a continuity with an Italian tradition of financial operations of this kind.) Above all, however, Italy succeeded in reorganizing itself along different political lines after the Second World War, and the post-war governments insisted on industry playing the role of the driving force of the entire Italian economy.

Processes of economic growth, therefore, need to be judged over a sufficiently long period of time: twenty or forty years are not sufficient to be able to come up with a reliable model of the development of a country. I think a century, or even a century and a half, are more suitable time-spans over which to measure growth, and the case-study of each country should be based on such a time-span, beginning from the initial phases, bearing in mind that the growth of one country is not necessarily synchronized with that of other countries. History has taught us that it is not only the initial stage of the economic development of a nation that is out of step with similar developmental stages of other nations. Later development is also different, due to the Gerschenkronian substitutive factors, to the Pollardian differentials of contemporaneousness, and to the various technological eras spanned, as well as to the diverse local historical traditions existing in each geographical area prior to industrialization. History has also taught us that the mechanism whereby an economic growth process automatically regenerates itself, that is, becomes self-propelling, is not enough to guarantee a trouble-free future. The developmental process follows a wavelike path, and each period consists of new challenges, which in turn require fresh commitment and fresh imagination. It can happen that the same factors which contribute to a country's leading position during one phase of development can slow that same country down during another phase and vice versa. One needs to utilize the 'right' factors at the 'right' time, and to change direction when they prove to be no longer of use.

The emphasis in this book has been on continuity between one wave and another rather than discontinuity—both on the home front and internationally. The reason for this is that I believe that the fundamental feature of all processes of economic expansion is the ability to accumulate capital, both of a physical and human variety, and to utilize this capital in response to the new challenges thrown up by each historical period. Sometimes this accumulation process has its roots way back in history; for example, Italian industrial districts such as Prato are of medieval origin, and they have only recently been revitalized after having lain dormant for centuries; or the 'forced' building-up of heavy industry between the First and the Second World Wars allowed that industry, converted with some difficulty, to become part of the foundations of the so-called 'economic miracle'. Those countries that either fail to accumulate capital, or delude themselves into thinking that it is better to 'start all over again', wiping the accumulation slate clean, cannot hope to go very far.

Of course, accumulation by itself is not enough to guarantee a level of economic growth that can keep pace with that of the world's economic leaders. It is also necessary to risk one's capital in the 'right' kinds of economic project, that is, in those projects conceived with the future in mind. Continuity is not incompatible with technological, managerial, and economic flexibility. One can learn from past mistakes, and from other countries' innovations. In Italy's case, a great many choices proved to be either unsuitable or hopelessly wrong, and I have gone to great lengths to point this out in this book; however, the fact that Italy managed to make up lost ground in relation to other industrial nations means that these other nations must have also made wrong or inappropriate choices, some of which were to have extremely dramatic consequences—consequences such as the slow decline of the British economy, the numerous crises in France, the Great Depression of 1929 in the USA and Germany, as well as the terrible phenomenon of German aggression, which ended with the aggressor beaten and on its knees. It is certainly no consolation that other countries too had their problems, but it does serve to underline the fact that the process of industrial development is everywhere a troublesome one, and to show that those countries which have yet to industrialize, and which aim at imitating this process, have an extremely difficult task in front of them.

The fact that the Italian economic success story has not been very widely acclaimed is also partly due to Italy's failure to create anything very original. In fact, until now Italy has proved to be a very able and innovative imitator among advanced countries, but it has never produced a model to imitate. Germany invented the 'mixed bank'; France produced the efficient State; the USA established the large managerially run corporation; Japan created an integrated business network (being internally integrated, and having each company connected to and interacting with other companies), which enables industry to produce long-term plans and guarantees the best product quality possible. Italy has imitated, and continues to imitate, more or less everything that has been invented by the others; not even its famous industrial districts are original; they already existed in England, as Alfred Marshall observed.

This could perhaps be considered to be the distinctive feature of the Italian case; that is, its limitless flexibility, typical of small businesses, but which can—though not without difficulty—also be adapted to suit the larger industrial corporation when there are no other alternatives available. Some people have claimed that the Italian model of industrial development has been, and still is, characterized by a particularly strong intervention of the State. I personally do not agree with this thesis, as there are a number of other countries, including Germany, France, and Japan, which have witnessed high levels of state intervention in the economy, even if these cases differ from the Italian one in terms of methods employed and timing.

So, has Italy really moved from the periphery to the centre? It would be too easy to reply in the affirmative simply because Italy can now boast the same per capita income levels as Great Britain, and is close on the heels of France and Germany (average income in the newly unified Germany could well be below that of the Italian average). The fact is that the 'centre' of the world economy moved some time ago away from Europe and towards the USA, and then more recently towards Japan (all European countries are some way behind these two now). Europe, the birthplace of the Industrial Revolution, remained associated for too long with a level of conflict which was totally incompatible with smooth social and economic progress. Europe now possesses the means to overcome its relative disadvantage, but an increase in the degree of co-operation between countries is necessary. Italy as an important member of the European community has its part to play in the building of a united Europe, which is going to require a considerable amount of energy.

However, even if the unification of Europe, together with the elimination of the threat of war from European territory, were to enable Europe (and with it Italy) to take its place once more at the centre of the economic stage, this would certainly not mean the end of the history. The 'centre', in fact, is not a fixed point. There are no limits to the capacity mankind has for improvement, but this is dependent upon there being no obstacles deliberately placed to prevent it. Unfortunately, such obstacles do exist, and they are due to the power of conservatism and individual greed to corrupt politics and institutions, to put off fundamentally important decisions, to stand in the way of the growth of new forces, and to exacerbate the seriousness of those new problems that arise and that need to be resolved.

When we reflect on these obstacles, we realize just how mistaken the idea of self-sustained economic growth is. A country's economy cannot exist in isolation, separated from its social and political framework. This is perhaps the most obvious difference between Italy's first and second economic revivals. The first revival, known throughout the world as the Renaissance, was accompanied by a very strong cultural, artistic, and social movement, which was to form the basis for subsequent civilization. Today, on the other hand, many people (and not only in Italy) believe that it is possible to continue economic development without at the same time having to worry too much about cultural, civil, and social improvement. It remains to be seen whether the present 'civilization' will prove to be as solid and as long-lasting as the Renaissance inheritance was.

APPENDIX 1

Politics and Administration, 1815–1985

5 June 1815 The Vienna Congress founded the new political order of Restoration Italy: Lombardy and the Veneto are given to Austria; the Kingdom of Sardinia, comprising Piedmont, Liguria, and Sardinia, remains independent; the two smallish Grand Duchies of Parma/Piacenza (where Napoleon's second wife Maria Luisa is made Governess) and Modena/Reggio are allowed to survive; the Grand Duchy of Tuscany is to be governed by the Lorena family from Austria; the Papal States are reintegrated with the regions of Romagna, the Marches, Umbria, and Latium; the Kingdom of the Two Sicilies is given back to the Bourbons.

2 July 1820 Popular revolts in Naples (put down on the 23 March 1821).

10 March 1821 Liberal revolts in the Kingdom of Sardinia (put down).

1831 Revolutionary revolts in Romagna, the Marches, and Umbria (crushed).

1845 More revolts in Romagna (put down).

1847 Liberalization moves in the Kingdom of Sardinia, Tuscany, and the Papal States.

4 March 1848 Passing of the Statute of the Kingdom of Sardinia.

14 March 1848 Passing of the Constitution of the Papal States.

20 March 1848 First War of Independence (lost on 6 August 1849). The Kingdom of Sardinia is the only one to keep a constitutional government.

4 November 1852 Prime Minister Cavour in the Kingdom of Sardinia.

14 April 1856 Cavour gets promise of support from Napoleon III in the event of war with Austria.

23 April 1859 Second War of Independence (ends in partial victory; Lombardy given to France, who passes it on to Italy in exchange for Nice and Savoy, 10 November 1859).

27 April 1859 Revolts in Tuscany—the Grand Duke leaves the State.

March 1860 Tuscany, Romagna, and Parma are annexed.

5 May 1860 Garibaldi's 'Expedition of the Thousand', aimed at liberating the Kingdom of the Two Sicilies.

11 September 1860 Piedmontese troops invade the Papal States.

2 November 1860 Former Kingdom of the Two Sicilies annexed.

4 November 1860 The Marches and Umbria are annexed.

17 March 1861 Vittorio Emanuele II proclaimed King of Italy; Turin is the temporary capital; the first governments of the Historical Right.

June 1865 Florence becomes the capital.

20 June 1866 Third War of Independence, ends in partial victory and the cession of the Veneto to the new Italian Kingdom.

20 September 1870 Occupation of Rome—end of the Papal State.

2 July 1871 Rome becomes the capital.

25 March 1876 Depretis (Historical Left) becomes Prime Minister.

9 January 1878 Umberto I becomes King of Italy.

21 December 1881 Italy joins the Triple Alliance (treaty signed 20 May 1882).

21 January 1882 Electoral reform—suffrage extended from 2 to 7% of the population.

5 February 1885 Beginning of Italian colonialism in Somalia, Eritrea, and Abyssinia. After a series of unsuccessful moves, Italy takes control of Eritrea and part of Somalia in 1896.

6 October 1887 Crispi's first cabinet.

August 1892 Foundation of the Partito Socialista Italiano (PSI).

October 1893 Uprising of the Sicilian 'fasci'.

May 1898 Uprisings in Milan, and failed attempt by Pelloux to pass special laws limiting political freedom.

29 July 1900 Umberto I assassinated; Vittorio Emanuele III made king.

November 1903 First Giolitti cabinet (beginning of the Giolitti years).

3 December 1910 Corradini sets up the Partito Nazionalista.

28 September 1911 War with Libya, ending with Italian domination of the country.

25 May 1912 Universal male suffrage.

24 May 1915 Italy enters the First World War on the side of the Allies. War ends with the annexation of Trentino, Alto Adige, Trieste, and Istria, together with Fiume and a part of Dalmatia in 1924).

18 January 1919 Foundation of the Partito Popolare (PP) by Don Sturzo.

23 March 1919 Mussolini sets up his Fascist squads.

January 1921 Partito Communista Italiano (PCI) founded at Leghorn.

28 October 1922 Fascist march on Rome.

29 October 1922 First government led by Mussolini.

April 1924 Last elections.

26 November 1925 All other political parties disbanded by the Fascists.

October 1925 Palazzo Vidoni pact with the industrialists, leaving only one (Fascist) trade union.

April 1927 Labour Charter passed by the regime (based on corporative lines introduced later, but the 'corporazioni' were not introduced until 1934).

11 February 1929 Pacts 'Lateranensi' between the Catholic Church and the State.

2 October 1935 Invasion of Ethiopia.

October 1936 Rome–Berlin Axis.

May 1939 Steel pact with Hitler signed.

10 June 1940 Italy enters the Second World War.

10 July 1943 Allies land in Sicily.

25 July 1943 Mussolini removed from power and arrested.

3 September 1943 Armistice agreement with the Allies.

12 September 1943 Mussolini escapes from prison with German help, and sets up his 'Republic of Salo' (Repubblica Sociale Italiana). Beginning of the war between resistance fighters and Nazi/Fascist troops.

25 April 1945 Liberation of Italy. Mussolini killed on 28 May 1945.

2 June 1946 Institutional referendum. Universal suffrage extended to women. Italy becomes a Republic.

January 1947 Foundation of the Partito Socialista dei Lavoratori (PSLI, later PSDI), a social democratic party.

31 May 1947 End of National Solidarity governments—first Christian Democrat (DC) government (the Democrazia Cristiana had taken over the role of Don Sturzo's Partito Popolare back in 1943).

1 January 1948 New Italian Constitution becomes law.

18 April 1948 Defeat of the Fronte Popolare (PCI and PSI), and victory of the DC: beginning of coalition governments between DC and parties of the centre.

August 1948 Division of the trade unions into three main branches, according to political affiliation: CGIL (mainly Communist), CISL (mainly Christian Democrat), and UIL (mainly Social Democrat).

3 April 1949 Italy joins NATO.

14 December 1955 Italy admitted to the United Nations.

30 July 1957 Parliament ratifies Italy's membership of the EEC.

4 December 1963 Beginning of Centre–Left coalition governments, with the inclusion of the PSI.

September 1969 The 'Hot Autumn' of social protest, strikes, etc. begins.

December 1969 The first bomb explodes in Milan, and marks the beginning of the 'strategy of tension' by right-wing and left-wing extremists (Red Brigades), as well as by the secret masonic lodge (P2).

12 May 1974 Referendum on divorce—anti-divorce lobby defeated.

16 March 1978 DC government, with external support from the PCI (historical compromise, which was to last until January 1979).

March–May 1978 Kidnap and murder of Aldo Moro (DC leader) by the Red Brigades, causing a very strong reaction which enables the State to get the upper hand over left-wing extremism.

18 May 1981 Anti-abortion referendum defeated.

2 June 1981 First member of another party (other than of the DC) to lead a government cabinet (Spadolini, member of the Partito Repubblicano Italiano (PRI), a centre party).

APPENDIX 2
Economics and Society, 1815–1990

1822 Foundation of the first Cassa di Risparmio, in the Veneto.

12 June 1823 Foundation of the Cassa di Risparmio delle Province Lombarde (Cariplo) in Milan.

3 October 1839 Opening of the first railway line in Italy between Naples and Portici.

14 December 1849 Foundation of the Banca Nazionale degli Stati Sardi (after unification to become the Banca Nazionale nel Regno d'Italia).

30 August 1857 Work begins on the Frejus tunnel (completed in 1871).

3 November 1859 Casati Law reorganizes the educational system.

21 August 1862 Common land is sold off.

17 January 1863 Trade treaties with France introducing free trade.

17 May 1863 Cassa Depositi e Prestiti (Cassa DDPP) is set up.

28 March 1864 Foundation of the first Banca Popolare (in Lodi, near Milan).

15 July 1864 Introduction of income tax.

14 May 1865 Railways sold off to private companies.

December 1865 Constitution of the Latin Monetary Union.

1 May 1866 Introduction of banknotes' inconvertibility.

15 August 1867 Regulations concerning the sale of Church lands.

7 July 1868 Introduction of the tax on the milling of flour (reduced in 1879, and repealed in 1884).

24 August 1868 The tobacco monopoly is managed by a private company (until 1883).

29 May 1870 Industrial survey is begun (completed in 1874).

September 1872 Work begins on the Gothard pass (opened on the 27 December 1881).

27 May 1875 Postal savings banks founded.

15 March 1877 Agricultural survey organized by Jacini (completed in 1884).

26 December 1877 Treasury is founded.

30 May 1878 First changes (mildly protectionist) made to customs duties.

24 March 1881 Survey of the merchant navy (completed in 1883).

7 April 1881 End of inconvertibility (effectively reached in 1883).

25 June 1882 Baccarini Law on land-reclamation and drainage.

1 March 1886 Work starts on the new national land-register (completed in 1956).

14 July 1887 First protectionist customs duty introduced.

22 December 1888 Health Act passed.

17 July 1890 Charities Law.

1 May 1891 Opening of the first 'Camere del Lavoro'.

10 October 1893 Banking Act and foundation of the Bank of Italy (which began work on 1 January 1894).

30 November 1893 Credito Mobiliare goes bankrupt, followed by Banca Generale a few months later.

21 February 1894 Lira convertibility suspended.

17 March 1894 Compulsory insurance against accidents at work.

31 March 1904 Basilicata law (followed by other special laws concerning other southern regions).

8 July 1904 Special legislation for the city of Naples.

22 April 1905 Nationalization of the railways.

1 July 1906 Interest conversion on public debt.

May 1907 The 1907 international economic crisis hits Italy.

17 July 1910 Introduction of compulsory maternity insurance.

August 1911 Salvage operation in the steel industry.

4 June 1912 Foundation of the Istituto Nazionale Assicurazioni (INA).

20 December 1914 Creation of Consorzio Sovvenzioni su Valori Industriali (CSVI).

26 June 1915 Beginning of the industrial war effort.

April 1919 Foundation of the Cassa Nazionale Assicurazioni Sociali (CNAS, then INFPS in 1933, and finally INPS after the fall of Fascism).

May 1921 ILVA crisis.

1 July 1921 Introduction of new protectionist customs duties.

3 December 1921 Crisis in the Ansaldo Company.

29 December 1921 Banca Italiana di Sconto (BIS) goes bankrupt.

March 1922 Salvage operation at the Banco di Roma begins (it is to last for several years).

August 1923 Gentile educational reforms.

December 1925 Volpi negotiations aimed at the settlement of Italy's foreign debt.

April 1926 AGIP founded.

18 August 1926 'Quota 90'—and the reintroduction of the gold standard (later abandoned on 5 October 1936).

24 December 1928 Integral Land Reclamation Programme.

3 December 1931 Foundation of the Istituto Mobiliare Italiano (IMI).

January 1933 Foundation of the Istituto per la Ricostruzione Industriale (IRI).

18 November 1935 League of Nations introduces sanctions against Italy (which last until 4 August 1936).

12 March 1936 Banking act puts an end to the 'mixed banks'.

July 1947 Introduction of the 'Einaudi line', aimed at stabilizing the Italian lira.

September 1947 Setting up of the Fondo Industrie Meccaniche (FIM, transformed in 1962 into the public holding company EFIM).

29 June 1948 Marshall Plan introduced.

February 1950 Italy joins the European Payments Union.

May 1950 Partial agrarian reform.

10 August 1950 Cassa per il Mezzogiorno set up.

April 1951 Italy joins the European Coal and Steel Community.

21 January 1951 Establishment of the Ente Nazionale Idrocarburi (ENI).

March 1955 Vanoni plan presented.

December 1956 Ministry for State shareholdings introduced.

25 March 1957 EEC Treaty signed in Rome.

6 December 1962 Nationalization of the electrical energy industry, and creation of ENEL.

14 May 1970 Workers' Statute passed by Parliament.

March 1971 Industrial Shareholdings Authority (Ente Gestione Partecipazioni Industriali—GEPI) established.

1 January 1973 Introduction of VAT.

1 January 1974 Tax reform law.

8 April 1974 The CONSOB, a body regulating stock-exchange activity, is set up.

25 January 1975 Agreement on wage-indexing between Confindustria and the Labour unions, which leads to a rise in inflation.

7 April 1977 Abolition of the EGAM (set up in 1958 to manage state-owned companies of the mining and hotel industries), with companies absorbed into IRI and ENI.

23 December 1978 National Health Service set up.

13 March 1979 Italy enters the European Monetary system (EMS).

14 October 1980 40,000 Fiat white-collar workers demonstrate against the existing policy of the trade unions, marking a turn-around in union politics—with a move towards a less conflictual position *vis-à-vis* the employers.

14 February 1984 The government, led by the socialist leader Craxi, waters down the agreement on wage indexation. The PCI later promoted a referendum asking for the abrogation of the new law, but the results demonstrated popular support for the governmental line, 10 June 1985.

4 July 1986 The CASMEZ is abolished, and a new Agency for Southern Development is set up.

10 October 1990 Introduction of anti-trust legislation (and controlling body).

APPENDIX 3
Biographies

CAVOUR, CAMILLO BENSO (Turin, 1810–Turin, 1861); aristocrat, well-educated man who travelled extensively abroad, involved himself in politics after the introduction of Constitution in Piedmont; in 1847 he directed the paper *Risorgimento*; MP in 1848, he became Prime Minister in 1852 and was the impresario of Italian unification.

COLOMBO, GIUSEPPE (Milan, 1836–Milan, 1921); graduated in mathematics, travelled abroad, taught at the SIAM and at the newly founded Milan Polytechnic, of which he became director in 1897. MP in 1886, Finance Minister in the 1890s, he is especially famous for his activities in Milanese industry.

CRISPI, FRANCESCO (Ribera, Sicily, 1818–Naples, 1901); lawyer, travelled abroad, collaborated with Mazzini, but later on supported the monarchy, organized the uprising of Sicily in connection with Garibaldi's expedition; elected MP, became minister under Depretis and Prime Minister between 1887–96 (with intervals between periods of office). He strongly supported the Triple Alliance and launched colonial ventures without much success.

DE GASPERI, ALCIDE (Pieve di Tesino, Trento, 1881–Sella di Valsugana, Trento, 1954); graduated in philosophy in Vienna, fought for the annexation of Trentino by Italy; elected as MP for the Popular Party, he was persecuted by the Fascists and took refuge in the Vatican as a librarian. In 1943 he reconstituted a Catholic party under the name of Christian Democracy (DC) and participated in all the democratic governments, becoming himself Prime Minister from 15 December 1945 to July 1953. He was an anti-Fascist, a democrat, and a Europeanist.

DEPRETIS, AGOSTINO (Mezzana Bottarone, Lombardy, 1813–Stradella, 1887); lawyer, Prime Minister 1876–87. He is well known for having been the first representative of the 'Historical Left' and having led his governments according to the principles of 'trasformismo' (transformism), i.e. *ad hoc* parliamentary majorities on each political project, cutting across party lines in Parliament.

EINAUDI, LUIGI (Carrù, Piedmont, 1874–Rome, 1961); professor of public finance, journalist, representative of the free-trade school in Italy; he became governor of the Bank of Italy (1945–6); Treasury Minister in 1947; President of the Republic 1948–55.

GIOLITTI, GIOVANNI (Mondovì, Piedmont, 1842–Cavour, 1928); lawyer, deputy in 1882, Prime Minister, with interruptions, 1903–13 and again during the troubled year June 1920–June 1921. He was an enlightened representative of the Italian liberals, supported industry, granted more freeedom of expression to the working-class movement and introduced universal male voting.

LUZZATTI, LUIGI (Venice, 1841–Rome, 1927); lawyer, representative of the 'socialism of the chair'; MP from 1870, he was the promoter of several bills in the socio-economic field; Minister of the Treasury on various occasions between 1891 and 1910.

MAGLIANI, AGOSTINO (Laurino, Campania 1824–Rome, 1891); lawyer, civil servant under the Bourbons; Senator from 1871, Finance Minister 1877–88, he reintroduced the gold standard in Italy, but was severely criticized for his management of public finances.

MARCONI, GUGLIELMO (Bologna, 1874–Rome, 1937); physicist, inventor of radio in 1895, Nobel prize winner in 1909.

MINGHETTI, MARCO (Bologna, 1818–Rome, 1886); aristocrat, well-educated man with a first-hand knowledge of foreign countries, active in the constitutional governments of the Papal State, went to Piedmont when the Pope withdrew the Constitution, collaborated with Cavour and then was Minister of Finance and Prime Minister on various occasions between 1862 and 1876. He pushed for a more decentralized organization of the new Kingdom without success.

MUSSOLINI, BENITO (Davia di Predappio, Romagna, 1883–border with Switzerland, 1945); schoolmaster, anarcho-socialist, he was called to direct the official socialist paper *Avanti* in 1914, but then expelled from the party as a result of his sudden about-turn, from a strictly neutral position to a position favouring the entry of Italy into the First World War; on 14 November 1914, he published the first issue of his nationalistic paper *Popolo d'Italia*, and on 23 March 1919 created the Fasci di Combattimento (Fighting Fasces). Having inspired the March on Rome on 28 October 1922 (in which he did not participate in person), he was called to form his first government the following day: the Fascist era began. Mussolini was shot dead 28 April 1945, while attempting to escape to Switzerland.

NITTI, FRANCESCO SAVERIO (Melfi, Basilicata, 1868–Rome, 1953); lawyer, he studied economics and public finance, and became professor of public finance. MP in 1904, then minister in several governments and Prime Minister in the difficult year June 1919–June 1920. During Fascism he lived in exile in France; in the new republic, he was still politically active. He is a representative of the 'southern' school of thought that advocated public intervention in the South.

PARETO, VILFREDO (Paris 1848–Céligny 1923); son of a Piedmontese follower of Mazzini, graduated in engineering in Turin and directed a metal works in Italy for 20 years. In the 1890s dedicated himself to economic studies and in 1893 took over Walras's chair of Political Economy in Lausanne, writing many famous works. Wrote for the *Giornale degli economisti* 1890–1905. After leaving his Chair in 1906, he spent the rest of his life in Switzerland.

SELLA, QUINTINO (Sella di Mosso, Piedmont, 1827–Biella, 1884); engineer, professor of mineralogy at the school for engineers in Turin; between 1862 and 1875 he was several times made Minister of Finance and as such he gave shape to the Italian financial system, together with Marco Minghetti.

STRINGHER, BONALDO (Udine, Veneto, 1854–Rome, 1930); graduated in economics at

Venice, became director general in the Ministry of Finance and then inspector general of the Treasury; in 1900 he was appointed director general of the Bank of Italy, a position he retained until 1930. He is the author of several important studies on applied economics.

TOGLIATTI, PALMIRO (Genoa, 1893–Yalta, USSR, 1964); lawyer, he collaborated with Gramsci in the foundation of the *Ordine Nuovo*, of which he became chief editor; in 1921 he was among the founders of the Italian Communist Party; persecuted by Fascism, he lived in France, in Spain, then in the USSR (1940–4). After Mussolini's downfall, he was a member of the democratic governments; his party went into opposition in the middle of 1947, but he was never to advocate revolution even after the attempt on his life on 14 June 1948, which he survived.

INDEX OF NAMES

INDEX OF ORGANIZATIONS

INDEX OF SUBJECTS